The Rust Programming Handbook

An end-to-end guide to mastering Rust fundamentals

Francesco Ciulla

The Rust Programming Handbook

Portfolio Director: Kunal Chaudhari
Relationship Lead: Dhruv J. Kataria
Project Manager: K. Loganathan
Content Engineer: Deepayan Bhattacharjee
Technical Editor: Irfa Ansari
Copy Editor: Safis Editing
Indexer: Manju Arasan
Proofreader: Deepayan Bhattacharjee
Production Designer: Shantanu Zagade
Growth Lead: Vinishka Kalra

First published: December 2025

Production reference: 1171225

Published by Packt Publishing Ltd.
Grosvenor House
11 St Paul's Square
Birmingham
B3 1RB, UK.

ISBN 978-1-83620-887-7

www.packtpub.com

To my parents, for their endless support

– Francesco Ciulla

Contributors

About the author

Francesco Ciulla is a Content Creator and a Docker Captain (since 2021) from Rome, Italy. Starting his career as a computer scientist, he transformed his passion for technology into a mission of teaching and sharing knowledge.

Francesco is a strong believer in the developer community, which he considers the best in the world. He has been a highly active international public speaker since 2022 and was recognized with the Microsoft Most Valuable Professional (MVP) award in 2024. Before dedicating himself fully to content creation, he gained significant experience as a full stack developer working on the Copernicus project for the **European Space Agency** (**ESA**).

Driven by the conviction that teaching is the highest form of understanding, Francesco shares his expertise in Rust and DevOps with over 340,000 subscribers on YouTube (as of December 2025). You can watch his latest tutorials at `https://www.youtube.com/FrancescoCiulla`.

I would like to extend a special thanks to my amazing girlfriend and future wife, Giulia, for her support, encouragement, and patience throughout the entire writing process.

Thanks to Rahul Nair for giving me the opportunity to write this edition, which has been a very enriching experience.

Special thanks to the entire content team, including Deepayan Bhattacharjee, K. Loganathan, Evgeni Pirianov, and Ruby Rose, for their valuable input and time reviewing this book.

Finally, thank you to the entire Packt team for their continuous support during the course of writing this book.

About the reviewers

Evgeni Pirianov is a Senior Rust Software Engineer specializing in backend technologies, Web3, and blockchain systems. A graduate of Imperial College London with a degree in Engineering, Evgeni began his career developing non-linear solvers in C++ before transitioning to become an architect and implementer of both centralized and decentralized applications across diverse software domains.

As a technical auditor for programming books, Evgeni brings rigorous expertise to reviewing Rust and lately Zig content, ensuring accuracy, clarity, and adherence to best practices. His deep understanding of systems programming, combined with hands-on experience building production-grade applications, allows him to identify not just technical errors but also pedagogical gaps that might hinder learners.

Evgeni's passion for Rust is unmatched: he is a fervent advocate for the language's bright future and believes in its transformative potential across the entire software engineering landscape. His commitment to the Rust ecosystem extends beyond writing code to creating courses and helping others learn it correctly and effectively.

Evgeni has served as technical auditor for Asynchronous Programming in Rust by Carl Fredrik Samson (ISBN: 978-1805128137) and Rust Web Programming by Maxwell Flitton (Packt Publishing, ISBN: 978-1803234694).

Ruby Rose is a software engineer currently working in the field of databases. She has 10+ years of software engineering experience, solving problems in the cloud, distributed systems, fintech, security, and privacy. She has contributed to and worked on several developer guides for cloud-managed web services.

Join us on Discord!

Read this book alongside other users, developers, experts, and the author himself.

Ask questions, provide solutions to other readers, chat with the authors via Ask Me Anything sessions, and much more. Scan the QR or visit the link to join the community.

https://packt.link/deep-engineering-rust

Table of Contents

Chapter 3: Functions in Rust 65

Chapter 5: Composite Types in Rust and the Module System 115

Chapter 7: Polymorphism and Lifetimes 209

Chapter 9: Thinking Functionally in Rust 275

Chapter 10: Testing in Rust 299

Chapter 11: Smart Pointers and Memory Management 343

Chapter 14: Rust for Web Development: Building Full-Stack Applications 493

Preface

If you are holding this book, you are probably curious about Rust. Maybe you heard about it from a colleague who wouldn't stop talking about how great it is. Maybe you read an article about it online. Or, perhaps you have been following my content for a while and finally decided to see what all the excitement is about. Whatever brought you here, I am glad you made it.

This book has two main goals. We will master the fundamentals and examine real, practical examples. In my extensive experience as a teacher, I have found that these two things work best when combined. We will not just look at theory in a vacuum. We will use it to build things.

Rust has incredible potential for the future. I honestly believe it will become the best language for the era of **Artificial Intelligence** (**AI**). When we code with AI, we need the final result to be high-performance, but we also need something that is easy to read and modify. Rust hits that perfect balance between speed and clarity.

You will also get very familiar with the famous Rust compiler. I like to describe the compiler as an "annoying grandma." She is grumpy, picky, moves a bit slowly, and is always complaining about what you are doing. It can be frustrating at first! But you have to remember that, just like a grandma, she only complains because she wants the best for you. She wants you to be safe.

Be prepared for some mind-blowing moments during this learning process. Rust does not just feel different. It *is* different. This is especially true when discussing memory management. It requires a shift in how you think, but I will save the details of that for the later chapters.

The journey ahead will be challenging at times, but it will also be rewarding. You are learning about a tool that will make you a better developer, no matter what language you use in the future.

So, grab a coffee, open your laptop, and let's get started. Let's crush it!

Who this book is for

This book is designed for developers familiar with languages such as Java, JavaScript, or Python who are interested in transitioning to Rust. If that describes you, you'll appreciate the book's pace and level of detail.

Beginners are also welcome, but please note that the learning curve may be steeper. To keep the book focused and manageable (and avoid creating a massive encyclopedia), I have assumed a basic understanding of common programming concepts. If you come across topics, such as web architecture, that aren't explained in depth, I recommend pausing to research those concepts before continuing.

What this book covers

Chapter 1, Getting Started with Rust, introduces the Rust programming language, details the installation process, and guides you through writing your first program using the Cargo toolchain.

Chapter 2, Rust Syntax and Functions, explores variable declarations, data types, and control structures, and demonstrates how Rust handles functions and ownership principles.

Chapter 3, Functions in Rust, focuses on structuring code effectively by defining functions and organizing them into modules to manage visibility and reusability across your projects.

Chapter 4, Ownership, Borrowing, and References, dives into Rust's revolutionary memory management approach, explaining how these interlinked concepts prevent common errors such as dangling pointers and data races.

Chapter 5, Composite Types in Rust and the Module System, covers the use of structs and enums to construct well-organized data structures, including how to handle variants with pattern matching and apply traits.

Chapter 6, Introduction to Error Handling, dives into Rust's error handling mechanisms, explaining how to use Result, Option, and panic handling to build safe and reliable applications.

Chapter 7, Polymorphism and Lifetimes, introduces polymorphism in Rust, demonstrating how to use generics for flexible data types, traits to define shared behavior, and validating references with lifetimes.

Chapter 8, Object-Oriented Programming in Rust, examines how Rust supports object-oriented principles such as encapsulation and polymorphism using the trait system and structs introduced in the previous chapter.

Chapter 9, Thinking Functionally in Rust, emphasizes iterators and closures, exploring how these features enable powerful, concise, and expressive code that leverages Rust's performance.

Chapter 10, Testing in Rust, highlights how Rust makes it easy and enjoyable to write tests, helping you ensure your code works correctly and the quality remains high over time.

Chapter 11, Smart Pointers and Memory Management, focuses on tools such as Box, Rc, and Arc, explaining how they are used to manage memory for shared ownership and thread-safe access.

Chapter 12, Managing System Resources, details the efficient management of memory and processor resources, discussing low-level handling without a garbage collector.

Chapter 13, Concurrency and Parallelism, covers powerful features for concurrent programming, ensuring thread safety and preventing bugs such as data races and deadlocks.

Chapter 14, Rust for Web Development: Building Fullstack Applications, demonstrates how to build fullstack applications, seamlessly integrating backend and frontend components using Rust's ecosystem.

Chapter 15, System Programming in Rust: Concrete Examples, provides practical examples of low-level development, such as interacting with file I/O, networking, and hardware.

Chapter 16, Dockerization and Deployment of Rust Applications, focuses on the practical aspects of containerizing Rust applications with Docker and implementing CI/CD strategies for reliable deployment.

Appendix, Common Pitfalls in Rust Programming (online), addresses typical challenges and mistakes encountered by developers, offering community insights and best practices to avoid them.

To get the most out of this book

I have written this book assuming you have some prior coding experience. To smoothly follow the examples and projects, you should be comfortable with the following:

- Programming fundamentals: You should be familiar with core programming concepts such as variables, loops, conditional statements, and functions. Experience with at least one other language (such as Python, JavaScript, Java, or C++) is highly recommended.
- Command-line basics: Rust relies heavily on the terminal. You should be comfortable navigating folders and running basic commands in a shell (Bash, PowerShell, or Zsh).

- System requirements: You can run the code examples on Windows, macOS, or Linux.
    - Rust toolchain: I will guide you through installing Rust using rustup in *Chapter 1*.
    - Code editor: I recommend Visual Studio Code (VS Code) with the rust-analyzer and Even Better TOML extensions for a lightweight, extensible experience. Alternatively, RustRover (by JetBrains) is an excellent dedicated IDE for Rust, offering a more robust environment. But you can follow along with any IDE you want.
    - Docker: For the deployment chapters (specifically, *Chapter 16*), you will need Docker installed on your machine.
    - Internet access: You will need an active internet connection to download Rust crates (dependencies) via Cargo.

Download the example code files

The code bundle for the book is hosted on GitHub at `https://github.com/FrancescoXX/rustcrab/tree/main/book-compendium`. We also have other code bundles from our rich catalog of books and videos available at `https://github.com/PacktPublishing`. Check them out!

Download the color images

We also provide a PDF file that has color images of the screenshots/diagrams used in this book. You can download it here: `https://packt.link/gbp/9781836208877`.

Conventions used

There are a number of text conventions used throughout this book.

`CodeInText`: Indicates code words in text, database table names, folder names, filenames, file extensions, pathnames, dummy URLs, user input, and Twitter handles. For example:

"The `.clone()` method on `String` creates a new allocation on the heap and copies the content (`"hello"`) into it."

A block of code is set as follows:

```
fn main() {
    {
        let espresso = String::from("Delicious");
        println!("{}", espresso);
    }
}
```

Any command-line input or output is written as follows:

```
docker --version
```

Bold: Indicates a new term, an important word, or words that you see on the screen. For instance, words in menus or dialog boxes appear in the text like this. For example: "At its core, an **HTTP request** consists of the following:"

Warnings or important notes appear like this.

Tips and tricks appear like this.

Get in touch

Feedback from our readers is always welcome.

General feedback: If you have questions about any aspect of this book or have any general feedback, please email us at `customercare@packt.com` and mention the book's title in the subject of your message.

Errata: Although we have taken every care to ensure the accuracy of our content, mistakes do happen. If you have found a mistake in this book, we would be grateful if you reported this to us. Please visit `http://www.packt.com/submit-errata`, click **Submit Errata**, and fill in the form.

Piracy: If you come across any illegal copies of our works in any form on the internet, we would be grateful if you would provide us with the location address or website name. Please contact us at `copyright@packt.com` with a link to the material.

If you are interested in becoming an author: If there is a topic that you have expertise in and you are interested in either writing or contributing to a book, please visit `http://authors.packt.com/`.

Share your thoughts

Once you've read *The Rust Programming Handbook*, we'd love to hear your thoughts! Scan the QR code below to go straight to the Amazon review page for this book and share your feedback.

https://packt.link/r/1836208871

Your review is important to us and the tech community and will help us make sure we're delivering excellent quality content.

Free Benefits with Your Book

This book comes with free benefits to support your learning. Activate them now for instant access (see the "*How to Unlock*" section for instructions).

Here's a quick overview of what you can instantly unlock with your purchase:

PDF and ePub Copies

- Access a DRM-free PDF copy of this book to read anywhere, on any device.
- Use a DRM-free ePub version with your favorite e-reader.

Next-Gen Web-Based Reader

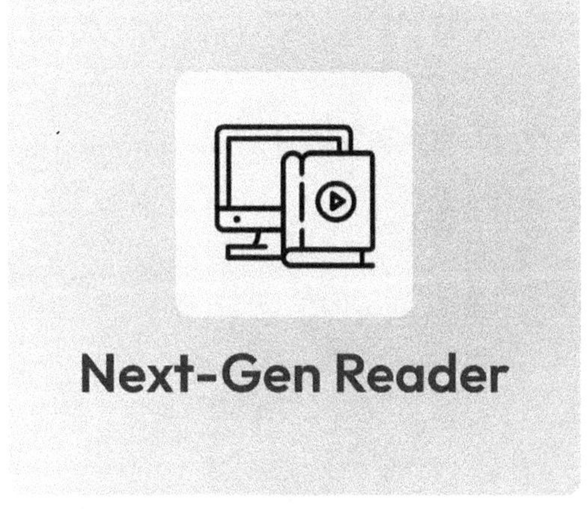

- **Multi-device progress sync:** Pick up where you left off, on any device.
- **Highlighting and notetaking:** Capture ideas and turn reading into lasting knowledge.
- **Bookmarking:** Save and revisit key sections whenever you need them.
- **Dark mode:** Reduce eye strain by switching to dark or sepia themes.

How to Unlock

UNLOCK NOW

Scan the QR code (or go to `packtpub.com/unlock`). Search for this book by name, confirm the edition, and then follow the steps on the page.

***Note:** Keep your invoice handy. Purchases made directly from Packt don't require one.*

1

Getting Started with Rust

Welcome to the realm of Rust programming!

If you've found your way here, you're probably intrigued by Rust's reputation as a robust, contemporary language specialized in systems programming, focusing on safety, speed, and reliability.

This book is for anyone who wants to learn Rust, from experienced developers looking to expand their skills to beginners exploring new technologies or those who are just curious. In the Stack Overflow 2024 Developer Survey, Rust was voted the "most admired programming language" by ~83% of developers. This is because it offers a rare combination of performance, memory safety, and a strong, welcoming community. It eliminates entire classes of bugs, such as null pointer dereferences and data races, while delivering the speed of a systems language. Learning Rust is a great way to write safer, more efficient code and future-proof your skills.

In this chapter, we start our journey by understanding the essence of Rust programming. We'll dive deep into the core principles defining Rust and explain why it shines among other programming languages. Rust has some unique features that really make it "special" among other languages. Following that, we'll set up your development environment together, ensuring you're fully equipped to dive into Rust coding right away. Finally, we'll start with the practical side of Rust by walking you through creating your first Rust program. To make it accessible to everyone, we will begin with a simple CLI tool, ensuring you grasp Rust's fundamental concepts before moving to more advanced projects such as a web server. This structured approach will help you build confidence in Rust step by step.

By the end of this chapter, you'll have a solid understanding of what makes Rust unique and why so many developers appreciate it. You'll get familiar with its core principles and how it differs from other programming languages. This foundation will give you the confidence to start exploring Rust and writing your first programs.

Let's get started!

> **Free Benefits with Your Book**
>
> Your purchase includes a free PDF copy of this book along with other exclusive benefits. Check the *Free Benefits with Your Book* section in the *Preface* to unlock them instantly and maximize your learning experience.

Technical requirements

You can use any operating system you want, but it is highly recommended that you have Git, the system versioning system. All the code examples are available in the `` `book-compendium` `` folder of the GitHub repository.

You will also need an IDE. Any IDE works, but for this book, I will use VS Code, with a couple of extensions.

- **GitHub**: `https://github.com/FrancescoXX/rustcrab/tree/main/book-compendium`
- **Git**: `https://git-scm.com/downloads`
- **VS Code (or any other IDE)**: `https://code.visualstudio.com/download`

What is Rust?

According to Wikipedia, "*Rust is a general-purpose programming language emphasizing performance, type safety, and concurrency. It enforces memory safety, meaning that all references point to valid memory, without a garbage collector. To simultaneously enforce memory safety and prevent data races, its 'borrow checker' tracks the object lifetime of all references in a program during compiling.*"

This definition sounds fascinating, but can also be quite confusing. This brief explanation alone isn't enough to fully grasp what Rust is and what makes it unique!

Let's break down this definition and explain each part:

- **General-purpose programming language**: Rust is a versatile language that excels in various domains, from system-level programming to modern web development. It's used in embedded systems, operating systems, backend engineering, and even high-frequency, low-latency applications. Rust also plays a significant role in frontend development with **WebAssembly (Wasm)** and is gaining traction in decentralized systems such as blockchain. Its ability to adapt across different fields makes it truly unique.
- **Emphasizing performance, type safety, and concurrency**: Rust is designed with three main goals in mind:
    - **Type safety**: Rust ensures that your code adheres to strict type rules, reducing bugs and making it easier for you and other developers to understand and maintain
    - **Performance**: Rust allows you to write high-performance software that runs as fast as programs written in C or C++
    - **Concurrency**: Rust provides powerful tools for writing concurrent code, allowing you to take full advantage of multi-core processors without the risk of data races
- **Enforces memory safety without a garbage collector**: Memory safety means that all pointers (references) point to valid memory. Rust achieves this without a garbage collector, which is typically used in other languages such as Java or Go to manage memory automatically. Instead, Rust uses a system of ownership with rules that the compiler checks at compile time.
- **The borrow checker**: To enforce memory safety and prevent data races, Rust employs a mechanism known as the "borrow checker." This system tracks the lifetime of all references in a program during compilation, ensuring that references are always valid and that multiple threads do not unexpectedly modify data.

No worries!

If some of these concepts sound complex or unfamiliar right now, don't worry! Throughout this book, we'll explore these topics in depth, providing clear explanations and practical examples to help you understand and master Rust programming.

By the end of the book, any doubts you have now will be resolved, and you'll be confident in your ability to use Rust effectively.

What is Rust good for?

So, what is Rust good for? Overall, Rust is versatile and excels in many areas, from system-level programming to web development. It provides the tools and guarantees necessary to build robust and efficient software, making it a valuable addition to any developer's skill set.

Rust is valued for its high performance, security, and ability to handle concurrency. These qualities matter more than ever, as software must be fast, scalable, and vulnerable to vulnerabilities. It's especially well-suited for systems programming, where speed and reliability are critical.

Rust is well-suited for developing low-level system components such as operating systems, device drivers, and embedded systems. Its memory safety features help prevent crashes and security vulnerabilities, making it a dependable choice for critical software where stability and performance are essential. But don't worry! We will start with something much simpler to help you become familiar with the syntax quickly.

Rust's robust concurrency model and expressive type system make it exceptionally well-suited for creating scalable and resilient network services, web servers, and concurrent applications. In fact, many real-world applications, such as the Firefox browser engine, Dropbox's file storage backend, and Cloudflare's performance-critical systems, currently use Rust.

In a recent communication from the US government, the White House recommended memory-safe programming languages and security-by-design principles to prevent cyberattacks. Rust was highlighted as a key example of such a language. While Rust doesn't make your application secure by default, it enforces strict rules that require developers to handle memory safely and efficiently.

The biggest challenge for developers learning Rust is adapting to its distinctive approach to memory management. This requires a mindset different from that of many other programming languages. The good news is that once you grasp these concepts, you'll be able to write safer and more efficient code with confidence. Unlike C and C++, where developers manually manage memory or languages with garbage collection, Rust requires you to adopt a different mindset. Be open-minded and ready to embrace this new way of thinking.

Key features of Rust

What makes Rust stand out compared to other programming languages is its unique features and design principles:

- **Expressiveness**: Rust's expressive syntax and powerful type system allow developers to write clear, concise, and maintainable code, making it easier to reason about complex systems. For instance, Rust's pattern matching makes decision-making elegant and enjoyable:

```
fn developer_mood(caffeine_level: u8) -> &'static str {
    match caffeine_level {
        0 => "I can't work without coffee! ☕",
        1..=2 => "Alright, I can write a few functions.",
        3..=5 => "Productivity mode: ON! 🚀",
        _ => "Too much coffee! I'm rewriting the entire project in
Rust! 🔥"
    }
}

fn main() {
    println!("{}", developer_mood(4));
    // Output: Productivity mode: ON! 🚀
}
```

- **Memory safety**: Rust guarantees memory safety while maintaining high performance by implementing strict rules during compile time. These checks help prevent common programming errors such as null pointer dereferencing and out-of-bounds array indexing before the code is executed. As a result, many potential bugs are identified early on, reducing the likelihood of crashes and enhancing the reliability of Rust programs, all without the necessity for garbage collection.
- **Concurrency**: Rust offers robust abstractions for writing concurrent code, enabling developers to fully utilize modern multi-core processors while minimizing concerns about data races and deadlocks. Features such as ownership-based threading and the `async/await` system ensure that concurrency is both safe and efficient. This allows developers to create fast, parallel code without encountering the typical challenges associated with concurrent programming.
- **Performance**: Rust provides performance that is comparable to low-level programming languages such as C and C++ by eliminating runtime overhead. Its zero-cost abstractions guarantee that high-level code compiles into efficient machine instructions without incurring additional performance penalties. Furthermore, Rust offers precise control over memory management, enabling developers to write fast and predictable code without compromising safety.

The Rust ecosystem

Rust not only boasts essential language features but also has a dynamic ecosystem of libraries, tools, and frameworks that enhance its functionality and simplify development. Notable crates such as Serde for data serialization, Tokio for asynchronous programming, and Axum for web development make Rust a strong option for various applications. This extensive ecosystem enables developers to create efficient and reliable software while taking advantage of Rust's safety and performance guarantees.

Rust's ecosystem caters to various industries and use cases, such as web development, system programming, data analysis, and gaming. One of Rust's most significant strengths lies in its ability to handle data processing tasks efficiently, which has become a cornerstone of its industrial applications. Rust's memory safety guarantees, combined with its performance comparable to C and C++, make it an excellent choice for building data-intensive systems. Developers use Rust to create high-performance data pipelines, process large-scale datasets, and implement real-time analytics applications. Its growing library ecosystem, including crates such as Polars, is a fast, multithreaded DataFrame library for Rust and Python, designed for efficient data manipulation and analysis. It is optimized for performance, using Apache Arrow's columnar memory format to handle large datasets efficiently. Polars is often compared to pandas, but it is significantly faster, especially for big data and parallel processing tasks.

You can check it out here: `https://crates.io/crates/polars`.

This versatility makes Rust a natural fit for demanding scenarios, such as optimizing database query engines or building distributed systems capable of processing petabytes of data. Beyond data processing, Rust excels in high-performance web servers and efficient system utilities, offering developers a robust toolkit across a range of domains.

The Rust community is very welcoming and committed to being open source. The Rust language itself is an open source project!

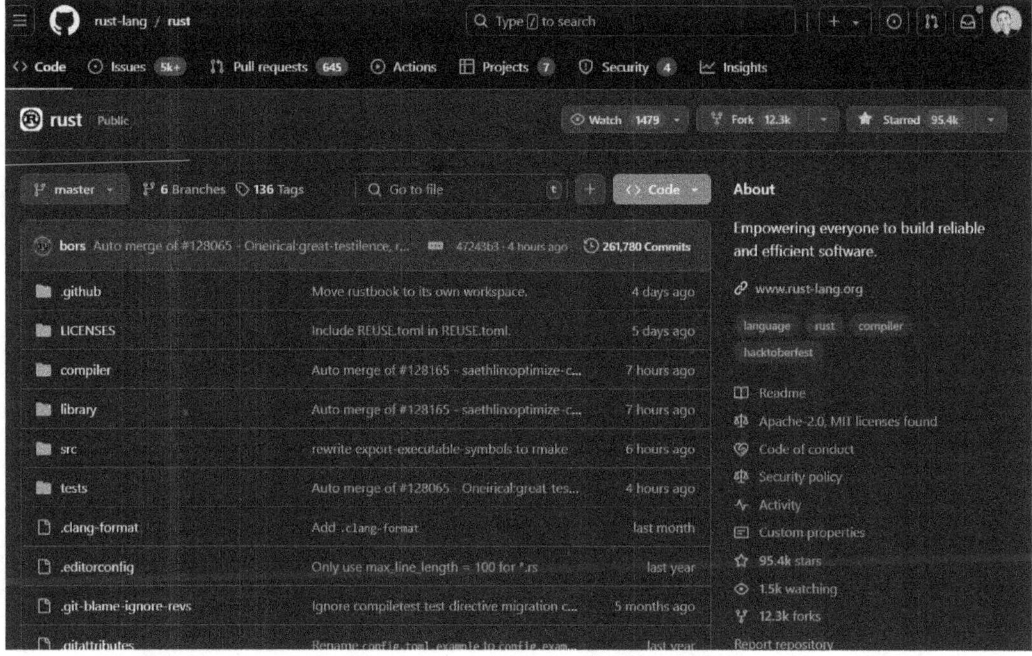

Figure 1.1: The official Rust repository

This is the perfect environment to grow a robust and solid language with a solid basis and a bright future.

Why learn Rust?

As a developer, learning Rust offers several advantages:

- **Enhanced productivity**: Rust's strict compiler checks and powerful tooling assist developers in catching bugs early and writing more reliable code, which reduces both development time and debugging efforts. For instance, Rust prevents the use of uninitialized variables at compile time:

```
fn main() {
    let x: i32;
    println!("{}", x); // ❌ Error: use of possibly-uninitialized variable `x`
}
```

- **Career opportunities**: Rust is gaining popularity in industries such as systems programming, cloud computing, and cybersecurity, opening up exciting career opportunities for developers. More and more companies are using Rust for performance-critical applications, secure backend services, and infrastructure tooling. This creates demand for different roles, such as systems engineers, backend developers, security engineers, and embedded systems developers. If you're looking for a language that's both future-proof and in high demand, Rust is a very strong choice for your career.
- **Personal growth**: Learning Rust goes beyond simply adding another language to your skill set; it transforms your approach to memory management, safety, and concurrency. It challenges your problem-solving abilities and enhances your understanding of how computers operate. By mastering Rust, you become a more well-rounded developer, enabling you to write efficient and reliable software. And let's face it, overcoming the borrow checker feels like a great achievement!

Installation and Hello World

This chapter will cover the essential steps to install Rust on your system and write your first Rust program.

We'll start by guiding you through the installation process, followed by a demonstration of compiling and running a `"Hello World"` program in Rust.

Installing Rust

Before diving into Rust programming, you must set up your development environment by installing the Rust toolchain.

You can download and install Rust by visiting `https://www.rust-lang.org/tools/install` and following the instructions for your operating system.

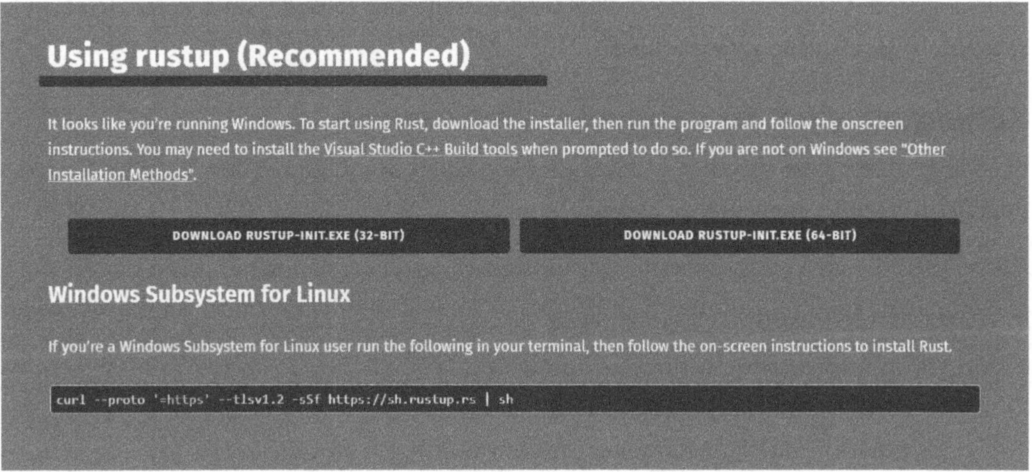

Figure 1.2: How to install Rust on different operating systems

Rust provides convenient installation options for different platforms, ensuring a smooth setup process:

- **Linux/Unix**: The official installer or package manager can install Rust on Linux and Unix-based systems
- **macOS**: Rust is well-supported on macOS, and you can install it using the official installer or Homebrew package manager
- **Windows**: Rust offers a straightforward installation experience through the official installer or Chocolatey package manager

Verifying the installation

Once Rust is installed on your system, you can verify the installation by opening a terminal or command prompt and running the following command:

```
rustc --version
```

This command should display the installed version of the Rust compiler, confirming that Rust is successfully installed on your machine.

Setting up your development environment

In addition to the Rust compiler, you'll need a text editor or **integrated development environment (IDE)** to write and edit Rust code.

A good IDE enhances productivity with features such as syntax highlighting, code completion, and debugging support. The most popular options for Rust development include the following:

- **Visual Studio Code (VS Code)**: A lightweight and highly customizable code editor with excellent Rust support via extensions
- **RustRover by IntelliJ IDEA:** A powerful, full-featured IDE specifically designed for Rust development, offering deep code analysis, refactoring tools, and seamless Cargo integration
- **Neovim**: A customizable, terminal-based editor with Rust support via plugins

Setting up VS Code for Rust (recommended)

VS Code is one of the most popular editors for Rust development due to its lightweight design, extensibility, and excellent Rust support.

To get started, download and install VS Code from the official website at `https://code.visualstudio.com/`:

1. Choose the version for your operating system (Windows, macOS, or Linux).
2. Follow the installation prompts.
3. Once installed, open VS Code.

For a smooth Rust development experience, install the following essential extensions:

- **Rust Analyzer** (`https://marketplace.visualstudio.com/items?itemName=rust-lang.rust-analyzer`): This provides intelligent code completion, error checking, go-to definitions, and code formatting. To install it, follow these steps:
    - Open VS Code.
    - Press *Ctrl* + *Shift* + *X* (or *Cmd* + *Shift* + *X* on macOS) to open the Extensions Marketplace.
    - Search for `Rust Analyzer` and click **Install**.
- **Even Better TOML** (`https://marketplace.visualstudio.com/items?itemName=tamasfe.even-better-toml`): This adds syntax highlighting and validation for `.toml` files, which are used in `Cargo.toml`.
- **(Optional) Crates** (`https://marketplace.visualstudio.com/items?itemName=serayuzgur.crates`): This helps manage dependencies by showing the latest versions of crates directly inside `Cargo.toml`.

Hello World

With Rust installed and your development environment set up, you can write your first Rust program.

For our first program, we'll use the Rust compiler (`rustc`) directly, even if this is not recommended for creating a project. We will do this just once to understand how the Rust compiler works. For all future projects, we will use a package manager that will compile all our project files for us.

Open your preferred text editor or IDE and create a new file named `hello.rs`. In this file, enter the following code:

```
fn main() {
    println!("Hello, Rust!");
}
```

The code is available here: `https://github.com/FrancescoXX/rustcrab/blob/main/book-compendium/chapter-1/hello_world.rs`.

This simple Rust program consists of a single function named `main`, which prints the message `"Hello, Rust!"` to the console using the `println!` macro. Similar to the `main` function in other programming languages, the `main` function serves as the entry point for all Rust programs.

Note

In Rust, a macro is a way of writing code that generates other code, this is known as metaprogramming. The `println!` macro is used to print text to the console, similar to how `console.log` works in JavaScript or print in Python.

Here is an example comparison:

- **Rust:** `println!("Hello, Rust!");`
- **JavaScript:** `console.log("Hello, Rust!");`

Compiling and running your Hello World

To compile and run your Rust program, open a terminal or command prompt, navigate to the directory containing your `hello.rs` file, and execute the following command:

```
rustc hello.rs
```

This command compiles your Rust source code into an executable binary named `hello` (or `hello.exe` on Windows). By default, Rust compiles your code in debug mode, which includes additional debugging information and performs fewer optimizations to make development easier:

```
./hello # (or hello.exe on Windows)
```

You should see the message `"Hello, Rust!"` printed on the console, indicating that your Rust program was executed successfully.

Note

While using `rustc` directly is useful for understanding how Rust compiles code, this is not the standard way to build Rust projects. In real-world development, Rust programmers use Cargo, Rust's official package manager and build system.

Why use Cargo instead of `rustc`?

- Simplifies project management (automates builds, dependencies, and tests)
- Handles multiple source files efficiently (unlike `rustc`, which requires compiling each file manually)
- Supports optimized builds (`cargo build --release`) for production-ready applications

In the next chapters, we'll explore how Cargo makes Rust development easier and dive into its powerful features for building, testing, and distributing Rust applications.

Using Cargo and Crates.io

Cargo is Rust's package manager and build system, designed to streamline developing, building, and managing Rust projects.

Crates.io is the official repository for Rust crates, where you can find and share libraries and tools written in Rust.

This is what the `https://crates.io/` website looks like:

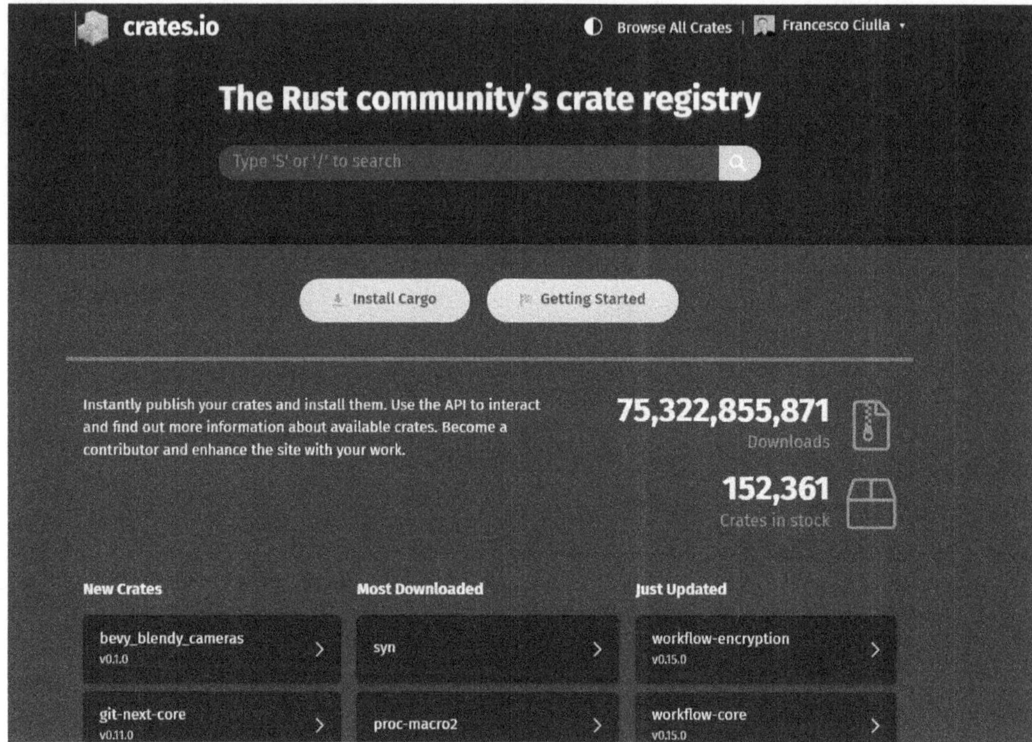

Figure 1.3: crates.io website

Verifying Cargo installation

Before we use Cargo and Crates.io, let's ensure that your system has Rust and Cargo installed:

```
cargo --version
```

If you see something like this, you are good to go; otherwise, check the installation procedure:

```
Francesco ~
$ cargo --version
cargo 1.77.0-nightly (add15366e 2024-01-02)
```

Figure 1.4: Check cargo version on your machine

What is Cargo?

Cargo is an essential tool for Rust development. It simplifies project management, from building and running programs to managing dependencies and publishing packages.

Cargo automates many tasks that would otherwise require manual configuration, making development more efficient. Instead of compiling each file individually, Cargo organizes and builds entire projects with a single command. It also ensures that dependencies are downloaded and used correctly.

Cargo's main features

Cargo provides several built-in commands for common development tasks:

1. **Creating a new project**: Cargo can generate a project structure with the necessary files:

   ```
   cargo new my_project
   ```

   This creates a folder with `Cargo.toml` (which manages dependencies) and a `src` directory for code.

2. **Building and running code**: Instead of compiling files manually, Cargo compiles the entire project:

   ```
   cargo build      # Compiles the project (debug mode)
   cargo run        # Compiles and runs the project
   ```

   For optimized performance, use the `release` mode:

   ```
   cargo build --release
   ```

   This produces a faster executable by applying optimizations.

3. **Managing dependencies**: Cargo makes it easy to add external libraries (called "crates"):

   ```
   cargo add serde
   ```

   This updates `Cargo.toml` and downloads the required dependencies automatically.

4. **Running tests**: Cargo includes a built-in testing framework:

   ```
   cargo test
   ```

   This runs all test functions in the project.

5. **Checking code without full compilation**: For quick feedback on potential errors, use the following:

```
cargo check
```

This is much faster than `cargo build` and helps catch issues early.

Stable versus Nightly Rust

Cargo also manages different versions of Rust. The default version is Stable Rust, which receives updates every six weeks and is recommended for most projects.

For developers who need access to experimental features, Cargo supports Nightly Rust, which can be installed with the following:

```
rustup install nightly
rustup default nightly
```

Nightly Rust includes features that may become part of future stable versions. However, it may be less stable than the default version.

Creating a new Rust project

With Rust and Cargo installed, you can create a new Rust project using the `cargo new` command. Open your terminal or command prompt and navigate to the directory where you want to create your project. Then, run the following command:

```
cargo new my_project
```

Replace `my_project` with the desired name of your project. This command will create a new directory named `my_project` containing the files and folders necessary for a basic Rust project.

Managing dependencies with Cargo.toml

When you create a new Rust project with Cargo, it generates a file named `Cargo.toml`. This file serves as the manifest for your project and contains metadata about your project, including its name, version, authors, and dependencies.

The `.toml` extension is used for configuration files in Rust projects because **TOML (Tom's Obvious, Minimal Language**, `https://toml.io/en/`) provides a human-readable format that is easy to write and understand. This makes it ideal for specifying project dependencies, build settings, and other configuration details concisely and intuitively.

Let's take a look at an example `Cargo.toml` file:

```
[package]
name = "my_project"
version = "0.1.0"
authors = ["Your Name <your@email.com>"]
edition = "2024"

[dependencies]
```

In the `[dependencies]` section, you can specify the dependencies required by your project. You can add dependencies manually by editing the `Cargo.toml` file, or you can use Cargo commands to manage dependencies automatically.

Installing dependencies from Crates.io

To install the dependencies, you usually just modify the `Cargo.toml` file.

An alternative is to use the `cargo add` command. For example, to add the `rand` crate, which provides random number generation functionality, run the following command:

```
cargo add rand
```

This command will automatically update your `Cargo.toml` file to include the `rand` crate as a dependency and fetch the latest version from `Crates.io`.

Cargo.lock: keeping dependencies consistent

When Cargo installs dependencies, it locks the exact versions in a file called `Cargo.lock`. This ensures that all developers working on the project use the same dependency versions, avoiding unexpected updates.

`Cargo.lock` is similar to `package-lock.json` in `npm` or `Pipfile.lock` in Python, as it records the resolved versions of all dependencies and their subdependencies.

Cargo automatically updates `Cargo.lock` when dependencies change, so you don't need to edit it manually.

To update dependencies explicitly, use the following:

```
cargo update
```

This will fetch the latest compatible versions based on the constraints in `Cargo.toml` and update `Cargo.lock` accordingly.

Building your project

Once you've set up your project and added any necessary dependencies, you can build and run your project using Cargo commands. By default, Cargo builds in debug mode, which includes additional debugging information and fewer optimizations.

To build your project, navigate to your project directory in the terminal and run the following:

```
cargo build
```

This generates a debug binary inside the `target/debug/` directory. Debug mode is useful for development because it compiles faster and provides better error messages.

For an optimized build with full compiler optimizations, use the following:

```
cargo build --release
```

This produces a release binary inside `target/release/`, which is faster but takes longer to compile.

Running your project with Cargo

Instead of manually executing the compiled binary after using `cargo build` or `cargo build --release`, Cargo provides a more efficient way to compile and run your project in a single step:

```
cargo run
```

This command automatically compiles the project if necessary and then runs the binary from `target/debug/`. If no changes were made since the last build, Cargo skips recompilation and executes the existing binary.

Initializing a new Rust project with cargo init

When starting a new Rust project, you have two main commands to choose from: `cargo new` and `cargo init`. Both simplify the setup process by generating the necessary files and directories for your project, but they serve slightly different purposes:

- `cargo new`: Used to create a brand-new project in a new directory. It's ideal when starting a project from scratch.
- `cargo init`: Used to initialize a Rust project in an existing directory. This is useful if you already have a folder set up and want to turn it into a Rust project.

For example, if you're working in a pre-existing directory, navigate to it in your terminal and run the following:

```
cargo init
```

This command generates two key components:

- `Cargo.toml`: The manifest file containing project metadata such as the name, version, and dependencies
- **The `src/` directory**: Contains your Rust source code, including a `main.rs` file for binary (executable) projects

If you're starting from scratch and want Cargo to create a new directory for you, use the following:

```
cargo new your_project_name
```

This creates a new folder named `your_project_name` with the same structure as `cargo init`, which, by default, generates a binary (executable) project containing a `main.rs` file.

Choose the command that fits your workflow: `cargo new` for a fresh start, or `cargo init` for existing directories. Either way, you can jump right into coding once the project is set up.

Creating a library with cargo init --lib

Alternatively, if you intend to create a Rust library (a reusable crate) instead of a binary project, you can utilize the `--lib` option with the `cargo init` command. This option tells Cargo to generate a library project structure instead of a binary project.

To create a new Rust library project, execute the following command:

```
cargo init --lib your_library_name
```

Cargo generates a project structure tailored for a library with the `--lib` option. This structure includes a `src/` directory with a file named `lib.rs`, which contains the initial code for your library.

This tells Cargo to generate a library project structure instead of a binary project. The key differences are as follows:

- Library (`--lib`) versus binary (`cargo init` default):
    - A binary project (default) creates a `src/main.rs` file, which acts as the entry point for execution
    - A library project (`--lib`) creates a `src/lib.rs` file instead, which contains reusable functions and modules but no main function

- Purpose:
    - Binary crates: Used for building applications that run as standalone programs
    - Library crates: Used for writing reusable Rust code that can be imported into other Rust projects via `Cargo.toml`
- How it's used:
    - A binary crate runs with `cargo run`
    - A library crate is imported into other Rust projects with the following:

    ```
    extern crate your_library_name;
    ```

Your first real Rust program: a CLI calculator

While a `"Hello, World!"` program is an excellent first step, it only touches the surface of what Rust is capable of. Let's take it a step further by building a simple command-line calculator that can perform basic arithmetic operations based on user input.

This small project will introduce you to key concepts in Rust, including the following:

- Handling user input using `std::io`
- Using functions to organize code efficiently
- Error handling with match expressions
- Working with numbers and string parsing using the `parse()` method

Step 1: Setting up your project

First, create a new Rust project using Cargo:

```
cargo new cli_calculator
cd cli_calculator
```

Open `src/main.rs` in your favorite IDE and let's start coding!

Step 2: Writing the calculator logic

We will build a simple calculator that does the following:

- Prompts the user for two numbers
- Asks for an operation (+, -, *, or /)
- Performs the calculation and displays the result

Here's the complete code, followed by a deeper explanation (Don't worry if you don't fully understand the code below. This is just to get used to the Rust code. We will get into all the concepts and constructs used in the example below in the upcoming chapters. Take this as a trailer!):

```
// Import the standard input/output library to handle user input
use std::io;

fn main() {
    // Display a welcome message to introduce the program
    println!("Welcome to the Rust CLI Calculator!");

    // Prompt the user to enter the first number
    // We use a helper function `get_number` to handle input validation
    let num1 = get_number("Enter the first number: ");

    // Prompt the user to enter the second number
    let num2 = get_number("Enter the second number: ");

    // Prompt the user to enter an operation
    println!("Enter an operation (+, -, *, /):");

    // Create a mutable string to store the user's input
    let mut operation = String::new();

    // Read the user's input and store it in `operation`
    io::stdin().read_line(&mut operation).expect("Failed to read input");

    // Trim any whitespace (e.g., newline) from the input
    let operation = operation.trim();

    // Perform the calculation based on the chosen operation
    let result = match operation {
        "+" => Some(num1 + num2), // Addition
        "-" => Some(num1 - num2), // Subtraction
        "*" => Some(num1 * num2), // Multiplication
        "/" => {
            // Before dividing, check that the second number is not zero
            if num2 != 0.0 {
```

```
                Some(num1 / num2) // Division
            } else {
                println!("Error: Division by zero is not allowed.");
                None // Return None if division by zero is attempted
            }
        }
        _ => {
            // If the user enters an invalid operation, print an error
message
            println!("Invalid operation. Please enter +, -, *, or /.");
            None // Return None to indicate an invalid operation
        }
    };

    // If the result is valid (not None), print the result
    if let Some(res) = result {
        println!("Result: {}", res);
    }
}

// This function prompts the user to enter a number and ensures valid
input
fn get_number(prompt: &str) -> f64 {
    loop { // Infinite loop until valid input is provided
        println!("{}", prompt); // Display the prompt message

        let mut input = String::new(); // Create a new mutable string for
user input
        io::stdin().read_line(&mut input).expect("Failed to read input");
// Read input

        // Try to convert the input string into a floating-point number
(f64)
        match input.trim().parse::<f64>() {
            Ok(num) => return num, // If parsing succeeds, return the
number
```

```
            Err(_) => println!("Invalid number. Please enter a valid
numeric value."), // If parsing fails, prompt again
        }
    }
}
```

Let's look at a detailed explanation:

- **Handling user input** (`io::stdin().read_line()`):
    - Reads input as a string, which is then trimmed to remove extra spaces and newlines
    - Used for both numbers and the operation selection
- **Validating numeric input** (the `get_number()` function):
    - Uses a loop to repeatedly ask the user for input until a valid number is provided
    - `parse::<f64>()` converts the input string into a floating-point number
    - If the input is not a number, it prints an error message and retries
- **Using `match` for decision-making**:
    - Determines which arithmetic operation to perform
    - Prevents division by zero, an important safety check
    - Returns `None` for invalid operations, preventing incorrect calculations
- Displaying the result (`if let Some(res) = result`):
    - If a valid result exists (`Some(value)`), it prints it
    - If an error occurred (e.g., invalid operation, division by zero), no incorrect result is shown

Step 3: Running the program

Now, compile and run your calculator:

```
cargo run
```

Try entering different numbers and operations. If you enter invalid input, the program will prompt you until a valid number is provided.

What you learned

This simple CLI calculator introduced several fundamental Rust concepts:

- Handling user input using `std::io::stdin()`
- Using functions to keep the code modular and readable
- Error handling with `match` expressions and loops for input validation
- String parsing and working with numbers using `.trim()` and `.parse()`

This is just the beginning! Don't worry if you don't understand everything now; this was meant to give you an idea of what Rust code looks like and to help you become familiar with the Rust syntax!

Functions

In this final section of the chapter, we'll explore functions, a fundamental building block of Rust programs. Functions allow you to encapsulate and reuse logic throughout your code, making it more modular and easier to maintain. Defining and using functions is essential for writing effective Rust programs.

Functions in Rust are defined using the `fn` keyword, followed by the function name, parameters, and the function body. Let's define a simple function to see how it works.

Functions example

In Rust, functions can be defined globally (outside `main`) or locally (inside another function). This example shows both approaches:

```
// Global function (available everywhere)
fn add(a: i32, b: i32) -> i32 {
    a + b
}

fn main() {
    // Local function (only available inside main)
    fn greet(name: &str) {
        println!("Hello, {}!", name);
    }
```

```
    // Call the local function
    greet("Alice");
    greet("Bob");

    // Call the global function
    let sum = add(1, 2);
    println!("The sum is: {}", sum);
}
```

In this example, we see both the function definition and the function invocation:

- **Function definition:**
    - The `greet` function takes a single parameter name of the `&str` type (a string slice), and prints a greeting message. This demonstrates how to define a function and use parameters.
    - The `add` function takes two parameters (`a` and `b`) of the `i32` type (32-bit integers) and returns their sum. This demonstrates how to define a function that returns a value.
- **Function invocation:**
    - We call the `greet` function twice with different arguments (`"Alice"` and `"Bob"`), demonstrating how to pass arguments to functions.
    - We call the `add` function with arguments of `5` and `7`, store the result in the variable sum, and print it.

These are just a few of the core syntax concepts in Rust. In this chapter, we've introduced the basics of Rust programming, including variables and mutability, data types, control flow, and functions. Each of these topics is crucial for building a solid foundation in Rust.

As we progress through the book, we'll explore more advanced topics and dive deeper into Rust's syntax and features. Each chapter will provide detailed explanations, practical examples, questions, and assignments to help you master Rust programming. By the end of this book, you'll have a comprehensive understanding of Rust and be well equipped to tackle complex programming challenges confidently.

Summary

In this opening chapter, we took our first steps into Rust programming. We explored why Rust has become such a hot topic among developers and how its unique features make it stand out in various fields, such as system programming and web development.

Getting practical, we talked about setting up your Rust development environment. We ensured that you're all set to start writing code, from installing Rust to initializing your first project.

We also introduced you to Cargo, Rust's trusty package manager and build system. We showed you how to use it for project management, handling dependencies, and publishing your work.

As we wrap up this chapter, you now understand Rust's basics and practical tools. Armed with this knowledge, you can confidently start your Rust journey. So, let's dive in and explore what Rust has to offer!

Questions

Before we proceed to the next chapter, let's take a moment to reflect on a few key questions. Note that the answers to the questions can be found in Appendix B (Online).

These questions reinforce the concepts discussed in this chapter and ensure a solid understanding as we move forward:

1. What key features of Rust make it stand out among other programming languages?
2. How does Rust ensure memory safety and prevent common programming errors?
3. What is Cargo, and what role does it play in Rust development?
4. Can you provide examples of projects or domains where Rust is commonly used?
5. Considering its unique features and syntax, how can beginners approach learning Rust effectively?

2

Rust Syntax and Functions

In this chapter, we will dive deep into the foundational aspects of Rust programming, focusing on the language's syntax and functions. Understanding these basics is crucial as they form the building blocks for more advanced Rust programming concepts. This chapter aims to provide a comprehensive overview of variable declarations, data types, functions, control flow constructs, and error handling in Rust. By the end of this chapter, you will have a solid understanding of how to write basic Rust programs, manipulate data, and handle errors effectively.

Rust is known for its strict and expressive syntax, which enforces safety and correctness in your code. By learning Rust's syntax, you will not only write more reliable programs but also gain a deeper understanding of how Rust ensures memory safety and performance. We will start with the fundamental concept of variable declarations and mutability, exploring how Rust handles data storage and manipulation. This foundation will help you appreciate the language's design philosophy and how it guides you towards writing safe and efficient code.

Next, we will dive into Rust's data types and structures, which are essential for organizing and managing data. Rust provides a rich set of built-in data types, including integers, floating-point numbers, booleans, and characters. Additionally, Rust's compound types, such as tuples and arrays, allow you to group multiple values together. Understanding these types and how to use them effectively is crucial for building robust applications.

Functions are another critical aspect of Rust programming. We will explore how to define and use functions in Rust, including how Rust's ownership model affects data passing in and out of functions. This section will cover the syntax for function definitions, parameter passing, and return values, providing you with the tools to write modular and reusable code.

Control flow constructs such as `if`, `else`, loops, and pattern matching are vital for writing dynamic and responsive programs. We will examine how Rust implements these constructs and how you can use them to control the flow of your programs effectively. Understanding control flow is key to writing programs that can respond to different conditions and inputs.

Finally, we will discuss Rust's approach to error handling. Rust's robust error handling mechanisms, including the `Result` and `Option` types, allow you to write programs that gracefully handle unexpected conditions. We will also look at the `panic!` macro, which provides a way to handle unrecoverable errors. Mastering Rust's error handling strategies will enable you to build reliable and resilient applications.

Throughout this chapter, we will provide detailed explanations, examples, and exercises to help you grasp these concepts and apply them in your own Rust projects. By the end of this chapter, you will have a strong foundation in Rust syntax and functions, preparing you for more advanced topics in subsequent chapters.

Variable declarations and mutability

One of the first concepts you'll encounter in Rust is how it handles variables, and this reveals a core piece of its design philosophy. In Rust, variables are **immutable by default**. This might feel different if you're coming from languages such as Python, JavaScript, C++, or Java, where variables are typically mutable unless you explicitly mark them as constant (e.g., with `const` or `final`). Rust flips this convention on its head: you must **explicitly** opt in to mutability. This design choice is intentional; it encourages a safer programming style by preventing accidental or unintended changes to a variable's value, which is a common source of bugs.

This emphasis on immutability makes your code easier to reason about, as you know that most variables won't change their value after being initialized. However, Rust is a practical language and understands that mutability is often necessary. For those situations, it provides the `mut` keyword, allowing you to declare a variable as mutable when you truly need its value to change. This way, any mutation in your code is a deliberate, clearly marked action.

Immutable variables

In Rust, you declare an immutable variable using the `let` keyword. Immutable variables are a cornerstone of Rust's safety guarantees, ensuring that values do not change unexpectedly, which can help avoid many common programming errors.

```
fn main() {
    let x = 5;
```

```
    println!("The value of x is: {}", x);
    // x = 6; // This line would cause a compile-time error because x is
immutable
}
```

In the preceding example, x is declared as an immutable variable with a value of 5. Any attempt to modify x will result in a compile-time error, enforcing the immutability guarantee.

Rust's preference for immutability by default helps in maintaining a clear and predictable state throughout your program. This makes it easier to track how data changes over time, reducing the likelihood of bugs caused by unintended modifications.

Mutable variables

While immutability is the default, there are cases where you need to change a variable's value. Rust allows you to declare mutable variables using the `mut` keyword. Mutable variables provide the flexibility to update and manage state as needed while maintaining control over when and where changes can occur.

```
fn main() {
    let mut x = 5;
    println!("The value of x is: {}", x);
    x = 6; // This is allowed because x is mutable
    println!("The value of x is: {}", x);
}
```

In this example, x is declared as mutable, allowing its value to be changed from 5 to 6. Using `mut` gives you the flexibility to modify variables while still adhering to Rust's safety principles.

Shadowing

Rust also supports a feature known as shadowing, where you can declare a new variable with the same name as a previous variable. The new variable shadows the previous one, effectively creating a new variable while retaining the name.

A real-world analogy for understanding shadowing in Rust is the concept of "overwriting" a draft on a whiteboard.

Imagine you are a teacher writing on a whiteboard. You start by writing the number 5 on the board:

1. You write "5" on the whiteboard.
2. Then, you decide to update this number by adding 1 to it. Instead of erasing the original number, you write a new number "6" on top of the old one, effectively "shadowing" the original number.

In this analogy:

- The whiteboard represents the variable name
- The numbers you write represent the values assigned to the variable
- Each time you write a new number, you are creating a new value while keeping the same name (the whiteboard)

This way, you can keep updating the value without changing the original number directly, similar to how shadowing works in Rust. Each new value is a fresh start, but it uses the same name, allowing you to transform the value step by step while maintaining immutability.

Let's see an example:

```
fn main() {
    let x = 5;
    let x = x + 1; // This shadows the previous x
    println!("The value of x is: {}", x);
}
```

In this example, the second declaration of x shadows the first one. This allows you to reuse variable names in a safe way, enabling transformations and updates without mutability.

Shadowing is useful in situations where you want to perform a transformation on a value and maintain immutability. Each shadowed variable is a new variable, allowing you to apply transformations step by step without modifying the original value.

Understanding variable declarations and mutability is the first step in mastering Rust's syntax. With these concepts, you can start to write more complex and expressive Rust code, building a solid foundation for further exploration of the language's features.

Data types and structures

Rust provides a rich set of built-in data types that allow you to store and manipulate data efficiently. Understanding these types is essential for effective Rust programming. Rust's data types can be broadly categorized into scalar types and compound types.

Scalar types

Scalar types represent a single value. Rust's scalar types include integers, floating-point numbers, Booleans, and characters.

Integers

Integers are whole numbers, and Rust provides a variety of types for them, giving you precise control over memory and data representation. Each integer type is defined by its **size** (the number of bits it uses, such as 8, 16, 32, 64, or 128) and whether it is **signed** (can be negative, starts with i) or **unsigned** (only zero and positive, starts with u). For example, an i8 can hold numbers from -128 to 127, while a u8 can hold numbers from 0 to 255. Choosing the appropriate type allows you to optimize memory usage and ensure your variables can hold the range of values you expect.

The special types `isize` and `usize` have a size that matches the architecture of the target machine (e.g., 64 bits on a 64-bit system) and are the idiomatic choice for indexing collections such as arrays.

These types differ in size and whether they can represent negative values.

```
fn main() {
    let signed_int: i32 = -42;
    let unsigned_int: u32 = 42;
    println!("Signed integer: {}, Unsigned integer: {}", signed_int,
unsigned_int);
}
```

Floating-point numbers

Rust provides two floating-point types, `f32` and `f64`, for representing decimal numbers. The default type is `f64` because it is more precise.

```
fn main() {
    let float_num: f64 = 3.14;
    println!("Floating-point number: {}", float_num);
}
```

Booleans

The boolean type `bool` represents a value that can be either true or false.

```
fn main() {
    let is_rust_fun: bool = true;
    println!("Is Rust fun? {}", is_rust_fun);
}
```

Characters

The character type `char` represents a single Unicode scalar value, which can be used to store a wide range of characters, including letters, numbers, and symbols.

```
fn main() {
    let letter: char = 'R';
    let emoji: char = '😊';
    println!("Letter: {}, Emoji: {}", letter, emoji);
}
```

Compound types

Compound types can group multiple values into one type. The two primary compound types in Rust are tuples and arrays.

Tuples

Tuples are a simple way to group together a fixed number of values with a variety of types into a single compound type. Once declared, a tuple's length cannot change. They are great for bundling a few related pieces of data without the need to create a full struct.

There are two primary ways to access the elements inside a tuple: **destructuring** and **direct indexing.**

```
fn main() {
    // A tuple holding an integer, a float, and a character.
    let my_tuple: (i32, f64, char) = (500, 6.4, 'R');

    // Method 1: Destructuring with a `let` binding.
    // This is a form of pattern matching that breaks the tuple into
separate variables.
    let (x, y, z) = my_tuple;
```

```
    println!("Destructured values: x = {}, y = {}, z = {}", x, y, z);

    // Method 2: Direct access using dot notation and the element's index.
    // Indices start from 0.
    let first_element = my_tuple.0;
    let second_element = my_tuple.1;
    println!("Direct access: First element is {}, second is {}", first_
element, second_element);
}
```

One of the most common and idiomatic uses for tuples in Rust is to return multiple values from a function. This is often cleaner and more lightweight than defining a new struct just for a single function's return type.

```
// This function calculates a sum and a product and returns both in a
tuple.
fn calculate_sum_and_product(a: i32, b: i32) -> (i32, i32) {
    (a + b, a * b) // The last expression in a function is its return
value
}

fn main() {
    let input1 = 10;
    let input2 = 5;

    // Call the function and destructure the returned tuple directly into
variables.
    let (sum_result, product_result) = calculate_sum_and_product(input1,
input2);

    println!("For {} and {}:", input1, input2);
    println!("  Sum: {}", sum_result);         // Output: 15
    println!("  Product: {}", product_result); // Output: 50
}
```

As you can see, tuples provide a convenient way to handle small, fixed-size collections of heterogeneous data. While the `let` binding is a simple form of pattern matching, you'll see later, in the *Control flow constructs* section, how the `match` statement can be used for even more powerful pattern matching on tuples.

Arrays

Arrays are collections of multiple values that must all have the same type. In Rust, an array is an **owned type**, which means the data it contains is stored directly as part of the array itself (usually contiguously on the stack). A key characteristic of arrays is that they have a fixed length, which is known at compile time and cannot be changed once declared.

```
fn main() {
    let array: [i32; 3] = [1, 2, 3];
    println!("Array values: {} {} {}", array[0], array[1], array[2]);
}
```

Arrays are beneficial when you need to store a fixed-size list of elements. However, their fixed length can be a limitation in scenarios where you need a dynamically sized list.

Slices

Slices provide a way to reference a contiguous sequence of elements within a collection (such as an array or a Vec) without needing to copy the data. A slice is a **view** or a **borrowed reference** into a portion of that collection. Crucially, slices **do not own** the data they point to; the ownership remains with the original collection. This makes them an incredibly safe and efficient way to work with sub-sections of data.

To better visualize this, imagine an array in memory:

```
Array: [ 10, 20, 30, 40, 50 ]
Index: 0, 1, 2, 3, 4
```

If we create a slice that refers to the elements at index 1 and 2, the slice is simply a "view" pointing to that specific portion of the original array's data:

```
Slice:    &[ 20, 30 ]
              ^   ^
              |   |
```

Points to index 1 and 2 of the original array.

This is how you create a slice in code:

```
fn main() {
    let array = [10, 20, 30, 40, 50];
    // Create a slice that references elements from index 1 up to (but not
including) index 3.
```

```
    // The type of `slice` is `&[i32]`.
    let slice = &array[1..3];
    println!("Original array: {:?}", array);
    println!("Slice (a view into the array): {:?}", slice); // Output:
[20, 30]
}
```

Slices are especially useful for working with parts of arrays or other collections without copying data.

They provide a safe and efficient way to access sub-sections of data.

Strings

Strings in Rust are a bit more complex than simple scalar types. Rust has two main types of strings: `String` and `&str` (string slice).

String

This is a growable, heap-allocated data structure. It is mutable and can store a dynamic number of characters.

```
fn main() {
    let mut s = String::from("Hello");
    s.push_str(", world!");
    println!("{}", s);
}
```

&str

This is an immutable reference to a string slice. It can refer to a part of a `String` or a string literal.

```
fn main() {
    let s = "Hello, world!"; // string literal
    println!("{}", s);
}
```

Understanding and using these data types and structures effectively will enable you to organize and manage your data efficiently in Rust. As you become more familiar with these types, you'll be able to write more complex and efficient Rust programs.

With a solid understanding of Rust's variable declarations, mutability, and data types, we can now move on to exploring how Rust handles functions, including syntax, parameter passing, and return values. This will include a look at how Rust's ownership model applies to data passed into and out of functions.

Structs

Structs are a fundamental feature in Rust that allow you to create custom data types. Structs group together related data, allowing you to create complex data structures with named fields.

Rust has three types of structs: classic structs, tuple structs, and unit structs.

Classic structs

Classic structs are the most commonly used type of struct. They allow you to define a data structure with named fields. Each field in a struct can have a different type, and you can access these fields using dot notation. We will see structs in more details in *Chapter 5*.

```
struct User {
    username: String,
    email: String,
    sign_in_count: u64,
    active: bool,
}

fn main() {
    let user1 = User {
        username: String::from("someusername123"),
        email: String::from("someone@example.com"),
        sign_in_count: 1,
        active: true,
    };

    println!("Username: {}", user1.username);
    println!("Email: {}", user1.email);
    println!("Sign in count: {}", user1.sign_in_count);
    println!("Active: {}", user1.active);
}
```

In this example, the `User` struct has four fields: `username`, `email`, `sign_in_count`, and `active`. The `main` function creates an instance of `User` and prints the values of its fields.

Tuple structs

Tuple structs are similar to classic structs but use unnamed fields. They are useful when you want to group a few values together without needing named fields.

```
struct Color(i32, i32, i32);
fn main() {
    let black = Color(0, 0, 0);

    println!("Black: ({}, {}, {})", black.0, black.1, black.2);
}
```

In this example, the `Color` struct is defined with three unnamed fields. The fields are accessed using dot notation with indices.

Unit structs

Unit structs are the simplest form of structs and do not have any fields. They are useful for creating types that don't need to store data but still need to implement certain traits.

```
struct AlwaysEqual;

fn main() {
    let _subject = AlwaysEqual;
}
```

In this example, the `AlwaysEqual` struct has no fields. It can be used to implement traits or mark specific types in your code.

Note

A struct can either hold its own data or borrowed data.

Struct initialization and update syntax

When creating instances of structs, you can use the struct update syntax to create a new instance based on an existing one. This is especially useful when most of the fields in the new instance have the same values as an existing instance.

```
struct User {
    username: String,
```

```
    email: String,
    sign_in_count: u64,
    active: bool,
}

fn main() {
    let user1 = User {
        username: String::from("user1"),
        email: String::from("user1@example.com"),
        sign_in_count: 1,
        active: true,
    };

    let user2 = User {
        email: String::from("user2@example.com"),
        ..user1 // Copies the remaining fields from user1
    };

    println!("Username: {}", user2.username);
    println!("Email: {}", user2.email);
    println!("Sign in count: {}", user2.sign_in_count);
    println!("Active: {}", user2.active);
}
```

In this example, the `user2` instance is created using the struct update syntax, copying the `username`, `sign_in_count`, and `active` fields from `user1` and providing a new value for the `email` field.

Methods and associated functions

Methods

You can define methods and associated functions for structs to provide behavior associated with your data types. Methods are defined within an `impl` block.

```
struct Rectangle {
    width: u32,
    height: u32,
}
```

```
impl Rectangle {
    fn area(&self) -> u32 {
        self.width * self.height
    }

    fn can_hold(&self, other: &Rectangle) -> bool {
        self.width > other.width && self.height > other.height
    }
}

fn main() {
    let rect1 = Rectangle {
        width: 30,
        height: 50,
    };

    let rect2 = Rectangle {
        width: 10,
        height: 40,
    };

    let rect3 = Rectangle {
        width: 60,
        height: 45,
    };

    println!("The area of rect1 is {} square pixels.", rect1.area());
    println!("Can rect1 hold rect2? {}", rect1.can_hold(&rect2));
    println!("Can rect1 hold rect3? {}", rect1.can_hold(&rect3));
}
```

In this example, the `Rectangle` struct has two methods: `area` and `can_hold`. The `area` method calculates the area of the rectangle, and the `can_hold` method checks if the rectangle can contain another rectangle.

Associated functions

Associated functions are functions that are associated with a struct but do not take `self` as a parameter. They are often used to define constructors or other functions that are related to the struct but do not operate on a specific instance.

```
impl Rectangle {
    fn square(size: u32) -> Rectangle {
        Rectangle {
            width: size,
            height: size,
        }
    }
}

fn main() {
    let sq = Rectangle::square(3);
    println!("The area of the square is {} square pixels.", sq.area());
}
```

In this example, the `square` function is an associated function of the `Rectangle` struct. It creates a new `Rectangle` instance with equal width and height.

Understanding and using structs effectively will allow you to define and manage complex data structures in Rust, providing a solid foundation for building robust applications. With a comprehensive grasp of variable declarations, data types, and structs, you are now ready to explore functions in Rust, including syntax, parameter passing, and how Rust's ownership model affects data passing.

Enums

Enums, short for enumerations, are a powerful feature in Rust that allow you to define a type by enumerating its possible variants. Enums are particularly useful when you need to work with a value that can be one of several distinct types. We will explore more enums in *Chapter 5*.

Enums can also hold data, making them extremely versatile for various programming scenarios.

Defining enums

Enums can hold different types of data. Each variant of an enum can have associated data of different types and structures, much like a struct. This is one of the features that makes enums in Rust so powerful.

Let's use a Color enum to see this in action. A color can be represented in multiple ways—for example, as an RGB triplet or by a name. An enum is a perfect way to model this.

```
#[derive(Debug)]
enum Color {
    // A variant that holds a tuple of three 8-bit unsigned integers
    Rgb(u8, u8, u8),
    // A variant that holds a single String
    Named(String),
}

fn main() {
    let red = Color::Rgb(255, 0, 0);
    let custom_color = Color::Named(String::from("Forest Green"));

    println!("An RGB color: {:?}", red);
    println!("A named color: {:?}", custom_color);
}
```

In this example, the Color enum has two variants that each hold different types of data. The Rgb variant holds a tuple of three u8 values, perfect for representing a standard RGB color, while the Named variant holds a String to represent a color by its name. This demonstrates the versatility of Rust enums: a single Color type can elegantly represent different ways of defining a color, each with its own associated data.

Matching with enums

One of the most powerful features of enums is pattern matching. The match expression allows you to execute code based on which variant of the enum you have.

We will see the match statement later in *Chapter 5*. For now, you can just consider it as a switch statement on steroids.

```
enum Message {
    Quit,
    Move { x: i32, y: i32 },
    Write(String),
    ChangeColor(i32, i32, i32),
}
```

```
fn main() {
    let msg = Message::Move { x: 10, y: 20 };

    match msg {
        Message::Quit => println!("Quit message"),
        Message::Move { x, y } => println!("Move to x: {}, y: {}", x, y),
        Message::Write(text) => println!("Write message: {}", text),
        Message::ChangeColor(r, g, b) => println!("Change color to red:
{}, green: {}, blue: {}", r, g, b),
    }
}
```

In this example, the `Message` enum has four variants, each capable of holding different types of data. The `match` expression checks which variant is present and executes the corresponding code block.

Enum methods

Enums, like structs, can have methods associated with them. Methods are defined within an `impl` block.

```
enum Message {
    Quit,
    Move { x: i32, y: i32 },
    Write(String),
    ChangeColor(i32, i32, i32),
}

impl Message {
    fn call(&self) {
        match self {
            Message::Quit => println!("Quit message"),
            Message::Move { x, y } => println!("Move to x: {}, y: {}", x,
y),
            Message::Write(text) => println!("Write message: {}", text),
            Message::ChangeColor(r, g, b) => println!("Change color to
red: {}, green: {}, blue: {}", r, g, b),
        }
    }
}
```

In this example, we define a method call for the `Message` enum that matches on `self` and prints a message based on the variant. This encapsulates the behavior associated with each variant within the enum itself.

Enums provide a powerful way to define types that can be one of a few different variants. This makes your code more expressive and type-safe, reducing the likelihood of errors and making your intentions clear.

Beyond representing data such as colors, enums are also excellent for modeling different kinds of actions or commands that a program might need to process.

This allows you to handle a variety of operations in a structured and type-safe way. For example, you could define a `Command` enum to represent different user actions.

We can then use a `match` statement (which we'll explore in detail in the control flow section) to execute different code depending on which command is received.

```
enum Command {
    Start,
    Stop,
    Move(i32, i32),
}

fn process_command(command: Command) {
    match command {
        Command::Start => println!("Starting..."),
        Command::Stop => println!("Stopping..."),
        Command::Move(x, y) => println!("Moving to coordinates: x = {}, y
= {}", x, y),
    }
}

fn main() {
    process_command(Command::Start);
    process_command(Command::Move(10, 20));
    process_command(Command::Stop);
}
```

Functions in Rust

Functions are a core component of Rust programming. They provide the means to organize your code into reusable blocks. Functions encapsulate logic, making your code more modular, maintainable, and easier to understand. We will explore more function in *Chapter 3*, but I want to give you a quick overview now.

This section will explore Rust's function syntax, parameter passing, return values, and how Rust's ownership model impacts functions.

Function syntax

In Rust, functions are defined using the `fn` keyword, followed by the function name, a list of parameters, and the function body enclosed in curly braces. Functions can take zero or more parameters and return a value.

```
fn main() {
    println!("Hello, world!");
}

fn greet(name: &str) {
    println!("Hello, {}!", name);
}

fn add(a: i32, b: i32) -> i32 {
    a + b
}
```

Let's break down the preceding example:

- `main` is the entry point of a Rust program and does not take any parameters
- `greet` takes a single parameter of type `&str` (a string slice) and prints a greeting message
- `add` takes two parameters of type `i32` and returns their sum. The return type is specified after the `->` symbol

Parameter passing

Rust supports passing parameters to functions by value, by reference, and by mutable reference. Understanding how these different modes of parameter passing work is crucial for managing data ownership and borrowing in Rust.

Passing by value

When you pass a parameter to a function "by value," what happens depends on the type of data.

For simple, fixed-size types that are stored entirely on the stack (such as integers, booleans, and floating-point numbers), Rust makes a full, bit-for-bit copy of the value. This means the function gets its own independent copy, and the original variable in the calling scope remains valid and unchanged.

```
fn takes_value_copy(mut some_integer: i32) {
    some_integer += 1;
    println!("Value inside function: {}", some_integer);
}

fn main() {
    let x = 5;
    takes_value_copy(x);
    println!("Original value of x after function call: {}", x); // x is
still 5
}
```

However, for more complex types that manage data on the heap (such as `String` or `Vec<T>`), passing by value results in an **ownership transfer**, also known as a **move**. The function takes ownership of the value, and the original variable in the calling scope is no longer valid and cannot be used. This is a key part of Rust's memory safety, as it prevents multiple owners from trying to modify or deallocate the same data. We will discuss this in an upcoming chapter.

Passing by reference

Often, you want a function to use a value without taking ownership of it. This is called **borrowing**, and you do it by passing a **reference** (`&T`). A reference allows a function to access the data without owning it, which is highly efficient as it avoids copying large amounts of data. An immutable reference (`&T`) allows the function to read the data but not modify it.

```
// This function borrows a String and calculates its length.
fn calculate_length(s: &String) -> usize {
```

```
    s.len()
} // `s` goes out of scope here, but since it doesn't have ownership, the
data is not dropped.

fn main() {
    let s1 = String::from("hello");

    // We pass a reference to s1 using the `&` operator.
    // s1 is borrowed, not moved.
    let len = calculate_length(&s1);

    println!("The length of '{}' is {}.", s1, len);
    // `s1` is still valid here because its ownership was never
transferred.
}
```

Passing by mutable reference

Passing a parameter by mutable reference allows the function to borrow and modify the parameter. This is useful for allowing functions to update data.

```
fn main() {
    let mut s = String::from("hello");
    takes_mutable_reference(&mut s);
    println!("s in main: {}", s); // s is modified by the function
}

fn takes_mutable_reference(some_string: &mut String) {
    some_string.push_str(", world");
}
```

In this example, `takes_mutable_reference` borrows s mutably, allowing it to modify the original `String`.

Return values

Functions in Rust can return values, and the return type is specified after the `->` symbol. The return value can be any type, including custom types such as structs and enums.

```
fn main() {
    let sum = add(5, 3);
```

```
    println!("The sum is: {}", sum);
}

fn add(a: i32, b: i32) -> i32 {
    a + b
}
```

In this example, the add function returns the sum of its two parameters. The return value is specified as i32 after the -> symbol.

Ownership and functions

Rust's ownership model, which we will explore in great detail in *Chapter 4*, plays a significant role in how functions handle data. When you pass a parameter to a function, the ownership of that parameter can change depending on how it's passed. Understanding these rules is essential for writing safe and efficient Rust code.

Let's look at a simple example that illustrates the difference between moving ownership and copying a value:

```
// This function takes ownership of the String passed to it.
fn takes_ownership(some_string: String) {
    println!("Inside takes_ownership: {}", some_string);
} // `some_string` is dropped here, and its memory is freed.

// This function takes a copy of the integer.
fn makes_copy(some_integer: i32) {
    println!("Inside makes_copy: {}", some_integer);
} // `some_integer` goes out of scope, but nothing special happens.

fn main() {
    let s = String::from("hello");
    // `s`'s value is moved into the function...
    takes_ownership(s);
    // ...so `s` is no longer valid here.
    // The next line would cause a compile-time error:
    // println!("Trying to use s after move: {}", s);

    let x = 5;
```

```
    // `x`'s value is copied into the function...
    makes_copy(x);
    // ...so `x` is still valid and can be used here.
    println!("x is still valid after makes_copy: {}", x);
}
```

In this example, when we pass the `String` s to `takes_ownership`, ownership is moved. After the function call, s is no longer valid in `main`. However, when we pass the i32 x to `makes_copy`, a copy is made because `i32` is a simple type with a known size that is stored on the stack.

This raises a common question: what if you want to give a function an owned value like a `String` but still need to use the original variable afterward? For types that support it, you can create an explicit "deep copy" using the `.clone()` method. This creates a brand-new instance of the data, allowing you to move the clone into the function while retaining ownership of the original.

Be mindful that cloning can have a performance cost for large data structures.

```
fn takes_ownership(some_string: String) {
    println!("Function received ownership of: {}", some_string);
}

fn main() {
    let s1 = String::from("hello");

    // We pass a clone of `s1`. The function takes ownership of the clone,
    // not the original `s1`.
    takes_ownership(s1.clone());

    // Because we only moved a clone, `s1` is still valid and can be used
here.
    println!("We can still use s1 after cloning: {}", s1);
}
```

Control flow constructs

Control flow constructs are essential in any programming language, as they allow you to dictate the flow of execution in your programs. Rust provides a variety of control flow mechanisms, including conditional statements (`if` and `else`), loops (`loop`, `while`, and `for`), and pattern matching (`match`). These constructs enable you to build dynamic and responsive applications by controlling how and when different parts of your code are executed.

if and else statements

Conditional statements in Rust allow you to execute code based on certain conditions. The most common conditional statements are `if` and `else`.

```
fn main() {
    let number = 7;

    if number < 5 {
        println!("The number is less than 5");
    } else if number > 5 {
        println!("The number is greater than 5");
    } else {
        println!("The number is exactly 5");
    }
}
```

In this example, the `if` statement checks if `number` is less than 5, greater than 5, or exactly 5, and executes the corresponding block of code.

Rust requires that the condition in an `if` statement be a boolean expression. This ensures clarity and reduces potential errors that can arise from using non-boolean conditions.

Loop constructs

Rust provides several types of loops for repeating code: `loop`, `while`, and `for`. Each type of loop is suited to different use cases.

The loop keyword

The `loop` keyword creates an infinite loop that will run forever until you explicitly tell it to stop. You can exit the loop using the `break` statement.

```
fn main() {
    let mut counter = 0;

    loop {
        counter += 1;
        println!("Counter is now: {}", counter);
        if counter == 5 {
            break; // Exits the loop
```

```
        }
    }
    println!("Loop finished.");
}
```

In this example, the loop runs until the `break` statement is executed when `counter` reaches `5`.

In addition to `break`, Rust provides the `continue` keyword to control loop flow. While `break` exits the loop entirely, `continue` skips over the rest of the current iteration and immediately starts the next one. This is useful when you want to bypass processing for certain values but keep the loop running.

Let's look at an example using a `for` loop (which we'll cover next) to see `continue` in action.

```
fn main() {
    for number in 1..=10 {
        // If the number is odd, skip the println! and go to the next
iteration.
        if number % 2 != 0 {
            continue;
        }
        // This line only runs for even numbers.
        println!("Found an even number: {}", number);
    }
}
```

In this example, the `for` loop iterates from 1 to 10. The `if` statement checks if a number is odd. If it is, `continue` is called, and the loop immediately proceeds to the next number, skipping `println!`. As a result, only the even numbers are printed.

In summary, `break` and `continue` give you fine-grained control over your loops: use `break` to stop the loop entirely and `continue` to skip the current iteration and move to the next.

The while keyword

The `while` keyword creates a loop that runs as long as a condition is true.

```
fn main() {
    let mut number = 3;

    while number != 0 {
        println!("{}!", number);
```

```
        number -= 1;
    }
    println!("Liftoff!");
}
```

In this example, the `while` loop runs until `number` is 0, printing each countdown number.

The for keyword

The `for` keyword creates a loop that iterates over a collection of items, such as an array or a range.

```
fn main() {
    let a = [10, 20, 30, 40, 50];

    for element in a.iter() {
        println!("The value is: {}", element);
    }
}
```

In this example, `a.iter()` creates an iterator over the elements of the array a. The `for` loop then iterates over each element, printing its value.

Using ranges with the for loop

Rust's `range` syntax is highly versatile, allowing you to define both inclusive and exclusive ranges. This is particularly useful for looping a specific number of times without needing to manually manage loop counters.

```
fn main() {
    for number in 1..5 {
        println!("Exclusive range value: {}", number);
    }

    for number in 1..=5 {
        println!("Inclusive range value: {}", number);
    }
}
```

In the first `for` loop, the range `1..5` is exclusive, meaning it includes numbers from 1 to 4. In the second `for` loop, the range `1..=5` is inclusive, meaning it includes numbers from 1 to 5.

Nesting loops

You can also nest `for` loops to iterate over multiple collections or ranges simultaneously. This is useful for multidimensional data structures such as matrices or grids.

```
fn main() {
    let matrix = [
        [1, 2, 3],
        [4, 5, 6],
        [7, 8, 9],
    ];

    for row in matrix.iter() {
        for element in row.iter() {
            print!("{} ", element);
        }
        println!();
    }
}
```

In this example, the outer `for` loop iterates over each row of the matrix, and the inner `for` loop iterates over each element within the row, printing the matrix in a grid format.

Pattern matching with match

Pattern matching with the `match` statement is one of Rust's most powerful features. It allows you to handle complex control flow by matching values against patterns and executing code based on which pattern is matched. The `match` statement can match literals, variables, and wildcards, and can even destructure structs and enums.

Matching literals

You can match literals directly in a `match` statement. This is useful for handling specific values differently.

```
fn main() {
    let number = 1;

    match number {
        1 => println!("One"),
        2 => println!("Two"),
```

```
        3 => println!("Three"),
        _ => println!("Other"),
    }
}
```

In this example, the match statement matches the value of number against the literals 1, 2, and 3. The underscore _ serves as a catch-all pattern for any value that does not match the specified literals.

Matching with variables

You can bind values to variables within a match statement, which is useful for extracting parts of a complex value.

```
fn main() {
    let pair = (2, -2);

    match pair {
        (x, y) if x == y => println!("The numbers are equal"),
        (x, y) if x + y == 0 => println!("The numbers are opposites"),
        (x, y) => println!("Different numbers: ({}, {})", x, y),
    }
}
```

In this example, the match statement matches the tuple pair and binds its elements to x and y. The additional if conditions (called guards) allow for more complex matching logic.

Destructuring enums

Pattern matching is particularly powerful with enums, allowing you to destructure and handle each variant differently.

```
enum Message {
    Quit,
    Move { x: i32, y: i32 },
    Write(String),
    ChangeColor(i32, i32, i32),
}

fn main() {
    let msg = Message::Move { x: 10, y: 20 };
```

```
    match msg {
        Message::Quit => println!("Quit message"),
        Message::Move { x, y } => println!("Move to x: {}, y: {}", x, y),
        Message::Write(text) => println!("Write message: {}", text),
        Message::ChangeColor(r, g, b) => println!("Change color to red:
{}, green: {}, blue: {}", r, g, b),
    }
}
```

In this example, the `Message` enum has four variants, each capable of holding different types of data. The `match` expression checks which variant is present and executes the corresponding block of code.

Combining patterns

Rust allows you to combine multiple patterns in a `match` arm using the | operator, which acts like "or." This lets you execute the same code for several possible values without duplicating logic.

```
fn main() {
    let x = 1;

    match x {
        1 | 2 => println!("The number is one or two"),
        3 => println!("The number is three"),
        _ => println!("It's some other number"),
    }
}
```

In this example, the pattern `1 | 2` will match if the value of x is either 1 or 2.

Adding conditional logic with match guards

Sometimes, a pattern alone isn't specific enough. You might want to execute a `match` arm only if an additional condition is met. For this, Rust provides **match guards**, which are `if` conditions that can be added after a pattern. The code for that arm will only be executed if both the pattern matches *and* the match guard's condition evaluates to true.

Let's look at an example where we only want to match `Point` if it lies on one of the axes, but we also want to check if its coordinates are within a certain range.

```
struct Point {
    x: i32,
    y: i32,
}

fn main() {
    let point = Point { x: 0, y: 10 };

    match point {
        // This arm matches only if x is 0 AND the guard `if y < 5` is
true.
        Point { x: 0, y } if y < 5 => {
            println!("On the y-axis, but close to the origin (y < 5).");
        }
        // This arm matches for any other point where x is 0.
        Point { x: 0, y } => {
            println!("On the y-axis at y = {}", y);
        }
        // This arm matches only if y is 0 AND the guard `if x > 5` is
true.
        Point { x, y: 0 } if x > 5 => {
            println!("On the x-axis, far from the origin (x > 5).");
        }
        // This arm matches for any other point where y is 0.
        Point { x, y: 0 } => {
            println!("On the x-axis at x = {}", x);
        }
        // This arm matches any other point.
        Point { x, y } => {
            println!("Point is at ({}, {})", x, y);
        }
    }
}
```

In this example, the `if y < 5` and `if x > 5` expressions are match guards. They allow you to add more complex conditional logic to your patterns, making `match` an even more expressive and powerful tool for controlling your program's flow.

Matching ranges

You can also match ranges of values using the `..=` syntax.

```
fn main() {
    let x = 5;

    match x {
        1..=5 => println!("One through five"),
        _ => println!("Something else"),
    }
}
```

In this example, the pattern `1..=5` matches if `x` is any value from `1` to `5` inclusive.

Pattern matching with Option

The `Option` type is a commonly used enum in Rust, representing a value that can be either `Some` (containing a value) or `None` (no value).

```
fn main() {
    let some_number = Some(5);
    let absent_number: Option<i32> = None;

    match some_number {
        Some(x) => println!("The number is: {}", x),
        None => println!("No number"),
    }

    match absent_number {
        Some(x) => println!("The number is: {}", x),
        None => println!("No number"),
    }
}
```

In this example, the `match` statements handle both `Some` and `None` variants of the `Option` type, demonstrating how to work with optional values safely.

Understanding and effectively using control flow constructs in Rust will enable you to write dynamic and responsive programs. With these tools, you can control how and when different parts of your code are executed, making your programs more flexible and robust.

Next, we will explore Rust's approach to error handling using the `Result` and `Option` types, as well as the `panic!` macro. This will help you build reliable applications that gracefully handle errors and unexpected conditions.

Understanding Rust's approach to error handling

Before we wrap up this chapter, I want to dedicate some time to understanding a very important aspect and feature of Rust: error handling. We will dive deeper into error handling in *Chapter 6*, but I want to give you an overview of it in this chapter.

Error handling is crucial to building robust and reliable applications. Rust provides a powerful and flexible approach to error handling that ensures your programs can gracefully manage unexpected conditions and recover from errors. In this section, we'll explore Rust's primary error handling tools: the `Result` and `Option` types and the `panic!` macro.

This short section will give you a basic understanding of these concepts, but error handling in Rust is rich and multifaceted.

We will dedicate an entire chapter to diving deeper into these topics later in the book.

For now, let's scratch the surface and get acquainted with Rust's fundamental error handling mechanisms.

Fundamentals of error handling

In Rust, some operations are not guaranteed to succeed. For example, trying to convert a piece of text such as "hello" into a number will fail. When faced with an operation that might fail, you have a choice. For now, we'll look at the simplest, most direct approach: deciding that if an operation fails, it's an unrecoverable error and the program should stop immediately. This is called a **panic**.

Rust provides a couple of helper methods that are shortcuts for this "succeed or panic" logic. You'll often see these in examples and simple programs:

- `.unwrap()`: This method is called on the result of an operation. If the operation was successful, `.unwrap()` gives you the `successful` value. If the operation failed, it will cause your program to panic and crash.

- `.expect("error message")`: This works exactly like `.unwrap()`, but it lets you provide a custom error message that will be displayed when the program panics. This is more helpful for debugging.

These methods are useful when you are confident that an operation will not fail, and a failure would indicate a bug in your program.

```
fn main() {
    // This string can be successfully parsed into a number.
    let number_str = "42";
    // .parse() attempts the conversion. .unwrap() gets the successful 
value.
    let number = number_str.parse::<i32>().unwrap();
    println!("Successfully parsed number: {}", number);

    // This string CANNOT be parsed into a number.
    let invalid_str = "hello world";

    // The line below would cause the program to panic and crash.
    // We use .expect() to provide a clear message upon failure.
    // let invalid_number = invalid_str.parse::<i32>()
    //     .expect("Failed to parse the string into a number!");

    // Because the line above is commented out, this program will run 
without error.
    // If you uncomment it, the program will panic and this line will not 
be reached.
    println!("This line will not be reached if the expect() call 
panics.");
}
```

While `unwrap()` and `expect()` are convenient, they should be used with care because they can make your program crash. In the chapter dedicated to error handling, we will explore much more robust ways to handle operations that can fail without panicking.

The Result type

The `Result` type is a powerful tool for error handling in Rust. It is an enum that can be either `Ok` or `Err`, representing success and failure, respectively. The `Result` type is commonly used for functions that can return an error.

```
fn divide(dividend: f64, divisor: f64) -> Result<f64, String> {
    if divisor == 0.0 {
        Err(String::from("Cannot divide by zero"))
    } else {
        Ok(dividend / divisor)
    }
}

fn main() {
    match divide(10.0, 2.0) {
        Ok(result) => println!("Result: {}", result),
        Err(e) => println!("Error: {}", e),
    }

    match divide(10.0, 0.0) {
        Ok(result) => println!("Result: {}", result),
        Err(e) => println!("Error: {}", e),
    }
}
```

In this example, the `divide` function returns `Result<f64, String>`. If the division is successful, it returns `Ok` with the result. If the divisor is zero, it returns `Err` with an error message. The `match` statement in `main` handles both cases, ensuring the program responds appropriately.

The Option type

The `Option` type is used when a value can be either something or nothing. It is an enum with two variants: `Some` (containing a value) and `None` (no value). The `Option` type is useful for functions that might not return a value, providing a safe way to handle absence without resorting to null values.

The most exhaustive way to handle `Option` is with a `match` statement, which forces you to handle both the `Some` and `None` cases.

```
fn find_element(arr: &[i32], target: i32) -> Option<usize> {
    for (index, &element) in arr.iter().enumerate() {
        if element == target {
            return Some(index); // Found it, return Some(index)
        }
    }
```

```
    None // Didn't find it, return None
}

fn main() {
    let numbers = [1, 2, 3, 4, 5];

    // Case 1: The element is found
    match find_element(&numbers, 3) {
        Some(index) => println!("Using match: Found element at index: {}",
index),
        None => println!("Using match: Element not found"),
    }

    // Case 2: The element is not found
    match find_element(&numbers, 6) {
        Some(index) => println!("Using match: Found element at index: {}",
index),
        None => println!("Using match: Element not found"),
    }
}
```

In this example, the `find_element` function returns `Option<usize>`. If the target element is found in the array, it returns `Some` with the index. If the target is not found, it returns `None`. The `match` statement in `main` handles both cases.

In this example, the `find_element` function returns `Option<usize>`. The `match` statement in `main` safely handles both the `Some` and `None` outcomes.

For common scenarios where you want to get the value inside `Some` or use a default value if it's `None`, Rust provides a convenient method called `unwrap_or()`. This can make your code more concise than a full `match` block.

```
fn main() {
    let maybe_number: Option<i32> = Some(5);
    // If maybe_number is Some(5), `number` becomes 5.
    // If it were None, `number` would become 0.
    let number = maybe_number.unwrap_or(0);
    println!("Using unwrap_or: The number is: {}", number);
```

```
    let nothing: Option<i32> = None;
    // Since `nothing` is None, `default_number` becomes 10.
    let default_number = nothing.unwrap_or(10);
    println!("Using unwrap_or: The default number is: {}", default_
number);
}
```

Error destructuring

Error destructuring is the process of extracting the specific error information contained within the `Err` variant of a `Result` type. When an operation fails, the `Err` variant holds a value that describes the error. By using pattern matching with `match` or `if let`, you can "destructure" the `Err` to bind this inner value to a variable, allowing you to inspect it, log it, or handle it in a specific way.

For example, in the following code, `Err(e)` is the pattern that destructures `Result`. It matches the `Err` variant and binds the error value inside it to the variable e, which we can then print.

```
let failed_parse: Result<i32, _> = "hello".parse();

match failed_parse {
    Ok(number) => println!("Success: {}", number),
    Err(e) => println!("Failed to parse. The error was: {}", e), // Here,
'e' is the destructured error.
}
```

The panic! macro

The `panic!` macro is used to indicate a program failure and immediately terminate execution. It is typically used in scenarios where the program cannot continue due to an unrecoverable error.

```
fn main() {
    let result = divide(10.0, 0.0);
    if let Err(e) = result {
        panic!("Application error: {}", e);
    }
}

fn divide(dividend: f64, divisor: f64) -> Result<f64, String> {
```

```
    if divisor == 0.0 {
        Err(String::from("Cannot divide by zero"))
    } else {
        Ok(dividend / divisor)
    }
}
```

In this example, if the `divide` function returns an error, the program will panic and terminate. While `panic!` is useful for handling unrecoverable errors, it should be used sparingly and only when absolutely necessary.

Understanding these basic error handling mechanisms is essential for writing robust Rust programs. While this section provides an introduction, we will dive deeper into Rust's error handling capabilities in a dedicated chapter later in this book. There, we will explore more advanced techniques and best practices for managing errors in Rust.

Summary

In this chapter, we covered the fundamental aspects of Rust syntax and functions, focusing on variable declarations, data types, structs, enums, control flow constructs, and error handling. Here's a quick recap:

- **Variable declarations and mutability**: Understanding the importance of immutability by default and the use of the `mut` keyword for mutable variables. The concept of shadowing to safely reuse variable names.
- **Data types and structures**: A comprehensive look at Rust's scalar and compound types, including integers, floating-point numbers, booleans, characters, tuples, arrays, and slices.
- **Structs and enums**: Defining and using custom data types with structs and enums, including methods and associated functions.
- **Control flow constructs**: Utilizing `if` and `else` statements, loops (`loop`, `while`, and `for`), and pattern matching with `match` to manage the flow of your programs.
- **Error handling**: An introduction to Rust's approach to error handling with the `Result` and `Option` types, and the `panic!` macro.

By understanding these foundational elements, you are now well-equipped to write basic Rust programs that are both robust and efficient. These concepts form the building blocks for more advanced Rust programming techniques, which we will explore in subsequent chapters. In the next chapter, we will examine functions and modules.

Questions and assignments

Note that the answers to the questions and assignment solutions can be found in Appendix B (Online).

Questions

Variable declarations and mutability

1. How do you declare a variable in Rust?
2. What is the difference between immutable and mutable variables?
3. What is shadowing, and how does it differ from mutability?

Data types and structures

1. What are the basic scalar types in Rust?
2. How do you define and use a tuple in Rust?
3. What is the difference between arrays and slices in Rust?
4. How do you define a struct in Rust, and what are the methods and associated functions for structs?
5. What is an enum, and how can you use it to define different types of values?

Control flow constructs

1. How do you use `if` and `else` statements in Rust?
2. What are the different types of loops in Rust, and how do you use them?
3. How does pattern matching with `match` work in Rust?
4. What is the purpose of the `if let` and `while let` constructs?

Functions in Rust

1. What is the basic syntax for defining a function in Rust?
2. How do you handle parameters and return values in functions?
3. How do ownership and borrowing affect function parameters and return values?

Assignments

Assignment 2.1: Variable declarations and mutability

Write a Rust program that declares an immutable variable and then shadows it with a new value. Also, declare a mutable variable and change its value.

Assignment 2.2: Data types and structures

Create a struct to represent a rectangle with width and height. Implement a method to calculate the area of the rectangle.

3

Functions in Rust

Welcome to *Chapter 3*! Now that we've covered Rust's basic data types, let's explore how to make them *do* things. In this chapter, we'll focus on **functions**, the primary way to organize code and behavior in Rust. Think of them as the named recipes of your program: they bundle up logic into reusable blocks that you can call whenever you need them, which is fundamental to writing clean and maintainable software. By breaking down a complex problem into smaller, named pieces, your code becomes much easier to read, debug, and update.

While the basic idea of a function might be familiar if you've worked with other languages, its behavior in Rust is deeply connected to its most unique feature: the ownership system. A very important part of this chapter will be understanding how data is passed to and returned from functions. We will look at the difference between moving ownership, making a copy of data, and borrowing data with references. Getting a good handle on this is a huge step in your journey to becoming a proficient Rust programmer.

We'll start with the basic anatomy of a function, including its syntax and how it returns values. Then we'll spend a good amount of time on how functions interact with ownership. Finally, we'll get a quick preview of more advanced concepts, such as closures, to set the stage for later chapters.

Let's get started!

Importance of understanding functions

Understanding why functions are so important is key to appreciating how to structure good software.

By breaking down a large, complex problem into smaller, named, and more manageable pieces, your code immediately becomes easier to read and understand.

For example, when you suspect a bug, it's much simpler to debug a small function with a clear purpose than to hunt through hundreds of lines of tangled logic. Functions also allow you to write a piece of code once and reuse it in many different places, which reduces repetition and makes your programs easier to update.

This practice of encapsulating logic into well-defined units is fundamental to writing clean and maintainable code in any language, and Rust is no exception.

With that in mind, let's look at how you actually define and call a function in Rust.

Defining and calling functions

Functions are fundamental to programming in Rust, allowing you to encapsulate logic, promote code reuse, and create modular programs.

Before we dive into the syntax, it's worth mentioning a community convention: function and variable names in Rust are written in **snake_case**, where all letters are lowercase and words are separated by underscores (e.g., `calculate_area`).

While the compiler doesn't enforce this, following this convention is strongly recommended as it makes your code more readable and idiomatic, especially when working with others.

With that in mind, this section will cover the basics of defining and calling functions, including their syntax, how they handle parameters, and how they return values.

Basic function syntax

A function in Rust is defined using the `fn` keyword, followed by the function name, a list of parameters enclosed in parentheses, and the function body enclosed in curly braces. Here's a simple example:

```
fn main() {
    let width = 10;
    let height = 5;
    let area = calculate_area(width, height);
```

```
    println!("The area of the rectangle is: {}", area);
}

fn calculate_area(width: i32, height: i32) -> i32 {
    width * height
}
```

In this example, note the following:

- The `main` function is the entry point of the program. It calls the `calculate_area` function, passing `width` and `height` as arguments.
- The `calculate_area` function takes two parameters of type `i32` and returns an `i32`. The return type is specified after the `->` symbol.
- The function body contains the logic to calculate the area and returns the result.

Tip: How to run this example

Want to try this code on your own machine? It's easy with Cargo!

2. **Create a new project:** Open your terminal and run `cargo new functions_example --bin`. This command creates a new directory called `functions_example` with all the necessary files for a Rust program.
3. **Navigate into the project:** Run `cd functions_example`.
4. **Add the code:** Open the `src/main.rs` file and replace its contents with the code from the preceding example.
5. **Run it!** In your terminal, just run `cargo run`. Cargo will compile your code and then execute it, and you should see the output printed directly to your console.

Parameters and return values

In Rust, you must declare the type of each function parameter.

A function can also return a value, and if it does, you must declare the return type after an arrow, `->`.

Let's look at a function that takes two parameters and returns a string:

```
fn greet(name: &str, age: u32) -> String {
    format!("Hello, {}! You are {} years old.", name, age)
}
```

```
fn main() {
    let message = greet("Alice", 30);
    println!("{}", message);
}
```

Here is an explanation of the `greet` function:

- It takes two parameters: `name` (a string slice, `&str`) and age (a 32-bit unsigned integer, `u32`)
- It declares a return type of `String` after the `->` character
- The `format!` macro builds a new string and, because it's the last expression in the function, it's automatically returned

Functions that don't return a value

What about functions that just perform an action and don't return a meaningful value, such as `println!`? In Rust, a function that doesn't explicitly return a value is said to return the **unit type**, which is written as `()`.

The unit type is an empty tuple and represents the absence of a value.

When you write a function without a `->` return type, the compiler implicitly understands that it returns `()`.

For clarity, especially when learning, you can also write this explicitly. Both of the following functions are identical in behavior.

Let's see an example:

```
// This function implicitly returns the unit type ().
fn log_message_implicit(message: &str) {
    println!("[LOG] {}", message);
    // No return value, so () is returned implicitly.
}

// This function explicitly returns the unit type ().
// It is functionally identical to the one above.
fn log_message_explicit(message: &str) -> () {
    println!("[LOG] {}", message);
    // We could write `return ();` here, but it's not necessary.
}
```

```
fn main() {
    log_message_implicit("System online.");
    log_message_explicit("User logged in.");

    // You can see the unit type in action if you assign the result to a
variable.
    let result = log_message_implicit("Task finished.");
    // The type of `result` is `()`.
    // Printing it with debug formatting will show "()".
    println!("The result of a function returning the unit type is: {:?}",
result);
}
```

- `log_message_implicit` has no `->` arrow, so its return type defaults to `()`.
- `log_message_explicit` explicitly states `-> ()`, which does the exact same thing.
- As shown in `main`, the "return value" of such a function is `()`, the unit type. This is Rust's way of being explicit about functions that perform actions but don't return data.

Functions with no parameters and no return values

Functions can also be defined without parameters and without return values. These functions perform actions but do not produce a value to return to the caller:

```
fn main() {
    print_greeting();
}

fn print_greeting() {
    println!("Hello, world!");
}
```

In this example, the `print_greeting` function takes no parameters and returns no value. It simply prints a greeting message to the console.

Function syntax and best practices

Now that we've covered the basic syntax for defining functions, let's discuss some common practices and conventions that will help you write clear, maintainable, and idiomatic Rust code. Adhering to these practices makes your code easier for others (and your future self!) to read and understand:

- **Use descriptive names in snake_case**: As a strong convention in the Rust community, function and variable names are written in snake_case, where all letters are lowercase and words are separated by underscores. Choose names that clearly describe the function's purpose. For example, `calculate_area` is much clearer than `calc_ar` or `area`. Similarly, parameter names should be descriptive, such as width: `u32` instead of just `w: u32`.
- **Keep functions small and focused**: A function should ideally do one thing and do it well. If you find a function is becoming very long or is handling multiple distinct tasks, it's often a good idea to break it down into smaller, more focused helper functions. This makes your code more modular, easier to test, and easier to reason about.
- **Prefer pure functions when possible**: A "pure" function is one whose output depends only on its inputs, and that has no observable side effects (such as printing to the console, modifying a global variable, or writing to a file). While not all functions can be pure, favoring them where possible makes your code more predictable and easier to test, as you don't have to worry about hidden state changes.
- **Document functions with doc comments**: Rust has excellent built-in support for documentation. You should document your public functions using **documentation comments**, which start with `///`. These comments support Markdown and have special sections for describing parameters, return values, and even panics. This documentation can be automatically converted into beautifully rendered HTML documentation by running `cargo doc`.

Here is an example of a well-documented function that follows these practices:

```
/// Calculates the area of a rectangle.
///
/// This function takes the width and height of a rectangle and returns
its area.
/// It demonstrates good naming conventions and clear documentation.
///
/// # Parameters
///
```

```
/// * `width`: A `u32` representing the width of the rectangle. Must be
positive.
/// * `height`: A `u32` representing the height of the rectangle. Must be
positive.
///
/// # Returns
///
/// A `u32` representing the calculated area of the rectangle.
///
/// # Panics
///
/// This function will panic if either `width` or `height` is zero, as a
rectangle
/// with a zero dimension is considered invalid in this context.
pub fn calculate_rectangle_area(width: u32, height: u32) -> u32 {
    if width == 0 || height == 0 {
        panic!("Both width and height must be non-zero.");
    }
    width * height
}

fn main() {
    let area = calculate_rectangle_area(10, 20);
    println!("The calculated area is: {}", area);
}
```

In the preceding example, the doc comments clearly explain the function's purpose, its parameters (under `# Parameters`), what it returns (`# Returns`), and under what conditions it will panic (`# Panics`).

This level of documentation, combined with descriptive naming and a focused purpose, makes the function robust and easy to use correctly.

Function ownership and borrowing

In Rust, the concepts of ownership and borrowing are integral to understanding how data is passed to and returned from functions. These concepts ensure memory safety without a garbage collector, making Rust both efficient and reliable. This section will explain how ownership and borrowing apply to function parameters and return values.

Important: Ownership and Borrowing will be covered in detail in the next *Chapter 4*, so don't worry if you don't understand everything below. After reading *Chapter 4*, feel free to come back here and learn more about ownership specifically related to functions!

Ownership in functions

When you pass a parameter to a function, Rust's ownership model determines whether the function takes ownership of the parameter or borrows it. By default, parameters passed by value transfer ownership to the function:

```
fn main() {
    let s = String::from("hello");
    takes_ownership(s);
    // println!("{}", s); // This line would cause a compile-time error
because s is no longer valid
}

fn takes_ownership(some_string: String) {
    println!("{}", some_string);
}
```

In this example, note the following:

- The `takes_ownership` function takes ownership of the `some_string` parameter
- After the function call, s is no longer valid in the `main` function, and attempting to use it results in a compile-time error

When a function takes ownership of a value, it is responsible for cleaning up the value when it goes out of scope. This transfer of ownership helps prevent memory leaks and other common issues in systems programming.

Borrowing in functions

To allow a function to use a value without taking ownership, you can pass a reference to the value. This is known as borrowing. Borrowing allows multiple parts of your code to access a value without transferring ownership.

Immutable borrowing

When you pass an immutable reference to a function, the function can read the value but cannot modify it. Immutable references are created using the & symbol:

```
fn main() {
    let s = String::from("hello");
    takes_reference(&s);
    println!("{}", s); // s is still valid here
}

fn takes_reference(some_string: &String) {
    println!("{}", some_string);
}
```

In this example, note the following:

- The `takes_reference` function borrows the `some_string` parameter by taking an immutable reference to it
- The original s variable remains valid in the `main` function after the function call

Mutable borrowing

When you pass a mutable reference to a function, the function can modify the value. Mutable references are created using the `&mut` symbol:

```
fn main() {
    let mut s = String::from("hello");
    takes_mutable_reference(&mut s);
    println!("{}", s); // s has been modified
}

fn takes_mutable_reference(some_string: &mut String) {
    some_string.push_str(", world");
}
```

In this example, note the following:

- The `takes_mutable_reference` function borrows the `some_string` parameter by taking a mutable reference to it
- The original s variable can still be used in the `main` function and reflects the modifications made by the function

Rust enforces a strict rule to prevent data races: you can only have **one mutable reference** to a particular piece of data in a particular scope at any given time. You also cannot have any immutable references if a mutable reference exists. The compiler will stop you if you try to break this rule. This is one of Rust's most important safety guarantees.

Returning values and ownership

Functions can also return values, and the ownership of these values follows the same rules. If a function returns a value, the caller takes ownership of that value:

```
fn main() {
    let s1 = gives_ownership();
    let s2 = String::from("hello");
    let s3 = takes_and_gives_back(s2);

    println!("s1: {}", s1);
    // println!("s2: {}", s2); // This line would cause a compile-time
error because s2 has moved
    println!("s3: {}", s3);
}

fn gives_ownership() -> String {
    let some_string = String::from("hello");
    some_string
}

fn takes_and_gives_back(a_string: String) -> String {
    a_string
}
```

In this example, note the following:

- The `gives_ownership` function returns a string, and the caller (`main`) takes ownership of it
- The `takes_and_gives_back` function takes ownership of its parameter and then returns it, transferring ownership back to the caller

Understanding ownership and borrowing in the context of functions is crucial for writing safe and efficient Rust code. These concepts prevent common programming errors, such as null pointer dereferences and data races, ensuring your programs are both reliable and performant.

In the next section, we will explore advanced function features, including closures, higher-order functions, and anonymous functions, to write more flexible and expressive Rust code.

Advanced function features

Rust offers several advanced features that enhance function flexibility and expressiveness. These include closures, higher-order functions, and anonymous functions.

These features allow you to write more concise and powerful code, capturing the surrounding environment, passing functions as arguments, and returning functions from other functions.

Closures

In Rust, a **closure** is an anonymous function that you can define inline, store in a variable, pass as an argument, or return from another function.

If you have experience with "lambda expressions" or "lambdas" from languages such as Python, Java, or C++, or "arrow functions" in JavaScript, you'll find that Rust's closures serve a very similar purpose. They are incredibly useful for short, one-off operations, especially when working with higher-order functions such as iterator methods.

The key feature that makes closures powerful is their ability to **capture** variables from their surrounding scope or "environment." While lambdas in other languages also do this, in Rust, this process is governed by the same strict ownership and borrowing rules that apply everywhere else, giving you compile-time safety for this powerful functional feature.

The basic syntax uses vertical bars, `| |`, for parameters, followed by the closure body. Type annotations are often optional, as the compiler is excellent at inferring them from the context.

Here is an example:

```
fn main() {
    // The compiler infers that `x` is an i32 and the return type is i32.
    let add_one = |x| x + 1;
    println!("5 + 1 = {}", add_one(5));

    // You can also add explicit type annotations for clarity.
    let multiply = |a: i32, b: i32| -> i32 {
        a * b
    };
    println!("3 * 4 = {}", multiply(3, 4));
}
```

Capturing the environment

This is where closures truly shine. They can "capture" variables from the scope in which they are defined. The compiler automatically determines how to capture each variable based on how it's used inside the closure. There are three ways a closure can capture a variable:

- **By immutable reference (&T)**: If the closure only reads the variable
- **By mutable reference (&mut T)**: If the closure modifies the variable
- **By taking ownership (T)**: If the closure consumes the variable

```
fn main() {
    let my_name = String::from("Alice");
    let mut counter = 0;
    let data = vec![1, 2, 3];

    // 1. Captures `my_name` by immutable reference (&String)
because it only reads it.
    let greet = || println!("Hello, {}!", my_name);
    greet();
    // `my_name` is still valid here.
    println!("`my_name` can still be used: {}", my_name);

    // 2. Captures `counter` by mutable reference (&mut i32) because
it modifies it.
    let mut increment = || {
```

```
            counter += 1;
            println!("Counter is now: {}", counter);
        };
        increment();
        increment();
        // `counter` has been modified.
        println!("Final counter value: {}", counter);

        // 3. Captures `data` by taking ownership (Vec<i32>) because of
    the `move` keyword.
        // We'll discuss `move` next.
        let consume_data = move || {
            println!("Consumed data: {:?}", data);
            // `data` is dropped when this closure ends.
        };
        consume_data();
        // The line below would cause a compile error because `data` was
    moved.
        // println!("Can we use data after move? No: {:?}", data);
    }
```

The move keyword

Sometimes, you need to explicitly force a closure to take ownership of the variables it captures, even if it could just borrow them. You do this with the `move` keyword. This is most often necessary when a closure will outlive the scope of the captured variable, a common scenario when spawning new threads.

The `move` keyword ensures the closure has its own copy of the data and won't be left with a dangling reference:

```
use std::thread;

fn main() {
    let message = String::from("Data for the new thread");

    // `thread::spawn` requires a closure that can live for the entire
program ('static).
    // If we didn't use `move`, the closure would try to borrow `message`,
but the compiler
```

```
    // can't prove that `message` will live as long as the new thread.
    let handle = thread::spawn(move || {
        // The `move` keyword forces the closure to take ownership of
`message`.
        println!("Thread received: {}", message);
    });

    // `message` is no longer valid in the main thread.
    handle.join().unwrap();
}
```

The closure traits: Fn, FnMut, and FnOnce

The way a closure captures its environment determines which of three special traits it implements: `FnOnce`, `FnMut`, or `Fn`. These traits specify *how* the closure can be called. When you write a higher-order function that accepts a closure, you use these traits as bounds to specify what kind of closure you need:

- **FnOnce**: This trait is for closures that can be called *at least once*. All closures implement `FnOnce`. A closure that consumes the variables it captures (by taking ownership) can *only* be called once, so it will only implement `FnOnce`. The name signifies that the closure consumes itself when called.
- **FnMut**: This trait is for closures that might mutate the variables they capture. These closures can be called multiple times. Any closure that implements `Fn` also implements `FnMut`, and any closure that implements `FnMut` also implements `FnOnce`.
- **Fn**: This trait is for closures that only immutably borrow values from their environment (or don't capture anything). These closures can also be called multiple times without changing their environment.

The compiler will always infer the most permissive trait that a closure can implement. For example, a closure that only reads a variable will implement all three traits (`Fn`, `FnMut`, and `FnOnce`), allowing it to be used in the widest range of situations.

Closures in action: Higher-order functions and iterators

Closures are most powerful when used with **higher-order functions**, functions that take other functions (or closures) as arguments. The most common place you'll see this in Rust is with **iterators**. Iterator methods such as `map`, `filter`, and `fold` are higher-order functions that take closures to define their behavior.

This pattern is very similar to chaining methods such as `.map()` and `.filter()` on arrays in JavaScript:

```
fn main() {
    let numbers = vec![1, 2, 3, 4, 5, 6, 7, 8, 9, 10];

    // Let's find the sum of the squares of all even numbers greater than
3.
    let result: i32 = numbers
        .iter() // Create an iterator that yields references (&i32)

        // Use a closure with `filter` to keep only even numbers greater
than 3.
        // `n` here is `&&i32`, so we need to dereference it twice.
        .filter(|&&n| n > 3 && n % 2 == 0)

        // Use a closure with `map` to square each remaining number.
        // `n` here is `&i32`, so we dereference it once.
        .map(|&n| n * n)

        // Use `sum()` to consume the iterator and add up the results.
        .sum();

    // The chain of operations would be:
    // Original: [1, 2, 3, 4, 5, 6, 7, 8, 9, 10]
    // After filter: [4, 6, 8, 10]
    // After map: [16, 36, 64, 100]
    // After sum: 216

    println!("The sum of the squares of even numbers greater than 3 is:
{}", result);
}
```

- **filter(|&&n| n > 3 && n % 2 == 0)**: The `filter` method takes a closure that must return `true` or `false`. We pass it `|&&n| n > 3 && n % 2 == 0`, an anonymous function that checks our condition.
- **map(|&n| n * n)**: The `map` method takes a closure that transforms each element. We pass it `|&n| n * n` to square each number.

- **Concise and expressive:** This "iterator chain" style, powered by closures, allows you to express complex data transformations in a very clear, readable, and efficient way, without needing to write manual loops and `if` statements. This is a cornerstone of idiomatic, functional-style Rust.

Anonymous functions and iterator methods

Rust supports **anonymous functions**, which are functions defined inline without a specific name. If you've worked with other languages, you'll recognize these as **lambda expressions** or, in JavaScript, often as **arrow functions**. They are most powerfully used with higher-order functions, especially the methods found on Rust's iterators.

For developers coming from a JavaScript background, this pattern will feel very familiar. Just as you might chain methods such as `.map()`, `.filter()`, and `.reduce()` on an array in JavaScript, you can do the same with iterators in Rust. Let's look at a few common methods that take closures (our anonymous functions) as arguments:

- `map`: Transforms each element
- `filter`: Keeps elements based on a condition
- `fold`: Accumulates a single value from all elements (similar to reduce in JavaScript)
- `for_each`: Executes an action for each element

Here's an example showing `map` and `fold` in action:

```
fn main() {
    let numbers = vec![1, 2, 3, 4, 5];

    // Use an anonymous function `|x| x * 2` with the map method.
    let doubled: Vec<i32> = numbers.iter().map(|x| x * 2).collect();
    println!("Doubled numbers: {:?}", doubled); // Output: [2, 4, 6, 8,
10]

    // Use an anonymous function `|acc, &x| acc + x` with the fold method
to sum the values.
    // The first argument to fold (0) is the initial value for the
accumulator (`acc`).
    let sum = numbers.iter().fold(0, |acc, &x| acc + x);
    println!("Sum of numbers: {}", sum); // Output: 15
}
```

In this example, `|x| x * 2` is an anonymous function passed to `map` to transform each element. Similarly, `|acc, &x| acc + x` is passed to `fold` to define the accumulation logic. Using these inline, anonymous functions with iterator methods allows you to write data processing logic that is highly expressive, concise, and often more efficient than writing manual loops.

Summary

In this chapter, we've taken a deep dive into functions, the fundamental building blocks for organizing logic and behavior in any Rust program. We started with the basics of defining functions using the `fn` keyword, specifying typed parameters, and understanding how Rust's expression-based nature allows for concise return values without an explicit `return` keyword. By mastering these essentials, you've learned how to break down complex problems into smaller, reusable, and more manageable pieces, which is a cornerstone of writing clean and maintainable code.

A central theme of this chapter was the critical interaction between functions and Rust's ownership system. We explored the important distinction between passing simple types that are copied (such as `i32`) and passing owned types (such as `String`), which results in a move, transferring ownership into the function. We also saw how to use references (`&T` and `&mut T`) to allow functions to *borrow* data, either immutably for reading or mutably for modification, all without taking ownership. Grasping these concepts of moving, copying, and borrowing is one of the most significant steps in writing safe and efficient idiomatic Rust.

You are now well equipped with the knowledge to define and use functions effectively, managing data flow and ownership with confidence.

These skills are essential, as nearly every Rust program you write will be built upon them. In the next chapter, we will explore Rust's ownership and borrowing system in even greater detail, providing a comprehensive understanding of how Rust ensures memory safety and performance.

Questions and assignments

Questions

Defining functions

1. What is the syntax for defining a function in Rust?
2. How do you specify parameters and return types in a function?
3. What are the common practices for naming functions and parameters?

Function ownership and borrowing

1. How does Rust handle ownership when passing parameters to a function?
2. What is the difference between passing a parameter by value and by reference?
3. How can you modify a value inside a function without taking ownership of it?

Advanced function features

1. What are closures in Rust, and how do they differ from regular functions?
2. How can you pass a function as an argument to another function?
3. What is a higher-order function, and how can it be used in Rust?

Assignments

These questions and assignments will help reinforce your understanding of functions and modules in Rust, providing practical experience with these essential concepts.

Assignment 3.1: basic function implementation

Write a function called `calculate_triangle_area` that takes the base and height of a triangle as parameters and returns the area. Call this function from `main` and print the result.

Assignment 3.2: ownership and borrowing in functions

Modify the `calculate_triangle_area` function to take references to the base and height instead of values. Ensure the function works without taking ownership of the arguments.

Assignment 3.3: using closures

Create a closure that takes two `i32` parameters and returns their sum. Use this closure in a function that applies the closure to two numbers and prints the result.

4

Ownership, Borrowing, and References

Welcome to *Chapter 4*. In this chapter, you'll learn about some of Rust's most important concepts: **ownership**, **borrowing**, and **references**. These fundamental ideas are not just features; they form the foundation of Rust's commitment to memory safety and efficiency!

One of the things that makes Rust different from other programming languages, and one of the reasons why I find it fascinating, is its unique approach to handling memory. Instead of relying on a garbage collector or manual memory management, Rust enforces a set of rules at compile time. This helps you avoid common issues such as null pointer dereferences, buffer overflows, double-free memory issues, dangling references, and data races.

Initially, this model might feel unfamiliar, especially if you come from languages such as Java, Python, or C++. However, this approach is what gives Rust its impressive combination of safety and performance. While these concepts can take a little time to get used to, rest assured that the effort is worthwhile, as mastering them is the key to writing the incredibly safe and efficient code that Rust is famous for. In this chapter, we will explore these concepts thoughtfully through practical, beginner-friendly examples.

You'll see how they function in real code, giving you the confidence to apply them to your own projects. Let's embark on this exciting journey together!

Let's get started!

Objective

These principles govern memory management in Rust programs, guaranteeing that resources are utilized safely and efficiently without the need for a garbage collector. Whether you come from a background in languages with manual memory management, such as C or C++, or from languages that use garbage collection, such as Java or Python, these concepts may initially seem unfamiliar. However, grasping these ideas will unlock your full Rust developer potential.

This chapter aims to offer a comprehensive understanding of Rust's unique ownership system. We will explore the mechanics of borrowing and references; no worries, there will be practical examples that illustrate how these concepts work together to ensure safe memory management.

By the end of this chapter, you will have a solid foundation in these critical Rust features, enabling you to write more efficient and safe code as you continue your Rust journey.

Practical examples will demonstrate how these concepts ensure safe memory management. By the end of the chapter, you will be equipped to write efficient and safe Rust code, thanks to a solid understanding of these key features.

What is ownership?

Ownership is a defining feature of Rust and a fundamental aspect of its memory management and safety approach. Unlike many traditional programming languages, Rust does not solely rely on garbage collection or manual memory management. Instead, it uses a unique concept called **ownership** to handle resource allocation and deallocation efficiently and safely.

At its core, ownership establishes clear rules about how and when memory is allocated, used, and freed. Every value in Rust has a single owner responsible for its life cycle, from creation to cleanup. This ownership model helps prevent common memory-related issues, such as memory leaks, double-free errors, dangling pointers, and data races, by ensuring that each piece of data has exactly one responsible owner at any given time.

Understanding ownership is essential for writing effective Rust code, as it significantly influences data structure, function interactions, and system design. By clearly defining boundaries and responsibilities for data management, ownership equips developers with a powerful tool to create robust, safe, and efficient software.

Understanding ownership

Understanding ownership in Rust is fundamental to managing data effectively. A few key principles govern ownership in Rust:

- **Each value has a single owner**: In Rust, every piece of data has exactly one owner at any given moment. This owner is typically a variable (like a pet has a specific owner). Once assigned to that variable, the variable has full control over that data until ownership is transferred or the variable goes out of scope.

  Take the following example:

  ```
  let name = String::from("Mario");
  // `name` is now the owner of the data "Mario"
  ```

- **Only one owner at a time**: Rust's ownership model ensures that no two variables can own the same data simultaneously. If you assign one variable to another (for types that manage memory, such as a string), Rust *moves* the ownership rather than creating a shallow copy. This is a critical safety feature that prevents a dangerous bug called a "double free," where two variables might try to deallocate the same memory, leading to corruption. By enforcing a single owner, Rust always knows exactly which variable is responsible for cleaning up the data, eliminating this confusion and guaranteeing memory safety.

  Here is an example:

  ```
  let pasta = String::from("Carbonara");
  let dinner = pasta; // ownership moves from `pasta` to `dinner`

  // println!("{}", pasta); // ❌ Error! `pasta` no longer owns the
  data
  println!("{}", dinner); // ✅ "Carbonara"
  ```

  After the ownership moves to `dinner`, the `pasta` variable can no longer access the data.

- **When the owner goes out of scope, the value is dropped**: When the owner variable reaches the end of its scope (such as the end of a function), Rust automatically cleans up the associated data and frees the memory. You don't have to manually call any kind of `free()` or `delete()` function, Rust handles this automatically at compile time, ensuring memory safety and reducing bugs.

  The following is an example:

```
fn main() {
    {
        let espresso = String::from("Delicious");
        println!("{}", espresso); // ☑ "Delicious"
    } // `espresso` goes out of scope here; Rust automatically drops
its value

    // println!("{}", espresso); // ✕ Error! `espresso` doesn't
exist anymore
}
```

The automatic dropping of values helps prevent memory leaks and makes your programs safer and easier to reason about.

These rules ensure that memory is managed automatically, avoiding common issues such as double-free errors or dangling pointers and data races, which are often seen in languages such as C and C++.

Ways variables interact: Move, copy, and clone

We've established that every value in Rust has a single owner. This naturally leads to an important question: what happens when you assign one variable to another, such as `let y = x;`?

This would create a simple copy in many languages, but Rust is more precise.

Depending on the data type, Rust handles this interaction in one of three ways: **move, copy**, or **clone**.

The default behavior: Moving ownership

For complex types that manage resources on the heap, such as `String` (which owns its text data), `Vec<T>` (which owns its elements), and `Box<T>` (which owns the data it points to), Rust's default behavior upon assignment is to **move** ownership.

A "move" is not a deep copy of the data. Instead, it's a very fast, shallow copy of the pointer, length, and capacity information that resides on the stack. The large block of data on the heap is not touched at all. Crucially, after the move, Rust invalidates the original variable to ensure there is still only one owner. This compile-time check is how Rust guarantees that only one variable is responsible for freeing the memory, thus preventing "double-free" errors.

Let's visualize this with a string:

```
fn main() {
    // s1 is on the stack and owns the "hello" data on the heap.
    let s1 = String::from("hello");

    // The `let s2 = s1;` line performs a move.
    // The pointer, length, and capacity from s1 are copied to s2.
    // Ownership of the heap data is transferred to s2.
    let s2 = s1;

    // After the move, s1 is no longer considered valid by the compiler.
    // Uncommenting the line below would cause a compile-time error.
    // println!("This will not compile: {}", s1);

    println!("s2 holds the value: {}", s2);
}
```

Let's visualize the move:

- **Initial state**: `s1` owns the string data on the heap.

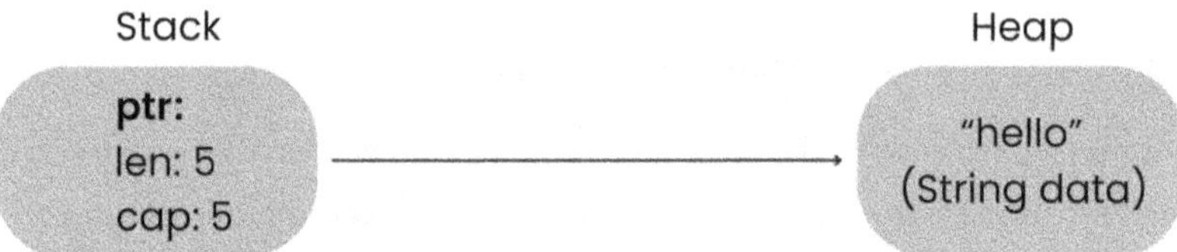

Figure 4.1: A String variable s1 on the stack, pointing to its heap-allocated data

- **Final state (after let s2 = s1;)**: Ownership has moved to `s2`. The `s1` is invalidated.

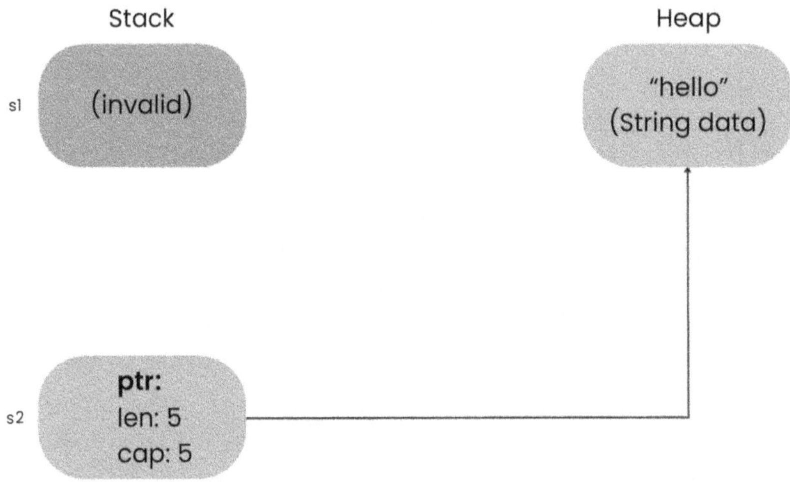

Figure 4.2: After let s2 = s1;, ownership of the heap data has moved to s2, and s1 is invalidated

This move-by-default behavior for owned types is a cornerstone of Rust's safety and performance.

The exception: Automatic copying with the Copy trait

You might have noticed that simple code such as `let x = 5; let y = x;` *doesn't* invalidate `x`. You can still use both `x` and `y` afterward. Why doesn't ownership move here?

This is because simple scalar types such as integers (`i32`), floating-point numbers (`f64`), Booleans (`bool`), and characters (`char`) implement a special trait called `Copy`. The `Copy` trait is a marker that tells Rust that it's okay to make a simple, bit-for-bit copy of a value instead of moving it.

This exception exists for types that are stored entirely on the stack and have no special resource management needs (such as a pointer to heap memory that needs to be freed). For these types, making a cheap, full copy of the data is no different from the shallow copy that happens during a move, so Rust allows the original variable to remain valid.

Types with the `Copy` trait include:

- All integer types (`u8`, `i32`, `usize`, etc.).
- All floating-point types (`f32`, `f64`).
- The Boolean type (`bool`).
- The character type (`char`).
- Tuples, if they *only* contain types that are also `Copy`. For example, `(i32, bool)` is `Copy`, but `(i32, String)` is not.

Types that own resources, such as `String`, `Vec<T>`, and `Box<T>`, *do not* and *cannot* implement the `Copy` trait, because that would lead to multiple owners of the same resource, breaking Rust's safety guarantees.

```
fn main() {
    // `x` is an i32, which implements the `Copy` trait.
    let x = 5;

    // Because `x`'s type is `Copy`, a bit-for-bit copy of the value 5
    // is made and assigned to `y`. `x` is not moved or invalidated.
    let y = x;

    println!("x = {}, y = {}", x, y); // Both x and y are valid and can be
used.

    // Let's look at a non-Copy type for contrast.
    let s1 = String::from("hello");
    // `String` does not implement `Copy`, so this is a move.
    let s2 = s1;

    // The line below would cause a compile-time error because s1 was
moved.
    // println!("s1 = {}, s2 = {}", s1, s2);
    // error[E0382]: borrow of moved value: `s1`
}
```

In summary, for types that implement Copy, assignment creates a copy, and the original variable remains valid. For all other types, assignment performs a move, and the original variable is invalidated. This distinction is a key part of Rust's predictable and safe memory management.

Explicit duplication: The Clone trait

So, what do you do when you have an owned type that isn't Copy (such as String or Vec<T>), but you genuinely need to create a duplicate of it? For this, Rust provides the Clone trait.

The Clone trait provides a method called .clone(), which is used to create an explicit, and often "deep," copy of a value. Unlike Copy, which is an implicit, bit-for-bit copy, clone() is a method you must call yourself. This makes the act of duplicating potentially expensive data a very deliberate one.

For a type such as String, calling .clone() will allocate new memory on the heap and copy the character data from the original string into the new allocation. This can be a relatively expensive operation in terms of performance and memory, especially for large strings or vectors.

```
fn main() {
    // `s1` is a String, which does not implement the `Copy` trait.
    let s1 = String::from("hello");

    // To create an independent duplicate of `s1`, we must explicitly call
.clone().
    // This performs a deep copy of the string data on the heap.
    let s2 = s1.clone();

    // Because we cloned `s1`, the original variable `s1` is still valid
and retains ownership
    // of its own data. `s2` is a brand new String that owns its own copy
of the data.
    println!("s1 = {}, s2 = {}", s1, s2);

    // We can modify one without affecting the other.
    // let mut s3 = s1.clone();
    // s3.push_str(", world!");
    // println!("s1 = {}, s3 = {}", s1, s3);
}
```

The following is an explanation of using `.clone()`:

- **Explicit call**: We must call `s1.clone()` to create `s2`. A `let s2 = s1;` assignment would have been a move.
- **Deep copy**: The `.clone()` method on `String` creates a new allocation on the heap and copies the content (`"hello"`) into it. `s1` and `s2` are now completely independent variables pointing to different memory locations.
- **Ownership**: `s1` retains ownership of its original data, and `s2` becomes the owner of the new, duplicated data. Both are valid and can be used after the clone.
- **Performance**: Remember that cloning can be costly. The idiomatic Rust approach is to prefer moving or borrowing whenever possible and to use `.clone()` only when you truly need a separate, owned copy of the data.

It's also worth noting that any type that implements `Copy` must also implement `Clone`. For `Copy` types, the implementation of `.clone()` is trivial and just performs the same cheap, bit-for-bit copy that happens implicitly on assignment.

Key rules of ownership in Rust

Each value has a single owner

In Rust, each value has a unique owner responsible for the value's life cycle, including its access and cleanup. This exclusive ownership prevents ambiguous or conflicting references to the same data, thus avoiding the memory errors found in other languages.

The following is an example:

```
fn main() {
    let book_title = String::from("The Rust Programming Guide");
    println!("{}", book_title); // book_title is valid here

    {
        let another_title = String::from("Rust and Beyond");
        println!("{}", another_title); // another_title is valid here
    } // another_title goes out of scope and is dropped here
} // book_title goes out of scope and is dropped here
```

In this example, both `book_title` and `another_title` have their own scope and owner. When the scope ends, the values are dropped, and the memory is automatically freed.

Ownership can be transferred (moved)

Ownership can be transferred from one variable to another. This process is called "moving." When a value is moved, the original owner no longer owns the value, and it becomes invalid. The new owner now controls the value's life cycle.

Take the following example:

```
fn main() {
    let original_owner = String::from("Rustacean");
    let new_owner = original_owner; // Ownership moves to new_owner

    // println!("{}", original_owner); // Error: original_owner is invalid
    println!("{}", new_owner); // new_owner is now the owner
}
```

In this example, the ownership of the `"Rustacean"` string is moved from `original_owner` to `new_owner`. After the move, `original_owner` is no longer valid, and attempting to use it will result in a compile-time error.

The owner is responsible for cleaning up the value

When the owner of a value goes out of scope, Rust automatically drops the value and frees the memory. This rule eliminates common issues such as memory leaks and ensures that memory is managed efficiently. The concept of "dropping" a value means that when a value's owner goes out of scope, the value is automatically cleaned up (similar to `dealloc` in C), preventing memory from being wasted.

Here is an example:

```
fn main() {
    {
        let temp_owner = String::from("Temporary");
        println!("{}", temp_owner); // temp_owner is valid here
    } // temp_owner is dropped here, and the memory is freed
    // println!("{}", temp_owner); // Error: temp_owner is invalid
}
```

In this example, `temp_owner` is created and dropped within a block. Once the block ends, `temp_owner` is no longer valid, and the memory is freed.

These ownership rules form the core of Rust's memory management strategy, ensuring that data is always handled safely and predictably. By following these rules, Rust eliminates many common programming errors, such as double frees, dangling pointers, and data races. Understanding and applying these rules in your programs is key to mastering Rust and writing efficient, safe code.

Moving ownership

In Rust, the concept of ownership extends beyond just the initial creation and destruction of variables; it also governs how values are transferred between different parts of a program. When a value is assigned from one variable to another, Rust performs a "move," which transfers ownership from the original variable to the new one. After a move, the original variable is no longer valid, preventing any further use and ensuring that no two variables can inadvertently share ownership of the same data.

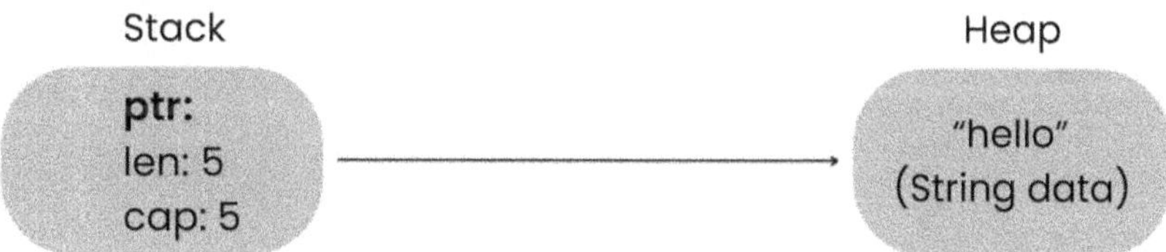

Figure 4.3: A String's memory layout: stack-allocated metadata (ptr, len, cap) pointing to its heap-allocated data

Moving ownership occurs when you transfer the ownership of a value from one variable to another. This happens in several scenarios, such as when you assign a value to another variable or when you pass it as an argument to a function. Once ownership is moved, the original variable becomes invalid, and attempting to use it results in a compile-time error. This is a key feature of Rust's safety guarantees.

The following is an example of a basic move:

```
fn main() {
    let first_owner = String::from("Hello, Rust!");
    let second_owner = first_owner;

    // The line below would cause a compile-time error
    // println!("{}", first_owner);

    println!("{}", second_owner); // This works because second_owner now
owns the value
}
```

In this example, the "Hello, Rust!" string is initially owned by first_owner. When ownership is moved to second_owner, the first_owner is no longer valid. If you try to use first_owner after the move, Rust will throw a compile-time error, enforcing the ownership rules.

Why move ownership?

Rust's move semantics ensure that data is not accidentally accessed or modified in unsafe ways. By enforcing strict ownership rules, Rust prevents common programming errors such as use-after-frees, double frees, and data races, which are prevalent in languages such as C and C++.

Moving ownership is particularly useful when dealing with large data structures that you don't want to copy. For instance, consider a function that processes a large collection of data, such as a vector containing millions of numbers. If the function takes ownership of the vector, the operation is extremely fast. Only the small amount of data on the stack (a pointer to the heap data, its length, and capacity) is moved.

The large block of data on the heap is not touched at all.

```
// A function that takes ownership of a large vector (a "move").
// This is very fast because only the pointer, length, and capacity are
moved.
fn process_large_data_by_move(data: Vec<i32>) {
    // Imagine some processing happens here.
    println!("Processing data by move. First element: {}, Length: {}",
data[0], data.len());
    // `data` is dropped here, and its heap memory is freed.
}

// A function that takes a clone of a large vector.
// This is much slower because it must allocate new memory and copy all
elements.
fn process_large_data_by_clone(data: &Vec<i32>) {
    let data_clone = data.clone();
    println!("Processing data by clone. First element: {}, Length: {}",
data_clone[0], data_clone.len());
    // `data_clone` is dropped here, and its heap memory is freed.
}

fn main() {
```

```
    // Create a large vector with one million integers.
    let large_vector: Vec<i32> = (0..1_000_000).collect();
    // Create another one for the clone example.
    let another_large_vector: Vec<i32> = (0..1_000_000).collect();

    println!("--- Demonstrating a move ---");
    // Ownership of `large_vector` is moved to the function. This is a
cheap operation.
    process_large_data_by_move(large_vector);
    // `large_vector` is no longer valid here and cannot be used.
    // println!("Can we use large_vector again? No."); // This would be a
compile error.

    println!("\n--- Demonstrating a clone ---");
    // We pass a reference and clone it inside the function.
    // This is an expensive operation, as it copies 1,000,000 integers.
    process_large_data_by_clone(&another_large_vector);
    // `another_large_vector` is still valid here because it was only
borrowed.
    println!("We can still use another_large_vector again. Length: {}",
another_large_vector.len());
}
```

In contrast, if we needed to keep the original vector and pass a copy to the function, we would have to use `.clone()`, as shown in the `process_large_data_by_clone` example. This would trigger a new heap allocation and a deep copy of all one million integers, a significantly more expensive operation in both time and memory. By choosing to move the data when the original is no longer needed, we transfer responsibility for it efficiently and safely, avoiding these costly duplications.

Moving in function calls

When you pass a value to a function, ownership of that value is typically moved to the function. This means that the value is no longer accessible in the original scope once the function call is made.

The following is an example of moving in functions:

```
fn main() {
    let data = String::from("Important data");

    process_data(data);
```

```
    // This line would cause a compile-time error
    // println!("{}", data);
}

fn process_data(input: String) {
    println!("Processing: {}", input);
}
```

In this example, the ownership of `data` is moved to the `process_data` function when it is called. After the function call, `data` is no longer accessible in the `main` function.

Advantages of moving ownership

The concept of moving ownership is fundamental to how Rust achieves its guarantees of safety and efficiency.

The primary *safety* advantage of a move is that it *invalidates the original variable.* Once ownership of a value has been moved, the Rust compiler statically prevents the original variable from being used again.

This compile-time check makes it impossible to accidentally access data through an old handle, which is a direct and powerful prevention against "use-after-free" bugs. Furthermore, because only one variable is considered the valid owner at any given time, only that variable will be responsible for cleaning up the data when it goes out of scope, which completely eliminates the risk of "double-free" errors.

The **efficiency** advantage is most apparent with large data structures. A move operation for heap-allocated data (such as a large `Vec<T>` or `String`) only involves copying a few bytes of stack data (the pointer, length, and capacity), not the potentially megabytes or gigabytes of data on the heap. This makes transferring ownership of large amounts of data an extremely fast operation, avoiding the significant performance cost of deep copying.

Ownership and functions

Ownership in Rust extends to how values are passed to functions. When a value is passed to a function, ownership of that value can be transferred (moved) to the function, or the function can borrow the value, either immutably or mutably, depending on the function's requirements. Understanding how ownership works with functions is crucial to writing safe and efficient Rust code.

Ownership transfer in function calls

When you pass a value to a function by value, the function takes ownership of that value (this is the default behavior). This means that the original variable in the calling function loses ownership and becomes invalid. After the function finishes execution, the value is dropped unless it is returned.

The following is an example of ownership transfer:

```
fn main() {
    let my_string = String::from("Hello, world!");

    take_ownership(my_string);

    // This line would cause a compile-time error
    // println!("{}", my_string);
}

fn take_ownership(s: String) {
    println!("Taking ownership: {}", s);
}
```

In this example, the `take_ownership` function takes ownership of `my_string`. After the function call, `my_string` is no longer valid in the `main` function because its ownership has been transferred to the `take_ownership` function.

Returning ownership

Sometimes, you might want a function to take ownership of a value, do some processing, and then return ownership to the caller. Rust allows you to return ownership from a function to the calling context.

The following is an example of returning ownership:

```
fn main() {
    let my_string = String::from("Hello, Rust!");

    let my_string = return_ownership(my_string);

    println!("{}", my_string); // Now this is valid
}
```

```
fn return_ownership(s: String) -> String {
    s
}
```

In this example, ownership of my_string is transferred to return_ownership, but then it is returned to the caller. This way, my_string remains valid after the function call, because ownership was returned to it.

Borrowing and references

Borrowing is one of Rust's most powerful and unique features, enabling data management that is both safe and highly efficient. While Rust's ownership model guarantees each value has a single owner, there are many cases where you need a function or another part of your program to temporarily access data without permanently taking ownership. This is where borrowing becomes crucial. It allows you to provide access to data without the performance cost of copying it, which is especially important for large data structures such as vectors or strings.

When you borrow a value, you create a reference to it. A reference, indicated by the & symbol, is a type that acts like a pointer, storing the memory address where the data resides, but with a crucial difference: it is governed by Rust's strict compile-time borrow checker. This means that while a reference allows you to access data without taking full responsibility for it, the compiler guarantees that the reference will always be valid and will not lead to dangerous situations such as data races.

Rust has some clear borrowing rules: at any one time, you can have either one mutable reference (&mut T) or many immutable references (&T), but not both. These guidelines are really important because they help avoid a lot of common bugs, such as data races, dangling pointers, and unsafe memory access, and all of this is checked during compilation to keep your code safe.

Borrowing, therefore, offers the best of both worlds: it guarantees memory safety through the borrow checker's rules and boosts performance by avoiding unnecessary data duplication and movement. It enables different parts of your program to safely share access to the same data while clearly indicating how that data is used throughout your code base. A thorough understanding of borrowing and references will greatly affect your ability to write safe, concurrent, and efficient Rust applications, making it a key concept in mastering Rust's ownership model.

Immutable borrowing

Immutable borrowing allows you to create read-only references to data. This means that while you can access the data, you cannot modify it. Multiple immutable references to the same data can exist simultaneously, allowing various parts of your code to read the data concurrently.

```
fn main() {
    let book = String::from("Rust Programming");

    let len = calculate_length(&book); // Borrow book immutably
    println!("The length of '{}' is {}.", book, len);

    // book is still valid here
}

fn calculate_length(s: &String) -> usize {
    s.len()
}
```

In this example, `calculate_length` borrows book immutably. The & symbol denotes that a reference is being passed. The original book variable remains valid and unchanged after the function call, allowing it to be used elsewhere in the code.

Mutable borrowing

Mutable borrowing lets you create a single, read-write reference to data, enabling you to modify the value it references.

However, this power comes with a critical rule that Rust's compiler strictly enforces: you can have **exactly one** mutable reference to a piece of data in any particular scope. This restriction is not arbitrary; it is the fundamental mechanism by which Rust prevents **data races** at compile time. A data race occurs when multiple references try to read and write to the same memory location simultaneously, leading to unpredictable and often disastrous bugs!

```
fn main() {
    let mut article = String::from("Rust is awesome");
    update_article(&mut article); // Borrow article mutably
    println!("Updated article: {}", article);
    // article is still valid here
}
```

```
fn update_article(s: &mut String) {
    s.push_str(" for system programming!");
}
```

Here, `update_article` borrows `article` mutably using `&mut`, allowing it to modify the original string. After the modification, the `article` variable is still valid in the `main` function.

Borrowing rules

Rust enforces several rules for borrowing to ensure safety and prevent data races:

- You can have either one mutable reference or multiple immutable references, but not both simultaneously.
- References must always be valid.

```
fn main() {
    let mut note = String::from("Rust is fast");

    let r1 = &note; // Immutable borrow
    let r2 = &note; // Immutable borrow
    // let r3 = &mut note; // Error: cannot borrow as mutable
because it is also borrowed as immutable

    println!("Note: {}, {}", r1, r2);

    let r3 = &mut note; // Mutable borrow is allowed here because no
immutable borrows are active
    r3.push_str(" and safe");
    println!("Updated note: {}", r3);
}
```

In this example, Rust prevents mutable borrowing while immutable references are active. The compiler is smart enough to see where the last use of the immutable references (`r1` and `r2`) occurs. After that point, their "borrow" is considered over, and a new mutable borrow is allowed.

This leads us to the second fundamental rule of borrowing: *all references must be valid.* This means that a reference must never point to memory that has been deallocated or has gone out of scope. In other languages, this dangerous bug is known as a "dangling reference" or "dangling pointer" and is a common source of crashes and security vulnerabilities.

Rust's compiler prevents this entire class of bugs at compile time through its analysis of **lifetimes**. The compiler ensures that the data a reference points to will live at least as long as the reference itself. If there's any possibility that a reference could outlive its data, the program will simply refuse to compile.

Consider this example, which Rust will correctly reject:

```
// This function attempts to return a reference to data that will be
deallocated.
// Rust's compiler will prevent this with a lifetime error.
fn get_dangling_reference() -> &String {
    let s = String::from("hello");

    &s // We are trying to return a reference to `s`.
} // But `s` goes out of scope and is dropped here, so the memory is
freed.
  // The returned reference would be "dangling" - pointing to invalid
memory.

fn main() {
    // let reference_to_nothing = get_dangling_reference();
    // If the code above were allowed to compile, `reference_to_nothing`
    // would be a dangling reference, and using it would be undefined
behavior.
}
```

Together, these two rules—(1) you can have either one mutable reference or any number of immutable references, and (2) all references must always be valid—form the core of Rust's **borrow checker**. This is the static analysis tool that allows Rust to guarantee memory safety without needing a garbage collector.

Borrowing in functions

In Rust, functions can borrow variables immutably or mutably depending on the required access. This allows functions to use or modify data without taking ownership, preserving the original variable's validity outside the function:

```
fn main() {
    let framework = String::from("Actix");
```

```
    display_framework(&framework); // Borrow framework immutably
    println!("Framework: {}", framework); // framework is still valid here
}

fn display_framework(s: &String) {
    println!("Using framework: {}", s);
}
```

In this example, `display_framework` borrows `framework` immutably, allowing it to be used elsewhere in the `main` function after the function call.

```
fn main() {
    let mut title = String::from("Rust Basics");

    modify_title(&mut title); // Borrow title mutably
    println!("Modified title: {}", title); // title is still valid here
}

fn modify_title(s: &mut String) {
    s.push_str(" - Advanced Topics");
}
```

Here, `modify_title` borrows `title` mutably, allowing it to modify the original string.

Practical example: Managing a library

Let's consider a more complex example of managing a library of books. We want to be able to add new books and print the list of books without transferring ownership:

```
struct Library {
    books: Vec<String>,
}

impl Library {
    fn new() -> Library {
        Library { books: Vec::new() }
    }

    fn add_book(&mut self, book: String) {
        self.books.push(book);
```

```
    }

    fn print_books(&self) {
        for book in &self.books {
            println!("{}", book);
        }
    }
}

fn main() {
    let mut library = Library::new();

    library.add_book(String::from("Rust Programming"));
    library.add_book(String::from("Advanced Rust"));

    library.print_books(); // Immutable borrow to print books
}
```

In this example, the `Library` struct has methods to add and print books. The `add_book` method mutably borrows `self` to modify the list of books, while the `print_books` method immutably borrows `self` to read the list of books.

In Rust, borrowing and references are key tools for safe and efficient data handling. Immutable borrowing allows multiple read-only references to a value, keeping data unchanged across different parts of the program.

Mutable borrowing allows data modification but grants exclusive access, meaning no other references, either mutable or immutable, can exist during a mutable borrow. This strict rule helps Rust prevent data races before runtime.

Common patterns and idioms in Rust: Ownership, borrowing, and references

Now that we have learned the basics, in this section, we will explore some practical examples and common patterns related to ownership, borrowing, and references in Rust. These patterns will help you to write safe and efficient code, taking advantage of all of Rust's powerful memory management features!

Borrowing for read-only access

Immutable data borrowing enables different parts of your code to read the same data simultaneously without the risk of modification. Here is an example of borrowing a reference to a struct:

```
struct Book {
    title: String,
    author: String,
}
fn print_book_title(book: &Book) {
    println!("The book title is: {}", book.title);
}
fn main() {
    let my_book = Book {
        title: String::from("Rust Programming"),
        author: String::from("John Doe"),
    };
    print_book_title(&my_book); // Borrowing the struct immutably
    println!("The book author is: {}", my_book.author); // The original
data is still accessible
}
```

In this example, the `print_book_title` function borrows the `Book` struct immutably. This allows the function to read the book's title without taking ownership, ensuring that the original data remains accessible in the `main` function.

The following are the key points:

- Multiple immutable references can coexist
- Data remains accessible and unmodified after borrowing
- There's no risk of data races as no mutation occurs

Mutable borrowing for modification

Mutable borrowing allows functions to modify data while the caller retains ownership. Rust's strict rules ensure that only one mutable reference exists at a time, which prevents data races.

Example: Mutable borrowing in a function

```
struct Account {
    balance: f64,
```

```
}

fn deposit(account: &mut Account, amount: f64) {
    account.balance += amount;
    println!("Deposited ${:.2}, new balance is ${:.2}", amount, account.
balance);
}

fn main() {
    let mut my_account = Account { balance: 1000.0 };

    deposit(&mut my_account, 200.0); // Mutably borrowing the struct
    println!("Final balance is ${:.2}", my_account.balance); // The
original data is modified
}
```

In this example, the `deposit` function mutably borrows the `Account` struct, allowing it to modify the `balance`. The `main` function retains ownership of the struct, but the balance is updated.

The following are the key points:

- Only one mutable reference can exist at a time
- Mutable borrowing allows data modification while retaining ownership
- This pattern is crucial for functions that need to modify data

Returning references with borrowing

Returning references from functions while maintaining ownership of the caller is a powerful pattern. This allows you to give controlled access to parts of your data without transferring ownership or needing to copy data.

Example: Returning a reference to the longest string

```
fn longest<'a>(x: &'a str, y: &'a str) -> &'a str {
// Lifetime annotation '<'a>' ensures that the returned reference
// lives at least as long as the shortest of the input references.
    if x.len() > y.len() {
        x
    } else {
        y
```

```
    }
}
fn main() {
    let string1 = String::from("Rust");
    let result; // Declare 'result' outside the inner scope
    {
        let string2 = String::from("Programming");
        result = longest(&string1, &string2);
        println!("The longest string is {}", result); // 'result' is valid
here because
        // it borrows either 'string1' or 'string2',
        // and both are still in scope.
    } // 'string2' goes out of scope and is dropped here.
    println!("The longest string is {}", result); // This is fine because
'result' borrows from 'string1'
    // which is still valid.
    println!("String 1 is {}", string1); // 'string1' is still valid
}
```

Here, the `longest` function returns a reference to the longer of two strings. This approach allows you to return data efficiently without transferring ownership or duplicating the data.

The following are the key points:

- References can be returned from functions while maintaining the original data ownership
- This is useful when you need to provide access to data without copying or transferring ownership

In this section, we've explored several common patterns in Rust that involve ownership, borrowing, and references. Here is a quick recap:

- **Borrowing for read-only access**: Safely share data across your program without modifying it
- **Mutable borrowing for modification**: Modify data through a single mutable reference while retaining ownership
- **Returning references with borrowing**: Efficiently return parts of data from functions without transferring ownership

Pitfalls and how to avoid them

As you start applying ownership, borrowing, and references in your Rust programs, you'll likely encounter some common pitfalls. These mistakes happen frequently when you're learning, but being aware of them can help you avoid frustration and write cleaner code.

Let's see some of the most common pitfalls.

Forgetting ownership has moved

One frequent mistake is trying to access a value after its ownership has moved to another variable:

```
let pizza = String::from("Margherita");
let lunch = pizza;

// println!("{}", pizza); // ✕ Error: pizza no longer owns the data!
println!("{}", lunch); // ☑ Works fine!
```

The key to avoiding this pitfall is to internalize Rust's "move by default" behavior for owned types. Always remember that when you assign a variable that owns its data (such as `String`, `Vec<T>`, or `Box<T>`) to another variable, you are not creating a copy; you are **transferring ownership**.

After this move, the original variable is no longer valid, and the compiler will prevent you from using it.

If you find that you genuinely need two separate, independent copies of the data, you should use the `.clone()` method explicitly. This creates a "deep copy" of the data, meaning it duplicates the data on the heap. While this allows both the original and the new variable to be used, it's important to be mindful of performance. Calling `.clone()` on large data structures, such as a big vector, can be an expensive operation in terms of both time and memory, as it requires allocating new memory and copying all the elements.

Therefore, the idiomatic Rust approach is to prefer moving ownership or borrowing with references whenever possible, and to use `.clone()` only when you have a clear reason to duplicate the data.

Multiple mutable references

Rust does not allow more than one mutable reference at the same time:

```
let mut gelato = String::from("Pistachio");

let ref1 = &mut gelato;
// let ref2 = &mut gelato; // ❌ Error: cannot borrow `gelato` as mutable
more than once

ref1.push_str(" & Chocolate");
println!("{}", gelato);
fn main() {
    let mut greeting = String::from("Hello"); // `greeting` owns the
String
    {
        let read1 = &greeting; // Immutable borrow: Can read `greeting`
        let read2 = &greeting; // Another immutable borrow: OK to have
        many readers
        println!("Immutable read 1: {}", read1);
        println!("Immutable read 2: {}", read2);
        // `read1` and `read2` are no longer used after this block
    } // `read1` and `read2` go out of scope here, so they're no longer
    borrowing `greeting`
    let write1 = &mut greeting; // Mutable borrow: Can modify `greeting`
    write1.push_str(", Rust!"); // Modify the string
    println!("Mutable write: {}", write1);
    println!("Original greeting: {}", greeting); // `greeting` is still
valid
}
```

This is how to avoid this issue:

- Keep mutable references short-lived and scoped narrowly
- Only create mutable references when truly necessary

Dangling references

Rust's borrow checker protects you from dangling references (references to data that no longer exists):

```
// This will NOT compile!
fn return_reference() -> &String {
    let s = String::from("Espresso");
    &s // ❌ Error: returning reference to local variable
}
```

This is how to avoid this issue:

- The fundamental rule is that you cannot return a reference to a value that was created *inside* the function, as that value will be deallocated when the function ends. While it is possible for functions to return references in Rust, those references must point to data that was passed *into* the function, not data it owns locally. This involves a concept called "lifetimes," which ensures the data lives long enough.
- For now, the safest and most common approach is to *return an owned value* (such as `String`, `Vec<T>`, etc.) from your function. This moves ownership of the value to the caller, guaranteeing it will remain valid.

Unnecessary clones

Beginners sometimes clone excessively to please the borrow checker:

```
fn print_pasta(pasta: &String) {
    println!("Pasta: {}", pasta);
}

let spaghetti = String::from("Carbonara");
print_pasta(&spaghetti.clone()); // ❌ Unnecessary clone!
```

The best way to avoid unnecessary clones is to think in terms of Rust's preferred modes of data access, which prioritize efficiency and safety.

Your first and most common choice should be to pass a reference (`&T`) to functions whenever possible. If a function only needs to read data, an immutable reference is perfect. If it needs to modify the data, a mutable reference (`&mut T`) is the right tool. Borrowing is always the most efficient option as it avoids any data duplication.

Only when a function truly needs to consume the data and take ownership should you move it. If, after moving, you find you still need the original variable, that's the signal to consider an explicit, and potentially expensive, clone. Therefore, you should only call `.clone()` when you have a clear and deliberate need for a separate, independent copy of the data and are willing to accept the potential performance cost.

Summary

In this chapter, we've explored the core concepts of ownership, borrowing, and references in Rust. These foundational principles are key to understanding how Rust ensures memory safety and prevents common programming errors without the need for a garbage collector.

The following are the key takeaways from this chapter:

- **Ownership**: Understanding how Rust manages memory through ownership, where each value has a single owner. We discussed how ownership can be transferred and the implications of this on memory management.
- **Borrowing and references**: We explained how Rust allows you to borrow data through references, either immutably or mutably, enabling safe access to data without transferring ownership.
- **Common patterns**: We explored common Rust patterns, including borrowing for read-only access and mutable borrowing for modification, providing practical examples of how to use these patterns effectively.
- **Pitfalls and solutions**: We identified common pitfalls related to ownership and borrowing, such as dangling references and conflicting borrows, and provided strategies for avoiding these issues.

Questions and assignments

Congratulations on completing this chapter!

Before we conclude this chapter, let's solidify what you've learned with some review questions and practical exercises.

These questions will help strengthen your understanding of ownership, borrowing, and references, while the exercises offer hands-on practice to apply these concepts directly.

Spending some time on these activities is important, as they will significantly improve your grasp of Rust's memory management principles.

Questions

1. What is the primary purpose of Rust's ownership system, and how does it differ from garbage collection in other languages?
2. How does borrowing allow you to use data without transferring ownership, and what are the rules governing immutable and mutable borrowing?
3. Explain the concept of a dangling reference and how Rust prevents this issue.
4. In what scenarios would you use mutable borrowing, and why does Rust enforce the rule of having only one mutable reference at a time?
5. What are some common patterns when using borrowing and references, and how do they contribute to safe and efficient Rust code?

Assignments

Assignment 4.1: ownership in action

Write a Rust program that creates a string and transfers ownership of it to another function. The second function should print the string. Observe how the original function can no longer use the string after the transfer.

Assignment 4.2: playing with borrowing

Create a Rust program that demonstrates both immutable and mutable borrowing. Set up a scenario where both types of borrowing are attempted simultaneously. Observe the compiler's response, then adjust your code to satisfy Rust's borrowing rules. This will help your understanding of how Rust handles borrowing to ensure memory safety.

5

Composite Types in Rust and the Module System

Welcome to *Chapter 5*! Having explored Rust's powerful ownership and borrowing system in the previous chapter, we now turn our attention to how Rust helps us structure and organize our data. Primitive types such as integers and Booleans are useful, but real-world applications often require grouping multiple values into a single, meaningful unit.

This is where Rust's **composite types** come into play. They provide a robust way to manage more complex data, forming the building blocks for sophisticated applications.

In this chapter, we'll dive deep into Rust's primary composite types. We will cover the following topics:

- **Structs**: How to define custom types to group related data fields, and how to add behavior using methods. We'll also look at variations such as tuple structs and unit-like structs.
- **Enums**: Defining types that can represent one of several possible variants, which is crucial for modeling different states or kinds of data, and how variants can hold data themselves.
- **Tuples**: A simple way to group a fixed number of potentially different types together. We'll explore these concepts with clear examples, connecting them back to Rust's core principles, such as ownership, and finish with practical exercises. By the end of this chapter, you'll be equipped to design and use custom data structures effectively in your Rust projects.

After discussing these types, we will explain the module system in Rust, which is essentially how Rust manages multiple files in a project.

Let's begin!

Structs: Named-field collections

Structs are one of Rust's fundamental custom data types, allowing you to create blueprints for grouping related values under a single type name.

If you've encountered classes in object-oriented languages, structs might feel somewhat familiar, though Rust handles associated behavior (methods) distinctly using `impl` blocks, which we'll explore shortly.

Structs are incredibly useful for modeling real-world entities (such as `User`, `Product`, or `BlogPost`) or abstract concepts by bundling different pieces of data into one logical unit.

Mastering structs is very important to write organized and meaningful Rust code.

Defining structs

Defining a struct in Rust is straightforward. You use the `struct` keyword, followed by the name you choose for your custom type (using PascalCase by convention), and then curly braces `{}` enclosing the fields.

Each field consists of a name (using snake_case by convention) and its data type. Structs are highly versatile, enabling you to represent anything from simple configuration settings to complex domain objects.

Let's define a simple `User` struct to represent a user in a system:

```
// We use the `derive` attribute to give our struct useful default
functionality.
// - `Debug`: Allows us to print the struct for debugging purposes using
`{:?}`.
// - `PartialEq`: Allows us to compare two `User` instances for equality
using `==`.
#[derive(Debug, PartialEq)]
struct User {
   // Note: Unlike tuples, you access struct fields by name, so the order
    // in which you declare or instantiate them doesn't matter.
    active: bool,
    username: String,
    email: String,
    sign_in_count: u64,
}
```

Here, our `User` struct logically groups four pieces of information: an active status (a Boolean, `bool`), a username and email (both owned Strings), and `sign_in_count` (a 64-bit unsigned integer, `u64`).

Adhering to the PascalCase for struct names and snake_case for field names is standard Rust practice and significantly improves code readability.

By adding `#[derive(Debug, PartialEq)]`, we've equipped our `User` struct with two important capabilities right from the start. `Debug` is essential for printing out instances of our struct while we're developing and debugging. `PartialEq` is incredibly useful for testing, as it allows us to use assertion macros such as `assert_eq!(user1, user2);` to check whether two instances are identical. For `#[derive(PartialEq)]` to work, all the fields within the struct must also support equality comparison, which is true for most common types.

We'll see more of these `derive` attributes throughout the book.

Creating instances of structs

Once you have defined a struct, you can create instances of it to store and manipulate data. Creating an instance of a struct involves specifying values for each of its fields.

Initializing structs

Once a struct is defined (the blueprint), you can create instances of it (actual objects built from the blueprint). Creating an instance involves using the struct's name, followed by curly braces, `{}`, containing `key: value` pairs for each field. You must provide a value for every field defined in the struct.

Let's create an instance of our `User` struct:

```
// Assuming the User struct is defined as above
fn main() {
    let user1 = User {
        email: String::from("someone@example.com"),
        username: String::from("someusername123"),
        active: true,
        sign_in_count: 1,
    };

    // We'll see how to access these fields next
    println!("Created user with email: {}", user1.email);
}
```

In this code, the `user1` variable holds an instance of our `User` struct. To create this instance, we provide concrete values for each field. It's important to notice that for the username and email fields, we use `String::from("...")`. This is a crucial detail related to Rust's ownership system.

Our `User` struct is defined to hold owned `String` types, not borrowed string slices (`&str`). This is a common and important design choice. For an instance of `User` to be a self-contained, independent piece of data, it needs to *own* all of its data. If it held `&str` references instead, the validity of the `User` instance would be tied to the lifetime of whatever data those references were borrowing.

By using `String`, the `User` instance manages its own string data on the heap, and this data will live exactly as long as the `User` instance does. `String::from()` is the standard way to create a new, owned `String` from a string literal (`&str`), which is why it's used here to provide the necessary owned data for the struct's fields.

Field initialization shorthand

Rust offers a convenient *field init shorthand* syntax. If you have variables in scope with the exact same names as the struct fields you want to initialize, you can simply write the variable name instead of `field_name: variable_name`.

This reduces repetition and makes initialization cleaner, especially when creating structs from function parameters.

Consider this example where variable names match field names:

```
// Assuming the User struct is defined
fn build_user(email: String, username: String) -> User {
    User {
        email, // Shorthand for email: email
        username, // Shorthand for username: username
        active: true,
        sign_in_count: 1,
    }
}

fn main() {
    let user_email = String::from("shorthand@example.com");
    let user_name = String::from("shorthand_user");
    let user2 = build_user(user_email, user_name);
```

```
    println!("User 2 active status: {}", user2.active);
}
```

Inside `build_user`, because the `email` and `username` parameters match the field names, we can use the shorthand.

Rust *understands* that this means `email: email` and `username: username`. Next, we'll discuss how to access and modify the fields of a struct instance.

Accessing struct fields

Once you have a struct instance, you'll often need to read the values stored in its fields. Rust uses the familiar dot notation (`.`) for this purpose. To read a field's value, use the instance name followed by a dot and the field name.

Reading field values

To read the value of a field in a struct, you use dot notation. Here's an example:

```
// Assuming the user1 instance from earlier
fn main() {
    let user1 = User {
        email: String::from("someone@example.com"),
        username: String::from("someusername123"),
        active: true,
        sign_in_count: 1,
    };
    // Accessing fields using dot notation
    println!("The username is: {}", user1.username);
    println!("Is the user active? {}", user1.active);
}
```

As shown, `user1.username` accesses the `username` field, and `user1.active` accesses the active `field`, providing direct read access to the data within the instance.

Modifying struct fields

What if you need to change a field's value after creating an instance? Remember Rust's default immutability! To allow modification, you must declare the `struct` instance variable as mutable using the `mut` keyword when you create it.

Tip: A common pitfall: forgetting let mut

A very common error for newcomers is trying to modify a field on a struct instance that was declared with just `let`. Remember, immutability in Rust applies to the entire binding. If you need to change *any* field on a struct instance, the instance itself must be declared as mutable when you create it.

```
// This will NOT compile:
let user = User { active: true, ... };
user.active = false; // Error: cannot assign to field `active` of
immutable binding

// This is the correct way:
let mut user = User { active: true, ... };
user.active = false; // This is allowed!
```

Then, you can use dot notation with the assignment operator (=) to change a field's value.

```
// ... assuming the `User` struct is defined ...

fn main() {
    // Declare user1 as mutable to allow its fields to be changed.
    let mut user1 = User {
        email: String::from("someone@example.com"),
        username: String::from("someusername123"),
        active: true,
        sign_in_count: 1,
    };

    println!("Original Email: {}", user1.email);

    // Modify fields of the mutable struct instance.
    user1.email = String::from("new.email@example.com");
    user1.sign_in_count += 1;

    println!("Updated Email: {}", user1.email);
    println!("Updated sign_in_count: {}", user1.sign_in_count);
}
```

Here, `let mut user1` is crucial. It allows us to later assign a new string to `user1.email` and increment `user1.sign_in_count`.

Without `mut`, the compiler would issue an error preventing these modifications.

Updating struct instances

Often, you might want to create a new struct instance that is mostly the same as an existing one, but with a few different values. Instead of manually specifying all the unchanged fields again, Rust provides the convenient **struct update syntax**.

This syntax lets you specify only the fields you want to change and tells Rust to either *copy* (for types that implement the `Copy` trait) or *move* (for owned types like `String`) the rest of the values from another instance.

Struct update syntax

The struct update syntax uses `..` to indicate that the remaining fields should be copied from another instance. Here's an example:

```
#[derive(Debug)]
struct User {
    username: String,
    email: String,
    sign_in_count: u64,
    active: bool,
}

fn main() {
    let user1 = User {
        username: String::from("original_user"),
        email: String::from("original@example.com"),
        sign_in_count: 50,
        active: true,
    };

    // Create user2 based on user1, but with a new email.
    let user2 = User {
        email: String::from("new_user@example.com"),
        ..user1 // Handle remaining fields
```

```
    };

    // The line below would now fail to compile because `user1.username`
(a String)
    // was *moved* to `user2`. The rest of `user1`'s fields (`sign_in_
count` and `active`)
    // were copied because they implement the `Copy` trait, but since part
of `user1`
    // was moved, the whole instance cannot be used like this anymore.
    // println!("Original User 1 after move: {:?}", user1);

    println!("New User 2 Details:");
    println!(" - username: '{}' (Moved from user1)", user2.username);
    println!(" - email: '{}' (Newly specified)", user2.email);
    println!(" - sign_in_count: {} (Copied from user1, as u64 is Copy)",
user2.sign_in_count);
    println!(" - active: {} (Copied from user1, as bool is Copy)", user2.
active);
}
```

In this example, when we create `user2` using `..user1`, Rust checks each field we didn't explicitly set. For `sign_in_count` (`u64`) and `active` (`bool`), which implement the `Copy` trait, the values are simply copied.

However, for `username` (`String`), which does not implement `Copy`, ownership is *moved* from `user1` to `user2`.

Because `user1` has had one of its fields moved away, the `user1` variable as a whole is no longer considered fully valid and cannot be used afterward, as shown by the commented-out line that would cause a compile error.

Cloning struct instances

When using the struct update syntax, it's important to remember that Rust's ownership rules apply to each field individually. The behavior depends on whether a type implements the `Copy` trait.

The `Copy` trait is a special marker for types whose values can be duplicated with a simple bit-for-bit copy without any special handling. This is true for simple types that are stored entirely on the stack, such as integers (`i32`), Booleans (`bool`), and tuples containing only other `Copy` types.

Types that manage resources, such as `String`, which owns data on the heap, do not implement `Copy`. A simple bitwise copy of `String` would result in two variables pointing to and believing they own the same heap memory, which would lead to a "double-free" error when both are dropped. For these non-`Copy` fields, the struct update syntax performs a move, transferring ownership.

If you need to keep the original struct valid after the update, you must explicitly clone its non-`Copy` fields to create a deep copy for the new instance.

Here is an example:

```
fn main() {
    let user1 = User {
        username: String::from("someusername123"),
        email: String::from("someone@example.com"),
        sign_in_count: 1,
        active: true,
    };

    let user2 = User {
        email: String::from("newemail@example.com"),
        username: user1.username.clone(),
        ..user1
    };

    println!("Username: {}", user2.username);
    println!("Email: {}", user2.email);
    println!("Sign-in Count: {}", user2.sign_in_count);
    println!("Active: {}", user2.active);
}
```

We explicitly set `email` and `active` for `user2`.

The `..user1` syntax instructs Rust to use the values from `user1` for any fields not explicitly set in `user2` (in this case, `username` and `sign_in_count`).

Important note on ownership: Remember Rust's ownership rules from *Chapter 4*!

The `..other_instance` struct update syntax behaves like assignment for the fields it copies. If a field's type implements the `Copy` trait (such as `u64` or `bool`), the value is copied. But if a field's type does *not* implement `Copy` (such as `String`), ownership of that field's data is moved from `other_instance` to the new instance. In our `User` example, using `..user1` moves ownership of `user1.username` (a string) to `user2`. Consequently, `user1` becomes partially moved, and you can no longer access `user1.username` after `user2` is created this way.

```
// Continuing from the previous example...
    // If username was moved via ..user1:
    // println!("User 1 Username after move: {}", user1.username); // ✕
Compile Error! Value moved

    // If you need user1 to remain fully usable, you must explicitly
.clone()
    // the non-Copy fields before the update syntax moves them:
    let user3 = User {
        email: String::from("user3@example.com"),
        username: user1.username.clone(), // Explicitly clone the String
        ..user1 // Copies 'active' and 'sign_in_count' (as they are Copy)
    };

    // Now user1 is still fully usable because its username was cloned,
not moved.
    println!("User 1 Username after clone: {}", user1.username); // ☑ OK!
    println!("User 3 Username: {}", user3.username); // ☑ OK!
```

In this example, we create `user2` by providing new, explicit values for the `email` and `sign_in_count` fields. The `..user1` syntax then handles the remaining fields. It's important to remember that this syntax performs a *move* for any fields that do not implement the `Copy` trait (such as `username: String`), while it performs a *copy* for fields that do implement `Copy` (such as `active: bool`).

Because `user1.username` was moved to `user2`, the `user1` variable as a whole can no longer be used after `user2` is created.

Methods for structs

Structs are great for organizing data, but often you'll want to associate *behavior* or *actions* directly with that data. In Rust, you achieve this by defining *methods* within an `impl` (implementation) block specifically tied to your struct type.

This keeps data and the operations on that data closely related, which is great.

Defining methods

An `impl` block allows you to define functions associated with your struct. Functions defined within an `impl` block are called *methods* if their first parameter is named `self`, which can appear in three forms:

- `&self`: Borrows the instance immutably (read-only access)
- `&mut self`: Borrows the instance mutably (read-write access)
- `self`: Takes ownership of the instance (consumes it)

Let's define a `Rectangle` struct and implement methods for it:

```
#[derive(Debug)] // Added for printing later
struct Rectangle {
    width: u32,
    height: u32,
}

// Implementation block for Rectangle
impl Rectangle {
    // Method to calculate the area (needs read-only access)
    fn area(&self) -> u32 {
        // Access fields using self.field_name
        self.width * self.height
    }

    // Method to check if width is greater than 0 (read-only)
    fn has_valid_width(&self) -> bool {
        self.width > 0
    }

     // Method that modifies the instance (needs read-write access)
    fn double_width(&mut self) {
        self.width *= 2;
    }
}
```

Here, inside `impl Rectangle`, we defined the following:

- `area()` and `has_valid_width()`: These take `&self`, borrowing the `Rectangle` immutably to read data
- `double_width()`: This takes `&mut self`, borrowing the `Rectangle` mutably, allowing it to change `self.width`

Calling methods

Once methods are defined, you call them on an instance of the struct using dot notation, just like accessing fields: `instance.method_name(arguments)`.

Rust handles the borrowing (`&self` or `&mut self`) automatically through a feature called **automatic referencing and dereferencing**:

```
// Assuming Rectangle struct and its impl block are defined as above
fn main() {
    let mut rect1 = Rectangle { width: 30, height: 50 }; // 'mut' needed
for double_width

    // Call methods using dot notation
    println!("The area of rect1 is {}.", rect1.area()); // Calls
area(&rect1)
    println!("Does rect1 have valid width? {}", rect1.has_valid_width());
// Calls has_valid_width(&rect1)

    println!("Original width: {}", rect1.width);
    rect1.double_width(); // Calls double_width(&mut rect1)
    println!("Width after doubling: {}", rect1.width);
    println!("New area: {}", rect1.area()); // Call area() again on
modified rect1
}
```

Notice how cleanly methods are called. When you write `rect1.area()`, Rust automatically passes `&rect1` as the `&self` parameter.

Similarly, `rect1.double_width()` automatically passes `&mut rect1` as `&mut self`.

Associated functions intro

Besides methods that operate on an instance (taking `&self` or `&mut self`), `impl` blocks can also contain **associated functions**. These are functions that are associated with the struct type itself but do not take `self` as their first parameter. They are often used as constructors or "factory functions" to create new instances of the struct.

Associated functions are called using the struct's name followed by `::`, such as `Rectangle::square(3)`:

```
// To print our struct with `{:?}`, we need to derive the Debug trait.
#[derive(Debug)]
struct Rectangle {
    width: u32,
    height: u32,
}

impl Rectangle {
    // An associated function, often called `new`, used as a constructor.
    // It returns `Self`, which is an alias for the type `Rectangle`
inside this impl block.
    fn new(width: u32, height: u32) -> Self {
        Rectangle { width, height }
    }

    // Another associated function to create a square.
    fn square(size: u32) -> Self {
        Rectangle { width: size, height: size }
    }

    // A method to calculate the area, for use in main.
    fn area(&self) -> u32 {
        self.width * self.height
    }
}

fn main() {
    // Call associated functions using the `StructName::function_name()`
syntax.
```

```
    let rect_from_new = Rectangle::new(10, 20);
    let square_rect = Rectangle::square(15);

    // We use `{:?}` to print `rect_from_new` because we derived the Debug
trait.
    println!("Rectangle from new: {:?}", rect_from_new);
    println!("Area of square: {}", square_rect.area());
}
```

- **Associated functions versus methods**: Notice that `new` and `square` do not take `self` as their first parameter. This is what makes them associated functions, not methods. They are associated with the `Rectangle` type, but not a specific instance of it.
- **The self keyword**: Inside an `impl` block, the `Self` keyword (with a capital *S*) is an alias for the type the block is implementing. So, `-> Self` is the idiomatic way of saying `-> Rectangle`. This makes the code more concise and easier to refactor if you ever rename the struct.
- **A note on {:?} and #[derive(Debug)]**: In the `println!` macro, the `{}` formatter uses a trait called `Display`, which is for user-facing output. To print a struct for debugging purposes, we use the `{:?}` formatter, which uses a trait called `Debug`. To automatically provide a `Debug` implementation for our `Rectangle` struct, we add the `#[derive(Debug)]` attribute directly above its definition. This is a common and very useful practice for easily inspecting your custom types during development.

Unit-like structs

Rust also allows defining *unit-like structs*, which are structs with no fields at all. They are declared using the `struct` keyword, a name, and an immediate semicolon, `;`.

They are useful when you need a type simply for its identity or to implement a trait, without needing to store any data.

Defining unit-like structs

Unit-like structs are defined using the `struct` keyword followed by the struct name without any fields. Here's an example:

```
struct Marker; // A unit-like struct

trait MyTrait {
    fn description(&self) -> &'static str;
```

```
}

// We can implement traits for unit-like structs
impl MyTrait for Marker {
    fn description(&self) -> &'static str {
        "This is a marker instance."
    }
}

fn main() {
    let m = Marker; // Create an instance (it holds no data)
    println!("{}", m.description()); // Call method from the implemented
trait
}
```

Here, `Marker` serves primarily to implement `MyTrait`. Instances such as `m` occupy no memory at runtime beyond their type information. They are often used with marker traits or in advanced generic programming.

Use cases for unit-like structs

Unit-like structs are typically used in situations where the existence of a type is more important than the data it holds. Some common use cases include the following:

- **Marker traits**: Sometimes you want to mark types with a specific trait to indicate that they conform to a particular behavior. Unit-like structs can be used to implement such traits without storing any data.
- **Type-level programming**: In more advanced Rust programming, unit-like structs can be used in type-level computations and generic programming scenarios where the type itself carries meaning.

Here's an example of using a unit-like struct with a marker trait:

```
struct MyStruct;

trait MyMarker {}

impl MyMarker for MyStruct {}

fn main() {
```

```
    let instance = MyStruct;
    // Now instance has the MyMarker trait
}
```

In this example, `MyStruct` is a unit-like struct, and `MyMarker` is a marker trait. We implement the `MyMarker` trait for `MyStruct`, and now any instance of `MyStruct` is marked with `MyMarker`.

Tuple structs

Tuple structs are another struct variant, blending features of tuples and regular structs. They get a unique type name like a struct, but their fields are unnamed and accessed by index like a tuple. Define them with `struct Name(Type1, Type2, ...);`. They are useful when naming the whole structure is important but naming individual fields feels redundant, such as for simple `Color` or `Point` types.

Defining tuple structs

Here's how you can define a tuple struct:

```
// Define tuple structs
struct Color(u8, u8, u8); // RGB
struct Point(i32, i32);   // 2D coordinates

fn main() {
    // Instantiate like tuples, but with the type name
    let red = Color(255, 0, 0);
    let origin = Point(0, 0);

    // Access fields using dot notation and index
    println!("Red's green component: {}", red.1); // Accesses the second
field (index 1)

    // They define distinct types
    // let point_tuple: (i32, i32) = origin; // Error: mismatched types
Point != (i32, i32)

    // Can be destructured
    let Point(x, y) = origin;
    println!("Origin coordinates: x={}, y={}", x, y);
}
```

Key points to note are that they create a new named type, fields are unnamed, and access is via `instance.index`. They offer a concise way to create simple, distinct types. In this example, note the following:

- `Dimensions` is a tuple struct with three `f64` fields representing length, width, and height
- `Coordinates` is a tuple struct with two `i32` fields representing *x* and *y* coordinates

Creating instances of tuple structs

You can create instances of tuple structs just like you create instances of tuples:

```
fn main() {
    let box_dimensions = Dimensions(30.5, 20.0, 15.0);
    let point = Coordinates(10, 20);

    println!("Box dimensions: {:?}", box_dimensions);
    println!("Point coordinates: {:?}", point);
}
```

Accessing tuple struct fields

Tuple struct fields are accessed using dot notation and their index:

```
fn main() {
    let box_dimensions = Dimensions(30.5, 20.0, 15.0);
    let point = Coordinates(10, 20);

    println!("Box dimensions - Length: {}, Width: {}, Height: {}", box_
dimensions.0, box_dimensions.1, box_dimensions.2);
    println!("Point coordinates - x: {}, y: {}", point.0, point.1);
}
```

Practical example: Using tuple structs in a function

Let's use tuple structs to represent the dimensions of a package and calculate its volume:

```
struct Dimensions(f64, f64, f64); // Represents length, width, and height

fn calculate_volume(dimensions: Dimensions) -> f64 {
    dimensions.0 * dimensions.1 * dimensions.2
}
```

```
fn main() {
    let package = Dimensions(30.5, 20.0, 15.0);

    println!("Package dimensions: Length: {}, Width: {}, Height: {}",
package.0, package.1, package.2);
    println!("Package volume: {} cubic units", calculate_volume(package));
}
```

In this example, note the following:

- We define a `Dimensions` tuple struct with three `f64` fields
- We create a `calculate_volume` function that calculates the volume of a package
- We create an instance of `Dimensions` and use the `calculate_volume` function to calculate its volume

Tuple structs provide a way to name and work with tuples in a more structured manner without needing to name each field.

They are useful for creating simple, lightweight data structures that benefit from having a named type.

Empty tuples

It's also important to understand the **unit type**, written as `()`, which is essentially an empty tuple. In Rust, functions that don't explicitly return a value are said to return the unit type. This is how Rust represents the concept of "no return value" in its type system.

You'll see this frequently in error handling, particularly with the `Result<(), Error>` type. This signature signifies a function that can fail (returning an `Err`), but on success, it simply signals completion without providing any data (`Ok(())`).

Think of `Ok(())` as a way of saying, "The operation succeeded, and there's no value to give back."

Structs and ownership

Ownership is a central concept in Rust that ensures memory safety without needing a garbage collector. Understanding how ownership works with structs is very important for managing data in Rust programs.

This section will briefly cover how ownership affects struct fields and how to work with borrowed and owned data.

Ownership of struct fields

When you create an instance of a struct, each field of the struct takes ownership of the data assigned to it.

This means that the struct instance owns its fields, and the ownership rules apply to these fields just as they do to any other data in Rust.

Here is an example:

```
struct User {
    username: String,
    email: String,
    sign_in_count: u64,
    active: bool,
}

fn main() {
    let user1 = User {
        username: String::from("someusername123"),
        email: String::from("someone@example.com"),
        sign_in_count: 1,
        active: true,
    };

    let user2 = user1; // Moves ownership of user1 to user2

    // println!("Username: {}", user1.username); // This would cause a
compile-time error
    println!("Username: {}", user2.username); // Accessing user2 is fine
}
```

In this example, the ownership of `user1` is moved to `user2`. After the move, `user1` can no longer be used, as it no longer owns its data. Attempting to use `user1` after the move results in a compile-time error.

Borrowing struct fields

Borrowing allows you to reference data without taking ownership of it. This is useful when you want to read or modify the data of a struct without transferring ownership.

Here's how you can borrow struct fields:

```
fn main() {
    let user1 = User {
        username: String::from("someusername123"),
        email: String::from("someone@example.com"),
        sign_in_count: 1,
        active: true,
    };

    let user_ref = &user1; // Borrowing user1
    println!("Username: {}", user_ref.username); // Reading borrowed data
    // user1 can still be used because user_ref is just a reference
    println!("Email: {}", user1.email);
}
```

In this example, `user_ref` is a reference to `user1`. Borrowing `user1` with `&user1` allows you to access the fields of `user1` without transferring ownership. This means `user1` can still be used after being borrowed.

Mutable borrowing

If you need to modify the fields of a struct, you can use mutable borrowing. Mutable borrowing allows you to borrow a mutable reference to the data, enabling you to make changes.

Here's an example of mutable borrowing:

```
fn main() {
    let mut user1 = User {
        username: String::from("someusername123"),
        email: String::from("someone@example.com"),
        sign_in_count: 1,
        active: true,
    };

    let user_ref = &mut user1; // Mutable borrowing of user1
```

```
    user_ref.email = String::from("newemail@example.com"); // Modifying
borrowed data

    println!("Updated Email: {}", user1.email);
}
```

In this example, user_ref is a mutable reference to user1. Borrowing user1 with &mut user1 allows you to modify the email field of user1.

Debugging with structs

Debugging is an essential part of software development, and Rust provides tools to make debugging easier. One of these tools is the Debug trait, which allows you to print your structs in a readable format.

By default, Rust's standard library includes a Debug implementation for most types, but you need to explicitly opt into it for your custom types.

Implementing the Debug trait

To enable the Debug trait for your struct, you use the #[derive(Debug)] attribute. This automatically provides a basic implementation of the Debug trait for your struct, allowing you to print it using the println! macro with the {:?} format specifier.

The following is an example:

```
#[derive(Debug)]
struct User {
    username: String,
    email: String,
    sign_in_count: u64,
    active: bool,
}

fn main() {
    let user1 = User {
        username: String::from("someusername123"),
        email: String::from("someone@example.com"),
        sign_in_count: 1,
        active: true,
    };
```

```
    println!("{:?}", user1);
}
```

In this example, we add `#[derive(Debug)]` above the `User` struct definition. This enables the `Debug` trait for `User`, allowing us to print `user1` using `println!("{:?}", user1)`.

Customizing debug output

While `#[derive(Debug)]` is often all you need, Rust gives you the power to completely customize the debug output for your structs. This is done by manually implementing the `Debug` trait.

This process involves syntax for implementing traits (`impl Trait for Struct`), a powerful feature we will cover in great detail in a dedicated chapter later on.

However, for those who are curious or have a specific need for custom formatting now, here's a quick look at how it works:

```
use std::fmt;

struct User {
    username: String,
    email: String,
    sign_in_count: u64,
    active: bool,
}

impl fmt::Debug for User {
    fn fmt(&self, f: &mut fmt::Formatter) -> fmt::Result {
        write!(
            f,
            "User {{ username: {}, email: {}, sign_in_count: {}, active:
{} }}",
            self.username, self.email, self.sign_in_count, self.active
        )
    }
}

fn main() {
    let user1 = User {
```

```
        username: String::from("someusername123"),
        email: String::from("someone@example.com"),
        sign_in_count: 1,
        active: true,
    };

    println!("{:?}", user1);
}
```

In this example, we manually implement the `Debug` trait for the `User` struct. This allows us to customize the output format when printing the struct.

Practical example: User profile

To bring together the concepts we've covered so far, let's create a practical example. We'll define a `UserProfile` struct, add methods to it, and implement the `Debug` trait.

Defining the UserProfile struct

We'll start by defining a `UserProfile` struct with fields for the username, email, age, and active status. We'll also derive the `Debug` trait so we can print the struct:

```
#[derive(Debug)]
struct UserProfile {
    username: String,
    email: String,
    age: u32,
    active: bool,
}
```

Adding methods to UserProfile

Next, we'll add methods to the `UserProfile` struct. These methods will include a constructor to create new user profiles and methods to deactivate and reactivate a user profile:

```
impl UserProfile {
    fn new(username: String, email: String, age: u32) -> UserProfile {
        UserProfile {
            username,
            email,
            age,
```

```
            active: true,
        }
    }

    fn deactivate(&mut self) {
        self.active = false;
    }

    fn reactivate(&mut self) {
        self.active = true;
    }
}
```

In this `impl` block, note the following:

- The `new` function is an associated function that creates a new `UserProfile` instance
- The `deactivate` method sets the `active` field to `false`
- The `reactivate` method sets the `active` field to `true`

Using the UserProfile struct

Let's use the `UserProfile` struct in the `main` function to create a new user, deactivate and reactivate the user, and print the user profile at each step:

```
fn main() {
    let mut user = UserProfile::new(
        String::from("johndoe"),
        String::from("johndoe@example.com"),
        30,
    );

    println!("{:?}", user);

    user.deactivate();
    println!("After deactivation: {:?}", user);

    user.reactivate();
    println!("After reactivation: {:?}", user);
}
```

In the `main` function, note the following:

- We create a new user profile using the `UserProfile::new` function
- We print the user profile using `println!("{:?}", user)`
- We deactivate the user profile using the `deactivate` method and print the updated profile
- We reactivate the user profile using the `reactivate` method and print the updated profile again

This example demonstrates how to define a struct, add methods, and use the `Debug` trait to print the struct.

Structs: Exercises and assignments

To reinforce your understanding, try the following exercises:

1. **Extend the UserProfile struct**: Add additional fields such as `phone_number` and `address`. Implement methods to update these fields.
2. **Implement more methods**: Add methods to update the email and age of the user profile.
3. **Debug output customization**: Manually implement the `Debug` trait for `UserProfile` to customize the debug output.

Structs: Summary

In this section, explored Rust's composite types, focusing primarily on structs. We've covered how to define structs, create instances, access and modify fields, update instances, add methods, and implement the `Debug` trait. We've also worked through a practical example to apply these concepts in a real-world scenario, reinforcing our understanding of how to manage complex data in Rust programs effectively.

Next, we'll explore another crucial composite type in Rust: **enums**. Enums allow you to define a type by enumerating its possible variants, providing a way to represent different kinds of data with the same type. We'll cover how to define and use enums, as well as pattern matching, providing practical examples to illustrate their usage.

Enums: One of several possibilities

Now, let's explore Rust's second major composite type: *enums* (enumerations). While structs group related fields *together*, enums define a type that can be *one of several possible variants*. Think of modeling states (e.g., *Loading, Success, Error*) or choices (*Red, Green, Blue*).

Enums allow you to encode these possibilities into the type system, ensuring a value can only be one of the defined variants, making your code safer and more expressive.

Defining and using enums

Define an enum using the `enum` keyword, a PascalCase name, and curly braces, `{}`, containing the PascalCase names of the possible variants. Instances are created using the `EnumName::VariantName` syntax.

The `match` expression is ideal for handling different enum variants exhaustively.

Let's see an example:

```
// Define an enum for different kinds of web events
enum WebEvent {
    PageLoad,                       // Simple variant with no data
    PageUnload,                     // Simple variant with no data
    KeyPress(char),                 // Tuple-like variant holding a char
    Click { x: i64, y: i64 },       // Struct-like variant holding named
data
}

// A function to process different web events
fn inspect(event: WebEvent) {
    match event {
        WebEvent::PageLoad => println!("Page loaded"),
        WebEvent::PageUnload => println!("Page unloaded"),
        // Destructure the data from the variant
        WebEvent::KeyPress(c) => println!("Key pressed: '{}'.", c),
        WebEvent::Click { x, y } => println!("Clicked at coordinates:
x={}, y={}.", x, y),
    }
}

fn main() {
    let load_event = WebEvent::PageLoad;
    let click_event = WebEvent::Click { x: 20, y: 80 };
    let key_event = WebEvent::KeyPress('x');

    inspect(load_event);
```

```
    inspect(click_event);
    inspect(key_event);
}
```

Here, `WebEvent` can be one of four distinct kinds, and some of these variants hold data. This example demonstrates two different styles for including data, and the choice between them is a matter of clarity:

- **Tuple-like variants (KeyPress(char))**: This style is concise and works well when the meaning of the data is clear from the type alone or when there's only one data value. Since `KeyPress` holds a single character, its purpose is obvious.
- **Struct-like variants (Click { x: i64, y: i64 })**: This style is preferred when a variant holds multiple pieces of data and giving them names improves readability. By naming the fields `x` and `y`, the code becomes more self-documenting; it's immediately clear that these are coordinates, which is more explicit than `Click(i64, i64)`.

The `match` statement elegantly handles each case, destructuring and extracting the data where present.

This ability for enum variants to hold different types and structures of data is what makes them incredibly powerful and flexible.

Enum variants can hold data

One of the most powerful features of Rust enums is that their variants can store data directly. This goes beyond simply listing possibilities; it allows each variant to carry specific information relevant to that particular case.

This makes enums incredibly versatile for modeling complex states or messages where the *kind* of information differs depending on the situation. Each variant can hold different types and amounts of data.

Let's illustrate this with a classic example: defining an enum to represent different kinds of messages or events that might occur in an application. Some events might be simple signals, while others need to carry associated values:

```
enum Message {
    Quit,                       // Variant with no associated data
    ChangeColor(u8, u8, u8),    // Variant holding three u8 values (like a
tuple)
```

```
    Move { x: i32, y: i32 },    // Variant holding named fields (like a
struct)
    Write(String),              // Variant holding a single String
}

fn process_message(msg: Message) {
    match msg {
        Message::Quit => {
            println!("Received Quit message: The program should
terminate.");
        }
        // Destructure the tuple-like data directly in the pattern
        Message::ChangeColor(r, g, b) => {
            println!("Received ChangeColor: Changing color to RGB({}, {},
{}).", r, g, b);
        }
        // Destructure the struct-like data directly in the pattern
        Message::Move { x, y } => {
            println!("Received Move: Moving to coordinates ({}, {}).", x,
y);
        }
        // Bind the contained String to the variable 'text'
        Message::Write(text) => {
            println!("Received Write: Message content is '{}'.", text);
        }
    }
}

fn main() {
    // Create instances of different variants, providing data where needed
    let msg1 = Message::Quit;
    let msg2 = Message::ChangeColor(255, 0, 0); // Red
    let msg3 = Message::Move { x: 100, y: 50 };
    let msg4 = Message::Write(String::from("Rust enums are powerful!"));

    // Process each message using our function
    process_message(msg1);
    process_message(msg2);
```

```
        process_message(msg3);
        process_message(msg4);
    }
```

In this `Message` enum, note the following:

- `Quit` is a simple variant, holding no data
- `ChangeColor` bundles three `u8` values, similar to a tuple struct
- `Move` uses named `x` and `y` fields, just like a regular struct definition
- `Write` contains a single string

The real magic happens in the `process_message` function. The `match` expression doesn't just identify the variant; it simultaneously *destructures* the associated data.

Notice how `Message::ChangeColor(r, g, b)` binds the three `u8` values to `r`, `g`, and `b`, and `Message::Move { x, y }` binds the field values to the `x` and `y` variables. This combination of enumeration, data storage, and pattern matching is central to writing idiomatic and safe Rust code.

Enum methods/functions intro

Enum methods example

Just like structs, you can define behavior associated with your enums using `impl` blocks. This allows you to add methods that operate on enum instances or **associated functions** that relate to the enum type itself. Associated functions don't take `self` as a parameter and are often used as constructors, providing a controlled way to create instances.

Let's create a `TrafficLight` enum with an associated `from_str` function that attempts to create an instance from a string. Since the input string might not be a valid color, this operation can fail. In Rust, the idiomatic way to handle operations that might return a value or nothing at all is with the `Option<T>` enum.

An enum is one of the most important types in Rust for handling the potential absence of a value. It has two variants:

- `Some(T)`: Represents the presence of a value of type `T`
- `None`: Represents the absence of a value

By returning `Option<TrafficLight>`, our `from_str` function makes it explicit that the conversion might not succeed, forcing the caller to handle the `None` case:

```
#[derive(Debug)] // Add derive for printing
enum TrafficLight {
    Red,
    Yellow,
    Green,
}

impl TrafficLight {
    // Associated function (like a constructor) that can fail.
    // It returns an Option<TrafficLight>.
    fn from_str(color: &str) -> Option<TrafficLight> {
        match color.to_lowercase().as_str() {
            "red" => Some(TrafficLight::Red),
            "yellow" => Some(TrafficLight::Yellow),
            "green" => Some(TrafficLight::Green),
            _ => None, // Return None for any invalid input string
        }
    }
}

fn main() {
    let green_light = TrafficLight::from_str("green");
    let invalid_light = TrafficLight::from_str("purple");

    println!("'green' -> {:?}", green_light); // Output: Some(Green)
    println!("'purple' -> {:?}", invalid_light); // Output: None

    // Using 'if let' is a concise way to handle the Some case.
    if let Some(light) = TrafficLight::from_str("Red") {
       println!("Successfully created from 'Red': {:?}", light);
    } else {
       // This part would run if from_str returned None.
       println!("Could not create light from 'Red'.");
    }
}
```

In this example, we define a method, `is_safe_to_go`, for the `TrafficLight` enum. This method checks whether the traffic light is green, returning `true` if it is and `false` otherwise.

The `is_safe_to_go` method takes an immutable reference, `&self`, and uses `match` to check the current variant. It returns `true` only if the light is `Green`. Encapsulating this logic within the `impl` block makes the enum more self-contained and easier to use correctly.

Using enums with structs

Structs and enums often work together beautifully. A common pattern is to include an enum as a field within a struct.

This allows you to represent an object that has some fixed data (the other `struct` fields) but also exists in one of several possible states or configurations (represented by the `enum` field).

Defining structs with enum fields

You can define a struct that includes an enum as one of its fields. This allows you to model more intricate relationships between data.

Let's model a network device that has an ID and name, but can be in various operational states:

```
#[derive(Debug)] // For printing Status
enum Status {
    Online,
    Offline,
    Connecting { attempts: u32 }, // Status with data
    Maintenance,
}

#[derive(Debug)] // For printing Device
struct Device {
    id: u32,
    name: String,
    status: Status, // Enum used as a field
}

impl Device {
    fn new(id: u32, name: String) -> Device {
        Device {
```

```
            id,
            name,
            status: Status::Offline, // Default status
        }
    }

    // Method to update the device status
    fn set_status(&mut self, new_status: Status) {
        self.status = new_status;
    }

    // Method to get a descriptive status message
    fn get_status_message(&self) -> String {
        match &self.status { // Match on a reference to the status field
            Status::Online => format!("Device '{}' (ID {}) is online.",
self.name, self.id),
            Status::Offline => format!("Device '{}' (ID {}) is offline.",
self.name, self.id),
            Status::Connecting { attempts } => format!("Device '{}' is
connecting (attempt {})...", self.name, attempts),
            Status::Maintenance => format!("Device '{}' ({}) is under
maintenance.", // <--- Added '{}' for the ID self.name, self.id),
        }
    }
}

fn main() {
    let mut router = Device::new(101, String::from("Main Router"));

    println!("{}", router.get_status_message());

    router.set_status(Status::Connecting { attempts: 1 });
    println!("{}", router.get_status_message());

    router.set_status(Status::Online);
    println!("{}", router.get_status_message());
```

```
    println!("Current device state: {:?}", router); // Debug print the
whole struct
}
```

Here, the Device struct holds id, name, and a status field of type Status (our enum). The set_status method allows changing the device's state, and get_status_message uses match on the status field (note the &self.status borrow) to provide a user-friendly description, handling the data within the Connecting variant correctly. This combination allows for flexible and type-safe state management within our Device objects.

Enums: exercises and assignments

To reinforce your understanding, try the following exercises:

1. **Extend the Device struct**: Add additional fields such as ip_address and location. Implement methods to update these fields.
2. **Implement more methods for enums**: Add methods to the Status enum that return different messages or perform different actions based on the current status.
3. **(Advanced) Create a network management system**: Combine structs and enums to create a simple network management system that can track devices and their statuses and perform operations such as bringing devices online or offline.

Enums: summary

In this section, we've explored Rust's enums and their powerful capabilities.

We covered how to define and use enums, how to handle data within enums, and how to combine enums with structs to create complex data structures.

We also looked at adding associated functions and methods to enums and using pattern matching to handle different enum variants.

Tuples: simple ordered groups

Beyond structs and enums, Rust provides a simpler composite type: the **tuple**. Tuples offer a lightweight way to group a fixed number of values, potentially of different types, into a single compound value.

Define them using parentheses, (), containing comma-separated values. Unlike structs, tuple elements lack names, identified only by their zero-based index.

Let's see an example, so everything will look easier to understand:

```
fn main() {
    // Define a tuple with type annotation
    let basic_tuple: (i32, f64, bool) = (100, 3.14, true);

    // Define a tuple with type inference
    let mix_tuple = ("Rust", 2015, '🦀'); // Type: (&str, i32, char)

    // Print tuples (Debug is usually available)
    println!("Basic tuple: {:?}", basic_tuple);
    println!("Mixed tuple: {:?}", mix_tuple);
}
```

Tuples are handy for quick, temporary groupings or returning multiple values from functions efficiently. There are two main ways to access their elements:

1. **Direct indexing**: Use dot notation followed by the zero-based index (e.g., `basic_tuple.0`, `mix_tuple.1`):

   ```
   // Continuing main...
   let first_val = basic_tuple.0; // 100 (i32)
   let second_val = basic_tuple.1; // 3.14 (f64)
   println!("First: {}, Second: {}", first_val, second_val);
   ```

2. **Destructuring**: Break the tuple into individual variables using a pattern in a `let` statement. This is often more readable:

   ```
   // Continuing main...
   let (language, year, mascot) = mix_tuple; // Destructure mix_tuple
   println!("Language: {}, Year: {}, Mascot: {}", language, year,
   mascot);

   // Ownership: If mix_tuple contained non-Copy types (like String),
   // destructuring would move ownership into 'language', 'year',
   'mascot'.
   // The original tuple might become unusable.
   ```

A common use case is returning multiple results from a function:

```
// Function returning (String, u32) tuple
fn get_server_info() -> (String, u32) {
    (String::from("192.168.1.100"), 8080)
}

fn main() { // Separate main for this example
    // Call function and destructure the returned tuple
    let (ip_address, port) = get_server_info();
    println!("Connect to server {}:{}", ip_address, port);

    // 'ip_address' now owns the String returned by the function.
}
```

Tuples provide fixed-size, ordered collections, which are great when the element positions provide enough meaning.

Using tuples

Tuples can be used to group related data items, making them easier to pass around and manage in your code. Here's an example where we use a tuple to return multiple values from a function:

```
fn get_person_info() -> (String, u32, bool) {
    let name = String::from("Alice");
    let age = 30;
    let is_active = true;
    (name, age, is_active)
}

fn main() {
    let person_info = get_person_info();
    println!("Name: {}, Age: {}, Active: {}", person_info.0, person_
info.1, person_info.2);
}
```

In this example, note the following:

- The `get_person_info` function returns a tuple containing a `String`, `u32`, and `bool`
- We call `get_person_info` in the `main` function and print each element of the returned tuple using positional indexing

Tuples are particularly useful for the following:

- Returning multiple values from a function without the need to define a struct
- Grouping related values for iteration or other operations where the context makes their meaning clear
- Passing multiple values as a single parameter to a function

Accessing tuple elements

Once you have defined a tuple, you can access its elements using positional indexing. Each element in a tuple is accessed using a zero-based index, which indicates its position in the tuple.

Accessing elements by index

Here's how to access the elements of a tuple using their indices:

```
fn main() {
    let tuple: (i32, f64, bool) = (42, 6.7, true);

    let int_value = tuple.0;
    let float_value = tuple.1;
    let bool_value = tuple.2;

    println!("Integer value: {}", int_value);
    println!("Float value: {}", float_value);
    println!("Boolean value: {}", bool_value);
}
```

In this example, note the following:

- `tuple.0` accesses the first element (`i32`)
- `tuple.1` accesses the second element (`f64`)
- `tuple.2` accesses the third element (`bool`)

Using positional indexing, we can extract and use the values stored in a tuple.

Practical example: employee record

Let's consider a practical example where we use a tuple to store an employee's record:

```
fn main() {
    let employee: (u32, String, f64) = (1001, String::from("John Doe"),
75000.0);

    let id = employee.0;
    // We take a reference (&) to the String because String is not a
`Copy` type.
    // This borrows the value without moving it, so `employee` can still
be used.

    let name = &employee.1;
    let salary = employee.2;

    println!("Employee ID: {}", id);
    println!("Employee Name: {}", name);
    println!("Employee Salary: ${}", salary);
}
```

In this example, note the following:

- We define an `employee` tuple with an `ID` (`u32`), `name` (`String`), and `salary` (`f64`)
- We access each element of the tuple using positional indexing and print the values

This demonstrates how to work with tuples effectively in a real-world scenario.

Next, we'll explore how to destructure tuples to extract multiple values simultaneously.

Destructuring tuples

Destructuring tuples allows you to extract multiple values simultaneously in a concise and readable way. This technique can be particularly useful when you need to work with multiple elements of a tuple at once.

Destructuring tuples

Here's how to destructure a tuple into individual variables:

```
fn main() {
    let tuple: (i32, f64, bool) = (42, 6.7, true);

    let (int_value, float_value, bool_value) = tuple;

    println!("Integer value: {}", int_value);
    println!("Float value: {}", float_value);
    println!("Boolean value: {}", bool_value);
}
```

In this example, note the following:

- We destructure the tuple into three separate variables: `int_value`, `float_value`, and `bool_value`
- Each variable corresponds to an element in the tuple, in order

Practical example: destructuring function return values

Let's use destructuring to handle multiple return values from a function:

```
fn calculate(a: i32, b: i32) -> (i32, i32, i32) {
    let sum = a + b;
    let difference = a - b;
    let product = a * b;
    (sum, difference, product)
}

fn main() {
    let (sum, difference, product) = calculate(10, 5);

    println!("Sum: {}", sum);
    println!("Difference: {}", difference);
    println!("Product: {}", product);
}
```

In this example, note the following:

- The `calculate` function returns a tuple containing the sum, difference, and product of two integers
- In the `main` function, we destructure the returned tuple into three separate variables: `sum`, `difference`, and `product`

Destructuring helps keep the code concise and readable when working with multiple values.

Destructuring in a loop

Destructuring can also be used in a loop to iterate over a collection of tuples:

```
fn main() {
    let points = vec![(0, 0), (1, 2), (3, 4)];

    for (x, y) in points {
        println!("Point at ({}, {})", x, y);
    }
}
```

In this example, note the following:

- We have a vector of tuples representing points
- We use a `for` loop to destructure each tuple into x and y coordinates and print them

Returning tuples from functions

Tuples are particularly useful for returning multiple values from functions without needing to define a more complex struct. This can simplify your code and make functions more flexible.

Returning multiple values

Here's an example of a function that returns a tuple with multiple values:

```
fn calculate(a: i32, b: i32) -> (i32, i32, i32) {
    let sum = a + b;
    let difference = a - b;
    let product = a * b;
    (sum, difference, product)
}
```

```
fn main() {
    let result = calculate(10, 5);
    println!("Sum: {}", result.0);
    println!("Difference: {}", result.1);
    println!("Product: {}", result.2);
}
```

In this example, note the following:

- The calculate function returns a tuple containing the sum, difference, and product of two integers
- In the main function, we call calculate and access each element of the returned tuple using positional indexing

Destructuring function return values

You can also destructure the returned tuple directly into individual variables:

```
fn main() {
    let (sum, difference, product) = calculate(10, 5);

    println!("Sum: {}", sum);
    println!("Difference: {}", difference);
    println!("Product: {}", product);
}
```

In this example, we destructure the tuple returned by `calculate` into `sum`, `difference`, and `product`. This makes the code more readable and easier to work with.

Practical example: splitting a full name

Let's create a practical example where we use a function to split a full name into first and last names:

```
fn split_name(full_name: &str) -> (&str, &str) {
    let parts: Vec<&str> = full_name.splitn(2, ' ').collect();
    (parts[0], parts[1])
}

fn main() {
```

```
    let full_name = "John Doe";
    let (first_name, last_name) = split_name(full_name);

    println!("First Name: {}", first_name);
    println!("Last Name: {}", last_name);
}
```

In this example, note the following:

- The `split_name` function takes a full name as a string slice and returns a tuple containing the first and last names
- We destructure the returned tuple in the `main` function to access and print the first and last names

Using tuples to return multiple values from functions makes your code more flexible and reduces the need for complex data structures.

Practical example: point in 3D space

To demonstrate the versatility and practical use of tuples, let's create a function that calculates the distance between two points in 3D space. Each point will be represented as a tuple containing three `f64` values for the x, y, and z coordinates.

Calculating the distance between points

The formula for the distance between two points, (x1,y1,z1) and (x2,y2,z2), in 3D space is as follows:

$distance = sqrt((x\_2 - x\_1)^\wedge 2 + (y\_2 - y\_1)^\wedge 2 + (z\_2 - z\_1)^\wedge 2)$

Here's how you can implement this in Rust:

```
fn distance(point1: (f64, f64, f64), point2: (f64, f64, f64)) -> f64 {
    let (x1, y1, z1) = point1;
    let (x2, y2, z2) = point2;

    ((x2 - x1).powi(2) + (y2 - y1).powi(2) + (z2 - z1).powi(2)).sqrt()
}

fn main() {
    let point1 = (0.0, 0.0, 0.0);
    let point2 = (3.0, 4.0, 0.0);
```

```
    println!("The distance between points is: {}", distance(point1,
point2));
}
```

In this example, note the following:

- We define a function, `distance`, that takes two tuples as parameters, each representing a point in 3D space
- We destructure the tuples into their respective coordinates
- We calculate the distance using the Euclidean distance formula and return the result

Practical usage

This example showcases how tuples can be used to represent complex data structures in a simple and efficient manner. By using tuples, we avoid the need for more complex structs, keeping the code concise and readable.

Tuples: exercises and assignments

To further solidify your understanding of tuples, try the following exercises:

1. **Extend the distance function**: Modify the `distance` function to handle points in 2D space (x, y) as well as 3D space.
2. **Create a color tuple**: Define a tuple to represent a color with **red, green, blue** (**RGB**) values, and write a function that converts it to a hexadecimal string.
3. **Employee information**: Write a function that returns an employee's ID, name, and salary as a tuple, and then destructure the tuple in the `main` function to print the employee's details.
4. **Point transformation**: Write a function that takes a 3D point (x, y, z) and a tuple representing a translation vector (dx, dy, dz). The function should return a new point that is the result of applying the translation vector to the original point.

Tuples: summary

We've explored tuples in Rust, including their definition, element access, destructuring, and use as function return types. A practical example showed calculating distances between 3D points using tuples.

Understanding tuples allows for the efficient grouping of values without complex structs. This concludes our discussion on Rust's composite types: structs, enums, and tuples.

Using structs, enums, and tuples together

The real power often comes from combining these different composite types. You can have structs containing enums, enums containing structs or tuples, structs containing other structs, and so on.

This allows you to model complex real-world data relationships accurately and safely within Rust's type system.

Practical example: modeling a user profile

Let's revisit the vehicle fleet idea, showing structs and enums working together:

```
#[derive(Debug)]
struct Point(i32, i32); // Tuple struct for coordinates

#[derive(Debug)]
enum VehicleKind {
    Car { passengers: u8 },
    Truck { capacity_tons: f32 },
    Bicycle { gears: u8 },
}

#[derive(Debug)]
struct Vehicle {
    id: u32,
    kind: VehicleKind, // Enum field
    location: Point, // Tuple struct field
}

fn main() {
    let delivery_truck = Vehicle {
        id: 101,
        kind: VehicleKind::Truck { capacity_tons: 2.5 },
        location: Point(50, -30),
    };

    let commuter_bike = Vehicle {
        id: 205,
        kind: VehicleKind::Bicycle { gears: 18 },
```

```
        location: Point(10, 15),
    };

    println!("Vehicle 1: {:?}", delivery_truck);
    println!("Vehicle 2: {:?}", commuter_bike);

    // We can match on the kind field
    match &delivery_truck.kind {
        VehicleKind::Truck { capacity_tons } => {
            println!("Truck {} has capacity: {} tons", delivery_truck.id,
capacity_tons);
        }
        _ => { // Handle other kinds if necessary
             println!("Vehicle {} is not a truck.", delivery_truck.id);
        }
    }
}
```

This example uses a tuple struct, `Point`, an enum, `VehicleKind` (where variants hold specific data), and a main struct, `Vehicle`, that contains both a `VehicleKind` enum and a `Point` tuple struct.

This demonstrates how you can layer these types to build expressive data models representing complex entities and their varying attributes or states.

Managing complexity with the module system

Packages and crates

To get a good grasp on organizing a project, let's start by looking at the physical artifacts Cargo creates.

When you run '`cargo new`', you're creating a Package, basically, a directory with a Cargo.toml file that explains how to build your code. Think of it as the main container for everything. Inside this package, your actual code lives in Crates.

What is a crate? A crate is just the smallest piece of code that the Rust compiler works on at a time. Usually, you'll be dealing with binary crates (which turn into a program you can run) or library crates (which hold code shared across projects). A package can have many binaries, but it will only have one library.

The Package layout

A Package essentially functions as a project bundle. When you run '`cargo new my_project`' in your terminal, you're creating a package. The key element of a package is the Cargo.toml file, serving as a manifest. This file offers Cargo the necessary instructions to compile your code, oversee dependencies, and manage software versioning.

Inside this package, you include your actual code in the form of crates. The package enforces specific rules about what it can contain. It must include at least one crate, whether that is a library or a binary. While a package can include as many binary crates as you want, it can only contain at most one library crate.

Binary crates vs. library crates

A **Crate** is the smallest amount of code that the Rust compiler considers at one time. Crates come in two distinct forms.

Binary crates Programs that you can compile into an executable and run, such as a command-line tool or a server, are often called crates. These crates need to include a function called main, which tells the program where to start. Usually, if your package has a file named src/main.rs, that file is considered the main entry point of a binary crate.

Library crates Most of these files usually don't include a main function, and they don't compile directly into an executable. Instead, they serve as a way to share functionality with other projects. When folks in the Rust community mention "crate," they're often talking about a library crate. Typically, if your package has a src/lib.rs file, Cargo recognizes this as the main part of your library crate. A package can have several binary crates, but it can only have one library crate.

```
my-project/
├── Cargo.toml
├── src/
│   ├── main.rs       <-- Root of the binary crate
│   └── lib.rs        <-- Root of the library crate
│   └── bin/
│       └── another.rs  <-- Root of another binary crate
```

Controlling scope and privacy with modules

Modules allow us to organize the code inside a crate into groups for readability and easy reuse. Modules also control the *privacy* of items, which is how we decide whether an item can be used by outside code (public) or is an internal implementation detail (private).

Defining the module tree

We define a module by starting with the mod keyword and then giving it a name. Inside the curly brackets, we can define other modules, as well as structs, enums, constants, traits, and functions.

By nesting modules inside other modules, we create a structure called the module tree.

Here is an example of how we might organize a library that models a restaurant:

```
mod front_of_house {
    mod hosting {
        fn add_to_waitlist() {}
        fn seat_at_table() {}
    }

    mod serving {
        fn take_order() {}
        fn serve_order() {}
    }
}
```

In this example, the crate root is the parent of the `front_of_house` module. The `front_of_house` module is the parent of hosting and serving. This tree structure allows you to keep related functionality together rather than having everything in a single flat list.

The rules of privacy (the pub keyword)

Rust carefully manages who can see and use different parts of your code, making sure everything stays secure and well-structured. By default, everything inside a module is private, so only the code within that module can access it. This helps keep your inner workings safe from accidental misuse. It's interesting to note that while child modules can reach into their parent modules, the reverse isn't automatically allowed: parents can't access items in their children without explicit permission.

To help external code access an item, you simply use the pub keyword. Think of it as opening a door to that module or function. In the example below, we've added pub to both the module and the function, allowing `eat_at_restaurant` to reach them easily.

```
mod front_of_house {
    // We add 'pub' to the module so the parent can see it
    pub mod hosting {
```

```
        // We add 'pub' to the function so it can be called
        pub fn add_to_waitlist() {}
    }
}

pub fn eat_at_restaurant() {
    // This works because 'hosting' and 'add_to_waitlist' are now public
    crate::front_of_house::hosting::add_to_waitlist();
}
```

Referring to items via paths

To show Rust where to find an item in the module tree, we use a path, similar to navigating a filesystem.

To call a function, specify its path with double colons :: as separators.

A path can be absolute or relative, like in a file system.

Absolute paths

An absolute path starts from the crate root or, if from an external crate, with that crate's name. For code within the current crate, it begins with the keyword crate. This approach is preferred as item definitions are less likely to move than calling code.

```
pub fn eat_at_restaurant() {
    // Absolute path starting with 'crate'
    crate::front_of_house::hosting::add_to_waitlist();
}
```

Relative paths and the super keyword

A relative path starts from the current module instead of the crate root. It uses self, super, or an identifier available in the current scope. This is often useful when the definition of the item and the code calling it are likely to be moved around the project together.

The super keyword allows you to reference the parent module. This is exactly like using .. in a filesystem path to go up one directory level. In the example below, the `fix_incorrect_order` function is inside the `back_of_house` module. To call `serve_order`, which is defined in the parent crate root, we use super.

```
fn serve_order() {}

mod back_of_house {
    fn fix_incorrect_order() {
        cook_order();
        // We use super to go up one level to the parent module
        super::serve_order();
    }
    fn cook_order() {}
}
```

Simplifying scope with the use keyword

Writing out a full path to a function repeatedly can be tedious and makes code harder to read.

Rust allows you to bring a path into scope once with the use keyword, enabling you to call the item as if it were local.

Think of this similar to creating a symbolic link or shortcut in your filesystem. By including a line with use at the beginning of your file, you create a shortcut to that particular module or item. In the example below, we bring the hosting module into scope. Now, whenever we want to access `add_to_waitlist`, we only need to specify hosting:: instead of the full path from the crate root.

```
mod front_of_house {
    pub mod hosting {
        pub fn add_to_waitlist() {}
    }
}

// Bring the module into scope
use crate::front_of_house::hosting;
```

```
pub fn eat_at_restaurant() {
    // Now we can use the shorter path
    hosting::add_to_waitlist();
}
```

Idiomatic use paths

You might wonder why we included the hosting module earlier instead of directly using `add_to_waitlist`. The reason is Rust convention: it's more idiomatic to bring the parent module into scope for functions. This makes your code clearer, showing that the function isn't in the current file.

However, when it comes to working with structs, enums, and other items, the usual convention is a bit different. Typically, we like to bring the entire item into scope so we can use it directly, which helps keep our code clean and concise. For instance, instead of just bringing in collections, we bring HashMap directly into scope.

```
// Idiomatic: Bring the function's parent module into scope
use crate::front_of_house::hosting;

// Idiomatic: Bring the full struct into scope
use std::collections::HashMap;

fn main() {
    // It is clear this function comes from the hosting module
    hosting::add_to_waitlist();

    // We can use the struct directly
    let mut map = HashMap::new();
}
```

Handling naming conflicts with "as"

Sometimes, you need to use items with identical names from different modules. If you attempt to bring both into scope with use, Rust won't know which one you're referencing and will fail to compile. To fix this, you can use the as keyword to create an alias, giving a new local name to the type and avoiding conflicts.

In the example below, we use the Result type from both the fmt module and the io module. By renaming `io::Result` to `IoResult`, we avoid confusion and can use both in the same file.

```
use std::fmt::Result;
use std::io::Result as IoResult;

fn function1() -> Result {
    // Returns std::fmt::Result
    Ok(())
}

fn function2() -> IoResult<()> {
    // Returns std::io::Result
    Ok(())
}
```

Physical organization: separating modules into files

As modules grow, managing all definitions in src/lib.rs becomes challenging. Moving definitions into separate files improves navigation. Rust enables extracting modules into different files without altering your crate's external API; the code structure changes, but the module tree remains logically consistent.

The module filesystem mapping

To move a module to its own file, we change how we declare it in the parent file. Instead of using a block with curly brackets, we declare the module with a semicolon. This tells Rust that the module exists but its definition is located in another file with the same name.

For example, to move the front_of_house module out of src/lib.rs:

1. In src/lib.rs, we replace the full module block with `pub mod front_of_house;`.
2. We create a new file named src/front_of_house.rs.
3. We paste the content of the module into the new file. Note that we do not need to wrap the code in a mod block inside the new file because the file itself acts as the module container.

File: src/lib.rs

```
// Rust looks for src/front_of_house.rs
pub mod front_of_house;
```

```
pub fn eat_at_restaurant() {
    crate::front_of_house::hosting::add_to_waitlist();
}
```

File: src/front_of_house.rs

```
pub mod hosting {
    pub fn add_to_waitlist() {}
}
```

Summary

Well done!

We've journeyed through Rust's essential composite data types, learning how to structure data beyond simple primitives. We started with **structs**, understanding how to define custom types with named fields, create instances, access and modify data, and add behavior using **methods** and associated functions within `impl` blocks. We also touched upon variations such as concise **tuple structs** and field-less **unit-like structs**.

Next, we explored **enums**, discovering how they allow us to define a type that can be one of several distinct **variants**. Crucially, we saw how these variants can hold associated data, making enums incredibly powerful for modeling different states, choices, or message types, often paired elegantly with Rust's exhaustive `match` expression for safe handling. Finally, we looked at **tuples** as a simple, lightweight way to group a fixed number of values together, which is particularly useful for returning multiple values from functions or for temporary data bundling.

Mastering structs, enums, and tuples is crucial for organizing data effectively in Rust. By combining these types and understanding how they interact with core concepts such as ownership and borrowing (which we covered in *Chapter 4*), you gain the tools to build complex, expressive, and safe data models for your applications. Keep practicing, and these fundamental building blocks will become second nature.

We also addressed the structural side of Rust programming by introducing the module system. We explored how to organize code into logical groups using packages, crates, and modules, and how to control the privacy of that code using the pub keyword. We also covered how to navigate the module tree using paths, which is essential for splitting code across multiple files and managing complexity as your projects grow.

In the next chapter, we'll explore another of Rust's most important safety features: a powerful and explicit system for handling errors.

Questions and assignments

Congratulations on completing this exploration of Rust's composite types! To ensure these concepts stick, let's reinforce your learning with some review questions and hands-on coding assignments. Tackling these will significantly strengthen your grasp of how to structure data effectively in Rust.

Questions

1. In your own words, what is the core difference between a struct and an enum? Provide a scenario where a struct is clearly more appropriate, and another where an enum is the better choice.
2. What are the three forms of `self` that a method's first parameter can take, and what does each signify in terms of ownership and mutability for the instance the method is called on?
3. Explain the purpose and syntax of an associated function (such as `::new()`) within an `impl` block. How does calling it differ from calling a method?
4. When defining an enum variant that holds data, what are the different ways you can structure that data (e.g., a tuple, a struct)?
5. What is the struct update syntax (`..`), and why is it important to consider ownership (and the `Copy` trait) when using it?
6. Why might you choose to use a tuple struct, such as `struct Color(u8, u8, u8);`, instead of a regular tuple `(u8, u8, u8)` or a regular struct, such as `struct Color { red: u8, green: u8, blue: u8 }`?
7. How can you make your custom struct or enum printable for debugging using `println!`?

Assignments

Assignment 5.1: order system

1. Define a `Product` struct with the `id` (`u32`), `name` (`String`), and `price` (`f32`) fields.
2. Define an `OrderStatus` enum with `Pending`, `Processing`, `Shipped`, `Delivered`, and `Cancelled` variants.
3. Define an `Order` struct with the `order_id` (`u32`), `product` (`Product`), `quantity` (`u32`), and `status` (`OrderStatus`) fields.
4. Implement `#[derive(Debug)]` for all structs and the enum.

5. Create an associated function, `Order::new(order_id: u32, product: Product, quantity: u32) -> Order`, that creates a new order with the `Pending` status.
6. Implement an `update_status(&mut self, new_status: OrderStatus)` method for the `Order` struct.
7. In `main`, create a `Product`, create a new order using `Order::new`, print the order, update its status to `Shipped`, and print it again.

Assignment 5.2: geometric shapes enhanced

1. Define a tuple struct, `Point(f64, f64)`, representing a 2D point.
2. Define a `Shape` enum with the following variants:
    - `Circle { center: Point, radius: f64 }`
    - `Rectangle { top_left: Point, width: f64, height: f64 }`
3. Implement `#[derive(Debug)]` for `Point` and `Shape`.
4. Implement an `impl` block for `Shape`. Add an `area(&self) -> f64` method that calculates and returns the area based on the shape variant (Area of circle = π * radius^2; Area of rectangle = width * height). Use `std::f64::consts::PI` for π.
5. In `main`, create a `Circle` and a `Rectangle`. Store them in a `Vec<Shape>`. Iterate through the vector and print both the debug representation (`{:?}`) and the calculated area for each shape.

6

Introduction to Error Handling

Welcome to *Chapter 6*!

After exploring composite types in the previous chapter, we now turn to a very important aspect of building robust and reliable software: **error handling**. In Rust, effectively handling errors isn't just good practice; it's a *core* part of mastering the language.

It ensures our programs can gracefully manage unexpected situations, maintaining stability and predictability.

Why error handling matters

But why dedicate an entire chapter to error handling? There are several fundamental reasons:

- **Robustness**: Programs must handle unexpected inputs, system issues (such as missing files or denied permissions), and other anomalies without crashing. Good error handling makes software more resilient.
- **User experience**: Clearly reporting errors helps users (and fellow developers!) understand what went wrong and potentially how to fix it.
- **Maintainability**: A consistent approach to error handling makes code easier to read, understand, and modify over time.

Rust's approach to errors

Rust takes a distinctive approach to error handling, heavily focused on safety and clarity, avoiding many common pitfalls found in other languages (such as unchecked exceptions or unhandled null/nil values). In Rust, errors primarily fall into two categories:

- **Recoverable errors**: These are problematic situations the program can anticipate and potentially handle or recover from, such as trying to open a file that doesn't exist. Rust encourages explicit handling of these, usually via the `Result<T, E>` type.
- **Unrecoverable errors (panic)**: These indicate serious, unexpected problems, typically bugs in the program (such as accessing an array index out of bounds), from which recovery isn't expected. In these cases, Rust enters a panic state (using the `panic!` macro), which, by default, unwinds the stack and quits the current thread.

Core tools: Result and Option

To manage these categories, Rust provides two fundamental enum types, which we've had a glimpse of before and will now explore thoroughly:

- **Result<T, E>**: Used for operations that might succeed (returning a value of type `T` in the `Ok` variant) or fail (returning an error of type `E` in the `Err` variant). It's the primary tool for recoverable errors.
- **Option<T>**: Used when a value might be present (the `Some(T)` variant) or absent (the `None` variant). It doesn't necessarily signify an error, but rather the absence of an expected value, such as when a search yields no results.

These types make the possibility of failure or absence an explicit part of a function's signature, forcing callers to consider these cases and dramatically improving code reliability.

In this chapter, we'll explore Rust's error-handling mechanisms in detail.

We will cover the following:

- **The Result and Option types**: How to use these enums effectively
- **Handling Result and Option**: Safe ways to extract values or handle `Err` and `None` cases (e.g., `match`, `unwrap_or`)
- **Propagating errors with ?**: Simplifying error handling in call chains
- **Custom error types**: Creating specific error types for your application.

- **Useful crates:** Introducing `thiserror` and `anyhow` for further simplification
- **Logging errors:** Techniques for recording useful information during execution
- **Practical examples and best practices:** Applying what we learn in realistic scenarios

Mastering error handling is essential for writing robust Rust software. This chapter will equip you with the tools and knowledge to do so effectively. Let's get started!

Introduction to Result and Option

As mentioned, `Result` and `Option` are the cornerstones of handling errors and potentially missing values in Rust. They are both enum types defined in the standard library.

Understanding their operation deeply is the first step toward writing safe and clear Rust code.

Let's start with `Result`.

The Result type

The `Result` type is Rust's primary tool for handling operations that can fail. It is an enum defined in the standard library with two variants: `Ok`, which represents success and contains a value, and `Err`, which represents failure and contains an error value.

The definition is as follows:

```
enum Result<T, E> {
    Ok(T),  // Success: contains a value of type T
    Err(E), // Failure: contains an error value of type E
}
```

Here, `T` is the type of the value in the success case (`Ok`), and `E` is the type of the error in the failure case (`Err`).

It's important to note that `T` and `E` are **generic type parameters.**

This means you can use `Result` with any combination of success and error types, making it incredibly flexible. `T` stands for the type of the value that will be returned in a success case, and `E` stands for the type of the error that will be returned in a failure case.

For example, a function that parses a string into a number might return `Result<i32, ParseIntError>`, while a function that opens a file might return `Result<File, std::io::Error>`.

Let's look at a classic example – a division function that must handle division by 0:

```
// Function returning a Result: Ok with an f64 result, or Err with a
String error message.
fn divide(numerator: f64, denominator: f64) -> Result<f64, String> {
    if denominator == 0.0 {
        // If denominator is zero, return an error (Err)
        Err(String::from("Error: division by zero!"))
    } else {
        // Otherwise, return the result successfully (Ok)
        Ok(numerator / denominator)
    }
}

fn main() {
    let result1 = divide(10.0, 2.0); // Successful call
    let result2 = divide(5.0, 0.0);  // Failing call

    // Use 'match' to handle both cases of the Result
    match result1 {
        Ok(value) => println!("Division 10/2 succeeded: {}", value), //
Output: 5.0
        Err(message) => println!("Error in division 10/2: {}", message),
    }

    match result2 {
        Ok(value) => println!("Division 5/0 succeeded: {}", value),
        Err(message) => println!("Error in division 5/0: {}", message), //
Output: Error: division by zero!
    }
}
```

In this example, the `divide` function declares that it returns `Result<f64, String>`. If the operation is valid, it wraps the `f64` result in `Ok`.

If division by 0 is attempted, it wraps a `String` error message in `Err`.

The calling code (in `main`) uses `match` to inspect the `Result` and act differently depending on whether it's `Ok` or `Err`, extracting the value or the error message accordingly.

The Option type

The `Option<T>` type is used when a value might be present or absent.

It's defined as follows:

```
enum Option<T> {
    Some(T), // Value is present: contains a value of type T
    None,    // Value is absent
}
```

Here, `T` is the type of the potentially present value. `Option` is very useful for functions that might not find what they're looking for, or for representing optional fields in structs.

Option example

Let's see an example involving searching for a substring:

```
// This function searches for a word in a sentence.
// It returns Option<usize>: Some(index) if the word is found, or None
otherwise.
fn find_word_index(haystack: &str, needle: &str) -> Option<usize> {
    // The built-in .find() method on string slices already returns
Option<usize>,
    // which is very convenient.
    haystack.find(needle)
}

fn main() {
    let famous_phrase = "The quick brown fox jumps over the lazy dog.";
    let word_to_find = "fox";
    let word_not_present = "cat";

    // --- Test Case 1: Word is found ---
    println!("Searching for '{}'...", word_to_find);
    match find_word_index(famous_phrase, word_to_find) {
```

```
        Some(index) => println!("Success! Found at index {}.", index),
        None => println!("Failure: Word not found."),
    }

    println!("---");

    // --- Test Case 2: Word is NOT found ---
    println!("Searching for '{}'...", word_not_present);
    match find_word_index(famous_phrase, word_not_present) {
        Some(index) => println!("Success! Found at index {}.", index),
        None => println!("Correctly determined that the word was not 
found."),
    }
}
```

The `find_word_index` function uses the string slice's built-in `.find()` method, which perfectly illustrates the use of `Option<usize>` by returning `Some(index)` if the substring is found, or `None` otherwise.

Our single `main` function then demonstrates how to call this function and use a `match` statement to safely handle both the success (`Some`) and failure (`None`) cases, printing an appropriate message for each outcome.

When to use Result versus Option

Choosing between `Result` and `Option` depends on the meaning you want to convey about the absence of a value:

- Use `Result<T, E>` when an operation can fail for a specific reason you want to communicate to the caller via the error type, `E`. It's for recoverable errors.
- Use `Option<T>` when the absence of a value is a possible and normal outcome (e.g., search failed or optional data not provided), and the reason for absence isn't important or is implicit.

It's also worth noting that from a programming perspective, Rust makes it very easy to convert between `Option` and `Result`, allowing you to adapt a function's return type to the specific needs of your error-handling logic.

Getting a good handle on `Result` and `Option` is really important. They encourage you to think about failure or missing values, which helps make Rust code clearer and much safer compared to languages that depend on unchecked exceptions or nulls.

In the next section, we will start exploring how to implement error handling in Rust. We will gradually move from the simplest methods to the most advanced ones. There is no single way to do this, but of course, using the most advanced techniques makes your code more robust and less prone to errors.

It also helps you better understand what went wrong and why, instead of just failing.

Handling Result and Option (unwrapping and alternatives)

Unrecoverable errors: Understanding panic!

Before we look at the different ways to handle `Result` and `Option`, it's important to understand Rust's mechanism for dealing with **unrecoverable errors**. These are errors that indicate a bug or a state from which your program cannot safely continue. The primary tool for this is the `panic!` macro.

When `panic!` is called, your program will, by default, stop execution immediately, unwind the stack (cleaning up memory as it goes), and print an error message. A panic signifies that something has gone so wrong that it's impossible to proceed. This is Rust's way of failing "loudly and early" rather than continuing with potentially corrupt data.

You can call `panic!` directly in your code to signal an unrecoverable error state:

```
fn check_critical_value(value: i32) {
    if value < 0 {
        // If the value is negative, it's an unrecoverable state for this
function.
        panic!("Critical value cannot be negative! Received: {}", value);
    }
    println!("Value {} is valid.", value);
}

fn main() {
    check_critical_value(10); // This will run fine.
```

```
    // The line below will cause the program to panic and terminate.
    // check_critical_value(-5);

    // This line will not be reached if the panic occurs.
    println!("Program finished successfully.");
}
```

While you can trigger a panic yourself, you'll more often encounter panics when using methods that are shortcuts for this behavior, such as `unwrap()` and `expect()`.

It's helpful to remember that these methods are purposely designed to trigger a panic upon failure, which is an important aspect to keep in mind when using them effectively.

Introduction to unwrapping

We've seen that `match` is a powerful and safe way of handling `Result` and `Option`. However, sometimes you might *know* with certainty (or near certainty) that a value is present (`Ok` or `Some`) and want to access that value directly.

Rust provides methods for this, but it's important to use them cautiously.

Using unwrap and expect

The most direct methods for extracting the value are `unwrap` and `expect`:

- **unwrap()**: If `Result` is `Ok(value)` or `Option` is `Some(value)`, it returns `value`. If it's `Err` or `None`, the program will panic (crashing the current thread):

  ```
  // A simple function that returns a Result, for context.
  fn divide(a: f64, b: f64) -> Result<f64, String> {
      if b == 0.0 {
          Err("Division by zero".to_string())
      } else {
          Ok(a / b)
      }
  }
  ```

```
fn main() {
    // --- Success Case ---
    let ok_result = divide(10.0, 5.0);

    // Print the Result before unwrapping to show its Ok(value)
state.
    println!("The Result before unwrap: {:?}", ok_result); //
Prints: Ok(2.0)

    // .unwrap() extracts the value from the Ok variant.
    let value = ok_result.unwrap();
    println!("The value after unwrap: {}", value); // Prints: 2.0

    // --- Panic Case ---
    // let err_result = divide(10.0, 0.0); // This would be
Err("Division by zero")
    // println!("The Result before panic: {:?}", err_result);
    //
    // // Calling .unwrap() on an Err variant will cause the program
to panic.
    // let value_panic = err_result.unwrap(); // This line would
PANIC!
}
```

- **expect("error message")**: Works like `unwrap`, but if it panics, it will use the provided message as part of the panic output. It's slightly better than `unwrap` as it lets you specify why you expected a value:

```
let non_existent_file: Result<String, std::io::Error> =
std::fs::read_to_string("file_no_exist.txt");
// This will panic with the specified message
// non_existent_file.expect("Expected the file to definitely
exist!");
```

Caution: unwrap and expect turn a potentially recoverable error (Err or None) into an unrecoverable one (panic). Use them only when there is a logic bug in your program from which there's no sensible recovery path, or in prototypes/examples where a crash is acceptable. In most production code, prefer safer methods.

If you were to run a program with the .expect() call on a failing operation, the output would look something like this, clearly showing your custom message:

```
thread 'main' panicked at 'Expected the file to definitely exist!:
Os { code: 2, kind: NotFound, message: "No such file or directory"
}', src/main.rs:4:5
note: run with `RUST_BACKTRACE=1` environment variable to display a
backtrace
```

Safe unwrapping with defaults

To access the value or provide a safe alternative without risking panic, Rust offers unwrap_or and unwrap_or_else:

- **unwrap_or(default_value):** Returns the contained value if Ok/Some. If Err/None, it returns the provided default_value (which must be of the same type as the Ok/Some value):

```
let err_result = divide(10.0, 0.0); // This is Err(...)
let value_or_default = err_result.unwrap_or(0.0); // Doesn't panic,
returns 0.0
println!("Value or default: {}", value_or_default);

let none_option: Option<i32> = None;
let option_value = none_option.unwrap_or(100); // Returns 100
println!("Option or default: {}", option_value);
```

- **unwrap_or_else(closure):** Similar to unwrap_or, but if the value is Err/None, it executes the provided *closure* (anonymous function) and returns the result of that closure. This is useful if the default value requires computation:

```
let err_result = divide(10.0, 0.0); // Err(...)
```

```
let value_or_computed = err_result.unwrap_or_else(|err_msg| {
    println!("Error during division: {}. Using fallback value.",
err_msg);
    -1.0 // Value computed/returned by the closure
});
println!("Value or computed: {}", value_or_computed);
```

These methods are much safer and more common alternatives to `unwrap`/`expect` in robust code.

Using combinators

While `match` is powerful, Rust provides several convenient methods on `Result` and `Option` called **combinators** that allow you to chain operations together in a more concise, functional style.

These methods can often replace a `match` statement for common patterns. Let's look at a few of the most common ones for `Result`:

- **map()**: This applies a function to the contained `Ok` value. The `map` method takes a closure and applies it to the value inside an `Ok`, leaving an `Err` value untouched. The closure takes the success value (`T`) and returns a new value (`U`), and `map` returns `Result<U, E>`:

```
fn main() {
 let successful_parse: Result<i32, _> = "10".parse();
// If successful_parse is Ok(10), the closure |x| x * 2 is called
with 10.
// The result is Ok(20).
let doubled_result = successful_parse.map(|x| x * 2);
println!("Doubled result: {:?}", doubled_result); // Prints: Ok(20)
 }
```

- **and_then**: This chains another operation that might fail. The `and_then` method is used when you want to perform a subsequent operation that *also* returns a `Result`. If the initial `Result` is `Ok`, `and_then` calls the closure with the success value. The closure itself must return a new `Result`. If the initial `Result` is `Err`, the closure is not called, and the error is propagated:

```
    // A function that only succeeds for even numbers.
    fn check_if_even(n: i32) -> Result<i32, String> {
```

```
        if n % 2 == 0 {
            Ok(n)
        } else {
            Err("Number is not even".to_string())
        }
    }
    fn main() {
        let successful_parse: Result<i32, _> = "10".parse();
        let failed_parse: Result<i32, _> = "7".parse();

        // Chain the parsing with the even check.
        let even_result = successful_parse.and_then(check_if_even);
        println!("Result for '10': {:?}", even_result); // Prints:
Ok(10)

        let odd_result = failed_parse.and_then(check_if_even);
        println!("Result for '7': {:?}", odd_result); // Prints:
Err("Number is not even")
    }
```

- **or_else**: This provides a fallback operation that might also fail. The `or_else` method is used to handle an `Err` case by trying an alternative operation. If the initial `Result` is `Ok`, `or_else` does nothing and returns the `Ok` value. If it's `Err`, it calls the closure with the error value. *Crucially, the closure passed to or_else must itself return a Result<T, E> of the same type.* This allows you to provide a fallback that could either succeed (`Ok`) or produce a different error (`Err`):

```
    fn main() {
        // First attempt fails to parse.
        let first_attempt: Result<i32, _> = "hello".parse();
        // Second attempt will succeed.
        let second_attempt: Result<i32, _> = "42".parse();

        // Use or_else to try the second attempt if the first one
fails.
        // The closure `|_| second_attempt` is called because first_
attempt is Err.
        // It returns the second_attempt Result.
```

```
        let final_result = first_attempt.or_else(|_| second_
attempt);

        println!("Final result after fallback: {:?}", final_result);
// Prints: Ok(42)
    }
```

These combinators allow for more expressive and concise error handling, enabling you to chain operations and handle errors inline.

By mastering these techniques for unwrapping and handling `Result` and `Option` types, you'll make your Rust code more reliable and easier to read. It helps ensure that errors are managed in a smooth and proper way, making your coding experience more confident and stress-free.

While combinator methods are excellent for handling a single `Result` or `Option`, a common challenge in Rust is managing errors within a function that calls multiple other functions that might fail.

Propagating errors with ?

To solve this problem and avoid deeply nested match statements, Rust provides a powerful and concise piece of syntactic sugar for error propagation: the question mark (?) operator.

The problem of manual propagation

Often, a function might call other functions that return `Result` or `Option`. If one of these inner calls fails (returns `Err` or `None`), we might want our outer function to also fail immediately, returning that specific error or `None` to its caller. Handling this manually with `match` at every step can become verbose:

```
// Verbose example without '?'
fn read_then_divide(file_path: &str, divisor: f64) -> Result<f64, String>
{
    let content_result = std::fs::read_to_string(file_path);
    let content = match content_result {
        Ok(c) => c,
        Err(e) => return Err(format!("File read error: {}", e)), // Manual
propagation
    };
```

```
    let number_result = content.trim().parse::<f64>();
    let number = match number_result {
        Ok(n) => n,
        Err(e) => return Err(format!("Number parse error: {}", e)), //
Manual propagation
    };

    match divide(number, divisor) { // Using our previous 'divide'
function
        Ok(result) => Ok(result),
        Err(e) => Err(e), // Manual propagation (simpler here)
    }
}
```

This code works, but the `match` blocks used solely for error propagation add noise.

The ? operator for Result

Rust offers an elegant solution: the ? (question mark) operator. Placed at the end of an expression that returns a `Result`, it does exactly what the propagation `match` blocks did:

- If the `Result` is `Ok(value)`, it unwraps `value` from the `Ok`, and execution continues
- If the `Result` is `Err(error)`, the ? operator *immediately halts* the execution of the current function and returns that `Err(error)` to the function's caller

Important: The ? operator can only be used inside functions that themselves return a compatible `Result` (the error type, `E`, of the inner `Result` must be convertible into the error type, `E`, of the `Result` returned by the current function, typically via the `From` trait).

Example: the ? operator for Result with Result

Let's rewrite the previous example using ?:

```
use std::fs;
use std::num::ParseFloatError; // Specific error type for parse::<f64>
use std::io; // For io::Error
```

```
// Define a custom error type for our function
#[derive(Debug)] // Implement Debug for printing
enum ReadDivideError {
    Io(io::Error),
    Format(ParseFloatError),
    Math(String), // For the error from our 'divide' function
}

// Implement `From` trait to allow '?' to automatically convert errors
impl From<io::Error> for ReadDivideError {
    fn from(err: io::Error) -> ReadDivideError {
        ReadDivideError::Io(err)
    }
}

impl From<ParseFloatError> for ReadDivideError {
    fn from(err: ParseFloatError) -> ReadDivideError {
        ReadDivideError::Format(err)
    }
}
// We also need a way to convert the String error from 'divide'
impl From<String> for ReadDivideError {
     fn from(err: String) -> ReadDivideError {
        ReadDivideError::Math(err)
    }
}


// Our original 'divide' function (could also return ReadDivideError
directly)
fn divide(numerator: f64, denominator: f64) -> Result<f64, String> {
     if denominator == 0.0 { Err(String::from("Division by zero!")) } else
{ Ok(numerator / denominator) }
}
```

```
// Function using '?' - Note it now returns our custom error type
fn read_then_divide_with_qmark(file_path: &str, divisor: f64) ->
Result<f64, ReadDivideError> {
    // '?' handles io::Error, converting it via From into
ReadDivideError::Io
    let content = fs::read_to_string(file_path)?;

    // '?' handles ParseFloatError, converting it via From into
ReadDivideError::Format
    let number = content.trim().parse::<f64>()?;

    // '?' handles the String error from divide, converting via From into
ReadDivideError::Math
    let result = divide(number, divisor)?;

    Ok(result) // If all OK, return Ok(...)
}

fn main() {
    // Create a dummy file for testing
    fs::write("number.txt", "100.5").expect("Cannot write file");

    match read_then_divide_with_qmark("number.txt", 2.0) {
        Ok(r) => println!("Result with '?': {}", r), // Output: 50.25
        Err(e) => println!("Error with '?': {:?}", e),
    }

     match read_then_divide_with_qmark("number.txt", 0.0) { // Test
division by zero
        Ok(r) => println!("Result with '?': {}", r),
        Err(e) => println!("Error with '?': {:?}", e), // Output:
Math("Division by zero!")
    }

     match read_then_divide_with_qmark("non_existent_file.txt", 2.0) { //
Test missing file
        Ok(r) => println!("Result with '?': {}", r),
```

```
        Err(e) => println!("Error with '?': {:?}", e), // Output: Io(Os {
code: 2, kind: NotFound, message: "No such file or directory" })
    }

    fs::remove_file("number.txt").ok(); // Clean up dummy file
}
```

Note: We implemented the `From` trait manually here. Later, we'll see how the `thiserror` crate can generate these implementations automatically.

The code is now significantly cleaner and more readable! The ? operator hides the repetitive error propagation logic.

The ? operator for Option

The ? operator works analogously with `Option<T>`:

- If the `Option` is `Some(value)`, it unwraps `value`, and execution continues
- If the `Option` is `None`, the ? operator *immediately halts* the execution of the current function and returns `None` to the function's caller

It can only be used in functions that return `Option`.

Let's see an example:

```
// Function that finds the first number in a slice satisfying a condition
// and possibly performs an operation on it.
fn find_and_operate(slice: &[i32], operation: fn(i32) -> Option<i32>) ->
Option<i32> {
    // Find the first element > 10. '?' propagates None if not found.
    let found_element = slice.iter().find(|&&x| x > 10)?; // find returns
Option<&i32>

    // Perform the operation on the found element.
    // The operation itself might return None. '?' propagates this None
too.
```

```
    let operation_result = operation(*found_element)?; // Dereference
found_element (*...)

    Some(operation_result) // If all OK, return Some(...)
}

// Example operation: double if even, otherwise None
fn double_if_even(n: i32) -> Option<i32> {
    if n % 2 == 0 {
        Some(n * 2)
    } else {
        None
    }
}

fn main() {
    let numbers1 = [5, 12, 8, 15, 6];  // First > 10 is 12 (even)
    let numbers2 = [5, 8, 13, 9];     // First > 10 is 13 (odd)
    let numbers3 = [1, 2, 3];        // No number > 10

    println!("Operation result on {:?}: {:?}", numbers1, find_and_
operate(&numbers1, double_if_even)); // Output: Some(24)
    println!("Operation result on {:?}: {:?}", numbers2, find_and_
operate(&numbers2, double_if_even)); // Output: None (because 13 is odd)
    println!("Operation result on {:?}: {:?}", numbers3, find_and_
operate(&numbers3, double_if_even)); // Output: None (no number > 10
found)
}
```

This example demonstrates how ? can chain `Option`-returning operations, short-circuiting the chain as soon as `None` is encountered.

When to use the ? operator

The ? operator is a fantastic tool for reducing boilerplate when working with `Result` and `Option`. It's the idiomatic choice when you want to quickly propagate an error or a `None` up the call stack.

However, it's not always the right choice: if a function needs to handle a specific error differently (e.g., log a special message or try an alternative operation), then `match` or other methods such as `map_err` might be more appropriate for that local error-handling logic.

The ? operator is incredibly effective for propagating errors, but its power is fully realized when the errors being propagated are more descriptive than just a simple string.

Custom error types

While `Result<T, String>` or generic errors such as `std::io::Error` suffice for simple cases, more complex applications greatly benefit from defining **custom error types**. This allows you to do the following:

- **Distinguish** between different application-specific failure modes
- **Encapsulate** additional information relevant to the error
- **Implement** more structured and meaningful error-handling logic

Defining custom error types with an enum

The most common and flexible way to create custom error types in Rust is using an enum. Each variant of the enum can represent a distinct class of error.

Here is an example:

```
use std::num::ParseIntError; // Error from parsing integers

// Our custom enum for data processing errors
#[derive(Debug)] // Allows printing the error with :?
enum DataProcessingError {
    FileNotFound(String), // Contains the name of the missing file
    InvalidFormat(ParseIntError), // Contains the original parsing error
    NegativeValue(i32), // Contains the negative value found
    IoError(std::io::Error), // Contains a generic I/O error
}

// We can implement methods or traits for our error enum
impl DataProcessingError {
    fn user_message(&self) -> String {
        match self {
```

```
            DataProcessingError::FileNotFound(name) => format!("Error:
Could not find file '{}'", name),
            DataProcessingError::InvalidFormat(_) => String::from("Error:
Invalid data format, expected an integer."),
            DataProcessingError::NegativeValue(val) => format!("Error:
Found negative value {}, expected positive.", val),
            DataProcessingError::IoError(_) => String::from("Error:
Problem during reading/writing."),
        }
    }
}
```

Here, `DataProcessingError` defines four possible failure causes, some carrying specific data (such as `FileNotFound` or `NegativeValue`). We also added a `user_message` method for more user-friendly descriptions.

Implementing standard error traits

To best integrate custom error types with the Rust ecosystem (e.g., to work smoothly with ? and third-party libraries), it's good practice to implement two standard traits: `std::fmt::Display` (for user-friendly string representation) and `std::error::Error` (for advanced features such as error "sourcing"):

```
use std::{fmt, error}; // Import the traits

// ---- Enum defined as before ----
#[derive(Debug)]
enum DataProcessingError {
    FileNotFound(String),
    InvalidFormat(ParseIntError),
    NegativeValue(i32),
    IoError(std::io::Error),
}

// Implement Display for user-friendly output (e.g., with {})
impl fmt::Display for DataProcessingError {
    fn fmt(&self, f: &mut fmt::Formatter) -> fmt::Result {
```

```
        match self {
            DataProcessingError::FileNotFound(name) => write!(f, "Could
not find file '{}'", name),
            DataProcessingError::InvalidFormat(e) => write!(f, "Invalid
data format: {}", e),
            DataProcessingError::NegativeValue(val) => write!(f, "Found
negative value {}, expected positive.", val),
            DataProcessingError::IoError(e) => write!(f, "I/O error: {}",
e),
        }
    }
}

// Implement the Error trait
impl error::Error for DataProcessingError {
    // The 'source()' method is optional but useful. It returns the
underlying
    // error that caused this error, if any.
    fn source(&self) -> Option<&(dyn error::Error + 'static)> {
        match self {
            // If our error is InvalidFormat, the source is ParseIntError
            DataProcessingError::InvalidFormat(ref e) => Some(e),
            // If our error is IoError, the source is std::io::Error
            DataProcessingError::IoError(ref e) => Some(e),
            // Our other errors don't have a standard underlying cause
            _ => None,
        }
    }
}
```

In the `DataProcessingError::IoError(ref e)` pattern, the `ref` keyword is used to create a **reference** to the `io::Error` value inside the enum variant, rather than moving it. Because the source method only has a reference to itself (`&DataProcessingError`), Rust's ownership rules prevent us from moving `io::Error` out of it. Using `ref e` solves this by borrowing the error, which is exactly what we need to return a reference from the function.

Implementing `Display` allows printing the error with `println!("{}", err)`. Implementing `Error` (especially `source`) enables features such as printing an error's cause chain.

Using custom errors in functions

Now we can use our `DataProcessingError` as the `E` type in `Result<T, E>` within our functions:

```
use std::fs;

// Function that reads a number from a file, validates it's positive
fn read_positive_number(path: &str) -> Result<i32, DataProcessingError> {
    let content = fs::read_to_string(path)
        // Manual error mapping needed here (for now)
        .map_err(|e| DataProcessingError::IoError(e))?;

    let number = content.trim().parse::<i32>()
        // Manual error mapping needed here (for now)
        .map_err(|e| DataProcessingError::InvalidFormat(e))?;

    if number < 0 {
        Err(DataProcessingError::NegativeValue(number))
    } else {
        Ok(number)
    }
}

fn main() {
     // Test with non-existent file (simulated)
    match read_positive_number("non_existent_data.txt") {
        Ok(n) => println!("Number read: {}", n),
        Err(e) => println!("Error: {}", e), // Uses Display impl
                     // Output: Error: I/O error: No such file or
directory ...
    }

    // Test with invalid format
    fs::write("invalid_data.txt", "abc").unwrap();
    match read_positive_number("invalid_data.txt") {
```

```
        Ok(n) => println!("Number read: {}", n),
        Err(e) => println!("Error: {}", e), // Output: Error: Invalid data
format: invalid digit found in string
    }
    fs::remove_file("invalid_data.txt").ok();

    // Test with negative value
    fs::write("negative_data.txt", "-10").unwrap();
     match read_positive_number("negative_data.txt") {
        Ok(n) => println!("Number read: {}", n),
        Err(e) => println!("Error: {}", e), // Output: Error: Found
negative value -10, expected positive.
    }
    fs::remove_file("negative_data.txt").ok();

     // Test success
    fs::write("valid_data.txt", "123").unwrap();
     match read_positive_number("valid_data.txt") {
        Ok(n) => println!("Number read: {}", n), // Output: Number read:
123
        Err(e) => println!("Error: {}", e),
    }
    fs::remove_file("valid_data.txt").ok();
}
```

Note: Error conversion using `map_err` is still manual here. We'll simplify this next.

Using custom error types makes the code clearer about potential failures and allows for more targeted error handling by the calling code.

Simplifying custom errors with thiserror and anyhow

Manually implementing the `Display` and `Error` traits for every custom error type can become repetitive. Fortunately, the Rust community has created excellent *crates* (libraries) to streamline this process. The two most popular crates for error handling are `thiserror` and `anyhow`.

The thiserror crate

The `thiserror` crate drastically reduces the boilerplate code needed for custom errors. By using the `#[derive(Error)]` macro and attributes such as `#[error("...")]` and `#[from]`, you can automatically generate `Display` and `Error` trait implementations, making your error types both ergonomic and powerful.

The `#[from]` attribute is particularly useful as it generates `From` trait implementations, allowing the ? operator to automatically convert source errors (such as `io::Error` or `ParseIntError`) into the appropriate variant of your custom error enum.

Let's see a practical example with a `main` function that handles the various errors our function can produce.

First, add `thiserror` to your `Cargo.toml`:

```
[dependencies]
thiserror = "2.0"
```

Then, redefine your error using the #[derive(Error, Debug)] macro and the #[error(...)] and #[from] attributes:

```
use thiserror::Error;
use std::num::ParseIntError;
use std::io;
use std::fs;
use std::path::Path;

#[derive(Error, Debug)]
pub enum DataProcessingError {
    #[error("Invalid data format in file")]
    InvalidFormat(#[from] ParseIntError),

    #[error("Value '{0}' is negative and cannot be processed")]
    NegativeValue(i32),

    #[error("I/O error when accessing file")]
    Io(#[from] io::Error),
```

```
}

/// Reads a number from a file and ensures it's not negative.
fn read_positive_number(path: &Path) -> Result<i32, DataProcessingError> {
    // The '?' operator automatically converts io::Error into
    // DataProcessingError::Io thanks to the #[from] attribute.
    let content = fs::read_to_string(path)?;

    // The '?' operator automatically converts ParseIntError into
    // DataProcessingError::InvalidFormat thanks to the #[from] attribute.
    let number = content.trim().parse::<i32>()?;

    if number < 0 {
        // We create this error variant manually.
        Err(DataProcessingError::NegativeValue(number))
    } else {
        Ok(number)
    }
}

fn main() {
    // --- Setup dummy files for demonstration ---
    fs::write("valid_number.txt", "123").unwrap();
    fs::write("invalid_format.txt", "abc").unwrap();
    fs::write("negative_number.txt", "-42").unwrap();

    // --- Test different scenarios ---
    println!("--- Test Case 1: Success ---");
    let path_valid = Path::new("valid_number.txt");
    match read_positive_number(path_valid) {
        Ok(n) => println!("Successfully read positive number: {}", n),
        Err(e) => eprintln!("An unexpected error occurred: {}", e),
    }

    println!("\n--- Test Case 2: File Not Found ---");
    let path_nonexistent = Path::new("no_such_file.txt");
    match read_positive_number(path_nonexistent) {
```

```
        Ok(n) => println!("Read number: {}", n),
        Err(e) => eprintln!("Error: {}", e), // Will print "I/O error when
accessing file"
    }

    println!("\n--- Test Case 3: Invalid Format ---");
    let path_invalid_format = Path::new("invalid_format.txt");
    match read_positive_number(path_invalid_format) {
        Ok(n) => println!("Read number: {}", n),
        Err(e) => eprintln!("Error: {}", e), // Will print "Invalid data
format in file"
    }

    println!("\n--- Test Case 4: Negative Value ---");
    let path_negative = Path::new("negative_number.txt");
    match read_positive_number(path_negative) {
        Ok(n) => println!("Read number: {}", n),
        Err(e) => eprintln!("Error: {}", e), // Will print "Value '-42' is
negative..."
    }

    // --- Cleanup ---
    fs::remove_file("valid_number.txt").ok();
    fs::remove_file("invalid_format.txt").ok();
    fs::remove_file("negative_number.txt").ok();
}
```

This example demonstrates a more realistic use case. The `main` function acts as the entry point of an application that calls our `read_positive_number` function and handles its potential failures.

- **Error enum:** `DataProcessingError` defines the specific ways our operation can fail. The `#[from]` attribute on the `Io` and `InvalidFormat` variants allows the `?` operator in `read_positive_number` to automatically convert `io::Error` and `ParseIntError` into our custom error type.
- **main function logic:** The `main` function sets up several test files to simulate different scenarios (success, file not found, bad data, and invalid value). It then calls `read_positive_number` for each case and uses a `match` statement to handle the `Result`.

- **Error output:** When an `Err` is returned, `eprintln!("Error: {}" e)` prints the user-friendly message defined by the `#[error("...")]` attribute in our enum, demonstrating how `thiserror` automatically implements the `Display` trait.

The anyhow crate

`anyhow` takes a different approach, primarily aimed at **applications** (or binaries). It provides a single, generic error type, `anyhow::Error`, designed to wrap *any* other error type that implements `std::error::Error`.

Its goal is to simplify application-level error handling, where you often don't need to *distinguish* between dozens of different error types programmatically, but just want to know that something went wrong and get a good error report (with context and a cause chain).

Add `anyhow` to `Cargo.toml`:

```
[dependencies]
anyhow = "1.0"
```

Then, you can use `anyhow::Result<T>` (which is an alias for `Result<T, anyhow::Error>`) as your return type and use ? freely. `anyhow::Error` implements `From` for most common error types:

```
use anyhow::{Context, Result, bail}; // Import Result, Context, bail
use std::fs;

// The function now returns anyhow::Result
fn read_positive_number_anyhow(path: &str) -> Result<i32> {
    let content = fs::read_to_string(path)
        // context() adds contextual information to the original error
        .context(format!("Failed to read file '{}'", path))?;

    let number = content.trim().parse::<i32>()
        .context("File content is not a valid integer")?;

    if number < 0 {
        // bail! is an easy way to create and return an anyhow::Error
        bail!("The number read ({}) must be positive.", number);
    }
```

```
    Ok(number)
}

// main can also return anyhow::Result<()> for easy error propagation
fn main() -> Result<()> {
    fs::write("valid_data_ah.txt", "789").unwrap();
    let number = read_positive_number_anyhow("valid_data_ah.txt")?;
    println!("Success with anyhow: {}", number);
    fs::remove_file("valid_data_ah.txt").ok();

    // Test with error (negative value)
    fs::write("negative_data_ah.txt", "-5").unwrap();
    match read_positive_number_anyhow("negative_data_ah.txt") {
        Ok(_) => println!("This shouldn't happen"),
        Err(e) => {
             // anyhow formats the error including context and cause chain
            println!("Error with anyhow: {:?}", e);
            // Output (approx): Error: The number read (-5) must be
positive.
        }
    }
     fs::remove_file("negative_data_ah.txt").ok();

     // Test with error (file not found)
      match read_positive_number_anyhow("nonexistent_ah.txt") {
        Ok(_) => println!("This shouldn't happen"),
        Err(e) => {
            println!("Error with anyhow: {:?}", e);
            // Output (approx):
            // Error: Failed to read file 'nonexistent_ah.txt'
            //
            // Caused by:
```

```
            //      No such file or directory (os error 2)
        }
    }

    Ok(()) // main returns Ok if everything succeeded
}
```

The following are key features of anyhow:

- Use `anyhow::Result<T>` (or `Result<T, anyhow::Error>`)
- The ? operator automatically converts most errors into `anyhow::Error`
- The `.context("...")` method easily adds context to errors as they propagate
- The `bail!("...")` macro is a convenient way to create and return an `anyhow::Error` from a specific point
- `anyhow::Error` provides excellent formatting for display (`{:?}`), including context and the full cause chain

`anyhow` is great for application code (such as `main`, web handlers, and CLI tools) where you want simple error handling and good reporting, without needing to define dozens of custom error enums or manage complex conversions.

When to use thiserror versus anyhow

- Use `thiserror` in libraries to define a stable, specific set of errors that library consumers can handle programmatically (e.g., with `match`)
- Use `anyhow` in applications to simplify error handling and reporting, especially when you don't need to programmatically distinguish between specific error types but just want to log/display a detailed error

Both crates are extremely useful and often used together: a library might use `thiserror` to define its errors, and an application using that library might use `anyhow` to handle those errors alongside others from various sources.

Handling errors with `Result` is crucial for program correctness, but for debugging and monitoring, it's equally important to record when and why these errors occur using a structured logging system.

Logging errors

Importance of logging

Error handling often doesn't stop at just returning a `Result`.

Especially in complex applications or long-running services, having a **logging** system is important for tracking important events, warnings, and, critically, errors. Logging helps us do the following:

- **Diagnose** problems after they occur (post-mortem debugging)
- **Monitor** the application's health in production
- **Understand** execution flow and identify bottlenecks or unexpected behavior

The log crate and implementations

The Rust ecosystem has a de facto standard logging facade crate called `log`. This crate defines a common logging API (macros such as `info!`, `warn!`, and `error!`) that libraries and applications can use to emit log messages.

However, the `log` crate itself doesn't *do* anything with the messages; it doesn't write them anywhere. It needs a logging **implementation** backend that actually filters the messages and writes them to the console or a file, or sends them to an external service.

One of the simplest and most common implementations to get started with is `env_logger`, which configures logging based on environment variables.

Basic setup with env_logger

To use `log` and `env_logger`, add them to your `Cargo.toml`:

```
[dependencies]
log = "0.11"
env_logger = "0.9" # Or latest version
anyhow = "1.0" # Often useful alongside logging
```

Then, initialize the logger at the start of your application (usually in `main`):

```
use log::{info, warn, error, debug, trace, LevelFilter}; // Import macros
and LevelFilter
use env_logger::{Builder, Env};
```

```
use anyhow::Result; // Using anyhow for simplicity in examples

fn main() -> Result<()> {
    // Initialize env_logger. By default, reads RUST_LOG env var.
    // We can set a default level if RUST_LOG is not defined.
    Builder::from_env(Env::default().default_filter_or("info")) // Default
to 'info' if RUST_LOG isn't set
        .init();

    info!("Application started."); // Logged at INFO level

    match risky_operation(10) {
        Ok(_) => info!("Operation successful."),
        Err(e) => {
            // Log the error at ERROR level. {:?} with anyhow shows the
cause chain.
            error!("Operation failed: {:?}", e);
        }
    }

     match risky_operation(-5) {
        Ok(_) => info!("Operation (negative) successful."),
        Err(e) => {
            error!("Operation (negative) failed: {:?}", e);
        }
    }

    debug!("This is detailed debug information."); // Only visible if
RUST_LOG=debug or trace
    trace!("This message is very verbose."); // Only visible if RUST_
LOG=trace

    info!("Application finished.");
    Ok(())
}

fn risky_operation(value: i32) -> Result<()> {
    if value < 0 {
```

```
        // Log a warning before returning the error
        warn!("Attempting operation on negative value: {}", value);
        anyhow::bail!("Value cannot be negative: {}", value);
    }
    debug!("Performing operation on value: {}", value);
    // ... operation logic ...
    Ok(())
}
```

Logging levels and configuration

With env_logger, you don't control log levels directly in your Rust code; instead, you control them from your terminal by setting the RUST_LOG environment variable before running your program. This is a powerful feature because it allows you or users of your application to change the log verbosity for debugging without needing to recompile the code.

The general pattern in your terminal is VARIABLE=value command. For a Rust project managed with Cargo, the command is typically cargo run. Let's look at some examples:

```
# In your terminal, in your project's root directory:

# Run your program, showing only INFO, WARN, and ERROR messages (a good default).
RUST_LOG=info cargo run

# Show more detailed DEBUG messages and everything above (info, warn, error).
RUST_LOG=debug cargo run

# Show only WARNING and ERROR messages.
RUST_LOG=warn cargo run

# Show DEBUG messages only for your own crate's code, keeping libraries quieter.
# Replace 'your_crate_name' with the actual name of your package from Cargo.toml.
```

```
RUST_LOG=your_crate_name=debug cargo run

# Show everything (can be very verbose, useful for deep debugging).
RUST_LOG=trace cargo run
```

The most useful feature here is the ability to set log levels on a per-crate basis. For instance, `RUST_LOG=my_web_app=debug` (where `my_web_app` is the name of your crate from `Cargo.toml`) is incredibly helpful for seeing detailed logs from *your* application code while keeping the output from libraries you're using (such as Actix Web or Diesel) at a less verbose level. This helps you focus on the logs that matter most for your immediate debugging task.

Logging errors with Context

When logging an error (especially using `error!`), it's crucial to include as much context as possible. If you're using `anyhow`, the `{:?}` format specifier on `anyhow::Error` is excellent because it automatically includes context added via `.context()` and the chain of causes:

```
use anyhow::{Context, Result};
use log::error;
// ... (other imports and Logger init) ...

fn read_config(path: &str) -> Result<String> {
    std::fs::read_to_string(path)
        .context(format!("Unable to read configuration file from '{}'",
path))
}

fn main() -> Result<()> {
    // ... init Logger ...
    match read_config("config.toml") {
        Ok(config) => log::info!("Configuration read: {} bytes", config.
len()),
        Err(e) => {
            // Log the error using anyhow's detailed formatting
            error!("Failed to read configuration: {:?}", e);
            // Example Log output:
```

```
            // ERROR [my_app] Failed to read configuration: Unable to read
configuration file from 'config.toml'
            // Caused by:
            //     No such file or directory (os error 2)
        }
    }
    Ok(())
}
```

Good error logging is indispensable for maintaining and diagnosing complex Rust applications.

Practical examples and error handling best practices

We've covered the fundamental mechanisms (`Result`, `Option`, `?`, `match`, custom errors, and logging). Now, let's consolidate this with a more integrated example and summarize key best practices for error handling in Rust.

Practical example: File data processing

Imagine a program that reads numbers from a file (one per line), validates them (must be positive), and calculates their sum. It needs to handle I/O errors, number format errors, and validation errors:

```
use std::fs::File;
use std::io::{self, BufRead, BufReader};
use thiserror::Error; // Using thiserror for specific processing errors
use anyhow::{Context, Result}; // Using anyhow for app level and context
use log::{info, warn, error};

// Specific error for this processing logic
#[derive(Error, Debug)]
enum ProcessingError {
    #[error("Invalid number format on line {line_num}: '{content}'")]
    InvalidFormat {
        line_num: usize,
        content: String,
        #[source] // Original source error
        source: std::num::ParseIntError,
    },
```

```
    #[error("Negative number {number} not allowed on line {line_num}")]
    NegativeNumber {
        line_num: usize,
        number: i32,
    },
    // Could add other specific errors here
}

// Function to process a single line
fn process_line(line_content: &str, line_num: usize) -> Result<i32,
ProcessingError> {
    let number = line_content.trim().parse::<i32>()
        .map_err(|e| ProcessingError::InvalidFormat {
            line_num,
            content: line_content.to_string(),
            source: e, // Include original parse error
        })?;

    if number < 0 {
        Err(ProcessingError::NegativeNumber { line_num, number })
    } else {
        Ok(number)
    }
}

// Main file processing function
fn process_file_and_sum(filename: &str) -> anyhow::Result<i32> {
    info!("Starting file processing: {}", filename);

    let file = File::open(filename)
        .context(format!("Failed to open file '{}'", filename))?; //
Anyhow context
    let reader = BufReader::new(file);
    let mut total_sum = 0;
    let mut lines_processed = 0;

    for (index, line_result) in reader.lines().enumerate() {
        let line_num = index + 1;
```

```
        let line = line_result.context(format!("Failed reading line {}", 
line_num))?; // Anyhow context for I/O

        match process_line(&line, line_num) {
            Ok(number) => {
                total_sum += number;
                lines_processed += 1;
            }
            Err(e) => {
                // Log the specific error but continue with other lines
                warn!("Error processing line {}: {} - Skipping line.", 
line_num, e);
                // Could also choose to stop here by returning Err(e.
into())
                // which works if ProcessingError impls Error, as 
anyhow::Error impls From<E: Error>
            }
        }
    }

    info!("File processing complete. Lines processed: {}. Total sum: {}", 
lines_processed, total_sum);
    Ok(total_sum)
}


fn main() -> anyhow::Result<()> {
    env_logger::Builder::from_env(env_logger::Env::default().default_
filter_or("info")).init();

    // Create a test file
    use std::io::Write;
    let mut file = File::create("test_data.txt")?;
    writeln!(file, "10")?;
    writeln!(file, "25")?;
    writeln!(file, "-5")?; // Error: negative
```

```
    writeln!(file, "abc")?; // Error: format
    writeln!(file, "15")?;
    drop(file); // Ensure file is closed

    match process_file_and_sum("test_data.txt") {
        Ok(sum) => {
            info!("Final sum calculated: {}", sum); // Should be 10 + 25 +
15 = 50
            assert_eq!(sum, 50); // Add a check
            println!("Sum calculated successfully: {}", sum);
        }
        Err(e) => {
            // Errors here would likely be I/O errors opening the file,
            // as internal errors are logged but not propagated by
process_file_and_sum
            error!("Critical error during file processing: {:?}", e);
        }
    }

     std::fs::remove_file("test_data.txt")?; // Clean up test file
    Ok(())
}
```

This example combines several concepts:

- Defining a custom error (`ProcessingError`) with `thiserror` for specific processing failures.
- Using `anyhow::Result` and `.context()` for the main `process_file_and_sum` function, handling I/O errors, and adding context.
- The `process_line` function returns the specific `ProcessingError`.
- In the loop within `process_file_and_sum`, specific errors from `process_line` are caught using `match`. Here, we choose to log them as `warn!` and *continue* processing subsequent lines, rather than halting everything (a common design choice).
- Logging (`info!`, `warn!`, and `error!`) tracks progress and reports issues.

Summary

Great job getting through *Chapter 6*!

Error handling can seem intimidating, but as you've seen, Rust gives you a clear and powerful toolkit to manage it with confidence.

In this chapter, we learned that Rust thinks about errors in two main ways: recoverable errors (such as a file not being found) and unrecoverable errors (bugs that would crash the program).

Here's a quick recap of the main tools we added to our belt:

- **Result<T, E>**: Our go-to for any operation that might fail, letting us handle both the `Ok(value)` and `Err(error)` cases
- **Option<T>**: The perfect tool for values that might be absent, safely handling `Some(value)` and `None`
- **panic!**: The big red button for unrecoverable errors, which we saw is what methods such as `.unwrap()` and `.expect()` use under the hood

We then explored the most common patterns for working with these types. We started with the exhaustive `match` statement and then saw how to make our code more concise with the **? operator**, which is a fantastic way of propagating errors cleanly. Finally, we saw how to make our errors even better by creating **custom error types** (especially with awesome crates such as `thiserror` and `anyhow`) and the importance of **logging** to keep an eye on our application's health.

Questions and assignments

Now that we've covered the concepts and best practices for error handling in Rust, it's time to test your knowledge with some exercises and assignments.

Questions

1. What is the fundamental difference in meaning between returning `Result<T, E>` versus `Option<T>` from a function? Describe a scenario where each would be the more appropriate choice.
2. Explain what a "panic" is in Rust. When is it appropriate to let a program panic (e.g., by using `.unwrap()` or `.expect()`) instead of returning a `Result`?
3. What does the **?** operator do when used on a `Result`? What is the main requirement for the function in which you use the ? operator?

4. Why would you create a custom error enum instead of just returning `Result<T, String>` with a descriptive error message?
5. What is the primary difference in use cases between the `thiserror` and `anyhow` crates? When would you choose one over the other?
6. What does the `.unwrap_or(default_value)` method on an `Option` do, and how does it help prevent a panic?
7. Why is structured logging (using a crate such as `log`) considered an important part of a robust error-handling strategy?

Assignments

Assignment 6.1: File reading with detailed error handling

1. Write a `read_content(path: &str) -> Result<String, std::io::Error>` function.
2. Use `std::fs::read_to_string`.
3. In `main`, call `read_content` for both an existing and a non-existent file.
4. Use `match` in `main` to print the content on `Ok`, or a specific error message (e.g., "File not found" or "Permission denied") on `Err`. (Hint: Inspect the `err.kind()` of the `io::Error`.)

Assignment 6.2: Division function with custom errors (using thiserror)

1. Define a `DivisionError` enum using `thiserror`. It should have at least a `DivisionByZero` variant.
2. Implement a `safe_divide(a: f64, b: f64) -> Result<f64, DivisionError>` function.
3. In `main`, call `safe_divide` with valid cases and a `division-by-zero` case.
4. Use `match` to handle the `Result` and print appropriate messages using the `Display` implementation generated by `thiserror`.

Assignment 6.3: Finding elements with Option and ?

1. Write a `find_first_greater_than_ten(slice: &[i32]) -> Option<i32>` function.
2. Use iterator methods (`iter()`, `find()`, and `copied()`) to find the *value* of the first element greater than 10.
3. (Optional advanced): Write a second function, `sum_first_and_last_even(slice: &[i32]) -> Option<i32>`, that uses `?` to find the first even number and the last even number, returning their sum, or `None` if either is not found.

7

Polymorphism and Lifetimes

We have spent the previous chapters defining concrete types such as structs and enums. These are excellent for modeling specific data, but real-world software often requires more flexibility! In real-world scenarios, we often need functions that can accept different types of data as long as they behave in a certain way.

In computer science, this concept is known as **polymorphism**. In Rust, we achieve this primarily through **traits** and **generics**. We will also cover **lifetimes**, which are a special form of generics that ensures references remain valid while our code becomes more abstract.

Ad hoc polymorphism: defining behavior with traits

The first step toward writing flexible code is changing how we view our data. Instead of focusing on the concrete details of what a type *is*, we focus on what it *can do*.

In Rust, traits are used to define shared behaviors for different types, functioning as a contract between the programmer and the compiler. When a struct indicates that it implements a trait, it commits to providing the specific functions outlined by that trait. While similar to "interfaces" in other languages, Rust traits offer distinctive capabilities and flexibility, which we will examine in this section.

Defining a trait

To define a trait, we use the `trait` keyword followed by the name we want to give it. Inside the curly brackets, we list the method signatures that describe how the types that implement this trait will behave. Imagine we are creating software for a classic Italian coffee bar.

We have a variety of machines, such as a simple Moka pot and a professional espresso machine. Although they are physically very different, they share one fundamental function: they both brew coffee. To represent this shared ability, we can define a trait called `Brew`:

```
pub trait Brew {
    // We only define the signature here, followed by a semicolon.
    // We do not define the body implementation yet.
    fn extract(&self) -> String;
}
```

In the definition, we return a `String` type. While this requires memory allocation, we choose it here to allow flexibility for formatting dynamic messages (such as specific temperatures) without complicating the code with lifetimes yet.

Leaving the body empty and ending with a semicolon clearly indicates to the compiler that any type meant to be a `Brew` type needs to provide its own implementation of the `extract` method. The compiler diligently enforces this rule to help ensure you remember to implement the method properly.

Method signatures versus default implementations

A trait does not always require the user to write new code from scratch. Sometimes, a behavior is so typical that we can provide a default implementation directly within the trait definition itself. This is incredibly useful for keeping your code **DRY** (which stands for **Don't Repeat Yourself**).

If a type implements the trait, it automatically gets this default behavior without needing to write a single line of code for it. However, if a specific type requires a unique approach, it can simply override the default.

For example, let's add a `clean` method to our `Brew` trait.

For most simple coffee makers (such as the Moka pot), cleaning is just a matter of rinsing them with water. We can make this the default. However, a professional espresso machine has a complex self-cleaning cycle that requires a specific implementation:

```
// src/lib.rs
pub trait Brew {
    fn extract(&self) -> String;

    // This is a default implementation.
```

```
    // If a type doesn't define this method, it gets this version
automatically.
    fn clean(&self) -> String {
        String::from("Cleaning with a simple hot water rinse.")
    }
}

pub struct Moka;
pub struct EspressoMachine;

impl Brew for Moka {
    fn extract(&self) -> String {
        String::from("Bubbling up some coffee...")
    }
    // We don't implement clean() here.
    // Moka automatically uses the default "hot water rinse".
}

impl Brew for EspressoMachine {
    fn extract(&self) -> String {
        String::from("Pressurizing water...")
    }

    // We override the default because this machine is complex.
    fn clean(&self) -> String {
        String::from("Running automatic descaling program.")
    }
}
```

Abstracting behavior

Designing with traits encourages a fresh perspective. Instead of focusing on what specific data a type contains, think about the actions it can perform. This approach is really empowering because it separates your functions from the nitty-gritty details of the types they work with. Imagine a computer sending a document to a peripheral: what it truly needs is a device that can print.

It doesn't matter whether it's a laser printer, an inkjet, or a thermal receipt printer, as long as the device can handle the `Print` action, the computer can send the job effortlessly. By focusing on these capabilities rather than specific structs, your code becomes more adaptable, making it easy to support new types in the future without having to overhaul your existing logic.

Implementing traits

Defining a trait is just the beginning! To really make it work for us, we need to apply it to our specific data types. This step is known as "implementing" the trait. We do this using the `impl TraitName` syntax for `TypeName`, which clearly signals to the compiler that our particular struct has the behaviors outlined by the trait.

Implementing custom types

Now, let's return to our coffee example. We start by defining a simple `Moka` struct:

```
// src/lib.rs
pub struct Moka {
    pub size: u8, // Capacity in cups
}
```

At this stage, our `Moka` struct is just a container for data. It doesn't know how to behave like a coffee maker yet. If we try to call the `extract` method immediately, the Rust compiler will stop us:

```
// src/main.rs
fn main() {
    let pot = Moka { size: 3 };

    // ⚠ This causes an error!
    let coffee = pot.extract();
}
```

The compiler will produce an error similar to this: `no method named 'extract' found for struct 'Moka' in the current scope.`

To fix this and make the Moka usable as a coffee maker, we must explicitly implement the `Brew` trait we defined earlier. Notice how the following implementation logic is specific to the Moka pot. It mentions bubbling on a stove, whereas an espresso machine implementation would likely involve high pressure:

```
// src/lib.rs
impl Brew for Moka {
```

```
    fn extract(&self) -> String {
        format!("Bubbling on the stove... ready to serve {} cups of rich
coffee!", self.size)
    }
}
```

Now that the trait is implemented, the compiler knows exactly what to do when we call `.extract()`.

The orphan rule (where implementation is allowed)

One important restriction to keep in mind is the **orphan rule**. We already mentioned it in the previous chapter, but let's look at the details.

Rust has a helpful rule: *you cannot implement an external trait on an external type*. This keeps things orderly. Think of it like renovation laws: you're free to renovate your own house (a local type) or build a new structure if you have the blueprints (a local trait). But, just like you can't walk up to a public monument and repaint it, you can't add an external trait to an external type. This rule is in place to prevent chaos and ensure that different crates don't conflict by adding the same method to a standard type, such as `Vec`.

There is a workaround: the **Newtype pattern**. If you encounter this restriction, there is a standard way to circumvent it: use a wrapper type (often called the Newtype pattern). By wrapping the external type (such as `Vec<i32>`) inside a struct defined in your crate (such as `struct MyVec(Vec<i32>)`), Rust treats the wrapper as a **local type**, allowing you to implement any trait you want:

```
// src/lib.rs
use std::fmt;

// --- ALLOWED SCENARIOS ---

// 1. Implementing a LOCAL trait (Brew) on an EXTERNAL type (String).
// This is allowed because we own the trait "Brew".
impl Brew for String {
    fn extract(&self) -> String {
        String::from("Pour-over coffee")
    }
}
```

```
// 2. Implementing an EXTERNAL trait (Display) on a LOCAL type (Moka).
// This is allowed because we own the type "Moka".
impl fmt::Display for Moka {
    fn fmt(&self, f: &mut fmt::Formatter) -> fmt::Result {
        write!(f, "Moka pot size {}", self.size)
    }
}

// --- FORBIDDEN SCENARIO (The Orphan Rule) ---

/*
// ⚠ ERROR: Implementing an EXTERNAL trait on an EXTERNAL type.
// You cannot implement Display for Vec<i32> because you own neither!
impl fmt::Display for Vec<i32> {
    fn fmt(&self, f: &mut fmt::Formatter) -> fmt::Result {
        write!(f, "Vector content...")
    }
}
*/

// --- THE SOLUTION (Newtype Pattern) ---

// We wrap the external type in a local struct.
pub struct MyIntList(pub Vec<i32>);

// Now MyIntList is LOCAL, so we can implement Display!
impl fmt::Display for MyIntList {
    fn fmt(&self, f: &mut fmt::Formatter) -> fmt::Result {
        // We access the wrapped Vec using .0
        write!(f, "List: {:?}", self.0)
    }
}
```

Trait objects

Sometimes we need to work with multiple different types at the same time, treating them all as a single abstract concept. Imagine a waiter holding a tray. The tray might contain a cappuccino, an espresso, and a latte.

These are all different physical drinks, but they all share the property of being a "beverage." In Rust, a standard collection such as a `Vec` is restricted to holding only one specific type. You cannot mix a `Moka` struct and an `EspressoMachine` struct in the same list because they have different sizes in memory. To solve this, Rust provides **trait objects**.

Note

We will cover Smart Pointers such as `'Box'` in detail in *Chapter 11*. For now, just know that `'Box'` allows us to store these different types in the same list by putting them behind a pointer of a fixed size.

Using the `dyn` keyword allows us to instruct the compiler to ignore the specific concrete type (such as `Moka`) and treat the item merely as "something that implements this trait." This is called a trait object.

Because the compiler cannot know the size of a trait object in advance (it could be a tiny Moka pot or a massive espresso machine), we must access it through a pointer:

- **`Box<dyn Brew>`**: We use `Box` when we want to **own** the data. `Box` puts the specific struct on the heap and gives us a predictable pointer size on the stack.
- **`&dyn Brew`**: We can also use a simple reference if we only need to **borrow** the trait object without taking ownership.

In the following example, we use `Box` so we can store mixed types inside a single vector:

```
// src/main.rs

// 1. Setup: Let's define the types and implementations first.
// (Moka was defined previously, but we define EspressoMachine here).

pub struct Moka { pub size: u8 }

impl Brew for Moka {
    fn extract(&self) -> String {
        format!("Bubbling up {} cups.", self.size)
    }
}
```

```
pub struct EspressoMachine { pub pressure: u8 }

impl Brew for EspressoMachine {
    fn extract(&self) -> String {
        format!("Extracting at {} bars of pressure.", self.pressure)
    }
}

// 2. The Main Event: Storing mixed types using Trait Objects.
fn main() {
    // We can store mixed types because they both satisfy 'dyn Brew'.
    // 'Box' puts the data on the heap, so the vector just stores pointers
    // of the same size.
    let machines: Vec<Box<dyn Brew>> = vec![
        Box::new(Moka { size: 6 }),
        Box::new(EspressoMachine { pressure: 9 }),
    ];

    for machine in machines {
        println!("Coffee shop says: {}", machine.extract());
    }
}
```

Static versus dynamic dispatch

When you use trait objects with dyn, you are choosing to use what is called **dynamic dispatch.** This means the compiler does not know exactly which method to call at compile time. Instead, it creates code that finds the correct function at runtime using a specialized table of function pointers called a **vtable** (which stands for **virtual method table**).

This flexibility comes with a performance cost. In standard generics (**static dispatch**), the compiler generates a specific version of the function for each concrete type, often "inlining" the code directly to maximize speed.

With dynamic dispatch, the compiler cannot do this. Every time you call a method on a trait object, the program must perform a pointer dereference to look up the address in the vtable before it can execute the code.

This extra layer of indirection not only adds a small runtime overhead but, more importantly, prevents the compiler from performing aggressive optimizations such as inlining.

However, despite the overhead, dynamic dispatch is the only way to achieve true polymorphism, allowing you to store different types (such as `Moka` and `EspressoMachine`) in the same container.

Parametric polymorphism: abstracting with generics

Now that we've explored how traits set shared behaviors, let's move on to the next exciting concept: generics. Think of generics as a way to make your code adaptable, regardless of the types you're working with, much like having a versatile tool that fits many jobs.

In computer science, this idea is known as **parametric polymorphism**, and you may have encountered it in action with collections such as `Vec<i32>` and `Vec<String>`. These collections employ the same logic for adding, removing, or accessing items, regardless of the data type contained within.

Thanks to generics, we can create functions and structs with placeholders for types, which means we write the code once and it's ready to handle any data type you need. Isn't that wonderful?

The problem of duplication

Let's consider why generics can be so helpful. Imagine you're working on a function that finds the biggest number in a list of integers. You name it `largest_i32`. Later, you realize you also need the same function for a list of characters. So, you copy the code, change the signature, and rename it `largest_char`. The core of the function remains the same, iterating through the list and comparing values, but now you have two separate pieces of code just because the input types are different. This kind of repetition can be tedious and prone to mistakes. Plus, if you find a bug in your logic later, you'll need to fix it in every version you've copied, which can be a real hassle.

Writing the same function for different types

To see why generics are important, consider the alternative. Imagine you need to write a function that finds the largest number in a list of integers. You create a function called `largest_i32`. Later, you realize you need the same functionality for a list of characters. You copy and paste the code, change the signature, and rename it `largest_char`.

The core of the function remains the same. It goes through the list and compares values.

But you're forced to duplicate the code just because the input types are different. This method is tedious and prone to errors. If you find a bug later, you have to remember to fix it in every copy.

```
// We are forced to write two functions with identical logic
fn largest_i32(list: &[i32]) -> i32 {
    let mut largest = list[0];
    for &item in list {
        if item > largest {
            largest = item;
        }
    }
    largest
}

fn largest_char(list: &[char]) -> char {
    let mut largest = list[0];
    for &item in list {
        if item > largest {
            largest = item;
        }
    }
    largest
}
```

The <T> type parameter

To avoid this duplication, we use a placeholder instead of a specific type. In Rust, this is declared using angle brackets containing a type parameter, usually named `T`. Think of `T` as a variable, but for types rather than values. When defining the function, we specify that it works for any `T` type rather than just integers or characters. We add `<T>` immediately after the function name, which signals to the compiler that `T` is a generic type.

It will be replaced with a specific type, such as `i32` or `String`, later when the function is called:

```
// We read this as: "largest is a function generic over some type T"
fn largest<T>(list: &[T]) -> T {
    let mut largest = list[0];
    for &item in list {
        // NOTE: This specific line will cause a compiler error right now!
        // We will explain why and fix it in the next section.
```

```
        if item > largest {
            largest = item;
        }
    }
    largest
}
```

Bounded parametric polymorphism (trait bounds)

This idea serves as a welcoming bridge, linking traits and generics seamlessly. While generics give us the freedom to accept any type, we sometimes want to make sure that the type we choose has specific abilities.

Limiting generics with traits (T: Trait)

If you tried to compile the largest function from the previous section, you would encounter an error. The compiler complains because the greater-than operator, >, is not available for every possible type in the universe. For example, it makes no sense to ask whether one generic *file handle* is mathematically larger than another.

To fix this, we need to restrict the generic `T` type. We must tell the compiler that we only accept types that know how to be compared. We do this using **trait bounds.**

By changing the signature to `fn largest<T: PartialOrd + Copy>(...)`, we indicate that `T` can be any type that implements the `PartialOrd` trait for comparison and the `Copy` trait, so we can move the value out of the slice:

```
// src/main.rs
// We restrict T: It must be comparable (PartialOrd) and copyable (Copy)
// We return Option<T> to handle the case where the list is empty.
fn largest<T: PartialOrd + Copy>(list: &[T]) -> Option<T> {
    if list.is_empty() {
        return None;
    }
    let mut largest = list[0];

    for &item in list {
        if item > largest {
            largest = item;
        }
```

```
    }
    Some(largest)
}
```

The where clause for complex constraints

Sometimes, a single function requires several generic types, each with its own set of traits. Writing all of this within the angle brackets can make the function signature quite lengthy and difficult to follow. It starts to resemble a crowded legal disclaimer rather than a neat and clear function definition. Luckily, Rust offers a helpful solution with the `where` clause.

This enables you to place constraints at the end of the signature, separating the function name and arguments from the specific type requirements. As a result, the code becomes easier to scan and understand:

```
use std::fmt::{Debug, Display};

// Hard to read: The bounds clutter the function name
fn compare_prints<T: Display + Clone, U: Clone + Debug>(t: &T, u: &U) { }

// Easier to read: The bounds are moved to the 'where' clause
fn compare_prints<T, U>(t: &T, u: &U)
where
    T: Display + Clone,
    U: Clone + Debug,
{
    // Function body...
}
```

Returning types that implement traits

We can also use traits in return positions. Instead of returning a concrete type such as `i32` or `String`, we can declare that a function returns `impl Trait`. This indicates to the caller that they will receive some type that implements the specified trait, but they don't need to know exactly which one.

This is especially useful when working with complex types such as iterators or closures, where writing out the full type signature can be difficult or impossible. It's similar to a vending machine: you press a button for soda, and you get a can.

You don't need to know the specific brand or manufacturing details, only that it satisfies the `Drinkable` interface:

```
use std::fmt::Display;

// The caller doesn't know this is a String, only that it can be
displayed.
fn get_status() -> impl Display {
    "System All Green"
}

// NOTE: This feature has a limit!
// You cannot return distinct types conditionally.
// This will NOT compile because the compiler needs one concrete type
hidden behind the trait.
fn invalid_return(flag: bool) -> impl Display {
    if flag {
        "Success" // This is a &str
    } else {
        100        // This is an i32
    }
}
```

Monomorphization

Performance can sometimes be a worry when working with high-level abstractions. In many programming languages, generic code may lead to some runtime overhead because the program needs to frequently verify the type of data it handles.

Rust avoids this entirely through a process called **monomorphization.**

This term originates from Greek, meaning "single form." It refers to the process the compiler uses to transform your versatile, generic code into specific machine instructions. Instead of relying on one generic function that attempts to manage everything at runtime, the compiler decomposes it into specialized functions during compilation.

How Rust optimizes polymorphism (zero-cost)

The result of this process is what we call a **zero-cost abstraction**. When you compile your code, Rust examines every instance where you used a generic function and generates a separate version of that function for the specific types you actually used.

If you call a generic function with an integer and later with a float, the compiler silently creates two separate copies of that function in the binary. This means your generic code runs exactly as fast as if you had manually copied and pasted the function for each type. You get the benefits of clean, abstract code without any performance cost during execution.

And now we have finally arrived at the topic that keeps many new Rustaceans up at night: lifetimes. Often cited as the single hardest concept to grasp in the language, lifetimes are the secret sauce that allows Rust to manage memory safely without a garbage collector. If you've heard horror stories about *fighting the borrow checker*, this is usually the battlefield, but rest assured: the logic behind it is more straightforward than it seems.

Lifetimes: polymorphism for scope

Let's explore the third fascinating feature of Rust's polymorphism: lifetimes. While traits help us manage behavior and generics handle different types, lifetimes are all about scope. Every reference in Rust has a lifetime, which is simply how long that reference remains valid.

Usually, these are implicit and inferred, so you might not notice them. But when we write functions that work with references from different sources, it's important to explicitly tell the compiler how those lifetimes relate. This helps us ensure that we never accidentally use data that has already been cleaned up.

The necessity of lifetimes

Lifetimes are more than just a syntax rule; they are a key part of how Rust keeps your memory safe without needing a garbage collector. Their primary role is to prevent **dangling references**, which occur when a program attempts to use data that has already been deleted or modified. In languages such as C or C++, this can often lead to crashes and security vulnerabilities because the compiler may allow you to access memory that's no longer valid. Rust helps prevent these problems by ensuring that every reference remains valid for as long as it's needed.

The dangling reference problem

Lifetimes avoid a bug known as a dangling reference, which occurs when a program references data that has been deleted or reassigned. In C++, this can lead to crashes or security vulnerabilities because pointers direct to invalid memory locations. Rust prevents this by disallowing references to variables that no longer exist after a function finishes, thereby ensuring that references remain valid and do not point to invalid data:

```
fn main() {
    let reference_to_nothing;
    {
        let x = 5;
        // Error: 'x' only lives inside this block
        reference_to_nothing = &x;
    } // 'x' is dropped here
    // This would crash if Rust allowed it!
    println!("r: {}", reference_to_nothing);
}
```

In this example, the x variable is created inside the inner set of curly brackets. This specific area where the variable is valid is known as its **scope**.

In Rust, memory management is tied strictly to these scopes. As soon as the code execution reaches the closing bracket, }, of the inner block, x goes out of scope. When this happens, Rust automatically performs a cleanup process called **dropping**.

Dropping means that the value of 5 is removed from memory, and the resources it occupied are returned to the system. Consequently, `reference_to_nothing` is left holding a reference to a memory address that no longer contains valid data. If Rust allowed us to run the final `println!`, we would be trying to read garbage memory, which leads to crashes or unpredictable bugs. The compiler catches this lifetime mismatch immediately.

How the borrow checker validates scopes

To ensure that references are valid, the Rust compiler uses a component called the **borrow checker**.

This acts like a strict auditor that runs during compilation. It compares the scope of a variable (how long it lives) with the scope of any references to it. If the borrow checker sees that a reference tries to outlive the data it points to, it stops the compilation immediately. This prevents the program from ever running with invalid pointers:

```
// src/main.rs
fn main() {
    let r;                  // ---------+-- 'a (Outer scope: Long duration)
    {                       //          |
        let x = 5;          // -+-- 'b  | (Inner scope: Short duration)
        r = &x;             //  |       |
    }                       // -+       | <--- 'b ends here (x is dropped)

    println!("r: {}", r);   //          |
}                           // ---------+ <--- 'a ends here

// Error: The reference 'r' has lifetime 'a, but refers to 'x' which has
lifetime 'b.
// Because the scope 'b is shorter (ends earlier) than 'a, 'r' is left
pointing to invalid memory.
```

In this diagram, the vertical lines represent the duration, or scope, of each variable. We label the outer scope `'a` and the inner scope `'b`.

Visually, you can see that `'b` is strictly shorter than `'a`. This creates a conflict because `r` (which lives for the long duration, `'a`) tries to hold a reference to `x` (which only exists for the short duration, `'b`). When the inner scope, `'b`, ends, `x` is dropped, but `r` is still alive and trying to look at it.

Rust forbids this: the data being referenced must always live at least as long as the reference itself.

Generic lifetime annotations

In most cases, Rust manages lifetimes automatically, so you don't need to worry about them.

However, the compiler sometimes cannot infer reference lifetimes automatically. This often occurs when a function takes multiple references and returns one. In such cases, the compiler is unsure whether the returned reference borrows from the first or second argument. Because it checks function signatures rather than implementation, we need to assist it by explicitly specifying the lifetimes.

The <'a> syntax

Lifetime annotations differ slightly from the generic types we saw earlier. They always begin with an apostrophe (`'`). The names are arbitrary, so you could call a lifetime `'pizza` if you wanted to. However, the Rust community prefers very short, lowercase names such as `'a`, `'b`, and `'c`.

These declarations are enclosed in angle brackets, just like generic types. It's very important to understand that adding these annotations doesn't change how your code runs. It doesn't make a variable live longer. Instead, it labels the relationships between the lifetimes of different references so the compiler can verify them:

```
&i32        // a reference
&'a i32     // a reference with an explicit lifetime 'a
&'a mut i32 // a mutable reference with an explicit lifetime 'a
```

Annotating functions holding references

Let's examine a practical example where this is necessary.

Imagine a function that takes in two string slices and gives back the longer one. If you try to compile this without annotations, Rust will gently remind you with an error.

The compiler notices that the function returns a reference, but it's not quite sure whether that reference belongs to the first or second argument. This can be a bit confusing because the two inputs might have different lifespans. To clarify, we introduce a generic lifetime, 'a, and specify it for both the input parameters and the return type.

This signature tells Rust: "There is some lifetime, 'a, that both x and y satisfy." In practice, when you call this function, Rust determines 'a to be the overlap of the two input scopes.

This means the returned reference is guaranteed to be valid only as long as the **shorter** of the two inputs:

```
// We declare 'a and say that x, y, and the return value all share this
lifetime. // Crucially, this means the return value is valid only as long
as the // SHORTER of the two input lifetimes.
fn longest<'a>(x: &'a str, y: &'a str) -> &'a str {
    if x.len() > y.len() {
        x
    } else {
        y
    }
}
```

The relationship between input and output lifetimes

When we specify the same lifetime, `'a`, for multiple parameters, we're basically setting a shared constraint based on where those references live. Think of `'a` as representing the *overlap* (or intersection) of all the input lifetimes. So, if you pass in a reference that lasts the whole program and another that only exists briefly in a small part of the code, the return value will be limited to that small part.

This is the contract we sign with the compiler. We promise that the returned reference will not outlive the shortest-lived input, making sure we never accidentally access data that has been cleaned up.

Lifetimes in data structures

Until now, we have only defined structs that own their data. For example, a struct containing a `String` or `Vec<i32>` type is straightforward because the struct and its data are created and destroyed together. However, in some cases, it is more efficient for a struct to store a reference to data managed by another entity.

This situation is common when creating parsers or views, where copying large text blocks is undesirable. Since the struct does not own the data, the compiler requires assurance that the struct won't outlive the referenced data. We ensure this safety by including lifetime annotations in the struct definition.

Structs with references

To define a struct that contains a reference, we need to add a lifetime annotation in two places:

- First, we declare the lifetime parameter inside angle brackets immediately after the struct name
- Second, we assign that lifetime to the specific field that holds the reference

This creates a binding contract. It informs the compiler that an instance of this struct cannot outlive the data it points to. If the original data is dropped (cleaned up from memory) while this struct is still trying to use it, the compiler will instantly flag an error.

This guarantees you never accidentally access "dead" data or dangling pointers:

```
// src/main.rs
// This struct holds a reference, so it needs a lifetime 'a
struct ImportantExcerpt<'a> {
    part: &'a str,
```

```
}

fn main() {
    let novel = String::from("Call me Ishmael. Some years ago...");

    // The instance 'first_sentence' cannot outlive 'novel'
    let first_sentence = ImportantExcerpt {
        part: &novel[0..15],
    };

    // If 'novel' were dropped here, 'first_sentence' would become
invalid.
}
```

The impl block for lifetime-bound structs

When you decide to add methods to a struct that holds references, the syntax might seem a bit repetitive initially because you see the lifetime annotation twice. However, this is necessary because we are separating **declaration** from **usage**.

First, we must write `impl<'a>` to **declare** the lifetime parameter. This tells the compiler, "I am about to use a generic lifetime symbol named `'a` inside this block." Second, we write `Highlight<'a>` to **use** that specific lifetime, applying it to the struct we are targeting. Since the lifetime is part of the struct's type identity, we cannot implement methods for just `Highlight`; we must implement them for `Highlight<'a>`:

```
struct Highlight<'a> {
    part: &'a str,
}

// 1. impl<'a>: We DECLARE the lifetime parameter here so the compiler
knows it exists.
// 2. Highlight<'a>: We USE it here to select the specific struct type.
impl<'a> Highlight<'a> {
    fn announce(&self) {
        println!("Attention to: {}", self.part);
    }
}
```

Advanced lifetime concepts

We have discussed the strict syntax where we manually label every reference. However, if this were always necessary for every function, writing Rust would become extremely tedious. Luckily, the language includes smart features to automatically handle the most common patterns.

Now, we will explore how the compiler can often determine lifetimes on its own without help. We will also look at a special reserved lifetime for data that remains valid for the entire duration of the program.

Lifetime elision rules

In early versions of Rust, every function that used a reference needed explicit lifetime annotations. This made the code cluttered and repetitive. The Rust team saw that developers kept writing the same lifetime patterns repeatedly. To fix this, they embedded these common patterns directly into the compiler as **elision rules**. This isn't magic; it's just a set of predictable assumptions.

For example, if your function takes exactly one reference as input, the compiler automatically assigns that same lifetime to the output reference. You only need to add annotations manually when there is ambiguity, such as when a function accepts multiple references and the compiler can't determine which one is being returned:

```
// What you write (Elided):
// This works automatically ONLY because there is exactly one input
reference.
// If there were multiple inputs, elision would fail.
fn get_part(s: &str) -> &str { ... }

// What the compiler actually understands (Explicit):
fn get_part<'a>(s: &'a str) -> &'a str { ... }
```

The static lifetime ('static)

The language reserves a special lifetime name called `'static`, which means the data stays accessible throughout the whole program run. Interestingly, you've been using this lifetime quite often without realizing it. For example, every string literal, such as `"Hello World"`, is stored right in the program's binary. Since this binary is loaded into memory whenever the program runs, those strings are always available for you to use.

Therefore, they have the `'static` lifetime. While this can be helpful, it's important not to overuse it. Many new Rust programmers try to fix lifetime errors by making everything `'static`, but this is usually not the right approach. It tends to hide the real problem by keeping data in memory longer than necessary instead of properly managing how references are used.

```
// This string data is baked into the executable.
// It is valid from the moment the program starts until it exits.
let s: &'static str = "I have a static lifetime.";
```

We have analyzed the tools individually; now it is time to see them in action.

Applied polymorphism: a project

In this chapter, we've explored the three main pillars of Rust's flexible architecture: traits, generics, and lifetimes. While it's helpful to understand each one on its own, their true strength really shines when you see them working together. In everyday Rust development, you'll find these concepts usually mixing and matching rather than standing alone.

In this final section, we'll bring together everything we've learned into a single, clear example. This will demonstrate how these features work together to enable us to write code that is safe, fast, and easy to reuse. You'll often come across generic structs constrained by traits that hold references with specific lifetimes, and understanding how they fit into this bigger picture will make your coding journey even more rewarding.

Building a zero-copy configuration parser

To illustrate these abstract ideas clearly, we will create a "zero-copy configuration loader."

The aim is to develop a system that accepts input from any source, such as custom text formats or JSON, without requiring the core logic to be rewritten. This involves traits to define the common behavior. Additionally, we want it to be highly efficient. Rather than creating new strings for each configuration key, which consumes extra memory, the configuration struct should directly reference the original input data.

This particular requirement necessitates using lifetimes to guarantee safety. Additionally, we aim for the system to be adaptable to any type of configuration structure, which calls for generics.

Defining the capability (the Parse trait)

Let's start by setting up the interface in a clear and straightforward way. We want a simple method to turn raw text into a structured Rust object, no matter the format. To achieve this, we'll define a trait called `Parse`. Think of this trait as a kind of agreement: any type that adopts it must include a `parse` method. This method takes in a string slice with the raw data and produces an instance of that type.

It's also important that we specify a lifetime, `'a`, on the trait itself. This detail is essential for our zero-copy approach, as it informs the compiler that the created object might hold references directly to the input string, sharing their lifecycles:

```
// We define a lifetime 'a so the returned Self can hold references to
'input'
trait Parse<'a> {
    fn parse(input: &'a str) -> Self;
}
```

Abstracting the input (using generics)

Now that we have this trait, we can build a function around it that's really versatile. We're aiming for a single loader function that can handle any kind of configuration, whether it's for a database, a web server, or something else. That's where generics really come in handy.

So, we'll create a function called `load_configuration`, but instead of tying it to a specific struct, we'll make it work with any `T` type. Of course, we can't just accept any type; we need to set some rules. We do this by adding a trait bound, making sure `T` implements our `Parse` trait.

This way, we know that every type passing through this function will have the `parse` method we need to turn a string into a struct:

```
// This function works for ANY type T that implements Parse
// The <'a> ensures that the returned T cannot outlive the input string.
fn load_configuration<'a, T>(input: &'a str) -> T
where
    T: Parse<'a>,
{
    println!("Loading configuration...");
    T::parse(input)
}
```

The safety guarantee

Because we linked the 'a lifetime of the input string to the `T: Parse<'a>` trait bound, Rust enforces a strict safety contract. If we try to drop the original input string while holding onto the configuration struct, the compiler will stop us:

```
// This function works for ANY type T that implements Parse
// The <'a> ensures that the returned T cannot outlive the input string.
fn load_configuration<'a, T>(input: &'a str) -> T
where
    T: Parse<'a>,
{
    println!("Loading configuration...");
    T::parse(input)
}
```

Validating references (integrating lifetimes)

Finally, we put the logic into a concrete struct. We create a `ServerConfig` struct that keeps references to the input string, so we avoid copying the data into new `String` objects.

This is where the lifetimes do their essential work. We need to declare 'a on the struct and incorporate it into the implementation block. This links the input of the parse function to the fields of the struct. By doing this, we achieve **zero-copy parsing**.

Instead of allocating new memory on the heap for the address and port, our struct simply holds "views" (slices) into the original configuration string.

If the original configuration string is released from memory, the compiler will ensure that our `ServerConfig` struct is immediately invalidated, ensuring that we never accidentally read a port number from memory after it has been cleared:

```
// src/lib.rs

struct ServerConfig<'a> {
    address: &'a str,
    port: &'a str,
}

impl<'a> Parse<'a> for ServerConfig<'a> {
    fn parse(input: &'a str) -> Self {
```

```
        // We look for a space to separate the address and port.
        // Example Input: "localhost 8080"
        let index = input.find(' ').unwrap_or(input.len());

        // ZERO-COPY MAGIC:
        // We use slicing syntax to create references that point directly
        // into the original 'input' memory buffer.
        // No new strings are allocated here!
        ServerConfig {
            address: &input[..index],      // Borrow the first part
            port: &input[index + 1..],     // Borrow the second part
        }
    }
}
```

Summary

In this chapter, we moved beyond defining concrete types and explored how to write code that is flexible, reusable, and safe. We started by examining traits, which allow us to define shared behavior across different types. We learned that by focusing on what a type *can do* rather than what it *is*, we can write functions that accept any data capable of performing a specific action, similar to interfaces in other languages. We also covered the orphan rule for implementations and the trade-offs between static dispatch and dynamic dispatch using trait objects.

Next, we introduced generics as the primary tool for reducing code duplication. By using type parameters such as `<T>`, we saw how to write a single function or struct that works with any data type. We discussed how trait bounds allow us to restrict these generics to ensure they support the operations we need. Crucially, we learned about monomorphization, the compiler process that generates specific code for each concrete type, ensuring that our high-level abstractions act as "zero-cost" features that do not slow down our program at runtime.

Finally, we tackled lifetimes, which act as a form of polymorphism for scope. We saw that lifetimes are the mechanism the borrow checker uses to prevent dangling references and ensure memory safety. While the compiler often infers these for us through elision rules, we learned how to manually annotate functions and structs using syntax such as `<'a>` when relationships are ambiguous. By combining traits, generics, and lifetimes, we built a zero-copy configuration parser, demonstrating how these three pillars work together to create efficient and robust software.

With the powerful combination of traits and generics in our toolkit, we're ready to tackle a question that puzzles many developers transitioning from languages such as Java or C++: Does Rust actually support object-oriented programming? The short answer is: yes.

Questions and assignment

Questions

1. In Rust, what is the primary purpose of a trait?
2. What is the process called where the Rust compiler generates specific code for each concrete type used in a generic function?
3. Explain the orphan rule regarding trait implementations.
4. When defining a `fn largest<T>(list: &[T])` generic function, why might you need to add a bound such as `T: PartialOrd`?
5. What is the specific problem that Rust's lifetimes are designed to prevent?
6. What is the correct syntax to declare a `Highlight` struct that holds a string slice reference with a lifetime, `'a`?
7. What does the keyword `dyn` indicate in Rust, for example, in `Box<dyn Brew>`?
8. What is the `'static` lifetime?
9. Why do we sometimes need to specify lifetimes such as `<'a>` in function signatures?
10. What is the purpose of the `where` clause in a generic function definition?

Assignment

The universal media player

Your task is to build a simple system for a media application that can handle different types of content using the polymorphic tools we learned in this chapter:

1. **Define a trait**: Create a trait named `Playable`. It should have one method signature: `play(&self)`.
2. **Create types**: Define two distinct structs: `AudioBook` (with fields such as `title` and `author`) and `VideoGame` (with fields such as `name` and `platform`).
3. **Implement behavior**: Implement the `Playable` trait for both structs. The `AudioBook` implementation should print `"Now playing book: [Title]..."`, and the `VideoGame` implementation should print `"Launching game: [Name]..."`.

4. **Write a generic function:** Write a generic function named `consume_media`. It should accept any `T` type that implements `Playable` and call the `.play()` method on it.
5. **Lifetimes (bonus)**: Create a struct named `Metadata<'a>` that holds a reference to a string slice (e.g., a description). Instantiate this struct in your main function, pointing to a string literal, ensuring that the lifetime logic is valid.

8

Object-Oriented Programming in Rust

Welcome to *Chapter 8*!

In previous chapters, we've enjoyed exploring Rust's core features like ownership and error handling together. Now, let's warmly dive into how concepts from **Object-Oriented Programming (OOP)** connect with Rust.

Although Rust isn't a traditional OOP language like Java or C++, you'll discover that it thoughtfully includes many of the same principles, all woven into its own unique, safety-focused approach to achieving object-oriented goals.

This distinctive approach isn't by chance; it's a natural result of Rust's motivations: ensuring memory safety without a garbage collector, enabling fearless concurrency by preventing data races, and delivering performance comparable to C.

These foundational goals have guided specific design decisions, such as choosing traits for shared behavior instead of traditional inheritance.

Understanding OOP principles

Rust isn't a traditional object-oriented language, but it offers features that let you write code in an object-oriented style, crafted around its core values of safety and performance.

- **Encapsulation**: Instead of using classes, Rust employs structs and enums to hold data, and you can add behavior with `impl` blocks. Access control is managed through Rust's module system and the `pub` keyword, which keeps things private by default.

- **Polymorphism**: Rust mainly uses traits for polymorphism. Traits let you define shared behavior that different structs and enums can implement. This allows you to write versatile code that works with any type implementing a specific trait (static dispatch), or you can use trait objects (`dyn` Trait) for runtime polymorphism (dynamic dispatch).
- **No class inheritance**: Rust intentionally skips implementation inheritance, where a struct would inherit fields and methods from a parent struct. Instead, it prefers composition over inheritance, sharing behavior through traits or building complex types from simpler ones. This design avoids common issues with deep inheritance hierarchies in traditional OOP, such as the "fragile base class problem," and encourages more flexible, loosely connected designs.

How Rust approaches OOP differently

Rust implements OOP concepts differently, prioritizing memory safety and performance, often without direct equivalents to traditional OOP features:

- **Data encapsulation:** Rust uses structs and enums (as seen in *Chapter 5*) to define custom data structures. Encapsulation (controlling access) is achieved through Rust's module system and privacy rules (pub, private by default), which we'll explore.
- **Behavior encapsulation:** Methods are associated with structs/enums using `impl` blocks, bundling data and behavior.
- **Abstraction and polymorphism (via traits):** Instead of classes and inheritance, Rust uses **traits**. Traits define shared interfaces (a set of method signatures) that different types can implement. This allows for polymorphism (treating different types implementing the same trait uniformly) through generics (static dispatch) and trait objects (dynamic dispatch).
- **No class inheritance:** Rust deliberately omits implementation inheritance (inheriting fields and method implementations directly from a superclass). It favors **composition** and **trait-based code reuse**, which often leads to more flexible and maintainable designs.

Rust's approach provides many benefits of OOP while avoiding common pitfalls such as complex inheritance hierarchies, null pointer issues, and data races, thanks to its ownership and borrowing system.

Encapsulation: structs, methods, and privacy

As we learned in *Chapter 5*, structs allow us to define custom data types by grouping related fields. Associating behavior with this data is done using `impl` blocks, where we define methods.

A deeper look at privacy: pub(crate) and pub(super)

While pub makes an item fully public, Rust offers more control over visibility, useful in larger projects.

- pub(crate): Visible within the same crate but private outside, ideal for internal helpers shared across your library.
- pub(super): Visible to the parent module, suitable for encapsulating implementation details. These features, which we'll explore later, highlight Rust's precise control over code visibility.

This combination of data (`struct` fields) and behavior (`impl` methods) is Rust's primary way of achieving the OOP principle of **encapsulation**: bundling data and the operations that act upon it into a cohesive unit.

A key part of encapsulation is controlling access. By default in Rust, `struct` fields are **private** to the module they are defined in. This prevents external code from directly accessing or modifying the internal state of a struct, promoting data integrity. Methods defined in an `impl` block are also private by default. To allow external access, we use the pub keyword.

Let's illustrate with an `AveragedCollection` that maintains a list of numbers and their average, ensuring the average is always correct.

```
// Define the struct in its own scope (like a module would provide)
pub mod math_utils { // Using a module to demonstrate privacy

    #[derive(Debug)] // Allow printing the struct
    pub struct AveragedCollection {
        list: Vec<i32>, // Private: External code cannot directly modify
the list
        average: f64,   // Private: External code cannot directly set the
average
    }
```

```
impl AveragedCollection {
    // Public constructor (associated function)
    pub fn new() -> AveragedCollection {
        AveragedCollection {
            list: Vec::new(),
            average: 0.0,
        }
    }

    // Public method to add an element, updating the average correctly
    pub fn add(&mut self, value: i32) {
        self.list.push(value);
        self.update_average(); // Call private helper method
    }

    // Public method to remove an element (if present)
    pub fn remove(&mut self) -> Option<i32> {
        let result = self.list.pop(); // pop() returns Option<i32>
        match result {
            Some(_) => {
                self.update_average(); // Update average if removal
happened
                result
            }
            None => None, // List was empty
        }
    }

    // Public method to get the current average (read-only access)
    pub fn average(&self) -> f64 {
        self.average
    }

    // Private helper method to recalculate the average
    // Not marked 'pub', so only usable within this module/impl block
    fn update_average(&mut self) {
        let total: i32 = self.list.iter().sum();
```

```
                self.average = if self.list.is_empty() {
                    0.0
                } else {
                    total as f64 / self.list.len() as f64
                };
            }
        }
} // end module math_utils

fn main() {
    // We need 'use' to bring the public items into scope
    use math_utils::AveragedCollection;

    let mut collection = AveragedCollection::new();

    // We can only interact via public methods
    collection.add(10);
    collection.add(20);
    collection.add(30);
    println!("Average after adds: {}", collection.average()); // Output:
20.0

    // Cannot do this - fields are private:
    // collection.list.push(100); // Compile Error!
    // collection.average = 50.0; // Compile Error!

    collection.remove();
    println!("Average after remove: {}", collection.average()); // Output:
15.0

    // Cannot call private methods:
    // collection.update_average(); // Compile Error!

    println!("Final collection state: {:?}", collection);
}
```

In this `AveragedCollection` example, the following happens:

- The `list` and `average` fields are private because they lack the `pub` keyword. Code outside the `math_utils` module cannot access them directly. This isn't just a convention; it's a strict rule enforced by the Rust compiler. By catching these invalid access attempts at compile time, Rust prevents common bugs, such as accidental data corruption, which might only appear as hard-to-debug runtime errors in less encapsulated languages.
- Methods such as `add`, `remove`, `average`, and the `new` constructor are explicitly marked `pub`, forming the public API of the struct.
- The `update_average` method is private (no `pub`), serving as an internal implementation detail. It can only be called by other methods within the same `impl` block (such as `add` and `remove`). This enforces encapsulation: the internal state (`list`, `average`) is protected, and modifications can only happen through the public methods, ensuring the average remains consistent with the list's contents. This is a common and recommended pattern in Rust.

Shared behavior with traits

While structs encapsulate data and specific behavior, how do we define *shared* behavior across different types? In traditional OOP, this is often done via inheritance or interfaces. Rust's answer is **traits**. In the previous chapter, we already introduced traits, but we will discuss them again here with more examples.

A trait defines a collection of method signatures (and sometimes associated types or constants) that declare a set of capabilities needed to perform some task. Think of them as defining an "interface" or a "contract" that types can agree to implement.

Defining and implementing traits

You define a trait using the `trait` keyword, followed by the trait name and the method signatures within curly braces. To make a specific type adhere to the trait's contract, you implement the trait for that type using an `impl` TraitName for Type block, providing concrete implementations for the required methods.

```
// Define a trait for things that can provide a summary
pub trait Summarizable {
    fn summary(&self) -> String; // Method signature: takes &self, returns
String
```

```
    // Traits can also have default method implementations
    fn default_summary(&self) -> String {
        String::from("(Read more...)") // Default implementation
    }
}

// Define some structs
pub struct NewsArticle {
    pub headline: String,
    pub location: String,
    pub author: String,
    pub content: String,
}

pub struct Tweet {
    pub username: String,
    pub content: String,
    pub reply: bool,
    pub retweet: bool,
}

// Implement the trait for NewsArticle
impl Summarizable for NewsArticle {
    fn summary(&self) -> String {
        format!("{}, by {} ({})", self.headline, self.author, self.
location)
    }
    // We don't need to implement default_summary, we can use the default
}

// Implement the trait for Tweet
impl Summarizable for Tweet {
    fn summary(&self) -> String {
        format!("{}: {}", self.username, self.content)
    }
```

```
    // We can override the default implementation if we want
    fn default_summary(&self) -> String {
        if self.retweet {
            format!("Retweeted: {}", self.summary())
        } else {
            self.summary() // Or just call the required method
        }
    }
}

fn main() {
    let tweet = Tweet {
        username: String::from("rustacean"),
        content: String::from("Traits are cool!"),
        reply: false,
        retweet: false,
    };

    let article = NewsArticle {
        headline: String::from("Rust 1.XX Released!"),
        location: String::from("Online"),
        author: String::from("The Rust Team"),
        content: String::from("A new version of Rust brings many
improvements..."),
    };

    println!("Tweet summary: {}", tweet.summary());
    println!("Article summary: {}", article.summary());
    println!("Tweet default summary: {}", tweet.default_summary());
    println!("Article default summary: {}", article.default_summary());
}
```

Traits for polymorphism: impl Trait

One of the main benefits of traits is enabling polymorphism. We can write functions that accept any type implementing a specific trait. The simplest way is to use `impl` Trait syntax in the parameter type. This uses **static dispatch** (monomorphization) – the compiler generates specialized code for each concrete type used.

```
// This function accepts any type that implements Summarizable
pub fn notify(item: &impl Summarizable) {
    // Using `impl Trait` syntax
    println!("Breaking news! {}", item.summary());
}

// Main function calling notify with different types
fn main() {
    // ... (tweet and article definitions from previous example) ...

    let tweet = Tweet {
        username: String::from("rustacean"),
        content: String::from("Traits are cool!"),
        reply: false,
        retweet: false,
    };

    let article = NewsArticle {
        headline: String::from("Rust 1.XX Released!"),
        location: String::from("Online"),
        author: String::from("The Rust Team"),
        content: String::from(
            "A new version of Rust brings many improvements..."
        ),
    };

    notify(&tweet);
    notify(&article);
}
```

Traits for polymorphism: trait bounds

An alternative, more verbose syntax for the same static dispatch is using **trait bounds** with generic type parameters.

This is necessary in more complex scenarios, such as when multiple parameters need the same generic type or when implementing traits for generic types.

Let's see an example:

```
// Equivalent to the previous notify function, using trait bounds
pub fn notify_generic<T: Summarizable>(item: &T) { // Using generic T with
trait bound
    println!("Breaking news (generic)! {}", item.summary());
}

// Can also use the 'where' clause for more complex bounds
pub fn notify_complex<T>(item1: &T, item2: &T)
    where T: Summarizable + std::fmt::Debug // Requires T to implement
both traits
{
    println!("Item 1: {} ({:?})", item1.summary(), item1);
    println!("Item 2: {} ({:?})", item2.summary(), item2);
}

// main function would call notify_generic similarly to notify
// (Need to add #[derive(Debug)] to Tweet and NewsArticle for notify_
complex)
```

Both `impl` Trait and trait bounds `<T: Trait>` achieve polymorphism via static dispatch, which is highly performant as the compiler optimizes the calls for each specific type at compile time.

Both `fn notify(item: &impl Summarizable)` and `fn notify_generic<T: Summarizable>(item: &T)` achieve the same goal, but choosing one depends on context.

The `impl` Trait syntax is preferred for simplicity, enhancing readability. The more verbose generic syntax, such as `<T: Trait>` or the `where` clause, is better in the following situations:

- Ensuring multiple parameters have the exact same type, as in `notify_complex<T: Summarizable>(item1: &T, item2: &T)`. The `<T: ...>` syntax enforces this, unlike `(item1: &impl Summarizable, item2: &impl Summarizable)`, which allows different types.

- When the generic type is used in the return type, requiring `<T: Trait>` syntax.
- For complex trait bounds involving multiple traits, where a `where` clause improves clarity over inline bounds.

A common pitfall: impl Trait versus "Any" Trait

It's important to clarify a common point of confusion about `impl` Trait.

When you see `fn notify(item: &impl Summarizable)`, it means the function can be called with a reference to *any single, concrete type* that implements `Summarizable`. For example, you can call it with `&Tweet` or call it with `&NewsArticle`.

However, it does not mean you can mix different concrete types within the same data structure. The compiler resolves `impl` Trait to a specific, single type at compile time for each use case. This means you cannot, for example, create a Vec that holds both `Tweets` and `NewsArticles` and pass it to a function expecting `Vec<impl Summarizable>`.

```
// This is fine:
// notify(&my_tweet);
// notify(&my_article);

// This will NOT compile:
// let items: Vec<&impl Summarizable> = vec![&my_tweet, &my_
article];
// error: `impl Trait` not allowed in path parameters
```

The compiler needs to know the exact size of the elements in the Vec at compile time, and `Tweet` and `NewsArticle` are different types with different sizes. To handle collections of different types that share a trait, you need dynamic dispatch using trait objects (`&dyn Summarizable`), which we will cover in the next section.

Understanding static dispatch (monomorphization)

When you write a generic function with a trait bound in Rust, such as `fn process<T: MyTrait>(item: T)`, you're essentially creating a template rather than just one function.

During compilation, the compiler produces specialized versions for each specific type you use, a process known as monomorphization. In the end, only concrete functions are left, which makes static dispatch fast: calls go directly, without any lookup delays, and this allows for optimizations such as inlining.

Here's a simple example to illustrate this:

```
use std::fmt::Debug;
use std::ops::Add;

// A generic function that takes any type `T` that can be added to itself
// and can be printed with the Debug trait.
// The `Copy` trait is needed so `value` can be used after being moved
into the `+` operation.
fn add_and_print<T>(value: T)
where
    T: Add<Output = T> + Copy + Debug,
{
    let result = value + value; // `value` must implement `Add` and `Copy`
    println!("[Generic Function] {:?} + {:?} = {:?}", value, value,
result);
}

fn main() {
    let my_integer: i32 = 10;
    let my_float: f64 = 5.5;

    // When the compiler sees this call, it generates a specialized
version of `add_and_print` for `i32`.
    // It's as if you had written a function `add_and_print_i32(value:
i32)`.
    add_and_print(my_integer);
```

```
    // When the compiler sees this call, it generates another specialized
version for `f64`.
    // It's as if you had written a function `add_and_print_f64(value:
f64)`.
    add_and_print(my_float);
}
```

Behind the scenes, the compiler effectively generates something like this for the main function:

```
// Conceptual code generated by the compiler (monomorphization)

fn add_and_print_i32(value: i32) {
    let result = value + value;
    println!("[Generic Function] {:?} + {:?} = {:?}", value, value,
result);
}

fn add_and_print_f64(value: f64) {
    let result = value + value;
    println!("[Generic Function] {:?} + {:?} = {:?}", value, value,
result);
}

fn main() {
    let my_integer: i32 = 10;
    let my_float: f64 = 5.5;

    // The call is replaced with a direct call to the specialized
function.
    add_and_print_i32(my_integer);

    // This call is also replaced with a direct call.
    add_and_print_f64(my_float);
}
```

This process of monomorphization is what allows Rust's generics to have zero runtime cost compared to non-generic code, making them a powerful tool for writing abstract code without sacrificing performance.

The trade-off is a potentially larger binary size, as code is duplicated for each concrete type used.

Static dispatch is very efficient, but since it needs to know specific types at compile time, it can't, for example, allow you to have a collection with different types like `Tweet` and `NewsArticle`, even if they both implement `Summarizable`.

To add more flexibility during runtime, Rust provides an alternative kind of polymorphism: dynamic dispatch.

Dynamic polymorphism with trait objects

When you're managing a collection of items that are of different types but share the same behavior, it's helpful to defer the method call decision from compile time to runtime. Rust handles this beautifully with trait objects: pointers that can hold any type implementing a trait.

This makes it possible to have diverse collections and creates more flexible, dynamic code that adapts to various needs.

Introduction to trait objects

Static dispatch via generics (`impl` Trait or `<T: Trait>`) works when the compiler knows the concrete types involved at compile time.

But what if you need a collection (like a Vec) that holds items of *different* concrete types, as long as they all implement the same trait? Or, if you need to return different types implementing a trait from a function? This requires **dynamic dispatch**, where the specific method to call is determined at *runtime*.

Rust achieves this using **trait objects**.

Creating trait objects: dyn Trait

A trait object is created by taking a reference (or a smart pointer like `Box` or `Rc`) to an instance of a type that implements a trait and specifying the type as `&dyn Trait` or `Box<dyn Trait>`. The `dyn` keyword indicates that method calls on this object will use **dynamic dispatch**.

When you want to create a collection that holds different types that all share the same trait, like a Vec containing both `NewsArticle` and `Tweet`, you must use a smart pointer like `Box`. This is a fundamental requirement of Rust's memory model. Rust needs to know the exact size of every element in a Vec at compile time to allocate memory for it on the stack. However, `NewsArticle` and `Tweet` are different structs and have different sizes.

This is the problem that `Box<dyn Trait>` solves. `Box` is a smart pointer, and the pointer itself has a known, fixed size, regardless of how big the data it points to is. By wrapping our differently sized objects in `Box`, we place them on the heap and store the consistently sized `Box` pointers in our Vec. This satisfies Rust's size requirements and allows us to create a heterogeneous collection.

```
// Using the Summarizable trait and types from before
pub trait Summarizable { fn summary(&self) -> String; }
pub struct NewsArticle { pub headline: String, pub location: String, pub
author: String, pub content: String }
impl Summarizable for NewsArticle { fn summary(&self) -> String {
format!("{}, by {} ({})", self.headline, self.author, self.location) } }
pub struct Tweet { pub username: String, pub content: String, pub reply:
bool, pub retweet: bool }
impl Summarizable for Tweet { fn summary(&self) -> String { format!("{}:
{}", self.username, self.content) } }

fn main() {
    let article = NewsArticle {
        headline: String::from("New Rust Feature"),
        location: String::from("Blog"),
        author: String::from("Dev Team"),
        content: String::from("..."),
    };
    let tweet = Tweet {
        username: String::from("user123"),
        content: String::from("Learning Rust traits!"),
        reply: false,
        retweet: false,
    };

    // Create a vector that holds trait objects.
```

```
    // We use Box<dyn Summarizable> because the concrete types
(NewsArticle, Tweet)
    // have different sizes, so we need an indirection (Box puts them on
the heap).
    let items_to_summarize: Vec<Box<dyn Summarizable>> = vec![
        Box::new(article), // Box::new creates a Box<NewsArticle>, which
converts to Box<dyn Summarizable>
        Box::new(tweet),   // Box::new creates a Box<Tweet>, which
converts to Box<dyn Summarizable>
    ];

    // We can iterate and call methods via the trait object
    for item in items_to_summarize {
        // item here is Box<dyn Summarizable>
        println!("Summary: {}", item.summary()); // Dynamic dispatch
happens here
    }
}
```

This code demonstrates **dynamic polymorphism.** It defines a `Summarizable` trait that two different structs, `NewsArticle` and `Tweet`, both implement. To store these different-sized structs in the same Vec, each is wrapped in `Box` (a smart pointer), creating a `Vec<Box<dyn Summarizable>>`.

When the code iterates through this vector and calls `.summary()` on each item, Rust determines the correct method to run at runtime, this is dynamic dispatch in action.

Dynamic versus static dispatch recap

Dynamic dispatch, achieved through trait objects, determines the method to call at runtime.

This is different from static dispatch, where the method to call is determined at compile time.

- **Static dispatch** (`impl` Trait, `<T: Trait>`):
    - Compiler generates specific code for each concrete type.
    - No runtime lookup cost; calls can often be inlined.
    - Requires knowing concrete types at compile time. Cannot store different types in the same homogeneous collection directly.

- **Dynamic dispatch** (`&dyn Trait`, `Box<dyn Trait>`):
    - Compiler uses a *vtable* (virtual method table) pointer stored alongside the data pointer to find the correct method implementation at runtime.
    - Incurs a small runtime lookup cost; prevents inlining.
    - Allows storing different types implementing the same trait together (e.g., in `Vec<Box<dyn Trait>>`).

Choose static dispatch when possible for performance. Use dynamic dispatch when you need the flexibility to handle heterogeneous collections or return different implementing types.

Object safety

Not all traits can be made into trait objects. For a trait to be used with `dyn Trait`, it must be **object-safe**. This is a set of rules that ensures the compiler can work with the trait when the concrete type is unknown at compile time. The main rules for object safety are that all methods in the trait must meet the following criteria:

1. Have a receiver (`self`, `&self`, or `&mut self`) as the first parameter.
2. Not use `Self` as a return type or in parameter types (except for the receiver).
3. Not have generic type parameters.

Most common traits are object-safe. However, let's look at a simple example of a trait that is **not** object-safe to understand why these rules exist. The `Clone` trait is a perfect example from the standard library that is not object-safe because its `clone` method returns `Self`.

Let's create our own version to see the problem:

```
// A trait that is NOT object-safe because its method returns `Self`.
pub trait Cloneable {
    fn clone_self(&self) -> Self;
}

// Let's implement it for our Tweet struct from earlier.
#[derive(Debug)] // Added for printing
pub struct Tweet {
    pub username: String,
    pub content: String,
}
```

```
impl Cloneable for Tweet {
    fn clone_self(&self) -> Self {
        Tweet {
            username: self.username.clone(),
            content: self.content.clone(),
        }
    }
}

fn main() {
    let tweet = Tweet {
        username: "rustacean".to_string(),
        content: "Object safety is important!".to_string(),
    };

    // This is fine, because the compiler knows the concrete type is
Tweet.
    let tweet_clone = tweet.clone_self();
    println!("Cloned tweet: {:?}", tweet_clone);

    // Now, let's try to create a trait object.
    // The line below will cause a compile-time error.
    // let cloneable_object: Box<dyn Cloneable> = Box::new(tweet);
    //
    // The compiler error would be something like:
    // error[E0038]: the trait `Cloneable` cannot be made into an object
    //    --> src/main.rs:31:31
    //     |
    // 31  |     let cloneable_object: Box<dyn Cloneable> =
Box::new(tweet);
    //     |                               ^^^^^^^^^^^^^ `Cloneable`
cannot be made into an object
    //     |
    // note: for a trait to be "object-safe" it must not have any methods
that return `Self`
    //    --> src/main.rs:5:28
    //     |
```

```
    // 5    |       fn clone_self(&self) -> Self;
    //      |                              ^^^^ ...because `Self` is treated
as a type parameter
}
```

The compiler will let you know if a trait isn't object-safe when you try to create a trait object from it.

The reason that `fn clone_self(&self) -> Self;` breaks object safety is because of the way trait objects work. When you have a trait object such as `Box<dyn Cloneable>`, Rust doesn't know the exact type inside `Box` at compile time, just that it's some type that implements `Cloneable`.

If you call `clone_self()` on this trait object, Rust needs to create and return a new value of that unknown specific type. But how much memory should it allocate for this return? It doesn't know the size of the concrete type (such as `Tweet`, but it could be something else!!).

Because the size of `Self` isn't known at runtime in a trait object, the compiler can't generate the proper code to handle the return value, so it blocks creating the trait object in the first place.

Simulating inheritance patterns

Composition over inheritance

As emphasized before, Rust intentionally omits traditional class-based inheritance.

Instead, it warmly promotes the idea of composition, creating complex types by including other types, such as structs and enums, as fields, and using traits to share behaviors.

This approach often results in more flexible and adaptable designs compared to deep inheritance hierarchies.

This preference for composition is a deliberate design choice that Rust developers generally favor. It is particularly effective for modeling **"has-a" relationships**, where one type contains another as a component (for example, a car *has an* engine). Compared to inheritance (which models an "is-a" relationship), composition often leads to designs with **less tight coupling** between components.

This modularity provides **greater flexibility**, as you can easily swap out different implementations of a component, and makes your code **easier to test** because each small, focused part can be tested in isolation.

Sharing behavior via traits

The primary way to share *behavior* (methods) is by defining that behavior in a trait and having multiple structs implement it.

We saw this with the `Summarizable` trait implemented by both `NewsArticle` and `Tweet`.

Each type provides its own data and its own implementation of the shared behavior.

Default implementations

Traits can offer default implementations for some or all of their methods, making code reuse easier and more efficient. It's helpful to see how this differs from traditional inheritance. In Rust, default implementations let you reuse behavior, such as the logic inside methods, without sharing data, such as `struct` fields. This is quite different from many object-oriented languages, where subclasses typically inherit both methods and data from their parents.

By keeping data and behaviors separated, Rust promotes more flexible and loosely connected designs. Types that implement a trait can simply use the default methods or choose to create their own custom versions if needed.

```
trait Clickable {
    fn click(&self); // Required method

    // Method with a default implementation
    fn hover_text(&self) -> String {
        String::from("Click me!") // Default text
    }
}

struct Button {
    label: String,
}
impl Clickable for Button {
    fn click(&self) {
        println!("Button '{}' clicked!", self.label);
    }
    // Uses the default hover_text()
}
```

```
struct ImageLink {
    src: String,
}
impl Clickable for ImageLink {
    fn click(&self) {
        println!("Navigating to image link '{}'...", self.src);
    }
    // Overrides the default hover_text()
    fn hover_text(&self) -> String {
        format!("View image: {}", self.src)
    }
}

fn main() {
    let button = Button { label: "Submit".into() };
    let image = ImageLink { src: "logo.png".into() };

    button.click();
    println!("Button hover: {}", button.hover_text()); // Uses default

    image.click();
    println!("Image hover: {}", image.hover_text()); // Uses override
}
```

Trait bounds as "subclassing" constraints: supertraits

You can require that a type implementing one trait must also implement another. This is done by specifying a supertrait in the trait definition using the `: Trait` syntax.

This setup resembles an "is-a" relationship, similar to inheritance, and helps you build upon existing trait agreements. While this is a powerful way to create layered abstractions, it's usually best to keep these trait hierarchies simple and not too deep, as overly complex bounds can sometimes make your code more difficult to understand and work with.

```
use std::fmt::Display; // Import the standard Display trait

// Define a trait that REQUIRES the implementing type to also implement
Display
```

```
trait PrintableSummary: Display { // PrintableSummary is a sub-trait of
Display
    fn print_summary(&self);
}

struct Report {
    title: String,
    content: String,
}

// To implement PrintableSummary, Report MUST first implement Display
impl Display for Report {
    fn fmt(&self, f: &mut std::fmt::Formatter<'_>) -> std::fmt::Result {
        write!(f, "Report: '{}'", self.title)
    }
}

// NOW we can implement PrintableSummary
impl PrintableSummary for Report {
    fn print_summary(&self) {
        println!("--- Summary ---");
        println!("{}", self); // We can use Display methods because of the
trait bound
        println!("Content length: {}", self.content.len());
        println!("---------------");
    }
}

fn main() {
    let report = Report {
        title: "Q1 Results".into(),
        content: "Sales were strong...".into(),
    };
    report.print_summary();
}
```

Here, `PrintableSummary: Display` means any type implementing `PrintableSummary` *must* also implement `Display`. This allows methods within `PrintableSummary` (such as `print_summary`) to rely on the methods provided by `Display` (such as printing `self` directly).

Requiring multiple traits with +

In addition to specifying supertraits, you can also require a generic type to implement *multiple* traits using the + syntax. This is very common in function signatures.

For example, if you wanted a function to take any item that is both printable for debugging (`Debug`) and can be cloned (`Clone`), you would write the following:

```
use std::fmt::Debug;

// This function accepts any type `T` that implements both `Debug` and
`Clone`.
fn process_item<T: Debug + Clone>(item: T) {
    let item_clone = item.clone();
    println!("Processing item: {:?}", item);
    println!("And its clone: {:?}", item_clone);
}
```

`T: Debug + Clone` is a **trait bound** that enforces multiple requirements on the type T.

While not inheritance, traits, default methods, composition, and supertrait bounds provide powerful tools for code reuse and structuring behavior in Rust.

Associated types

Sometimes, a trait needs to refer to a specific related type that isn't chosen until the trait is actually implemented. We achieve this using associated types.

While it's possible to use generic type parameters on the trait for a similar purpose, like in `Iterator<T> { fn next(&mut self) -> Option<T>; }`, associated types are often preferred, especially for traits like `Iterator`. The main reason is that a type can only implement a trait with a particular set of associated types once, which helps prevent confusion. For example, `Vec<i32>` can only be an iterator over one kind of item, which is `i32`.

By using an associated type `Item`, we clarify this one-to-one relationship, making the type system more intuitive and supporting both the compiler and programmers.

In fact, the standard Iterator trait also uses an associated type to indicate the kind of item it produces!

```
// Simplified Iterator-like trait
pub trait SimpleIterator {
    // 'Item' is an associated type. Each implementor specifies what Item
is.
    type Item;

    // next() returns an Option of the associated Item type
    fn next(&mut self) -> Option<Self::Item>;
}

// Implement the trait for a simple counter
struct Counter {
    current: u32,
    max: u32,
}

impl SimpleIterator for Counter {
    // Specify that for Counter, the Item type is u32
    type Item = u32;

    fn next(&mut self) -> Option<Self::Item> { // Returns Option<u32>
        if self.current < self.max {
            let val = self.current;
            self.current += 1;
            Some(val)
        } else {
            None
        }
    }
}

fn main() {
    let mut counter = Counter { current: 0, max: 3 };
```

```
    // We can call next() and get Option<u32>
    println!("{:?}", counter.next()); // Some(0)
    println!("{:?}", counter.next()); // Some(1)
    println!("{:?}", counter.next()); // Some(2)
    println!("{:?}", counter.next()); // None
}
```

In the `SimpleIterator` trait, `type Item;` declares an associated type.

When `Counter` implements `SimpleIterator`, it specifies `type Item = u32;`. This links the `Item` placeholder to the concrete type `u32` *for that specific implementation.*

The next method can then refer to `Self::Item` (which means `u32` when implemented for `Counter`) in its signature.

Associated types are crucial for defining generic abstractions such as iterators, futures, and collections, where the trait needs to work with types determined by the implementor.

Now that we have our toolkit of structs, enums, and powerful traits, let's explore how they can come together to beautifully implement some of the most effective and commonly used object-oriented design patterns in a genuinely idiomatic Rust style.

Object-oriented design patterns in Rust

Introduction to patterns in Rust

While Rust isn't traditionally OOP, many common software design patterns can be effectively implemented by leveraging traits, enums, and composition. What makes this particularly powerful is how Rust's core features often lead to more robust and type-safe versions of these patterns than in other languages.

For example, Rust's expressive enums are perfect for creating compile-time verified state machines (the State pattern), while the ownership system provides a natural and safe way to manage resource construction (the Builder pattern).

The borrow checker adds another layer of safety, preventing invalid state mutations at compile time. This means you can implement familiar patterns with a higher degree of confidence in their correctness.

Builder pattern

The **Builder** pattern is useful when constructing an object with many fields, especially if many are optional or require complex setup.

For the reader and user of your code, this pattern dramatically improves API usability and readability. Instead of confronting them with a single, complex constructor function with a long, confusing list of parameters, the builder provides a clean, step-by-step, and self-documenting process.

Each optional parameter is set with a descriptive method call (e.g., `.with_feature_x()`, `.set_timeout()`), making it immediately clear which specific options are being configured for the new object.

```
#[derive(Debug)] // To allow printing the final struct
pub struct WindowConfig {
    title: String,
    width: u32,
    height: u32,
    is_resizable: bool,
    has_decorations: bool,
}

// The builder struct
pub struct WindowConfigBuilder {
    title: String, // Required field
    width: Option<u32>,
    height: Option<u32>,
    is_resizable: Option<bool>,
    has_decorations: Option<bool>,
}

impl WindowConfigBuilder {
    // Start building with the required field(s)
    pub fn new(title: String) -> Self {
        WindowConfigBuilder {
            title,
            width: None,
            height: None,
```

```
            is_resizable: None,
            has_decorations: None,
        }
    }

    // Methods to set optional fields, consuming and returning self
(fluent interface)
    pub fn width(mut self, width: u32) -> Self {
        self.width = Some(width);
        self
    }

    pub fn height(mut self, height: u32) -> Self {
        self.height = Some(height);
        self
    }

    pub fn resizable(mut self, resizable: bool) -> Self {
        self.is_resizable = Some(resizable);
        self
    }

     pub fn decorations(mut self, decorations: bool) -> Self {
        self.has_decorations = Some(decorations);
        self
    }


    // Finalize the build, providing defaults for unset options
    pub fn build(self) -> WindowConfig {
        WindowConfig {
            title: self.title,
            width: self.width.unwrap_or(800), // Default width
            height: self.height.unwrap_or(600), // Default height
            is_resizable: self.is_resizable.unwrap_or(true), // Default
resizable
            has_decorations: self.has_decorations.unwrap_or(true), //
Default decorations
```

```
        }
    }
}

fn main() {
    let basic_window = WindowConfigBuilder::new("My App".to_string())
        .build(); // Uses all defaults

    let custom_window = WindowConfigBuilder::new("Game Window".to_
string())
        .width(1024)
        .height(768)
        .resizable(false)
        .build(); // Sets some fields, uses defaults for others

    let fullscreen_window = WindowConfigBuilder::new("Fullscreen".to_
string())
        .decorations(false) // Only set decorations
        .build();

    println!("Basic Window: {:?}", basic_window);
    println!("Custom Window: {:?}", custom_window);
    println!("Fullscreen Window: {:?}", fullscreen_window);
}
```

The `WindowConfigBuilder` provides a clear, step-by-step way to construct a `WindowConfig`, handling optional fields and defaults cleanly.

State pattern/typed states

Another common pattern involves handling an object whose behavior depends on its internal state. While many languages use flags or string fields (e.g., `if post.status == "draft"`), this approach can be a bit fragile and might lead to runtime errors if the state isn't checked before calling a method.

Rust's enums and match system offer a wonderfully powerful and safe way to implement the State pattern. Instead of relying on simple flags, you can encode the various states of an object directly within the type system, making your code both robust and clear.

This enables the Rust compiler to double-check state changes and make sure that certain methods are only called when the object is in the right state. It helps catch potential bugs early, during compilation instead of at runtime.

```
// Define the states and the context
struct DraftPost { content: String }
struct PendingReviewPost { content: String }
struct PublishedPost { content: String }

// The main object holding the current state
enum PostState {
    Draft(DraftPost),
    PendingReview(PendingReviewPost),
    Published(PublishedPost),
}

pub struct Post {
    state: PostState,
}

impl Post {
    pub fn new() -> Post {
        Post { state: PostState::Draft(DraftPost { content: String::new()
}) }
    }

    pub fn add_text(&mut self, text: &str) {
        // Only allowed in Draft state
        if let PostState::Draft(ref mut draft) = self.state {
             draft.content.push_str(text);
        } else {
            println!("Cannot add text in current state.");
            // In a real app, might return Result<(), Error>
```

```
        }
    }

    pub fn request_review(&mut self) {
        // Transition from Draft to PendingReview
        if let PostState::Draft(draft) = std::mem::replace(&mut self.
state, PostState::Draft(DraftPost{content: String::new()})) { // Temporary
replace to take ownership
            self.state = PostState::PendingReview(PendingReviewPost {
content: draft.content });
        } else {
            println!("Post must be in Draft state to request review.");
        }
    }

    pub fn approve(&mut self) {
        // Transition from PendingReview to Published
        if let PostState::PendingReview(pending) = std::mem::replace(&mut
self.state, PostState::Draft(DraftPost{content: String::new()})) {
            self.state = PostState::Published(PublishedPost { content:
pending.content });
        } else {
            println!("Post must be Pending Review to approve.");
        }
    }

    pub fn content(&self) -> &str {
        // Access content based on current state
        match &self.state {
            PostState::Draft(s) => &s.content,
            PostState::PendingReview(s) => &s.content,
            PostState::Published(s) => &s.content,
        }
    }
}

fn main() {
```

```
    let mut post = Post::new();

    post.add_text("Learning about state patterns in Rust. ");
    println!("Content (Draft): {}", post.content());

    post.request_review();
    post.add_text("This won't be added."); // Tries adding text in wrong
state

    post.approve();
    println!("Content (Published): {}", post.content());

    post.request_review(); // Tries invalid transition
}
```

This `Post` example uses an enum (`PostState`) to represent the possible states. The main `Post` struct holds the *current* state. Methods on `Post` check the current state (using `if let` or `match`) and only allow valid actions or transitions.

This enforces the state machine logic at compile time to a large degree, preventing invalid operations based on the current state.

You may have noticed the use of `std::mem::replace` in transition methods such as `request_review`; this is a handy technique used to temporarily take ownership of the state from `&mut self.state`. It allows us to move the `Draft` variant out so we can use its data to construct the new `PendingReview` state, all while upholding Rust's ownership rules.

This is often considered more robust than using simple boolean flags or string-based states.

Rust's features enable implementing many design patterns effectively, often with enhanced type safety compared to traditional OOP languages.

Observer pattern

The Observer pattern is a helpful way for objects to stay connected and communicate smoothly. It creates a one-to-many relationship, so when the main object, called the subject, changes, all the dependents, known as observers, are easily notified and updated.

This makes it perfect for building event-driven systems where different parts of an app can respond to changes without being tightly tied to the object that changes. In Rust, this pattern is often put into practice using traits and smart pointers.

The main idea is to define an `Observer` trait with a method such as `update()`. Then, the `Subject` struct keeps a collection of objects that follow this trait. To manage shared ownership and allow observers to change their state after being notified, this collection is usually a Vec of smart pointers, such as `Vec<Rc<RefCell<dyn Observer>>>` for single-threaded environments or `Vec<Arc<Mutex<dyn Observer>>>` when working with multiple threads.

```
use std::rc::Rc;
use std::cell::RefCell;

// The trait that all observers must implement.
trait Observer {
    // The subject calls this method to notify the observer of a change.
    fn update(&self, new_state: &str);
}

// The subject holds the state and a list of observers.
struct Subject {
    state: String,
    // We use Rc<RefCell<...>> to allow shared ownership and interior
mutability of the observers list.
    observers: RefCell<Vec<Rc<dyn Observer>>>,
}

impl Subject {
    fn new(initial_state: &str) -> Self {
        Subject {
            state: initial_state.to_string(),
            observers: RefCell::new(Vec::new()),
        }
    }

    // Add a new observer to the list.
    fn attach(&self, observer: Rc<dyn Observer>) {
```

```
        self.observers.borrow_mut().push(observer);
    }

    // Change the state and notify all observers.
    fn set_state(&mut self, new_state: &str) {
        self.state = new_state.to_string();
        println!("\nSubject: State changed to '{}'. Notifying 
observers...", self.state);
        // We borrow the observers list immutably to iterate and notify.
        for observer in self.observers.borrow().iter() {
            observer.update(&self.state);
        }
    }
}

// A concrete observer that logs updates.
struct Logger {
    name: String,
}

impl Observer for Logger {
    fn update(&self, new_state: &str) {
        println!("[Logger {}]: Received update! New state is: '{}'", self.
name, new_state);
    }
}

// Another concrete observer that might perform a different action.
struct Notifier {
    email: String,
}

impl Observer for Notifier {
    fn update(&self, new_state: &str) {
        println!("[Notifier]: Sending email to {}. Subject: State changed 
to '{}'", self.email, new_state);
    }
}
```

```
fn main() {
    let mut subject = Subject::new("Initial State");

    // Create observers. We wrap them in Rc to manage shared ownership.
    let logger = Rc::new(Logger { name: "FileLogger".to_string() });
    let notifier = Rc::new(Notifier { email: "admin@example.com".to_
string() });

    // Attach the observers to the subject.
    subject.attach(Rc::clone(&logger) as Rc<dyn Observer>);
    subject.attach(Rc::clone(&notifier) as Rc<dyn Observer>);

    // Change the subject's state. This should trigger notifications.
    subject.set_state("State A");
    subject.set_state("State B");
}
```

- **Observer trait:** Defines the common interface with an update method that the subject will call.
- **Subject struct:** Holds its own state and the list of observers.
- **RefCell<Vec<Rc<dyn Observer>>>:** This is the core data structure for the observers list:
    - **Rc:** Enables shared ownership, allowing multiple parts of the application to hold a reference to an observer.
    - **RefCell:** Provides interior mutability, allowing the list of observers to be modified (e.g., adding a new observer) even through an immutable reference to the Subject.
    - **dyn Observer:** A trait object that allows the Vec to store different concrete types of observers (such as `Logger` and `Notifier`) as long as they all implement the `Observer` trait.
- **Concrete observers:** These are the specific structs (`Logger`, `Notifier`) that implement the `Observer` trait, each providing its own unique logic for the `update` method.

- **Execution flow**: The `main` function creates a `Subject` instance and one or more observer instances (wrapped in `Rc`). It then attaches the observers to the subject. When the subject's `set_state()` method is called, it iterates through its list of observers and calls the `update()` method on each one.

Strategy pattern

The Strategy pattern is a helpful behavioral design pattern that allows you to pick an algorithm while your program is running. It involves creating a set of interchangeable algorithms, each housed in its own type, so you can easily swap them out.

This pattern is especially handy when you have a task that can be done in multiple ways, giving you the flexibility to select or switch the specific method (the "strategy") without changing the rest of your code.

In Rust, this pattern is typically implemented with traits. You define a common `Strategy` trait that all different algorithm types will share. The main object (the "context") can then hold a reference to any object that implements this trait, making it easy to switch strategies on the fly. This is often done using a `trait` object (`Box<dyn Strategy>`).

```
// The trait that defines the common interface for all our strategies.
trait TextFormattingStrategy {
    fn format(&self, text: &str) -> String;
}

// A concrete strategy: formats text to all uppercase.
struct UpperCaseFormatter;

impl TextFormattingStrategy for UpperCaseFormatter {
    fn format(&self, text: &str) -> String {
        text.to_uppercase()
    }
}

// Another concrete strategy: formats text to all lowercase.
struct LowerCaseFormatter;

impl TextFormattingStrategy for LowerCaseFormatter {
```

```
    fn format(&self, text: &str) -> String {
        text.to_lowercase()
    }
}

// The "context" that uses a formatting strategy.
// It holds a trait object, allowing the strategy to be changed at
runtime.
struct TextProcessor {
    strategy: Box<dyn TextFormattingStrategy>,
}

impl TextProcessor {
    // Creates a new processor with an initial strategy.
    fn new(strategy: Box<dyn TextFormattingStrategy>) -> Self {
        TextProcessor { strategy }
    }

    // Allows swapping the strategy at runtime.
    fn set_strategy(&mut self, strategy: Box<dyn TextFormattingStrategy>)
{
        self.strategy = strategy;
    }

    // Executes the current strategy on the given text.
    fn process(&self, text: &str) -> String {
        self.strategy.format(text)
    }
}

fn main() {
    // Start with an uppercase formatting strategy.
    let mut processor = TextProcessor::new(Box::new(UpperCaseFormatter));

    let text = "Hello, Strategy Pattern!";
```

```
    let uppercase_result = processor.process(text);
    println!("Using uppercase strategy: {}", uppercase_result);

    // Now, change the strategy to Lowercase at runtime.
    processor.set_strategy(Box::new(LowerCaseFormatter));

    let lowercase_result = processor.process(text);
    println!("Using lowercase strategy: {}", lowercase_result);
}
```

- -**TextFormattingStrategy Trait**: This defines the common contract for all formatting algorithms. Any strategy we create must provide a format method.
- **Concrete strategies (UpperCaseFormatter, LowerCaseFormatter)**: These are the individual, interchangeable algorithms. Each is a simple struct that implements the `TextFormattingStrategy` trait with its own specific logic.
- **TextProcessor (The Context)**: This struct is the user of the strategy. It holds a strategy field of type `Box<dyn TextFormattingStrategy>`.
    - **Box<dyn TextFormattingStrategy>**: This is a `trait` object. It allows the `TextProcessor` to hold *any* concrete type that implements `TextFormattingStrategy`, without the `TextProcessor` needing to know which specific strategy it is. This is what enables dynamic, runtime selection.
- **Execution flow**: In `main`, create a `TextProcessor` with an `UpperCaseFormatter` and call `.process()` to see the result. Then, use `.set_strategy()` to switch to a `LowerCaseFormatter` and call `.process()` again. The code remains unchanged; only its `strategy` object changes.

Summary

This chapter gently guided us through the fascinating ways Rust integrates core object-oriented programming ideas.

We discovered that encapsulation is like wrapping data in structs or enums and connecting behavior with `impl` blocks, making everything neat and organized. Rust's module system and privacy rules help us control access, adding a layer of security.

When it comes to abstraction and polymorphism, traits come into play as Rust's way of defining shared interfaces, enabling both static and dynamic dispatch, kind of like versatile tools for different tasks. Instead of relying on traditional inheritance, Rust embraces composition and uses traits with default methods and supertrait bounds to promote code reuse and build hierarchical relationships smoothly.

All these features work together beautifully, allowing us to implement popular OOP design patterns, such as the Builder and State patterns, with perhaps even better type safety and confidence!

Now that we've seen how to define behavior on individual data structures, get ready to explore Rust's functional side, where we'll learn how to process entire sequences of data with the power and elegance of iterators and closures.

Questions and assignments

Questions

1. In Rust, what two fundamental components are used to achieve the OOP principle of encapsulation by bundling data and associated methods?
2. If a function accepts a parameter using the syntax item: &impl Summarizable, what kind of method dispatch (static or dynamic) will the compiler use for method calls on item?
3. What is the Box<dyn Trait> syntax necessary for when creating a Vec that needs to hold different concrete types (e.g., NewsArticle and Tweet)?
4. Instead of traditional implementation inheritance, what two main mechanisms does Rust favor for code reuse and sharing behavior?
5. What is the purpose of a supertrait (e.g., trait PrintableSummary: Display) in a trait definition?
6. The process where the compiler generates specialized, concrete versions of a generic function for each type it is used with is known as what?
7. What kind of pointer-based mechanism does dynamic dispatch use at runtime to find the correct method implementation?
8. If a trait method uses Self as a return type (like fn clone_self(&self) -> Self;), why does this prevent the trait from being object-safe?
9. In the Builder pattern (e.g., WindowConfigBuilder), what technique is used for the methods that set optional fields (like .width()) to allow method chaining?
10. In the Observer pattern, the Subject holds its observer list using RefCell. What problem in Rust's ownership system does RefCell solve in this context?

Assignments

Assignment 8.1: The private bank account (encapsulation)

Goal: Practice creating a struct with private data and a public method to modify it safely.

Define a module: Create a module named finance so you can test privacy rules (or just imagine it's in a separate file).

Create a struct: Inside the module, define a struct named `BankAccount` with one field: `balance: i32`.

Crucial step: Do not make the balance field public (do not put pub in front of balance). This ensures external code cannot change it directly.

Add a method: Use an `impl` block to add a public method called `deposit(&mut self, amount: i32)`.

This method should add the amount to `self.balance`.

Add a constructor: Add a public new() function that returns a `BankAccount` starting with 0 balance.

Test in Main:

1. Create a new account using `BankAccount::new()`.
2. `Call .deposit(100)`.

Try (and fail): Attempt to print `account.balance` directly. It should fail to compile because the field is private.

Fix: Add a public `get_balance(&self)` method to read the value safely, and print that instead.

Assignment 8.2: Animal sounds (basic traits)

Goal: Practice defining a shared behavior (trait) and implementing it for two different things.

Define a trait: Define a trait named Voice with one method signature: `fn speak(&self);`.

Create structs: Create two empty structs: Dog and `Cat`.

Implement the trait:

1. Implement Voice for Dog. Inside speak, `print "Woof!"`.
2. Implement Voice for Cat. Inside speak, `print "Meow!"`.

Test in Main:

1. Create an instance of Dog and Cat.
2. Call `.speak()` on both of them to see their different behaviors.

Subscribe to Deep Engineering

Join thousands of developers and architects who want to understand how software is changing, deepen their expertise, and build systems that last.

Deep Engineering is a weekly expert-led newsletter for experienced practitioners, featuring original analysis, technical interviews, and curated insights on architecture, system design, and modern programming practice.

Scan the QR or visit the link to subscribe for free.

`https://packt.link/deep-engineering-newsletter`

Thinking Functionally in Rust

Let's take a moment to appreciate another wonderful aspect of Rust: its support for functional programming ideas.

Functional programming is a style where we treat computation as we do evaluating mathematical functions, often preferring immutable data and steering clear of side effects.

Even though Rust isn't solely a functional language (it's actually multi-paradigm), it adopts many helpful concepts from this style because they bring so many benefits.

Using these functional techniques often makes your code cleaner, more declarative, and easier to understand and debug.

And by reducing side effects, these patterns can make it simpler to develop correct and efficient concurrent code, which is one of Rust's key strengths. When you combine these ideas with Rust's other powerful features, you get the ability to write code that is not only concise and expressive but also robust and reliable!

Let's get started!

Rust and functional programming

You don't need to go "all-in" on functional programming to enjoy these features in Rust. The language smoothly combines functional ideas with its imperative and systems-level features, making them useful tools for your development.

This multi-paradigm nature allows you to, for instance, use a concise iterator chain (a functional style) to process data before applying a mutable state update within a loop (an imperative style), giving you the best of both worlds.

In this chapter, we'll focus on some of the most impactful functional features Rust offers:

- **Iterators**: For processing sequences of data lazily and efficiently
- **Closures**: For creating flexible, anonymous functions that can capture their environment
- **Higher-order functions**: How functions that take other functions as arguments, such as iterator methods, enable expressive code

Let's see how these can make your Rust code shine.

Iterators: Processing sequences lazily

At the core of functional-style data processing in Rust are iterators.

What is an iterator? It's a tool that generates a sequence of values. What's unique about Rust's iterators is that they are **lazy**. This means they don't produce all values at once; instead, they generate them one by one, only when you ask for them. This laziness makes them extremely efficient.

For example, imagine you must find the first line containing an error in a huge, multi-gigabyte log file that might not fit into memory. An iterator lets you process it line by line, stopping as soon as you find what you're looking for, without ever loading the entire file. This demonstrates the power of doing work only when it's needed.

Creating and consuming iterators with next()

Most collection types in Rust provide ways to create iterators. The most basic way to interact with an iterator is by calling its `next()` method repeatedly. `next()` returns an `Option<Item>`, giving `Some(value)` when the next item is available and `None` when the sequence is exhausted:

```
fn main() {
    let fruits = vec!["apple", "banana", "cherry"];

    // Create an iterator over references to the elements in the vector.
    // The iterator variable must be `mut` because calling `.next()`
advances
    // the iterator and changes its internal state.
    let mut fruit_iterator = fruits.iter();
```

```
    // Call next() manually
    println!("First call: {:?}", fruit_iterator.next()); // Some("apple")
    println!("Second call: {:?}", fruit_iterator.next()); //
Some("banana")
    println!("Third call: {:?}", fruit_iterator.next()); // Some("cherry")
    println!("Fourth call: {:?}", fruit_iterator.next()); // None
(sequence finished)

    // Note: Once an iterator returns None, it will always return None
afterwards.
    println!("Fifth call: {:?}", fruit_iterator.next()); // None
}
```

In this example, `fruits.iter()` creates an iterator that yields immutable references (`&str`) to the elements in the fruits vector. We store it in a `mut` variable because calling `next()` advances the iterator's internal state, thus modifying it. Each call to `next()` gives us the next fruit wrapped in `Some`, until the vector runs out, at which point `next()` returns `None`.

Three ways to iterate

Before we explore methods that use iterators, let's first get to know the three main ways to create an iterator from a collection. Each method has its own way of handling ownership and mutability, so understanding them will help you use iterators more effectively.

Three ways to iterate: iter(), iter_mut(), and into_iter()

Collections in Rust typically offer three main methods to create an iterator, distinguished by how they handle the collection's data:

- **iter() (immutable borrowing)**:
    - **Signature:** `fn iter(&self)`.
    - **Behavior:** This method borrows the collection immutably. The iterator it produces yields **immutable references** (`&T`) to the items.
    - **Use case:** This is the most common way to iterate. You use it when you only need to read the elements without changing them. The original collection remains untouched and can be used after the loop.

- **iter_mut() (mutable borrowing)**:
    - **Signature:** `fn iter_mut(&mut self)`.
    - **Behavior:** This method borrows the collection mutably. The iterator it produces yields **mutable references** (`&mut T`), allowing you to modify the items in place.
    - **Use case:** Use this when you need to iterate through a collection and change its elements. The collection itself must be declared as `mut`.
- **into_iter() (taking ownership)**:
    - **Signature:** `fn into_iter(self)`.
    - **Behavior:** This method consumes the collection and takes ownership of it. The iterator it produces yields the **owned values** (`T`) themselves.
    - **Use case:** Use this when you want to move the elements out of the collection, consuming it in the process. After using `into_iter()`, the original collection is no longer valid.

Let's see all three in action:

```
fn main() {
    // --- 1. iter() - Immutable Borrows ---
    let names = vec!["Alice", "Bob", "Charlie"];
    for name in names.iter() {
        // `name` here is of type `&&str` (a reference to a string slice)
        println!("Hello, {}!", name);
    }
    // `names` is still valid and can be used here.
    println!("The names vector is still available: {:?}\n", names);


    // --- 2. iter_mut() - Mutable Borrows ---
    let mut numbers = vec![10, 20, 30];
    for num in numbers.iter_mut() {
        // `num` here is of type `&mut i32` (a mutable reference)
        *num *= 2; // We dereference `num` to modify the value it points
to
    }
    // `numbers` has been modified in place.
```

```
    println!("The numbers vector has been modified: {:?}\n", numbers);

    // --- 3. into_iter() - Taking Ownership ---
    let messages = vec![String::from("First"), String::from("Second")];
    for msg in messages.into_iter() {
        // `msg` here is of type `String` (the owned value)
        println!("Processing message: {}", msg);
    }
    // The `messages` vector has been moved and is no longer valid.
    // The line below would cause a compile-time error.
    // println!("Can we use messages again? No: {:?}", messages);
}
```

This example clearly shows the three different iteration methods and their effect on the original data:

- The `names.iter()` loop *borrows* the data immutably, allowing you to read each name while leaving the original names vector available for later use
- In contrast, the `numbers.iter_mut()` loop *borrows* the data mutably, giving you a mutable reference (`&mut i32`) to each `num` so you can modify the numbers vector in place
- Finally, `messages.into_iter()` takes full *ownership* of the messages vector, moving each string into the loop; after this, the messages vector can no longer be used

The role of consumers

I hope you are getting a clear idea of what iterators are.

So far, you've only used them inside `for` loops or called `.next()` manually. The true magic happens when you chain methods together. But remember, iterators are lazy; they don't do any work until you ask them to. That's where consuming adaptors, or just called consumers, come into play.

Think of it like this: methods such as `.map()` and `.filter()` (which we'll explore soon) are like the different steps in a recipe.

The consumer is the final step, the "bake" or "serve," that actually runs the recipe and gives you the finished dish. These methods are what drive the iterator forward, pulling items through the entire chain of your operations.

A fun thing to remember about a consumer is that it takes ownership of the iterator. That means once you call a consuming method such as `.collect()` or `.sum()`, the iterator is considered "used up," and you can't use it again. This aligns perfectly with Rust's ownership model, making it clear that producing a final value is the last step.

Common consumers: collect(), sum(), and fold()

While there are many consuming methods, a few stand out as everyday tools for working with iterators. These methods provide powerful ways to transform your lazy iterator into a concrete, final value:

- `collect()`: This versatile consumer gathers all items from an iterator into a new collection, with the type annotation specifying the collection type you want to create.
- `sum()`: This is a simple consumer for iterators that generate numbers. It smoothly goes through all the items and calculates their total sum, making it easy to get the combined value.
- `fold()`: This is a flexible and versatile tool for gathering a single value, kind of like what's called "reduce" in many other programming languages. You start with an initial value, known as the "accumulator," and then use a closure that takes the current accumulator and the next item to produce a new accumulator value. It's especially useful for tasks such as calculating a product or creating other custom aggregations.

Let's see them in action with an example:

```
fn main() {
    let numbers = vec![1, 2, 3, 4, 5];

    // --- Using collect() ---
    // Here, we filter for numbers greater than 2 and collect them into a
new Vec.
    // We use a type annotation `Vec<_>` to tell collect what to build.
    let greater_than_two: Vec<_> = numbers
        .iter()
        .filter(|&&n| n > 2)
        .collect();
    println!("Numbers greater than 2: {:?}", greater_than_two); // Output:
[3, 4, 5]
```

```
    // --- Using sum() ---
    // We can sum the numbers in a range.
    let total: i32 = (1..=10).sum(); // The iterator is the range (1..=10)
    println!("The sum of numbers from 1 to 10 is: {}", total); // Output:
55

    // --- Using fold() ---
    // Let's calculate the product of the numbers in our vector.
    // We start with an initial accumulator value of 1.
    let product = numbers
        .iter()
        .fold(1, |accumulator, &item| accumulator * item);
    println!("The product of the numbers is: {}", product); // Output: 120
}
```

Iterator adapters: Transforming sequences

The real power of iterators comes from *iterator adapters*. These are methods defined on the `Iterator` trait that take an iterator and return a *new*, transformed iterator without consuming the original one immediately. Because adapters return new iterators, you can chain multiple adapters together to perform complex operations in a readable way. Since iterators are lazy, no actual computation happens until you call a consuming method (such as `collect()` or `sum()`) at the end of the chain.

The map adapter

One of the most popular and handy adapters you might come across is `.map()`. It's a really useful tool for transforming data: it takes an iterator and creates a new one by applying a simple function to each item, turning each into something new. It's great for converting data types, doing calculations on every number in a sequence, or changing every string in a list.

The way you close the `.map()` function really shows how each item will be changed:

```
fn main() {
    let numbers = vec![1, 2, 3, 4];

    // Create an iterator, map a closure to square each number,
    // and then collect the results.
    let squares: Vec<i32> = numbers.iter() // Iterator yields &i32
                                   .map(|x| x * x) // Closure takes &i32,
squares it, returns i32
```

```
                                .collect(); // Collects the i32 results

    println!("Original: {:?}", numbers);    // Output: [1, 2, 3, 4]
    println!("Squares: {:?}", squares); // Output: [1, 4, 9, 16]

    // Example with Strings
    let names = vec!["alice", "bob", "charlie"];
    let upper_names: Vec<String> = names.iter() // Iterator yields &str
                                     .map(|name| name.to_uppercase())
// Closure returns String
                                     .collect(); // Collects the
Strings

    println!("Upper names: {:?}", upper_names); // Output: ["ALICE",
"BOB", "CHARLIE"]
}
```

The map adapter takes a closure (the part like `|x| x * x`). For each element, x, produced by the original iterator (`numbers.iter()`), map calls the closure with that element and produces the closure's return value in the *new* iterator it creates. Notice that the original numbers vector remains unchanged. The computation (`x * x` or `name.to_uppercase()`) only happens when `collect()` requests the values.

The filter adapter

Another essential adapter is `filter`. It takes a closure that returns a Boolean (`true` or `false`). `filter` creates a new iterator that only yields elements from the original iterator for which the closure returns `true`:

```
fn main() {
    let numbers = vec![1, 2, 3, 4, 5, 6, 7, 8, 9, 10];

    // Create an iterator, filter for even numbers, and collect.
    let evens: Vec<i32> = numbers.iter() // Iterator yields &i32
                                 // Closure takes &i32, returns true if
even.
                                 // We need *x because filter gets a
reference (&i32)
                                 .filter(|&&x| x % 2 == 0) // Note the
double reference `&&x`
```

```
                                        .copied() // Convert the iterator of &i32
to i32
                                        .collect(); // Collects the i32 results

    println!("Original: {:?}", numbers); // Output: [1, 2, ..., 10]
    println!("Evens: {:?}", evens);   // Output: [2, 4, 6, 8, 10]
    // Chaining map and filter
    let scores = vec![85, 42, 95, 60, 77];
    // Get scores above 70, and add a 5-point bonus
    let adjusted_high_scores: Vec<i32> = scores.iter()
                                                  .filter(|&&score| score >
70) // Keep scores > 70
                                                  .map(|&score| score + 5) //
Add 5 to the filtered scores
                                                  .collect();

    println!("Adjusted high scores: {:?}", adjusted_high_scores); //
Output: [90, 100, 82]
}
```

The `filter` adapter takes a closure (e.g., `|&&x| x % 2 == 0`). For each element, `x`, from the original iterator, it calls the closure. If the closure returns `true`, the element is included in the new iterator produced by `filter`; otherwise, it's skipped.

Tip: What's with all the &s? Understanding |&x| versus |&&x|

Ever wonder why you sometimes see `|&x|` and other times `|&&x|` in iterator closures? Think of it like layers of wrapping:

1. When you call `.iter()` on a collection, it gives you an iterator of references (`&T`), which is like one layer of wrapping around each item.
2. Methods such as `.filter()` often pass a reference *to that item* to your closure, which can add a *second* layer of wrapping, resulting in `&&T`.

The `|&&x|` pattern provides a convenient way to destructure or "unwrap" both layers at once, so the `x` inside your closure is the actual value you want to work with. Similarly, `|&x|` unwraps a single layer of reference. It's just a quick pattern match to access the data directly!

Other useful adapters and consumers

Rust provides a variety of helpful iterator adapters, such as `take`, `skip`, `rev`, `zip`, `enumerate`, and `flat_map`, along with useful consumers such as `position`, `any`, and `all`. It's a good idea to check out the `std::iter::Iterator` trait documentation to discover all the available tools. Among these, `fold` and `find` stand out as especially powerful options.

The `fold` method is a versatile tool that helps you combine all elements in a sequence into a single, meaningful value, whether you're calculating a product or creating other detailed summaries.

The `find` method is great for searching; it goes through each element and returns an option with the first element that meets your specified condition:

```
fn main() {
    let numbers = [1, 2, 3, 4, 5];

    // Use fold to calculate the product
    // Starts with an initial accumulator value (1)
    // The closure takes the accumulator (acc) and the current element
(&x)
    let product = numbers.iter().fold(1, |acc, &x| acc * x);
    println!("Product: {}", product); // Output: 120

    // Use find to get the first element satisfying a condition
    // find returns an Option<&Item>
    let first_even = numbers.iter().find(|&&x| x % 2 == 0);
    match first_even {
        Some(n) => println!("First even number: {}", n), // Output: 2
        None => println!("No even numbers found."),
    }

    // find returns a reference; use copied() if you need the value
     let first_gt_3_value: Option<i32> = numbers.iter()
                                              .find(|&&x| x > 3) // Find
first > 3 (&i32)
                                              .copied();         //
Convert Option<&i32> to Option<i32>
     println!("First > 3 value: {:?}", first_gt_3_value); // Output:
Some(4)
}
```

`fold` takes an initial accumulator value and a closure. The closure receives the current accumulator and the next element, returning the *new* accumulator value. This repeats for all elements. `find` takes a predicate closure and returns an option containing a *reference* to the first element for which the predicate returns `true`, or `None` if no such element exists. Remember to use `.copied()` or `.cloned()` after `find` if you need the value itself rather than a reference.

You may have noticed that all our powerful iterator methods, such as `.map()` and `.filter()`, have one thing in common: that compact `|parameter|` expression syntax we've been passing to them. These powerful, inline anonymous functions are called **closures**, a cornerstone of idiomatic Rust. In the next section, we'll take a much deeper look at what they are, how they work, and why they are so flexible.

Closures: Capturing the environment

We've touched on closures briefly with iterator adapters such as `map` and `filter` before. Now, let's explore them in a more friendly way. Closures are simply anonymous functions that you can define right where you're using them. They're perfect for quick, one-time logic without the fuss of creating a full, named function with `fn`. What really makes closures special is their ability to "pick up" variables from the surrounding scope, or their "environment." This feature makes them incredibly handy for crafting small, context-aware functions whenever you need them, right on the spot!

Defining closures

Here's a friendly explanation of closures: the basic syntax uses vertical bars, `| |`, for parameters, followed by the body of the closure, which can be a single expression or a block in curly braces, `{}`. One of the great things about closures is that the Rust compiler is really good at figuring out types, so in many cases, you don't need to explicitly specify the parameter or return types.

Of course, you can add type annotations for clarity, such as `|a: i32, b: i32|`, but it's quite common to leave out the return type. If your closure's body is just a single expression, Rust will automatically determine the return type based on that expression.

It's still good practice to include a return type annotation, such as `-> i32`, especially in more complex closures, but often, the compiler can handle it without:

```
fn main() {
    // Basic closure, type inference works
    let add_one = |x| x + 1;
    println!("5 + 1 = {}", add_one(5)); // Output: 6
```

```
    // Closure with explicit type annotations
    let multiply = |a: i32, b: i32| -> i32 {
        a * b // No semicolon needed if it's the return expression
    };
    println!("3 * 4 = {}", multiply(3, 4)); // Output: 12

    // Closure with a block body
    let complex_closure = |x: i32| {
        println!("Calculating for input: {}", x);
        let result = x * x + 2 * x + 1;
        // 'return' keyword is optional for the last expression in a block
        result
    };
    println!("Complex result for 3: {}", complex_closure(3)); // Output:
Calculating... 16
}
```

Closures are written as `|param1, param2, ...| body`. The compiler figures out the types of x in add_one and the return type based on their first usage, which here is with an `i32`. For `multiply` and `complex_closure`, we include explicit type annotations to make things clearer. Using a block, `{}`, enables us to include multiple statements inside the closure.

Capturing the environment

This is the key feature! Closures can access variables from the scope they are defined in. How they capture these variables (by immutable reference, by mutable reference, or by taking ownership) determines which *closure trait* they implement:

```
fn main() {
    let factor = 10;
    let threshold = 50;

    // This closure captures 'factor' by immutable reference (&)
    // It implements the Fn trait
    let multiply_by_factor = |n| n * factor;
    println!("5 times factor: {}", multiply_by_factor(5)); // Output: 50

    // ---
```

```
    let mut items_processed = 0;
    // This closure captures 'items_processed' by mutable reference (&mut)
    // because it modifies it. It implements the FnMut trait.
    let mut process_item = |item_id| {
        println!("Processing item {}", item_id);
        items_processed += 1; // Modifies captured variable
    };
    process_item(101);
    process_item(102);
    println!("Items processed: {}", items_processed); // Output: 2

    // ---

    let data_to_own = vec![1, 2, 3];
    // This closure takes ownership of 'data_to_own' because of the 'move'
keyword.
    // It implements the FnOnce trait (can only be called once).
    let consume_data = move || {
        println!("Consuming data: {:?}", data_to_own);
        // data_to_own is dropped when consume_data goes out of scope
    };
    consume_data();
    // println!("{:?}", data_to_own); // Error! data_to_own was moved

    // --- Using closures with iterators often involves capturing
    let numbers = vec![1, 2, 3, 4, 5, 6];
    let greater_than_threshold: Vec<i32> = numbers.into_iter() // into_
iter() takes ownership
                                              // Captures 'threshold'
by reference
                                              .filter(|&num| num >
threshold)
                                              .collect();
    // Note: threshold is still usable here because filter only needed a
reference.
    println!("Numbers > {}: {:?}", threshold, greater_than_threshold); //
Output: [] (if threshold=50)
}
```

- `multiply_by_factor` only *reads* `factor`, so it captures by immutable reference (&).
- `process_item` *modifies* `items_processed`, so it captures by mutable reference (`&mut`). We needed `mut process_item` because calling it modifies its captured state.
- `consume_data` uses the `move` keyword, forcing it to take *ownership* of `data_to_own`. Without `move`, it might try to borrow, but `move` is often used when the closure needs to outlive the captured variable's original scope (e.g., sending it to another thread).
- The `filter` closure captures the threshold by reference to perform the comparison.

A common pitfall: Using data after a move

Be mindful of Rust's ownership rules when using move closures! Once a closure takes ownership of a variable, that variable is no longer valid in its original scope. The compiler will prevent you from using it, which is a key safety feature:

```
let data = vec![1, 2, 3];

// This closure takes ownership of `data`.
let consume_data = move || {
    println!("Closure has data: {:?}", data);
};

consume_data(); // `data` is moved here.

// The line below would cause a compile-time error because
`data`
// has been moved and is no longer owned by this scope.
// println!("Main scope can no longer access data: {:?}",
data);
// error[E0382]: borrow of moved value: `data`
```

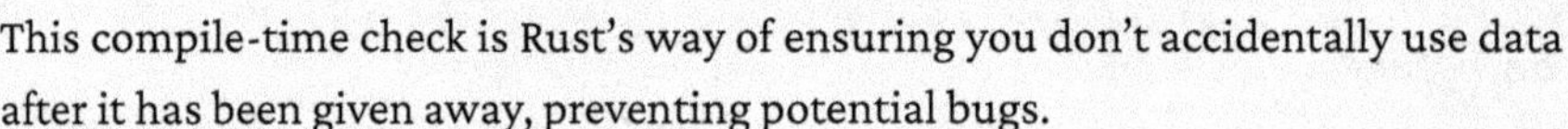

This compile-time check is Rust's way of ensuring you don't accidentally use data after it has been given away, preventing potential bugs.

Closure traits: Fn, FnMut, and FnOnce

The way a closure captures its environment dictates which of three special traits it implements: `FnOnce`, `FnMut`, or `Fn`. These traits define *how* the closure can be called. When you write a higher-order function that accepts a closure, you use these traits as bounds to specify what kind of closure you need:

- `FnOnce`: This trait is for closures that can be called *at least once*. A closure that consumes the variables it captures (by taking ownership) can *only* be called once, so it will only implement `FnOnce`. The name signifies that the closure consumes itself when called.
- `FnMut`: This trait is for closures that might mutate the variables they capture. These closures can be called multiple times. Any closure that implements `Fn` also implements `FnMut`.
- `Fn`: This trait is for closures that only immutably borrow values from their environment. These closures can also be called multiple times without changing their environment.

The compiler will always infer the most permissive trait that a closure can implement. For example, a closure that only reads a variable will implement all three traits (`Fn`, `FnMut`, and `FnOnce`), allowing it to be used in the widest range of situations.

Let's see this in action with higher-order functions that accept different kinds of closures:

```
// This function accepts closures that only need immutable access (`Fn`).
fn call_reporter<F>(reporter: F)
where
    F: Fn() -> String, // Trait bound: must implement Fn
{
    println!("Report: {}", reporter());
}

// This function accepts closures that might mutate their environment
(`FnMut`).
fn call_mutator<F>(mut mutator: F) // Note the `mut` here
where
    F: FnMut(), // Trait bound: must implement FnMut
{
    // We can call it multiple times.
```

```
    mutator();
    mutator();
}

// This function accepts any closure but consumes it (`FnOnce`).
fn call_once<F>(consumer: F)
where
    F: FnOnce(), // Trait bound: must implement FnOnce
{
    consumer();
    // Calling `consumer()` again here would cause a compile error.
}

fn main() {
    let message = String::from("System status OK");
    // This closure captures `message` by reference, so it implements
`Fn`.
    let report_closure = || message.clone();
    call_reporter(report_closure);

    let mut counter = 0;
    // This closure captures `counter` by mutable reference, so it
implements `FnMut`.
    let mut increment_closure = || {
        counter += 1;
        println!("Counter is now: {}", counter);
    };
    // We pass ownership of the closure to `call_mutator`.
    call_mutator(increment_closure);

    let data = String::from("Consume me");
    // This closure moves `data`, so it implements `FnOnce`.
    let consume_closure = || {
        println!("Consumed: {}", data);
    };
    call_once(consume_closure);
}
```

Let's explain the `FnMut` case.

The `call_mutator` function is a great example of a common point of confusion. Let's break it down:

- **Why mut mutator: F?** The `FnMut` trait's call method takes `&mut self`, so calling an `FnMut` closure mutably borrows the closure. This allows `mutator()` to change the closure's internal state, including captured variables such as `counter`. Therefore, mutator must be declared as `mut` inside `call_mutator`.
- **Passing ownership**: In our `main` function, we call `call_mutator(increment_closure)`, moving ownership of the closure into `call_mutator`, which is the most common way to pass `FnMut` closures. The function now owns and can mutate the closure. If the signature were `fn call_mutator<F: FnMut()>(mutator: &mut F)`, you'd pass a mutable reference (`&mut increment_closure`), but taking ownership with `mut F` is more common.

With a solid understanding of how to use closures to define behavior, let's now turn to another powerful feature that is often used alongside them, especially when working with enums and iterators: **pattern matching**.

Pattern matching

Closures beautifully shape behavior in a clear way, especially when working with iterators. Rust's pattern matching adds even more expressive power to our code. Having already looked at the `match` statement, let's now take a dive into it from a functional perspective, seeing how it neatly destructures data and guides our control flow, perfectly complementing closure-based transformations.

Pattern matching in functional style

We saw `match` used extensively in error handling (*Chapter 6*) and with enums (*Chapter 5*). Pattern matching is also a key feature often associated with functional programming languages, and Rust's implementation is particularly powerful. It allows you to destructure data types and control program flow based on the *shape* of the data, not just its value.

Destructuring structs and enums

`match` arms can directly destructure structs and enums, binding parts of their data to variables within the arm's scope:

```
enum Message {
    Quit,
    Write(String),
    ChangeColor(u8, u8, u8),
```

```
    Move { x: i32, y: i32 },
}

struct User {
    id: u32,
    name: String,
    active: bool,
}

fn process_message(msg: Message) {
    match msg {
        Message::Quit => println!("Quitting."),
        // Bind the String inside Write to 'text'
        Message::Write(text) => println!("Message to write: {}", text),
        // Bind the RGB values
        Message::ChangeColor(r, g, b) => println!("Change color to R:{}
G:{} B:{}", r, g, b),
        // Destructure the struct variant, binding fields
        Message::Move { x, y } => println!("Move to ({}, {})", x, y),
    }
}

fn describe_user(user: User) {
     match user {
        // Match specific field values and bind others
        User { id: 1, name, active: true } => println!("Admin user '{}' is
active.", name),
        // Match based on a field value, ignore others with '..'
        User { active: false, .. } => println!("User {} is inactive.",
user.id), // Can still use 'user' here
         // Match any other user
        User { id, name, .. } => println!("Regular user #{} is '{}'.", id,
name),
     }
}

fn main() {
    process_message(Message::ChangeColor(255, 0, 128));
```

```
    process_message(Message::Move { x: 10, y: -5 });

    let user1 = User { id: 1, name: "Alice".to_string(), active: true };
    let user2 = User { id: 2, name: "Bob".to_string(), active: false };
    let user3 = User { id: 3, name: "Charlie".to_string(), active: true };

    describe_user(user1);
    describe_user(user2);
    describe_user(user3);
}
```

The `match` arms directly mirror the structure of the enum variants or struct definition. You can bind values within the variants/structs to new variables (such as `text`, `r`, `g`, `b`, `x`, `y`, `name`, or `id`). You can also match specific literal values (such as `id: 1`, `active: true`). The `..` syntax ignores any fields not explicitly mentioned in the pattern for structs.

This same destructuring pattern is especially powerful when working with Rust's standard `Result` and `Option` enums, allowing you to handle success, failure, or absence while directly accessing the contained values:

```
fn process_input(input: &str) {
    let result: Result<i32, _> = input.parse();

    match result {
        Ok(number) => {
            // Destructured `Ok`, binding the i32 to `number`.
            println!("Successfully parsed number: {}", number);
        }
        Err(error) => {
            // Destructured `Err`, binding the ParseIntError to `error`.
            println!("Failed to parse. Error: {}", error);
        }
    }
}

fn main() {
    let maybe_name: Option<String> = Some(String::from("Alice"));
```

```
    match maybe_name {
        Some(name) => {
            // Destructured `Some`, binding the String to `name`.
            println!("Found a name: {}", name);
        }
        None => {
            println!("No name was provided.");
        }
    }

    process_input("123");
    process_input("abc");
}
```

if let and while let

Sometimes, you're only interested in matching a single specific pattern and prefer to overlook all others. Using `match` for this can feel a bit lengthy because you'll still need a catch-all `_ => {}` arm. Rust offers more streamlined options, such as `if let` and `while let`, which are perfect for these single-pattern situations.

`if let` is a shorter way to write a `match` that handles only one case.

`while let` is especially handy for looping as long as a pattern keeps matching. It's commonly paired with methods that return an option, such as an iterator's `.next()` or a vector's `.pop()`, which are used to process items until a `None` is encountered, signaling a smooth ending. In advanced async programming, this pattern processes stream items or polls futures until ready:

```
fn main() {
    let maybe_value: Option<i32> = Some(10);

    // Instead of match maybe_value { Some(x) => ..., None => ... }
    if let Some(value) = maybe_value {
        println!("Got a value using if let: {}", value);
    } else {
        println!("No value found.");
    }
```

```
    let mut data_stack = vec![Some(1), Some(2), None, Some(3)];

    // Instead of loop { match data_stack.pop() { Some(Some(x)) => ..., _
=> break } }
    // Process items from the stack as long as they are Some(Some(value))
    while let Some(Some(value)) = data_stack.pop() {
        // The outer `Some` matches the `Option` from `pop()`.
        // The inner `Some` matches the `Option<i32>` that was inside the
`Vec`.
        // The loop continues as long as we successfully pop a
`Some(value)`.
        println!("Processing value from stack: {}", value);
    }
    // Loop stops when pop() returns None or Some(None)

    println!("Stack processing finished. Remaining: {:?}", data_stack); //
Output: [Some(1), Some(2)] (or reversed depending on pop order)
}
```

`if let` provides a neat way to handle a single `match` arm, optionally with an `else`. `while let` is perfect for loops that should continue as long as a certain pattern matches, often used for consuming iterators or processing collections until a specific condition (such as `None` or `Err`) is met. They make code that only cares about one successful pattern much cleaner.

Summary

In this chapter, we explored the wonderful functional programming features that make Rust such an expressive and powerful language.

We discovered that while Rust is a multi-paradigm language, it thoughtfully incorporates core functional ideas such as immutability and treating functions as first-class values, which helps us write cleaner and more reliable code. The heart of this functional style is Rust's lazy iterators, offering an efficient way to process sequences of data.

We learned how to create them in different ways (`iter()`, `into_iter()`, and `iter_mut()`), how to transform them with powerful iterator adapters such as `map()` and `filter()`, and how to get a final result using consumers such as `collect()` and `fold()`.

These iterator methods are powered by closures, which are flexible anonymous functions that can capture variables from their environment. We explored their syntax, how they handle ownership through the `Fn`, `FnMut`, and `FnOnce` traits, and how they enable concise, inline logic.

Finally, we revisited pattern matching with `match`, `if let`, and `while let`, highlighting how beautifully it can destructure data types, perfectly fitting into the functional style. By combining iterators, closures, and pattern matching, you can approach many programming challenges in Rust with remarkable elegance and safety.

Don't hesitate to explore the wealth of methods available on the `Iterator` trait; they are truly fundamental to idiomatic Rust!

Questions and assignments

Let's put these functional concepts into practice! These questions and assignments will help you get comfortable using iterators, closures, and pattern matching in Rust.

Questions

1. What does it mean for Rust's iterators to be "lazy"? Briefly describe one advantage of this laziness.
2. Explain the difference between the three main iterator creation methods: `iter()`, `iter_mut()`, and `into_iter()`. Describe what kind of value each one yields (e.g., owned value, mutable reference, or immutable reference).
3. What is the difference between an iterator adapter (such as `.map()` or `.filter()`) and a consuming adaptor (such as `.collect()` or `.sum()`)?
4. What is a closure in Rust? What is the key feature that makes them different from regular functions defined with `fn`?
5. Briefly explain the purpose of the `move` keyword when used with a closure, especially in the context of spawning a new thread.
6. What are the three `Fn` traits (`Fn`, `FnMut`, and `FnOnce`), and what do they represent about how a closure interacts with its environment?
7. When would you choose to use `if let` instead of a full `match` statement?
8. Describe a common use case for the `while let` construct, particularly with a method that returns an option.

Assignments

Assignment 9.1 (easy): Simple data filtering and transformation

Goal: Practice using basic iterator adapters such as `filter` and `map` in a chain.

Task:

1. Create a function named `process_names` that takes a `Vec<&str>` as input.
2. Inside the function, use an iterator chain to perform the following transformations on the input vector:
   - Filter out any names that have five or fewer characters
   - Convert the remaining names to uppercase strings
3. The function should return a `Vec<String>` containing the final, processed names.
4. In your `main` function, create a sample vector of names, call `process_names`, and print the result to verify that it works correctly.

Example: If the input is `vec!["Alice", "Bob", "Charlie", "David", "Eve"]`, the output should be `["CHARLIE", "DAVID"]`.

Assignment 9.2 (advanced): Implementing a custom Fibonacci iterator

Goal: Get a deeper understanding of how iterators work by implementing the `Iterator` trait for a custom struct.

Task:

1. Create a struct named `Fibonacci` that holds the current state needed to generate the sequence (e.g., `curr: u32`, `next: u32`).
2. Implement a `new()` associated function for `Fibonacci` that initializes it to the start of the sequence (current value: `0`, next value: `1`).

3. Implement the `Iterator` trait for your `Fibonacci` struct:
    - The type `Item` should be `u32`.
    - In the `next(&mut self)` method, implement the logic to do the following:
        - Return the current Fibonacci number
        - Update the struct's internal state to the next numbers in the sequence
        - Return `None` if the next number would exceed a certain limit (e.g., if it would overflow `u32`, or you can add a `max` field to your struct)
4. In your `main` function, create a new Fibonacci iterator. Use it in a `for` loop to print the first 10 Fibonacci numbers. Then, use iterator methods such as `.take(5).collect::<Vec<_>>()` to demonstrate that your custom type works just like any other iterator.

10

Testing in Rust

Welcome to *Chapter 10*!

After defining data, managing errors, and exploring functional concepts, we now arrive at a crucial practice for any software developer: **testing.**

This chapter highlights how Rust makes it easy and enjoyable to write tests, helping you ensure your code works correctly and the quality remains high over time. Rust doesn't just support testing; it actively encourages it with fantastic built-in tools, making testing a seamless and natural part of your development journey.

Think of this chapter as learning how to build a robust safety net for all the awesome Rust code you will write!

But before we proceed, let's start with a question most of you might have now.

Why ever bother with testing?

Why bother with testing?

You might think, "Okay, testing sounds good, but is it necessary, especially when I'm just starting or working on smaller projects?" That's a fair question! Investing a bit of time in writing tests, even for simpler projects, pays off handsomely. Here's why it's a big deal:

- **Catching bugs early**: It's far less painful (and less expensive) to find and fix a bug when you've just written the code than weeks or months later when it's buried under layers of new features. Tests act like an early warning system.

- **Confidence to refactor and change**: Code evolves. When you need to refactor (restructure existing code) or add new features, a good set of tests gives you the confidence that you haven't accidentally broken something else. You can make changes, run your tests, and breathe a little easier if they pass!
- **Documentation by example**: Tests are, in a way, a form of living documentation. They show exactly how a piece of code is intended to be used and its expected outputs for given inputs. This is invaluable for yourself later, or for anyone else trying to understand your code.
- **Preventing regressions**: A "regression" is when a previously fixed bug reappears or a new change breaks existing functionality. Once you write a test for a bug, that test helps ensure the bug stays fixed.
- **Better code design**: Often, thinking about how to test a piece of code encourages you to write it in a more modular, decoupled, and, thus, better-designed way. If something is hard to test, it might indicate that its design could be improved.

So, while it might seem like extra work upfront, testing is a fundamental practice that leads to more reliable, maintainable, and, ultimately, more professional software.

Note

All these benefits connect to an important idea called test coverage. Think of test coverage as a way to see how much of your production code is actually run when you execute your test suite. Even though reaching 100% coverage isn't always realistic, aiming for a high percentage helps you feel more confident that your code has been carefully checked. It's a helpful way to spot parts of your application that haven't been tested yet and might have bugs waiting to be found.

We won't go into detail about specific coverage tools in this chapter, but the concept is straightforward: the more of your code that your tests cover, the stronger and more reliable your safety net becomes.

Types of tests in Rust's ecosystem

When we talk about testing in Rust, especially using its built-in capabilities, we're generally focusing on a few key categories. It's good to know the lingo:

- **Unit tests:** These are the most detailed tests. They focus on checking small, individual parts of your code in isolation, usually a single function, a method, or a very specific section of a module. The goal is to make sure that each "unit" works correctly on its own. In Rust, these are often located in a `mod tests` submodule within the same file as the code they test.
- **Integration tests:** These tests take a broader view. Instead of testing individual units in isolation, they check how different parts of your library or application work *together*. They typically test the public API of your crate, simulating how an external user or another part of a larger system would interact with it. Rust has a special `tests` directory at the root of your project for these.
- **Documentation tests (doc tests):** This is a rather neat feature in Rust! Code examples that you write directly within your documentation comments (using `///` or `//!`) can be automatically compiled and run as tests. This is fantastic for ensuring that your examples are always correct and up to date, providing reliable documentation for users of your code.

While other testing forms, such as end-to-end or performance testing, exist, this chapter mainly focuses on Rust's strong support for unit, integration, and documentation tests with `cargo test`.

These form the backbone of most Rust testing strategies!

Unit tests: The building blocks

Now that we understand why testing is essential, let's get practical and explore unit tests.

These are the first line of defense in ensuring the quality of your code.

Think of them as small, focused checks for the individual components, the "units" of your program.

What are unit tests?

Unit tests are designed to verify the smallest testable parts of your application in isolation. Typically, this means testing a single function or a method on a struct or enum. The goal is to confirm that a specific piece of logic behaves correctly given a known set of inputs, producing the expected outputs or side effects (though pure functions with no side effects are often easiest to unit test!).

Because they are isolated, unit tests have a few great characteristics:

- **Fast**: They usually run very quickly, allowing you to run them frequently during development
- **Precise**: When a unit test fails, it generally points to a very specific area of your code, making debugging much easier
- **Independent**: Ideally, unit tests don't rely on external systems, such as databases, networks, or even other parts of your own application, being in a particular state

In Rust, the convention is to place unit tests in the same file as the code they are testing, grouped within a submodule. Let's see how.

Writing your first unit test

Rust makes writing unit tests quite straightforward.

You'll typically create a submodule named `tests` within your source file, annotate it with `#[cfg(test)]` so it's only compiled during testing, and then write functions within that module marked with the `#[test]` attribute.

Let's imagine that we have a utility function that capitalizes the first letter of a string slice and leaves the rest lowercase:

```
// In src/lib.rs or your relevant module file
pub fn capitalize_first_letter(s: &str) -> String {
    if s.is_empty() {
        return String::new();
    }
    let mut chars = s.chars();
    match chars.next() {
        None => String::new(), // Should be covered by is_empty, but good
for robustness
        Some(first_char) => {
            first_char.to_uppercase().to_string() + chars.as_str().to_
lowercase().as_str()
        }
    }
}

// This is where our tests will go
```

```
#[cfg(test)] // Only compile this module when running tests
mod tests {
    // Import items from the parent module (where capitalize_first_letter
is)
    use super::*;

    #[test] // Marks this function as a test case
    fn test_capitalize_basic_string() {
        let input = "hello";
        let expected = "Hello";
        assert_eq!(capitalize_first_letter(input), expected);
    }

    #[test]
    fn test_capitalize_already_capitalized() {
        assert_eq!(capitalize_first_letter("World"), "World");
    }

    #[test]
    fn test_capitalize_mixed_case() {
        assert_eq!(capitalize_first_letter("rUsT"), "Rust");
    }

    #[test]
    fn test_capitalize_empty_string() {
        assert_eq!(capitalize_first_letter(""), "");
    }

    #[test]
    fn test_capitalize_single_char_string() {
        assert_eq!(capitalize_first_letter("a"), "A");
        assert_eq!(capitalize_first_letter("Z"), "Z");
    }

    #[test]
    fn test_capitalize_with_numbers_and_symbols() {
        assert_eq!(capitalize_first_letter("1st place!"), "1st place!");
```

```
        assert_eq!(capitalize_first_letter("!leadingSymbol"),
"!leadingsymbol");
    }
}
```

Let's break down the key parts of the test setup:

- `pub fn capitalize_first_letter(...)`: This is the function we intend to test. Notice it's marked `pub`, so it can be accessed from other modules if this were part of a library.
- `#[cfg(test)]`: This attribute is a conditional compilation flag. It tells the Rust compiler, "Only compile the following module (`mod tests`) if we are running tests (e.g., via `cargo test`)." This ensures your test code doesn't end up in your final release binary, keeping it lean.
- `mod tests { ... }`: This declares a new submodule named `tests`. It's a strong convention in Rust to put unit tests for a module, `foo`, in a submodule, `foo::tests`.
- `use super::*;`: Inside the `tests` module, this line imports all items (functions, structs, etc.) from its parent module (which is the module containing `capitalize_first_letter`). The `super` keyword refers to the parent module. The * character is a glob import, bringing everything in. This allows us to call `capitalize_first_letter` directly in our tests.
- `#[test]`: This attribute, placed above a function, signals to Rust's test runner that this particular function is a test case. Test functions are typically plain functions that don't take arguments and don't return values.
- Assertion macros: Inside the test functions (such as `test_capitalize_basic_string`), we use macros such as `assert_eq!`. These macros check whether a certain condition is true. If the condition is false, the macro will cause the test function to panic, which the test runner interprets as a test failure. We'll look at common assertion macros next.

Tip: Better test diffs with pretty_assertions

For much clearer test failures when comparing large structs or multi-line strings, the popular `pretty_assertions` crate replaces the standard `assert_eq!` output with a colorful, git-style "diff." To use it, simply add it as a `[dev-dependency]` in your `Cargo.toml` and then import its macro (e.g., use `pretty_assertions::assert_eq;`) in your test module. It's a drop-in replacement that can make debugging much faster.

Running your tests with cargo test

Once you've written some tests, how do you run them? It's remarkably simple with Cargo, Rust's build system and package manager. Just open your terminal in the root directory of your Rust project and execute the following:

```
cargo test
```

`cargo test` is great for running all tests, but flags give more control in larger projects with multiple crates or binaries.

Common ones include `cargo test --lib` for library tests, `cargo test --bin` for specific binaries, and `cargo test --package` for a single crate in a workspace. These help focus testing efforts without running the entire suite!

Cargo will then do the following:

1. Compile your main code.
2. Compile your test code (including modules marked `#[cfg(test)]` and functions marked `#[test]`).
3. Run each test function.
4. Report the results, telling you how many tests ran, how many passed, how many failed, how many were ignored, and so on.

You'll get a comforting green "ok" if all tests pass. If any test fails (due to a panicking assertion), Cargo will print details about the failure, including the filepath, line number, and any message provided to the assertion macro. This makes it easy to pinpoint what went wrong.

Go ahead and create a new library project using `cargo new string_utils --lib`, replace the contents of `src/lib.rs` with the `capitalize_first_letter` function and its tests from previously, and then run `cargo test`. You should see all tests passing! For fun, try introducing a bug in `capitalize_first_letter` (e.g., make it always return an empty string) and run `cargo test` again to observe a test failure.

The test failure should look like this:

```
running 6 tests
test test_capitalize_already_capitalized ... ok
test test_capitalize_empty_string ... ok
test test_capitalize_mixed_case ... ok
test test_capitalize_single_char_string ... ok
test test_capitalize_with_numbers_and_symbols ... ok
test test_capitalize_basic_string ... FAILED

failures:

---- test_capitalize_basic_string stdout ----
thread 'main' panicked at src/lib.rs:21:9:
assertion failed: `left == right`
  left: `""`,
 right: `"Hello"`
note: run with `RUST_BACKTRACE=1` environment variable to display a
backtrace

failures:
    test_capitalize_basic_string

test result: FAILED. 5 passed; 1 failed; 0 ignored; 0 measured; 0 filtered
out; finished in 0.00s

error: test failed, to rerun pass `--lib`
```

Common assertion macros

The core of most tests involves checking that some condition holds true or that an actual value matches an expected value. Rust's standard library provides a few essential macros for this, which all cause a panic (and thus a test failure) if their condition isn't met:

- `assert!(expression, ...optional_message_args...)`: This is the most basic assertion. It checks whether the given Boolean expression evaluates to true. If it's false, the test panics:

```
#[test]
fn is_string_long_enough() {
    let my_string = "Rustacean";
    assert!(my_string.len() > 5, "String '{}' should be longer than
5 chars", my_string);
}
```

- `assert_eq!(left, right, ...optional_message_args...)`: This macro checks whether the left and right expressions are equal (using the == operator, so the types must implement `PartialEq`). If they are not equal, it panics, helpfully printing both the left and right values. This is probably the most common assertion you'll use:

```
#[test]
fn values_should_be_equal() {
    let calculated_value = 2 + 2;
    let expected_value = 4;
    assert_eq!(calculated_value, expected_value, "Checking simple
addition");
}
```

- `assert_ne!(left, right, ...optional_message_args...)`: The opposite of `assert_eq!`. It checks that `left` and `right` are not equal (using the != operator, requiring `PartialEq`). It panics if they are equal:

```
#[test]
fn values_should_not_be_equal() {
    let value_a = "apple";
    let value_b = "orange";
    assert_ne!(value_a, value_b, "Different fruits should not be
equal");
}
```

All these assertion macros can take additional arguments after the main condition/values. These extra arguments are passed to the `format!` macro to create a custom panic message if the assertion fails.

Providing clear, contextual failure messages can be a huge help when a test breaks, especially if it's not immediately obvious why from the code itself.

Testing Result and Option types

Many Rust functions, especially those performing operations that might fail or not find a value, return `Result<T, E>` or `Option<T>`.

Testing these types involves checking for the correct variant (`Ok`, `Err`, `Some`, or `None`) and often inspecting the contained value or error:

```
// A function that might fail if input is empty
fn create_greeting(name: &str) -> Result<String, String> {
    if name.trim().is_empty() {
        Err("Name cannot be empty".to_string())
    } else {
        Ok(format!("Hello, {}!", name))
    }
}

// A function that returns an Option
fn find_even_number(numbers: &[i32]) -> Option<i32> {
    for &num in numbers {
        if num % 2 == 0 {
            return Some(num); // Return the first even number found
        }
    }
    None // No even number found
}


#[cfg(test)]
mod tests {
    use super::*;

    #[test]
    fn test_create_greeting_success() {
        let result = create_greeting("Rustacean");
        assert!(result.is_ok(), "Greeting should be Ok for valid name");
```

```
        // Once we know it's Ok, it's generally safe to unwrap in a test
        assert_eq!(result.unwrap(), "Hello, Rustacean!");
    }

    #[test]
    fn test_create_greeting_failure_empty_name() {
        let result = create_greeting("");
        assert!(result.is_err(), "Greeting should be Err for empty name");
        // We can also check the specific error message
        assert_eq!(result.unwrap_err(), "Name cannot be empty");
    }

    #[test]
    fn test_create_greeting_failure_whitespace_name() {
        let result = create_greeting("   ");
        assert!(result.is_err(), "Greeting should be Err for whitespace-
only name");
    }

    #[test]
    fn test_find_even_number_some_found() {
        let numbers = [1, 3, 4, 5, 7];
        let result = find_even_number(&numbers);
        assert!(result.is_some(), "Should find an even number");
        assert_eq!(result.unwrap(), 4);
    }

    #[test]
    fn test_find_even_number_none_found() {
        let numbers = [1, 3, 5, 7, 9];
        let result = find_even_number(&numbers);
        assert!(result.is_none(), "Should return None if no even number is
present");
    }

    #[test]
    fn test_find_even_number_empty_slice() {
        let numbers: [i32; 0] = []; // Empty slice
```

```
        let result = find_even_number(&numbers);
        assert!(result.is_none(), "Should return None for an empty
slice");
    }

    // Using assert!(matches!(...)) for more precise checks (Rust 1.42+)
    #[test]
    fn test_greeting_with_matches_macro() {
        let result_ok = create_greeting("Pat");
        assert!(matches!(result_ok, Ok(ref s) if s == "Hello, Pat!"),
"Expected Ok(\"Hello, Pat!\"), got {:?}", result_ok);

        let result_err = create_greeting(" ");
        assert!(matches!(result_err, Err(ref s) if s == "Name cannot be
empty"), "Expected specific error, got {:?}", result_err);
    }
}
```

For `Result<T, E>`, the `is_ok()` and `is_err()` methods are very useful for asserting the outcome. If you've checked that `Result` is `Ok`, it's generally considered safe to call `.unwrap()` within a test to get the value for further assertions. Similarly, `.unwrap_err()` can be used to get the error value after checking `is_err()`.

For `Option<T>`, `is_some()` and `is_none()` serve the same purpose, with `.unwrap()` being used to get the value from a `Some`.

The `matches!(expression, pattern)` macro (stable since Rust 1.42) is a powerful tool. It allows you to assert that an expression matches a given pattern without needing to unwrap or write a full `match` statement. You can even include guards in the pattern (such as `Ok(ref s) if s == "Hello, Pat!"`). This is often cleaner than multiple `is_ok/unwrap/assert_eq` chains.

Testing for panics

Sometimes, the correct behavior of your code *is* to panic, for example, when an unrecoverable error occurs due to invalid input that signifies a programming error, or an internal state becomes inconsistent. Rust allows you to explicitly test for these panic conditions.

You do this by adding the `#[should_panic]` attribute to your test function:

```
pub struct ScoreKeeper {
    scores: Vec<u32>,
```

```
    max_scores: usize,
}

impl ScoreKeeper {
    pub fn new(max_scores: usize) -> Self {
        if max_scores == 0 {
            panic!("Cannot create a ScoreKeeper with zero capacity!");
        }
        ScoreKeeper { scores: Vec::with_capacity(max_scores), max_scores }
    }

    pub fn add_score(&mut self, score: u32) {
        if self.scores.len() >= self.max_scores {
            panic!("Cannot add score: ScoreKeeper is full!");
        }
        self.scores.push(score);
    }

    pub fn get_scores(&self) -> &[u32] {
        &self.scores
    }
}

#[cfg(test)]
mod tests {
    use super::*;

    #[test]
    fn can_add_scores_within_limit() {
        let mut keeper = ScoreKeeper::new(2);
        keeper.add_score(100);
        keeper.add_score(95);
        assert_eq!(keeper.get_scores(), &[100, 95]);
    }

    #[test]
    #[should_panic] // This test will pass if the code inside it panics
```

```
    fn adding_score_to_full_keeper_panics() {
        let mut keeper = ScoreKeeper::new(1);
        keeper.add_score(80);
        keeper.add_score(70); // This line should cause a panic
    }

    #[test]
    #[should_panic(expected = "ScoreKeeper is full")] // Checks if panic
message contains this text
    fn adding_to_full_keeper_panics_with_specific_message() {
        let mut keeper = ScoreKeeper::new(1);
        keeper.add_score(88);
        keeper.add_score(99); // Panics here
    }

    #[test]
    #[should_panic(expected = "zero capacity")] // Checks the constructor
panic
    fn new_score_keeper_with_zero_capacity_panics() {
        ScoreKeeper::new(0); // This should panic
    }
}
```

If you annotate a test function with `#[should_panic]`, the test will *pass* if the code inside the function panics. If the code *doesn't* panic, the test will *fail*.

You can make this more precise by providing an expected string to the attribute: `#[should_panic(expected = "substring of the panic message")]`.

In this case, the test only passes if the code panics *and* the panic message produced by the `panic!` macro contains the specified substring.

This is useful to ensure you're panicking for the correct reason, not just random panic.

Controlling test execution

`cargo test` is quite versatile.

By default, it runs all your tests (unit, integration, and doc tests) in parallel to speed things up. It also captures any output printed by passing tests, so you typically only see output from failing tests, which helps keep the test results clean.

Here are some common command-line options to customize test execution:

- **Running specific tests**:
    - `cargo test test_function_name`: Runs only the test function with that exact name.
    - `cargo test module_name`: Runs all tests within a specific module (e.g., `cargo test tests` would run all unit tests if your module is named `tests`).
    - `cargo test substring`: Runs all tests whose names contain a substring. For instance, `cargo test capitalize` would run all tests such as `test_capitalize_basic_string` and `test_capitalize_empty_string`, from our earlier example.
- **Showing output**:
    - `cargo test -- --show-output`: This will display the output (e.g., from `println!`) for all tests, even passing ones. The `--` characters are used to separate arguments for `cargo test` itself from arguments for the test binary it compiles and runs.
- **Running tests sequentially**:
    - `cargo test -- --test-threads=1`: This tells the test runner to use only one thread, effectively running your tests one after another. This can be useful if your tests might interfere with each other (though ideally they shouldn't!) or if you're trying to debug an issue where parallel execution complicates things.
- **Ignoring tests:** Sometimes, you might have tests that are very slow or require a specific setup that's not always available. You can mark such tests with the `#[ignore]` attribute:

```
#[test]
#[ignore]
fn very_resource_intensive_and_slow_test() {
    // ... some very slow operations ...
    assert!(true);
}
```

By default, `cargo test` will skip ignored tests. To run *only* the ignored tests, you can use `cargo test -- --ignored`.

To run *all* tests, including ignored ones, use `cargo test -- --include-ignored`.

These options give you fine-grained control over your testing workflow, allowing you to focus on specific areas or manage different types of tests effectively.

Integration tests: Checking how parts fit together

While unit tests are really great for making sure each part of your code works well on its own, remember that software is often more than just separate pieces.

Components need to work together, modules need to communicate smoothly, and your library's public interface should do exactly what users expect. Everything should come together seamlessly for the best experience.

This is where **integration tests** come into play. They verify that different parts of your project correctly "integrate" and work together.

Purpose of integration tests

So, what is an integration test's main job, and how does it differ from a unit test?

- **Focus on interactions**: Integration tests check the connections between components, mostly testing the public API functions, structs, and methods marked `pub` for external use.
- **External perspective**: Unlike unit tests, which can access private functions and internal details within a module, integration tests use your crate like any other external crate. They can only call public API functions. This makes them excellent for ensuring your library's interface is correct and usable.
- **Broader scope**: They naturally cover more code than a single unit test. A successful integration test implies that several components are working together correctly.
- **Catching different bugs**: Integration tests can catch bugs that unit tests might miss, such as issues arising from incorrect assumptions about how different modules interact, problems with data flow between components, or misunderstandings about how an API is meant to be used.

You can think of it this way: unit tests ensure each actor knows their lines, while integration tests ensure the actors perform the scene together correctly.

Setting up integration tests

Rust has a very clear convention for where integration tests live, and Cargo knows exactly how to find and run them:

1. **Create a tests directory**: At the root of your project (alongside your `src` directory and `Cargo.toml` file), create a new directory named `tests`.

2. **Add .rs files:** Each Rust source file (e.g., `my_feature_test.rs`) you place directly inside this `tests` directory will be compiled by Cargo as a separate, individual crate. This is a key point: each test file is its own little program that links against your main library crate.
3. **Import your crate:** Because each test file is a separate crate, you need to import the library you want to test using use `your_crate_name;`. The `your_crate_name` is the name specified in your `Cargo.toml` file under `[package]`.
4. **Write test functions:** Inside these files, you write functions annotated with `#[test]` just like you do for unit tests. You don't need an enclosing `mod tests {}` or `#[cfg(test)]` because Cargo already knows these are tests due to their location.

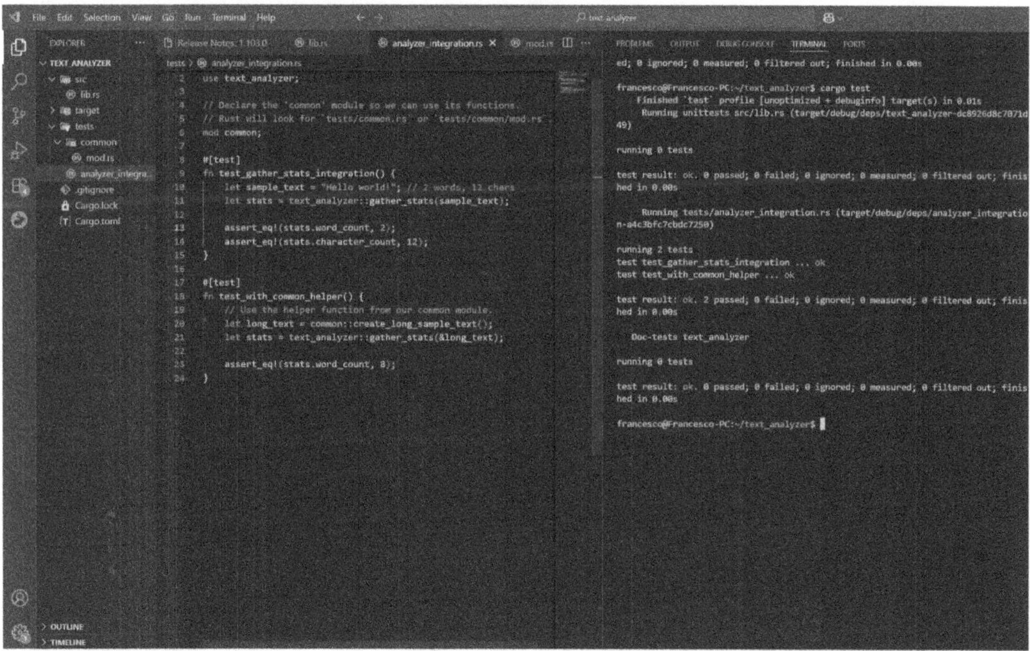

Figure 10.1: Example of the directory structure and code for integration tests in VS Code

Let's consider a small library that provides some simple text manipulation utilities.

Our library code (src/lib.rs)

Here is the library code:

```
// src/lib.rs
// Assume our crate name in Cargo.toml is "text_analyzer"

pub mod analysis {
```

```
    pub fn count_words(text: &str) -> usize {
        if text.is_empty() {
            return 0;
        }
        text.split_whitespace().count()
    }

    pub fn contains_profanity(text: &str, banned_words: &[&str]) -> bool {
        let lower_text = text.to_lowercase();
        for word in banned_words {
            if lower_text.contains(word) {
                return true;
            }
        }
        false
    }
}

pub struct TextStats {
    pub word_count: usize,
    pub character_count: usize,
}

pub fn gather_stats(text: &str) -> TextStats {
    TextStats {
        word_count: analysis::count_words(text), // Uses the module
        character_count: text.chars().count(),
    }
}
```

Now, let's write an integration test for this. First, create the `tests` directory:

```
mkdir tests
```

Then, create a file named `tests/analyzer_integration.rs`.

Integration test file (tests/analyzer_integration.rs)

Here is the test code:

```
// tests/analyzer_integration.rs

// Import the crate we want to test.
// The name "text_analyzer" must match the `name` field in Cargo.toml
use text_analyzer;

#[test]
fn test_word_count_integration() {
    let sample_text = "This is a sample sentence.";
    // Call the public function from our library's public module
    let count = text_analyzer::analysis::count_words(sample_text);
    assert_eq!(count, 5, "Word count should be 5");
}

#[test]
fn test_profanity_checker_integration() {
    let sample_text_clean = "A lovely day for a walk.";
    let sample_text_profane = "This is a darn naughty sentence.";
    let banned = ["darn", "naughty"];

    assert!(!text_analyzer::analysis::contains_profanity(sample_text_
clean, &banned), "Clean text should not contain profanity");
    assert!(text_analyzer::analysis::contains_profanity(sample_text_
profane, &banned), "Profane text should be detected");
}

#[test]
fn test_gather_stats_integration() {
    let sample_text = "Hello world!"; // 2 words, 12 chars
    let stats = text_analyzer::gather_stats(sample_text);

    assert_eq!(stats.word_count, 2);
    assert_eq!(stats.character_count, 12);
    // We can also access public fields of structs returned by public
functions
```

```
}

#[test]
fn test_empty_string_stats() {
    let stats = text_analyzer::gather_stats("");
    assert_eq!(stats.word_count, 0);
    assert_eq!(stats.character_count, 0);
}
```

Helper functions in integration tests

Sometimes, your integration tests might require common setup routines, data, or utility functions that you want to share across multiple test functions or even multiple test files within the `tests` directory.

If you have helper functions that are only used within a single integration test file (e.g., `tests/analyzer_integration.rs`), you can simply define them as regular (non-`#[test]`) functions within that same file.

However, if you want to share helper code *between different integration test files* (e.g., between `tests/analyzer_integration.rs` and `tests/advanced_analysis.rs`), you can't just put it in another `.rs` file directly in the `tests` directory, because Cargo will try to compile that helper file as a separate test crate.

The common way to handle this is to create a submodule within the `tests` directory, as follows:

1. Create a subdirectory: `tests/common/`.
2. Inside this subdirectory, create a `mod.rs` file: `tests/common/mod.rs`.
3. Put your shared helper functions (marked `pub`) inside `tests/common/mod.rs`.

Example shared helper (tests/common/mod.rs)

Code:

```
// tests/common/mod.rs

pub fn create_sample_long_text() -> String {
    "This is a very long string that we might want to use in multiple
integration tests for various analysis purposes. It contains several
words and punctuation marks like commas, and even exclamation points!".
to_string()
```

```
}

pub fn common_banned_words_list() -> Vec<&'static str> {
    vec!["heck", "darn", "gosh"]
}
```

Now, you can use these helpers in your actual integration test files.

Using shared helpers (tests/analyzer_integration.rs)

```
// tests/analyzer_integration.rs

// Declare the 'common' module. Rust will look for tests/common.rs or
tests/common/mod.rs
mod common;

use text_analyzer; // Your main library crate

#[test]
fn test_long_text_word_count() {
    let long_text = common::create_sample_long_text();
    let count = text_analyzer::analysis::count_words(&long_text);
    // You'd assert a specific count here, e.g., based on manual counting
    assert!(count > 10, "Expected more than 10 words in the long sample
text");
}

#[test]
fn test_profanity_with_common_list() {
    let text_with_profanity = "Oh heck, this is not good.";
    let banned_list = common::common_banned_words_list();
    assert!(text_analyzer::analysis::contains_profanity(text_with_
profanity, &banned_list));
}
```

By placing shared code into `tests/common/mod.rs` (or `tests/common.rs`), you create a regular module that other integration test files can then use via `mod common;` and `common::your_helper_function()`.

This is an efficient way to prevent duplicating setup code or utility logic across your integration tests. Remember that for functions in this common module to be accessible from other test files, they must be made visible. You can do this by marking them as `pub`, which makes them fully public.

However, a more idiomatic and precise choice is often to use `pub(crate)`.

This makes the helper functions visible to all other code within the same crate, and since Cargo compiles all your integration tests as part of a single test crate, `pub(crate)` is enough to share helpers among them while keeping them properly internal to your test suite.

Integration tests are a vital part of ensuring your library or application is robust and that its public contract is upheld. They complement unit tests by verifying how the pieces work in concert.

Documentation tests: Keeping examples correct

One of Rust's rather unique and incredibly useful features is its built-in support for **documentation tests**. These aren't just about checking your code's logic in isolation or how parts integrate; they are about ensuring that the code examples you provide in your documentation are actually correct and stay correct as your code evolves.

What are documentation tests?

Simply put, documentation tests (often called "doc tests") are code examples embedded directly within your comments (specifically, your *documentation comments*) that `cargo test` can automatically extract, compile, and run.

Why is this so valuable?

- **Accuracy**: It guarantees that your documented examples actually work. There's nothing more frustrating for a user of your library than trying an example from the documentation only to find that it's outdated or incorrect. Doc tests prevent this.
- **Living documentation**: Because the examples are tested, they evolve with your code. If you change a function in a way that breaks an example, the doc test will fail, prompting you to update the documentation.
- **Usability**: They provide clear, runnable demonstrations of how to use your library's API, directly alongside the API's description.
- **Encourages good examples**: Knowing your examples will be tested encourages you to write clear, concise, and correct examples in the first place.

Rust's commitment to documentation tests reflects its broader philosophy of providing tools that help developers write high-quality, reliable software. It's a small feature with a big impact on the ecosystem.

Writing documentation tests

Writing a documentation test is as simple as including a Rust code block within your doc comments. Doc comments are those that start with `///` (for items such as functions, structs, enums, or modules) or `//!` (for documenting the enclosing item, often a module or crate itself).

Inside these comments, you create a fenced code block using triple backticks. If you specify `rust` after the opening backticks (or leave it blank, as `rust` is the default), `cargo test` (or specifically `cargo test --doc`) will treat it as a testable example.

Let's create a small utility function and document it with a testable example:

````
// In src/lib.rs or your relevant module file
// Let's assume our crate name in Cargo.toml is "string_formatter"

/// Formats a name and an age into a greeting string.
///
/// This function takes a name (a string slice) and an age (an unsigned
32-bit integer)
/// and returns a nicely formatted greeting.
///
/// # Examples
///
/// ```
/// // This code block will be run as a test!
/// use string_formatter::format_greeting; // Assuming this is how users
would import
///
/// let name = "Alice";
/// let age = 30;
/// let greeting = format_greeting(name, age);
/// assert_eq!(greeting, "Hello, Alice! You are 30 years old.");
/// ```
///
/// You can have multiple examples:
/// ```
````

```
/// use string_formatter::format_greeting;
///
/// let greeting_bob = format_greeting("Bob", 42);
/// assert!(greeting_bob.contains("Bob"));
/// assert!(greeting_bob.contains("42"));
/// ```
pub fn format_greeting(name: &str, age: u32) -> String {
    format!("Hello, {}! You are {} years old.", name, age)
}

// To make the `use string_formatter::format_greeting;` line in the doc
test work easily
// when `cargo test --doc` is run from the crate root, `format_greeting`
needs to be
// part of the public API accessible via `string_formatter::format_
greeting`.
// If this code IS `src/lib.rs` of a crate named `string_formatter`, it
should work.
// Alternatively, inside the doc test, you could use `crate::format_
greeting`
// if you don't want to simulate an external user's import path.
```

- The comments starting with `///` are documentation comments for the `format_greeting` function.
- The `# Examples` section is a common convention for showing usage.
- The code within the ` ``` ` (or ` ```rust`) block is the actual documentation test.
- Inside this block, we can write any Rust code, including use statements (often needed to bring the item being tested into scope, as a user would) and, crucially, **assertion macros** such as `assert_eq!` or `assert!`.
- When you run `cargo test` (or `cargo test --doc` to run *only* doc tests), Cargo will extract this code block, effectively wrap it in an `fn main() { ... }` function, compile it, and run it. If any assertion fails, or if the code doesn't compile, the doc test fails.

Important note on paths in doc tests

The way you refer to items from your own crate within a doc test can sometimes be a bit tricky:

- If you're writing a doc test for a public item in your library's root (`src/lib.rs`), and you want to show how an external user would use it, you'd typically write use `your_crate_name::your_item;`, as shown previously. `cargo test --doc` is usually smart enough to make this work.
- If the example is very internal or you want to avoid ambiguity, you can sometimes use use `crate::your_item;` to refer to items from the current crate's root.
- The test runner implicitly adds extern crate self as `your_crate_name;`, which makes `your_crate_name::` available.

Controlling doc test behavior

Just like regular tests, you can control how doc tests behave using annotations within the code block's opening fence:

Ignore:

````
/// ```ignore
/// // This example will be compiled but not run by `cargo test --doc`
/// // unless you use `cargo test --doc --ignored`
/// println!("This is an ignored example.");
/// ```
````

Useful for examples that might be slow or require specific external setup.

should_panic:

````
/// ```should_panic
/// // This test passes if the code inside panics.
/// // For example, documenting a function that should error on bad input.
/// // imagine_a_function_that_panics_on_zero(0);
/// panic!("This example is expected to panic");
/// ```
````

This works just like #[should_panic] on a regular test function. You can also add (expected = "substring") if you want to check the panic message.

no_run:

```
/// ```no_run
/// // This code will be compiled to ensure it's valid Rust,
/// // but it will not be executed. Useful for examples that
/// // demonstrate something that shouldn't actually run in a test,
/// // like starting a web server or modifying files.
/// // start_web_server();
/// ```
```

This is great for illustrating APIs that have side effects that you don't want to trigger during routine testing.

Hiding lines from documentation output but not from the test

Sometimes you need setup code for an example that isn't relevant to what you're trying to show the user. You can prefix such lines with #. These lines will be executed by the test runner but won't appear in the rendered HTML documentation:

```
/// ```
/// # fn get_important_config() -> String { "config_value".to_string() }
/// // Users will only see this part in the docs:
/// let config = get_important_config();
/// assert_eq!(config, "config_value");
/// ```
```

Documentation tests are a powerful way to ensure your examples remain accurate and serve as a first line of defense against documentation rot. They are a strong encouragement to write helpful, working examples for anyone using your code.

A brief look at Test-Driven Development (TDD)

So far, we've discussed writing tests for code that might already exist or that you're designing alongside the tests. There's also a popular software development methodology called **Test-Driven Development (TDD)**, which flips this on its head: you write your tests *before* you write the actual implementation code.

While a full exploration of TDD is extensive, it's worth understanding its core principles as it can be a very effective way to develop software, and Rust's testing framework supports it well.

TDD cycle

TDD operates on a short, iterative cycle, often referred to as red-green-refactor:

1. **Red:**
    - **Write a test:** Before writing any implementation code for a new feature or piece of functionality, you first write an automated test that defines what that new functionality should do.
    - **Run all tests:** At this point, the new test *must fail* (hence "red") because the code it's trying to test doesn't exist or isn't implemented yet. If it passes, your test is likely not testing what you think it is, or the functionality already exists!
2. **Green:**
    - **Write the code:** Write the *minimum amount of implementation code* necessary to make the failing test (and all other existing tests) pass. The goal here is just to get to "green," not to write perfect or highly optimized code.
    - **Run all tests:** Verify that all tests now pass.
3. **Refactor:**
    - **Clean up the code:** Now that you have passing tests acting as a safety net, you can refactor the implementation code you just wrote. This is where you improve its structure, remove duplication, enhance readability, or optimize performance, all while ensuring the tests continue to pass.
    - You might also refactor the test code itself if it can be made clearer or more efficient.

Once this cycle is complete for one small piece of functionality, you pick the next small piece and start the cycle again: write a new failing test, make it pass, then refactor.

TDD benefits and a micro example

Adopting TDD can bring several benefits:

- **Ensures test coverage:** By writing tests first, you guarantee that every piece of new functionality has corresponding tests.
- **Drives design:** Thinking about how to test a feature often forces you to design it in a more modular, decoupled, and testable way from the outset. The tests define the "contract" the code must fulfill.

- **Reduces bugs**: Catching issues at the "red" stage or during the "green" stage is much quicker than finding them later.
- **Provides a safety net for refactoring**: The comprehensive test suite built through TDD gives you high confidence when making changes or improvements to the code base.
- **Focuses on requirements**: Writing a test first forces you to clearly define what the code should accomplish before you dive into how it will accomplish it.

Let's walk through a tiny TDD example. Suppose we want to implement a function, `is_palindrome(s: &str) -> bool`, that checks whether a string is a palindrome (reads the same forward and backward, ignoring case and non-alphanumeric characters for simplicity here, though a real TDD cycle might add those requirements incrementally).

1. Red: Write a failing test

First, we add a test case to our `#[cfg(test)] mod tests { ... }`:

```
// In src/lib.rs or where our function will live

// We haven't written is_palindrome yet, so this will initially fail to compile,
// or fail at runtime if we provide a stub like `fn is_palindrome(_s: &str) -> bool { todo!() }`

#[cfg(test)]
mod tests {
    // Assuming is_palindrome will be in the parent module
    use super::is_palindrome; // This line might cause an error if is_palindrome doesn't exist yet

    #[test]
    fn test_empty_string_is_palindrome() {
        assert!(is_palindrome(""));
    }

    #[test]
    fn test_single_char_is_palindrome() {
        assert!(is_palindrome("a"));
    }
```

```
    #[test]
    fn test_simple_palindrome() {
        assert!(is_palindrome("madam"));
    }

    #[test]
    fn test_non_palindrome() {
        assert!(!is_palindrome("hello"));
    }
}
```

If `is_palindrome` doesn't exist, this won't even compile. Let's add a minimal stub so it compiles but fails the logic:

```
// In src/lib.rs
pub fn is_palindrome(_s: &str) -> bool {
    false // Simplest thing to make it compile; will fail most tests
}
```

Now, running `cargo test` should show `test_empty_string_is_palindrome`, `test_single_char_is_palindrome`, and `test_simple_palindrome` failing (red).

2. Green: Write minimal code to make tests pass

Let's implement `is_palindrome` to satisfy these tests:

```
// In src/lib.rs
pub fn is_palindrome(s: &str) -> bool {
    if s.is_empty() {
        return true; // Empty string is a palindrome
    }
    let forward_chars: Vec<char> = s.chars().collect();
    let reversed_chars: Vec<char> = s.chars().rev().collect();
    forward_chars == reversed_chars
}
```

Now, running `cargo test` should make all current tests pass (green).

3. Refactor: Improve the code

Our current implementation creates two new `Vec<char>`, which might be a bit inefficient for very long strings. We could refactor it to compare characters from both ends inward without extra allocations:

```
// In src/lib.rs - Refactored version
pub fn is_palindrome(s: &str) -> bool {
    let mut fwd_iter = s.chars();
    let mut rev_iter = s.chars().rev();

    // Loop as long as both iterators can produce an item
    // and the items are equal
    while let (Some(f_char), Some(r_char)) = (fwd_iter.next(), rev_iter.
next()) {
        // We only need to compare up to the middle.
        // If fwd_iter's current position "crosses" rev_iter's, we're
done.
        // The `next_back()` method on DoubleEndedIterator would be more
efficient here,
        // but for a simple `chars().rev()` this approach is okay.
        // A more robust way is to compare iterators up to half the
length,
        // or check if fwd_iter.size_hint().0 <= rev_iter.size_hint().0
        if f_char != r_char {
            return false;
        }
        // For simplicity, let's just rely on the loop eventually
consuming one iterator
        // faster if length is odd, leading to one `next()` being None.
        // This simple loop only works if we consume from both ends until
they meet or cross.
        // A more correct iterative comparison for non-allocating:
    }
    // If the loop completed without returning false, it's a palindrome
    true
}
```

The initial refactor attempt was a bit complex to explain simply. A more common and still efficient refactor without extra allocation for simple palindromes (ignoring case/non-alphanumeric for now, as per the TDD step) would be as follows:

```
// In src/lib.rs - A more common refactored version
pub fn is_palindrome(s: &str) -> bool {
    let s_cleaned: String = s.chars().collect(); // Simple case: works
with original string
    s_cleaned.chars().eq(s_cleaned.chars().rev())
}
```

This refactored version is concise and still passes all the original tests. We could then add new tests for case-insensitivity or ignoring non-alphanumeric characters, starting the red-green-refactor cycle again for those new requirements.

Next cycle: red (for case-insensitivity)

```
#[test]
    fn test_case_insensitive_palindrome() {
        assert!(is_palindrome("Madam"));
    }
```

This would fail. Then we'd go to green by modifying `is_palindrome` to handle casing, for example, by converting to lowercase before comparison.

TDD is a discipline. While the micro example is very basic, the cycle helps maintain a focus on requirements and ensures that code is always testable and tested as it's being written. It might feel slower initially, but many developers find that it leads to higher quality and more confidence in the long run.

TDD for an API handler

The same TDD principles apply to more complex components, such as API handlers. You can write a test that defines the expected response for a given request before implementing the handler's logic.

Let's imagine we need a handler that gsenerates a user profile as JSON.

1. Red: Write the failing test

We'll test the handler function directly. The test will check that for a valid user ID, we get the correct JSON, and for an invalid one, we get an error:

```
// This code would go in your tests module, e.g., in `src/handlers.rs`

#[cfg(test)]
mod tests {
    use super::*; // Assuming handlers are in the parent module

    // The test needs the User struct to compare against.
    // In a real project, this would be in a shared `models` module.
    #[derive(serde::Serialize)] // Needed for serde_json::to_string
    struct User {
        id: u32,
        username: String,
    }

    // A stub for the handler we are about to write.
    // This allows the test code to compile but fail.
    fn get_user_handler(id: u32) -> Result<String, String> {
        // todo!() would also work here and cause a panic.
        Err("Not implemented yet".to_string())
    }

    #[test]
    fn test_get_user_success() {
        let expected_user = User { id: 1, username: "Alice".to_string() };
        let expected_json = serde_json::to_string(&expected_user).
unwrap();

        let result = get_user_handler(1);
        assert!(result.is_ok());
        assert_eq!(result.unwrap(), expected_json);
    }
```

```
    #[test]
    fn test_get_user_not_found() {
        let result = get_user_handler(999); // An ID that doesn't exist
        assert!(result.is_err());
        assert_eq!(result.unwrap_err(), "User not found");
    }
}
```

Running `cargo  test` now would show failures (red) because our stub always returns `Not implemented yet`.

2. Green: Write minimal code to make the test pass

Now we implement the struct and the handler logic in our main source file (e.g., `src/handlers.rs`) just to satisfy our test cases:

```
// This code would go in your main source, e.g., in `src/lib.rs` or `src/
handlers.rs`

// We need serde for this example. Add `serde = { version = "1.0",
features = ["derive"] }`
// and `serde_json = "1.0"` to your Cargo.toml.
use serde::Serialize;

#[derive(Serialize)]
pub struct User {
    id: u32,
    username: String,
}

/// A simple handler that simulates fetching a user.
pub fn get_user_handler(id: u32) -> Result<String, String> {
    // In a real app, this would be a database lookup.
    // Here, we hardcode the logic to make the tests pass.
    match id {
        1 => {
            let user = User { id: 1, username: "Alice".to_string() };
```

```
            // serde_json::to_string also returns a Result, so we handle
it.
            serde_json::to_string(&user).map_err(|e| e.to_string())
        }
        _ => Err("User not found".to_string()),
    }
}
```

Now, if you update your `tests` module to import this real implementation, running `cargo test` will show all tests passing (green).

3. Refactor

With the tests passing, we could now refactor `get_user_handler`. For instance, instead of hard-coding users in a `match` statement, we could refactor it to fetch data from a database or another data source, confident that our tests will catch any regressions in the expected output format.

This brief example shows how the TDD cycle can guide the development of API logic, ensuring the contract with the client (the expected JSON response) is met from the very beginning.

Isolating tests with test doubles (mocks and stubs)

We've talked a lot about unit tests, focusing on small, isolated pieces of code. But what happens when the function or module you want to test depends on something else, like another complex part of your system, a database, a web service, or even the current time? If your unit test relies on these external factors, it can become unreliable, slow, or difficult to set up.

This is where **test doubles** come in.

The need for isolation

For unit tests to be truly effective, they should ideally test *only* the logic of the unit in question, without interference or variability from its dependencies. Here's why isolation is so important:

- **Reliability and determinism**: Tests that interact with external systems (such as a network service) can fail for reasons unrelated to your code (e.g., network outage). This makes tests "flaky"—sometimes they pass, sometimes they fail, without any changes to your code. Isolated tests are deterministic: given the same input, they always produce the same result.
- **Speed**: Real dependencies, especially those involving I/O (disk and network), are often slow. Unit tests should run very quickly so you can run them often. Slow tests get skipped, defeating their purpose.

- **Focus:** If a test fails, you want to know immediately that the bug is in the unit being tested, not in one of its dependencies. Isolation helps pinpoint failures.
- **Setup simplicity:** It can be complicated to set up real dependencies in a test environment (e.g., initializing a database with specific test data for every test run).

To achieve this isolation, we replace real dependencies with controlled, predictable stand-ins called **test doubles** during our unit tests.

What are test doubles? Stubs and mocks

A "test double" is a general term for any object or component that you use in a test to stand in for a real production dependency. There are various kinds of test doubles, but two common ones you'll hear about are stubs and mocks:

- **Stubs:** These provide canned answers to calls made during the test. They usually don't have much logic beyond returning predefined values. For example, a stub for a weather service might always return `Sunny, 25°C` regardless of the input, just to allow the code that *uses* the weather data to be tested.
- **Mocks:** These are more sophisticated. Like stubs, they provide canned responses, but they can also be programmed with *expectations* about how they will be used. For instance, a mock object might verify that its methods are called a certain number of times, in a particular order, or with specific arguments. If these expectations aren't met, the mock can cause the test to fail.

Let's see how we can create a simple stub manually in Rust.

Manual stubbing (with traits)

One common way to create a stub in Rust is to define a trait that represents the dependency, have your production code depend on that trait (using generics or trait objects), and then, in your tests, create a simple struct that implements the trait with stubbed behavior.

Imagine we have a service that sends notifications, and we want to test a piece of code that uses this service without actually sending real notifications:

```
// src/lib.rs (or your module)

// The trait defining our dependency
pub trait Notifier {
    fn send_alert(&self, user_id: &str, message: &str) -> Result<(),
String>;
```

```
}

// The component we want to test
pub struct EventProcessor<N: Notifier> {
    notifier_service: N, // Depends on the Notifier trait
    admin_user_id: String,
}

impl<N: Notifier> EventProcessor<N> {
    pub fn new(notifier_service: N, admin_user_id: String) -> Self {
        EventProcessor { notifier_service, admin_user_id }
    }

    pub fn process_critical_event(&self, event_details: &str) {
        println!("Processing critical event: {}", event_details);
        // Attempt to notify the admin
        let alert_message = format!("CRITICAL: {}", event_details);
        match self.notifier_service.send_alert(&self.admin_user_id,
&alert_message) {
            Ok(_) => println!("Admin notified successfully."),
            Err(e) => println!("Failed to notify admin: {}", e),
        }
        // ... other event processing logic ...
    }
}

#[cfg(test)]
mod tests {
    use super::*; // Import Notifier, EventProcessor

    // Our Stub implementation for the Notifier trait
    struct StubEmailNotifier {
        // We can add fields to control stub's behavior for different
tests
        should_succeed: bool,
        expected_user_id: String,
        expected_message_contains: String,
```

```
        call_count: std::cell::Cell<usize>, // To track calls (simple
mock-like behavior)
    }

    impl Notifier for StubEmailNotifier {
        fn send_alert(&self, user_id: &str, message: &str) -> Result<(),
String> {
            self.call_count.set(self.call_count.get() + 1); // Increment
call count

            println!("STUB: Attempting to send alert to '{}' with message
'{}'", user_id, message);
            assert_eq!(user_id, self.expected_user_id, "Stub called with
wrong user_id");
            assert!(message.contains(&self.expected_message_contains),
"Stub message content mismatch");

            if self.should_succeed {
                Ok(())
            } else {
                Err("StubNotifier: Simulated failure.".to_string())
            }
        }
    }

    #[test]
    fn critical_event_notifies_admin_successfully() {
        let stub_notifier = StubEmailNotifier {
            should_succeed: true,
            expected_user_id: "admin_001".to_string(),
            expected_message_contains: "CRITICAL: System Overload".to_
string(),
            call_count: std::cell::Cell::new(0),
        };

        let event_processor = EventProcessor::new(stub_notifier,
"admin_001".to_string());
        event_processor.process_critical_event("System Overload");
```

```
        // Check if the notifier was called (accessing our stub's field)
        // This makes our stub act a bit like a mock.
        assert_eq!(event_processor.notifier_service.call_count.get(), 1,
"Notifier should have been called once");
    }

    #[test]
    fn critical_event_handles_notification_failure() {
        let stub_notifier = StubEmailNotifier {
            should_succeed: false, // Simulate failure
            expected_user_id: "sys_alert_user".to_string(),
            expected_message_contains: "CRITICAL: Disk Full".to_string(),
            call_count: std::cell::Cell::new(0),
        };
        let event_processor = EventProcessor::new(stub_notifier, "sys_
alert_user".to_string());

        // We aren't asserting a panic here, just that the function runs
        // and internally would print the failure message.
        // A more robust test might have process_critical_event return a
Result.
        event_processor.process_critical_event("Disk Full");
         assert_eq!(event_processor.notifier_service.call_count.get(), 1,
"Notifier should have been called once, even on failure path");
    }
}
```

- We define a `Notifier` trait that abstracts the notification functionality.
- Our `EventProcessor` is generic over any type, `N`, that implements `Notifier`. This is key: it allows us to substitute different implementations.
- In the `tests` module, `StubEmailNotifier` is a simple struct that implements `Notifier`. Its `send_alert` method doesn't actually send an email; it just prints a message and returns a pre-programmed `Ok(())` or `Err(...)` based on its `should_succeed` field.

- We've also added `expected_user_id`, `expected_message_contains`, and `call_count` (using `std::cell::Cell` for interior mutability since `send_alert` takes `&self`) to our stub. This allows the stub to perform some basic checks on how it was called, blurring the lines a bit toward mock behavior. `Cell` is used here because `send_alert` takes `&self` but we want to modify `call_count` internally; for more complex scenarios, `RefCell` might be used, or the method could take `&mut self` if appropriate for the trait.
- In the tests, we create an `EventProcessor` with an instance of our `StubEmailNotifier`. This allows us to test the logic within `process_critical_event` (such as how it formats messages or handles errors from the notifier) without any real notification system being involved.

This manual approach is fine for simple cases. The "stub" here even has some light "mock" capabilities by checking arguments and counting calls.

Mocking libraries

For more complex scenarios where you need to verify intricate interactions, such as the order of method calls, the number of times a method is called, or asserting specific arguments for multiple calls, creating manual mocks can become quite cumbersome and error-prone.

This is where **mocking libraries** shine. Rust has a growing ecosystem of these, with `mockall` being one of the most popular and powerful. These libraries typically provide macros or procedural macros that can automatically generate mock implementations for your traits (or even structs, in some cases).

With a library such as `mockall`, you could define expectations on your mock object in your test setup:

- "I expect the `send_alert` method to be called exactly once"
- "I expect it to be called with `user_id == "admin_001"` and a message containing `CRITICAL`"
- "When it's called under these conditions, it should return `Ok(())`"

If the code under test doesn't meet these expectations, the mock object will cause the test to fail.

Our manual stub was handy but could get complicated if we needed to verify more, such as calling `send_alert` exactly three times or not at all. Adding more fields would become cumbersome.

Mocking libraries such as `mockall` simplify this by generating mock objects based on traits, which can be programmed with expectations.

This allows testing of complex scenarios by replacing real dependencies with controlled substitutes, keeping tests focused, fast, and reliable.

Best practices for writing good tests

Knowing how to write tests is a skill in itself, and while testing theory is a deep topic, a few key practices will make your Rust tests much more effective and maintainable:

- **Keep tests clear and focused:** Each test should verify a single, specific behavior. Give it a descriptive name (such as `fails_when_input_is_empty`), and use the optional message in assertion macros (`assert_eq!(a, b, "...")`) to explain *why* a failure occurred. This makes debugging much faster.
- **Ensure tests are independent and fast:** Tests should never depend on each other, as `cargo test` runs them in parallel by default. Keep unit tests quick to encourage frequent running; mark any slow, resource-intensive tests with the `#[ignore]` attribute and run them separately.
- **Test the edges, not just the "happy path":** The most valuable tests often check boundary conditions and error paths. Always test for empty inputs, zero values, what happens when a function should return `None` or `Err`, and conditions that should cause a `panic!` (using `#[should_panic]`).
- **Follow the "Arrange, Act, Assert" pattern:** A great way to structure your tests is to first *Arrange* any setup or data needed, then *Act* by calling the function or method you are testing, and finally, *Assert* that the outcome is correct. This makes tests easy to read and understand at a glance.

Adopting these habits will help you build a robust and valuable test suite that truly supports your development process, giving you confidence and helping you catch bugs before they cause bigger problems.

Summary

And that brings us to the end of *Chapter 10*!

We've explored the essential way of testing in Rust, a key part of creating software that is reliable, correct, and easy to maintain!

I hope you now see testing not as a chore but as a helpful partner in your development journey! Here is a recap of what we've covered:

- **The "why" of testing**: We started by reinforcing the critical *importance of testing*: how it boosts reliability, makes refactoring safer, acts as documentation, and helps catch bugs when they are cheapest to fix.
- **Types of tests in Rust**: We identified the main types of tests directly supported by Rust's ecosystem:
  - **Unit tests:** Small, focused tests for individual functions or modules, written within `mod tests {}` in the same file as the code
  - **Integration tests:** Tests that check how different parts of your library work together, focusing on the public API, and residing in a separate `tests` directory
  - **Documentation tests:** Runnable code examples embedded directly in your `///` doc comments, ensuring your examples stay correct
- **Writing unit tests**: We saw how to define test functions using the `#[test]` attribute, use assertion macros (`assert!`, `assert_eq!`, and `assert_ne!`) to verify conditions, and specifically test functions returning `Result` and `Option`. We also learned how to test for expected panics using `#[should_panic]`.
- **Running and controlling tests**: The `cargo test` command is your gateway to running all these tests, and we looked at options for running specific tests, showing output, and handling `#[ignore]`d tests.
- **Broader concepts**: We briefly touched upon TDD as a methodology where tests are written before code, and the use of **test doubles (stubs and mocks)** to isolate the code under test from its dependencies, often using traits for manual stubbing.
- **Best practices:** Finally, we summarized key best practices for writing effective tests, such as keeping tests focused and independent, writing clear names and failure messages, testing edge cases, and keeping tests fast.

By consistently applying these testing techniques, you're not just finding bugs; you're building a safety net that allows you to develop and evolve your Rust projects with much greater confidence and speed. As you write more Rust, make `cargo test` your frequent companion!

Questions and assignment

Testing concepts are never easy, especially for beginners.

Let's take a moment to review the key ideas from this chapter. The following questions are meant to help you assess your understanding of the essential testing concepts we've discussed, from the structure of different test types to the specific tools that Rust offers. If you can answer these confidently, you're well on your way to writing effective tests for your own Rust projects.

Questions

1. What are the three main types of tests that `cargo test` runs by default, and where are unit tests and integration tests typically located in a Rust project?
2. Explain the purpose of the `#[test]` attribute and the `#[cfg(test)]` attribute when writing a unit test module.
3. What is the difference between `assert!` and `assert_eq!`? Provide a simple example of a situation where you would use each.
4. You have a function that is designed to panic if given invalid input. How would you write a test to verify this panic behavior, and how could you make the test even more specific by checking the panic message?
5. What is the primary benefit of writing documentation tests in Rust?

Assignment

For this assignment, you'll create a very simple command-line task manager library and test it thoroughly.

1. **Project setup:**
    - **Create a new library crate:** `cargo new task_manager --lib`
2. **Define structs (src/lib.rs):**
    - `pub struct Task { pub id: u32, pub description: String, pub completed: bool }`
    - `pub struct TaskManager { tasks: Vec<Task>, next_id: u32 }`

3. **Implement methods for TaskManager (src/lib.rs):**

    - `pub fn new() -> Self`: Creates an empty `TaskManager` with `next_id` starting at 1.
    - `pub fn add_task(&mut self, description: String) -> u32`: Adds a new task with the given description (initially not completed), assigns it the `next_id`, increments `next_id`, and returns the new task's ID.
    - `pub fn mark_complete(&mut self, task_id: u32) -> Option<()>`: Marks the task with the given `task_id` as completed. Returns `Some(())` if the task was found and marked, and `None` otherwise.
    - `pub fn get_task(&self, task_id: u32) -> Option<&Task>`: Returns an immutable reference to the task with the given ID, or `None` if not found.
    - `pub fn list_pending_tasks(&self) -> Vec<&Task>`: Returns a vector of immutable references to all tasks that are not completed.
    - `pub fn remove_task(&mut self, task_id: u32) -> Option<Task>`: Removes the task with the given ID from the manager and returns it. If not found, returns `None`.

4. **Testing requirements:**

    Unit tests (in `mod tests {}` within `src/lib.rs`):

    - Test that `TaskManager::new()` ensures an empty task list and `next_id` is `1`.
    - Test that `add_task()` does the following:
        - Adds a task correctly
        - Assigns sequential IDs
        - New tasks are initially not completed
    - Test `mark_complete()` doing the following:
        - Mark an existing pending task as complete
        - Attempt to mark a non-existent task
        - Attempt to mark an already completed task (should still be `Some(())` if found)
    - Test get_task() doing the following:
        - Get an existing task
        - Get a non-existent task

- Test `list_pending_tasks()`:
    - With no tasks
    - With all tasks pending
    - With some tasks completed and some pending
    - With all tasks completed
- Test `remove_task()` doing the following:
    - Removing an existing task
    - Trying to remove a non-existent task
    - Ensure `next_id` is *not* affected by removal (new tasks should still get unique IDs)

Integration test (create tests/task_flow_tests.rs):

- Write a test function that simulates a user workflow:
    - Create a new `TaskManager`
    - Add a couple of tasks
    - List pending tasks and verify them
    - Mark one task as complete
    - List pending tasks again and verify the change
    - Get a specific task by ID and check its details
    - Remove a task
    - Try to get the removed task (should be `None`)
    - Add another new task and verify its ID is what you expect

11

Smart Pointers and Memory Management

Welcome to *Chapter 11*!

We are about to begin an exciting chapter: smart pointers!

If you're familiar with pointers in languages such as C or C++, you may have a particular perception of them.

But Rust's smart pointers are more than just memory addresses; they function like pointers but have additional metadata and features. They are essential in ensuring Rust's memory management is both safe and efficient. By the end of this chapter, you will have a solid understanding of smart pointers in general and how Rust utilizes them.

In simple terms, they can be described as granting you some "superpowers" when programming in Rust.

To understand these powerful tools, our exploration in this chapter will cover several key areas:

- We'll start by defining what **smart pointers** are and their crucial role in Rust's memory model
- We'll look at the simplest smart pointer, **Box<T>**, for straightforward heap allocation
- Next, we'll cover **Rc<T>** and **Arc<T>** for managing shared ownership of data in single-threaded and multi-threaded contexts
- Then, we'll dive into the **interior mutability** pattern with **RefCell<T>** and **Mutex<T>**
- Finally, we'll see how to combine and use these pointers effectively in practical scenarios

By the end, I hope you will have a solid understanding of smart pointers and how Rust utilizes them to write powerful, safe, and efficient code.

Let's dive in!

What are smart pointers, anyway?

Smart pointers are essentially **structs** that implement the `Deref` and `Drop` traits.

- The `Deref` trait lets a smart pointer struct act like a reference, enabling you to write code compatible with both references and smart pointers
- The `Drop` trait enables you to define the code executed when a smart pointer instance goes out of scope, which is vital for efficient resource management, such as memory deallocation

Think of smart pointers as wrappers around raw pointers that add additional functionalities. These functionalities may include automatic memory deallocation, reference counting for multiple data owners, and mechanisms for safe data mutation, even with immutable references. They are termed "smart" because they not only point to data but also manage it effectively.

The role of smart pointers in Rust's memory model

Rust is well-known for ensuring memory safety. This is primarily accomplished through its ownership system, which includes stringent rules regarding borrowing and lifetimes, all enforced at compile time.

Smart pointers help Rust go the extra mile by significantly enhancing the system's flexibility and extending its capabilities.

Enhancing safety beyond basic ownership

While the fundamental ownership rules are effective, they are built around a single-owner model, which can sometimes feel limiting in more complex situations.

For instance, imagine you have a configuration object that many different parts of an application need to share and access, or you're working on a data structure such as a graph where multiple nodes share ownership of another node. In such cases, you might also want to modify data that is otherwise borrowed immutably.

Smart pointers offer helpful solutions for these scenarios, making it safe and easy to handle shared ownership or runtime-checked borrowing, enhancing Rust's robust ownership system.

For example, you may need a single data element to be "owned" by several sections of your program or to alter data that is otherwise borrowed immutably.

Smart pointers offer methods to manage these situations safely, either through Rust's compile-time assurances or by implementing clearly defined runtime checks.

Performance implications

Rust's memory management approach plays a key role in delivering predictable and efficient performance. Smart pointers, through using the `Drop` trait, make sure memory is freed in a reliable way: that is, exactly when the owner goes out of scope. This means your program can run smoothly without unexpected pauses that might happen with a separate cleanup process, which is especially important for tasks that need top-tier performance and operate at the system level.

Smart pointers improve this by allowing for deterministic deallocation: memory is typically freed when the owning smart pointer goes out of scope, facilitated by the `Drop` trait.

This guarantees the absence of unpredictable GC pauses.

Enabling safe concurrency

Some smart pointers are tailored for concurrent programming.

They provide means to safely share data among threads or permit several threads to modify data, thereby preventing data races. This offers a considerable benefit for developing high-performance, concurrent applications with confidence.

Key ideas behind smart pointers

To appreciate how smart pointers provide these benefits, it's useful to see how they are built upon and interact with the core Rust concepts we've already learned about, such as ownership and traits.

Ownership and borrowing still apply

Smart pointers are values that conform to Rust's ownership and borrowing principles. For instance, a `Box<T>` (which we will explore shortly) owns the data it references on the heap. When the `Box<T>` is transferred, the ownership of that heap data follows suit.

Also, when borrowed, the standard borrowing rules pertain to the `Box<T>` itself.

Automatic cleanup

This is significant.

Most smart pointers implement the `Drop` trait. When a smart pointer instance goes out of scope, its `drop` method is triggered automatically.

This method usually includes the logic to deallocate memory or release other resources managed by the smart pointer. This automatic cleanup effectively prevents memory leaks in many scenarios and is referred to as RAII.

What is RAII?

RAII stands for **Resource Acquisition Is Initialization**. While the name may sound complex, the idea is simple and powerful: the lifetime of a resource (such as allocated memory, an open file, or a network connection) is tied to the lifetime of the object that owns it.

- **Acquisition**: You acquire the resource when the object is created (e.g., `File::open()` returns a `File` object)
- **Initialization**: The object is initialized, and it now owns the resource
- **Release**: When the object goes out of scope, its `Drop` implementation is automatically run, which releases the resource (e.g., closes the file)

This pattern guarantees that resources are always cleaned up correctly, which is fundamental to how Rust prevents resource leaks!

Reference counting for shared data

What if multiple parts of your program need to share ownership of the same data, which should only be cleaned up once the last owner is done using it?

This is a common situation in many applications, such as when several services in your program need to read from the same shared configuration object, or multiple parts of a UI need to display data from a shared cache.

To manage this, Rust offers smart pointers that enable shared ownership through reference counting. The main tools for this are `Rc<T>` (Reference Counted) for single-threaded cases, and its thread-safe counterpart, `Arc<T>` (Atomic Reference Counted).

These pointers handle shared data by keeping track of the number of active references, ensuring the data is only deallocated when the last reference is gone.

Interior mutability: bending the rules safely

Rust's borrowing rules generally indicate that a mutable reference cannot coexist with immutable references.

Nonetheless, there are times when you need to modify data that appears immutable from an external viewpoint.

The interior mutability pattern enables this functionality. Smart pointers such as RefCell<T> and Mutex<T> facilitate data mutation even when accessed through an immutable reference, by enforcing borrowing rules during runtime (in the case of RefCell) or by guaranteeing exclusive access (for Mutex).

A quick tour of Rust's smart pointer toolkit

Rust's standard library includes several important smart pointers, each tailored for specific use cases. We will look at them in detail, but here's a brief and quick overview of some of them:

- Box<T>: This is the most basic smart pointer. It allocates memory on the heap and provides a "box" containing a pointer to that memory. It's ideal for situations where you want to own data on the heap, transfer ownership of that data, or store a type with an unknown size at compile time within a struct that requires a known size (such as in recursive types).
- Rc<T>: Short for "Reference Counted," this permits multiple owners of the same heap data, limited to a single thread. It tracks the number of references and frees the data when the last reference is dropped.
- Arc<T>: Short for "Atomically Reference Counted," this is the thread-safe counterpart of Rc<T>, used when you need to share ownership of data across multiple threads.
- RefCell<T>: This offers interior mutability for single-threaded contexts. It allows mutable references to data to be borrowed even when RefCell<T> itself is immutable, by upholding Rust's borrowing rules at runtime (and will panic if those rules are broken). It's often used together with Rc<T>.
- Mutex<T>: This allows for interior mutability in a thread-safe manner (mutual exclusion). It guarantees that only one thread can access the data at any moment. It's typically used alongside Arc<T>.

There are other smart pointers, such as Cell<T>, Weak<T>, and Cow<T>, but these are the primary ones we will focus on. Grasping these will provide you with a robust toolkit for managing memory and data ownership safely and flexibly.

Box<T>: pointing to heap-allocated data

We've discussed smart pointers in general; now let's dive deep into specifics. The most straightforward smart pointer in Rust's standard library is `Box<T>`, commonly referred to as a "box."

Its main purpose is to enable you to store data on the heap rather than the stack, ensuring clear ownership and automatic deallocation.

Why use Box<T>?

To appreciate `Box<T>`, it's helpful to quickly recall the difference between the stack and the heap:

- **Stack**: Memory allocation is extremely fast. Data stored on the stack must have a known, fixed size at compile time. Local variables in functions usually reside on the stack. When a function finishes, its stack frame is removed, and the memory is reclaimed immediately.
- **Heap**: Memory allocation here is more flexible but comes with additional overhead. You request a certain amount of memory from the operating system, which finds a suitable location. This is where you store data whose size might not be known at compile time or data that needs to outlast the function that created it. Properly managing heap memory is crucial to avoid memory leaks or accessing deallocated memory.

So, why would you explicitly want to use a `Box<T>` to allocate something on the heap? Here are a few key reasons:

- **Storing large amounts of data**: When working with data on the stack, such as small structs of primitive types, Rust copies it fully when passing to functions or assigning. This is fast for small data but slow for large structures, such as those with massive arrays. Passing such structs duplicates the entire array, causing delays. Using a `Box<T>` stores data on the heap, with only a small pointer on the stack. Moving the `Box<T>` transfers just the pointer, not the data, making large data ownership transfers quick because the data stays on the heap.
- **Transferring ownership of data with unknown size at compile time:** Sometimes, you want a type to own some data, but the exact size of that data isn't known at compile time (e.g., when dealing with `trait` objects, which we'll discuss later). `Box<T>` can own this data on the heap, and the Box itself has a known size: it's just a pointer.
- **Recursive types:** For types that may include themselves in their own definition (such as nodes in a tree or a linked list), Rust needs a way to guarantee that the type has a finite size. `Box<T>` is critical in this scenario, as we'll see.

Box<T> offers the simplest method for achieving heap allocation with clear, single ownership. When the Box<T> goes out of scope, the memory it points to on the heap is automatically deallocated: no manual free calls are necessary!

Creating and using a Box<T>

Creating a Box<T> is straightforward using Box::new(value):

```
// It's standard practice to define structs outside the main function.
#[derive(Debug)]
struct Point {
    x: f64,
    y: f64,
}

fn main() {
    // Create a Box<i32> to store an integer on the heap.
    let heap_int = Box::new(5);
    println!("Value in a Box: {}", heap_int);

    // Create a Box<Point> to store a struct on the heap.
    let heap_point = Box::new(Point { x: 10.0, y: 20.5 });
    println!("Struct in a Box: {:?}", heap_point);

    // Explicitly dereference the Box to access the value.
    let value_from_box = *heap_int;
    println!("Explicitly dereferenced value: {}", value_from_box);

    // Access a field directly thanks to automatic dereferencing (Deref
coercion).
    println!("Accessing field via deref coercion: heap_point.x = {}",
heap_point.x);

    // When `heap_int` and `heap_point` go out of scope here, the memory
they manage
    // on the heap is automatically freed via the Drop trait.
}
```

- `Box::new(value)` takes a value, moves it to the heap, and returns a Box that "points" to this heap-allocated data.
- The `Box<T>` itself (the pointer) resides on the stack (unless it's part of another heap-allocated structure).
- You can access the data "inside" the box using the dereference operator *, such as `*heap_int`.
- Conveniently, Rust often performs automatic dereferencing (a feature called "Deref coercion" that we'll touch on more when we discuss the `Deref` trait). This is why you can call methods or access fields directly on a `Box<StructType>` such as `heap_point.x` without explicitly writing `(*heap_point).x`. `println!` also often handles dereferencing for you.
- It's important to note that `Box<T>` follows Rust's standard borrowing rules for mutability. It does not provide "interior mutability" like other smart pointers we'll see later. To get mutable access to the data inside the box, the `Box<T>` variable itself must be declared as `mut`.
- Crucially, `Box<T>` implements the `Drop` trait. When a `Box<T>` instance goes out of scope (e.g., at the end of the `main` function in the example), its `drop` method is called, which deallocates the heap memory it was managing. This ensures no memory leaks automatically.

Key use case: enabling recursive data structures

One of the key functions of `Box<T>` is facilitating the creation of recursive types. A recursive type is one in which a value can include another value of the same type as part of its definition. Common examples are linked lists and trees.

When attempting to define such a type directly in Rust, the compiler raises an error, as it cannot determine the size of the type at compile time. If a node contains another node, which also contains another node, this leads to an infinite size!

`Box<T>` addresses this by adding a layer of indirection. Rather than storing the recursive part directly, you store a Box that references the recursive component. A `Box<T>`, which is the pointer itself, always has a fixed size known at compile time, regardless of the size of `T`. This prevents the cycle of infinite size.

Now, let's create a simple recursive "expression" tree to represent basic arithmetic:

```
use std::fmt;

// A recursive enum representing a simple arithmetic expression.
// `Box<T>` is used to give the recursive variants a known size.
```

```
#[derive(Debug)]
enum Expression {
    Value(i32),
    Add(Box<Expression>, Box<Expression>),
    Multiply(Box<Expression>, Box<Expression>),
    Negate(Box<Expression>),
}

// A custom error type for our evaluation function.
#[derive(Debug)]
pub enum EvaluationError {
    Overflow,
}

// Implement Display for user-friendly error messages.
impl fmt::Display for EvaluationError {
    fn fmt(&self, f: &mut fmt::Formatter) -> fmt::Result {
        match self {
            EvaluationError::Overflow => write!(f, "Arithmetic overflow
occurred during evaluation"),
        }
    }
}

// Helper functions for building the expression tree ergonomically.
fn val(v: i32) -> Box<Expression> {
    Box::new(Expression::Value(v))
}
fn add(left: Box<Expression>, right: Box<Expression>) -> Box<Expression> {
    Box::new(Expression::Add(left, right))
}
fn multiply(left: Box<Expression>, right: Box<Expression>) ->
Box<Expression> {
    Box::new(Expression::Multiply(left, right))
}
fn negate(expr: Box<Expression>) -> Box<Expression> {
    Box::new(Expression::Negate(expr))
}
```

```
// A robust, recursive function to evaluate the expression tree.
// It now returns a Result to handle potential overflows.
fn evaluate(expr: &Expression) -> Result<i32, EvaluationError> {
    match expr {
        Expression::Value(v) => Ok(*v),
        Expression::Add(left, right) => {
            // Recursively evaluate sub-expressions, propagating errors
with `?`.
            let left_val = evaluate(left)?;
            let right_val = evaluate(right)?;
            // Use checked_add, which returns an Option, then convert to
Result.
            left_val.checked_add(right_val).ok_
or(EvaluationError::Overflow)
        }
        Expression::Multiply(left, right) => {
            let left_val = evaluate(left)?;
            let right_val = evaluate(right)?;
            // Use checked_mul for safe multiplication.
            left_val.checked_mul(right_val).ok_
or(EvaluationError::Overflow)
        }
        Expression::Negate(inner_expr) => {
            let val = evaluate(inner_expr)?;
            // Use checked_neg for safe negation.
            val.checked_neg().ok_or(EvaluationError::Overflow)
        }
    }
}

fn main() {
    // Build an expression for: (5 + 10) * -2
    let expr = multiply(
        add(val(5), val(10)),
        negate(val(2)),
    );
    println!("--- Expression 1: (5 + 10) * -2 ---");
```

```
    match evaluate(&expr) {
        Ok(result) => println!("Evaluated: {}", result), // Expected: -30
        Err(e) => println!("Error: {}", e),
    }

    // Build an expression for: -(3 + (4 * 5))
    let expr2 = negate(
        add(
            val(3),
            multiply(val(4), val(5)),
        )
    );
    println!("\n--- Expression 2: -(3 + (4 * 5)) ---");
    match evaluate(&expr2) {
        Ok(result) => println!("Evaluated: {}", result), // Expected: -23
        Err(e) => println!("Error: {}", e),
    }

    // Build an expression designed to overflow an i32
    let overflow_expr = add(val(i32::MAX), val(1));
    println!("\n--- Expression 3: i32::MAX + 1 (Overflow Test) ---");
    match evaluate(&overflow_expr) {
        Ok(result) => println!("Evaluated: {}", result),
        Err(e) => println!("Correctly caught error: {}", e), // Expected:
Arithmetic overflow...
    }
}
```

This example showcases how `Box<T>` is essential for defining recursive data structures such as our `Expression` enum.

- **Breaking the infinite loop**: Our `Expression` is recursive because variants such as `Add`, `Multiply`, and `Negate` contain other expressions. If we had defined them as `Add(Expression, Expression)`, the compiler would be unable to determine the size of an `Expression` at compile time, leading to an error. By using `Box<Expression>`, we are instead storing a smart pointer on the stack, which has a known, fixed size. This pointer points to the next `Expression` allocated on the heap, breaking the infinite sizing loop and allowing Rust to compile the code.

- **Robust evaluation with Result**: The `evaluate` function has been made more robust to handle potential arithmetic overflows, which would cause a panic in a release build.
    - It now returns `Result<i32, EvaluationError>`, explicitly stating that the operation can fail.
    - Instead of using standard operators such as + and *, it uses **checked arithmetic** methods such as `.checked_add()`. These methods do not panic on overflow; they return an `Option (Some(value)` on success or `None` on failure.
    - The `.ok_or(EvaluationError::Overflow)?` pattern is used to bridge this. `.ok_or()` converts the Option into a Result, turning `None` into the `Err` we specify. The ? operator then propagates this error up if it occurs.
- **Handling in main**: The `main` function now uses `match` to handle the Result returned by `evaluate`, allowing it to gracefully print either the successful result or the specific overflow error, as demonstrated by the `overflow_expr` test case.

Using `Box<T>` in this way is a basic building block for creating tree or list structures in Rust. Pairing it with `Result` helps you write safer and more reliable code, making your programs stronger and more dependable.

When to choose Box<T>: performance and ownership

So, when should `Box<T>` be your go-to smart pointer?

- **Single ownership of the heap**: `Box<T>` enforces a single owner for the heap-allocated data it controls. The data is also deallocated when `Box<T>` is dropped. Moving the `Box<T>` transfers ownership of the heap data accordingly. This aligns seamlessly with Rust's fundamental ownership principles.
- **Known size indirection**: As noted, this is crucial for recursive types. It also applies to trait objects (such as `Box<dyn MyTrait>`) since the size of the specific type implementing the trait is not determined at compile time, but Box provides a known size.
- **Efficiently transferring large data**: When dealing with a large struct and needing to transfer ownership to another function or store it in a collection, boxing it (`Box<MyLargeStruct>`) means that only the pointer is transferred, rather than the entire struct, enhancing efficiency.

Performance considerations:

- `Box<T>` entails a heap allocation, typically slower than stack allocation.
- Accessing data via `Box<T>` requires a single pointer dereference.
- Nonetheless, `Box<T>` does not introduce any additional runtime overhead aside from heap allocation/deallocation and pointer indirection. With no reference counting or locking mechanisms, it serves as a lightweight heap pointer when compared to `Rc<T>` or `Arc<T>`.

`Box<T>` serves as the essential tool for managing heap data with definitive ownership and automatic deallocation.

It is straightforward and efficient, playing a crucial role in the implementation of certain data structures in Rust.

Sharing data safely: Rc<T> and Arc<T>

With `Box<T>`, we handle heap data with a single owner that releases data when out of scope. But for shared, long-term access, reference-counting smart pointers are used: `Rc<T>` for single-threaded, and `Arc<T>` for multi-threaded environments.

The concept of shared ownership

In Rust, the main ownership rule is that each value can only have one owner. This helps us avoid many bugs, but sometimes it can feel a bit restrictive. For instance, imagine multiple data structures need to access the same configuration, or several nodes in a graph want to reference a common resource.

Using `Box<T>`, only one structure can own the data, which means others have to borrow it. This might not work well if their lifetimes are complex or if they need to "co-own" the resource together.

That's where reference counting comes in. It's a helpful technique that lets a piece of data have several "owners," or more accurately, multiple references that keep it alive. A smart pointer keeps track of how many references are pointing to the data. When a new reference is made, the count goes up, and when a reference is dropped or goes out of scope, the count goes down. The data is only cleaned up when the count hits zero. This approach makes it easier to share data widely without putting all the responsibility on a single owner.

Rc<T>: reference counting for single-threaded scenarios

The `Rc<T>` smart pointer, standing for Reference Counted, provides Rust with a mechanism for shared ownership in single-threaded environments. It monitors the number of references to a heap value, ensuring that the value is only deallocated when no references remain.

It's helpful to keep in mind that `Rc<T>` is designed mainly for single-threaded situations. Since it doesn't use atomic operations for updating its reference count, it tends to be faster than its thread-safe counterpart. But, it's important to remember that sharing or sending `Rc<T>` between threads isn't safe.

Creating Rc<T> instances and cloning references

First, you instantiate an `Rc<T>` with `Rc::new(value)`.

To generate more references that share ownership, invoke the `clone()` method on an existing `Rc<T>`. Importantly, `Rc::clone(&rc_instance)` doesn't execute a deep copy of the data `T` itself; rather, it merely generates another pointer to the same heap-allocated data while increasing the internal reference count.

```
use std::rc::Rc;

#[derive(Debug)]
struct SharedConfig {
    version: String,
    api_key: String,
}
struct ServiceA {
    id: u32,
    config: Rc<SharedConfig>,
}
struct ServiceB {
    name: String,
    config: Rc<SharedConfig>,
}

fn main() {
    // Create the shared configuration data wrapped in an Rc.
    let shared_config = Rc::new(SharedConfig {
        version: "v1.2.3".to_string(),
```

```
        api_key: "ABC123XYZ789".to_string(),
    });
    println!("Initial strong count: {}", Rc::strong_count(&shared_
config));
    // Create clones of the Rc to share ownership.
    // This only increments the reference count; it does not deep copy the
data.
    let service_a = ServiceA {
        id: 101,
        config: Rc::clone(&shared_config),
    };
    println!("After ServiceA created: strong count = {}", Rc::strong_
count(&shared_config));
    let service_b = ServiceB {
        name: "LoggerService".to_string(),
        config: Rc::clone(&shared_config),
    };
    println!("After ServiceB created: strong count = {}", Rc::strong_
count(&shared_config));
    println!("---");
    println!("Service A accesses config version: {}", service_a.config.
version);
    println!("Service B accesses API key: {}", service_b.config.api_key);
    println!("---");

    // Explicitly drop service_a to see the reference count decrease.
    drop(service_a);
    println!("After ServiceA is dropped: strong count = {}", Rc::strong_
count(&shared_config)); // Output: 2
    // Explicitly drop service_b.
    drop(service_b);
    println!("After ServiceB is dropped: strong count = {}", Rc::strong_
count(&shared_config)); // Output: 1
    // The final Rc (`shared_config`) will be dropped at the end of main's
scope.
    // At that point, the count will become 0, and the SharedConfig data
will be deallocated.
}
```

```
    Finished `dev` profile [unoptimized + debuginfo] target(s) in 0.44s
     Running `target/debug/rusttesting`
Initial strong count: 1
After ServiceA created: strong count = 2
After ServiceB created: strong count = 3
---
Service A accesses config version: v1.2.3
Service B accesses API key: ABC123XYZ789
---
After ServiceA is dropped: strong count = 2
After ServiceB is dropped: strong count = 1
francesco@Francesco-PC:~/workspace/rusttesting$
```

Figure 11.1: Output for the reference counting Smart pointer example

- We create a `SharedConfig` struct for use by various services.
- `Rc::new()` initializes our `SharedConfig` instance, placing it on the heap and setting its reference count to 1.
- `Rc::clone(&rc_pointer)` is crucial. It does not duplicate the `SharedConfig` data; instead, it produces a new `Rc` pointer to the same data while increasing the reference count. This operation is inexpensive.
- `Rc::strong_count(&rc_pointer)` indicates how many `Rc` instances (strong references) are currently referencing the data.
- When an `Rc<SharedConfig>` instance (such as `service_a.config`, `service_b.config`, or `shared_config_data` itself) exits its scope, its destructor executes, reducing the reference count.
- The `SharedConfig` data on the heap is deallocated only when the strong reference count reaches zero.

Arc<T>: atomic reference counting for multithreading

For now, we will focus on smart pointers. If you need to know more about concurrency, go to the next chapter and come back here later!

`Rc<T>` works well for single-threaded tasks, but if you're thinking about sharing data across multiple threads, things get trickier. You can't simply transfer an `Rc<T>` to another thread because its internal count isn't updated atomically, which can cause issues such as data races or memory corruption if multiple threads attempt to clone it simultaneously.

That's where `Arc<T>` comes in. It's like `Rc<T>` but with a safety net.

It utilizes atomic operations to maintain an accurate reference count, even when multiple threads are involved, making it the ideal choice for safe, shared ownership in concurrent programs.

Using Arc<T> to share data across threads

The API for `Arc<T>` is virtually identical to `Rc<T>`: you use `Arc::new(value)` to create one and `Arc::clone(&arc_instance)` to get another reference-counted pointer to the same data.

```
use std::sync::Arc;
use std::thread;
use std::time::Duration;
#[derive(Debug)]
struct SharedResource {
    id: u32,
    data: String,
}

fn main() {
    // Create shared data wrapped in an Arc
    let shared_resource_main = Arc::new(SharedResource {
        id: 1001,
        data: "This is some important data shared across threads.".to_
string(),
    });

    println!("Main thread: Initial strong count = {}", Arc::strong_
count(&shared_resource_main)); // Output: 1

    let mut thread_handles = vec![];

    for i in 0..3 { // Spawn 3 threads
        // Clone the Arc for each thread. This is crucial.
        // The cloned Arc is moved into the thread's closure.
        let shared_resource_for_thread = Arc::clone(&shared_resource_
main);
        println!("Main thread: Count before spawning thread {} = {}", i,
Arc::strong_count(&shared_resource_main));

        let handle = thread::spawn(move || {
```

```
            // This thread now has its own Arc pointing to the shared data
            println!("Thread {}: Started. Accessing resource ID: {}, Data: 
'{}'. Strong count here: {}",
                     i,
                     shared_resource_for_thread.id,
                     shared_resource_for_thread.data,
                     Arc::strong_count(&shared_resource_for_thread) // 
Count might be higher due to other clones
            );
            thread::sleep(Duration::from_millis(50)); // Simulate some 
work
            println!("Thread {}: Finished.", i);
            // When shared_resource_for_thread goes out of scope here, the 
count is decremented.
        });
        thread_handles.push(handle);
    }

    // The main thread still has its reference
    println!("Main thread: After spawning threads, strong count = {}", 
Arc::strong_count(&shared_resource_main));
    println!("Main thread: Resource data: {}", shared_resource_main.data);

    // Wait for all threads to complete
    for handle in thread_handles {
        handle.join().unwrap();
    }

    println!("Main thread: All threads finished. Final strong count 
(before shared_resource_main drops): {}", Arc::strong_count(&shared_
resource_main)); // Should be 1
    // When shared_resource_main drops, the count goes to 0, and 
SharedResource is deallocated.
}
```

- We create a `SharedResource` wrapped in `Arc::new()`.

- For each new thread we spawn, we first call `Arc::clone(&shared_resource_main)`. This increments the atomic reference count and provides the new thread with its own `Arc` pointer, which is then moved into the thread's closure. This is the standard pattern for sharing data with threads using `Arc`.
- Each thread can safely access the data through its `Arc`.
- When each thread finishes, its `Arc` instance is dropped, and the atomic reference count is decremented.
- The `SharedResource` data is only deallocated when the last `Arc` pointing to it (including the one in the main thread) is dropped.

The "atomic" in Arc<T>

The "atomic" aspect of `Arc<T>` pertains to atomic operations.

These are unique hardware instructions that ensure operations such as incrementing or decrementing the reference count are executed as a single, indivisible step, even when multiple CPUs or cores are attempting to access it simultaneously.

This helps prevent race conditions with the reference count, making `Arc<T>` safe to use across multiple threads, unlike `Rc<T>`. While this thread safety is a great feature, it does come with a slight performance cost compared to `Rc<T>`, because atomic operations are a bit more complex. So, the best approach is to use `Rc<T>` whenever possible and only choose `Arc<T>` when you need to share ownership between different threads.

Reference counting, Drop, and potential cycles

Both `Rc<T>` and `Arc<T>` happily ensure that data gets cleaned up when their strong reference count drops to zero. This smooth process, managed by the `Drop` trait for `Rc<T>` and `Arc<T>`, does a great job at preventing memory leaks. However, sometimes reference counting can lead to memory leaks when there's a reference cycle. This occurs when two or more `Rc<T>` (or `Arc<T>`) instances reference each other in a loop, causing their reference counts to stay high even when they're no longer needed from outside: for example:

- Object A holds an `Rc` to Object B (B's count is at least 1)
- Object B holds an `Rc` to Object A (A's count is at least 1)

So, even if all other references are gone, A and B keep each other's counts at 1, which stops them from being deallocated. This can, unfortunately, cause a memory leak.

How Weak<T> can break cycles

Rust handles reference cycles using weak references through `Weak<T>`, sourced from `std::rc::Weak` for `Rc` and `std::sync::Weak` for `Arc`. A `Weak<T>` serves as a non-owning reference that points to the data without increasing the strong reference count, meaning it cannot keep the data alive by itself.

To access the data through a `Weak<T>`, you need to attempt to "upgrade" it to an `Rc<T>` (or `Arc<T>`). This upgrade returns an `Option<Rc<T>>`: it yields `Some(rc)` if the data still exists (i.e., when its strong count is greater than `0`) or `None` if the data has already been deallocated.

In data structures where cycles can arise, such as graphs or doubly linked lists where a parent references a child and the child references back to the parent, one of the references is typically made "weak" (e.g., the child references the parent using `Weak<T>`) to break the cycle and facilitate proper deallocation.

While we won't explore `Weak<T>` in detail in this introductory chapter, it's important to recognize the potential for reference cycles with `Rc<T>` and `Arc<T>`, along with the fact that `Weak<T>` is the main tool for addressing them. `Rc<T>` and `Arc<T>` are essential when data needs to be accessed from multiple locations, with its lifetime linked to the existence of those access points rather than being confined to a single lexical scope.

Interior mutability: modifying data through shared references

So far, we've been following Rust's fundamental borrowing rule: at compile time, you can either have several immutable references (`&T`) to some data, or just one mutable reference (`&mut T`), but never both at the same time.

However, in some cases, compile-time enforcement may seem too restrictive. What if you want to change data accessed through an immutable reference or modify a value that has been immutably borrowed? This is when the interior mutability pattern becomes useful.

This principle is validated during compile time and is essential for Rust's memory safety.

Nonetheless, there are scenarios in which this compile-time enforcement can seem overly constraining. What if you have a seemingly immutable value externally (you only have an `&T`), but you need to alter some internal component of it?

This is where the **interior mutability** pattern comes into play.

What is interior mutability and why is it needed?

Interior mutability in Rust is a clever design pattern that lets you change data even when there are only immutable references to it. It might seem like it's breaking the rules, but that's not quite the case.

Instead of skipping Rust's safety checks, it moves the enforcement of borrowing rules from compile time to runtime for certain specific types. If these rules are broken at runtime, your program will crash, ensuring safety is still maintained.

Why would you need such a thing? Consider these scenarios:

- **Observer pattern or callbacks**: You might have a list of observers that need to be notified of an event. The list itself may be held within a structure that is otherwise immutable, but the act of notification might involve changing some state within each observer.
- **Caching**: A struct might have a method that performs an expensive computation. You could internally cache the result so that subsequent calls are faster. The method might only take `&self` (an immutable reference), but it needs to write to the internal cache.
- **Data structures with shared ownership**: When using `Rc<T>` to share data, `Rc<T>` only provides immutable access to `T` by default. If you need multiple owners and the ability to mutate the shared data, you'll need interior mutability.

Rust provides a few types in its standard library that enable interior mutability, primarily `Cell<T>` and `RefCell<T>` for single-threaded scenarios, and `Mutex<T>` and `RwLock<T>` for multi-threaded contexts. We'll focus on `RefCell<T>` and `Mutex<T>` as they are commonly used with smart pointers.

RefCell<T>: enforcing borrowing rules at runtime (single-threaded)

The `RefCell<T>` type is perfect for situations where you need to change data inside a single-threaded context. It allows you to get mutable references (`&mut T`) to its data, even if the `RefCell<T>` itself is immutable: for example, when you have an `&RefCell<T>`. Unlike compile-time checks, `RefCell<T>` makes sure Rust's borrowing rules (one mutable reference or multiple immutable ones) are followed at runtime. This check occurs whenever you call the `.borrow()` or `.borrow_mut()` methods, helping you use data safely and flexibly.

If you attempt to borrow in a way that violates these rules, such as calling `.borrow_mut()` while another `borrow` (mutable or immutable) is already active, the call will immediately cause your program to **panic**.

- To acquire an immutable reference, use the `borrow()` method, which returns a smart pointer, `Ref<T>`
- For a mutable reference, the `borrow_mut()` method is called, returning a smart pointer, `RefMut<T>`

If you breach the borrowing rules (e.g., invoking `borrow_mut()` while a `borrow()` is active, or calling `borrow_mut()` multiple times without the previous `RefMut<T>` going out of scope), your program will panic at runtime. This mechanism ensures safety, albeit checked at a different time.

`RefCell<T>` is frequently paired with `Rc<T>` to allow multiple ownership of mutable data. A common pattern is `Rc<RefCell<T>>`.

Using borrow() and borrow_mut()

Let's see an example:

```
use std::cell::RefCell;
use std::rc::Rc;

// A logger that uses interior mutability to track its state.
struct MessageLogger {
    message_count: RefCell<usize>,
    history: RefCell<Vec<String>>,
}

impl MessageLogger {
    fn new() -> Self {
        MessageLogger {
            message_count: RefCell::new(0),
            history: RefCell::new(Vec::new()),
        }
    }

    // This method takes &self but can modify internal state via RefCell.
    fn log(&self, message: &str) {
        let mut count = self.message_count.borrow_mut();
```

```
        *count += 1;

        self.history
            .borrow_mut()
            .push(format!("#{}: {}", *count, message));
    }
    fn get_count(&self) -> usize {
        *self.message_count.borrow()
    }
    fn print_history(&self) {
        println!("--- Log History ---");
        for entry in self.history.borrow().iter() {
            println!("{}", entry);
        }
        println!("-------------------");
    }
}

fn main() {
    // Wrap the MessageLogger in Rc to allow shared ownership.
    let shared_logger: Rc<MessageLogger> = Rc::new(MessageLogger::new());
    // Create multiple references to the same logger instance.
    let logger_clone1 = Rc::clone(&shared_logger);
    let logger_clone2 = Rc::clone(&shared_logger);

    // Log messages from different references.
    // Each call will mutate the same underlying MessageLogger instance.
    shared_logger.log("Main logger event.");
    logger_clone1.log("Event from clone 1.");
    logger_clone2.log("Event from clone 2.");
    // Check the final state from any of the references.
    println!("\nTotal messages logged: {}", shared_logger.get_count());
    shared_logger.print_history();
}
```

Here's the output:

```
Total messages logged: 3
--- Log History ---
#1: Main logger event.
#2: Event from clone 1.
#3: Event from clone 2.
-------------------
```

Figure 11.2: Using borrow() and borrow_mut()

- The `MessageLogger` struct consists of two fields: `message_count` and `history`, with types `RefCell<usize>` and `RefCell<Vec<String>>`, respectively. This indicates that the logger owns these `RefCell` types.
- The `log` method takes an immutable reference to `MessageLogger (&self)`. Despite this, it can call `self.message_count.borrow_mut()` and `self.history.borrow_mut()`, which return `RefMut`, a smart pointer providing mutable access to the `usize` count and `Vec<String>` history within the `RefCell`.
- Borrowing rules are enforced at runtime: If `borrow_mut()` is invoked while another `RefMut` `(mutable borrow)` or `Ref (immutable borrow)` exists for the same `RefCell`, the program will panic.
- If `borrow()` is attempted while a `RefMut` for the same `RefCell` exists, it will also panic.
- The `RefMut` (from `borrow_mut()`) and `Ref` (from `borrow()`) smart pointers automatically release their borrow when they exit their scope. This is essential for permitting subsequent borrows.
- The example with `Rc<MessageLogger>` illustrates a typical use case: `Rc<RefCell<T>>` enables multiple `Rc` pointers (shared ownership) to reference a `RefCell`, allowing for interior mutability of the data `T`.

Runtime panics on borrow rule violations

It's important to remember that `RefCell<T>` delays borrow checking until runtime. If used incorrectly, your program won't just fail to compile; it will panic when the problematic `borrow()` or `borrow_mut()` call is executed.

This runtime check is the trade-off for the flexibility of `RefCell<T>`. Although it still maintains safety by preventing data races in single-threaded code through panics, errors are caught later than with compile-time checks.

Mutex<T>: ensuring exclusive access in concurrent code

Imagine a `Mutex<T>` as a cozy public restroom with a single stall that has a lock on the door. The data `T` is the restroom itself, and the different threads are the people waiting happily outside. Before a thread can access the data, it simply needs to "acquire the lock" by calling `.lock()`, just like locking the stall door for privacy. While the lock is held, everyone else who tries to get in waits patiently in line. When the thread is done, the lock is released automatically as the "guard" object goes out of scope, much like someone unlocking the door when they leave and giving the next person a turn.

When you need interior mutability in a multi-threaded context, `RefCell<T>` is unsuitable because its runtime checks are not thread-safe. For this purpose, Rust provides `Mutex<T>`, which stands for Mutual Exclusion.

A `Mutex<T>` ensures that only one thread can access the data `T` at any given time.

Locking and unlocking with lock()

To access the data within a `Mutex<T>`, a thread must first "acquire the lock" by invoking the `lock()` method.

- The `lock()` method attempts to obtain the lock. If no other thread currently holds it, the current thread secures the `lock` and `lock()` returns a `LockResult<MutexGuard<T>>`.
- A `MutexGuard<T>` functions as a smart pointer that implements `Deref` and `DerefMut`, enabling mutable access to the data of type `T`.
- If another thread is already holding the lock, the `lock()` call will block the current thread until the lock becomes free.
- Once the `MutexGuard<T>` goes out of scope, the lock is automatically released, allowing other waiting threads to acquire it. This RAII pattern is quite handy and helps avoid deadlocks that may occur from forgetting to release a lock.

The `LockResult` returned by `lock()` is a Result because acquiring a lock can fail if the mutex is "poisoned." A mutex is considered poisoned if a thread panics while it is holding the lock.

For simplicity, many examples often use `unwrap()` on the result of `lock()`, which causes the current thread to panic if the mutex is poisoned. In more robust applications, you might want to handle a poisoned mutex more gracefully.

Combining Arc<T> and Mutex<T> for shared mutable state

Because `Mutex<T>` manages data access among multiple threads, it frequently needs to be shared among them.

The typical approach is to encapsulate the `Mutex<T>` within an `Arc<T>`, resulting in an `Arc<Mutex<T>>`.

The `Arc` facilitates the shared ownership of the mutex, while the mutex ensures synchronized access to the underlying data.

```
use std::sync::{Arc, Mutex};
use std::thread;
use std::time::Duration;

struct GlobalCounter {
    count: Arc<Mutex<u32>>, // Shared, mutable counter
}

impl GlobalCounter {
    fn new() -> Self {
        GlobalCounter { count: Arc::new(Mutex::new(0)) }
    }

    fn increment(&self) {
        // Acquire the lock. This blocks if another thread has the lock.
        // unwrap() here will panic if the mutex is poisoned.
        let mut num_guard = self.count.lock().unwrap();
        *num_guard += 1; // Mutate the data through the MutexGuard
        // Lock is released when num_guard goes out of scope
    }

    fn get_value(&self) -> u32 {
        *self.count.lock().unwrap() // Lock, get value, unlock
    }
}

fn main() {
```

```
    let global_counter = GlobalCounter::new();
    let mut handles = vec![];

    println!("Initial count: {}", global_counter.get_value()); // Output:
0

    // Spawn multiple threads that all increment the same counter
    for i in 0..5 {
        // Clone the Arc to give ownership to the new thread
        let counter_clone = Arc::clone(&global_counter.count);

        let handle = thread::spawn(move || {
            // This is a different way to use the Arc<Mutex<T>> directly
            // without the GlobalCounter struct, for illustration.
            for _ in 0..100 {
                let mut num = counter_clone.lock().unwrap();
                *num += 1;
                // Slight delay to make interleaving more likely
                thread::sleep(Duration::from_micros(1));
            }
            println!("Thread {} finished incrementing.", i);
        });
        handles.push(handle);
    }

    // Using the methods on our GlobalCounter struct from the main thread
    // (This is a bit contrived here as the struct methods would also
contend for the same lock
    //  if called concurrently with the threads above, but demonstrates
method usage)
    global_counter.increment(); // Main thread also increments

    // Wait for all spawned threads to finish
    for handle in handles {
        handle.join().unwrap();
    }
```

```
    println!("Final count: {}", global_counter.get_value()); // Expected:
5 * 100 + 1 = 501
}
```

```
Initial count: 0
Thread 1 finished incrementing.
Thread 3 finished incrementing.
Thread 4 finished incrementing.
Thread 0 finished incrementing.
Thread 2 finished incrementing.
Final count: 501
```

Figure 11.3: Combining Arc<T> and Mutex<T> for shared mutable state

Arc::new(Mutex::new(0)) creates a counter secured by a mutex and encapsulates it in an Arc for sharing across threads.

- Each thread uses Arc::clone(&global_counter.count) to generate a new Arc pointer to the same mutex, which is then transferred into the thread.
- Inside each thread, counter_clone.lock().unwrap() attempts to lock the mutex. At any time, only one thread can hold the lock. Once successful, the MutexGuard (referred to as num) allows for mutable access (*num += 1).
- When num (MutexGuard) goes out of scope at the end of the critical section, the lock is automatically released.
- This ensures that, although multiple threads are trying to increment count, these increments happen sequentially concerning the lock, thereby avoiding data races.

RefCell<T> and Mutex<T> (as well as RwLock<T>, which permits multiple readers or a single writer) are effective resources when Rust's compile-time borrow checking presents excessive limitations on your design. However, they do come with their own challenges (such as the risk of runtime panic in RefCell and the potential for blocking or deadlock in Mutex).

Use them judiciously where their unique functionalities are necessary.

RwLock for read-mostly data

While Mutex<T> is a great general-purpose tool for ensuring exclusive access, it can sometimes be too restrictive.

For data that is read very frequently by many threads but only written to occasionally (like a shared configuration cache), Rust provides a more specialized smart pointer: `RwLock<T>` (Read-Write Lock). Unlike a mutex, which always enforces a single lock, `RwLock<T>` allows for two kinds of locks: a shared read lock via its `.read()` method, which multiple threads can hold simultaneously, and an exclusive write lock via its `.write()` method, which only one thread can hold.

This "multiple readers or one writer" policy can significantly improve performance in read-heavy concurrent scenarios by allowing readers to proceed in parallel.

Here is a short example:

```
use std::sync::{Arc, RwLock};
use std::thread;

fn main() {
    // A shared configuration that many threads will read, but one will
update.
    let config = Arc::new(RwLock::new("Initial Config".to_string()));

    let mut handles = vec![];

    // --- Spawn multiple READER threads ---
    for i in 0..5 {
        let config_clone = Arc::clone(&config);
        handles.push(thread::spawn(move || {
            // Acquire a read lock. Multiple threads can hold this at the
same time.
            let config_guard = config_clone.read().unwrap();
            println!("Reader {}: sees config: '{}'", i, *config_guard);
        }));
    }

    // --- Spawn one WRITER thread ---
    let config_clone = Arc::clone(&config);
    handles.push(thread::spawn(move || {
        // Simulate some work before writing
        thread::sleep(std::time::Duration::from_millis(10));

        // Acquire a write lock. This will wait until all readers are
```

```
done.
        // Once held, no new readers or writers can get a lock.
        let mut config_guard = config_clone.write().unwrap();
        *config_guard = "Updated Config".to_string();
        println!("--- Writer: Updated config! ---");
    }));

    // Wait for all threads to finish
    for handle in handles {
        handle.join().unwrap();
    }

    println!("\nFinal config value: '{}'", *config.read().unwrap());
}
```

```
Reader 0: sees config: 'Initial Config'
Reader 1: sees config: 'Initial Config'
Reader 2: sees config: 'Initial Config'
Reader 3: sees config: 'Initial Config'
Reader 4: sees config: 'Initial Config'
--- Writer: Updated config! ---
```

Figure 11.4: RwLock for read-mostly data

Working effectively with smart pointers

Alright, that was a solid introduction.

Now that we've become familiar with the key smart pointers `Box<T>`, `Rc<T>`, `Arc<T>`, `RefCell<T>`, and `Mutex<T>`, let's explore some common patterns and interactions.

Smart pointers and method calls (the Deref trait in action)

In earlier examples, you may have noticed that smart pointers allow you to call methods directly, similar to how you would on the contained value (e.g., `my_box.some_method()` rather than `(*my_box).some_method()`).

This is made possible by the Deref trait and a feature known as "Deref coercion." The Deref trait is defined in the standard library as follows (simplified):

```
trait Deref {
    type Target: ?Sized; // The type that this pointer dereferences to
    fn deref(&self) -> &Self::Target;
}
```

A type that implements the Deref trait can be dereferenced with the * operator (for example, *my_box). More significantly for method invocations, if you possess a &MySmartPointer<T>, and MySmartPointer<T> implements Deref<Target = T>, Rust can automatically convert &MySmartPointer<T> to &T when attempting to invoke a method that exists solely on T.

This process is known as Deref coercion. This can occur multiple times if a type dereferences to another type that also utilizes Deref.

Additionally, there's a DerefMut trait for smart pointers that allow for mutable dereferencing (such as Box<T> and RefMut<T> from RefCell):

```
trait DerefMut: Deref {
    fn deref_mut(&mut self) -> &mut Self::Target;
}
```

This enables &mut MySmartPointer<T> to convert to &mut T. Most smart pointers we have covered (Box, Rc, Arc, Ref, RefMut, MutexGuard) implement Deref (and DerefMut where applicable).

```
struct MyValue {
    data: i32,
}

impl MyValue {
    fn display(&self) {
        println!("MyValue data: {}", self.data);
    }
}

fn main() {
    let b = Box::new(MyValue { data: 42 });
    let rc_val = std::rc::Rc::new(MyValue { data: 100 });
```

```
    // Calling display() on Box<MyValue>
    // 1. `b` is `Box<MyValue>`. `&b` is `&Box<MyValue>`.
    // 2. `Box<MyValue>` implements `Deref<Target = MyValue>`.
    // 3. So, `&Box<MyValue>` coerces to `&MyValue`.
    // 4. `display()` is called on `&MyValue`.
    b.display(); // Works due to deref coercion

    // Similarly for Rc<MyValue>
    rc_val.display(); // Works

    // Explicit dereference is also possible, but often not needed for
method calls
    (*b).display();
    (*rc_val).display();

    // With a String (which Box<String> and Rc<String> dereference to
&str)
    let name_box = Box::new("Rustacean".to_string());
    // String -> &str, so we can call &str methods
    println!("Is '{}' empty? {}", name_box, name_box.is_empty()); // .is_
empty() is a &str method

    // Deref coercion also works with function arguments
    fn print_str_slice(s: &str) {
        println!("Slice: {}", s);
    }
    print_str_slice(&name_box); // &Box<String> -> &String -> &str
}
```

```
     Running `target/debug/rusttesting`
MyValue data: 42
MyValue data: 100
MyValue data: 42
MyValue data: 100
Is 'Rustacean' empty? false
Slice: Rustacean
```

Figure 11.5: The Deref trait in action

Deref coercion significantly enhances the ergonomics of working with smart pointers. Typically, you don't have to explicitly dereference them (*smart_ptr) when invoking a method on the underlying type. Rust automates this process for you if the smart pointer supports Deref (and DerefMut for mutable methods).

This feature is applicable to Box<T>, Rc<T>, Arc<T>, and the guard types obtained through RefCell::borrow(), RefCell::borrow_mut(), and Mutex::lock().

Implementing methods on structs that own smart pointers

It's typical for your structs to manage data using smart pointers.

You can certainly create methods within these structs that work with the data contained in the smart pointer.

```
#[derive(Debug)]
struct ImportantData {
    id: u32,
    payload: String,
}

// This struct owns an ImportantData instance on the heap
struct DataOwner {
    name: String,
    // Box<T> is good when the struct needs to own T and T is large,
    // or T's size is unknown (like a trait object).
    data_ptr: Option<Box<ImportantData>>,
}

impl DataOwner {
    fn new(name: &str) -> Self {
        DataOwner {
            name: name.to_string(),
            data_ptr: None,
        }
    }

    fn initialize_data(&mut self, id: u32, payload: &str) {
        self.data_ptr = Some(Box::new(ImportantData {
            id,
```

```
            payload: payload.to_string(),
        }));
        println!("{} initialized data.", self.name);
    }

    fn update_payload(&mut self, new_payload: &str) {
        // self.data_ptr is an Option<Box<ImportantData>>
        // .as_mut() gives Option<&mut Box<ImportantData>>
        // .map() operates on the &mut Box if Some
        if let Some(boxed_data_mut_ref) = self.data_ptr.as_mut() {
            // boxed_data_mut_ref is &mut Box<ImportantData>
            // We can call methods on ImportantData thanks to DerefMut on
Box
            // or directly assign to fields if they are public.
            // Here, `payload` is public on `ImportantData`.
            boxed_data_mut_ref.payload = new_payload.to_string();
            println!("{} updated payload for ID {}.", self.name, boxed_
data_mut_ref.id);
        } else {
            println!("{} has no data to update.", self.name);
        }
    }

    fn display_data(&self) {
        // self.data_ptr is an Option<Box<ImportantData>>
        // .as_ref() gives Option<&Box<ImportantData>>
        if let Some(boxed_data_ref) = self.data_ptr.as_ref() {
            // boxed_data_ref is &Box<ImportantData>
            // We can access fields of ImportantData thanks to Deref on
Box
            println!("{}'s Data [ID: {}]: {}", self.name, boxed_data_ref.
id, boxed_data_ref.payload);
        } else {
```

```
            println!("{} has no data to display.", self.name);
        }
    }
}

fn main() {
    let mut owner1 = DataOwner::new("OwnerAlpha");
    owner1.display_data(); // No data

    owner1.initialize_data(101, "Initial crucial data");
    owner1.display_data();

    owner1.update_payload("Updated important information");
    owner1.display_data();
}
```

```
OwnerAlpha has no data to display.
OwnerAlpha initialized data.
OwnerAlpha's Data [ID: 101]: Initial crucial data
OwnerAlpha updated payload for ID 101.
OwnerAlpha's Data [ID: 101]: Updated important information
```

Figure 11.6: Implementing methods on structs that own smart pointers

- The `DataOwner` struct contains `ImportantData` within an `Option<Box>`.
- The `initialize_data` function allocates `ImportantData` on the heap and assigns the Box to `data_ptr`.
- The `update_payload` function requires mutable access. By using `self.data_ptr.as_mut()`, we obtain `Option<&mut Box>`. When it is `Some`, we retrieve `&mut Box`, and thanks to `DerefMut`, we can treat it as `&mut ImportantData` to update its payload.
- The `display_data` function needs immutable access. Utilizing `self.data_ptr.as_ref()` provides `Option<&Box>`. If it is `Some`, we get `&Box`, which `Deref` enables us to treat as `&ImportantData` to read its fields.

Combining smart pointers for complex scenarios

Rust's smart pointers can be combined to create complex ownership and mutability patterns. Two of the most potent and commonly used combinations are as follows:

- `Rc<RefCell<T>>`: This combination enables multiple owners (through `Rc<T>`) and also allows for interior mutability (using `RefCell<T>`) in a single-threaded environment
    - `Rc` manages shared ownership and reference counting
    - `RefCell` within `Rc` grants any `Rc` holder mutable access to `T` (with runtime borrow checking)
- `Arc<Mutex<T>>` (or `Arc<RwLock<T>>`): This serves as the thread-safe counterpart for shared, mutable data
    - `Arc` ensures thread-safe shared ownership
    - Mutex (or `RwLock`) within the `Arc` enables synchronized, mutable access to `T` across multiple threads

Now, let's examine an instance of `Rc<RefCell<T>>` in which multiple "observers" need to react to updates in a common subject.

These notifications may also require the observers to modify their own internal states, thus possibly necessitating interior mutability for them as well.

```
use std::rc::Rc;
use std::cell::RefCell;

fn main() {
    // 1. Create a shared, mutable list.
    //    RefCell allows mutation. Rc allows multiple owners.
    let shared_data = Rc::new(RefCell::new(Vec::new()));

    // 2. Create multiple owners (clones of the pointer, not the data).
    let owner1 = Rc::clone(&shared_data);
    let owner2 = Rc::clone(&shared_data);

    // 3. Mutate the data via the first owner.
    //    We use .borrow_mut() to get write access.
    owner1.borrow_mut().push("Data from Owner 1".to_string());
```

```
    // 4. Mutate the SAME data via the second owner.
    owner2.borrow_mut().push("Data from Owner 2".to_string());

    // 5. Read the data from the original owner.
    //    We use .borrow() to get read access.
    println!("Final data: {:?}", shared_data.borrow());
    // Output: ["Data from Owner 1", "Data from Owner 2"]
}
```

```
User 1 added. List: ["Hello from user 1"]
User 2 added. List: ["Hello from user 1", "User 2 was here"]
Main sees list: ["Hello from user 1", "User 2 was here"]
```

Figure 11.7: Combining smart pointers for complex scenarios

- Creating an empty vector with `Rc::new(RefCell::new(Vec::new()))` gives ownership to an `Rc`, allowing multiple owners, while being wrapped in a `RefCell` to enable mutation through an immutable `Rc` path.
- Both `list_user1` and `list_user2` receive `Rc` clones that reference the same `RefCell<Vec<String>>`.
- The `list_user1.borrow_mut().push(...)` expression acquires a mutable reference to the Vec (through the `RefCell` runtime checking) and updates it.
- Similarly, `list_user2.borrow_mut().push(...)` performs the same action. Since both `Rc` refer to the same `RefCell`, which in turn references the same Vec in heap memory, changes made via one `Rc` are observable by the others. This approach is crucial for many single-threaded situations requiring shared mutable state, such as GUI programming or managing graph-like structures.

Smart pointers and ownership transfer

Let's briefly summarize how various smart pointers function within Rust's ownership system, especially in relation to transfer.

- **Box<T> implies unique ownership**: When you have a `Box<T>`, it's the sole owner of the `T` on the heap.

  ```
  let b1 = Box::new(5);
  let b2 = b1; // Ownership of the Box (and the heap data 5) MOVES
  from b1 to b2.
  ```

```
// println!("{}", b1); // Error! b1 was moved.
println!("{}", b2); // Ok
```

- **Rc<T> and Arc<T> enable shared ownership:** Calling `clone()` on an `Rc<T>` or `Arc<T>` does *not* move ownership of the underlying data. Instead, it creates a new pointer to the same data and increments the reference count. The original `Rc`/`Arc` and the cloned one now co-own the data.

```
use std::rc::Rc;
let rc1 = Rc::new("hello".to_string());
let rc2 = Rc::clone(&rc1); // rc1 and rc2 now both point to "hello"
                           // Ownership of "hello" is shared.
println!("rc1: {}, rc2: {}", rc1, rc2); // Both are valid.
println!("Strong count: {}", Rc::strong_count(&rc1)); // Will be 2
```

It's very important to grasp this difference here!

Box transfers and `Rc`/`Arc` sharing occur through cloning.

Practical application: a simple graph with shared nodes (Rc<RefCell<Node>>)

A common data structure that requires shared ownership and potential mutability is a graph, in which nodes can point to other nodes, and multiple nodes may point to the same successor.

`Rc<RefCell<Node>>` is often an appropriate choice here for single-threaded graphs.

Let's see an example:

```
use std::rc::{Rc, Weak}; // Weak is included to hint at the solution for
cycles
use std::cell::RefCell;

#[derive(Debug)]
struct GraphNode {
    id: usize,
    name: String,
```

```
    // Using Rc<RefCell<...>> allows shared ownership and interior
mutability of edges.
    edges: RefCell<Vec<Rc<GraphNode>>>,
}

impl GraphNode {
    fn new(id: usize, name: &str) -> Rc<Self> {
        Rc::new(GraphNode {
            id,
            name: name.to_string(),
            edges: RefCell::new(Vec::new()),
        })
    }

    // Adds a directed edge from one node to another.
    fn add_edge(from: &Rc<GraphNode>, to: &Rc<GraphNode>) {
        from.edges.borrow_mut().push(Rc::clone(to));
    }

    fn print_connections(&self) {
        print!("Node '{}' (ID {}) connects to: ", self.name, self.id);
        if self.edges.borrow().is_empty() {
            print!("(none)");
        } else {
            for (i, node) in self.edges.borrow().iter().enumerate() {
                if i > 0 { print!(", "); }
                print!("{}", node.name);
            }
        }
        println!();
    }
}
```

```
fn main() {
    let node_a = GraphNode::new(1, "A");
    let node_b = GraphNode::new(2, "B");
    let node_c = GraphNode::new(3, "C");
    let node_d = GraphNode::new(4, "D");

    // Create connections for a directed acyclic graph:
    // A -> B
    // A -> C
    // B -> C
    // C -> D
    GraphNode::add_edge(&node_a, &node_b);
    GraphNode::add_edge(&node_a, &node_c);
    GraphNode::add_edge(&node_b, &node_c);
    GraphNode::add_edge(&node_c, &node_d);

    println!("--- Graph Connections ---");
    node_a.print_connections();
    node_b.print_connections();
    node_c.print_connections();
    node_d.print_connections();
    println!("------------------------");

    println!("\n--- Reference Counts ---");
    // Each node starts with a count of 1 from `main`'s ownership.
    // The count is incremented for each incoming edge from another node.
    println!("Node A strong_count: {}", Rc::strong_count(&node_a)); //
Output: 1 (owned by main)
    println!("Node B strong_count: {}", Rc::strong_count(&node_b)); //
Output: 2 (owned by main + edge from A)
    println!("Node C strong_count: {}", Rc::strong_count(&node_c)); //
Output: 3 (owned by main + edge from A + edge from B)
    println!("Node D strong_count: {}", Rc::strong_count(&node_d)); //
Output: 2 (owned by main + edge from C)
}
```

```
--- Graph Connections ---
Node 'A' (ID 1) connects to: B, C
Node 'B' (ID 2) connects to: C
Node 'C' (ID 3) connects to: D
Node 'D' (ID 4) connects to: (none)
-------------------------


--- Reference Counts ---
Node A strong_count: 1
Node B strong_count: 2
Node C strong_count: 3
Node D strong_count: 2
```

Figure 11.8: Output of a graph with shared nodes example

- Each GraphNode is wrapped in an Rc to enable multiple nodes to point to it (shared ownership).
- The edges field of a GraphNode, which stores its connections to other nodes, is a RefCell<Vec<Rc<GraphNode>>>.
- Vec<Rc<GraphNode>>: The vector contains Rc pointers to the neighboring nodes, sharing ownership of them.
- RefCell: This allows the edges vector to be modified (e.g., to add a new edge) even when we only have an immutable reference (&Rc<GraphNode>) to the node itself. The add_edge function takes &Rc<GraphNode> but can modify from_node.edges due to the RefCell.

Important note on cycles

This simple graph example using only Rc for edges can easily lead to reference cycles if, for instance, node D points back to node A with another Rc. Both A and D would then keep each other's reference count above zero indefinitely, causing a memory leak. In real graph implementations, you would typically use Weak<GraphNode> for some of the references (e.g., "back-edges" or parent pointers) to break these cycles and allow for deallocation. We're just showing the basic Rc<RefCell<T>> structure here.

This section has demonstrated how the Deref trait facilitates ergonomic method calls and how combining smart pointers such as Rc and RefCell (or Arc and Mutex) unveils powerful patterns for shared data and interior mutability, essential for many complex data structures and application designs.

Important note on cycles and Weak

While `Rc<T>` is excellent for managing shared ownership, it has a potential pitfall: **memory leaks from reference cycles.** A reference cycle occurs when two or more `Rc<T>` instances point to each other in a loop. Because each object is holding a strong reference to the other, their reference counts will never drop to zero, and their memory will never be deallocated, even if no other part of the program can access them.

Summary

We've concluded our exploration of Rust's smart pointers in this chapter! Understanding these tools is important for writing effective and safe Rust code, especially in complex areas such as memory management and concurrency. Smart pointers provide high-level conveniences while upholding Rust's core principles of safety and performance, connecting low-level control with high-level abstraction.

Let's recap what we've unpacked:

- **The "why" of smart pointers**: We began by recognizing that smart pointers are not merely raw memory addresses; they are structures that function as pointers but also offer additional features such as automatic resource management (through the `Drop` trait) and pointer-like behavior (using the `Deref` trait). They assist in managing data in ways that Rust's fundamental ownership and borrowing rules might make cumbersome.
- **Box<T>**: Our first focus was `Box<T>`, the most straightforward smart pointer for allocating heap data with clearly defined single ownership. We examined its use for placing large data on the heap, for types with sizes unknown at compile time (such as trait objects, which we only briefly covered), and, importantly, for enabling recursive data structures by resolving infinite sizing loops.
- **Rc<T> and Arc<T> for shared ownership**: We then dived deep into how to maintain multiple "owners" or persistent references to the same piece of data using reference counting.
    - **Rc<T> (Reference Counted)** is designed for single-threaded contexts. Cloning an `Rc<T>` increases a reference count, and the data is deallocated only when the count reaches zero.
    - **Arc<T> (Atomically Reference Counted)** offers similar functionality but is thread-safe due to atomic operations managing the reference count, making it suitable for sharing data among threads.
    - We also highlighted the risks of reference cycles with these types and briefly mentioned `Weak<T>` as a solution.

- **Interior mutability with RefCell<T> and Mutex<T>**: Next, we explored the interior mutability pattern, which permits data modification even through a seemingly immutable reference.
    - **RefCell<T>** applies Rust's borrowing rules (one mutable reference or multiple immutable ones) at runtime for single-threaded applications. It will panic if the rules are violated.
    - **Mutex<T> (Mutual Exclusion)** provides thread-safe interior mutability, ensuring that only one thread can access the data at a time using a locking mechanism.
- **Working effectively with smart pointers**: We learned how the `Deref` trait and Deref coercion make method calls on smart pointers more user-friendly. We also discussed patterns such as combining smart pointers (for instance, `Rc<RefCell<T>>` for shared mutable data in single-threaded contexts, or `Arc<Mutex<T>>` for multi-threaded scenarios) and reviewed a practical example using `Rc<RefCell<Node>>` to represent a graph structure.

Mastering smart pointers unlocks much of Rust's potential. While the core ownership system addresses many scenarios, these tools offer the flexibility required for more complex data structures, shared state, and concurrent programming, all while adhering to Rust's safety guarantees, either at compile time or, in the case of types such as `RefCell`, with clear runtime checks. As you continue to write Rust, you'll frequently find yourself utilizing these smart pointers!

In the next chapter, we will extend Rust's principles of safety and resource management beyond internal memory to the world outside our program, covering the essential and error-prone tasks of interacting with the file system and the network.

Questions and assignments

We've covered a lot of ground on smart pointers, from simple heap allocation with `Box<T>` to shared ownership with `Rc<T>` and `Arc<T>`, and even interior mutability with `RefCell<T>` and `Mutex<T>`.

These questions and assignments will help you review the key concepts of smart pointers discussed in this chapter.

Questions

1. What is the main purpose of a `Box<T>` smart pointer?
2. Which smart pointer would you use to allow multiple owners of some data, but only within a single thread?

3. What does the `Rc::clone(&my_rc)` function do, and is it a "deep" or "shallow" copy of the underlying data?
4. What is the thread-safe equivalent of `Rc<T>`?
5. Explain the concept of "interior mutability." Why is it sometimes necessary in Rust?
6. What is the key difference between how `RefCell<T>` and `Mutex<T>` provide interior mutability? When would you choose one over the other?
7. What does the `Deref` trait enable for smart pointers? Provide a simple example of where it makes code more convenient.
8. Why is `Box<T>` essential for defining recursive data structures such as a linked list enum?

Assignment

Goal: Get comfortable with the `Rc<T>` smart pointer for managing shared, read-only data in a single-threaded context.

Scenario: Imagine you are building a text editor application. Multiple parts of the application (e.g., the main text view, a word count panel, a spell checker) all need to access the same document's content without making expensive copies of it.

Task:

1. Define structs:
   - Create a simple struct named `Document` that contains content: String.
   - Create another struct named `TextViewer` that holds document: `Rc<Document>`.
   - Create a third struct named `WordCounter` that also holds document: `Rc<Document>`.
2. Create and share the document:
   - In your `main` function, create an instance of `Document` with some sample text.
   - Wrap this `Document` instance in an `Rc<Document>`.
   - Print the initial strong reference count (it should be 1).
3. Create "Viewers":
   - Create an instance of `TextViewer` and an instance of `WordCounter`.
   - For each one, pass it a **clone** of the `Rc<Document>` using `Rc::clone()`.
   - After creating each viewer, print the `strong_count` of the `Rc` again to see it increase.

4. Access the shared data:
    - From both the `TextViewer` and the `WordCounter` instances, access and print some information from the shared document (e.g., `viewer.document.content`, `counter.document.content.len()`). This demonstrates that both structs are pointing to the same data.
5. Observe cleanup (optional):
    - Use `drop()` on one of the viewers and the original `Rc` in main, printing the `strong_count` after each drop to see the count decrease.

12

Managing System Resources

Welcome to *Chapter 12*!

Let's look at another vital aspect of real-world applications: managing system resources. This includes things such as files on your disk, network connections, memory, and processor time.

Engaging with these resources really helps your program run smoothly, reliably, and at its best quality!

You might wonder, "Why is managing resources so important?" As applications become complex or handle heavy workloads, efficient resource handling is very important.

Here are a few reasons why:

- **Performance is key:** Disk I/O and network communication are often much slower than CPU operations. Inefficient handling can make your program sluggish. Efficient management minimizes unnecessary operations.
- **Stability and reliability**: Applications can crash from resource leaks, such as when they run out of file handles or consume all memory. Rust's ownership and RAII patterns help, but mindful design is essential.
- **Scalability matters**: Efficient resource management allows applications to support more users or larger datasets without failures.

- **Good system citizenship**: A well-behaved application limits its resource consumption to maintain system stability.
- **Cost considerations**: In cloud deployments, inefficient resource use can lead to higher operational costs. Using less CPU, memory, and bandwidth reduces bills.

Rust offers tools and a strong type system for safe resource management. However, you, the developer, must grasp the core principles.

In this chapter, we'll get practical with common system resources:

- **File I/O**: We'll explore file operations, including reading, writing, and file manipulation, focusing on efficiency and safety
- **Network programming**: You'll learn how to create TCP servers and clients to handle connections and data exchange while improving performance with buffered I/O
- **Secure network communication**: We'll look at enhancing network security with TLS using relevant Rust crates
- **Best practices and performance**: We'll discuss resource management strategies, memory efficiency, optimizing file/network performance, and security
- **Real-world examples**: We'll review comprehensive examples simulating real-world applications, illustrating resource management techniques

By the end of this chapter, you'll have a good understanding of how to manage system resources in Rust, which will help you build apps that are not only functional and fast but also reliable. We're excited to see you grow your skills and create amazing projects!

Let's dive into file I/O essentials!

Working with files in Rust (file I/O)

A program interacts with the system by reading and writing files, whether loading configuration, processing datasets, saving user work, or writing logs. File **I/O (Input/Output)** is essential. Rust's standard library, especially the `std::fs` and `std::io` modules, offers safe tools for these operations.

We'll explore common file tasks while emphasizing Rust's focus on error handling and resource management.

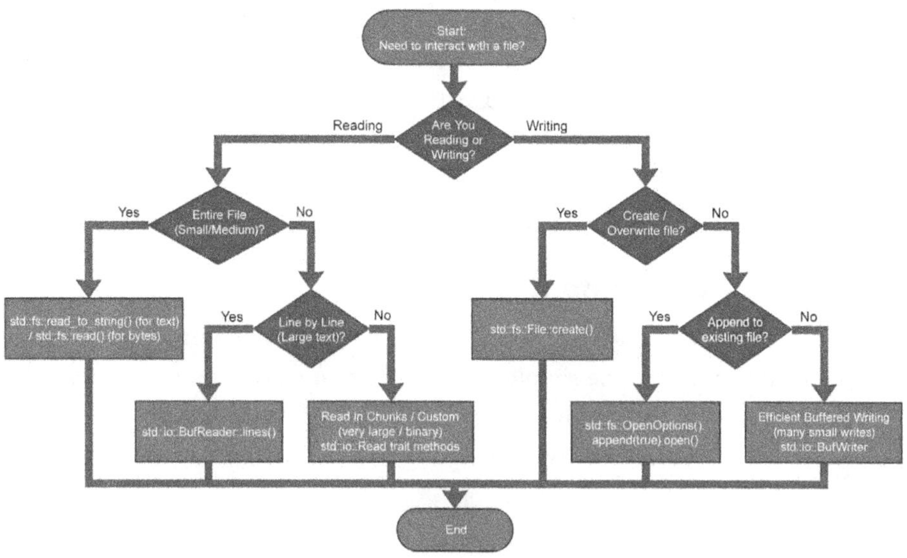

Figure 12.1: Flowchart for selecting the appropriate file I/O strategy in Rust

Core concepts of file operations

Before we jump into code, let's cover a few core ideas:

- **Files and paths:** Files are identified by paths. Rust's `std::path::Path` and `PathBuf` types help you work with file paths in a platform-independent way.
- **Opening files:** To read or write, you first need to "open" a file. This operation can fail (e.g., file doesn't exist, no permissions), so Rust's file opening functions typically return a result.
- **Reading and writing:** Once a file is open, you can read bytes from it or write bytes to it. These operations can also fail (e.g., disk full, network error for a remote file system).
- **Closing files:** When you're done with a file, it should be closed to free up system resources and ensure any buffered data is written to disk. In Rust, files are often represented by types such as `std::fs::File`, which implement the `Drop` trait. This means when an instance of `File` goes out of scope, its `drop` method is automatically called, which handles closing the file.
- This **RAII (Resource Acquisition Is Initialization)** pattern is a great way to help prevent resource leaks by naturally tying a resource's lifespan to the scope of its owning variable. In practice, it means that once a variable that owns a resource (like a File handle) goes out of scope, Rust ensures the resource is automatically cleaned up by calling its `Drop` implementation. This makes closing files or freeing memory smooth and predictable, so you don't have to worry about writing manual cleanup code.

- **Buffering**: I/O operations are often "buffered" for efficiency. Instead of processing one byte at a time, data is read/written in larger chunks to an in-memory buffer. This is commonly done using `std::io::BufReader` and `std::io::BufWriter`.

Reading from files

Depending on your needs, there are several ways to read data from a file in Rust. Let's see them.

Reading an entire file into a string

If a file isn't excessively large and you need all its content at once (perhaps it's a configuration file or a small text document), the simplest way is often to read it directly into a string. The `std::fs::read_to_string` function is perfect for this.

```
use std::fs;
use std::path::Path;
use std::process;

fn main() {
    let sample_path = Path::new("my_sample_file.txt");

    // --- Success Case: Read an existing file ---

    // First, let's create a file to ensure it exists for our success 
case.
    if let Err(e) = fs::write(sample_path, "Hello from a Rust test file!") 
{
        eprintln!("Setup failed: Could not write to sample file: {}", e);
        process::exit(1);
    }

    println!("--- Attempting to read '{}' ---", sample_path.display());
    match fs::read_to_string(sample_path) {
        Ok(contents) => {
            println!("Success! File contents: '{}'", contents);
        }
        Err(e) => {
            // This part shouldn't run if the file was created 
successfully.
            eprintln!("Unexpected error reading the file: {}", e);
```

```
        }
    }
    // Clean up the created file.
    let _ = fs::remove_file(sample_path);
    println!("\n--------------------------------\n");
    // --- Failure Case: Try to read a non-existent file ---

    let non_existent_path = Path::new("no_such_file.txt");
    println!("--- Attempting to read '{}' ---", non_existent_path.
display());
    match fs::read_to_string(non_existent_path) {
        Ok(_) => {
            // This should not happen.
            println!("Unexpectedly found a file that should not exist!");
        }
        Err(e) => {
            // This is the expected outcome.
            eprintln!("Correctly failed to read non-existent file. Error:
{}", e);
        }
    }
}
```

A note on safe file writing: avoiding overwrites

The `fs::write()` function (and `File::create()`) is really handy to use. However, it's good to keep in mind that it will always overwrite the destination file if it already exists. In real, everyday applications, especially command-line tools, this might accidentally cause data loss if a user points it at an important file. To be safer, consider checking if the file exists before writing. You can do this easily with the `Path::exists()` method.

```
use std::path::Path;
use std::fs;

fn safe_write(path: &Path, content: &str) {
    if path.exists() {
```

```
        // The file already exists. Decide what to do:
        // 1. Return an error.
        // 2. Ask the user for confirmation.
        // 3. Do nothing.
        eprintln!("Error: File '{}' already exists. Aborting to prevent 
overwrite.", path.display());
    } else {
        // The file doesn't exist, so it's safe to write.
        if let Err(e) = fs::write(path, content) {
            eprintln!("Error writing to new file: {}", e);
        } else {
            println!("Successfully wrote to new file '{}'", path.
display());
        }
    }
}
```

- **Success case:** We first use `fs::write` to ensure a sample file exists. Then, `fs::read_to_string(sample_path)` is called. The `match` statement handles the `Ok(contents)` variant by printing the file's content.
- **Failure case:** We define a path to a file we know doesn't exist. We then call `fs::read_to_string` on this path. The `match` statement handles the expected `Err(e)` variant by printing the I/O error message. This demonstrates the robust error handling required when working with files.

Reading a file line by line

For larger files, or when you want to process data as it comes in without loading everything into memory, reading line by line is more efficient.

This is typically done using `std::fs::File` to open the file, then wrapping it in a `std::io::BufReader` for efficient buffered reading, and then using the `.lines()` method.

```
use std::fs::{self, File};
use std::io::{self, BufRead, BufReader};
use std::path::Path;

fn main() -> io::Result<()> {
    let log_file_path = Path::new("events.log");
```

```
    // Setup: Create a dummy log file for the example.
    fs::write(log_file_path, "INFO: User logged in.\nWARN: Disk space is
low.\nERROR: Failed to fetch resource.")?;

    println!("--- Reading '{}' line by line ---", log_file_path.
display());

    // 1. Open the file. The '?' operator propagates errors.
    let file = File::open(log_file_path)?;

    // 2. Wrap the file in a BufReader for efficient, buffered reading.
    let reader = BufReader::new(file);

    // 3. Use the .lines() method to get an iterator over each line.
    for (index, line_result) in reader.lines().enumerate() {
        // Each line is a Result, as I/O can fail mid-read.
        // '?' will propagate the error if a line is malformed or read
fails.
        let line = line_result?;

        // Process the line.
        println!("[Line {}] Content: {}", index + 1, line);
    }

    // Cleanup: Remove the dummy file. .ok() ignores a potential error if
removal fails.
    fs::remove_file(log_file_path).ok();

    Ok(())
}
```

This memory-efficient approach is ideal for large files.

- `File::open(path)?`: First, we open the file, handling potential errors immediately with `?`.
- `BufReader::new(file)`: We wrap the file in a `BufReader`. This is a key performance optimization, as it reads the file in larger chunks into an internal buffer, minimizing slow system calls.

- `reader.lines()`: This method returns an iterator that yields each line from the buffer as an `io::Result<String>`. The result is necessary because an I/O error could occur at any point while reading.
- `let line = line_result?;`: Inside the loop, we use ? again to concisely get the string content from the result for each line. This makes the loop body clean while still handling potential errors correctly.

Writing to files

Just like reading, Rust provides several ways to write data to files for different needs.

Writing a string or bytes to a file

To write an entire string or a slice of bytes to a file, you can use `std::fs::write`. For more control, such as ensuring a file is created or truncated, you can open a file with `File::create` and then use its `write_all` method (from the `std::io::Write` trait).

```
use std::fs; // For fs::write and fs::read_to_string (for verification)
use std::fs::File; // For File::create
use std::io::{self, Write}; // For the Write trait and its methods like
write_all
use std::io::ErrorKind;
use std::path::Path;

fn save_report_to_file(report_path: &Path, report_content: &str) ->
io::Result<()> {
    // Method 1: Using fs::write (convenient for simple, complete writes)
    // This will create the file if it doesn't exist, or truncate and
overwrite it if it does.
    // fs::write(report_path, report_content)?;

    // Method 2: Using File::create and write_all for more explicit
control
    // File::create opens a file in write-only mode.
    // If the file already exists, its content is truncated (emptied).
    // If it does not exist, a new file is created.
    let mut output_file = File::create(report_path)?;

    // The write_all method takes a byte slice (&[u8]).
    // It will attempt to write the entire buffer to the file.
```

```
    output_file.write_all(report_content.as_bytes())?;

    println!("Successfully wrote report to '{}'", report_path.display());
    Ok(())
}

fn main() {
    let my_report_path = Path::new("financial_report.txt");
    let report_data = "Q1 Report:\nSales: $1,000,000\nExpenses: $400,000\
nProfit: $600,000\n";

    if let Err(e) = save_report_to_file(my_report_path, report_data) {
        eprintln!("Error writing report to file: {}", e);
    } else {
        // Verify by reading it back
        match fs::read_to_string(my_report_path) {
            Ok(content_read) => {
                println!("\n--- Report Read Back for Verification ---");
                println!("{}", content_read);
                println!("--- End of Verification ---");
            }
            Err(e) => eprintln!("Error reading back report for
verification: {}", e),
        }
    }

    // Clean up the dummy file
    if let Err(e) = fs::remove_file(my_report_path) {
         eprintln!("Cleanup error: Failed to remove report file '{}': {}",
my_report_path.display(), e);
    }
}
```

- `std::fs::write(path, content)` is a quick and convenient function if you need to write the entire contents of a string or byte slice to a file in one go. It handles opening (creating or truncating) and closing the file for you.
- `File::create(path)?` explicitly opens a file for writing. If the file exists, it is truncated (its current contents are erased). If it doesn't exist, it's created.

- The `Write` trait (brought into scope by using `std::io::Write;`) must be imported to use methods such as `write_all` on File instances.
- `output_file.write_all(report_content.as_bytes())?` takes the content (converted to a byte slice via `.as_bytes()`) and attempts to write every byte to the file. The `?` handles any potential `io::Error`.

Appending content to an existing file

Often, you don't want to overwrite a file but instead add new content to its end. You need to open the file with specific options, typically using `std::fs::OpenOptions`.

```
use std::fs::{self, OpenOptions};
use std::io::{self, Write};
use std::path::Path;--

/// Opens a file in append mode and writes a new line to it.
/// Creates the file if it doesn't exist.
fn append_line_to_file(file_path: &Path, line_to_append: &str) ->
io::Result<()> {
    // Use OpenOptions to configure how the file is opened.
    let mut file = OpenOptions::new()
        .append(true)  // Set to append mode.
        .create(true)  // Create the file if it does not exist.
        .open(file_path)?;

    // writeln! is convenient for writing a string followed by a newline.
    writeln!(file, "{}", line_to_append)?;

    Ok(())
}

fn main() -> io::Result<()> {
    let log_path = Path::new("application.log");

    // Start with a clean slate for the example.
    // .ok() converts Result to Option, so we ignore errors if file
doesn't exist.
match std::fs::remove_file(system_activity_log) {
    Ok(_) => {
```

```
            // Successfully removed the old file, we can optionally log this
            println!("Note: Removed old log file for a clean run.");
        }
        Err(e) if e.kind() == ErrorKind::NotFound => {
            // This is perfectly fine, the file just didn't exist.
            // We can do nothing and continue.
        }
        Err(e) => {
            // This is an unexpected error (like permission denied).
            // We'll print a warning but continue the program.
            eprintln!(
                "Warning: Could not remove old log file '{}': {}. Proceeding
anyway.",
                system_activity_log.display(), e
            );
        }
    }
        println!("Preparing to write to '{}'...", log_path.display());


        // Append several lines to the same file.
        append_line_to_file(log_path, "[INFO] Application started.")?;
        append_line_to_file(log_path, "[WARN] Low disk space detected.")?;
        append_line_to_file(log_path, "[INFO] User 'admin' logged in.")?;

        println!("Finished writing log entries.");

        // Verify the final contents of the file.
        let final_content = fs::read_to_string(log_path)?;
        println!("\n--- Final Contents of '{}' ---", log_path.display());
        println!("{}", final_content);
        println!("--------------------------------");
        // Clean up the created file.
        fs::remove_file(log_path)?;
        Ok(())
    }
```

- `OpenOptions::new()`: This builder creates a set of options for opening a file.
- `create(true)`: This option will create the file if it does not already exist.
- `.append(true)`: This is the key option. It ensures that when the file is opened for writing, the "cursor" is placed at the end of the file, so any new writes add to the existing content instead of overwriting it.
- `writeln!(file, "...")?`: This macro conveniently writes a formatted string, followed by a newline, to the file. It returns an `io::Result<()>`, allowing the `?` operator to be used for concise error handling.
- The `main` function calls `append_line_to_file` multiple times, reads the file back to show the aggregated result, and then cleans up.

Manipulating files and directories

The `std::fs` module provides functions for various file system operations beyond basic reading and writing. Key functions include the following:

- `fs::create_dir("path/to/new_dir")`: Creates a directory, failing if it exists or a parent doesn't.
- `fs::create_dir_all("path/to/possibly/nested/dirs")`: Creates a directory and necessary parents if they don't exist.
- `fs::remove_dir("path/to/empty_dir")`: Removes an empty directory; fails if it's not empty or doesn't exist.
- `fs::remove_dir_all("path/to/dir_with_contents")`: Removes a directory and all contents; use with caution!
- `fs::remove_file("path/to/file.txt")`: Deletes a file.
- `fs::rename("old/path/name.txt", "new/path/name.txt")`: Renames or moves a file/directory. Behavior may vary across platforms when moving between file systems.
- `fs::copy("source_file.txt", "destination_file.txt")`: Copies contents from one file to another, failing if the destination exists unless using `OpenOptions` carefully.
- `fs::read_dir("path/to/dir")`: Returns an iterator of entries (`DirEntry`) in the directory, with each item being a `Result<DirEntry, io::Error>`.
- `fs::metadata("path/to/item")`: Retrieves metadata about a file/directory, including size, permissions, and modification times. Most functions return an `io::Result` to handle potential errors such as "path not found," "permission denied," or "directory not empty."

```
use std::fs;
use std::path::{Path, PathBuf};
use std::io;

fn demonstrate_fs_operations() -> io::Result<()> {
    let playground_dir = PathBuf::from("my_temp_playground");

    // 1. Create a directory structure
    if playground_dir.exists() {
        // Clean up from previous run if necessary (use with
caution)
        fs::remove_dir_all(&playground_dir)?;
        println!("Cleaned up existing '{}'", playground_dir.
display());
    }
    fs::create_dir_all(&playground_dir)?;
    println!("Created directory: '{}'", playground_dir.display());

    let notes_subdir = playground_dir.join("notes");
    fs::create_dir(&notes_subdir)?;
    println!("Created subdirectory: '{}'", notes_subdir.display());

    // 2. Create and write to a file
    let important_file = notes_subdir.join("important.txt");
    fs::write(&important_file, "Initial notes for the project.")?;
    println!("Created and wrote to: '{}'", important_file.
display());

    let draft_file = notes_subdir.join("draft.md");
    fs::write(&draft_file, "# My Draft\n\nThis is a draft
document.")?;
    println!("Created and wrote to: '{}'", draft_file.display());

    // 3. List directory contents and get metadata
    println!("\nContents of '{}':", notes_subdir.display());
    for entry_result in fs::read_dir(&notes_subdir)? {
        let entry = entry_result?; // Each entry itself is a Result
        let path = entry.path();
```

```
            let metadata = fs::metadata(&path)?;

            let entry_type = if metadata.is_dir() {
                "DIR"
            } else if metadata.is_file() {
                "FILE"
            } else {
                "OTHER"
            };
            let size = if metadata.is_file() { metadata.len() } else { 0
};

            println!("  - [{}] {} (Size: {} bytes)",
                     entry_type,
                     path.file_name().unwrap_or_default().to_string_
lossy(),
                     size);
        }

    // 4. Copy and Rename a file
    let copied_file_path = playground_dir.join("important_backup.
txt");
    fs::copy(&important_file, &copied_file_path)?;
    println!("\nCopied '{}' to '{}'", important_file.display(),
copied_file_path.display());

    let renamed_draft_path = notes_subdir.join("final_ideas.md");
    fs::rename(&draft_file, &renamed_draft_path)?;
    println!("Renamed '{}' to '{}'", draft_file.display(), renamed_
draft_path.display());

    // 5. Clean up (remove the entire playground directory)
    // Use with caution in real applications!
    fs::remove_dir_all(&playground_dir)?;
    println!("\nSuccessfully cleaned up and removed directory:
'{}'", playground_dir.display());

    Ok(())
```

```
}

fn main() {
    if let Err(e) = demonstrate_fs_operations() {
        eprintln!("A file system operation failed: {}", e);
    }
}
```

Warning: Use fs::remove_dir_all with extreme caution!

The `fs::remove_dir_all` function is a very powerful tool, but it can also be quite dangerous. Think of it like running rm -rf on the command line: it deletes a directory and all its contents at once, and there's no way to undo it.

In our example, we use it carefully to clean up a temporary directory we've just created. However, it's really important to never use this function on a path that comes from a user input (such as from a command-line argument) unless you've added some safety checks first. In real-world applications, it's a good idea to include a confirmation prompt (such as "Are you sure you want to delete this? [y/N]") to help prevent accidental data loss.

- We use `PathBuf::from("...")` to create an owned path, which is often more flexible than `Path::new("...")` if you need to modify it (though `Path::new` is fine for fixed paths). `playground_dir.join("notes")` is a convenient, platform-aware way to construct subpaths.
- `fs::create_dir_all` is generally safer than `fs::create_dir` for ensuring a directory path exists, as it creates any necessary parent directories.
- `fs::read_dir` returns an iterator over `io::Result<DirEntry>`. You must handle the result for the iteration itself and for each `DirEntry` obtained.
- `fs::metadata` retrieves information about a file system item, such as its type (file/directory) and size.
- The example demonstrates creating directories, writing files, listing contents, copying, renaming, and finally, cleaning up by removing the top-level directory with `fs::remove_dir_all`.
- Always remember that these operations can fail for many reasons (permissions, path not found, disk issues), so robust error handling using the returned result is essential.

Key takeaways for file I/O in Rust

Working with files in Rust is designed to be both safe and reasonably ergonomic:

- **Error handling is explicit**: Most file operations return Result, compelling you to address potential errors. This is essential to Rust's reliability approach.
- **RAII for resource management**: File objects (and `BufReader`/`BufWriter` wrapping them) implement the `Drop` trait. This means their `drop` method is automatically called when these objects go out of scope, which ensures the underlying file is closed. This reduces the risk of resource leaks such as unclosed file handles.
- **Buffering for efficiency**: Use `std::io::BufReader` when reading files, especially line by line or in small chunks, and `std::io::BufWriter` when writing multiple small pieces of data. Buffering minimizes direct, costly system calls and can significantly improve performance.
- **Path types for portability**: Utilize `std::path::Path` (a borrowed slice) and `PathBuf` (an owned, string-like type) for working with file system paths. These types provide methods for path manipulation (such as `.join()`) that are aware of platform-specific differences (such as the path separators / versus \), making your code more portable. It's also important to distinguish between **absolute paths** (which start from a root, such as `/home/user` or `C:\Users`) and **relative paths** (such as `my_file.txt`), which are interpreted relative to your program's **current working directory**. Rust's standard library provides `std::env::current_dir()` to find this location, which is very helpful for resolving relative paths into absolute ones.

File I/O is a common source of runtime issues in many applications (files not existing, permission problems, disk full conditions, etc.).

Rust's strong emphasis on handling Result and its RAII pattern for automatic resource cleanup are significant aids in writing programs that can manage these situations gracefully and reliably.

Now that we have a solid understanding of how Rust interacts with local file system resources, let's explore how to manage another fundamental resource: communicating with other computers over a network.

Network programming essentials in Rust

Beyond manipulating files on a local disk, many applications require communication over a network, whether fetching data from a web API, interacting with a database server, or building a peer-to-peer application. Rust's standard library offers solid primitives for network programming, especially for working with TCP and UDP protocols.

In this section, we'll focus on the fundamentals of TCP networking by building a simple client and server to demonstrate these concepts in action.

The following one is not a detailed explanation, but more of a refresher (there are entire books and materials about networking). Also, if you are already familiar with these concepts, feel free to skip the following section.

Fundamentals of network communication

Before diving into Rust code, let's briefly touch upon some core networking concepts.

If you are already familiar with them, you can skip this.

- **IP addresses and ports**: To communicate, computers on a network need addresses. The **IP address** (such as `127.0.0.1` for your local machine, or `192.168.1.101` for a device on your local network) identifies a specific machine. Once you've found the machine, a **port number** (e.g., `80` for HTTP, `443` for HTTPS, or custom ports such as `7878`) identifies a specific application or service running on that machine. An IP address plus a port number creates a unique endpoint for communication, often called a **socket address**.
- **TCP (Transmission Control Protocol)**: This is one of the main protocols in the Internet protocol suite. TCP provides reliable, ordered, and error-checked delivery of a stream of bytes between applications running on hosts communicating via an IP network. It's a connection-oriented protocol, meaning a connection must be established between two endpoints (e.g., a client and a server) before data can be exchanged. Think of it like a phone call – you dial, the other person answers, and then you can talk. This is what we'll primarily use.
- **UDP (User Datagram Protocol)**: Another core protocol, UDP is connectionless and provides a simpler, faster, but unreliable datagram (packet) service. It doesn't guarantee delivery, order, or error checking in the same way TCP does. It's more like sending a postcard – quick, but no guarantees. UDP is often used for applications where speed is critical and some data loss is acceptable (e.g., streaming video, online games). We won't focus on UDP in this introductory section.

- **Sockets:** A socket is an internal endpoint for sending or receiving data at a single node in a computer network. Conceptually, it's one end of a two-way communication link between two programs running on the network. When you write network code, you're typically interacting with socket APIs provided by the operating system (which Rust's standard library wraps for you).
- **Client-server model:** This is a common architectural pattern. A **server** is a program that waits for incoming connection requests from other programs, called **clients**. Once a connection is established, the client can send requests to the server, and the server processes these requests and sends back responses.

With these basics in mind, let's see how to build a simple TCP server in Rust.

Building a basic TCP server

A TCP server's primary job is to "listen" on a specific IP address and port for incoming client connection attempts. When a client tries to connect, the server "accepts" the connection, creating a new communication channel (another socket) specifically for that client.

Listening for connections with TcpListener

Rust's `std::net::TcpListener` struct creates a TCP server socket that listens for incoming connections. You "bind" a `TcpListener` to a socket address (IP address and port).

Handling incoming client connections

Once bound, you can call the `incoming()` method on the `TcpListener`.

This method returns an iterator that blocks until a new connection is established. Each item this iterator produces is a `Result<TcpStream, std::io::Error>`. A `TcpStream` represents the established connection with a client; you can use it to read and write data from that client.

Reading requests and sending responses

After accepting a connection and getting a `TcpStream`, you typically want to do the following:

1. Read the request sent by the client from the `TcpStream`
2. Process the request
3. Write a response back to the client via the same `TcpStream`

The `Read` and `Write` traits (from `std::io`) are implemented by `TcpStream`, so you can use methods such as `read()` and `write_all()`.

Let's build a very simple "echo server." It will listen for connections, read whatever the client sends, and then send the same data right back to the client.

```
use std::net::{TcpListener, TcpStream};
use std::io::{Read, Write};

/// Handles a single client connection by reading from the stream and
echoing back.
fn handle_client(mut stream: TcpStream) -> std::io::Result<()> {
    println!("Accepted connection from: {}", stream.peer_addr()?);

    // A buffer to hold incoming data.
    // 1024 bytes (1KB) is a common size for simple examples. In a real
    // application, buffer size is a trade-off:
    // - Too small (e.g., 64 bytes) can lead to many system calls, which
is inefficient.
    // - Too large (e.g., 1MB) wastes memory, especially if you have many
    //   concurrent connections.
    // Common sizes for I/O buffers are often 4KB (4096) or 8KB (8192).
    let mut buffer = [0u8; 1024]; // A buffer to hold incoming data

    // Loop to read data and echo it back
    loop {
        // Read data from the client into the buffer
        let bytes_read = stream.read(&mut buffer)?;

        // If read() returns 0 bytes, the client has closed the connection
        if bytes_read == 0 {
            println!("Client disconnected.");
            return Ok(());
        }

        // Echo the received data back to the client
        stream.write_all(&buffer[..bytes_read])?;
        println!("Echoed {} bytes.", bytes_read);
    }
}
```

```
fn main() -> std::io::Result<()> {
    let listener_address = "127.0.0.1:8080";
    let listener = TcpListener::bind(listener_address)?;

    println!("Simple Echo Server listening on {}", listener_address);
    println!("Waiting for connections...");

    // listener.incoming() is an iterator that blocks until a new
connection arrives.
    // This loop processes one client connection fully before accepting
the next.
    for stream_result in listener.incoming() {
        match stream_result {
            Ok(stream) => {
                // A new client has connected successfully.
                if let Err(e) = handle_client(stream) {
                    eprintln!("Error handling client: {}", e);
                }
            }
            Err(e) => {
                // An error occurred while accepting a new connection.
                eprintln!("Failed to accept incoming connection: {}", e);
            }
        }
    }
    Ok(())
}
```

This server demonstrates the fundamental TCP server lifecycle:

- `TcpListener::bind(address)?`: This binds the server to a local IP address and port, making it ready to accept connections.
- `listener.incoming()`: This method returns an iterator that blocks and waits for new clients to connect. The `for` loop processes each incoming connection sequentially.
- `handle_client(stream)`: This function contains the logic for a single client session.

- `stream.read(&mut buffer)?`: This reads data from the client into a buffer. It's a blocking call that waits for data. If it returns `Ok(0)`, the client has closed the connection.
- `stream.write_all(&buffer[..bytes_read])?`: This takes the data that was just read (a slice of the buffer) and writes it back to the same client, effectively "echoing" it.
- **Error handling**: The ? operator is used for concise error handling. If any read or write operation fails, the error is propagated up, and a message is printed in main.
- **Limitation**: This simple server handles clients one at a time. The main loop is blocked until `handle_client` finishes, preventing other clients from connecting. We'll address this with threads in later examples.

Important: This server is sequential (one client at a time)

It's important to understand the limitation of this simple server: it is sequential. Because the `for stream_result in listener.incoming()` loop calls `handle_client(stream)` directly and *waits for that function to finish* before it can loop again to accept another connection, it can only handle one client at a time.

Imagine the server is a bank with only one teller. The process looks like this:

Sequential (Our current server):

- Client 1 arrives --> [Teller serves Client 1... (takes 5 minutes)] --> Client 1 leaves
- Client 2 arrives --> (Waits in line) --> [Teller serves Client 2... (takes 2 minutes)] --> Client 2 leaves

The key problem, as the reviewer noted, is that **Client 2 must wait for Client 1 to completely finish,** even if Client 2's request is very fast. If Client 1 is slow, the entire server is blocked for everyone else.

The multi-threaded version we'll build next is like opening more teller windows:

Concurrent (What we will build):

- Client 1 arrives --> [Teller 1 serves Client 1]
- Client 2 arrives --> [Teller 2 serves Client 2 (at the same time)]
- Client 3 arrives --> [Teller 3 serves Client 3 (at the same time)]

This concurrent approach is far more responsive and efficient. We will address this limitation in the very next section by spawning a new thread for each connection.

Creating a basic TCP client

We now have a server that listens for connections, so we need a client program to initiate connections and exchange data.

A TCP client actively connects to a TCP server at a specific address and port.

Once connected, it can send requests and receive responses based on the server's expected protocol. For our echo server, the "protocol" is simple: send some bytes and expect the same bytes back.

Connecting to a server with TcpStream::connect

The client also uses the `std::net::TcpStream` type used by the server to manage accepted connections to initiate a connection. The `TcpStream::connect(socket_address)` method establishes a TCP connection to the server at the specified `socket_address` (typically `127.0.0.1:8080`).

This call is blocking by default: the client program pauses here until the connection is established or an error occurs (e.g., the server isn't running, the address is wrong, or a firewall blocks the connection).

Like most I/O operations in Rust, `TcpStream::connect` returns a `Result<TcpStream, std::io::Error>`. If successful, you get `Ok(stream)`, where `stream` is the `TcpStream` for communication. If it fails, you receive an `Err` with details about the connection failure.

Sending data and receiving responses

Once the `TcpStream` is established, the client can send data to the server and receive responses. The `TcpStream` type implements the `std::io::Write` and `std::io::Read` traits, providing methods such as the following:

- `write_all(&buf)`: Sends data (a byte slice `&[u8]`) to the server, attempting to send all bytes.
- `read(&mut buf)`: Reads data from the server into a buffer and returns the number of bytes read.
- `flush()`: It's essential to `flush()` the stream to ensure all buffered data is sent. While `write_all` often attempts this, explicit flushing can be necessary in some scenarios. The client and server must agree on message structure or delimiters, whether messages are a fixed size, terminated by a newline character, or prefixed by their length. In our echo server example, if the server reads until a newline or echoes chunks, the client needs to send data in a processable format and be ready to read the echoed responses similarly. Let's write a client that connects to our echo server on port `8080`, sends a few lines of text, and prints the echoed responses.

```
use std::net::TcpStream;
use std::io::{self, Write, BufRead, BufReader};

fn main() -> io::Result<()> {
    let server_address = "127.0.0.1:8080";
    println!("Connecting to echo server at {}...", server_address);

    // 1. Connect to the server. The '?' operator handles connection
errors concisely.
    let mut stream = TcpStream::connect(server_address)?;
    println!("Connected! Type a message and press Enter. Type 'quit' to
exit.");

    // 2. Prepare for reading and writing.
    //    We can clone the stream to have separate handles for reading and
writing.
    //    This is a common pattern for more complex I/O.
    let mut reader = BufReader::new(stream.try_clone()?);

    loop {
        // Read a line of input from the user's keyboard.
        let mut input_line = String::new();
        io::stdin().read_line(&mut input_line)?;

        let message_to_send = input_line.trim(); // Trim whitespace and
newline
        if message_to_send == "quit" || message_to_send.is_empty() {
            break; // Exit loop if user types 'quit' or just presses Enter
        }

        // 3. Send the message to the server.
        // We add a newline so the server's `read_line` can process it.
        writeln!(stream, "{}", message_to_send)?;
        stream.flush()?; // Ensure the buffered data is sent immediately.

        // 4. Read the echo back from the server.
        let mut echoed_response = String::new();
        reader.read_line(&mut echoed_response)?
```

```
        print!("Server echoed: {}", echoed_response); // `read_line`
includes the newline
    }

    println!("Disconnecting from server.");
    Ok(())
}
```

- **Connection**: `TcpStream::connect(server_address)?` establishes the connection, propagating errors with `?`.
- **I/O setup**: In this example, we use `stream.try_clone()?` to create a duplicate handle to the `TcpStream`. This is a safe and efficient operation because `TcpStream` is designed to be cloned, allowing both the original handle and the new one to refer to the **same underlying network connection** (or socket). We then wrap this new read-handle in a `BufReader`, which lets us use the original stream handle exclusively for writing. While this is a robust pattern, it's worth noting that for simpler, strictly sequential communication (where you write a request, *then* read a response), you could often just reuse the *same* stream handle for both operations, perhaps by wrapping it in a `BufWriter` first, flushing, and then wrapping it in a `BufReader`.
- **The loop**: Inside the loop, the program reads a line of input from the user's terminal using `io::stdin().read_line()`, sends that message to the server using the `writeln!` macro, ensures it's sent immediately by calling `stream.flush()`, and then blocks until `reader.read_line()` receives the echoed response back from the server.
- **Termination**: The loop ends when the user types "quit" or enters an empty line. The `TcpStream` is automatically closed when stream and its clone go out of scope at the end of `main`.

Tip: Which I/O model should I use (blocking versus async)?

It can be confusing to know when to use timeouts, threads, or async. Here's a simple guide to the trade-offs:

1. **Basic blocking (what we're doing)**: Use this for simple clients or servers that only need to handle one connection at a time. It's easy to read but will freeze if the network is slow or if a second client tries to connect.
2. **Blocking with timeouts:** This is a more robust version of the preceding. You still handle one client at a time, but you add `.set_read_timeout()` and `.set_write_timeout()` to your `TcpStream`. This prevents your program from freezing *indefinitely* if the other end becomes unresponsive. This is a good, simple default for basic clients.
3. **Thread-per-client:** This is what we did in our multi-threaded server example. It's great for handling a moderate number of concurrent connections (e.g., 5-100) because it's relatively simple to understand. Its main drawback is that it can use a lot of memory and system resources, as each thread has its own stack.
4. **Asynchronous I/O (async/await)**: This is the most efficient and modern solution for handling *thousands* of connections at once (e.g., a high-performance web server or chat application). It uses a few threads to manage all connections by never blocking on I/O. It has a steeper learning curve but is the standard for high-performance I/O-bound applications.

For this chapter, we're focusing on the `std::net` methods (blocking and thread-per-client). Async/await is a more advanced topic we'll explore later.

Ensuring robust and secure network applications

Building network applications that "work" on the happy path is one thing; creating robust applications against network glitches, server issues, and security threats is another challenge.

This section discusses handling network errors gracefully and securing communication with **Transport Layer Security (TLS)**.

Graceful error handling in network code

As we've seen, almost every operation in `std::net` (such as `TcpStream::connect`, `read`, `write`, `TcpListener::bind`, `accept`) returns a `Result<T, std::io::Error>`. This is Rust compelling you to acknowledge that network operations are inherently fallible. Ignoring these results is a shortcut to an unreliable application!

Handling Result from network operations

We've already been using `?` and `match` to handle results in our examples. It's important to continue this practice diligently. Let's look at a more focused example on handling connection errors and preventing our program from hanging indefinitely.

```
use std::net::TcpStream;
use std::io::{self, Write, ErrorKind};
use std::time::Duration;

/// Attempts to connect to a server and returns a custom, more descriptive
error.
fn connect_to_server(server_addr: &str) -> Result<TcpStream, String> {
    // Set a timeout for the connection attempt itself.
    let timeout = Duration::from_secs(5);
    println!("Attempting to connect to {} (timeout: {:?})...", server_
addr, timeout);
    match TcpStream::connect_timeout(&server_addr.parse().unwrap(),
timeout) {
        Ok(stream) => {
            println!("Connection successful!");
            Ok(stream)
        }
        Err(e) => {
            // Match on the error kind to provide a better error message.
            let error_message = match e.kind() {
                ErrorKind::ConnectionRefused => {
                    "Connection refused. Is the server running on that
port?".to_string()
                }
                ErrorKind::TimedOut => {
                    "Connection timed out. Check network or firewall.".to_
```

```
string()
                }
                _ => {
                    format!("An unexpected error occurred: {}", e)
                }
            };
            Err(error_message)
        }
    }
}
fn main() {
    // This address is unlikely to have a server running, so it should
fail.
    let bad_address = "127.0.0.1:9999";
    println!("--- Testing connection to a non-existent server ---");
    if let Err(e) = connect_to_server(bad_address) {
        eprintln!("Operation failed as expected: {}", e);
    }

    // To test a success case, you would run one of the echo servers from
    // a previous example (e.g., on port 8080) and call:
    // connect_to_server("127.0.0.1:8080");
}
```

- `TcpStream::connect_timeout`: Instead of `connect`, which can block indefinitely, `connect_timeout` is used. It attempts a connection for a specified duration and returns a timeout error if it takes too long. This is a crucial technique for preventing your application from freezing.
- **Specific error handling**: The `match` block on the `Err` case inspects `e.kind()`. This allows us to provide more user-friendly and specific error messages for common problems, such as `ConnectionRefused` (server isn't running) or `TimedOut`.
- **Clearer function signature**: The `connect_to_server` function returns a `Result<TcpStream, String>`, abstracting the `io::Error` into a more descriptive String error message for the caller (`main` in this case) to use directly.

Timeouts and non-blocking operations

Network operations can hang indefinitely if the remote side is unresponsive or the network is down. Relying solely on blocking operations without any escape hatch can make your application freeze and become unusable.

- **Timeouts**: As demonstrated in the preceding code example, `TcpStream` provides methods such as `set_read_timeout(Option<Duration>)` and `set_write_timeout(Option<Duration>)`. Setting a timeout is a fundamental technique for robustness. It ensures that if a network read or write operation takes longer than the specified duration, the operation will be interrupted and return an `io::Error` (usually with `kind()` set to `ErrorKind::TimedOut`). This allows your program to regain control, log the issue, retry, or inform the user, instead of waiting forever. Passing `None` as the `Option<Duration>` will remove any previously set timeout, reverting to blocking behavior.
- **Non-blocking I/O**: A more advanced strategy for handling many network connections concurrently without dedicating a thread to each one is to use **non-blocking I/O**. You can configure a `TcpStream` to be non-blocking by calling `stream.set_nonblocking(true)`. In non-blocking mode:
    - `read()` and `write()` calls (and `connect()` or `accept()` for listeners) will return *immediately*.
    - If the operation could be completed without waiting (e.g., data was available to read, or there was space in the OS send buffer to write), they return `Ok(...)` with the number of bytes processed.
    - If the operation *would have blocked*, they instead return an `io::Error` with its `kind()` set to `ErrorKind::WouldBlock` (sometimes seen as EAGAIN or EWOULDBLOCK at the operating system level). This allows a single thread to attempt operations on many sockets, only processing those that are ready and skipping those that would block. This is the foundation of event loops and asynchronous programming frameworks (such as Tokio, async-std, or libraries such as mio for lower-level polling). While `std::net` supports setting non-blocking mode, effectively managing many non-blocking sockets directly often requires an event notification mechanism (such as epoll on Linux, kqueue on macOS, or IOCP on Windows), which is what async runtimes provide.

For now, the key takeaway is that using **timeouts** with your standard blocking `TcpStream` operations is a significant and relatively easy step towards making your network code more robust against unresponsive peers or network issues. Full non-blocking I/O with an event loop is a more advanced topic, often handled by dedicated async libraries.

Implementing secure connections with TLS

So far, our TCP client and server have been sending data "in the clear." This means anyone who can intercept the network traffic between them could potentially read or even modify the data. For many applications, especially those handling sensitive information such as passwords, personal details, or financial transactions, this is unacceptable. We need a way to make these connections secure. The standard solution for this on the internet is **Transport Layer Security** (**TLS**).

Introduction to TLS for secure communication

Transport Layer Security (**TLS**), the successor to the now-deprecated **Secure Sockets Layer** (**SSL**), is a cryptographic protocol designed to provide secure communication over a computer network. When you see "HTTPS" in your web browser's address bar, that "S" signifies that your connection to the website is secured by TLS.

TLS provides three main security benefits:

- **Encryption**: Data exchanged between the client and server is encrypted, making it unreadable to any third party who might intercept it. Only the client and server, with the correct cryptographic keys, can decrypt and understand the information.
- **Authentication**: TLS allows the client to verify the identity of the server (and optionally, for the server to verify the client's identity). This is typically done using digital certificates issued by trusted **Certificate Authorities** (**CAs**). When your browser connects to an HTTPS site, it checks the site's certificate to ensure it's genuine and issued to the correct domain. This prevents "man-in-the-middle" attacks, where an attacker might impersonate a legitimate server.
- **Integrity**: TLS ensures that the data sent between the client and server has not been tampered with or altered during transit. It uses **message authentication codes** (**MACs**) to detect any modifications.

In short, if your application needs to send or receive data over a network securely, especially over the public internet, using TLS is a must.

How TLS works

To secure a connection, two main handshakes must occur. First, as shown at the top of the following diagram, a **TCP handshake** (the "three-way handshake" using SYN, SYN ACK, and ACK) establishes a basic, raw connection. Think of this as simply getting a clear phone line. Second, the **TLS handshake** happens immediately after, *on top* of that TCP connection, to encrypt the line and verify who you're talking to. The following diagram illustrates this two-phase process:

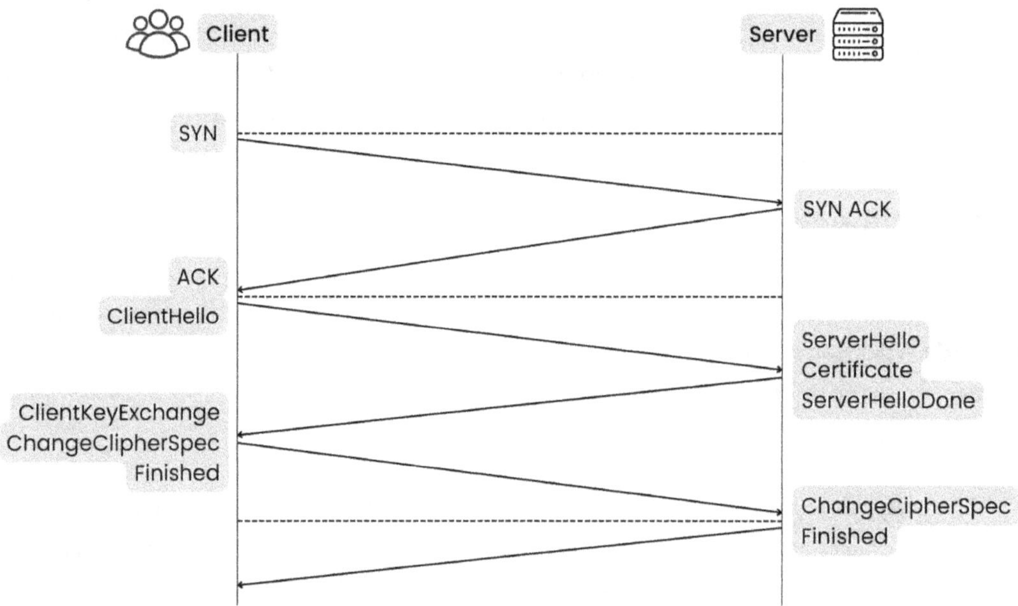

Figure 12.2: The TCP and TLS handshake sequence

Let's break down the important TLS steps from the diagram, as this is what crates like native-tls and rustls handle for you:

- `ClientHello`: This is the client's first message in the secure handshake. It tells the server what encryption methods it supports. Crucially, this message also contains the hostname (such as www.rust-lang.org) that the client is trying to reach. This is a vital feature called **Server Name Indication** (**SNI**), and it's what allows a single server IP address to host multiple secure websites.
- `ServerHello`, `Certificate`: The server replies. It agrees on an encryption method and sends its Certificate. Think of the certificate as the server's digital ID card, proving it is who it claims to be (e.g., "I am genuinely www.rust-lang.org").

- **Client-side verification (the most important step, not a packet)**: After receiving the certificate, your client (or the TLS library) performs the most critical security check: it verifies the certificate. It checks that the name on the certificate matches the SNI hostname it requested and, most importantly, that the certificate was signed by a trusted **Certificate Authority (CA)** (such as LetGood, Let's Encrypt, or DigiCert). Your operating system maintains a list of these trusted CAs. If this verification fails (e.g., the certificate is expired, for the wrong domain, or self-signed and untrusted), the connection is immediately aborted.
- `ClientKeyExchange`, `ChangeCipherSpec`, `Finished`: This is the final phase where the client and server use the server's public key (from the trusted certificate) to securely negotiate a brand-new, secret session key. Once both sides send `ChangeCipherSpec` and `Finished`, the handshake is complete.

From this point on, all application data (such as your HTTP requests and responses) sent over this `TcpStream` is encrypted using the secret session key that only the client and server know.

Using crates for TLS

Rust's standard library (`std::net`) provides the building blocks for TCP and UDP networking, but it does *not* include a TLS implementation directly. This is because TLS is a complex protocol with many cryptographic dependencies, and Rust prefers to keep its standard library lean, relying on the rich ecosystem of crates for more specialized functionality.

To add TLS capabilities to your Rust network applications, you'll use external crates. Two of the most prominent choices are as follows:

- `native-tls`: This crate provides a high-level API that acts as a wrapper around the native or OS-provided TLS library. For example, on Windows, it might use SChannel; on macOS, Secure Transport; and on Linux, it often uses OpenSSL (though this can vary).
    - **Pros**: Leverages well-vetted, platform-specific TLS implementations. Often easier to set up for basic use cases.
    - **Cons**: Introduces a dependency on system libraries (such as OpenSSL on Linux), which can sometimes complicate cross-compilation or deployment if those libraries aren't present or are the wrong version.
- `rustls`: This is a modern TLS library implemented entirely in Rust.
    - **Pros**: Being pure Rust, it avoids dependencies on C-based libraries such as OpenSSL, which can simplify building and deployment, and offers the memory safety benefits of Rust throughout the TLS stack. It's gaining a lot of traction.

- **Cons:** Might require a bit more configuration for certain advanced scenarios compared to `native-tls` if you're not using a higher-level library that integrates it (such as `hyper-rustls` for HTTP clients).

For integrating with asynchronous frameworks such as Tokio or `async-std`, you'll often find adapter crates such as `tokio-native-tls`, `tokio-rustls`, or `async-tls` that make these TLS libraries work smoothly in an async context.

For our first example of a blocking TLS client, `native-tls` can be quite straightforward to get started with.

Example: Setting up a basic TLS client or server

Let's write a simple client that connects to a public HTTPS server, such as www.rust-lang.org on port 443 (the standard port for HTTPS), and attempts to send a basic HTTP GET request. This will demonstrate how to layer TLS on top of a regular TCP connection.

First, you'll need to add `native-tls` to your Cargo.toml dependencies (you need pkg-config package for your OS):

```
[dependencies]
native-tls = "0.2" # Check crates.io for the latest version
# std::net and std::io are part of the standard library, no need to add
them.
```

Now, for the Rust code:

```
use native_tls::{TlsConnector, TlsStream}; // Key types from native-tls
use std::net::TcpStream;
use std::io::{self, Read, Write};

fn main() -> Result<(), Box<dyn std::error::Error>> { // Using Box<dyn
Error> for simple error handling
    let domain = "www.rust-lang.org";
    let port = 443; // HTTPS port
    let server_address = format!("{}:{}", domain, port);

    // 1. Create a TlsConnector builder and build the connector.
    //    TlsConnector::new() provides default settings which usually work
for
```

```
    //     connecting to public servers by using the system's certificate
trust store.
    let connector = TlsConnector::builder()
        // You could add custom configurations here if needed
        .build()
        .map_err(|e| format!("Failed to build TLS connector: {}", e))?;

    println!("Attempting TCP connection to {}...", server_address);
    // 2. Establish a regular TCP connection to the server.
    let tcp_stream = TcpStream::connect(&server_address)
        .map_err(|e| format!("TCP connect to '{}' failed: {}", server_
address, e))?;
    println!("TCP connection established.");

    println!("Attempting TLS handshake with domain '{}'...", domain);
    // 3. Wrap the TCP stream with the TlsConnector to perform the TLS
handshake.
    //     The `connect` method on the connector takes the domain name (for
SNI and certificate validation)
    //     and the existing TcpStream.
    let mut tls_stream: TlsStream<TcpStream> = connector.connect(domain,
tcp_stream)
        .map_err(|e| format!("TLS handshake with '{}' failed: {}", domain,
e))?;
    println!("TLS connection established successfully!");

    // 4. Now, the `tls_stream` can be used much like a regular TcpStream.
    //     It implements the `Read` and `Write` traits. Data written to it
will be
    //     encrypted, and data read from it will be decrypted.
    //     Let's send a very basic HTTP/1.1 GET request.
    let http_request = format!(
        "GET / HTTP/1.1\r\nHost: {}\r\nConnection: close\r\nUser-Agent:
RustBookClient/0.1\r\n\r\n",
        domain
    );

    println!("\nSending HTTP GET request...");
```

```
    tls_stream.write_all(http_request.as_bytes())
        .map_err(|e| format!("Failed to write HTTP request: {}", e))?;
    tls_stream.flush() // Ensure all data in the writer's buffer is sent
        .map_err(|e| format!("Failed to flush stream after request: {}",
e))?;
    println!("HTTP GET request sent.");

    println!("\nReading HTTP response (first part):");
    let mut response_buffer = Vec::new(); // Use a Vec for dynamic sizing
    // Note: For this simple example, we only perform *one* read to get
the
    // first chunk. A real-world HTTP client would need to parse
    // the response headers (which are in this first chunk) to find the
    // 'Content-Length' header, or loop .read() until it returns Ok(0)
    // (EOF) to get the entire response body.
    let mut temp_chunk = [0u8; 512]; // Read in chunks of 512 bytes

    // Read the server's response.
    // A real HTTP client would parse headers, status codes, content
length, etc.
    // This simple example just reads a chunk of the response.
    match tls_stream.read(&mut temp_chunk) {
        Ok(0) => {
            println!("Server closed connection without sending a response
after our request.");
        }
        Ok(bytes_read) => {
            response_buffer.extend_from_slice(&temp_chunk[..bytes_read]);
            println!("Read {} bytes from server.", bytes_read);

            // Attempt to print the received part as UTF-8.
            // HTTP responses usually start with text headers.
            match String::from_utf8(response_buffer) {
                Ok(response_str) => {
                    println!("--- Response Snippet (first {} bytes) ---",
bytes_read);
                    println!("{}", response_str.trim_end());
                    if bytes_read == temp_chunk.len() {
```

```
                println!("... (response might be longer)");
            }
            println!("--- End of Response Snippet ---");
        }
        Err(_) => {
            println!("Response data (first {} bytes) is not valid
UTF-8. Displaying as hex:", bytes_read);
            for byte_val in &temp_chunk[..bytes_read] {
                print!("{:02x} ", byte_val);
            }
            println!();
        }
    }
  }
  Err(e) => {
      eprintln!("Error reading HTTP response: {}", e);
      return Err(Box::new(e)); // Convert io::Error to Box<dyn
Error> for main
  }
 }
 // The TlsStream (and the underlying TcpStream) will be closed
automatically
 // when `tls_stream` goes out of scope due to the Drop trait.
 Ok(())
}
```

- **Dependency**: The example uses the `native-tls` crate, which you would add to your `Cargo.toml`.
- `TlsConnector`: We create a `TlsConnector::builder().build()?`. This object is responsible for setting up the parameters for a TLS connection, such as how to verify server certificates. The default `TlsConnector::new()` or `builder().build()` typically uses the operating system's trusted root certificate store, which is usually what you want for connecting to public websites.
- **Establish TCP connection:** First, a standard, unencrypted `TcpStream::connect()` is made to the server (e.g., www.rust-lang.org on port 443).

- **TLS handshake**: The most important step is connector.connect(domain, tcp_stream)?. This method takes the domain string (which is important for **Server Name Indication (SNI)** – allowing a server hosting multiple HTTPS sites on one IP to know which site you want – and for validating the server's certificate against that domain) and the existing tcp_stream. It performs the TLS handshake over the tcp_stream. This involves cryptographic negotiations, exchanging certificates, and establishing a shared secret key. If the handshake is successful, it returns a TlsStream<TcpStream>.
- **Using TlsStream**: The returned tls_stream now represents the secure, encrypted connection. It implements the Read and Write traits, just like a regular TcpStream. Any data you write to this tls_stream will be automatically encrypted by native-tls before being sent over the underlying TcpStream, and any data read from it will be automatically decrypted.
- **Sending an HTTP request**: We then craft a very basic HTTP/1.1 GET request as a string, convert it to bytes, and send it using tls_stream.write_all() followed by tls_stream.flush().
- **Reading the response**: We attempt to read a chunk of the server's response using tls_stream.read(). In a real HTTP client, this part would be much more sophisticated, involving parsing HTTP headers, status codes, content length, and potentially handling chunked transfer encoding. Our example just reads the first few hundred bytes and tries to print them.
- **Error handling**: All network and TLS operations can fail, so they return Result. The ? operator or map_err is used throughout to handle these potential errors. The main function returns Result<(), Box<dyn std::error::Error>> as a common way to allow different error types to be propagated up using ?.

This example demonstrates the fundamental layering: TCP provides the basic connection, and TLS (via a crate such as native-tls) adds the security layer on top. For most practical HTTP/HTTPS client needs, you would likely use a higher-level HTTP client library such as reqwest, ureq, or hyper, which handle the complexities of HTTP and TLS (often offering choices between native-tls and rustls backends) for you. However, understanding this underlying process is valuable.

We've now covered the mechanics of handling files and building secure network applications.

To tie all these concepts together, let's explore some essential best practices that ensure your Rust applications manage system resources not just correctly, but also efficiently, reliably, and securely!

Best practices for system resource management

We've now covered the mechanics of file I/O and basic TCP networking in Rust. While Rust's safety features and **Resource Acquisition Is Initialization** (**RAII**) via the `Drop` trait save us from many common pitfalls such as forgetting to close files, building truly robust and efficient applications requires a bit more thought.

Let's discuss some general best practices and performance considerations when your Rust programs interact with system resources.

Efficient memory usage with I/O operations

I/O operations, especially with files and networks, can often involve handling significant amounts of data. Being mindful of memory here is key:

- **Avoid reading entire large files into memory**: While `fs::read_to_string()` is convenient for small configuration files, using it for multi-gigabyte log files or datasets will likely exhaust your system's memory. Prefer line-by-line processing (with `BufReader`) or chunk-based processing for large files.
- **Stream when possible**: If you're reading data from one source (file/network) and writing it to another, try to stream it in chunks rather than loading the whole thing into a single large buffer in memory. This reduces your application's peak memory footprint.
- **Reuse buffers where appropriate**: If your program, especially in a loop, needs to repeatedly read data (e.g., from a file or network), allocating a new `Vec<u8>` or String for each read can be inefficient due to frequent memory allocations. A more performant pattern is to allocate the buffer once outside the loop and pass a mutable reference to it on each iteration. The read method will fill this existing buffer, and you can then process the valid data within it. Let's look at a practical example. We'll write a function that reads a file in 8 KB (8,192 bytes) chunks and counts how many zero-bytes (0x00) it contains, all while reusing the same buffer for every chunk.

```
use std::fs::{self, File};
use std::io::{self, Read, BufReader};
use std::path::Path;

// Define a standard chunk size for reading. 8KB is a common,
efficient size.
const CHUNK_SIZE: usize = 8 * 1024; // 8192 bytes
```

```
/// Reads a file in chunks, reusing a buffer to count zero bytes.
fn count_zero_bytes(file_path: &Path) -> io::Result<u64> {
    let file = File::open(file_path)?;
    // Wrap in a BufReader for efficiency, even though we read in
chunks.
    let mut reader = BufReader::new(file);

    // 1. Allocate the buffer *once*, outside the loop.
    // We use a Vec, which is heap-allocated, as a very large
    // stack-allocated array could cause a stack overflow.
    let mut buffer = vec![0u8; CHUNK_SIZE];
    let mut total_zero_bytes = 0;

    loop {
        // 2. Pass a mutable reference to the *existing* buffer to
`read`.
        let bytes_read = match reader.read(&mut buffer) {
            Ok(0) => break, // Ok(0) means End of File (EOF). We're
done.
            Ok(n) => n,     // `n` is the number of bytes actually
read.
            Err(ref e) if e.kind() == io::ErrorKind::Interrupted =>
continue, // Interrupted by a signal, retry.
            Err(e) => return Err(e), // A real I/O error occurred.
        };

        // 3. Process only the valid part of the buffer (`&buffer[..
bytes_read]`).
        // Our "processing" is just counting zero bytes.
        let count_in_chunk = buffer[..bytes_read]
            .iter()
            .filter(|&&b| b == 0x00)
            .count() as u64;

        total_zero_bytes += count_in_chunk;
    }

    Ok(total_zero_bytes)
```

```
}

fn main() {
    let test_file = Path::new("chunk_test.dat");

    // --- Setup: Create a dummy file with some zero bytes ---
    let mut content = vec![1, 2, 3, 4, 5, 0, 6, 7, 0, 8];
    content.resize(10_000, 1); // Make it ~10KB with mostly 1s
    content[2000] = 0; // Add a few more zeros
    content[9000] = 0;
    fs::write(test_file, &content).expect("Failed to create dummy
file");
    // We now have a file with 4 zero bytes.

    // --- Act: Run our function ---
    match count_zero_bytes(test_file) {
        Ok(count) => {
            println!("Found {} zero bytes in '{}'.", count, test_
file.display());
            assert_eq!(count, 4); // Check our logic
        }
        Err(e) => {
            eprintln!("Error processing file '{}': {}", test_file.
display(), e);
        }
    }

    // --- Cleanup ---
    fs::remove_file(test_file).ok();
}
```

- This function allocates a single 8 KB buffer *before* the loop starts, which is a key performance optimization. Inside the loop, `reader.read()` repeatedly fills this *same* buffer, and we process only the slice of valid data (`&buffer[..bytes_read]`) each time, completely avoiding the high cost of allocating new memory for every chunk.

- **Be mindful of string allocations**: When processing text data, frequent creation of new String objects (e.g., one for every line, one for every word) can lead to many small heap allocations. If performance is critical, consider techniques such as working with string slices (`&str`) as much as possible, or using specialized string interning libraries if you have many duplicate strings.

Optimizing file I/O performance

Disk I/O is often a bottleneck. Here's how to make it more efficient:

Buffering strategies recap

We've already emphasized this, but it bears repeating: always use `BufReader` when reading and `BufWriter` when writing files, especially if you're doing multiple small reads/writes or line-by-line processing.

They significantly reduce the number of direct, costly system calls by interacting with an in-memory buffer. Remember to `flush()` your `BufWriter` when you need to ensure data is persisted to disk!

Processing large files in chunks

For very large binary files or structured data files where line-by-line processing isn't appropriate, reading the file in manageable chunks (e.g., a few kilobytes or megabytes at a time) into a buffer is a common strategy. You process one chunk, then read the next, overwriting the buffer. This keeps memory usage constant regardless of file size.

```
use std::fs::File;
use std::io::{self, Read, BufReader};
use std::path::Path;

const CHUNK\_SIZE: usize = 8 \* 1024; // 8KB chunks

fn process\_large\_file\_in\_chunks(file\_path: \&Path) -\>
io::Result\<()\> {
    let file = File::open(file\_path)?;
    let mut reader = BufReader::new(file); // Buffering is still good\!
    let mut chunk = vec\![0u8; CHUNK\_SIZE];
    loop {
        // Attempt to fill the chunk buffer
        // reader.read() might not fill the whole buffer if EOF is
reached.
```

```
        let bytes_read = match reader.read(&mut chunk) {
            Ok(0) => break, // End of file
            Ok(n) => n,
            Err(ref e) if e.kind() == io::ErrorKind::Interrupted =>
continue, // Retry on interrupt
            Err(e) => return Err(e), // Other error
        };
        // Process the data in `&chunk[..bytes_read]`
        // For example, count occurrences of a byte, hash the chunk, etc.
        println!("Processed a chunk of {} bytes", bytes_read);
        // In a real app, you'd do something more useful here.
        if bytes_read < CHUNK_SIZE {
            break; // Likely reached EOF or a partial last chunk
        }
    }
    Ok(())
}

fn main() {
    // You'd need a large\_test\_file.dat for this to be meaningful
    // For now, let's just show the function definition and conceptual
call
    // if let Err(e) = process\_large\_file\_in\_chunks(Path::new("large\_
test\_file.dat")) {
    //     eprintln\!("Error processing large file: {}", e);
    // }

    println\!("Conceptual chunked file processing function defined.");
}
```

The `process_large_file_in_chunks` function demonstrates reading a file in fixed-size portions.

- A chunk buffer is allocated once.
- In a loop, `reader.read(&mut chunk)` attempts to fill this buffer; `read()` returns the number of bytes actually read, which might be less than `CHUNK_SIZE` if the end of the file is reached.
- `Ok(0)` from `read()` signals that the end of the file has been definitively reached.

- The `&chunk[..bytes_read]` slice contains the valid data for the current chunk to be processed. This approach ensures that memory usage remains constant and low, irrespective of the total file size.

Optimizing network I/O performance

Network latency and bandwidth are often critical performance factors.

Understanding asynchronous I/O for networking

While the thread-per-client model we just discussed works well, it's good to keep in mind that for applications handling many connections at once (such as large web servers or chat platforms), a more sophisticated approach called asynchronous I/O is often a better fit. We'll dive into this topic more deeply in *Chapter 13, Concurrency and Parallelism,* as it offers an effective alternative to assigning one OS thread per connection.

Async I/O allows a small number of threads to handle thousands of connections by not blocking when waiting for network events. Libraries such as tokio and async-std provide the runtimes and utilities for this in Rust.

While `std::net` provides blocking I/O, these async libraries build upon non-blocking primitives to offer much greater scalability for I/O-bound network applications.

Managing network buffers and packet sizes

- **Buffering (recap)**: Just like with files, `BufReader` and `BufWriter` are beneficial for `TcpStream` to reduce system call overhead.
- **TCP Nagle's algorithm and TCP_NODELAY**: By default, TCP often tries to bundle small outgoing packets together to improve network efficiency (Nagle's algorithm). This can introduce latency for applications that need to send small messages quickly (e.g., real-time games, some RPC protocols). `TcpStream` has a `set_nodelay(true)` method that can disable Nagle's algorithm, potentially reducing latency for small, frequent messages at the cost of slightly increased network overhead. Use it judiciously.
- **Application-level buffering**: Sometimes your application protocol involves messages of known or variable sizes. Managing your own buffers to assemble or parse these messages before writing to/after reading from the `TcpStream` can be more efficient than many small `read()`/`write()` calls on the stream itself.

General security principles for resource handling

When your application interacts with system resources, especially those influenced by external input (files from users, network data), security becomes a concern.

Validating inputs from external sources

- **File paths**: If your program takes file paths as input (e.g., from a user or a config file), be extremely careful. Maliciously crafted paths (e.g., containing `..` to traverse directories or pointing to sensitive system files) can lead to security vulnerabilities (path traversal attacks). Sanitize and validate any externally supplied paths before using them with `File::open` or other `fs` operations. Consider restricting operations to a specific base directory if possible.
- **Network data**: Data received over the network should never be trusted implicitly. Always validate its format, size, and content before processing it. For example, if you expect a number, parse it carefully and handle parsing errors. If you expect a certain message structure, verify it. This helps prevent crashes, denial-of-service, and other attacks.
- **Resource limits**: Impose limits on resource usage. For example, limit the maximum size of a file that can be uploaded or processed, the maximum number of concurrent network connections, or the maximum amount of data read from a socket in one go. This prevents a malicious client or a malformed file from exhausting system resources.

Principle of least privilege

When your application performs operations that require system privileges (such as writing to certain file locations or binding to low-numbered network ports), it should ideally only hold those privileges for the minimum time necessary. If possible, drop privileges after the privileged operation is complete.

While Rust itself doesn't manage OS-level user privileges directly in std, this is a good design principle to keep in mind for the overall application architecture, especially for system daemons or services.

Minimizing resource contention in concurrent scenarios

This topic ties directly into the concepts we will explore in *Chapter 13, Concurrency and Parallelism*. When multiple threads try to access shared system resources (such as a file or a network socket, though direct sharing of such OS handles is often complex and better managed through higher-level abstractions), you can run into contention.

- **Locking shared resources**: If multiple threads *must* write to the same file or send data over the same (non-thread-safe by default) network connection, you'd need to protect access with a mutex or similar synchronization primitive. As always, keep the locked sections short.
- **Dedicated I/O threads with message passing**: A common pattern is to dedicate one or a few threads to handle specific I/O tasks (e.g., a logging thread that writes to a file, a network thread that manages all socket communication) and have other worker threads communicate with these I/O threads via message-passing channels. This can serialize access to the resource and often simplifies reasoning about its state.
- **Connection pooling**: For resources such as database connections or outgoing network connections that are expensive to establish, using a "pool" of pre-established connections that threads can borrow from and return to can be much more efficient than each thread creating and tearing down its own connection repeatedly. Crates exist to help manage such pools.

By being mindful of these practices, you can build Rust applications that are correct and safe, and efficient and well-behaved citizens of the systems they run on.

Real-world scenarios and examples

We've covered a fair bit of ground on file I/O, basic networking, security considerations, and best practices for managing system resources.

Now, let's try to bring some of these concepts together by looking at a few more practical, albeit simplified, real-world-inspired scenarios.

Example 1: Building a more robust HTTP server

Earlier, we built a very basic TCP echo server and then a multi-threaded version. Let's refine that into a slightly more recognizable (though still very simple) multi-threaded HTTP server that can serve a couple of static HTML files and return a 404 error. This will combine TCP listening, multi-threading, file reading, and basic HTTP response formatting.

(This example will be more conceptual in its HTTP handling for brevity, focusing on resource management aspects such as concurrent connection handling and file reading per request.)

```
use std::fs;
use std::io::{Read, Write, BufReader, BufRead};
use std::net::{TcpListener, TcpStream};

/// Handles a single client connection, parses a simple GET request, and
serves a file.
/// This function will block until it is finished with the client.
fn handle_http_connection(mut stream: TcpStream) -> std::io::Result<()> {

    let client_addr = stream.peer_addr().unwrap_or_else(|_| "unknown".
parse().unwrap());
    println!("Handling connection from {}", client_addr);

    // Wrap the stream in a BufReader to read lines
    let mut reader = BufReader::new(&stream);

    // --- 1. Read the HTTP Request Line ---
    let mut request_line = String::new();
    if reader.read_line(&mut request_line).is_err() {
        eprintln!("Failed to read request line from {}", client_addr);
        return Ok(()); // Close connection on read error
    }

    println!("Request from {}: {}", client_addr, request_line.trim());

    // --- 2. Read (and ignore) HTTP Headers ---
    // A real HTTP request has headers after the request line,
    // ending in a blank line (e.g., "\r\n"). We must read them
    // to consume the full request, even if we don't use them.
    let mut header_line = String::new();
    loop {
        match reader.read_line(&mut header_line) {
            Ok(0) => { // Client disconnected prematurely
                eprintln!("Client disconnected during header read.");
                return Ok(());
```

```
            }
            Ok(_) => {
                // If the line is just "\r\n" or "\n", it's the end of the
headers.
                if header_line.trim().is_empty() {
                    break; // End of headers, break the loop
                }
                // We're just ignoring the header line in this simple
server.
            }
            Err(e) => {
                eprintln!("Error reading headers: {}", e);
                return Err(e);
            }
        }
        header_line.clear(); // Clear string for the next line
    }
    // At this point, we've consumed the headers.

    // --- 3. Very basic request routing ---
    let (status_line, filename) = if request_line.starts_with("GET /
HTTP/1.1") || request_line.starts_with("GET /index.html HTTP/1.1") {
        ("HTTP/1.1 200 OK", "index.html")
    } else if request_line.starts_with("GET /about.html HTTP/1.1") {
        ("HTTP/1.1 200 OK", "about.html")
    } else {
        ("HTTP/1.1 404 NOT FOUND", "404.html")
    };

    // --- 4. Read File Content and Send Response ---
    let file_contents = match fs::read_to_string(filename) {
        Ok(contents) => contents,
        Err(_) => {
            // If the specific file isn't found, try to send the generic
404 page
            println!("File '{}' not found for {}. Sending 404.", filename,
client_addr);
            let not_found_page = "404.html"; // Assume this one exists
```

```
            let generic_404_content = fs::read_to_string(not_found_page)
                .unwrap_or_else(|_| "<h1>404 Not Found</h1><p>The
requested resource was not found.</p>".to_string());

            let response = format!(
                "HTTP/1.1 404 NOT FOUND\r\nContent-Length: {}\r\n\r\n{}",
                generic_404_content.len(),
                generic_404_content
            );

            // Send 404 response
            if let Err(e) = stream.write_all(response.as_bytes()) {
                 eprintln!("Error sending 404 response to {}: {}", client_
addr, e);
            }
            if let Err(e) = stream.flush() {
                 eprintln!("Error flushing 404 response to {}: {}",
client_addr, e);
            }
            return Ok(());
        }
    };

    // --- 5. Construct and send the successful HTTP response ---
    let response = format!(
        "{}\r\nContent-Length: {}\r\n\r\n{}",
        status_line,
        file_contents.len(),
        file_contents
    );

    if let Err(e) = stream.write_all(response.as_bytes()) {
        eprintln!("Error sending response to {}: {}", client_addr, e);
    }
    if let Err(e) = stream.flush() {
         eprintln!("Error flushing response to {}: {}", client_addr, e);
    }
```

```
    println!("Response sent to {}. Closing connection.", client_addr);

    Ok(())
}

fn main() -> std::io::Result<()> {
    // --- Setup: Prepare dummy HTML files for the server to serve ---
    fs::write("index.html", "<h1>Welcome!</h1><p>This is the main page.</
p><p><a href=\"/about.html\">About Us</a></p>")?;
    fs::write("about.html", "<h1>About Us</h1><p>We are a Rust learning
example!</p><p><a href=\"/\">Home</a></p>")?;
    fs::write("404.html", "<h1>404 - Page Not Found</h1><p>Sorry, the page
you are looking for does not exist.</p><p><a href=\"/\">Go Home</a></
p>")?;

    let listener_address = "127.0.0.1:7878";
    let listener = TcpListener::bind(listener_address)?;
    println!("Simple HTTP Server listening on http://{}", listener_
address);

    // Accept connections one at a time (sequentially)
    for stream_result in listener.incoming() {
        match stream_result {
            Ok(stream) => {
                println!("Main: Accepted new connection. Handling...");
                // Handle the connection directly in the main thread.
                // The loop will block here until this client is done.
                if let Err(e) = handle_http_connection(stream) {
                    eprintln!("Connection error: {}", e);
                }
            }
            Err(e) => {
                eprintln!("Main: Failed to accept connection: {}", e);
            }
        }
    }
```

```
    // --- Cleanup (in a real server, this part wouldn't be reached) ---
    fs::remove_file("index.html")?;
    fs::remove_file("about.html")?;
    fs::remove_file("404.html")?;
    Ok(())
}
```

- **Setup**: Before main runs the listener, we create three dummy HTML files (`index.html`, `about.html`, `404.html`) in the current directory so the server has something to serve.
- **Listening and threading**: main sets up a `TcpListener` and then, for each incoming connection (stream), it spawns a new thread that calls `handle_http_connection(stream)`. This allows the server to handle multiple client requests concurrently.
- **Reads headers**: This server is more robust than our echo server because the `handle_http_connection` function now includes a loop to read and consume the HTTP headers (the lines after the first GET / line) until it finds the blank line (`\r\n`) that signifies the end of the header block. This is important for properly handling HTTP requests.
- **Basic routing**: It performs simple routing by checking the `request_line` and serves different files based on the requested path.
- **Serves files**: It uses `fs::read_to_string` to read the contents of the requested HTML file and sends it back to the client with the correct HTTP status line and Content-Length header.

Important limitation: sequential handling

Notice that in the main function, we call `handle_http_connection(stream)` directly inside the `for` loop. This server is sequential (or single-threaded in its handling).

This means it can only handle one client at a time.

If Client A connects and `handle_http_connection` is busy processing their request (e.g., reading a large file, or if the client is on a slow connection), Client B cannot connect. Client B's connection attempt will sit in a queue, and the server's main loop will be blocked until `handle_http_connection` for Client A finally finishes.

This is a major bottleneck for any real-world server. To solve this and handle multiple clients concurrently, we need to use the concurrency techniques we will explore in the next chapter, such as spawning a new thread for each connection.

Example 2: Command-line tool for file operations

Let's build a very simplified version of the wc (word count) utility that takes a file path as a command-line argument and prints out the number of lines, words, characters (UTF-8), and the total file size in bytes. This example combines argument parsing and file I/O in a practical CLI tool.

```
use std::env;
use std::fs::{self, File};
use std::io::{self, BufRead, BufReader};
use std::path::Path;
use std::process;

#[derive(Debug, Default)]
struct FileStats {
    lines: usize,
    words: usize,
    chars: usize,
}

fn main() -> io::Result<()> {
    // 1. Get file path from command-line arguments.
    let file_path_str = match env::args().nth(1) {
        Some(path) => path,
        None => {
            eprintln!("Usage: my_wc <file_path>");
            process::exit(1);
        }
    };
    let file_path = Path::new(&file_path_str);

    // 2. Open the file and prepare to read it line by line.
    let file = File::open(file_path)?;
    let reader = BufReader::new(file);

    // 3. Process the file to gather stats.
    let mut stats = FileStats::default();
```

```
    for line_result in reader.lines() {
        let line = line_result?; // Propagate I/O error if reading a line
fails
        stats.lines += 1;
        stats.words += line.split_whitespace().count();
        stats.chars += line.chars().count();
    }

    // 4. Get total file size in bytes from metadata for accuracy.
    let file_size_bytes = fs::metadata(file_path)?.len();

    // 5. Print the results.
    println!("\n--- Statistics for '{}' ---", file_path.display());
    println!("  Lines:      {}", stats.lines);
    println!("  Words:      {}", stats.words);
    println!("  Characters: {}", stats.chars);
    println!("  Bytes:      {}", file_size_bytes);
    Ok(())
}
```

- **Argument parsing**: `env::args().nth(1)` is used to directly get the first command-line argument after the program name. If it's `None`, we print a usage message and exit.
- **Error handling with ?**: The main function returns an `io::Result<()>`, allowing us to use the ? operator for concise error handling on file operations such as `File::open`, `fs::metadata`, and reading lines. If any of these fail, the program will exit, and the OS will typically print the I/O error.
- **Statistics calculation:**
- A loop over `reader.lines()` efficiently processes the file line by line
- `line.chars().count()` accurately counts Unicode characters
- `line.split_whitespace().count()` gives a simple word count
- **Accurate byte count**: Instead of approximating the byte count from string lengths, this version uses `fs::metadata(file_path)?.len()` to get the exact file size from the file system, which is more reliable.
- **Output**: The final statistics are printed in a clean format.

Next steps

The examples in this chapter, such as our simple HTTP server and my_wc tool, were intentionally built using *only* Rust's standard library. This was to help you understand the fundamentals of how Rust handles system resources such as TcpStreams and Files directly.

However, for building real-world, production-ready applications, you will almost always want to use the powerful, high-level crates that the Rust community has built. These frameworks handle much of the complex, boilerplate logic for you, allowing you to focus on your application's features.

- For a real **HTTP server**, you wouldn't build one from raw TcpStreams. Instead, you would use a mature web framework such as **Actix Web**, **Axum**, or **Rocket**.
- For a **command-line tool**, you wouldn't parse arguments manually with `std::env::args()`. You'd use a powerful crate such as **clap** or **argh** to define arguments and get robust parsing and help-message generation for free.
- For **secure networking (TLS)**, you would typically use a high-level HTTP client such as reqwest, which handles TLS internally, rather than using native-tls directly.

Frameworks and high-level libraries like these evolve much faster than the Rust standard library. This book emphasizes the stable fundamentals that remain relevant.

With your solid understanding of file I/O and networking, you're now ready to explore advanced crates and read their documentation to create powerful applications.

Summary

We have reached the end of *Chapter 12*, which covered managing system resources in Rust. It explored how Rust interacts with external resources, such as the file system and the network. Resource management is essential for building functional, efficient, reliable, and secure applications. Rust's design emphasizes safety through explicit error handling via the `Result` type and automatic resource cleanup using the `Drop` trait (RAII).

Recap:

- **Why resource management matters**: We emphasized managing resources such as files and network connections for performance, stability, scalability, and system health.
- **File I/O in Rust**:
    - We learned how to read files, loading them into strings for smaller files or processing line by line for larger files using `BufReader`

    - We explored writing data using `File::create` and `fs::write` for creating/overwriting, or `OpenOptions` for appending
    - We covered file system operations in `std::fs`, such as creating directories, renaming files, and reading contents
- **Network programming essentials (TCP)**:
    - We discussed TCP basics, including IP addresses, ports, and the client-server model
    - We used `TcpListener` to accept incoming connections and handled multiple clients by spawning threads for each `TcpStream`
    - For clients, `TcpStream::connect` was used to establish connections with read and `write_all` for communication
    - The benefits of `BufReader` and `BufWriter` for network I/O performance were highlighted
- Ensuring robust and secure network applications:
    - We emphasized careful error handling for all network operations returning `Result`
    - The importance of `set_read_timeout` and `set_write_timeout` on `TcpStream` was introduced to avoid indefinite blocking
    - We discussed **Transport Layer Security** (**TLS**), introducing external crates such as `native-tls`, `rustls`, and a basic TLS client example.
- Best practices for system resource management:
    - We covered strategies for efficient memory usage during I/O, optimizing file and network performance (e.g., buffering, chunking, and asynchronous I/O)
    - Key security principles, such as validating external inputs, were highlighted
    - We also briefly linked concurrency concepts to minimize resource contention
    - Real-world examples: We provided real-world examples to better understand how they are used

In this chapter, we looked at how to manage system resources such as files and network streams. Our simple server examples showed a key limitation: they can only handle one client at a time. To create more efficient applications that can manage several tasks simultaneously, we'll move on to the next chapter, *Concurrency and Parallelism*. There, we'll explore how to use threads, share data safely, and see why Rust's compile-time guarantees make this exciting feature known as "fearless concurrency" a term the Rust community often uses.

Questions and assignments

Questions

1. What are the main differences between `std::fs::read_to_string()` and using `File::open()` followed by `BufReader::new().lines()` for reading a text file? When would you prefer one over the other?
2. Explain the purpose of `File::create()` versus using `OpenOptions::new().append(true).create(true).open()`. What happens if the file already exists in each case?
3. What does `TcpListener::bind()` do, and what kind of errors might it return?
4. When handling a `TcpStream` on a server, why is it common to spawn a new thread for each accepted connection? What problem does this solve?
5. What is the role of `stream.flush()` after a `write_all()` call on a `TcpStream` or `BufWriter`? Why is it sometimes important?
6. Briefly explain why TLS is important for network communication and what main security benefits it provides.
7. What is "buffering" in the context of I/O, and why are `BufReader` and `BufWriter` useful?

Assignments

Assignment 12.1: Simple file copy utility

Goal: Get comfortable with basic file I/O and error handling.

Task:

1. Create a Rust command-line program that takes two arguments: a `source_file` path and a `destination_file` path.
2. The program should read the entire contents of the `source_file`.
3. It should then write those contents to the `destination_file`, creating it if it doesn't exist or overwriting it if it does.
4. Handle potential errors gracefully. If the source file cannot be read or the destination file cannot be written, print a clear error message to standard error (`eprintln!`) and exit with a non-zero status code (`std::process::exit(1)`).

Steps and hints:

- Use `std::env::args()` to get the command-line arguments.
- `std::fs::read()` can read the entire file into a `Vec<u8>` (a vector of bytes), which is good for handling any kind of file, not just text.
- `std::fs::write()` is a convenient way to write an entire byte slice (`&[u8]`) to a file.

Assignment 12.2: Simple key-value TCP server

Goal: Practice networking, basic protocol parsing, and in-memory state management.

Task: Implement a simple in-memory key-value store server that listens on a TCP port (e.g., `127.0.0.1:8989`). You do **not** need to build a separate client program; you can test your server using a tool such as netcat (nc) or telnet.

- **Server setup**:
    - The server should use a TcpListener to accept connections. For this assignment, handling clients one at a time (sequentially) is fine.
    - It should maintain an in-memory `HashMap<String, String>` to store the key-value pairs.
- **Command handling**:
    - For each connected client, the server should read commands line by line.
    - It must support two commands:
        - `SET <key> <value>`: Stores the value associated with the key. The server should respond with `OK\n`. If the key already exists, its value should be updated.
        - `GET <key>`: Retrieves the value for the key. If the key exists, the server should respond with `VALUE <value>\n`. If the key does not exist, it should respond with `NOT_FOUND\n`.
    - Any other command can be considered invalid, and the server might respond with INVALID_COMMAND\n.
- **Error handling**: The server should handle client disconnections gracefully without crashing.

Steps and hints:

- Use `BufReader::read_line()` to read commands from the `TcpStream`.
- Use `split_whitespace()` on the received line to parse the command and its arguments. Be sure to handle cases where not enough arguments are provided.
- Use a HashMap owned by your main loop or handler function to store the data.
- Use `writeln!` or `write_all` on the `TcpStream` to send responses back to the client. Remember to `flush()`!

13

Concurrency and Parallelism

Welcome to Chapter 13!

We've just seen how smart pointers such as Arc<T> and Mutex<T> provide tools for managing data in thread-safe ways. This was a deliberate setup for our next big topic: **concurrency**.

In this chapter, we'll explore how Rust enables you to write programs that can perform multiple tasks simultaneously.

This is a cornerstone of modern software development, allowing applications to be more responsive, effectively utilize modern multi-core processors, and handle many operations in parallel.

Rust's approach to concurrency is particularly noteworthy because of its strong emphasis on safety.

What are concurrency and parallelism?

Before discussing the "how," let's clarify two terms often used interchangeably but with distinct meanings: **concurrency** and **parallelism**:

- **Concurrency** is about *dealing* with multiple tasks at once. It's a way to structure a program to switch between different tasks, making progress on each. These tasks might not all be executing at the exact same instant, especially on a single-core processor, but they are managed in a way that allows them to overlap in time. Think of a chef juggling multiple orders in a kitchen: they switch between chopping vegetables for one order, checking the oven for another, and plating a third. They are *concurrently* handling multiple orders.
- **Parallelism** is about *doing* multiple tasks at the exact same time. This requires hardware with multiple processing units (such as multi-core CPUs). If our chef had two assistant chefs, they could, *in parallel*, chop vegetables, stir a sauce, and bake a dish.

A concurrent program *can* be parallel if you have the hardware to support it. Rust provides tools to write concurrent programs, and if you run that code on a multi-core processor, those concurrent tasks can often execute in parallel, leading to genuine performance gains.

Our main focus will be on writing concurrent code, which can then benefit from parallelism.

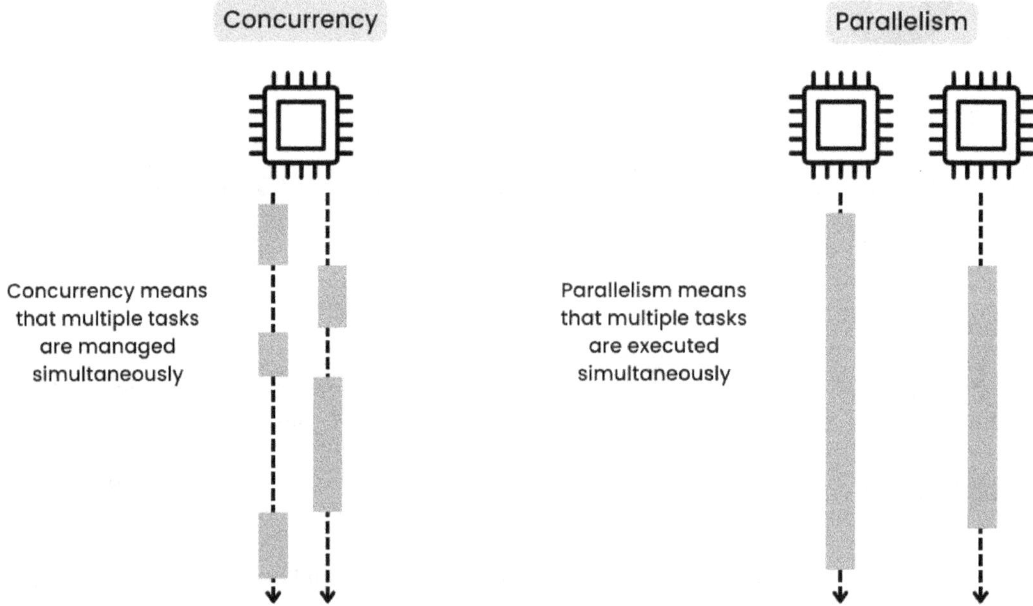

Figure 13.1: The difference between concurrency and parallelism

Why write concurrent programs?

Why go through the trouble of managing multiple tasks at once? There are several compelling reasons:

- **Performance through parallelism**: Most modern computers have CPUs with multiple cores. If your program only does one thing at a time, it's only using one of those cores, leaving a lot of processing power untapped. Concurrent programming allows you to break down a large task into smaller pieces that can be executed in parallel on different cores, significantly speeding up CPU-bound computations (such as complex calculations, image processing, or data analysis).

- **Responsiveness**: For applications with UIs (GUIs and web servers), concurrency is vital for responsiveness. Imagine a desktop application that needs to perform a long calculation. If it does this on its main thread without concurrency, the entire UI will freeze until the calculation is done. By running the calculation on a separate thread, the main thread can remain free to respond to user input, keeping the application feeling smooth and interactive. Similarly, a web server can handle multiple client requests concurrently, rather than making each client wait in a long queue.
- **Handling multiple I/O operations**: Programs often wait for **input/output** (**I/O**) operations, such as reading from a file, writing to a network socket, or waiting for user input. These operations can be slow. Concurrency allows a program to start an I/O operation and then switch to another task while waiting for the I/O to complete, rather than just sitting idle. This is key for efficient network services and applications dealing with many external resources.

The classic challenges: Race conditions and deadlocks

While concurrency offers significant benefits, it also introduces new categories of challenging bugs that are notoriously hard to find and fix. Two of the most infamous are the following:

- **Race conditions**: A race condition occurs when two or more threads access shared data concurrently, and at least one of them modifies the data. The final outcome depends on the unpredictable order in which the threads happen to execute their operations. This can lead to corrupted data, incorrect results, or crashes. For example, if two threads try to increment a shared counter (counter += 1) without proper synchronization, both might read the same initial value, both increment it, and both write back the same new value, effectively losing one of the increments.
- **Deadlocks**: A deadlock happens when two or more threads are blocked forever, each waiting for the other to release a resource. Imagine Thread A has locked Resource X and is waiting for Resource Y, while Thread B has locked Resource Y and is waiting for Resource X. Neither can proceed, and the program grinds to a halt.

These issues arise because of the complexities of managing shared mutable state and synchronizing access between threads. They are often difficult to reproduce because they depend on the precise timing of thread execution.

Rust's promise: Compile-time safety for concurrency

This is where Rust truly shines and offers a compelling reason to use it for concurrent programming. Rust's ownership and borrowing system, which we've seen ensuring memory safety, also extends to ensure **thread safety** at compile time for many common concurrency bugs, especially data races.

- **Preventing data races**: Rust's type system and borrow checker ensure that you cannot have a data race in safe Rust. A data race occurs when you have the following:
    1. Two or more pointers/references accessing the same memory location concurrently.
    2. At least one of them is for writing.
    3. There's no synchronization mechanism being used to control access. Rust's rules about mutable and immutable borrows (one &mut T XOR many &T) prevent this scenario from happening across threads for most types unless you use special synchronization primitives (such as mutex, which then enforces its own rules).
- **Clearer shared state management**: Types such as Arc<T> (for shared ownership across threads) and Mutex<T> or RwLock<T> (for controlled mutation of shared data) make the intent of sharing and mutation explicit in the type system.

While Rust can't magically prevent all concurrency bugs (such as all types of deadlocks, which are often a logic issue), it eliminates entire classes of very common and nasty bugs at compile time. This is what's often referred to as "fearless concurrency", the ability to write concurrent code with much greater confidence because the compiler is your ally in preventing many common pitfalls. This makes Rust an incredibly powerful tool for building high-performance, concurrent systems reliably.

Creating and managing threads

Now that we understand the "why" of concurrency, let's get to the "how" in Rust. The most fundamental way to achieve concurrency is by creating and managing **threads**.

What is a thread?

A thread is an independent path of execution within your program. Your operating system can schedule these threads to run, potentially in parallel on different CPU cores. Rust's standard library provides `std::thread`.

Spawning new threads with std::thread::spawn

The primary way to create a new thread in Rust is by calling the `std::thread::spawn` function.

This function takes a *closure* (an anonymous function) as an argument, and this closure contains the code that the new thread will execute.

Basic thread creation

When you call `thread::spawn`, it immediately returns a `JoinHandle`. The new thread starts executing its closure in the background, and your main thread (or the thread that called spawn) continues its own execution without waiting:

```
use std::thread;
use std::time::Duration;

fn main() {
    println!("Main thread: Starting up!");

    // Spawn a new thread
    let handle = thread::spawn(|| {
        // This code runs in the new thread
        for i in 1..=5 {
            println!("New thread: count {}", i);
            thread::sleep(Duration::from_millis(500)); // Pause for 0.5
seconds
        }
        println!("New thread: I'm done!");
    });

    // The main thread continues its work immediately
    for i in 1..=3 {
        println!("Main thread: working... {}", i);
        thread::sleep(Duration::from_millis(300)); // Pause for 0.3
seconds
    }

    println!("Main thread: Waiting for the new thread to finish...");
    // We'll see how to properly wait for the handle next.
    // For now, if main exits, the spawned thread might be killed.
```

```
    // To ensure the spawned thread finishes in this example, we can add a
longer sleep here,
    // but using join() is the correct way.
    // thread::sleep(Duration::from_secs(3)); // Temporary, to see spawned
thread output

    // The correct way to wait for the spawned thread:
    handle.join().unwrap(); // We'll explain join() shortly

    println!("Main thread: All done!");
}
```

The following is the output:

```
Main thread: Starting up!
Main thread: working... 1
New thread: count 1
Main thread: working... 2
New thread: count 2
Main thread: working... 3
Main thread: Waiting for the new thread to finish...
New thread: count 3
New thread: count 4
New thread: count 5
New thread: I'm done!
Main thread: All done!
```

Figure 13.2: Output of thread creation

- We use `std::thread` to bring the `spawn` function and other thread-related items into scope.
- `thread::spawn(|| { ... })` creates a new thread. The `|| { ... }` part is a closure containing the code for that new thread.
- Notice how the output from `Main thread` and `New thread` will likely be interleaved. This is because both threads are running concurrently (and potentially in parallel if you have multiple CPU cores).
- The `thread::sleep()` calls are just there to simulate work and make the interleaving more obvious.

- The handle returned by `thread::spawn` is a `JoinHandle`. We'll use this to manage the thread. The `handle.join().unwrap()` line at the end is crucial for ensuring the main thread waits for the spawned thread to complete before exiting.

Moving data into threads with the move closure

Often, the closure you pass to `thread::spawn` will need to use data that's defined in the scope of the thread that *creates* it (the parent thread). Rust's ownership rules are strict here to prevent data races.

If a spawned thread's closure tries to capture a variable from its environment by reference, the compiler might complain because it can't guarantee that the reference will remain valid for the entire lifetime of the new thread (the new thread might outlive the parent function's scope where the variable was defined).

To solve this, you typically use the `move` keyword before the closure. A `move || { ... }` closure takes ownership of the variables it captures from its environment:

```
use std::thread;
use std::time::Duration;

fn main() {
    let message = String::from("Hello from the main thread!");
    let important_number = 42;

    // The `move` keyword forces the closure to take ownership of
`message` and `important_number`.
    let handle = thread::spawn(move || {
        println!("Spawned thread received message: '{}'", message);
        println!("Spawned thread received number: {}", important_number);
        // `message` and `important_number` are now owned by this
closure's environment.
        // The original variables in main are no longer accessible if they
were moved (like String).
        // For Copy types like i32, a copy is moved.
    });

    // Attempting to use `message` here would cause a compile error:
    // println!("Main thread still has message: {}", message); // ERROR!
value borrowed here after move
```

```
    // `important_number` was an i32, which is Copy, so a copy was moved.
    // The original `important_number` in main is still valid.
    println!("Main thread still has important_number: {}", important_
number);

    // Wait for the thread to finish
    handle.join().unwrap();
    println!("Main thread: Spawned thread finished.");
}
```

- The `move` keyword before the `|| { ... }` closure tells Rust that any variables from the outer scope used inside the closure should be transferred into the closure's environment.
- For types that implement the `Copy` trait (such as `i32`, `bool`, etc.), moving means that a copy of the value is created. The original variable in the parent thread remains usable.
- For types that do not implement `Copy` (such as `String` and `Vec<T>`), moving transfers ownership. Consequently, the original variable in the parent thread becomes invalid and cannot be used after the closure is created. This is why attempting to use `message` in `main` after it has been moved to the spawned thread results in a compile error, as illustrated in the commented-out line.
- This ownership transfer is crucial for safety, ensuring that the spawned thread has valid ownership of the required data, even if the parent thread completes or the original variables go out of scope.

Waiting for threads to finish: JoinHandle and join()

When you spawn a new thread, it runs independently. Often, your main thread (or the spawning thread) will need to wait for the newly created thread to complete its work before proceeding or before the program exits. If the main thread exits while other threads are still running, those other threads are typically shut down abruptly.

`JoinHandle<T>` returned by `thread::spawn` provides a `join()` method for this purpose:

- Calling `handle.join()` on `JoinHandle` will block the current thread's execution until the thread associated with `handle` terminates.
- `join()` also allows you to get a value back from the thread, as it returns a `Result<T, E>`:

- If the spawned thread completes successfully, `join()` returns `Ok(value)`, where `value` is the value returned by the closure given to `spawn`. (Yes, spawned threads can return values!)
- If the spawned thread panics, `join()` returns `Err(error)`, where `error` contains information about the panic.

Handling thread panics gracefully

A key part of Rust's safety is that *a panic in one thread does not crash the entire program* (unless it's the main thread). The panic is isolated to that thread. The `JoinHandle` "catches" this panic, and `join()` will return an `Err` variant. This allows the main thread to detect and handle worker failures gracefully, instead of crashing along with them.

Let's see an example that shows both a successful thread and a panicking thread, and how to handle both outcomes with `match`:

```
use std::thread;
use std::time::Duration;

fn main() {
    println!("Main: Spawning a worker thread that will succeed...");
    let worker_handle = thread::spawn(|| {
        println!("Worker (Success): Starting computation...");
        thread::sleep(Duration::from_secs(1)); // Simulate work
        println!("Worker (Success): Computation finished.");
        42 // This is the return value
    });

    println!("Main: Spawning a worker thread that will panic...");
    let panicking_handle = thread::spawn(|| {
        println!("Worker (Panic): I'm about to panic!");
        panic!("The worker thread has panicked!");
    });

    // --- Wait for the successful worker ---
    println!("Main: Waiting for the successful worker...");
    match worker_handle.join() {
        Ok(result_from_worker) => {
            println!("Main: Successful worker joined and returned: {}",
```

```
result_from_worker);
        }
        Err(e) => {
            // This case won't be hit for worker_handle
            eprintln!("Main: Successful worker panicked (unexpected!):
{:?}", e);
        }
    }

    // --- Wait for the panicking worker ---
    println!("\nMain: Waiting for the panicking worker...");
    match panicking_handle.join() {
        Ok(_) => {
            // This case won't be hit for panicking_handle
            println!("Main: Panicking worker... returned Ok?
(unexpected!)");
        }
        Err(e) => {
            // This is the expected outcome.
            // The 'e' here is an `Any + Send + 'static` object
representing the panic.
            eprintln!("Main: Caught panic from worker thread as
expected!");
            // We can't print the panic message directly in a simple way,
            // but we've confirmed it was an `Err`.
        }
    }

    println!("\nMain: Program finished gracefully, even after a worker
panic.");
}
```

This example clearly demonstrates the two possible outcomes of calling `join()`:

- `Ok(value)`: The `worker_handle` completes its closure normally and returns the value 42. Our `match` statement catches this `Ok` variant and prints the successful result.

- `Err(e)`: The `panicking_handle` calls `panic!`. This terminates that specific worker thread, but *not the main thread*. When the main thread calls `.join()` on `panicking_handle`, the panic is "caught," and `join()` returns an `Err(e)`. Our `match` statement catches this `Err` variant, allowing us to log the error and continue execution. This isolation of panics is a key safety feature of Rust's concurrency model.

This is why you should prefer using `match` to handle the `Result` from `.join()` in production code. Using `.unwrap()` is just a shortcut that says, "If this thread panics, I want my main thread to panic too," which is often not the robust behavior you want for your application.

Thread panics and their effect

What happens if a spawned thread panics?

- By default, a panic in one thread *does not* bring down the entire program (unless it's the main thread). The panicking thread will unwind its stack and terminate.
- Other threads will continue running.
- As we saw, the `JoinHandle::join()` method will return an `Err` value if the thread it's waiting on has panicked. This allows the joining thread to detect and react to the panic if necessary.

This isolation of panics (by default) contributes to the robustness of concurrent Rust programs. You can configure the behavior on panic further, but the default is usually what you want, one misbehaving thread shouldn't necessarily crash everything.

Sharing data safely between threads

This is such an important aspect of concurrent programming! When you have multiple threads running, they often need to access or change the same data.

Without proper safeguards, this can lead to serious issues and bugs that can be extremely difficult to identify. Rust, with its strong focus on safety, offers great tools to help manage shared data safely and effectively.

The perils of unsafe shared state

Why is sharing data between threads so tricky? The core issue is **shared mutable state.** If multiple threads can read *and* write to the same memory location at the same time without any coordination, you can run into several problems, the most common being the following:

- **Data races:** This happens in the following cases:
    1. Two or more threads concurrently access a location in memory.
    2. At least one of the accesses is a write.
    3. The accesses are not synchronized. The result is unpredictable behavior because the final value depends on the exact, non-deterministic order in which thread operations interleave. Rust's compiler, remarkably, prevents data races in safe code!
- **Race conditions (broader term):** This is a more general term for situations where the behavior of a system depends on the sequence or timing of uncontrollable events (such as thread scheduling). Data races are a specific type of race condition. Even without data races in the Rust sense, you can have logical race conditions if operations aren't ordered correctly.
- **Inconsistent state:** If a thread reads data while another thread is in the middle of modifying it (and the modification isn't atomic or protected), the reading thread might see a partially updated, inconsistent state.

Traditional approaches to these problems often involve manual locking, semaphores, and careful programming, which are error-prone. Rust aims to make these patterns safer by integrating them into the type system.

Arc<T>: Sharing ownership atomically across threads

In *Chapter 11*, we learned about smart pointers and `Rc<T>` for reference-counted shared ownership. However, `Rc<T>` is *not thread-safe.*

Its internal reference count is not updated using atomic operations, so if multiple threads tried to clone or drop an `Rc<T>` simultaneously, you could get a data race on the count itself.

Recap: Why Rc<T> isn't enough

If you try to move an `Rc<T>` into a new thread using `thread::spawn` with a `move` closure, the Rust compiler will stop you with an error.

This is Rust's safety in action! It knows `Rc<T>` isn't safe to share this way.

Using Arc::clone() for thread distribution

The solution for sharing ownership of data across threads is `Arc<T>`, which stands for **Atomically Reference Counted.** It works conceptually just like `Rc<T>`:

- `Arc::new(value)` creates a new arc that owns value on the heap

- `Arc::clone(&my_arc)` creates another arc pointer to the *same* data and increments the reference count
- The data is dropped only when the last arc pointing to it is dropped

The key difference is that `Arc<T>` uses **atomic operations** to manage its reference count. Atomic operations are special CPU instructions that guarantee that updates (such as incrementing or decrementing the count) are indivisible and cannot be interrupted by other threads, thus preventing data races on the count itself. This makes `Arc<T>` safe to send and share between threads:

```
use std::sync::Arc;
use std::thread;
use std::time::Duration;

struct ImportantConfig {
    api_url: String,
    max_retries: u32,
}

fn main() {
    // Data we want to share (read-only) across multiple threads
    let config = Arc::new(ImportantConfig {
        api_url: "https://api.example.com/data".to_string(),
        max_retries: 5,
    });

    let mut handles = vec![];

    println!("Main thread: Initial Arc strong count = {}", Arc::strong_
count(&config));

    for i in 0..3 { // Spawn 3 threads
        // Clone the Arc for each thread. The clone is moved into the
thread.
        let config_clone = Arc::clone(&config);
        println!("Main thread: Count before thread {} spawn: {}", i,
Arc::strong_count(&config));

        let handle = thread::spawn(move || {
```

```
            // This thread now has its own Arc pointing to the same
ImportantConfig data
            println!("Thread {}: Started. Accessing resource API URL '{}'
with max_retries = {}. Current Arc count in this thread's scope (approx):
{}",
                     i,
                     config_clone.api_url, // Accessing data through Arc
                     config_clone.max_retries,
                     Arc::strong_count(&config_clone)
            );
            // Simulate some work
            thread::sleep(Duration::from_millis(100));
            println!("Thread {}: Finished.", i);
            // When config_clone goes out of scope here, the count is
decremented.
        });
        handles.push(handle);
    }

    println!("Main thread: Count after all threads spawned: {}",
Arc::strong_count(&config));
    println!("Main thread: Resource API URL: {}", config.api_url);

    // Wait for all threads to complete
    for handle in handles {
        handle.join().unwrap();
    }

    println!("Main thread: All threads finished. Final Arc strong count
(before main's Arc drops): {}", Arc::strong_count(&config));
    // When 'config' in main goes out of scope, the count drops to 0, and
ImportantConfig is deallocated.
}
```

- `Arc::new()` wraps the `ImportantConfig` data, making it shareable.

- `Arc::clone()` is called before spawning each thread. This is crucial. It creates a new arc pointer that shares ownership of the *same* underlying `ImportantConfig` data and atomically increments the reference count. This new arc is then moved into the closure for the new thread.
- Each thread can safely read from the `config_clone` because `Arc<T>` ensures the data lives as long as at least one arc points to it.
- The `Arc::strong_count()` method shows how many arc pointers are actively sharing the data.
- `Arc<T>` is for sharing *immutable* data by default (or data that uses interior mutability, which we'll see next). If you try to get `&mut T` from an `Arc<T>`, the compiler won't let you, because that would break the safety guarantee if multiple threads tried to mutate it simultaneously without further synchronization.

`Arc<T>` is your go-to when you need multiple threads to have shared, read-only access to some data, or when you need to set up shared ownership for data that will be mutated using other synchronization primitives, such as `Mutex<T>`.

A note on Arc::strong_count() and concurrency

You might notice that the exact reference counts printed from *inside* the threads vary slightly each time you run the program. This is perfectly normal! It's a result of the operating system's thread scheduler. For example, one thread might print a count of 3 just an instant before the main thread spawns another thread, which would immediately bump the count to 4.

Because the count can change at any moment, you should never use `Arc::strong_count()` for any program logic (such as `if Arc::strong_count(&my_arc) == 1 { ... }`). This would be a classic race condition. Think of `strong_count()` as a helpful tool for debugging and learning (like we're using it here), not as a reliable mechanism for production code.

Mutex<T>: Ensuring mutual exclusion for mutable data

`Arc<T>` solves shared ownership, but what if multiple threads need to *mutate* the shared data? If multiple threads tried to write to the same data without coordination, you'd have a data race. This is where `Mutex<T>` (which stands for mutual exclusion) comes in.

A `Mutex<T>` ensures that only one thread can access the data, `T`, it protects at any given time.

To access the data, a thread must first acquire the "lock" on the mutex.

Acquiring the lock with lock()

The primary method on a `Mutex<T>` is `lock()`:

- When a thread calls `data_mutex.lock()`, one of two things happens:
    - If the lock is not currently held by any other thread, the current thread acquires the lock, and `lock()` returns successfully
    - If the lock *is* held by another thread, the current thread will **block** (pause its execution) until the lock is released by the other thread
- `lock()` returns a `LockResult<MutexGuard<T>>` type. This is a `Result` because acquiring a lock can fail if the mutex is "poisoned" (meaning a thread that previously held the lock panicked). In many examples, you'll see `.unwrap()` called on this result for simplicity.

The role of MutexGuard

If `lock()` succeeds (i.e., returns `Ok(...)`), the value inside the `Ok` is a `MutexGuard<T>`. This is a smart pointer that does the following:

1. Implements `Deref` and `DerefMut`, so you can use it to get an `&T` or `&mut T` to the data protected by the mutex.
2. Crucially, it implements the `Drop` trait. When the `MutexGuard<T>` goes out of scope, its drop method is called, which *automatically releases the lock*. This RAII (which stands for Resource Acquisition Is Initialization) pattern is extremely helpful in preventing deadlocks caused by forgetting to release a lock.

Combining Arc<Mutex<T>> for shared mutable state

To allow multiple threads to access and potentially mutate the *same* piece of data protected by a mutex, you need to share the mutex itself across threads.

You do this by wrapping the `Mutex<T>` in an `Arc<T>`, resulting in the common `Arc<Mutex<T>>` pattern:

```
use std::sync::{Arc, Mutex};
use std::thread;

fn main() {
    // Create a counter, protected by a Mutex, and wrapped in an Arc for
sharing
    let counter = Arc::new(Mutex::new(0u32)); // Start with 0
```

```
    let mut handles = vec![];

    println!("Main: Initial counter value = {}", *counter.lock().
unwrap());

    for i in 0..5 { // Spawn 5 threads
        let counter_clone_for_thread = Arc::clone(&counter); // Clone Arc
for the thread

        let handle = thread::spawn(move || {
            // Each thread will try to increment the counter 10 times
            for _ in 0..10 {
                // Acquire the lock. This blocks if another thread has it.
                let mut num_guard = counter_clone_for_thread.lock().
unwrap();
                // We now have exclusive mutable access to the u32 inside
the Mutex.
                *num_guard += 1;
                // The lock is released automatically when num_guard goes
out of scope here.
            }
            println!("Thread {}: Finished incrementing.", i);
        });
        handles.push(handle);
    }

    // Wait for all threads to complete their work
    for handle in handles {
        handle.join().unwrap();
    }

    // Lock the mutex in the main thread to read the final value
    let final_value = *counter.lock().unwrap();
    println!("Main: All threads finished. Final counter value = {}",
final_value); // Expected: 50
}
```

- `Arc::new(Mutex::new(0))` creates an initial counter value of `0`, wraps it in a mutex to control access, and then wraps the mutex in an arc so the mutex itself can be shared across threads
- Each thread receives a *clone* of the arc, allowing them all to refer to the same mutex
- Inside each thread, `counter_clone_for_thread.lock().unwrap()` is called:
    1. `lock()` attempts to acquire exclusive access. If another thread holds the lock, this thread waits.
    2. `.unwrap()` is used here for simplicity; it would panic if another thread panicked while holding the lock (poisoning it).
    3. If successful, it returns a `MutexGuard` (here, `num_guard`).
- `*num_guard += 1;` dereferences the `MutexGuard` to get a mutable reference to the `u32` data and increments it. This operation is safe because only one thread can hold the lock (and thus have mutable access) at a time.
- When `num_guard` (the `MutexGuard`) goes out of scope at the end of the inner loop's iteration (or end of the block), the lock is automatically released.
- The final result should be `50` (5 threads each incrementing 10 times).

Arc<T> - Shared Ownership

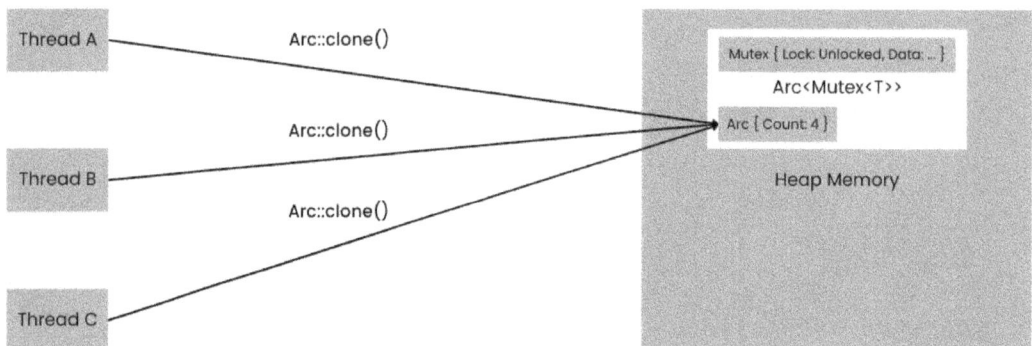

All threads use Arc::clone() to get a pointer to the same Mutex on the heap, increasing the reference count.

Figure 13.3: Shared ownership model using Arc<T>, allowing multiple threads to simultaneously hold references to the same data on the heap

Arc<Mutex<T>>: Mutual Exclusion in Action
Thread A
waiting...
Thread B
Thread C
waiting...
Mutex { Lock: Locked, Data: ... }
Arc<Mutex<T>>
Arc { Count: 4 }
Heap Memory
The Arc allows all threads to share a pointer to the same Mutex.
However, the Mutex's job is to ensure only one thread (like Thread B) can acquire the lock and get exclusive access to the data at a time. All other threads (like A and C) are blocked and must wait until Thread B is finished and releases the lock.

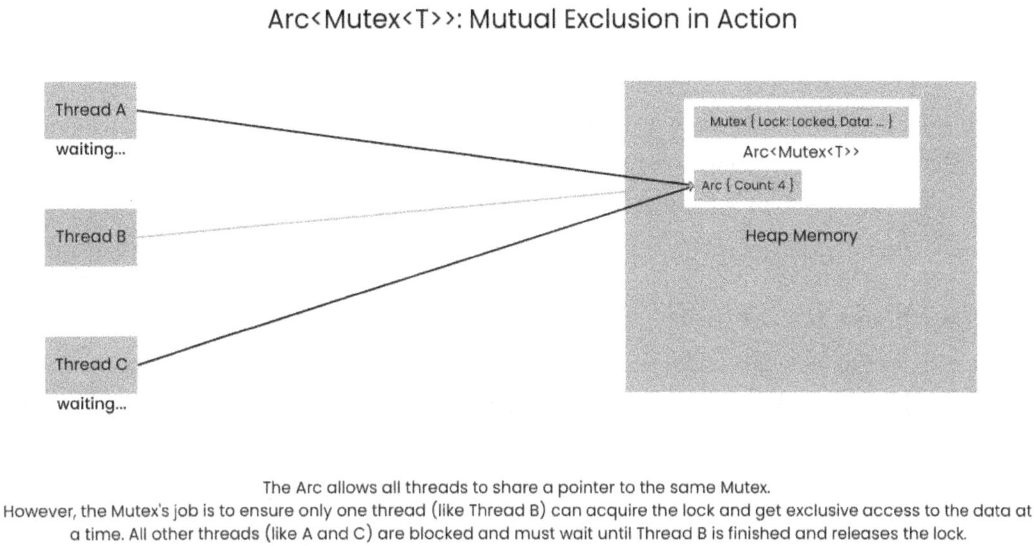

Figure 13.4: Mutual exclusion in action

Thinking about deadlocks

While `Mutex<T>` prevents data races, it introduces the possibility of **deadlocks**. A deadlock occurs if threads try to acquire multiple locks in different orders, leading to a situation where each thread is waiting for a lock held by another thread in the cycle. Take the following example:

- Thread A locks Mutex 1, then tries to lock Mutex 2.
- Thread B locks Mutex 2, then tries to lock Mutex 1. If both threads acquire their first lock and then block waiting for the second, they will wait forever.

Preventing deadlocks involves careful design, often by ensuring that all threads acquire locks in a consistent global order if they need multiple locks. Rust doesn't prevent deadlocks at compile time (it's a complex runtime problem), but its ownership system and explicit locking help you reason about them more clearly.

RwLock<T>: Allowing multiple readers or one writer

Sometimes, the "exclusive access" provided by a `Mutex<T>` is too restrictive. If you have data that is read much more often than it is written, a mutex would still force readers to wait for each other if only one reader can hold the lock at a time (which is true for a mutex).

For these "read-mostly" scenarios, Rust provides `RwLock<T>` (read-write lock). `RwLock<T>` allows the following:

- Any number of threads to acquire a **read lock** (`.read().unwrap()`) simultaneously, as long as no thread holds a write lock. This gives them immutable access (`&T`).
- Exactly one thread to acquire a **write lock** (`.write().unwrap()`) exclusively, as long as no other thread holds either a read or a write lock. This gives it mutable access (`&mut T`).

When to use RwLock<T> versus Mutex<T>

- Use `Mutex<T>` when you need simple exclusive access, or when writes are as common as reads, or when the critical sections are very short. A mutex is generally simpler and can sometimes be faster if contention is low.
- Use `RwLock<T>` in the following cases:
    - You have data that is read very frequently by many threads
    - Writes to the data are infrequent
    - The read operations are non-trivial (i.e., holding the lock for a read actually provides a benefit over just rapidly acquiring and releasing a mutex)

`RwLock<T>` can offer better performance in read-heavy concurrent scenarios by allowing multiple readers to proceed in parallel. However, it's slightly more complex than a mutex and has its own potential issues, such as "writer starvation" (if there's a constant stream of readers, a writer might have to wait a long time). Like `Mutex<T>`, you'd typically share an `RwLock<T>` across threads using `Arc<RwLock<T>>`:

```
use std::sync::{Arc, RwLock};
use std::thread;
use std::collections::HashMap;
use std::time::Duration;

fn main() {
    // A cache that is read often, written to occasionally
    let cache: Arc<RwLock<HashMap<String, String>>> =
Arc::new(RwLock::new(HashMap::new()));
    let mut handles = vec![];
```

```
    // Writer thread to populate the cache
    let cache_writer_clone = Arc::clone(&cache);
    let writer_handle = thread::spawn(move || {
        let mut cache_guard = cache_writer_clone.write().unwrap(); //
Acquire write lock
        println!("Writer: Acquired write lock. Populating cache...");
        cache_guard.insert("url1".to_string(), "Data for URL1".to_
string());
        cache_guard.insert("url2".to_string(), "Data for URL2".to_
string());
        thread::sleep(Duration::from_millis(100));
        println!("Writer: Cache populated. Releasing write lock.");
        // Write lock released when cache_guard goes out of scope
    });
    handles.push(writer_handle);

    // Multiple reader threads
    for i in 0..3 {
        let cache_reader_clone = Arc::clone(&cache);
        let reader_handle = thread::spawn(move || {
            thread::sleep(Duration::from_millis(20 * i as u64)); //
Stagger readers slightly
            let cache_guard = cache_reader_clone.read().unwrap(); //
Acquire read lock
            println!("Reader {}: Acquired read lock. Reading cache...",
i);
            if let Some(data1) = cache_guard.get("url1") {
                println!("Reader {}: Found data for url1: '{}'", i,
data1);
            }
            if let Some(data2) = cache_guard.get("url2") {
                println!("Reader {}: Found data for url2: '{}'", i,
data2);
            }
            thread::sleep(Duration::from_millis(50));
```

```
            println!("Reader {}: Releasing read lock.", i);
            // Read lock released when cache_guard goes out of scope
        });
        handles.push(reader_handle);
    }

    for handle in handles {
        handle.join().unwrap();
    }
    println!("Main: All threads finished.");
}
```

- We have a shared `HashMap` cache wrapped in `Arc<RwLock<...>>`.
- One thread acts as a "writer." It acquires an exclusive write lock using `cache.write().unwrap()`. While it holds this lock, no other thread (reader or writer) can access the cache.
- Multiple "reader" threads are spawned. Each attempts to acquire a shared read lock using `cache.read().unwrap()`. Multiple readers can hold a read lock simultaneously, allowing them to read the cache data in parallel, as long as no writer holds the write lock.
- If a writer tries to get a write lock while readers are active, it will wait. If readers try to get a read lock while a writer is active, they will wait.

These synchronization primitives, `Arc`, `Mutex`, and `RwLock`, are the fundamental building blocks in Rust for safely managing shared state in concurrent programs. They allow you to opt in to shared mutability where needed, with Rust ensuring that the access patterns are sound.

Message passing: Communicating between threads

So far, we've seen how to share data between threads using Arc for shared ownership and `Mutex` or `RwLock` for synchronizing access to mutable data. This is often called **shared-state concurrency**. While powerful, managing locks and shared memory can sometimes be complex and prone to issues such as deadlocks if not handled carefully.

Rust, like many modern languages, also offers another excellent model for concurrency: **message passing**. The core idea here is: "Do not communicate by sharing memory; instead, share memory by communicating." Threads send messages to each other over channels, transferring data ownership without needing complex locking mechanisms on the data itself.

An alternative to shared state: Channels

Instead of multiple threads trying to access and modify the same piece of memory (protected by locks), message passing involves one thread sending a piece of data to another thread. Once the data is sent, the sending thread often gives up ownership (or sends a copy), and the receiving thread takes ownership. This can lead to simpler designs because you're thinking about data flow rather than shared access patterns.

Rust's standard library provides **channels** as the primary mechanism for message passing. A channel can be thought of as a one-way conduit: you have a **transmitter** (or sender) end and a **receiver** end. You send messages in one end, and they pop out the other.

Introduction to std::sync::mpsc channels (multiple producer, single consumer)

The main channel implementation in Rust's standard library is found in the `std::sync::mpsc` module. `mpsc` stands for **multiple producer, single consumer**. This is what that means:

- Many threads (multiple producers) can send messages
- Only one thread (a single consumer) can receive messages

This is a common and useful pattern, for example, when you have multiple worker threads generating results that are all collected and processed by a single main or aggregator thread.

Creating a channel: channel()

You create a channel using the `mpsc::channel()` function. This function returns a tuple containing the sender and receiver: `(Sender<T>, Receiver<T>)`, where `T` is the type of data you want to send through the channel:

```
use std::sync::mpsc; // Import the mpsc module

fn main() {
    // Create a new channel. The type of data sent will be i32.
    let (tx, rx): (mpsc::Sender<i32>, mpsc::Receiver<i32>) =
mpsc::channel();

    // tx is the Sender (transmitter)
    // rx is the Receiver
```

```
    println!("Channel created successfully! Sender: {:?}, Receiver: {:?}",
tx, rx);
    // We'll see how to use tx and rx next.
}
```

The `mpsc::channel()` function is generic over the type of message `T` that will be sent. Here, we've explicitly annotated that we want to send `i32` values, so `tx` becomes an `mpsc::Sender<i32>` and `rx` becomes an `mpsc::Receiver<i32>`. The `println!` shows their (opaque) debug representations.

Sending data with Sender<T>

The `Sender<T>` half of the channel has a `send(value: T)` method. This method takes ownership of the value you're sending and attempts to put it onto the channel. `send()` returns a `Result<(), SendError<T>>`.

It will return `Err` if the receiver end of the channel has already been dropped (meaning no one is listening anymore):

```
use std::sync::mpsc;
use std::thread;
use std::time::Duration;

fn main() {
    let (tx, rx): (mpsc::Sender<String>, mpsc::Receiver<String>) =
mpsc::channel();

    // Spawn a thread that will send messages
    let sender_thread_handle = thread::spawn(move || {
        let messages_to_send = vec![
            String::from("Greetings"),
            String::from("from"),
            String::from("the producer"),
            String::from("thread!"),
        ];

        for msg_content in messages_to_send {
            println!("Sender Thread: Preparing to send '{}'", msg_
content);
            // Send the message. send() takes ownership of msg_content.
            if tx.send(msg_content).is_err() {
```

```
                // This error would occur if the receiver (rx) was
dropped.
                eprintln!("Sender Thread: Receiver has disconnected,
unable to send further messages.");
                break; // Exit the loop if we can't send
            }
            println!("Sender Thread: Message sent successfully.");
            thread::sleep(Duration::from_millis(200)); // Simulate some
work
        }
        println!("Sender Thread: All messages dispatched or receiver
gone.");
    });

    // Main thread will now try to receive.
    // The receiver (rx) is still in scope here.
    println!("Main Thread: Waiting for messages from sender thread...");
    for received_message in rx { // rx can be used as an iterator
        println!("Main Thread: Received: '{}'", received_message);
    }
    println!("Main Thread: Channel disconnected (all senders dropped).");

    // Wait for the sender thread to finish its execution completely
    sender_thread_handle.join().expect("Sender thread panicked!");
    println!("Main Thread: Sender thread has joined.");
}
```

- We establish a channel designed for `String` messages.
- The `Sender` end (`tx`) is moved into a newly spawned thread. This is a common pattern, as you often want to send data *from* one thread *to* another.
- Inside the spawned thread, `tx.send(msg_content)` dispatches each `String`. Because `send` consumes `T` by value, ownership of `msg_content` is transferred into the channel, making it unavailable in the sending thread afterward.
- The `if tx.send(...).is_err()` check demonstrates how a sender can detect whether the receiver is no longer available.
- In the main thread, we iterate over `rx` to receive messages. This loop will naturally end when all senders (in this case, just `tx` in the spawned thread) are dropped.

Receiving data with Receiver<T> (recv(), try_recv())

The `Receiver<T>` half has a couple of primary methods for getting messages:

- `recv()`: This method will block the current thread's execution until a message becomes available on the channel:
    - It returns a `Result<T, RecvError>`
    - `Ok(value)` means a message was successfully received
    - `Err(RecvError)` means the channel has closed because all senders have been dropped (so no more messages will ever arrive)
- `try_recv()`: This method is non-blocking. It attempts to receive a message immediately:
    - It returns a `Result<T, TryRecvError>`
    - `Ok(value)` if a message was available
    - `Err(TryRecvError::Empty)` if the channel is currently empty but still open
    - `Err(TryRecvError::Disconnected)` if the channel is empty *and* all senders have been dropped

A `Receiver<T>` can also be used directly as an iterator, which will yield messages until the channel is empty and disconnected. This is often the most idiomatic way to process all messages:

```
use std::sync::mpsc;
use std::thread;
use std::time::Duration;

fn main() {
    let (tx_main, rx_main): (mpsc::Sender<String>, mpsc::Receiver<String>)
= mpsc::channel();

    // Clone the sender to demonstrate multiple producers
    let tx_producer1 = tx_main.clone();

    // Producer thread 1
    let handle1 = thread::spawn(move || {
        tx_producer1.send("Message Alpha from Producer 1".to_string()).
unwrap();
        thread::sleep(Duration::from_millis(150));
        tx_producer1.send("Message Beta from Producer 1".to_string()).
```

```
unwrap();
        println!("Producer 1: All messages sent.");
        // tx_producer1 is dropped here when the thread ends
    });

    // Producer thread 2 (using the original tx_main, which was moved)
    let handle2 = thread::spawn(move || {
        tx_main.send("Message Gamma from Producer 2".to_string()).
unwrap();
        thread::sleep(Duration::from_millis(80));
        tx_main.send("Message Delta from Producer 2".to_string()).
unwrap();
        println!("Producer 2: All messages sent.");
        // tx_main is dropped here when the thread ends
    });

    println!("Main Thread (Consumer): Waiting for messages from
producers...");

    /* Using rx_main as an iterator in a for loop is a very clean and
idiomatic way to receive all messages. However, it's important to
understand how this loop behaves, as it's different from iterating over
a Vec. This loop will block if the channel is temporarily empty and wait
for the next message to arrive. It does not stop just because the channel
is empty. The loop will only terminate and allow the program to continue
to the next line when all Senders (tx and tx1 in our example) have been
dropped, which signals that no more messages will ever be sent.
    */
    for received_message_content in rx_main {
        println!("Main Thread (Consumer): Received: '{}'", received_
message_content);
    }

    println!("Main Thread (Consumer): Channel disconnected, all producers
have finished.");

    // Ensure both producer threads have completed their execution
    handle1.join().expect("Producer 1 thread panicked!");
```

```
    handle2.join().expect("Producer 2 thread panicked!");

    // Example demonstrating try_recv()
    let (tx_single_msg, rx_single_msg) = mpsc::channel::<i32>();

    // Attempt to receive when channel is empty
    match rx_single_msg.try_recv() {
        Ok(msg) => println!("try_recv (1): Unexpectedly got a message:
{}", msg),
        Err(mpsc::TryRecvError::Empty) => println!("try_recv (1): Channel
is confirmed empty."),
        Err(mpsc::TryRecvError::Disconnected) => println!("try_recv (1):
Channel is disconnected."),
    }

    // Send a message
    tx_single_msg.send(101).expect("Failed to send on single_msg
channel");

    // Attempt to receive again
    match rx_single_msg.try_recv() {
        Ok(msg) => println!("try_recv (2): Got the message: {}", msg), //
This will be executed
        Err(mpsc::TryRecvError::Empty) => println!("try_recv (2): Channel
is still empty (unexpected)."),
        Err(mpsc::TryRecvError::Disconnected) => println!("try_recv (2):
Channel is disconnected (unexpected)."),
    }

    // Drop the sender, then try_recv again
    drop(tx_single_msg);
    match rx_single_msg.try_recv() {
        Ok(msg) => println!("try_recv (3): Unexpectedly got a message
after drop: {}", msg),
        Err(mpsc::TryRecvError::Empty) => println!("try_recv (3): Channel
is empty after drop (unexpected)."),
```

```
        Err(mpsc::TryRecvError::Disconnected) => println!("try_recv (3): 
Channel correctly reported as disconnected."), // This
    }
}
```

- We create two producer threads. Note how `tx_main.clone()` is used to create `tx_producer1`, allowing both threads to send to the same receiver (`rx_main`).
- In the main thread (the consumer), the line for `received_message_content` in `rx_main` elegantly iterates through incoming messages. The `rx_main` receiver effectively acts as an iterator in this context. It will block on each iteration until a new message arrives or the channel is closed.
- This loop automatically terminates once all sender instances (`tx_producer1` and `tx_main` in their respective threads) have been dropped and no more messages can be sent.
- The `try_recv()` example demonstrates its non-blocking nature, returning `Err(TryRecvError::Empty)` if no message is immediately available and `Err(TryRecvError::Disconnected)` if the channel is closed.

Using channels for thread communication and synchronization

Channels are not just for shuttling complex data around; they are also a powerful tool for basic synchronization and coordinating the flow of work between threads:

- **Ownership transfer**: A beautiful aspect of Rust's channels is that when you send data via `sender.send(data)`, ownership of data is transferred to the receiving end. This inherently avoids many of the complexities and potential pitfalls of shared mutable state because the data isn't shared in the traditional sense; it's *moved*.
- **Signaling**: You can send simple "signal" messages. For example, `Sender<()>::send(())` (sending the unit type ()) can be used to indicate that a particular task is complete, an event has occurred, or a thread is ready to proceed.

- **Backpressure (bounded channels)**: While `mpsc::channel()` creates an *unbounded* channel (it can theoretically queue an infinite number of messages, limited only by system memory), the `mpsc` module also provides `mpsc::sync_channel(bound_size)`. A `sync_channel` is *bounded*; it can only hold up to `bound_size` messages. If a sender tries to send a message to a full bounded channel, the `send()` call will block until the receiver makes space by consuming messages. This naturally creates "backpressure," preventing a fast producer from overwhelming a slower consumer.

```
use std::sync::mpsc;
use std::thread;
use std::time::Duration;

fn main() {
    // Channel for the main thread to signal the worker to start
    let (start_tx, start_rx) = mpsc::channel::<()>(); // Using unit
type for a pure signal

    // Channel for the worker to send its result back to the main
thread
    let (result_tx, result_rx) = mpsc::channel::<String>();

    let worker_handle = thread::spawn(move || {
        println!("Worker Thread: Initialized and waiting for the
green light...");
        // Block until a () signal is received on start_rx
        start_rx.recv().expect("Failed to receive start signal from
main thread.");

        println!("Worker Thread: Green light received! Performing
complex task...");
        thread::sleep(Duration::from_secs(1)); // Simulate some work
        let computation_result = "Task completed successfully by
worker!".to_string();

        // Send the result back to the main thread
        result_tx.send(computation_result).expect("Failed to send
result to main thread.");
        println!("Worker Thread: Result sent, finishing up.");
    });
```

```
    println!("Main Thread: Performing some setup before signaling
worker...");
    thread::sleep(Duration::from_millis(500)); // Simulate setup
work

    println!("Main Thread: Setup complete. Sending start signal to
worker...");
    start_tx.send(()).expect("Failed to send start signal to
worker."); // Send the () signal

    // Block and wait for the worker thread to send back its result
    println!("Main Thread: Waiting for result from worker...");
    let worker_output = result_rx.recv().expect("Failed to receive
result from worker.");
    println!("Main Thread: Received from worker: '{}'", worker_
output);

    // Ensure the worker thread has fully completed its execution
    worker_handle.join().expect("Worker thread panicked during
execution!");
    println!("Main Thread: Worker thread has joined. Program
exiting.");
}
```

- We employ two distinct channels: `start_tx/start_rx` enables the main thread to signal the worker when it's okay to commence its primary task. `result_tx/result_rx` allows the worker thread to transmit its computational result back to the main thread.
- The worker thread's call to `start_rx.recv().expect(...)` is a blocking operation. The worker will pause at this line until the main thread dispatches a message (even an empty `()` "unit type" message, which is perfect for pure signals) on `start_tx`.
- This mechanism allows the main thread to perform preliminary setup or wait for specific conditions before "unleashing" the worker thread.
- Conversely, the `result_rx.recv().expect(...)` call in the main thread blocks it until the worker thread completes its task and sends back the outcome via `result_tx`.

Message passing via channels provides a structured and often easier-to-reason-about approach to concurrency compared to direct shared-state synchronization, especially when you need a clear transfer of data ownership or want to coordinate distinct phases of work between threads. It aligns beautifully with Rust's core ownership principles.

While operating system threads are a powerful tool for running code in parallel, they can be inefficient for applications that manage thousands of tasks that are mostly *waiting*, such as network connections. To handle these common I/O-bound scenarios, Rust provides another model for concurrency: asynchronous programming with async/await.

A glimpse into asynchronous programming with async/await

So far in this chapter, we've focused on concurrency using operating system threads. Threads are a powerful way to run multiple pieces of code in parallel or manage blocking tasks. However, operating system threads aren't always the most efficient solution, especially when dealing with a very large number of tasks that spend most of their time waiting for external events, such as network I/O.

This is where **asynchronous programming**, often using Rust's async/await syntax, offers an alternative approach.

When threads aren't always the best fit (I/O-bound tasks versus CPU-bound tasks)

Operating system threads come with some overhead:

- **Context switching**: When the operating system switches execution from one thread to another, there's a cost involved in saving the state of the current thread and loading the state of the next
- **Memory**: Each thread typically has its own stack, which consumes memory

For **CPU-bound tasks** (tasks that are busy doing computations, such as complex calculations or data processing), using a number of threads roughly equal to the number of CPU cores is often optimal. The overhead of threads is usually acceptable because the threads are doing significant work.

However, for **I/O-bound tasks** (tasks that spend most of their time waiting for external operations such as network requests, database queries, or filesystem operations to complete), operating system threads can be less efficient. If you have thousands of network connections to manage, creating a separate operating system thread for each one could overwhelm your system due to memory usage and context-switching overhead. Many of these threads would just be sitting idle, waiting for data to arrive.

Asynchronous programming provides a way to handle many such I/O-bound tasks concurrently on a smaller number of operating system threads (often just one per CPU core, or even a single thread for the whole async part of an application). It does this by allowing tasks to "yield" control when they encounter a blocking operation, letting other tasks run on the same thread until the awaited operation is ready to proceed. This is a form of cooperative multitasking.

Brief overview of the async and await keywords

Rust provides the async and await keywords to make writing asynchronous code feel more like writing regular synchronous code:

- `async fn`: When you declare a function with `async fn`, it doesn't execute its body immediately when called. Instead, it returns a value that implements the `Future` trait (e.g., `Future<Output = T>`). `Future` is a placeholder for a value that will be computed at some point in the... well, future! It represents an operation that might not be complete yet.
- `.await`: Inside an `async fn` (or an async block), you can use the `.await` operator on a `Future`. When execution reaches an `.await`, if the Future is not yet ready (e.g., the network data hasn't arrived), instead of blocking the entire operating system thread, the async function *pauses* its execution at that point. Control is yielded back to an "executor" or "runtime," which can then run other async tasks that are ready. When the awaited Future eventually completes, the runtime will schedule the paused async function to resume from where it left off.

Let's see a basic example.

First, update your `Cargo.toml` file, adding the dependency from `future`:

```
[dependencies] futures = "0.3"


use std::future::Future;
use std::time::Duration;
```

```
use std::thread::sleep; // We'll use this for a simple blocking sleep

// We need an executor to run our async functions.
// `block_on` is a simple one from the `futures` crate.
use futures::executor::block_on;

/// This is an async function. It returns a `Future`.
async fn fetch_simulated_data(task_id: u32) -> String {
    println!("Task {}: Starting fetch...", task_id);

    // In a real async function, we would .await an async operation here.
    // Since we don't have a full async runtime, we can't use an async
sleep.
    // We'll just use a normal sleep to simulate work *within* this
Future.
    // This is NOT true async, but it shows the structure.
    sleep(Duration::from_secs(1));

    println!("Task {}: Finished fetch.", task_id);
    format!("Data from task {}", task_id)
}

/// This is our main async logic.
async fn process_tasks_sequentially() {
    println!("Starting sequential processing...");

    // We call and .await the first task.
    let data1 = fetch_simulated_data(1).await;
    println!("Main: Received first data: '{}'", data1);

    // Only *after* the first task is complete, we call and .await the
second.
    let data2 = fetch_simulated_data(2).await;
    println!("Main: Received second data: '{}'", data2);

    println!("Sequential processing finished.");
}
```

```
/// We can't use `#[tokio::main]`, so we use a standard `fn main()`.
fn main() {
    // `process_tasks_sequentially()` creates a Future, but doesn't run
it.
    // `block_on` is an executor that takes a Future and blocks the
    // current thread until that Future (and any futures it .await's)
completes.
    block_on(process_tasks_sequentially());
}
```

The following is the output:

```
Starting sequential processing...
Task 1: Starting fetch...
Task 1: Finished fetch.
Main: Received first data: 'Data from task 1'
Task 2: Starting fetch...
Task 2: Finished fetch.
Main: Received second data: 'Data from task 2'
Sequential processing finished.
```

Figure 13.5: Sequential task output

- `futures::executor::block_on`: This is the key. It's a simple function that acts as a minimal executor. It takes one `Future` (the one returned by `process_tasks_sequentially()`) and *blocks the main thread* while it runs that `Future` to completion.
- `async fn` and `.await`: The syntax inside `process_tasks_sequentially` is the same. It calls `fetch_simulated_data(1)` and gets a `Future`, and the `.await` keyword waits for that `Future` to finish before moving on. `block_on` is what's actually driving this process.
- A note on `sleep`: Notice that we're still using `std::thread::sleep`. In this simple `block_on` executor, this will block the single thread it's running on. This example demonstrates the `async`/`await` syntax and structure, but to get the real non-blocking behavior (where one task pausing allows another to run), you need a more advanced, multi-threaded runtime, such as `tokio` or `async-std`.

This example is the absolute simplest, runnable way to show `async`/`await` in action without pulling in a large runtime.

Async runtimes (such as tokio or async-std)

A very important point is that Rust's async/await syntax itself only defines the *structure* of asynchronous operations (the futures).

It doesn't actually *execute* them or manage the switching between tasks.

To run async code, you need an **asynchronous runtime** (also called an "executor").

The async runtime is a library that does the following:

- Takes top-level futures (such as the one returned by calling `process_data()` in our example)
- Polls these futures to see whether they can make progress
- When a future is awaiting an operation and cannot proceed, the runtime suspends it and runs other futures that *are* ready
- Manages waking up suspended futures when their awaited operations complete (e.g., network data arrives)

Popular async runtimes in the Rust ecosystem include the following:

- `tokio`: A widely used, powerful runtime focused on network applications and providing a rich ecosystem of utilities for async I/O, timers, synchronization, and so on
- `async-std`: A runtime that aims to provide async equivalents of `std` library APIs, making the transition to async feel familiar
- Others exist for specific use cases (e.g., embedded systems or WebAssembly)

You typically add one of these runtimes as a dependency to your `Cargo.toml` and use a macro they provide (such as `#[tokio::main]` or `#[async_std::main]`) to set up your main function to run async code.

Let's see an example with `tokio`.

First, you add the dependency in the `Cargo.toml` file:

```
[dependencies]
tokio = { version = "1", features = ["full"] }
```

Here is the example:

```
use tokio::time::{sleep, Duration};

/// This is an async function. When called, it returns a `Future`
```

```
/// that will resolve to a String.
async fn fetch_simulated_data(task_id: u32) -> String {
    println!("Task {}: Starting fetch...", task_id);

    // This is an async-aware sleep.
    // Unlike `std::thread::sleep`, this does NOT block the whole thread.
    // It yields control back to the tokio runtime,
    // allowing other async tasks to run.
    sleep(Duration::from_secs(1)).await;

    println!("Task {}: Finished fetch.", task_id);
    format!("Data from task {}", task_id)
}

/// This function contains our main async logic.
async fn process_tasks_sequentially() {
    println!("Starting sequential processing...");

    // We call and .await the first task.
    // Our function's execution pauses here (non-blockingly)
    // until `fetch_simulated_data(1)` completes.
    let data1 = fetch_simulated_data(1).await;
    println!("Main: Received first data: '{}'", data1);

    // Only *after* the first task is complete, we call and .await the
second.
    let data2 = fetch_simulated_data(2).await;
    println!("Main: Received second data: '{}'", data2);

    println!("Sequential processing finished.");
}

/// The #[tokio::main] macro automatically:
/// 1. Creates a new Tokio runtime instance.
/// 2. Runs the `async fn main` on that runtime.
#[tokio::main]
async fn main() {
```

```
    // We .await the future returned by our main logic function.
    process_tasks_sequentially().await;
}
```

The following is the output:

```
Starting sequential processing...
Task 1: Starting fetch...
Task 1: Finished fetch.
Main: Received first data: 'Data from task 1'
Task 2: Starting fetch...
Task 2: Finished fetch.
Main: Received second data: 'Data from task 2'
Sequential processing finished.
```

Figure 13.6: Sequential task output using tokio

As you can probably tell, asynchronous programming is a substantial topic with its own set of concepts (such as futures, pinning, executors, streams, and wakers) and best practices. What we've covered here is truly just a "glimpse" to make you aware of its existence and purpose.

While async/await can offer significant benefits for I/O-bound workloads and highly concurrent services, it also introduces a different way of thinking about program flow and can have its own complexities. For many applications, especially those that are CPU-bound or have a manageable number of concurrent tasks, traditional operating system threads, as discussed earlier in this chapter, are perfectly adequate and often simpler to reason about.

Consider async/await as another powerful tool in Rust's concurrency toolkit, particularly suited for scenarios demanding high levels of I/O concurrency. It's definitely an area for further learning once you're comfortable with the fundamentals of Rust, including the threading and shared-state concurrency models we've covered.

We've covered tools for concurrent programming, such as threads, locks, message passing, and async/await. Let's review key best practices to write safe, efficient, and maintainable concurrent code.

Best practices for concurrent Rust

Writing concurrent code can be incredibly powerful, but it also comes with its own set of challenges. While Rust's compiler does an amazing job at preventing entire classes of concurrency bugs (especially data races), good design and thoughtful practices are still crucial for writing concurrent programs that are not only safe but also correct, efficient, and maintainable.

Prefer message passing for simplicity where possible

We've seen two main models for concurrency: shared-state (using `Arc`, `Mutex`, and `RwLock`) and message passing (using channels such as `mpsc`). While both are powerful, message passing often leads to simpler and easier-to-reason-about code, especially for complex interactions:

- **Clear ownership transfer**: When data is sent over a channel, ownership transfers to avoid shared mutable state complexities, so only one thread "owns" the data at a time, either the sender before sending or the receiver after
- **Reduced lock contention**: Relying less on locks can reduce the chances of performance bottlenecks due to lock contention (many threads waiting for the same lock) and can make deadlocks less likely (though not impossible if multiple channels are involved in complex ways)
- **Easier to reason about**: Thinking about data flowing through channels can often be more intuitive than tracking which thread has locked which piece of shared memory

When should you consider message passing first?

- When tasks can be largely independent and only need to communicate results or signals
- When you want to clearly define the "owner" of data at each stage of a process
- When you want to avoid the complexities of fine-grained locking

Of course, shared state with locks is sometimes necessary or more efficient, especially for data that truly needs to be accessed and modified by many threads frequently (such as a shared cache). But as a general guideline, if you can model your concurrency with message passing without significant contortions, it's often a good path to explore first. "Share memory by communicating" is a good mantra.

Keep critical sections (locks) short and sweet

When you *do* use locks (such as `Mutex` or `RwLock`), the section of code that executes while a lock is held is often called a **critical section**. It's vital to keep these critical sections as short as possible:

- **Minimize contention**: The longer a thread holds a lock, the longer other threads might have to wait to acquire it. This waiting is called lock contention and can severely degrade performance in a multithreaded application.

- **Reduce deadlock risk**: Holding multiple locks simultaneously increases the risk of deadlocks. If you can perform operations by acquiring only one lock at a time, or by ensuring all threads acquire multiple locks in the exact same order, you reduce this risk. Holding a lock for a very short duration means you're less likely to be holding it while trying to acquire another.

This is what to do inside a lock:

- Perform only the absolutely necessary operations on the shared data.
- Avoid long-running computations and, especially, any I/O operations (such as network calls or file access) while holding a lock. These operations can block for an unpredictable amount of time, starving other threads.

```
use std::sync::{Arc, Mutex};
use std::thread;
use std::time::Duration;

struct SharedData {
    value: i32,
    // some other complex data
}

fn main() {
    let shared_data = Arc::new(Mutex::new(SharedData { value: 0 }));
    let mut handles = vec![];

    for i in 0..2 {
        let data_clone = Arc::clone(&shared_data);
        let handle = thread::spawn(move || {
            // --- BAD: Long operation inside lock ---
            // let mut data_guard = data_clone.lock().unwrap();
            // data_guard.value += i + 1;
            // println!("Thread {}: Updated value to {}", i, data_
guard.value);
            // thread::sleep(Duration::from_secs(1)); // Simulate
long work WHILE HOLDING LOCK
            // println!("Thread {}: Releasing lock after long
work.", i);
            // Drop(data_guard) happens here
```

```
            // --- GOOD: Prepare data, then short lock ---
            let value_to_add = i + 1; // Prepare computation outside
lock
            let mut data_guard = data_clone.lock().unwrap(); //
Acquire lock
            data_guard.value += value_to_add; // Quick update
            println!("Thread {}: Updated value to {}. Releasing
lock.", i, data_guard.value);
            // Lock released as data_guard goes out of scope
immediately

            // If more work needs to be done with the new value, but
doesn't need the lock:
            let current_value_snapshot = data_guard.value; // Copy
value out if needed
            drop(data_guard); // Explicitly drop guard to release
lock early if needed

            // Now do other work without holding the lock
            thread::sleep(Duration::from_secs(1));
            println!("Thread {}: Finished other work with snapshot
value {}", i, current_value_snapshot);
        });
        handles.push(handle);
    }

    for handle in handles {
        handle.join().unwrap();
    }
    println!("Final value: {}", shared_data.lock().unwrap().value);
}
```

The GOOD pattern in the example shows calculating value_to_add *before* acquiring the lock. The lock is then held only for the brief period needed to update shared_data.value. If subsequent operations don't require the lock, the MutexGuard can be dropped (explicitly with drop() or implicitly when it goes out of scope) to release the lock sooner.

This minimizes the time other threads might be blocked.

Be mindful of lock ordering to avoid deadlocks

As briefly mentioned when discussing `Mutex<T>`, deadlocks are a serious concern when threads need to acquire multiple locks. A deadlock occurs when two or more threads are each waiting for a resource held by another thread in the group, forming a cycle of dependencies.

The most common way to prevent deadlocks is to establish a **global, consistent order** for acquiring locks. If all threads that need to acquire, say, Lock A and Lock B always acquire Lock A *before* attempting to acquire Lock B, a deadlock between A and B cannot occur.

- Identify all locks that might be acquired together
- Assign a unique order to these locks (e.g., based on memory address, a unique ID, or simply an arbitrary but consistent convention)
- Enforce that all threads acquire these locks strictly in that predefined order

If you cannot guarantee a strict order, you might need to use more advanced techniques such as `try_lock()` (which attempts to acquire a lock without blocking and returns immediately if it can't), timeouts on lock acquisition, or deadlock detection algorithms, but these are more complex. Sticking to a consistent locking order is the simplest and often most effective prevention.

Trust the compiler: Leverage Rust's safety guarantees

One of Rust's biggest selling points for concurrency is its "fearless concurrency" promise, largely delivered by the compiler. The ownership system, borrowing rules, and the `Send` and `Sync` marker traits play a huge role here:

- **Send trait**: A type `T` is `Send` if it's safe to transfer ownership of `T` to another thread. Most common types are `Send`. Notable examples of types that are *not* `Send` are `Rc<T>` and `RefCell<T>`.
- **Sync trait**: A type `T` is `Sync` if it's safe to have an immutable reference, `&T`, shared across multiple threads. Most types that are `Send` are also `Sync`. For example, `RefCell<T>` is `Send` but *not* `Sync` (you can send it to another thread, but then only that thread can use it; you can't share `&RefCell<T>` across threads and have them all call `borrow_mut()` because its internal checks aren't atomic). `Mutex<T>` *is* `Sync` because it internally handles synchronized access.

Type	Send? (Can move to new thread)	Sync? (Can share &T with threads)	Why?
i32, bool, f64	Yes	Yes	Simple, Copy types. Safe to
String, Vec<T>, Box<T>	Yes	Yes	Owned types. As long as T is
Rc<T>	No	No	The reference count is non-
RefCell<T>	Yes	No	You can move it to a new thread, but
Arc<T>	Yes	Yes	Arc is the thread-safe Rc. Its
Mutex<T>	Yes	Yes	Mutex is (like) the thread-safe

Figure 13.7: Summary of Send and Sync trait implementations for common Rust types

The compiler checks these traits automatically. If you try to send a non-`Send` type to another thread, or share a non-`Sync` type via `Arc<&T>`, your code won't compile. *This is a good thing!* The compiler is preventing potential data races.

Listen to the compiler. When it gives you errors related to `Send`, `Sync`, or lifetimes in a concurrent context, it's usually pointing to a genuine safety issue. Don't try to fight it with unsafe code unless you are an expert and know exactly what you're doing. Instead, rethink your data sharing or ownership strategy. Often, this means using `Arc` for shared ownership, `Mutex` or `RwLock` for interior mutability of shared data, or switching to message passing.

Consider the granularity of your parallelism

When breaking down work for threads, think about the "granularity" of the tasks:

- **Fine-grained parallelism:** Breaking work into many very small tasks:
    - **Pros:** Can potentially utilize cores very effectively if tasks are truly independent
    - **Cons:** The overhead of creating threads, managing them, and synchronizing/communicating can outweigh the benefits if the tasks are too small

- **Coarse-grained parallelism**: Breaking work into fewer, larger tasks:
  - **Pros**: Less overhead from thread management and synchronization
  - **Cons**: Might not utilize all cores effectively if one task is much longer than others, or if there aren't enough tasks to keep all cores busy

Finding the right balance depends on the nature of your problem. If tasks involve significant computation, coarser grains might be fine. If tasks are short but numerous and can be done independently, a thread pool or an async approach might be better than spawning a new operating system thread for each tiny task. Tools such as thread pools (from crates such as Rayon for data parallelism, or manually managed pools) can help manage the overhead of many short-lived tasks by reusing a fixed number of worker threads.

By keeping these practices in mind, you can write concurrent Rust code that is not only safe (thanks to the compiler) but also efficient, maintainable, and less prone to common concurrency pitfalls such as deadlocks and excessive contention.

Summary

Our exciting adventure into the world of concurrent programming with Rust! We've discovered how Rust tackles the sometimes intimidating challenge of making programs do multiple things at once, but with a confidence that sets it apart from many other languages. This idea of "fearless concurrency" isn't just a catchy phrase; it's a wonderful result of Rust's ownership and type systems working harmoniously to prevent many common concurrency bugs right during compilation. While concurrency can be tricky, Rust offers robust and surprisingly user-friendly tools to help manage that complexity with ease.

Let's briefly recap what we've explored:

- **Fundamentals of concurrency**: We started by distinguishing between **concurrency** (dealing with multiple tasks) and **parallelism** (doing multiple tasks simultaneously), and discussed the benefits such as improved performance and responsiveness, alongside the classic challenges such as **race conditions** and **deadlocks**. We highlighted Rust's core promise: to help prevent many of these issues before your code even runs.
- **Working with threads**: We learned how to create new execution paths using `std::thread::spawn`, how to safely move data into these threads with **move closures**, and the importance of waiting for threads to complete their work using `JoinHandle` and its `join()` method.

- **Safe data sharing**: A major focus was on how to share data between threads without inviting chaos:
    - `Arc<T>` emerged as the way to enable multiple threads to share ownership of read-only data (or data that will be mutated via interior mutability).
    - `Mutex<T>` and its sibling `RwLock<T>` provide mechanisms to allow controlled, synchronized mutable access to shared data, preventing data races by ensuring only one writer (or multiple readers for `RwLock`) can access the data at any given time. The common `Arc<Mutex<T>>` pattern became clear.
- **Message passing with channels**: We explored an alternative to shared-state concurrency: **message passing** using `std::sync::mpsc` channels. This "share memory by communicating" approach involves sending data (transferring ownership) between threads via the sender and receiver ends of a channel, often leading to simpler designs.
- **A glimpse into async**: We took a very brief peek at **asynchronous programming** with **async/await**, understanding it as a powerful technique for handling many I/O-bound tasks efficiently on a small number of threads, with the help of async runtimes such as `tokio` and `async-std`.
- **Best practices**: Finally, we covered essential best practices for concurrent programming in Rust, such as preferring message passing where it simplifies design, keeping locked critical sections short, being mindful of lock ordering to avoid deadlocks, and trusting Rust's compiler to guide us toward safe patterns.

Mastering concurrency is a very important step in becoming a professional Rust developer.

The tools and guarantees Rust provides make it a uniquely suitable language for building high-performance, concurrent systems with a degree of safety that is hard to match. As you build more complex applications, these concepts will become increasingly valuable.

Questions and assignment

Questions

1. What is the main difference between concurrency and parallelism?
2. What function from `std::thread` do you call to create a new thread, and what keyword must you use on its closure to pass owned data (such as a string) to it?
3. What is `JoinHandle` and what is the purpose of its `.join()` method?
4. If a spawned thread panics, does the main thread also panic? How does the `.join()` method inform you of a panic?

5. Why is `Arc<T>` needed for sharing ownership across threads, while `Rc<T>` (from *Chapter 11*) cannot be used?
6. What is the primary purpose of `Mutex<T>`? What does its `.lock()` method return, and what happens automatically when that returned object goes out of scope?
7. What is the most common data type pattern (using two smart pointers) for safely sharing a *mutable* value (such as a counter) across multiple threads?
8. Briefly, what is the main difference between `Mutex<T>` and `RwLock<T>`? In what scenario would `RwLock<T>` be more performant?
9. What does `mpsc` stand for in `std::sync::mpsc`? What is the main difference between the `Sender<T>` and `Receiver<T>` types?
10. What is a data race, and how does Rust's compiler (specifically the `Send` and `Sync` traits) prevent them in safe code?

Assignment: Concurrent file word counter

For this assignment, you'll build a command-line application that takes one or more file paths as arguments and counts the total occurrences of each word across all files, performing the counting for each file in parallel.

1. **Project setup**:
    - Create a new binary project: `cargo new concurrent_word_counter`
    - Add the clap crate (or `argh`, or just use `std::env::args()`) for command-line argument parsing to get file paths

    Note

    To complete this assignment, you'll need to combine concepts from several chapters. You'll need to read files (which we covered in *Chapter 12* using `std::fs` and `std::io::BufReader`), and you'll be using concurrency tools from this chapter, such as `std::thread::spawn` for the workers and `std::sync::mpsc` for sending results. You'll also likely want to use a HashMap (from `std::collections::HashMap`) to store the word counts.

2. **Core logic**:
    - The main function will get a list of file paths from the command-line arguments.
    - For each file path, do the following:

  - Spawn a new thread dedicated to processing that file
  - The thread should do the following:
  - Read the content of the file (handle potential `std::io::Errors`).
  - Convert the content to lowercase.
  - Split the content into words (you can define what a "word" is: `split_whitespace` is a good start, but you might want to filter out punctuation).
  - Count the frequency of each word within *that file*, storing it in a local `HashMap<String, u32>`.
  - Send this local HashMap back to the main thread using an `mpsc` channel.
- The main thread should do the following:
  - Create an `mpsc` channel before spawning threads. Sender clones will be moved into each thread.
  - Collect all the JoinHandles from the spawned threads.
  - Collect all the partial HashMaps sent back by the worker threads via the receiver end of the channel. (Remember to receive for each thread you spawned.)
  - Aggregate all the partial HashMaps into a single, final `HashMap<String, u32>` that contains the total word counts across all files.
  - Wait for all threads to complete using `join()`.
  - Print the top *N* (e.g., 10) most frequent words and their counts from the final aggregated map.

3. **Error handling:**
   - If a file cannot be read, the respective thread should send an error indication back to the main thread (e.g., wrap the HashMap in a `Result<HashMap<_,_>, String>`), or the main thread can log an error if `recv()` fails for a particular thread's expected result. For simplicity, you could have threads print an error message and send an empty HashMap if they fail to read their file.

14

Rust for Web Development: Building Full-Stack Applications

Now, let's dive into one of Rust's most practical and exciting applications.

This chapter explains why the Rust Language is a great choice for building modern, fast, reliable web applications. I believe it's one of the best ways to learn Rust: web development!

We'll take a full-stack approach, starting with a quick review of the fundamental web concepts, then moving on to building a backend API with the Axum framework.

We'll also connect this API to a PostgreSQL database using Docker (although we will introduce Docker properly in *Chapter 16*) and sqlx, and conclude with a fun peek at how Rust can even power frontend components using **WebAssembly** (**Wasm**).

Let's start!

Core web concepts: a quick refresher

Before we begin creating our first Axum server, let's take a moment to review some key technologies that form the foundation of the web.

This quick refresher on HTTP, JSON, and RESTful APIs will help ensure we're all on the same page.

If you're already familiar with these basics, you can proceed to the next section, *Getting started with Axum*.

The HTTP protocol: requests, responses, and methods

At its core, the web is powered by the **Hypertext Transfer Protocol** (HTTP).

It's a simple request-response system: a client, such as your browser or Rust application, makes a request to a server, which then responds with the information you need.

This process happens seamlessly, making the browsing experience smooth and easy.

Requests and responses

What is an HTTP request?

At its core, an **HTTP request** consists of the following:

- A **method** (or "verb") such as `GET`, `POST`, `PUT`, or `DELETE`, indicating the desired action.
- A **path** (or URL) identifying the resource on the server (e.g., /users/123).
- **Headers**, which are key-value pairs of metadata (e.g., Content-Type: application/json).
- An optional **body**, which contains data being sent to the server (e.g., a JSON payload).

An **HTTP response** consists of the following:

- A **status code** (e.g., 200 OK, 404 Not Found).
- **Headers** (e.g., Content-Length: 1234).
- An optional **body**, which contains the data being sent back to the client (e.g., an HTML page or JSON data).

Common HTTP methods

In this book, we'll focus on the four primary HTTP methods used for **CRUD** (**Create, Read, Update, Delete**) operations:

- **GET**: Used to **Read** data from a resource. It should be safe and idempotent (calling it multiple times has the same result as calling it once).
- **POST**: Used to **Create** a new resource. The data for the new resource is sent in the request body.
- **PUT** or **PATCH**: Used to **Update** an existing resource. PUT typically replaces the entire resource, while PATCH (which we'll use) applies a partial update.
- **DELETE**: Used to **Delete** a resource.

Status codes

The server's response status code is important for the client to understand what happened. The following list is not exhaustive, but the most important categories are as follows:

- **2xx (Successful):** The request was successful.
  - **200 OK**: The standard response for a successful GET, PUT, or PATCH
  - **201 Created**: The standard response for a successful POST that created a new resource
  - **204 No Content**: A successful response that has no body (often used for DELETE)
- **4xx (Client Error):** The client did something wrong.
  - **400 Bad Request**: The request was malformed (e.g., invalid JSON)
  - **404 Not Found**: The requested resource (e.g., /users/999) doesn't exist
- **5xx (Server Error):** The server failed to fulfill a valid request.
  - **500 Internal Server Error**: A generic "something went wrong" on the server (e.g., a database connection failed, or our code panicked)

Data formats: JSON and RESTful API design

When our client and server exchange data in the request and response bodies, they need to agree on a format.

JSON for APIs

The most common data format for modern web APIs is **JSON** (**JavaScript Object Notation**). It's a lightweight, human-readable format that easily maps to Rust structs and enums.

We're excited to use the serde crate, a powerful tool that helps us automatically convert our Rust structs into JSON responses and turn JSON requests back into structs with ease.

Brief on RESTful API design principles

We will be building a **RESTful API**. This is an architectural style that uses these web fundamentals in a predictable way.

Instead of creating custom function names in our URLs (such as `/getUserById`), we will identify "**resources**" (such as `/todos`) and use standard HTTP methods to operate on them.

1. **Resources and path parameters:** We use the URL path to identify *what* we are interacting with. If we need to target a specific item, we use a **path parameter** (usually an ID):
    - `GET /todos`: Get a list of all todos
    - `POST /todos`: Create a new todo
    - `GET /todos/1`: Get the specific todo with ID 1
    - `PATCH /todos/1`: Update the todo with ID 1
    - `DELETE /todos/1`: Delete the todo with ID 1
2. **Refining results with query parameters:** Sometimes, we need to provide extra instructions to the server, such as filtering a list, searching, or pagination, without changing the resource we are accessing. For this, we use **query parameters** (or "query strings").

These appear at the end of the URL, following a ? symbol, and are formatted as key-value pairs:

- `GET /todos?completed=true`: Get a list of todos, but *filter* to show only the completed ones
- `GET /todos?sort=title`: Get all todos, sorted alphabetically by title
- `GET /todos?page=2&limit=10`: Get the second page of results, limiting the list to 10 items

This combined approach – using **path parameters** for identity and **query parameters** for filtering – helps make our API predictable, standard, and easy for other developers to understand and use.

Getting started with Axum

With our web fundamentals refreshed, it's time to build our first web server.

We'll be using **Axum**, a modern, ergonomic web framework that's part of the Tokio ecosystem.

Axum is known for its simplicity, powerful "extractor" system (how it gets data from requests), and composable router.

This section guides you through setting up a new Rust project for Axum and getting a basic "Hello, Web!" server up and running.

Project setup and dependencies

First, let's create a new Rust binary project using Cargo.

Open your terminal and run the following:

```
cargo new my_axum_server --bin
cd my_axum_server
```

Axum is built on top of **Tokio**, an asynchronous runtime. Async/await in Rust requires a runtime to execute asynchronous code, and Axum is designed to work perfectly with Tokio.

We need to add both `axum` and `tokio` to our `Cargo.toml` dependencies.

We'll enable the "full" feature for `tokio` for this chapter, which gives us the `#[tokio::main]` macro and everything else we need.

Here's the `Cargo.toml` snippet:

```
[dependencies]
axum = "0.8" # Check crates.io for the latest
tokio = { version = "1", features = ["full"] }
```

After saving `Cargo.toml`, run `cargo build` to download and compile these crates.

"Hello, Web!" – Your first Axum server (*Getting started with Axum*)

Writing a "Hello, World!" server in Axum involves two main parts:

1. A **handler function** that defines what to do when a request is received.
2. A **main function** that sets up the **router**, binds to an address, and starts the server.

Let's look at the minimal code to get this running.

`src/main.rs` snippet (handler):

```
// This is a "handler" function.
// It's an async function that returns something that can be
// converted into an HTTP response. A simple &str works!
async fn hello_world_handler() -> &'static str {
    "Hello, Web!"
}
```

Conceptual `src/main.rs` snippet (`main` function):

```
// We need the tokio::main macro to run our async main function
#[tokio::main]
async fn main() {
    // build our application with a single route
    let app = Router::new().route("/", get(hello_world_handler));

    // run it
    let listener = tokio::net::TcpListener::bind("127.0.0.1:8080")
        .await
        .expect("Failed to bind to address 127.0.0.1:8080");

    println!("🚀 Server listening on http://{}", listener.local_addr().
unwrap());

    axum::serve(listener, app)
        .await
        .expect("Failed to start server");
}
```

Our project should look like this:

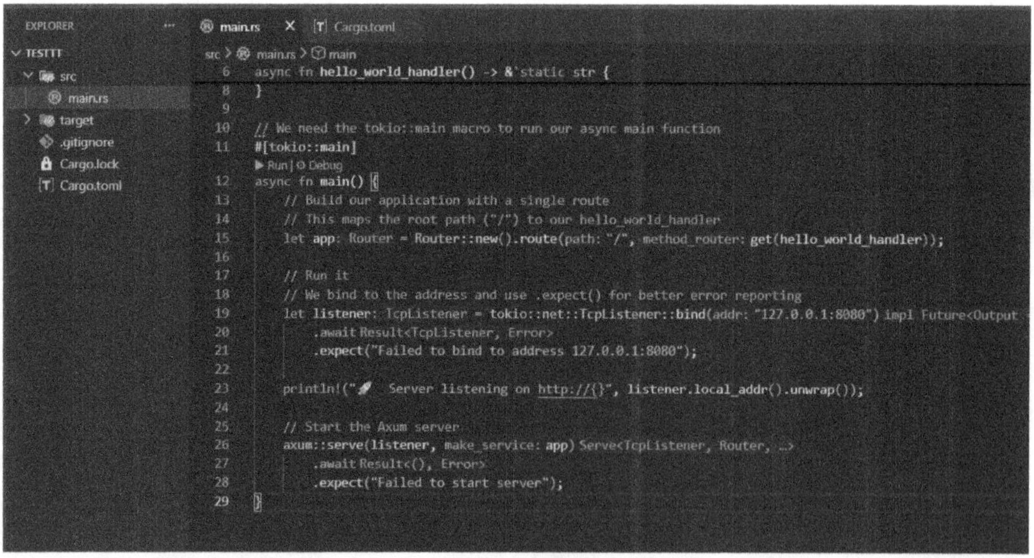

Figure 14.1: The complete src/main.rs file for the "Hello, Web!" server

If you were to combine these snippets and run `cargo run`, you could visit `http://127.0.0.1:8080` in your browser and see **Hello, Web!**.

Figure 14.2: Visiting http://127.0.0.1:8080 in the browser displays the response from our handler

Understanding handlers and the router

The preceding example introduced the two most important concepts in Axum: handlers and the router.

Defining handler functions

A **handler** is simply an asynchronous function (`async fn`) that takes zero or more arguments (called "extractors," which we'll look at soon) and returns a type that can be converted into an HTTP response (a type that implements Axum's `IntoResponse` trait).

The `hello_world_handler` handler is the simplest possible handler:

```
async fn hello_world_handler() -> &'static str {
    "Hello, Web!"
}
```

It doesn't require any arguments and returns `&'static str`, which Axum conveniently converts into a 200 OK response with your string as the body.

Handlers are the heart of your application, where all your main logic will be happily organized.

Registering routes with Router::route

Think of the router as the heart of your Axum app.

Its main role is to guide incoming HTTP requests, based on their path and method, to the right handler functions.

You can create a router easily by chaining together `.route()` methods, making your setup smooth and straightforward.

```
use axum::{routing::get, Router};

// Assume we have these two handlers defined:
async fn root_handler() -> &'static str { "This is the root." }
async fn about_handler() -> &'static str { "This is the about page." }

// Create a router that maps paths to handlers
let app = Router::new()
    .route("/", get(root_handler)) // Handles GET /
    .route("/about", get(about_handler)); // Handles GET /about
```

Here, `routing::get()` is a function that creates a "method router" for the GET HTTP method.

Axum provides similar functions for other methods, such as POST, PUT, DELETE, and so on.

Here is the complete, runnable `src/main.rs` file that puts all these pieces together, including multiple routes, so you have a fully functioning example to start with.

```
use axum::{
    routing::get, // Used to create a router for the GET method
    Router,
};
use std::net::SocketAddr;

/// This is our first handler function for the root path (`/`).
/// It's an async function that returns a type implementing
`IntoResponse`.
/// A static string slice (`&'static str`) is one of the simplest.
async fn root_handler() -> &'static str {
    "Welcome to our Axum server!"
}

/// This is a second handler function for the `/hello` path.
async fn hello_handler() -> &'static str {
```

```
    "Hello, Web!"
}
...
let app = Router::new()
    .route("/", get(root_handler))        // Handle requests to root
    .route("/hello", get(hello_handler)); // Handle requests to /hello
...
/// Refer to the GitHub repository for the complete code!
```

Building a RESTful API: an in-memory todo list

Now that we have a basic Axum server up and running, let's work on something more practical: building a RESTful API.

This is the foundation of many of today's web applications, making it easy for clients such as web browsers or mobile apps to communicate and share data seamlessly.

To keep our focus on the API logic, we'll create a simple "todo" list application that stores its data in memory. This way, we can get comfortable with handling HTTP methods, JSON data, and shared state before we move on to adding a database.

For this more advanced example, let's start a new project from scratch to keep everything tidy and easy to understand.

Don't forget to stop your current server because the next project will also use port `8080`!

Project setup for the API

Open your terminal and create a new binary Rust project.

We'll also `cd` into it and immediately create the module files we'll need for organization:

- `models.rs` (for our data structs)
- `handlers.rs` (for our API logic)

Let's initialize the project by running some commands on the terminal (the two files can also be created manually or with the help of an IDE).

```
cargo new todo_api --bin
cd todo_api
touch src/models.rs
touch src/handlers.rs
```

Next, open your `Cargo.toml` file and add `axum`, `tokio`, and `serde` (for JSON).

```
[package]
name = "todo_api"
version = "0.1.0"
edition = "2021"

[dependencies]
axum = "0.8"
tokio = { version = "1", features = ["full"] }
serde = { version = "1.0", features = ["derive"] }
```

Now we're ready to define our data structures.

Defining data models with serde for JSON

First, we need to define the *shape* of our data. We'll use Rust structs and `serde` to automatically handle conversions to and from JSON.

We'll define two structs in the `src/models.rs` file we just created: `Todo` for an existing item (which has an ID) and `NewTodo` for the data a client sends to create one (which doesn't include an ID yet).

```
use serde::{Deserialize, Serialize};

/// Represents a Todo item in the system.
#[derive(Debug, Serialize, Deserialize, Clone)]
pub struct Todo {
    pub id: u32,
    pub title: String,
    pub completed: bool,
}
```

```
/// Represents the payload for creating a new Todo.
#[derive(Debug, Deserialize)]
pub struct NewTodo {
    pub title: String,
}
```

Here's an explanation of the code:

- `#[derive(Serialize, Deserialize)]`: These macros from `serde` are key. `Serialize` allows us to convert our `Todo` struct *into* JSON to send as a response. `Deserialize` allows us to parse incoming JSON data *from* a request into our `NewTodo` struct.
- `Clone`: We derive `Clone` on `Todo` to make it easy to return copies of items from our in-memory store.
- `NewTodo`: We use a separate struct for creating a new `todo` because the client won't know the ID (the server will assign it), and we'll set `completed` to `false` by default.

Remember to declare this new module in your `src/main.rs` file by adding `pub mod models;` at the top.

Managing shared state

Our API needs a place to keep all our `todo` items organized.

For now, a simple in-memory `Vec<Todo>` will do the trick, but in a real app, we'd use a proper database (no worries – we will do it later!).

One thing to keep in mind is that Axum, like most high-performance Rust web frameworks, runs on an asynchronous runtime (Tokio). This means it can handle multiple requests simultaneously, even with just a few threads.

To keep everything running smoothly and avoid data races when multiple requests attempt to update our `Vec` simultaneously, we'll need to use synchronization techniques to protect our shared data.

Using Arc<Mutex<...>> for in-memory state

We will use a standard Rust concurrency pattern:

1. `std::sync::Mutex`: This "mutual exclusion" lock will wrap our `Vec<Todo>`. It ensures that only one thread can get mutable access to the vector at any given moment.

Note on performance

For read-heavy applications (such as an API where GET requests far outnumber POST requests), you might often see `std::sync::RwLock` used instead. While a mutex allows only one thread to access data at a time (whether reading or writing), `RwLock` allows **multiple readers** to access the data simultaneously, blocking only when a writer needs exclusive access. We are using `Mutex` here for simplicity, as `RwLock` introduces slightly more overhead for writes, but it is a great alternative to keep in mind for production.

2. `std::sync::Arc`: This is an "atomic reference counted" smart pointer. This allows our mutex-protected `Vec` to be safely shared (co-owned) by multiple threads (i.e., Axum's worker threads).

We'll define an `AppState` struct to hold this shared data, along with an atomic counter for generating new todo IDs.

Sharing state with the state extractor

Axum makes it very easy to share this `AppState` struct with all our handlers. We wrap our state in an `Arc` (Axum's `State` extractor works with `Arc`-wrapped types) and then add it to our router using the `.with_state()` method.

Any handler can then "extract" this shared state by simply adding `State<AppState>` as one of its arguments.

Let's set this up in `src/main.rs`.

```
use axum::{
    extract::State,
    response::Json,
    routing::get,
    Router,
};
```

```
use std::sync::{Arc, Mutex};
use std::sync::atomic::{AtomicU32, Ordering};
use tokio::net::TcpListener;

// Import our data models
pub mod models;
use models::Todo;

// --- 1. Define the AppState ---
// This struct will hold all shared state for our application.
// We use `Arc` to allow shared ownership across threads.
// We use `Mutex` for interior mutability for our in-memory `Vec`.
#[derive(Clone)]
struct AppState {
    db: Arc<Mutex<Vec<Todo>>>,
    next_id: Arc<AtomicU32>,
}

// Implement a simple constructor for our state
impl AppState {
    fn new() -> Self {
        Self {
            db: Arc::new(Mutex::new(Vec::new())), // Start with an empty Vec
            next_id: Arc::new(AtomicU32::new(1)), // Start IDs from 1
        }
    }
}

// A simple handler to show the state is working (we'll replace this soon)
async fn get_todos_placeholder(
    State(app_state): State<AppState>, // This is the `State` extractor
) -> Json<Vec<Todo>> {
    // Lock the mutex to get access to the inner Vec
    let todos = app_state.db.lock().unwrap();

    // Return a clone of the data as JSON
    Json(todos.clone())
```

```
}

#[tokio::main]
async fn main() {
    // --- 2. Create and initialize our AppState ---
    let app_state = AppState::new();

    // --- 3. Define the Router and add the state ---
    let app = Router::new()
        .route("/todos", get(get_todos_placeholder))
        // `.with_state()` makes the `app_state` available to all routes
        .with_state(app_state);

    // --- 4. Bind and Serve ---
    let listener = TcpListener::bind("127.0.0.1:8080")
        .await
        .expect("Failed to bind to address 127.0.0.1:8080");

    println!("🚀 Server listening on http://{}", listener.local_addr().
unwrap());

    axum::serve(listener, app)
        .await
        .expect("Failed to start server");
}
```

Here's an explanation of the code:

- `AppState` **struct:** This struct holds our shared data. `db` is an `Arc<Mutex<Vec<Todo>>>` (a thread-safe, shared, mutable vector). `next_id` is an `Arc<AtomicU32>` (a thread-safe, shared counter).
- `State` **extractor**: In our `get_todos_placeholder` handler, the `State(app_state): State<AppState>` argument tells Axum to find the `AppState` we registered and inject it. This is Axum's built-in dependency injection for shared state.
- `.with_state(app_state)`**:** In `main`, this method attaches our `app_state` instance to the router, making it available to all handlers that ask for it via the `State` extractor.
- `app.into_make_service()`**:** This is needed when using `.with_state()` to convert the router into a service that can be run by `axum::serve`.

Handling requests and extracting data

An API handler is almost useless if it can't receive data. A client might send data in several ways: as part of the URL path (e.g., `/todos/123`), as query parameters (e.g., `/search?completed=true`), or as a data payload in the request body (e.g., a JSON object).

Axum handles this using **extractors.**

Extracting path parameters with Path

An extractor is a type that you add as an argument to your handler function. Axum sees this argument and automatically tries to extract the corresponding data from the request. If it fails (e.g., the data is missing or in the wrong format), Axum will automatically return a 400 Bad Request or 404 Not Found response, which saves you from writing a lot of boilerplate validation code.

Let's look at the three most common extractors you'll use.

We often put unique identifiers directly in the URL path. Axum lets you capture these dynamic segments using the `Path` extractor.

1. **In your router:** You define a route with a placeholder, prefixed with a colon (`:`).

   ```
   // In main.rs, inside the Router:
   .route("/todos/{id}", get(get_todo_by_id))
   // The `{id}` is the placeholder
   ```

2. **In your handler:** You add an argument of type `Path<T>`, where `T` is the type you want Axum to parse the segment into (e.g., `u32`).

   ```
   // The Path<u32> argument tells Axum to extract the corresponding
   // segment from the URL (e.g., "1" from "/todos/1") and parse it as
   a u32.
   async fn get_todo_by_id(
       State(app_state): State<AppState>,
       Path(id): Path<u32>,
   ) -> Result<Json<Todo>, StatusCode> {
       // We can now use `id` directly in our logic
       let db = app_state.db.lock().unwrap();

       // ... logic to find todo by `id` ...
   }
   ```

Extracting query parameters with Query

Query parameters are key-value pairs that come after a ? in the URL (e.g., `/search?q=rust&lang=en`). They are often used for optional filters, sorting, or pagination. Axum uses the `Query` extractor, which deserializes parameters into a struct you define.

1. **Define a Query struct**: The struct must derive `serde::Deserialize`.

```
use serde::Deserialize;

#[derive(Deserialize)]
pub struct Pagination {
    pub page: Option<u32>,
    pub per_page: Option<u32>,
}
```

2. **In your handler:** Add an argument of type `Query<YourStruct>`.

```
use axum::{extract::Query, ...}; // Add Query to imports
use serde::Deserialize;

#[derive(Deserialize)]
pub struct SearchParams {
    // We can use Option for parameters that are not required
    pub completed: Option<bool>,
}

// Handler for GET /todos/search?completed=true
pub async fn search_todos(
    State(app_state): State<AppState>,
    Query(params): Query<SearchParams>, // The Query extractor
) -> Json<Vec<Todo>> {

        let db = app_state.db.lock().expect("Mutex was poisoned");

    // Start with an iterator over the todos
    let mut results = db.clone();

    // If the `completed` query param was provided, filter the
results
```

```
    if let Some(completed_status) = params.completed {
        results.retain(|todo| todo.completed == completed_status);
    }

    Json(results)
}
```

Extracting JSON bodies with JSON

For POST or PUT requests, data is usually sent in the request body, often as JSON. The `Json` extractor tells Axum to parse the request body as JSON and deserialize it into your chosen struct.

1. **You already have a struct:** We'll use the `NewTodo` struct we defined earlier, in `src/models.rs`, which derives `Deserialize`.
2. **In your handler:** Add an argument of type `Json<YourStruct>`.

Here's the code snippet for `src/handlers.rs`:

```
use axum::{extract::Json, http::StatusCode, ...}; // Add Json to imports
use crate::models::NewTodo;
// ... other imports

// Handler for POST /todos
pub async fn create_todo(
    State(app_state): State<AppState>,
    Json(payload): Json<NewTodo>, // The Json extractor
) -> (StatusCode, Json<Todo>) {


let mut db = app_state.db.lock().expect("Mutex was poisoned");
    let id = app_state.next_id.fetch_add(1, Ordering::SeqCst);

    let new_todo = Todo {
        id,
        title: payload.title,
        completed: false,
    };
```

```
    db.push(new_todo.clone());

    // Return 201 Created and the new todo
    (StatusCode::CREATED, Json(new_todo))
}
```

Using these three extractors (`Path`, `Query`, and `Json`), you can manage most data inputs in a typical RESTful API.

Axum's extractor system effortlessly performs parsing, type validation, and error handling, so you can concentrate on your application's core logic.

Implementing the CRUD API endpoints

We've already outlined the handlers for Create (POST) and Read (GET). Now, let's move on to adding the handlers for Update and Delete.

A truly effective API doesn't just perform the actions; it also makes sure to return the right data and HTTP status codes to keep everyone on the same page.

Returning JSON and HTTP status codes

Axum handlers use their return type to build an HTTP response. This system is very flexible. A handler can return the following:

- A simple `&'static str` (like our "Hello, Web!" example), which becomes a 200 OK response with a plain text body.
- `Json<T>`: This serializes the value `T` into a JSON string and sends a 200 OK response with the `Content-Type: application/json` header.
- `StatusCode`: You can return just a status code (e.g., `StatusCode::NOT_FOUND` for a 404).
- A tuple (`StatusCode, Json<T>`): This is a very common and powerful pattern. It allows you to specify a custom status code (such as `201 CREATED`) and a JSON body in one step.
- `Result<impl IntoResponse, StatusCode>`: This allows you to return `Ok(Json(data))` on success and `Err(StatusCode::NOT_FOUND)` on failure, and Axum will automatically turn them into the correct HTTP responses.

We'll use these patterns to complete our API.

First, let's create a new struct in `src/models.rs` to represent the payload for updating a todo. This is good practice as it allows for partial updates (e.g., only changing the title or the completed status).

`src/models.rs` (add this struct):

```
// In src/models.rs
use serde::{Deserialize, Serialize};

// ... (Existing Todo and NewTodo structs) ...

/// Represents the payload for updating an existing Todo.
/// All fields are optional.
#[derive(Debug, Deserialize)]
pub struct UpdateTodo {
    pub title: Option<String>,
    pub completed: Option<bool>,
}
```

Now, let's create the update and delete handlers in `src/handlers.rs`.

`src/handlers.rs` (add these functions):

```
use axum::{
    extract::{Path, State, Json as AxJson},
    http::StatusCode,
    response::IntoResponse,
    Json, // The response type for all successful bodies
};
use std::sync::atomic::Ordering;
use crate::models::{Todo, NewTodo, UpdateTodo};
use crate::AppState; // We assume AppState is defined in main.rs

// --- Create ---
/// Handler for POST /todos
/// Creates a new todo item.
pub async fn create_todo(
    State(state): State<AppState>,
    AxJson(payload): AxJson<NewTodo>, // The Json extractor (aliased for
clarity)
) -> (StatusCode, Json<Todo>) {
```

```
    // Lock the mutex safely
    let mut db = state.db.lock().expect("Mutex was poisoned");

    // Generate u32 ID from counter and cast it to i32 for the Todo 
struct.
    let id_u32 = state.next_id.fetch_add(1, Ordering::SeqCst);

    let new_todo = Todo {
        id: id_u32 as i32, // FIX: Cast u32 to i32 to match Todo struct/
PostgreSQL
        title: payload.title,
        completed: false,
    };

    db.push(new_todo.clone());

    // Return 201 Created and the new todo as JSON
    (StatusCode::CREATED, Json(new_todo))
}

// --- Read All ---
/// Handler for GET /todos
/// Returns a list of all todo items.
pub async fn get_all_todos(
    State(state): State<AppState>
) -> Json<Vec<Todo>> {

    // Lock the mutex for reading and clone the vector safely
    let todos = state.db.lock().expect("Mutex was poisoned").clone();

    Json(todos) // Return 200 OK with JSON body
}

// --- Read Single ---
/// Handler for GET /todos/{id} (Axum 0.8 Syntax)
/// Returns a single todo by its ID.
pub async fn get_todo(
    State(state): State<AppState>,
```

```
    Path(id): Path<i32>, // FIX: Change extractor type to i32
) -> Result<Json<Todo>, StatusCode> {

    let db = state.db.lock().expect("Mutex was poisoned");

    // Find the todo by its ID (i32 == i32 comparison is now valid)
    if let Some(todo) = db.iter().find(|t| t.id == id) {
        Ok(Json(todo.clone())) // Return 200 OK with the todo
    } else {
        Err(StatusCode::NOT_FOUND) // Return 404 Not Found
    }
}

// --- Update (Partial) ---
/// Handler for PATCH /todos/{id} (Axum 0.8 Syntax)
/// Updates a todo item (partial updates).
pub async fn update_todo(
    State(state): State<AppState>,
    Path(id): Path<i32>, // FIX: Change extractor type to i32
    AxJson(payload): AxJson<UpdateTodo>, // Use the UpdateTodo struct
) -> Result<Json<Todo>, StatusCode> {

    let mut db = state.db.lock().expect("Mutex was poisoned");

    // Find a mutable reference to the todo
    if let Some(todo) = db.iter_mut().find(|t| t.id == id) {
        // Update fields if they are provided in the JSON payload
        if let Some(title) = payload.title {
            todo.title = title;
        }
        if let Some(completed) = payload.completed {
            todo.completed = completed;
        }
        Ok(Json(todo.clone())) // Return 200 OK with the updated todo
    } else {
        Err(StatusCode::NOT_FOUND) // 404 Not Found
    }
```

```
}

// --- Delete ---
/// Handler for DELETE /todos/{id} (Axum 0.8 Syntax)
/// Deletes a todo item by its ID.
pub async fn delete_todo(
    State(state): State<AppState>,
    Path(id): Path<i32>, // FIX: Change extractor type to i32
) -> StatusCode {

    let mut db = state.db.lock().expect("Mutex was poisoned");

    let len_before = db.len();
    // Keep all todos *except* the one with the matching ID
    db.retain(|todo| todo.id != id);
    let len_after = db.len();

    if len_before > len_after {
        // We removed an item
        StatusCode::NO_CONTENT // 204 No Content (success, no body)
    } else {
        // No item was removed, so it wasn't found
        StatusCode::NOT_FOUND // 404 Not Found
    }
}
```

Here's an explanation of the code:

- `create_todo`: Now returns a tuple (`StatusCode, AxJson<Todo>`) to explicitly send a 201 CREATED status along with the new `Todo`.
- `get_todo`: Returns `Result<AxJson<Todo>, StatusCode>`. This is a powerful pattern in Axum. If we return `Ok(Json(todo))`, Axum sends 200 OK with the JSON. If we return `Err(StatusCode::NOT_FOUND)`, Axum automatically sends a 404 Not Found response.
- `update_todo`: We've changed this to use the PATCH method (which is more correct for partial updates) and the `UpdateTodo` struct. It finds a *mutable* reference to the todo (`.iter_mut().find(...)`) and updates only the fields that were provided (are `Some`) in the JSON payload.

- `delete_todo`: This handler uses `db.retain(...)` to efficiently remove the item. It returns a `StatusCode` directly: 204 NO_CONTENT on a successful deletion, and 404 NOT_FOUND if no item with that ID existed.

All the code for the RESTful API example

The following is all the code you need to make the preceding example work.

First, here are the dependencies you need in your `Cargo.toml` file:

File 1: Cargo.toml

```
[package]
name = "todo_api"
version = "0.1.0"
edition = "2024"

[dependencies]
axum = "0.8"
tokio = { version = "1", features = ["full"] }
serde = { version = "1.0", features = ["derive"] }
```

File 2: src/models.rs

Create this file to define your data structures.

```
use serde::{Deserialize, Serialize};

/// Represents a Todo item in the system.
/// We derive `FromRow` to allow sqlx to map database rows to this struct.
#[derive(Debug, Serialize, Deserialize, Clone)]
pub struct Todo {
    pub id: i32, // PostgreSQL SERIAL maps to i32
    pub title: String,
    pub completed: bool,
}

/// Represents the payload for creating a new Todo.
#[derive(Debug, Deserialize)]
pub struct NewTodo {
    pub title: String,
```

```
}

/// Represents the payload for updating an existing Todo.
/// All fields are optional to allow for partial updates.
#[derive(Debug, Deserialize)]
pub struct UpdateTodo {
    pub title: Option<String>,
    pub completed: Option<bool>,
}
```

File 3: src/handlers.rs

Create this file to hold all your API logic/handler functions.

```
use axum::{
    extract::{Path, State, Json as AxJson},
    http::StatusCode,
    response::IntoResponse,
    Json, // The response type for all successful bodies
};
use std::sync::atomic::Ordering;
use crate::models::{Todo, NewTodo, UpdateTodo};
use crate::AppState; // We assume AppState is defined in main.rs

// --- Create ---
/// Handler for POST /todos
/// Creates a new todo item.
pub async fn create_todo(
    State(state): State<AppState>,
    AxJson(payload): AxJson<NewTodo>, // The Json extractor (aliased for
clarity)
) -> (StatusCode, Json<Todo>) {

    // Lock the mutex safely
    let mut db = state.db.lock().expect("Mutex was poisoned");

    // Generate u32 ID from counter and cast it to i32 for the Todo struct.
    let id_u32 = state.next_id.fetch_add(1, Ordering::SeqCst);
```

```
    let new_todo = Todo {
        id: id_u32 as i32, // FIX: Cast u32 to i32 to match Todo struct/
PostgreSQL
        title: payload.title,
        completed: false,
    };

    db.push(new_todo.clone());

    // Return 201 Created and the new todo as JSON
    (StatusCode::CREATED, Json(new_todo))
}

// --- Read All ---
/// Handler for GET /todos
/// Returns a list of all todo items.
pub async fn get_all_todos(
    State(state): State<AppState>
) -> Json<Vec<Todo>> {

    // Lock the mutex for reading and clone the vector safely
    let todos = state.db.lock().expect("Mutex was poisoned").clone();

    Json(todos) // Return 200 OK with JSON body
}

// --- Read Single ---
/// Handler for GET /todos/{id} (Axum 0.8 Syntax)
/// Returns a single todo by its ID.
pub async fn get_todo(
    State(state): State<AppState>,
    Path(id): Path<i32>, // FIX: Change extractor type to i32
) -> Result<Json<Todo>, StatusCode> {

    let db = state.db.lock().expect("Mutex was poisoned");
```

```
    // Find the todo by its ID (i32 == i32 comparison is now valid)
    if let Some(todo) = db.iter().find(|t| t.id == id) {
        Ok(Json(todo.clone())) // Return 200 OK with the todo
    } else {
        Err(StatusCode::NOT_FOUND) // Return 404 Not Found
    }
}

// --- Update (Partial) ---
/// Handler for PATCH /todos/{id} (Axum 0.8 Syntax)
/// Updates a todo item (partial updates).
pub async fn update_todo(
    State(state): State<AppState>,
    Path(id): Path<i32>, // FIX: Change extractor type to i32
    AxJson(payload): AxJson<UpdateTodo>, // Use the UpdateTodo struct
) -> Result<Json<Todo>, StatusCode> {

    let mut db = state.db.lock().expect("Mutex was poisoned");

    // Find a mutable reference to the todo
    if let Some(todo) = db.iter_mut().find(|t| t.id == id) {
        // Update fields if they are provided in the JSON payload
        if let Some(title) = payload.title {
            todo.title = title;
        }
        if let Some(completed) = payload.completed {
            todo.completed = completed;
        }
        Ok(Json(todo.clone())) // Return 200 OK with the updated todo
    } else {
        Err(StatusCode::NOT_FOUND) // 404 Not Found
    }
}

// --- Delete ---
/// Handler for DELETE /todos/{id} (Axum 0.8 Syntax)
/// Deletes a todo item by its ID.
```

```
pub async fn delete_todo(
    State(state): State<AppState>,
    Path(id): Path<i32>, // FIX: Change extractor type to i32
) -> StatusCode {

    let mut db = state.db.lock().expect("Mutex was poisoned");

    let len_before = db.len();
    // Keep all todos *except* the one with the matching ID
    db.retain(|todo| todo.id != id);
    let len_after = db.len();

    if len_before > len_after {
        // We removed an item
        StatusCode::NO_CONTENT // 204 No Content (success, no body)
    } else {
        // No item was removed, so it wasn't found
        StatusCode::NOT_FOUND // 404 Not Found
    }
}
```

Note on JSON aliasing

We alias the inbound `Json` extractor as `AxJson` (`Json as AxJson`) to clearly distinguish it from the `Json` response type. This prevents confusion, as both are used in the signature for handlers such as `create_todo` (i.e., receiving `AxJson<NewTodo>` and returning `Json<Todo>`).

File 4: src/main.rs

Finally, this file ties everything together. It defines the modules, sets up the shared state, and builds the router.

```
use axum::{
    extract::State,
    http::StatusCode,
    response::{IntoResponse, Json}, // Json is now used for the response
body
```

```
    routing::{get, post, patch, delete},
    Router,
};
use std::net::SocketAddr;
use std::sync::{Arc, Mutex};
use std::sync::atomic::{AtomicU32, Ordering};
use tokio::net::TcpListener;
use tokio::signal; // Required for graceful shutdown

// --- Modules ---
pub mod models;
pub mod handlers;

// --- Imports from our modules ---
use models::Todo;
use handlers::{
    create_todo,
    get_all_todos,
    get_todo,
    update_todo,
    delete_todo
};

// --- Application State ---
#[derive(Clone)]
pub struct AppState {
    db: Arc<Mutex<Vec<Todo>>>,
    next_id: Arc<AtomicU32>,
}

impl AppState {
    fn new() -> Self {
        Self {
            db: Arc::new(Mutex::new(Vec::new())),
            next_id: Arc::new(AtomicU32::new(1)),
        }
    }
}
```

```
// Handler for the health check endpoint
async fn health_check() -> (StatusCode, &'static str) {
    (StatusCode::OK, "Service is healthy")
}

// --- Main Server Setup ---
#[tokio::main]
async fn main() {
    // Initialize our shared state
    let app_state = AppState::new();

    // Build our application router, registering all CRUD handlers
    let app = Router::new()
        .route("/health", get(health_check)) // Health check endpoint

        // Root resource CRUD methods
        .route("/todos",
            get(get_all_todos) // GET /todos
            .post(create_todo) // POST /todos
        )

        // Individual resource CRUD methods using Axum 0.8 syntax: {id}
        .route("/todos/{id}",
            get(get_todo)         // GET /todos/{id}
            .patch(update_todo)  // PATCH /todos/{id}
            .delete(delete_todo) // DELETE /todos/{id}
        )

        // Share the AppState with all handlers
        .with_state(app_state);

    // --- Bind and Serve ---
    // Use expect() for safer startup error handling
    let addr = SocketAddr::from(([127, 0, 0, 1], 8080));
    println!("🚀 Server listening on http://{}", addr);
```

```
    let listener = TcpListener::bind(addr).await.expect("Failed to bind to
address");

    // Run the server and enable graceful shutdown
    axum::serve(listener, app)
        .with_graceful_shutdown(shutdown_signal())
        .await
        .expect("Server failed to run");
}

// --- Graceful Shutdown Handler ---
async fn shutdown_signal() {
    let ctrl_c = async {
        signal::ctrl_c()
            .await
            .expect("Failed to install Ctrl+C handler");
    };

    #[cfg(unix)]
    let terminate = async {
        signal::unix::signal(signal::unix::SignalKind::terminate())
            .expect("Failed to install signal handler")
            .recv()
            .await;
    };

    // Use a pending future for non-Unix systems (like Windows)
    #[cfg(not(unix))]
    let terminate = std::future::pending::<()>();

    tokio::select! {
        _ = ctrl_c => {},
        _ = terminate => {},
    }

    println!("Graceful shutdown initiated.");
}
```

Testing our RESTful application

You can explore this application using various methods and tools, such as Postman, VS Code extensions, and others.

However, the simplest and most universal way is to use **curl** commands.

Give it a try and see how smoothly it works!

Step 1: Run your Axum server

In your terminal, navigate to your `todo_api` project directory (where your `Cargo.toml` file is) and run the server:

```
cargo run
```

You should see this output:

```
🚀 Server listening on http://127.0.0.1:8080
Your server is now running and waiting for requests.
```

Step 2: Open a new terminal

Leave your server running in the first terminal. Open a **second, separate terminal window**. You will use this new terminal to send commands to your server using curl, a common command-line tool for making HTTP requests.

Ensure that `'curl'` is a command available in this terminal.

Step 3: Test your API endpoints with curl

Run the following commands one by one in your **new** terminal to test each part of your CRUD API.

1. Create a new todo (`POST /todos`):

   ```
   # We send a POST request with a JSON body
   curl -X POST http://127.0.0.1:8080/todos -H "Content-Type:application/json" -d '{"title": "Learn Axum"}'
   ```

   Expected output:

   ```
   {"id":1,"title":"Learn Axum","completed":false} (with a 201 Created status)
   ```

2. Create a second todo (`POST /todos`):

```
curl -X POST http://127.0.0.1:8080/todos -H "Content-Type:
application/json" -d '{"title": "Write database chapter"}'
```

Expected output:

```
{"id":2,"title":"Write database chapter","completed":false}
```

3. Get all todos (`GET /todos`):

```
curl http://127.0.0.1:8080/todos
```

Expected output:

```
[{"id":1,"title":"Learn
Axum","completed":false},{"id":2,"title":"Write database
chapter","completed":false}]
```

4. Get a single todo by ID (`GET /todos/1`):

```
curl http://127.0.0.1:8080/todos/1
```

Expected output:

```
{"id":1,"title":"Learn Axum","completed":false}
```

5. Get a non-existent todo (`GET /todos/99`):

```
curl -I http://127.0.0.1:8080/todos/99
```

Expected output:

```
Not Found (or similar, with a 404 status)
```

6. Update a todo (`PATCH /todos/1`):

```
mark "Learn Axum" as completed
curl -X PATCH http://127.0.0.1:8080/todos/1 -H "Content-Type:
application/json" -d '{"completed": true}'
```

Expected output:

```
{"id":1,"title":"Learn Axum","completed":true}
```

7. Verify the update (`GET /todos/1` again):

```
curl http://127.0.0.1:8080/todos/1
```

Expected output:

```
{"id":1,"title":"Learn Axum","completed":true} (Note completed is
now true)
```

8. Delete a todo (`DELETE /todos/1`):

```
# -v shows verbose output, so we can see the 204 No Content status
curl -v -X DELETE http://127.0.0.1:8080/todos/1
```

Expected output: You won't see a body, but in the verbose output (`-v`), you should see `< HTTP/1.1 204 No Content`.

9. Verify the deletion (`GET /todos`):

```
curl http://127.0.0.1:8080/todos
```

Expected output:

```
[{"id":2,"title":"Write database chapter","completed":false}] (Item
1 is gone)
```

Following is a list of the commands I tried myself:

```
me@Francesco-PC MINGW64 /c/workspace/todo_api (master)
$ # We send a POST request with a JSON body
curl -X POST http://127.0.0.1:8080/todos \
     -H "Content-Type: application/json" \
     -d '{"title": "Learn Axum"}'
{"id":1,"title":"Learn Axum","completed":false}
$ curl -X POST http://127.0.0.1:8080/todos \
     -H "Content-Type: application/json" \
     -d '{"title": "Write database chapter"}'
{"id":2,"title":"Write database chapter","completed":false}
me@Francesco-PC MINGW64 /c/workspace/todo_api (master)
$ curl http://127.0.0.1:8080/todos
[{"id":1,"title":"Learn Axum","completed":false},{"id":2,"title":"Write database chapter","completed":false}]
me@Francesco-PC MINGW64 /c/workspace/todo_api (master)
$ curl http://127.0.0.1:8080/todos/1
{"id":1,"title":"Learn Axum","completed":false}
me@Francesco-PC MINGW64 /c/workspace/todo_api (master)
$ curl http://127.0.0.1:8080/todos/99

me@Francesco-PC MINGW64 /c/workspace/todo_api (master)
$ # Let's mark "Learn Axum" as completed
curl -X PATCH http://127.0.0.1:8080/todos/1 \
     -H "Content-Type: application/json" \
     -d '{"completed": true}'
{"id":1,"title":"Learn Axum","completed":true}
me@Francesco-PC MINGW64 /c/workspace/todo_api (master)
$ curl http://127.0.0.1:8080/todos/1
{"id":1,"title":"Learn Axum","completed":true}
me@Francesco-PC MINGW64 /c/workspace/todo_api (master)
$ # -v shows verbose output, so we can see the 204 No Content status
curl -v -X DELETE http://127.0.0.1:8080/todos/1
*   Trying 127.0.0.1:8080...
* Connected to 127.0.0.1 (127.0.0.1) port 8080
* using HTTP/1.x
> DELETE /todos/1 HTTP/1.1
> Host: 127.0.0.1:8080
> User-Agent: curl/8.14.1
> Accept: */*
>
< HTTP/1.1 204 No Content
< date: Tue, 04 Nov 2025 14:35:34 GMT
<
* Connection #0 to host 127.0.0.1 left intact

me@Francesco-PC MINGW64 /c/workspace/todo_api (master)
$ [200~curl http://127.0.0.1:8080/todos~
bash: [200~curl: command not found

me@Francesco-PC MINGW64 /c/workspace/todo_api (master)
$ curl http://127.0.0.1:8080/todos
[{"id":2,"title":"Write database chapter","completed":false}]
me@Francesco-PC MINGW64 /c/workspace/todo_api (master)
$
```

Figure 14.3: Testing the in-memory RESTful API endpoints using curl to confirm the functionality of all CRUD operations

Adding persistence with PostgreSQL

Storing data in an in-memory `Arc<Mutex<Vec<Todo>>>` is great for examples, but it has a major drawback: all our data is lost when the server restarts.

For a real application, we need **persistence**.

This means storing our data in a database. In this section, we'll refactor our API to use **PostgreSQL**, a powerful and popular open source relational database.

We'll use **sqlx**, a modern, pure-Rust, and async-native SQL toolkit.

Database setup

Before our Rust app can connect with a database, it's important to have a database server up and running.

Although you can install PostgreSQL directly on your computer, using Docker to run it inside a container is a much cleaner, more straightforward, and more consistent approach for development.

This method keeps the database isolated, avoids any conflicts, and makes cleanup a breeze. Just stop the container when you're done.

If you haven't installed Docker yet, you can download it easily from the official website: `https://www.docker.com/get-started`. (We'll go into more detail about Docker in *Chapter 16*, but for now, just ensure it's installed and running.)

Once Docker is up and running, starting a new PostgreSQL server is as simple as running a single command in your terminal.

```
docker run --name my_app_db_postgres -e POSTGRES_PASSWORD=password \
    -p 5432:5432 -d postgres:15-alpine
```

This should be obvious, but **NEVER** use `password` as a password for your production database! This is just an example to make something easy to remember!

This command will download the lightweight `postgres:15-alpine` image, start a container, set a password, and map the port so your Axum app (running on localhost) can communicate with it.

If you are curious about what the preceding command does exactly, here is a short explanation, if you are quite familiar with Docker:

- `docker run ... -d`: Runs the container in detached (background) mode.
- `--name my-todo-db`: Gives your container a memorable name for easy stopping/starting.
- `-e POSTGRES_PASSWORD=password`: Sets the required password for the postgres superuser inside the container.

- `-p 5432:5432`: Maps port 5432 on your host machine (localhost) to port 5432 inside the container. This is what allows your Axum app to connect to `localhost:5432`.
- `postgres:15-alpine`: The image to use: Postgres 15 on a minimal Alpine Linux base.

If you run the "`docker ps -a`" command on your terminal, you should see something like this:

```
CONTAINER ID   IMAGE                COMMAND                  CREATED          STATUS
PORTS                                        NAMES
1554feb9c28b   postgres:15-alpine   "docker-entrypoint.s…"   23 minutes ago   Up 23 minutes
0.0.0.0:5432->5432/tcp, [::]:5432->5432/tcp   my_app_db_postgres
francesco@Francesco-PC:~$
```

Figure 14.4: Running the postgres container with Docker

This means that your database is up and running (in a Docker container).

Integrating sqlx into the Axum project

Since our PostgreSQL database is running smoothly inside a Docker container, let's now move forward and incorporate the sqlx toolkit into our Axum project.

This exciting step involves three essential and straightforward tasks: adding the needed sqlx libraries to your `Cargo.toml` file, setting up your database connection URL in an `.env` file, and installing the `sqlx-cli` command-line tool to help manage your database schema effortlessly.

Let's proceed step by step.

Adding sqlx and dotenvy dependencies

Let's start by adding the `sqlx` crate to our project.

`sqlx` is a wonderful, async-native Rust SQL toolkit that works seamlessly with our Tokio runtime. We'll enable features for Postgres, the Tokio runtime, rustls for secure connections, and macros to ensure compile-time query checking.

Additionally, we'll include `dotenvy`, a reliable fork of `dotenv` (since `dotenv` is no longer maintained), to help us load our database connection string effortlessly from an `.env` file.

Open your `Cargo.toml` file and add these to your `[dependencies]` section:

```
[dependencies]
# ... (keep axum, tokio, serde)
sqlx = { version = "0.7", features = ["runtime-tokio-rustls", "postgres",
"macros", "chrono", "uuid"] }
dotenvy = "0.15"
```

Note

We've added `chrono` and `uuid` as common features you might need for database work, though for our simple `todos` table, they aren't strictly required. The macros feature is for the compile-time checked queries we'll see later.

Configuring DATABASE_URL

Both our application and `sqlx-cli` (which we'll install next) need to know how to connect to the PostgreSQL database we started in Docker.

The standard way to provide this information is through an environment variable named `DATABASE_URL`. We'll use the `dotenvy` crate we added earlier to load this variable from an `.env` file.

VERY IMPORTANT: you must add this .env file to your .gitignore! This file contains sensitive credentials (such as your database password) and should never be committed to source control.

`.gitignore`

```
..env
```

Create a new file named `.env` in the root directory of your `todo_api` project (the same directory as `Cargo.toml`). Then, add the following line. This connection string must match the settings (user `postgres`, password `password`, port `5432`, and database `postgres`) we used in our `docker run` command.

The `.env` file should look like this:

```
DATABASE_URL=postgres://postgres:password@localhost:5432/postgres
```

Installing and using sqlx-cli for migrations

To manage our database schema (such as creating tables), we'll use `sqlx-cli`, a command-line tool built by the sqlx team. Its most important feature is handling **migrations**.

You can install `sqlx-cli` using `cargo install`. A significant advantage of this tool is that it's a pure-Rust application and connects to the database in the same way as our app will.

```
cargo install sqlx-cli
```

Once installed, `sqlx-cli` will automatically read your `.env` file to find the `DATABASE_URL` and establish a connection to your database.

We'll use it in the next section to create and run our migrations.

Schema management with sqlx migrations

Now that we have `sqlx-cli` installed and our `.env` file is ready, we can define our database's structure. `sqlx-cli` uses **migrations** to manage changes to your database schema in a version-controlled way.

A migration is just a SQL file with a unique timestamped name.

This is a fantastic practice as it keeps a history of your schema and makes it easy to set up your database in any environment.

Creating and running migrations

First, we need to tell `sqlx-cli` to create the migration files.

In your terminal, from your project's root directory, run this:

```
sqlx migrate add create_todos_table
```

This command will do the following:

1. Connect to your database (using `DATABASE_URL` from `.env`) to ensure it's reachable.
2. Create a `migrations` folder in your project root.
3. Inside `migrations`, it will create a new file with a timestamp and the name you provided, such as `YYYYMMDDHHMMSS_create_todos_table.sql`.

Now, open that new `.sql` file. `sqlx-cli` migrations are simple: you write your "up" SQL (to create or alter tables) directly in the file. To add a "down" migration (to revert the change), you add `-- Add down migration` in a comment.

Let's edit the newly created `migrations/YYYY..._create_todos_table.sql` file:

```
CREATE TABLE todos (
    id SERIAL PRIMARY KEY,
    title VARCHAR NOT NULL,
    completed BOOLEAN NOT NULL DEFAULT FALSE
);

DROP TABLE IF EXISTS todos;
```

Reversibility note

The `DROP TABLE IF EXISTS todos;` command is the **DOWN migration.** If you ever need to completely undo this change, `sqlx-cli` will execute this command.

After saving this file, you can **apply** the migration to your database (which is running in Docker) with this command:

```
sqlx migrate run
```

`sqlx-cli` will connect to the database, see that this migration has not been run yet, execute the `up.sql` portion, and record the migration in a special `_sqlx_migrations` table it creates in your database.

To test it out, go to the terminal where you are running Docker commands and type the following:

```
docker exec -it my_app_db_postgres psql -U postgres
```

Then, type this command:

```
\dt
```

You should be able to see the `todos` table:

```
postgres=# \dt
              List of relations
 Schema |        Name        | Type  |  Owner
--------+--------------------+-------+----------
 public | _sqlx_migrations   | table | postgres
 public | todos              | table | postgres
(2 rows)
```

Figure 14.5: Check the todos table with docker exec and psql

Amazing!

But, let's say we type the following:

```
SELECT * FROM todos;
```

We can see that the table is empty.

```
postgres=# select * from todos;
 id | title | completed
----+-------+-----------
(0 rows)

postgres=#
```

Figure 14.6: The todos table is currently empty

Mapping Rust structs and using a connection pool

Now that our database has a todos table defined via migrations, we need to handle two important tasks to make it usable in our Axum app.

First, we must "map" our `Todo` struct to the `todos` table; this involves telling `sqlx` how to convert a database row into our struct.

Second, we need to create an efficient way to manage database connections (a "connection pool") and make it available to all our API handlers so they can actually run queries.

Using sqlx::PgPool for the connection pool

Creating a new database connection for every single incoming web request is extremely slow and inefficient.

The correct solution is a **connection pool**, which is a cache of database connections that your application maintains.

When a handler needs to talk to the database, it quickly "borrows" a connection from the pool, uses it, and then returns it.

sqlx provides an excellent, async-native connection pool called `sqlx::PgPool` (for Postgres). We'll create this pool when our server first starts up in `main.rs` by reading the `DATABASE_URL` from our `.env` file and using the `PgPoolOptions` builder.

`src/main.rs` (snippet for pool creation):

```
// Add these to your `use` statements at the top of src/main.rs
use dotenvy::dotenv;
use std::env;
use sqlx::postgres::PgPoolOptions;
use sqlx::PgPool; // Import the Pool type
```

```
// ...

#[tokio::main]
async fn main() {
    // Load environment variables from .env file (DATABASE_URL)
    dotenv().ok(); // .ok() ignores errors if .env is not found

    // Get the database URL from the environment
    let database_url = env::var("DATABASE_URL")
        .expect("DATABASE_URL must be set in .env file");

    // --- Create the Database Connection Pool ---
    let pool = PgPoolOptions::new()
        .max_connections(5) // Set a max of 5 connections for our pool
        .connect(&database_url)
        .await
        .expect("Failed to create database connection pool");

    println!("🚀 Database connection pool initialized.");

    // ... (rest of main function will go here) ...
}
```

Here's an explanation of the code:

- `dotenv().ok()`: We call this at the start of `main` to load our `.env` file
- `env::var("DATABASE_URL")`: This reads the connection string from the environment
- `PgPoolOptions::new()`: This is the builder for our sqlx connection pool
- `.connect(...).await`: This asynchronously connects to the database (running in Docker) and establishes the initial connections for the pool

Deriving FromRow for our Todo struct

Now that we have a pool, we need to tell sqlx how to map a row from our todos table into our `Todo` struct. We do this by adding the `sqlx::FromRow` derive macro.

We also need to ensure the `id` type is `i32`, as PostgreSQL's `SERIAL` type maps to a 32-bit signed integer.

`src/models.rs` (updated for sqlx):

```
use serde::{Deserialize, Serialize};
use sqlx::FromRow; // Import the FromRow derive macro

/// Represents a Todo item in the system.
/// We derive `FromRow` to allow sqlx to map database rows to this struct.
#[derive(Debug, Serialize, Deserialize, Clone, FromRow)]
pub struct Todo {
    pub id: i32, // PostgreSQL SERIAL maps to i32
    pub title: String,
    pub completed: bool,
}

/// Represents the payload for creating a new Todo.
#[derive(Debug, Deserialize)]
pub struct NewTodo {
    pub title: String,
}

/// Represents the payload for updating an existing Todo.
#[derive(Debug, Deserialize)]
pub struct UpdateTodo {
    pub title: Option<String>,
    pub completed: Option<bool>,
}
```

Here's an explanation of the code:

- `use sqlx::FromRow`: We import the necessary derive macro.
- `#[derive(..., FromRow)]`: By adding `FromRow` to `Todo`, sqlx can now automatically map the columns `id`, `title`, and `completed` from a query result directly to the fields of our `Todo` struct.
- `id: i32`: We've changed the `id` type from `u32` to `i32` to correctly match PostgreSQL's `SERIAL` type.

- `NewTodo` and `UpdateTodo`: These structs don't need `FromRow` because they are only deserialized from the client's JSON request body, not mapped from a database row.

Sharing the pool in Axum's AppState

Finally, we need to make our connection pool available to all our Axum handlers. The idiomatic way to do this is to store the pool in a shared `AppState` struct and use Axum's `.with_state()` method to "inject" it into our router.

`src/main.rs` (updated to share the pool):

```
use axum::{
    routing::get,
    Router,
    extract::State, // We'll need this in our handlers
};
use std::net::SocketAddr;
use tokio::net::TcpListener;
use dotenvy::dotenv;
use std::env;
use sqlx::postgres::PgPoolOptions;
use sqlx::PgPool; // Import the Pool type

// --- Modules ---
pub mod models;
pub mod handlers; // We'll create this in the next section
// pub mod schema; // NO LONGER NEEDED FOR SQLX

// --- Application State ---
// Define a struct to hold our shared state (the pool)
// We derive Clone so the state can be shared with all threads
#[derive(Clone)]
pub struct AppState {
    db_pool: PgPool,
}

#[tokio::main]
async fn main() {
    // Load environment variables from .env file (DATABASE_URL)
    dotenv().ok();
```

```
    let database_url = env::var("DATABASE_URL")
        .expect("DATABASE_URL must be set in .env file");

    // Create the Database Connection Pool
    let pool = PgPoolOptions::new()
        .max_connections(5)
        .connect(&database_url)
        .await
        .expect("Failed to create database connection pool");

    println!("🚀 Database connection pool initialized.");

    // Run SQLx migrations
    sqlx::migrate!()
        .run(&pool)
        .await
        .expect("Failed to run database migrations.");

    println!("🚀 Database migrations ran successfully.");


    // --- Create the AppState ---
    let app_state = AppState { db_pool: pool };

    // --- Build our application router ---
    let app = Router::new()
        .route("/", get(|| async { "Hello, World! (from database-backed
server)" }))
        // We will register our real CRUD handlers in the next section
        // .route("/todos", post(handlers::create_todo_db).
get(handlers::get_all_todos_db))
        // ... etc ...

        // Share the AppState with all handlers
        .with_state(app_state);

    // --- Bind and Serve ---
    let addr = SocketAddr::from(([127, 0, 0, 1], 8080));
```

```
    println!("🚀 Server listening on http://{}", addr);
    let listener = TcpListener::bind(addr).await.unwrap();

    // `.into_make_service()` is required when using `.with_state`
    axum::serve(listener, app.into_make_service()).await.unwrap();
}
```

- `AppState` **struct**: We've defined a simple `AppState` struct that holds our `PgPool`.
- `#[derive(Clone)]`: This is required by Axum's `with_state` method. `PgPool` is already cheap to clone (it's an `Arc` internally).
- `sqlx::migrate!()`: This macro, needing the `migrations` folder, automatically runs pending database migrations at server start, ensuring your database schema stays current with your code.
- `.with_state(app_state)`: This method connects our state (which includes the pool) to the router, making it accessible to all handlers.
- `app.into_make_service()`: When you use `.with_state`, you must call `.into_make_service()` on your router before passing it to `axum::serve`.

Refactoring handlers for async database persistence

We will now refactor the functions in `src/handlers.rs` to use the `DbPool` from our `AppState` instead of the in-memory `Arc<Mutex<Vec<Todo>>>`. A key advantage of sqlx is that it's **async-native**, designed to work perfectly with Tokio and Axum.

This means we **do not need** to use `tokio::task::spawn_blocking`. We can `.await` database queries directly in our async handlers, leading to cleaner and more efficient code.

Writing raw SQL queries

One of the most powerful features of sqlx is its ability to check your SQL queries at **compile time**. It does this by connecting to your database (using the `DATABASE_URL` in your `.env` file) during the build process and verifying that your SQL is valid and that the columns you're selecting can be correctly mapped to the fields of your Rust struct. This catches typos in your `SQL (SELECT *...)` or type mismatches (e.g., trying to map VARCHAR to `i32`) before your program even runs.

- `sqlx::query_as!(Todo, "...")`: We'll use this macro when we want to run a query and have sqlx automatically map the resulting rows into our `Todo` struct (which we've already derived `FromRow` for).
- `sqlx::query!("...")`: We'll use this simpler macro for queries where we want to execute a command and don't need to map the result to a full struct (such as our `DELETE` command).

Important note on compile-time checking

For this powerful feature to work, your **database must be running and accessible** when you run `cargo build` or `cargo run`. This is because the Rust compiler relies on live schema information to validate the queries and type mappings. If the database isn't available during compilation, the build will fail. Alternatively, you can use the sqlx `prepare` command to generate offline query metadata, allowing compilation without a live database connection.

Refactoring the CRUD endpoints to be fully async

We will now **replace the entire contents** of the `src/handlers.rs` file with this new, database-backed logic. (Check the 11_db_handlers.rs file for the complete code)

```
// ... imports and helper functions ...

// --- Reading Data (SELECT) ---
pub async fn get_all_todos_db(State(state): State<AppState>) -> impl
IntoResponse {
    // query_as! macros check SQL validity at compile time
    let result = sqlx::query_as!(
        Todo,
        "SELECT id, title, completed FROM todos ORDER BY id"
    )
    .fetch_all(&state.db_pool) // Returns Vec<Todo>
    .await;

    match result {
        Ok(todos) => (StatusCode::OK, Json(todos)).into_response(),
        Err(e) => internal_db_error(e).into_response(),
    }
}

// --- Writing Data (INSERT) ---
pub async fn create_todo_db(
    State(state): State<AppState>,
    AxJson(payload): AxJson<NewTodo>,
) -> impl IntoResponse {
```

```
    let result = sqlx::query_as!(
        Todo,
        "INSERT INTO todos (title) VALUES ($1) RETURNING *",
        payload.title
    )
    .fetch_one(&state.db_pool) // Returns a single Todo
    .await;

    match result {
        Ok(todo) => (StatusCode::CREATED, Json(todo)).into_response(),
        Err(e) => internal_db_error(e).into_response(),
    }
}

// ... Additional handlers (update, delete, get_one) follow this same
pattern ...
```

Here's an explanation of the code:

- **Fully async:** Notice that we **do not use** `tokio::task::spawn_blocking` anywhere! Because sqlx is async-native, we can `.await` its methods (such as `.fetch_one()`, `.fetch_all()`, and `.execute()`) directly within our async handlers. This is much cleaner and more efficient.
- **State injection:** All handlers receive the `State<AppState>` extractor to get access to the `db_pool`.
- `sqlx::query_as!` Macro: This is the most powerful feature of sqlx. The `query_as!(Todo, "SELECT ...")` macro does the following:
    1. Checks your SQL query string at **compile time.**
    2. Compares it against your database (using the `DATABASE_URL` at compile time) to ensure the query is valid and that the columns (`id`, `title`, `completed`) can be correctly mapped to the fields of your `Todo` struct.
    3. This prevents a whole class of runtime errors, such as typos in your SQL (`SELECT *`) or type mismatches.
- **Error handling:** We use a simple `internal_db_error` helper to map any `sqlx::Error` to a 500 Internal Server Error response. For specific cases such as `get_todo_db` (where "not found" is expected), we use `.fetch_optional()`, which returns an Option, allowing us to send a 404 NOT FOUND status code.

Finally, you must update `src/main.rs` to import these new handlers and register them in your router.

Complete project reference: Since the full code for a multi-file project structure (containing `Cargo.toml`, `src/models.rs`, `src/handlers.rs`, and `src/main.rs`) can be quite long, we have minimized it here.

For the entire, runnable project structure, including the graceful shutdown handler and module definitions, please check the project repository on GitHub.

```
// src/main.rs

// ... imports and AppState definition ...
// ... imports from handlers module ...

#[tokio::main]
async fn main() {
    // 1. Create Connection Pool and Table
    // ... pool and table creation logic ...

    let app_state = AppState { db_pool: pool };

    // 2. Build our final RESTful router
    let app = Router::new()
        .route("/todos",
            get(handlers::get_all_todos_db)
            .post(handlers::create_todo_db)
        )
        .route("/todos/:id",
            get(handlers::get_todo_db)
            .patch(handlers::update_todo_db)
            .delete(handlers::delete_todo_db)
        )
        .with_state(app_state);

    // 3. Bind and Serve
    // ... server startup logic ...
}
```

Testing the application

To test the new application, first run the following:

```
cargo run
```

The output should look like this:

```
🚀 Database connection pool initialized.
🚀 'todos' table is ready.
🚀 Server listening on http://127.0.0.1:8080
```

Figure 14.7: Axum application up and running

Now let's test the application using curl commands to keep it as universal as possible. But feel free to use tools such as Postman or a VS Code extension to make proper HTTP calls – whichever works best for you!

1. Get all todos (to verify it's empty):

   ```
   curl http://127.0.0.1:8080/todos
   ```

   Expected output:

   ```
   [] (An empty JSON array)
   ```

2. Create a new todo (`POST /todos`):

   ```
   curl -X POST -H "Content-Type: application/json" -d '{"title":
   "Learn sqlx"}' http://127.0.0.1:8080/todos
   ```

   Expected output:

   ```
   {"id":1,"title":"Learn sqlx","completed":false}
   ```

3. Create a second todo (`POST /todos`):

   ```
       curl -X POST -H "Content-Type: application/json" -d '{"title":
   "Test the API"}' http://127.0.0.1:8080/todos
   ```

   Expected output:

   ```
   {"id":2,"title":"Test the API","completed":false}
   ```

4. Get all todos (to see the new items):

```
curl http://127.0.0.1:8080/todos
```

Expected output:

```
[{"id":1,"title":"Learn
sqlx","completed":false},{"id":2,"title":"Test the
API","completed":false}]
```

5. Get a single todo (`GET /todos/1`):

```
curl http://127.0.0.1:8080/todos/1
```

Expected output:

```
{"id":1,"title":"Learn sqlx","completed":false}
```

6. Get a non-existent todo (`GET /todos/99`):

```
curl http://127.0.0.1:8080/todos/99
```

Expected output:

```
Todo not found
```

7. Update a todo (`PATCH /todos/1`):

```
curl -X PATCH -H "Content-Type: application/json" -d '{"completed":
true}' http://127.0.0.1:8080/todos/1
```

Expected output:

```
{"id":1,"title":"Learn sqlx","completed":true}
```

8. Delete a todo (`DELETE /todos/1`):

```
curl -v -X DELETE http://127.0.0.1:8080/todos/1
```

Expected output:

```
You won't see a body, but in the verbose output (-v), you should see
< HTTP/1.1 204 No Content.
```

9. Verify the deletion (`GET /todos`):

```
curl http://127.0.0.1:8080/todos
```

Expected output:

```
[{"id":2,"title":"Test the API","completed":true}]
```

Following is a recap of all the commands:

```
me@Francesco-PC MINGW64 ~
$ curl http://127.0.0.1:8080/todos
[]
me@Francesco-PC MINGW64 ~
$ curl -X POST -H "Content-Type: application/json" -d '{"title": "Learn sqlx"}' http://127.0.0.1:8080/todos
{"id":1,"title":"Learn sqlx","completed":false}
me@Francesco-PC MINGW64 ~
$ curl -X POST -H "Content-Type: application/json" -d '{"title": "Test the API"}' http://127.0.0.1:8080/todos
{"id":2,"title":"Test the API","completed":false}
me@Francesco-PC MINGW64 ~
$ curl http://127.0.0.1:8080/todos
[{"id":1,"title":"Learn sqlx","completed":false},{"id":2,"title":"Test the API","completed":false}]
me@Francesco-PC MINGW64 ~
$ curl http://127.0.0.1:8080/todos/1
{"id":1,"title":"Learn sqlx","completed":false}
me@Francesco-PC MINGW64 ~
$ curl http://127.0.0.1:8080/todos/99
Todo not found
me@Francesco-PC MINGW64 ~
$ curl -X PATCH -H "Content-Type: application/json" -d '{"completed": true}' http://127.0.0.1:8080/todos/1
{"id":1,"title":"Learn sqlx","completed":true}
me@Francesco-PC MINGW64 ~
$ curl -v -X DELETE http://127.0.0.1:8080/todos/1
*   Trying 127.0.0.1:8080...
* Connected to 127.0.0.1 (127.0.0.1) port 8080
* using HTTP/1.x
> DELETE /todos/1 HTTP/1.1
> Host: 127.0.0.1:8080
> User-Agent: curl/8.14.1
> Accept: */*
>
* Request completely sent off
< HTTP/1.1 204 No Content
< content-type: text/plain; charset=utf-8
< date: Wed, 05 Nov 2025 07:18:09 GMT
<
* Connection #0 to host 127.0.0.1 left intact

me@Francesco-PC MINGW64 ~
$ curl http://127.0.0.1:8080/todos
[{"id":2,"title":"Test the API","completed":false}]
me@Francesco-PC MINGW64 ~
$ |
```

Figure 14.8: Testing endpoints with curl

Verifying with psql

You can also directly check the database. In your testing terminal, run the following:

```
docker exec -it my_app_db_postgres -U postgres
```

Replace `my_app_db_postgres` with the name of your container.

To verify the current status of the database, you can type this:

```
SELECT * FROM TODOS;
```

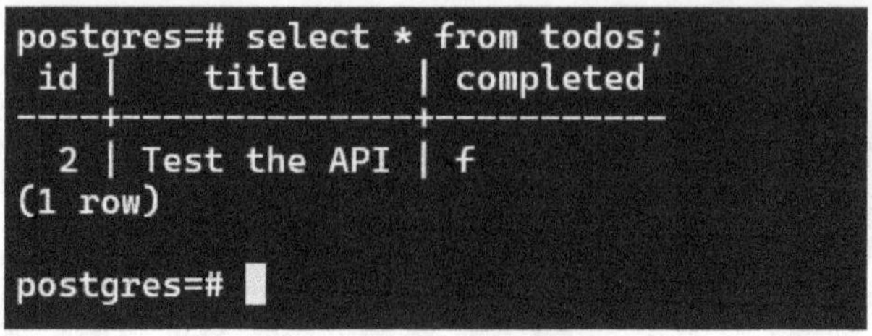

```
postgres=# select * from todos;
 id |    title     | completed
----+--------------+-----------
  2 | Test the API | f
(1 row)

postgres=#
```

Figure 14.9: Verification with psql

You should see the current state of your `todos` table. Type `\q` to exit psql.

That's it! Your API is now fully persistent and working.

A final backend step: enabling CORS

We've now updated all our handlers to be fully async and integrated the sqlx database.

Before we can connect our frontend JavaScript application to this API (which we'll cover in the next section), there's just one more important step for our backend: setting up a **CORS (Cross-Origin Resource Sharing)** policy. By default, web browsers adhere to a security principle known as the same-origin policy.

This means that code running on one domain, such as our development frontend at `http://localhost:8001`, would normally be blocked from making `fetch` requests to our API on another domain, such as `http://localhost:8080`.

To make our full-stack example work smoothly, we need to allow these cross-origin requests on our Axum server explicitly. We can do this easily by adding a "CORS layer" from the `tower-http` crate.

First, be sure to include `tower-http` in your `Cargo.toml` file.

```
[dependencies]
# ... (axum, tokio, serde, dotenvy, sqlx)
tower-http = { version = "0.5", features = ["cors"] }
```

The full, multi-file version is available on the GitHub repository.

We should highlight the CorsLayer setup and application:

```
// src/main.rs (CORS Setup Snippet)

use axum::{routing::get, Router};
use axum::http::Method;
use tower_http::cors::{Any, CorsLayer};
// ... other imports ...

#[tokio::main]
async fn main() {
    // ... Pool creation and AppState setup (Steps 1-3) ...

    // --- 4. Define CORS Policy ---
    let cors = CorsLayer::new()
        .allow_methods([Method::GET, Method::POST, Method::PATCH,
Method::DELETE])
        .allow_headers([axum::http::header::CONTENT_TYPE])
        .allow_origin(Any);

    // --- 5. Build our application router ---
    let app = Router::new()
        // ... route definitions ...
        .with_state(app_state)
        .layer(cors); // <-- Apply the CORS layer here!

    // ... Bind and Serve (Step 6) ...
}
```

Now, to test this, *before* we start creating any frontend code, we should use `curl`:

```
curl -v -X OPTIONS http://localhost:8080/todos \ -H "Origin: http://
localhost:8001" \ -H "Access-Control-Request-Method: POST" \ -H "Access-
Control-Request-Headers: content-type"
```

Because you used the `-v` (verbose) flag, curl will show you the headers in the server's response. If your CORS layer is working, you should see headers like this coming back from your Axum server:

```
me@Francesco-PC MINGW64 ~/wasm_greeter (master)
$ curl -v -X OPTIONS http://localhost:8080/todos \
     -H "Origin: http://localhost:8001" \
     -H "Access-Control-Request-Method: POST" \
     -H "Access-Control-Request-Headers: content-type"
* Host localhost:8080 was resolved.
* IPv6: ::1
* IPv4: 127.0.0.1
*   Trying [::1]:8080...
*   Trying 127.0.0.1:8080...
* Connected to localhost (127.0.0.1) port 8080
* using HTTP/1.x
> OPTIONS /todos HTTP/1.1
> Host: localhost:8080
> User-Agent: curl/8.14.1
> Accept: */*
> Origin: http://localhost:8001
> Access-Control-Request-Method: POST
> Access-Control-Request-Headers: content-type
>
< HTTP/1.1 200 OK
< access-control-allow-origin: *
< vary: origin, access-control-request-method, access-control-request-headers
< access-control-allow-methods: GET,POST,PATCH,DELETE
< access-control-allow-headers: content-type
< allow: GET,HEAD,POST
< content-length: 0
< date: Wed, 05 Nov 2025 08:58:07 GMT
<
* Connection #0 to host localhost left intact
```

Figure 14.10: Terminal output showing the successful CORS preflight check for the backend API

The most important line is `access-control-allow-origin: *` (or `http://localhost:8001` if you configured it to be specific).

- If you see `access-control-allow-origin: *`, congratulations, your CORS is working perfectly! Your backend is telling the "browser" (simulated by curl) that it will accept requests from any origin.
- If you do not see that header, it means your CORS layer isn't configured correctly or isn't being applied to that route.

Frontend: WebAssembly

So far, our Axum application is a powerful backend API, complete with a persistent sqlx database connection. But the "full-stack" promise of Rust also extends to the client side.

This is possible through **WebAssembly (Wasm)**, a high-performance binary format that runs in modern web browsers, allowing you to execute Rust code directly on the client for computationally intensive tasks or, as we'll do here, to build a simple, interactive frontend.

Getting a full grasp of WASM could fill a book on its own! But basically, it's a way to run non-JavaScript code in your browser very efficiently, almost at native speed.

This section provides a brief overview of this workflow to demonstrate how you can connect a Rust-powered frontend to the Rust backend we have just built.

Building and using a simple Wasm module

To get started, we need to create a new, separate **library** crate for our Wasm code. This project will be compiled into a Wasm module that our `index.html` file can load.

In your terminal, navigate **outside** of your `todo_api` project directory and run the following:

```
cargo new wasm_client --lib
cd wasm_client
```

Next, open the new `wasm_client/Cargo.toml` file. We need to tell Rust that this library is a "cdylib" (which is what Wasm compiles to) and add the dependencies for Wasm:

- `wasm-bindgen`: The core library that handles communication between Rust and JavaScript.
- `wasm-bindgen-futures`: A helper to let us use Rust async/await with JavaScript's Promises.
- `reqwest`: A popular HTTP client that can be compiled to Wasm (with its json feature) to make requests to our backend.
- `serde` / `serde_json`: To create the JSON payloads to *send* to our API.
- `web-sys`: To let our Wasm code log messages to the browser's console for debugging.

```
[package]
name = "wasm_client"
version = "0.1.0"
edition = "2024"

[lib]
```

```
crate-type = ["cdylib"] # Essential: specifies output as a dynamic
library for Wasm

[dependencies]
wasm-bindgen = "0.2"
wasm-bindgen-futures = "0.4" # For converting JS Futures to Rust
Futures
reqwest = { version = "0.12", features = ["json"] } # reqwest
supports Wasm!
serde = { version = "1.0", features = ["derive"] }
serde_json = "1.0"

# We also add web-sys for logging to the browser console
[dependencies.web-sys]
version = "0.3"
features = [
  'console',
]
```

Now, we'll write our Rust code in `wasm_client/src/lib.rs`. This code will define the functions that our JavaScript will call.

Notice that we redefine the `Todo` structs here. In a large project, you might put these in a shared "common" crate, but for our minimal example, redefining them is simpler.

Exposing Rust functions with #[wasm_bindgen]

Now, we'll write our Rust code in `wasm_client/src/lib.rs`. This code will define the functions that our JavaScript will call. Notice that we redefine the `Todo` structs here. In a large project, you might put these in a shared "common" crate, but for our minimal example, redefining them is simpler.

File: `wasm_client/src/lib.rs`

```
use wasm_bindgen::prelude::*;
use serde::{Deserialize, Serialize};

// --- We redefine our models here for the frontend ---
// (In a large project, this would be in a shared crate)
```

```
#[derive(Debug, Serialize, Deserialize, Clone)]
pub struct Todo {
    pub id: i32,
    pub title: String,
    pub completed: bool,
}

#[derive(Debug, Serialize)]
pub struct NewTodo {
    pub title: String,
}

// A simple macro to log to the browser console
macro_rules! log {
    ( $( $t:tt )* ) => {
        web_sys::console::log_1(&format!( $( $t )* ).into());
    }
}

// Our backend API URL
const API_URL: &str = "http://localhost:8080/todos";

/// Fetches the current list of todos from the backend API.
/// Returns the JSON as a `JsValue` (which will be a string).
#[wasm_bindgen]
pub async fn fetch_todos() -> Result<JsValue, JsValue> {
    log!("Wasm: Fetching todos from {}", API_URL);

    let client = reqwest::Client::new();
    let resp = client
        .get(API_URL)
        .send()
        .await
        .map_err(|e| JsValue::from_str(&e.to_string()))?;


    // use .text() to get the raw JSON string
```

```
    let json_text = resp
        .text()
        .await
        .map_err(|e| JsValue::from_str(&e.to_string()))?;

    // Convert the Rust String into a JavaScript String (JsValue)
    Ok(JsValue::from_str(&json_text))
}

/// Adds a new todo item by POSTing to the backend API.
#[wasm_bindgen]
pub async fn add_todo(title: String) -> Result<JsValue, JsValue> {
    log!("Wasm: Adding todo: {}", &title);
    let new_todo = NewTodo { title };

    let client = reqwest::Client::new();
    let resp = client
        .post(API_URL)
        .json(&new_todo) // Send our NewTodo struct as a JSON body
        .send()
        .await
        .map_err(|e| JsValue::from_str(&e.to_string()))?;

    // Use .text() here as well
    let json_text = resp
        .text()
        .await
        .map_err(|e| JsValue::from_str(&e.to_string()))?;

    // Convert the Rust String into a JavaScript String (JsValue)
    Ok(JsValue::from_str(&json_text))
}
```

Here's an explanation of the code:

- **Model redefinition**: We redefine the Todo and NewTodo structs. In a large production project, you would put these structs in a separate "common" crate that both your backend and frontend could depend on to avoid duplication, but redefining them here is simpler for our example.
- log! **macro**: This is a simple helper macro we've defined that uses web_sys::console::log_1 to print debug messages (such as Wasm: Fetching todos...) to the browser's developer console. This is very useful for debugging your Wasm code.
- #[wasm_bindgen]: This is the most important attribute. It "exposes" our pub async fn functions (fetch_todos and add_todo) to JavaScript, allowing our index.html file to call them by name.
- **Async functions**: Both fetch_todos and add_todo are async because they perform network I/O (using reqwest). wasm-bindgen-futures helps convert these Rust async functions into JavaScript Promises that our JavaScript code can await.
- reqwest::Client: We use the reqwest crate (which supports Wasm) to create an HTTP client and make GET and POST requests to our Axum backend's API_URL.
- **Returning** Result<JsValue, JsValue>:
    - **Success (**Ok(JsValue)**)**: Our functions don't return Vec<Todo>. Instead, they use resp.text().await to get the raw JSON **string** from the server's response. They then wrap this string in JsValue::from_str(...). This passes the JSON string to JavaScript.
    - **Error (**Err(JsValue)**)**: If reqwest fails (e.g., a network error, or our backend is down), .map_err(...) converts the Rust error into a simple JavaScript string (JsValue), which will be thrown as a JavaScript exception.
- **JavaScript's job**: Our index.html JavaScript will be responsible for calling these functions, awaiting the Promise, and then using JSON.parse() on the string it receives to get the actual JavaScript Todo objects.

Building the .wasm and JavaScript glue

We will use a handy command-line tool called wasm-pack to build our library.

It simplifies everything: compiling your Rust code into Wasm, generating the JavaScript "glue" code with wasm-bindgen, and packaging everything nicely for you.

If you haven't already, just install `wasm-pack` to get started:

```
cargo install wasm-pack
```

Then, from *inside your* `wasm_client` *directory* (the one with your Wasm code), run the `build` command.

We use the `--target web` flag to tell `wasm-pack` to generate code that's compatible with modern browser ES modules.

```
wasm-pack build --target web
```

This command compiles your code and creates a new `pkg` directory. Inside this `pkg` directory, you'll find the following:

- `wasm_client_bg.wasm`: Your compiled Rust code in WebAssembly format.
- `wasm_client.js`: The JavaScript "glue" file. This file knows how to load the `.wasm` file and provides the JavaScript `fetch_todos()` and `add_todo()` functions that call into your Rust code.
- `wasm_client.d.ts`: A TypeScript definition file, which is great for code completion if you use TypeScript.
- `package.json`: A file that describes this package to JavaScript build tools.

With this `pkg` directory generated, we now have everything we need to use our Rust code from a web page.

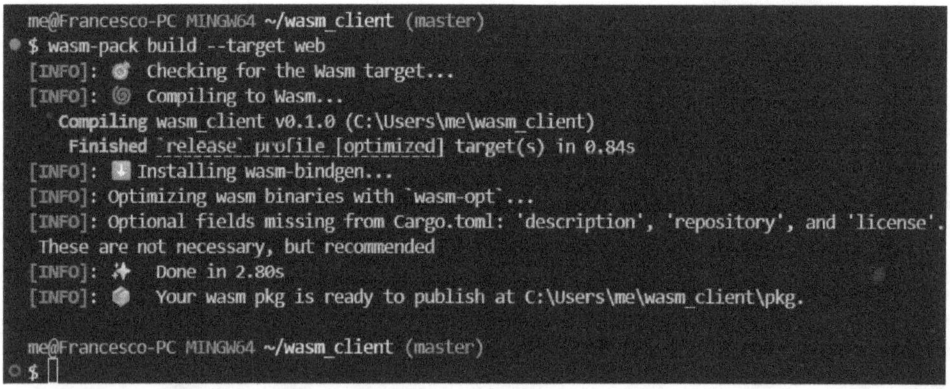

```
me@Francesco-PC MINGW64 ~/wasm_client (master)
$ wasm-pack build --target web
[INFO]: Checking for the Wasm target...
[INFO]: Compiling to Wasm...
   Compiling wasm_client v0.1.0 (C:\Users\me\wasm_client)
    Finished `release` profile [optimized] target(s) in 0.84s
[INFO]: Installing wasm-bindgen...
[INFO]: Optimizing wasm binaries with `wasm-opt`...
[INFO]: Optional fields missing from Cargo.toml: 'description', 'repository', and 'license'.
 These are not necessary, but recommended
[INFO]:  Done in 2.80s
[INFO]:  Your wasm pkg is ready to publish at C:\Users\me\wasm_client\pkg.

me@Francesco-PC MINGW64 ~/wasm_client (master)
$
```

Figure 14.11: The wasm-pack utility compiling Rust code, installing wasm-bindgen, and optimizing the Wasm binary for web consumption

Using the Wasm module from a simple web page

This is the final step where we connect all the pieces.

We'll create a minimal `index.html` file to be our user interface.

This file will contain a small amount of JavaScript to load our Wasm module and wire up the UI elements to call our exported Rust functions (`fetch_todos` and `add_todo`).

Following our plan, you should do the following:

1. Create a `www` directory *inside* your `wasm_client` project folder.
2. Move the pkg directory (that `wasm-pack` just created) *into* this new `www` directory.
3. Create the `index.html` file inside the `www` directory.

Repository reference: The full HTML structure, CSS styling, and the complete JavaScript event handlers are available in the GitHub repository file: `wasm_client/www/index.html`.

```
// The snippet focuses on the critical import and initialization logic.

<script type="module">
    // 1. Import Wasm functions from the generated 'pkg' directory
    import init, { fetch_todos, add_todo } from './pkg/wasm_client.js';

    // ... define DOM element references (todoList, titleInput, addButton)
...

    // --- Function to refresh the list of todos from the backend ---
    async function refreshTodos() {
        // ... UI update logic ...
        try {
            // Call our async Rust Wasm function!
            const todos_json_string = await fetch_todos();

            // Parse the JSON string received from Wasm
            const todos = JSON.parse(todos_json_string);

            // ... logic to render list items ...
        } catch (e) {
            console.error("Error fetching todos:", e);
```

```
            // ... error handling ...
        }
    }

    // --- Main function to run the app ---
    async function run() {
        // Initialize the Wasm module
        await init();

        // Load the initial list of todos
        await refreshTodos();

        // Wire up the "Add" button
        addButton.addEventListener('click', addNewTodo);
    }

    // Start the application
    run();
</script>
```

Here's an explanation of the code:

- `import init, { ... } from './pkg/wasm_client.js';`: This line is the bridge to our Rust code. It imports the default `init` function (which loads and initializes the `.wasm` file) and our two exported functions, `fetch_todos` and `add_todo`, from the JavaScript "glue" file created by `wasm-pack`. The `./pkg/wasm_client.js` path is relative to this `index.html` file.
- `async function run()`: This is the main entry point for our frontend. It first calls `await init()`. This is crucial; we must wait for the Wasm module to be fully loaded and initialized before we can call any of its functions. After initialization, it calls `refreshTodos()` to get the initial list and attaches the `addNewTodo` function to the button's click event.
- `async function refreshTodos()`: This function shows the "Wasm-to-Rust" communication for getting data.

1. It calls `await fetch_todos()`, which is our **async Rust function** running in Wasm.
2. This Rust function makes an HTTP GET request to our Axum backend (`http://localhost:8080/todos`).
3. Our Rust function returns a `JsValue` (which we designed to be a JSON string).
4. The JavaScript code then uses `JSON.parse()` to convert this string into a JavaScript array of objects.
5. Finally, it loops through the array to build and display the HTML `<li>` elements in the list.

- `async function addNewTodo()`: This function shows the "Wasm-to-Rust" communication for sending data.
    1. It gets the title from the input box.
    2. It calls `await add_todo(title)`, passing the JavaScript string to our **async Rust function.**
    3. The Rust function creates a `NewTodo` struct, serializes it to JSON, and makes an HTTP POST request to our Axum backend.
    4. Once the Wasm function completes, the JavaScript code clears the input box and calls `refreshTodos()` to show the updated list.

This simple HTML file, combined with our Wasm module, creates a complete client-side application that is fully powered by Rust, from its internal logic to its communication with our Rust-based backend.

Testing the frontend

1. To test the frontend, we need a simple **static file server** to serve the `index.html` file and the generated Wasm module. We'll use `miniserve`, a lightweight and easy-to-use utility written in Rust:

```
Cargo install miniserve
```

What is miniserve?

`miniserve` is a simple, command-line utility written in Rust, designed for serving local files over HTTP quickly. It is perfect for local development because it's fast, single-binary, and serves static content reliably.

Alternatives: You could achieve the same result using other static file servers, such as the following:

Python: `python3 -m http.server 8001`

Node.js: `npx serve -l 8001`

Any other locally running static server.

2. Then, to run the wasm application, run this command from the `wasm_client` folder:

```
miniserve www/pkg/ --index index.html --port 8001
```

```
me@Francesco-PC MINGW64 ~/wasm_client (master)
$ miniserve www/ --index index.html --port 8001
miniserve v0.32.0
Bound to [::]:8001, 0.0.0.0:8001
Serving path \\?\C:\Users\me\wasm_client\www
Available at (non-exhaustive list):
    http://127.0.0.1:8001
    http://172.27.64.1:8001
    http://192.168.1.213:8001
    http://[::1]:8001
    http://[2001:b07:a13:8e57:380e:e4a8:f861:9f70]:8001
    http://[2001:b07:a13:8e57:e672:db78:becb:d91e]:8001
```

Figure 14.12: Running the miniserve static file server to host the Wasm frontend on port 8001

You should see something like this:

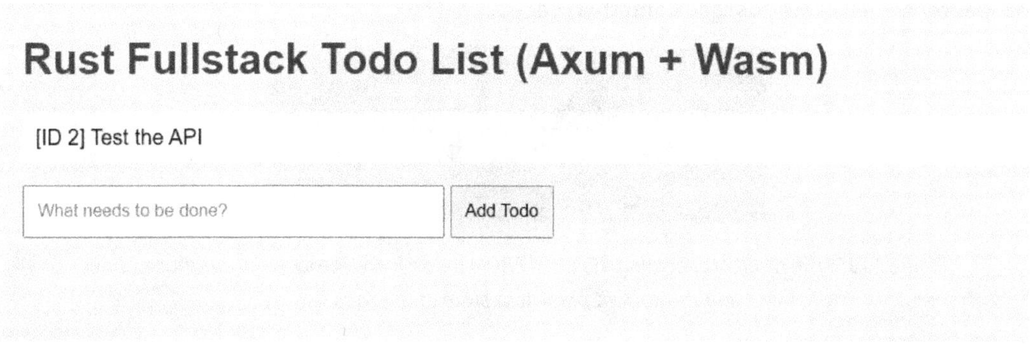

Rust Fullstack Todo List (Axum + Wasm)

[ID 2] Test the API

What needs to be done?

Add Todo

Figure 14.13: The Wasm frontend, served on port 8001, successfully loads the initial list item (ID 2: "Test the API") from the running Axum API on port 8080

3. Now you can try to add a new todo using the user interface:

    1. Write some input text.
    2. Click **Add Todo**.

    The UI should update, showing the updated list!

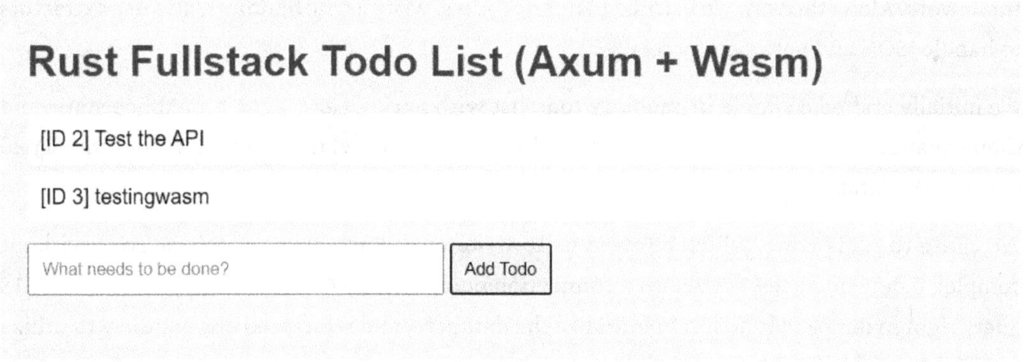

Rust Fullstack Todo List (Axum + Wasm)

[ID 2] Test the API

[ID 3] testingwasm

What needs to be done?

Add Todo

Figure 14.14: The updated frontend display after successfully adding a new todo item through the user interface

You can also check this directly in the postgres container, running `docker exec -it my_app_db_postgres psql -U postgres` and then `select * from todos;`.

```
postgres=# select * from todos;
 id |     title      | completed
----+----------------+-----------
  2 | Test the API   | f
  3 | testingwasm    | f
(2 rows)
```

*Figure 14.15: The result of executing SELECT * FROM todos; in the PostgreSQL database, showing the current persistent state of the Todo list*

Summary

And with that, we've successfully built a complete full-stack application in Rust!

Let's have a quick recap.

This chapter was an exciting, fast-paced adventure that brought everything we've learned together, from the backend to the browser!

We started by creating a backend API from scratch with Axum, a modern and user-friendly web framework. Along the way, we learned to define routes, write async handlers, and use extractors to handle JSON and path parameters.

We initially crafted a simple in-memory todo list with `Arc<Mutex<...>>` to manage state, and then enhanced it by making it persistent. To do this, we replaced the in-memory `Vec` with a real PostgreSQL database.

We chose the sqlx crate, which allowed us to write pure-Rust, async database code without complex C dependencies. We set up a connection pool, added a `CREATE TABLE IF NOT EXISTS` query right in our `main` function to initialize the database, and refactored our handlers to utilize compile-time checked `sqlx::query_as!` macros.

Finally, we linked everything to the frontend by building a small **WebAssembly (Wasm)** module.

We explored how to use `wasm-pack` and `#[wasm_bindgen]` to expose Rust functions that use `reqwest` to call our own Axum API, and then ran that Wasm module from a simple `index.html` file to create a fully functional, end-to-end application, all written in Rust.

That was a complete end-to-end full-stack application entirely written in Rust!

In the next chapter, we will dive deeper into the world of systems programming!

Questions and assignment

Questions

1. What is the purpose of the `#[tokio::main]` macro in a Rust web server? Why is it essential when working with Axum?
2. In Axum, what is a **handler**? How does a simple handler return a 200 OK response when its return type is just a plain `&'static str`?
3. When defining a route for dynamic data (e.g., fetching a todo by ID), how does the `Path<T>` extractor in the handler signature prevent the need for manual string parsing and error checking?
4. When building the in-memory API, why did we have to wrap the `Vec<Todo>` in both `Arc` and `Mutex`? Explain the distinct role of each smart pointer in this scenario.
5. What is the role of the `State<T>` extractor in Axum? How does it gain access to the shared data (such as the `AppState`)?
6. Explain the primary purpose of the `serde` crate when building a REST API. How do the `Serialize` and `Deserialize` traits apply to an HTTP POST request?
7. Why is using a **connection pool** (such as `sqlx::PgPool`) far more efficient than creating a new connection with every incoming request?
8. When using `sqlx`, what is the purpose of deriving the `FromRow` trait on the `Todo` struct?
9. We opted to use sqlx instead of a synchronous ORM. What is the fundamental advantage of using an **async-native** library such as sqlx when writing handlers for an asynchronous framework such as Axum? (Hint: Think about blocking threads.)
10. Why was it necessary to add the CORS layer to our Axum backend before the Wasm frontend could successfully communicate with it?

Assignment

Expanding the API and using basic extractors

Goal: Get hands-on with Axum's core routing, handler definition, and the simple use of extractors for shared state and path parameters.

Here's the task:

1. **Use your existing project:** Continue with the `todo_api` project you just completed.
2. **Add a new state check handler:** Create a new asynchronous handler function named `get_server_status`.

3. **Implement logic**: This handler should access the shared `AppState` and return a 200 OK response with a plain text body that says: `Server Status: OK. Database Pool Ready.`
4. **Add a dynamic route**: Register this new handler to the `/status` path.
5. **Add a Path parameter echo handler**: Create a second handler function named echo_path that takes a string path parameter (e.g., `/echo/:message`). This handler should extract the message and return it as the response body (e.g., returning `You sent: [message]`).
6. **Register routes:** Update your router in `main.rs` to include the `GET /status` and `GET /echo/:message` routes.

Here's what you will learn how to do from this:

- Define simple, new async handlers
- Use the `State<AppState>` extractor
- Use the `Path<String>` extractor
- Register routes with different paths and parameters

Example usage (using curl):

```
curl http://127.0.0.1:8080/status
# Expected: Server Status: OK. Database Pool Ready.

curl http://127.0.0.1:8080/echo/testing-123
# Expected: You sent: testing-123
```

15

System Programming in Rust: Concrete Examples

We've explored many of Rust's high-level features, including its impressive error handling and even its potential applications in web development and concurrency.

Now, let's turn our attention to something more hands-on: system programming with Rust. This is an area where Rust really shines, offering a powerful alternative to traditional languages such as C and C++.

We'll discover how Rust's core design principles give you a special edge when building software that works closely with the operating system and hardware.

Let's start!

What defines system programming?

System programming is about writing software that manages and controls computer hardware directly or provides a platform for other software to run.

Think of operating systems, device drivers, embedded systems, game engines, browsers, command-line utilities, network daemons, and even the core components of programming language runtimes themselves.

These kinds of programs often have stringent requirements:

- **Performance**: They need to be fast and efficient, often with predictable latency.
- **Control**: Developers need fine-grained control over memory layout, resource allocation, and hardware interaction.

- **Reliability and security**: System software forms the foundation for everything else. It must be extremely robust and fault-tolerant, but this goes beyond just preventing crashes. Mistakes in system-level code have severe **security implications**. A bug such as a buffer overflow isn't just an error; it's a potential vulnerability that could lead to **arbitrary code execution**, **privilege escalation**, and the complete compromise of the system.
- **Resource constraints**: Sometimes, system programs run in environments with limited memory or processing power (such as embedded devices).

Traditionally, languages such as C and C++ have dominated this space due to their low-level control and performance. However, they also come with well-known challenges related to memory safety (e.g., buffer overflows, dangling pointers, data races).

Why Rust is a strong candidate for systems work

Rust has emerged as a compelling language for system programming precisely because it offers a unique combination of control, performance, and safety:

- **Memory safety**: This is Rust's flagship feature. Its ownership and borrowing system, enforced at compile time, prevents common memory errors such as null pointer dereferences, buffer overflows, and data races in concurrent code, all without the runtime overhead of a garbage collector. This is huge for systems where predictable performance and reliability are paramount.
- **Performance on par with C/C++**: Rust compiles to efficient machine code and gives developers the control needed to optimize critical sections. It has no runtime or garbage collector to introduce unpredictable pauses, making it suitable for performance-sensitive applications.
- **Fearless concurrency**: As we saw in the previous chapter, Rust's type system helps prevent data races at compile time, making it much safer to write concurrent and parallel programs that can fully utilize modern multi-core processors.
- **Low-level control**: Rust provides abstractions but also allows you to drop down to a lower level when needed. Features such as raw pointers, unsafe blocks for operations the compiler can't guarantee, and control over memory layout (#[repr(C)]) give you the power you need for system tasks.
- **Excellent tooling**: Cargo (Rust's package manager and build system), rustup (for managing Rust versions), and a supportive community make the development experience pleasant and productive.

- **Foreign Function Interface (FFI)**: Rust has excellent support for interoperating with C code, allowing you to leverage existing C libraries or integrate Rust components into C/C++ projects.

These features make Rust an attractive choice for a new generation of system software that aims to be both high-performance and highly reliable.

The core tension: control versus abstraction

Before we dive into the mechanics of unsafe Rust and FFI, it's crucial to understand the central *philosophy* that makes Rust a world-class systems language. Your work as a systems programmer will always be defined by a fundamental tension: the trade-off between **high-level abstraction** and **low-level control**.

The systems programmer's dilemma

For decades, programming languages forced you to choose a side, each with a major compromise:

- **Maximum control (e.g., C/C++)**: You get full control. You can manually manage memory, lay out data structures precisely, and perform hyper-optimized operations.
    - **The cost**: This power is dangerous. You are 100% responsible for memory safety. A single mistake can lead to buffer overflows, dangling pointers, data races, or segfaults, which are not just bugs but critical security vulnerabilities.
- **Maximum abstraction (e.g., Python/Java/C#)**: You get a powerful, safe environment. A **garbage collector** (GC) manages memory for you, preventing leaks and use-after-free errors. Arrays are bounds-checked.
    - **The cost**: You lose control. You cannot predict *when* the GC will run, causing non-deterministic pauses (GC stutter). Abstractions have "hidden costs" in performance and memory, making them unsuitable for time-critical or resource-constrained environments such as kernels, drivers, or game engines.

Historically, systems programming had no choice but to pick "maximum control" and accept the danger.

Rust's solution: control without compromise

Rust is designed to systematically eliminate this tension. Its core premise is that you should not have to choose between safety and performance.

You get **both** by adhering to one central philosophy:

Zero-cost abstractions (ZCAs)

A zero-cost abstraction is a high-level feature (such as an iterator, an `Option` type, or a generic) that is as safe and convenient as a high-level language *but* compiles down to the *exact same* (or faster) machine code as the "manual control" version you would have written in C.

The "cost" (in CPU time or memory) is paid at **compile time**, not at runtime.

ZCA in practice: the iterator versus the for loop

Let's look at a classic example. A C programmer needing performance would write a manual `for` loop.

```
// The "Control" version: What you'd write in C/C++
let mut total = 0;
let my_vec = vec![1, 2, 3, 4, 5];

for i in 0..my_vec.len() {
    total += my_vec[i] * 2;
}
```

A Rust programmer can use a high-level, "abstracted" functional approach:

```
// The "Abstraction" version: Safe, clear, and high-level
let my_vec = vec![1, 2, 3, 4, 5];

let total: i32 = my_vec.iter()
                       .map(|x| x * 2)
                       .sum();
```

In a language such as Python, the abstracted version might run a lot slower, but in Rust, both versions compile down to the same efficient machine code. The compiler employs the borrow checker to verify the iterator's safety during compilation, and then it completely optimizes the high-level iterator chain, leaving behind only a quick and straightforward loop. This showcases the real strength of a ZCA.

The bridge to unsafe: when ZCAs aren't enough

This brings us to the "why" of this chapter.

Rust's philosophy is to make the safe, abstract way the default (such as `Vec<T>`, `std::fs::File`). These ZCAs cover 99% of your needs.

But what happens when you need to do something that the Rust compiler cannot verify as safe?

- What if you must call a function in a C library? (The compiler can't check C code.)
- What if you need to read from a specific memory address to control hardware? (The compiler can't know what's at that address.)
- What if you are implementing a new ZCA (such as `Vec<T>`) and need to manually manage raw memory?

For these rare but critical "maximum control" scenarios, Rust provides a clearly marked escape hatch: the `unsafe` keyword.

Using `unsafe` is a contract. You tell the compiler: "I am now stepping outside your verifiable safety rules. I have read the documentation, and I am manually guaranteeing that I will uphold the safety invariants for this specific operation." The rest of this chapter explains how, why, and, most importantly, when to use this escape hatch. We will learn the `unsafe` mechanics, use them to interface with C code, and see how to wrap this danger in our own new, safe abstractions.

Chapter roadmap: from low-level mechanics to practical builds

In this chapter, we'll put these ideas into practice. Our journey will include the following:

- **Revisiting low-level foundations**: We'll start by briefly recapping Rust's memory model and then take a closer look at unsafe Rust, understanding why it exists and how to work with raw pointers
- **Building command-line utilities**: We'll apply our knowledge to create practical command-line tools, a common system programming task
- **Interfacing with C code (FFI)**: You'll learn how to call C libraries from Rust and understand the basics of data marshalling between the two languages
- **A glimpse into kernel modules (optional)**: For the more adventurous, we'll offer a high-level look at what it takes to write a very simple kernel module in Rust, highlighting the unique challenges.

Through concrete examples, you'll gain a better appreciation for how Rust's features translate into building efficient and reliable system-level software.

Let's get started!

Low-level programming foundations in Rust

To write system-level software in Rust successfully, it's helpful to have a good understanding of how Rust handles memory management and how it enables you to perform more advanced operations, sometimes even by carefully stepping outside its usual safety features.

This section goes over some key memory concepts and then introduces unsafe Rust, an important tool for specific system programming tasks.

Rust's memory safety model: a systems perspective

We've touched upon Rust's memory management throughout this book, especially its ownership and borrowing system.

For system programming, a clear understanding of these mechanics, along with where your data lives (stack or heap), is doubly important.

Ownership and borrowing recap for control and safety

Here's a quick refresher:

- **Ownership**: Every value in Rust has a variable that's its "owner." There can only be one owner at a time. When the owner goes out of scope, the value is dropped (and its memory is deallocated if it was on the heap). This prevents "dangling pointers" (pointing to the freed memory) and "double free" errors.
- **Borrowing**: You can create references to data:
    - Multiple immutable references (`&T`) allow read-only access.
    - Only one mutable reference (`&mut T`) is allowed at any given time, preventing data races at compile time.
- **Lifetimes**: The compiler uses lifetimes to ensure that references are always valid and never outlive the data they point to.

This system is the bedrock of Rust's memory safety. For system programmers who might be used to manual memory management (such as malloc/free in C), Rust's approach takes some getting used to, but it automates many safety checks that would otherwise require meticulous manual effort.

Tip: need a deeper refresher?

The concepts of ownership, borrowing, and lifetimes are the most fundamental (and challenging!) parts of Rust. We are only summarizing them here. If any of these rules feel a bit fuzzy, we highly recommend flipping back to *Chapter 4, Ownership, Borrowing, and References*, for a full, in-depth explanation before you dive into the low-level topics ahead.

Stack versus heap: managing memory explicitly

Understanding where your data is stored is crucial for performance and control:

- **Stack**: This is a region of memory used for static memory allocation. It's very fast because it's a simple **LIFO** (**Last-In, First-Out**) structure. Local variables, function arguments, and return addresses are typically stored on the stack. Data on the stack *must* have a size known at compile time. When a function returns, its stack frame (containing its local variables) is popped off, instantly reclaiming the memory.

```
fn stack_example() {
    let x = 10; // x (an i32) is on the stack
    let y = true; // y (a bool) is on the stack
    // When stack_example returns, x and y are gone
}
```

- **Heap**: This is a region of memory used for dynamic memory allocation, where data can be allocated and deallocated at runtime. It's more flexible than the stack because the size of data doesn't need to be known at compile time, and data can live longer than the function that created it. However, heap allocation is generally slower than stack allocation due to the overhead of finding a suitable block of memory and managing its lifecycle.

```
fn heap_example() {
    let s1 = String::from("hello"); // String data ("hello") is on
the heap, s1 (ptr, len, cap) is on stack
    let v1 = vec![1, 2, 3];       // Vector data ([1,2,3]) is on the
heap, v1 (ptr, len, cap) is on stack
    // When s1 and v1 go out of scope, their Drop implementations
free the heap memory
}
```

In system programming, you often need to make conscious decisions about whether to use the stack for speed and simplicity or the heap for flexibility and larger data.

The role of smart pointers in memory management

As we explored in detail in *Chapter 11, Smart Pointers and Memory Management*, Rust provides **smart pointers** such as `Box<T>`, `Rc<T>`, and `Arc<T>` to manage heap-allocated data with clear ownership semantics and automatic deallocation.

- `Box<T>` is the most straightforward way to allocate a value on the heap and have a single owner. It's crucial for creating recursive data structures or owning data whose size isn't known at compile time (such as `trait` objects).
- `Rc<T>` and `Arc<T>` allow for shared ownership of heap-allocated data via reference counting, in single-threaded and multi-threaded contexts, respectively.

These smart pointers abstract away manual `malloc` and `free` (or `new` and `delete`) operations, integrating heap memory management directly into Rust's ownership and `Drop` system.

This significantly reduces the risk of memory leaks or use-after-free errors compared to manual management in languages such as C.

While you *can* do manual memory allocation in unsafe Rust (which we'll touch on), for most heap allocation needs in safe Rust, smart pointers are the idiomatic solution.

Venturing into unsafe Rust

One of Rust's primary goals is to provide strong memory safety guarantees, most of which are enforced by the compiler at compile time. However, certain operations are inherently "unsafe" in the sense that the compiler *cannot* statically verify their safety. For these situations, Rust provides the `unsafe` keyword.

This doesn't turn off all of Rust's safety checks (such as the borrow checker, which still operates), but it allows you to perform a few specific operations that are otherwise disallowed in safe Rust.

Using `unsafe` is a **contract**: you, the programmer, are telling the compiler, "I know what I'm doing here, and I've manually verified that this code is safe under these specific conditions."

When and why unsafe is necessary

You might wonder, if Rust is all about safety, why have an unsafe escape hatch at all? There are legitimate reasons:

- **Interfacing with other languages or hardware (FFI)**: When calling functions written in C (or other languages via a C ABI) through the FFI, Rust cannot guarantee the safety of the external code. Dereferencing raw pointers received from C, for instance, is an unsafe operation.
- **Low-level hardware interaction**: Writing device drivers or interacting directly with hardware registers often requires direct memory manipulation via raw pointers.
- **Implementing low-level data structures or abstractions**: Sometimes, to create safe, high-level abstractions, their internal implementation must use unsafe code. This applies to standard collection types such as `Vec<T>` and `String`, which manage raw, uninitialized memory, as well as many of the smart pointers we've discussed. Types such as `Rc<T>`, `RefCell<T>`, and `Mutex<T>` rely on unsafe code internally to perform their functions, such as manipulating reference counts or implementing runtime borrow checks in ways the compiler can't verify. In all these situations, the goal is the same: to wrap this complex, unsafe core in a public API that is entirely safe for the end user.
- **Performance-critical code**: In very rare, performance-critical sections, `unsafe` might be used to bypass certain checks if they are proven bottlenecks and the programmer can guarantee safety manually. This is rare and should be a last resort.

The key idea is that unsafe doesn't mean "this code is buggy"; it means "the compiler cannot verify the safety of these specific operations, so the programmer must."

The five superpowers of unsafe Rust

The `unsafe` keyword allows you to perform five main categories of operations that are usually forbidden in safe Rust.

These are often referred to as the "unsafe superpowers":

1. **Dereferencing a raw pointer**: Accessing the data pointed to by `*const T` or `*mut T`.
2. **Calling an unsafe function or method**: Functions or methods marked `unsafe` can only be called from within an `unsafe` block or another `unsafe` function.
3. **Accessing or modifying a mutable static variable**: Global mutable state is inherently risky for concurrency, so modifying it requires `unsafe`.
4. **Implementing an unsafe trait**: Some traits are marked `unsafe` to indicate that implementing them requires upholding certain invariants that the compiler can't check.
5. **Accessing fields of unions**: Unions allow multiple types to share the same memory location; accessing which field is active is unsafe, as Rust doesn't track it. (Unions are a more advanced topic, less common than the others.)

We'll focus primarily on the first three in our examples.

Working with raw pointers (*const T and *mut T)

Unlike Rust's references (`&T` and `&mut T`), which come with strong compile-time guarantees about validity and aliasing, **raw pointers** are a more primitive concept. Rust provides two types of raw pointers:

- `*const T`: An immutable raw pointer, meaning the data it points to should not be changed through this pointer
- `*mut T`: A mutable raw pointer, meaning the data it points to *can* be changed through this pointer

Here are the key characteristics of raw pointers that differentiate them from references:

- **Allowed to be dangling**: They can point to invalid memory or memory that has been deallocated
- **Allowed to be null**: They can explicitly point to no valid location
- **Do not have automatic cleanup**: They don't implement `Drop` in a way that cleans up the pointed-to memory when the pointer itself goes out of scope (unlike `Box<T>`)
- **Bypass borrowing rules**: You can have multiple mutable raw pointers to the same location, or mutable and immutable raw pointers simultaneously, without the compiler stopping you

Creating raw pointers is generally safe. For example, you can cast a reference to a raw pointer:

```
let my_num = 10;
let raw_ptr_const: *const i32 = &my_num;

let mut my_mut_num = 20;
let raw_ptr_mut: *mut i32 = &mut my_mut_num;
```

You can also create them from integer addresses, though this is highly platform-specific and usually only done for interacting with hardware or known memory layouts.

The critical part is that **dereferencing** a raw pointer (using the * operator to access the data it points to) is an unsafe operation. This is because the compiler cannot guarantee the pointer is valid. Therefore, any dereference must occur within an `unsafe` block, where you, the programmer, assert that the operation is safe under the current circumstances.

```
fn main() {
    let mut num = 5;

    // Create raw pointers from references. This part is safe.
    // r1 is an immutable raw pointer to num.
    let r1: *const i32 = &num as *const i32;
    // r2 is a mutable raw pointer to num.
    let r2: *mut i32 = &mut num as *mut i32;

    // --- WARNING: DANGEROUS OPERATION ---
    // The following code creates a raw pointer from an arbitrary memory
address.
    // This is NOT something you should do in normal application code.
    // Accessing random memory addresses is undefined behavior and will
    // almost certainly crash your program with a segmentation fault.
    // This is only done in very specific low-level programming, like
    // interacting with known, fixed hardware addresses.
    let arbitrary_address = 0x012345usize;
    let r3_arbitrary_ptr = arbitrary_address as *const i32;
    // --- END WARNING ---


    // To dereference raw pointers and access the data they point to,
    // we MUST use an `unsafe` block. We are telling the compiler
    // that we take responsibility for the pointer's validity at this
    // moment.
    unsafe {
        // Dereferencing r1 to read the value of num
        // This is safe because we know r1 was created from a valid
reference.
        println!("Value via r1 (immutable raw pointer): {}", *r1); //
Output: 5

        // Dereferencing r2 to write a new value to the memory location of
num.
        // This is safe because r2 was also created from a valid
reference.
        *r2 = 10; // Modifies `num` through the raw pointer
```

```
        println!("`num` has been changed via r2 to: {}", num); // Output:
10

        // r1 still points to `num`, so it will now see the new value.
        println!("Value via r1 after change via r2: {}", *r1); // Output:
10

        // --- DANGER: DO NOT DO THIS ---
        // Uncommenting the line below would attempt to dereference r3_
arbitrary_ptr.
        // This is EXTREMELY DANGEROUS because r3_arbitrary_ptr points to
an arbitrary,
        // likely invalid, memory location. It would almost certainly
crash your program.
        // println!("Attempting to read from arbitrary address r3: {}",
*r3_arbitrary_ptr);
        // --- END DANGER ---
    }

    // Creating a null pointer.
    let null_pointer: *const i32 = std::ptr::null();
    let mut_null_pointer: *mut i32 = std::ptr::null_mut();

    // It's crucial to check if a raw pointer is null before attempting to
dereference it.
    if !null_pointer.is_null() {
        // This block will not execute because null_pointer is indeed
null.
        unsafe {
            println!("This line should not be reached: {}", *null_
pointer);
        }
    } else {
        println!("null_pointer is confirmed to be null, not
dereferencing.");
    }
}
```

- **Creation**: Raw pointers (`*const T` for immutable, `*mut T` for mutable) can be created by casting references (e.g., `&num as *const i32`). This process is safe. They can also be formed from integer addresses, which is inherently unsafe unless you know exactly what that address represents (e.g., memory-mapped hardware). `std::ptr::null()` and `std::ptr::null_mut()` create null raw pointers.
- **Dereferencing (*)**: The act of accessing the data that a raw pointer points to (using the * operator, for either reading or writing) is **always an unsafe operation**. This is because the compiler cannot make any guarantees about the validity of the raw pointer (it could be null, dangling, or point to uninitialized/incorrectly typed memory). Therefore, dereferencing must occur within an `unsafe { ... }` block. By using this block, you are asserting to the compiler that you have ensured the pointer is valid at that point.
- **Mutability**: `*r1` reads the value pointed to by `r1`. `*r2 = 10;` writes `10` to the memory location pointed to by `r2`, thereby modifying the original `num`.
- **Null pointers**: Raw pointers can be null, so use `.is_null()` to check for nulls before dereferencing, particularly when the source is uncertain. Dereferencing a null pointer often leads to program crashes, which is undefined behavior.
- **Responsibility**: The `unsafe` block signifies that the programmer takes full responsibility for upholding memory safety for the operations contained within it. The usual compile-time guarantees are relaxed for these specific operations.

Best practices for encapsulating unsafe code

While `unsafe` provides necessary power for low-level programming, its use should be approached with caution and discipline. The primary goal when you *must* use `unsafe` is to **minimize its scope and encapsulate it within a safe abstraction**. This means that while the *internals* of a particular function or module might use unsafe operations, the interface it presents to the rest of your Rust code (and to other developers) should ideally be entirely safe.

Here are key practices for doing this effectively:

- **Keep unsafe blocks as small as possible**: The `unsafe { ... }` block should only contain the absolute minimum lines of code that *require* the unsafe superpowers. If you can perform setup, teardown, or checks outside the unsafe block, do so. This makes it easier to review and reason about the specific unsafe operations.

Bad: large unsafe block:

```
// unsafe fn some_complex_operation(ptr: *mut u32, len: usize,
value: u32) {
//     // ... lots of safe logic ...
//     unsafe {
//         // ... more safe logic ...
//         // The actual unsafe part:
//         for i in 0..len {
//             *ptr.add(i) = value + i as u32;
//         }
//         // ... even more safe logic ...
//     }
//     // ...
// }
```

Good: minimal unsafe block:

```
// fn some_complex_operation_safer(ptr: *mut u32, len: usize, value:
u32) {
//     // ... lots of safe logic to validate ptr, len, value ...
//     // The actual unsafe part, tightly scoped:
//     unsafe {
//         for i in 0..len {
//             *ptr.add(i) = value + i as u32;
//         }
//     }
//     // ... more safe logic using results ...
// }
```

- **Create safe abstractions around unsafe code:** This is the most important principle. If you use unsafe code to implement a data structure (such as `Vec<T>` or `String` in the standard library), a system call wrapper, or an FFI binding, strive to provide a public API for it that is entirely safe to use. The internal unsafe details are your responsibility to get absolutely right, verifying all preconditions and maintaining invariants, but users of your safe API shouldn't need to write unsafe code themselves or worry about the low-level details. The `increment_global_counter()` and `read_global_counter()` functions from our static `mut` example (in `ch15_mutable_static_vars_v3`) are small examples of this: they perform unsafe operations internally but present a safe interface.

- **Clearly document invariants and safety conditions**: If your unsafe code relies on certain conditions (invariants) being true for it to be safe, these conditions *must* be thoroughly documented.
    - If you expose an unsafe `fn` to users of your library, its documentation must clearly state the contract the caller *must* uphold to use it safely.
    - If you have an internal `unsafe` block, comments explaining *why* it's safe in that context (what conditions are being met) are crucial for maintainability and for other developers (including your future self).
- **Use debug_assert! for internal invariants (in unsafe blocks)**: While `debug_assert!` doesn't make unsafe code safe, it can help catch violations of your assumed invariants during development and testing. These assertions are compiled only in debug builds (`cargo build`) and are completely removed in release builds (`cargo build --release`), so they have zero performance cost in your production code. This makes them the perfect tool for checking preconditions inside an `unsafe` block. For example, if you're writing an unsafe function that assumes a pointer is non-null, you can add a `debug_assert!` to catch errors during testing.

```
/// # Safety
///
/// The caller *must* ensure that the pointer `ptr` is valid, non-
null,
/// and points to a valid `i32`.
pub unsafe fn do_something_with_ptr(ptr: *mut i32) {
    // This check runs only in debug builds. It helps catch
    // incorrect usage of this unsafe function during development.
    // In a release build, this check disappears, and passing a null
    // pointer would lead to undefined behavior.
    debug_assert!(!ptr.is_null(), "do_something_with_ptr called with
a null pointer!");

    // The actual unsafe operation
    *ptr += 1;
}

fn main() {
    let mut x = 5;
```

```
    let ptr = &mut x as *mut i32;

    unsafe {
        do_something_with_ptr(ptr);
    }

    println!("x is now: {}", x); // Output: x is now: 6

    // If you were to run this in a debug build:
    // unsafe {
    //     do_something_with_ptr(std::ptr::null_mut()); // This
would panic!
    // }
}
```

In this example, if someone (including yourself) accidentally calls `do_something_with_ptr` with a null pointer during a `cargo test` or `cargo run` (debug build), the `debug_assert!` will panic, immediately identifying the bug. In a release build, the check is removed, and the unsafe code runs at full speed.

- **Minimize the use of raw pointers when safe alternatives exist**: Don't reach for raw pointers and `unsafe` if a problem can be solved using safe Rust abstractions such as references, slices, `Box<T>`, `Vec<T>`, `Cell<T>`, `RefCell<T>`, `Mutex<T>`, and so on. `unsafe` is for when those abstractions are insufficient or when you are building those very abstractions.
- **Meticulously review unsafe code**: Code within `unsafe` blocks deserves the highest level of scrutiny during code reviews. Since the compiler's safety guarantees are partially lifted, the responsibility for correctness falls entirely on the developer. Consider edge cases, potential null pointers, dangling pointers, buffer overflows, data races (if static `mut` or shared raw pointers are involved), and alignment issues.

By following these practices, you can harness the power of unsafe Rust when needed, while still ensuring a high level of safety and reliability in your code base. The aim is to create robust, safe layers over any unavoidable unsafe foundations.

In the next section, we'll explore some real-world examples to show you how to build effective command-line interfaces.

Building practical command-line utilities

One of the most common and immediately rewarding applications of system programming is the creation of **command-line utilities** (CLI tools).

These are programs that users interact with through a text-based interface in their terminal or console. You use them every day: `ls` to list files, `grep` to search for text, `find` to locate files, `curl` to transfer data, or even `git` and `cargo` themselves! Rust's strengths in performance, safety, and memory management, and its excellent handling of strings and I/O make it a superb choice for crafting efficient, reliable, and powerful CLI applications.

In this section, we'll walk through the common steps and considerations involved in designing and implementing a simple but useful command-line tool.

Designing a useful CLI tool

Before a single line of code is written, it's good practice to clearly define what your CLI tool should accomplish and how users will interact with it. A little bit of design upfront can save a lot of time and effort later.

For our primary example in this section, let's decide to build a utility that searches for a specific text pattern within a given file. This will be a very simplified version of the popular `grep` command. Let's call our tool `mini_grep`.

Here's a breakdown of the desired functionality and user interaction for `mini_grep`:

- **Core functionality**:
    - Search for a given text query (a string) within the lines of a specified text file
    - Print every line from the file that contains the query
- **Command-line arguments**:
    - The tool should accept two mandatory arguments:
        - The query: The string pattern to search for
        - The `file_path`: The path to the file that needs to be searched
    - The expected usage from the command line would look something like this:

```
mini_grep "search_term" path/to/my/file.txt
```

- **Output**:
  - If the query is found in a line, that entire line should be printed to the standard output
  - If the query is not found in any line, the program should produce no output (or perhaps a message indicating "no matches found"; we can decide this)
  - Error messages (e.g., if the file doesn't exist or arguments are incorrect) should be printed to the standard error stream
- **Error handling**:
  - The tool must handle cases where the file specified by `file_path` cannot be opened (e.g., it doesn't exist, or the program lacks permission to read it)
  - It should handle cases where an incorrect number of command-line arguments is provided
  - In case of an error, it should print an informative message to standard error and exit with a non-zero status code (which is a convention for CLI tools to indicate failure)
- **Optional enhancements (to consider, maybe not for the first version)**:
  - A command-line flag to make the search case-insensitive (e.g., `-i` or `--ignore-case`)
  - Printing line numbers alongside matching lines
  - Searching in multiple files or standard input if no file is specified

For our initial implementation, we'll focus on the core functionality. Having this clear set of requirements helps guide the implementation process. We know we'll need to do the following:

- Parse command-line arguments
- Read a file line by line
- Perform string searching
- Print to standard output and standard error
- Manage potential errors from file operations and argument parsing

This design phase, even for a small tool, is crucial. It clarifies the "what" before you dive into the "how."

Parsing command-line arguments

When a user runs your CLI tool, they often provide input directly on the command line after the program's name, for example, `mini_grep "search_pattern" input.txt`.

Here, "search_pattern" and input.txt are command-line arguments. Your Rust program needs a way to access these values. Rust's standard library offers a basic mechanism for this, and for more complex needs, the ecosystem provides robust third-party crates like clap. For this example, we will stick to the standard library to understand the fundamentals.

Using std::env::args() for basic arguments

The simplest way to get command-line arguments in Rust is using the `std::env::args()` function.

This function returns an iterator that yields the arguments as String values.

The first argument (at index 0) is traditionally the program's name or path, and subsequent elements are the user's arguments.

```
use std::env; // Required to use args()

fn main() {
    // env::args() returns an iterator over the command-line arguments.
    // We can collect these into a Vec<String>.
    let arguments: Vec<String> = env::args().collect();

    println!("Total arguments passed: {}", arguments.len());

    // Print each argument along with its index.
    // args[0] is typically the path used to execute the program.
    for (index, argument) in arguments.iter().enumerate() {
        println!("Argument [{}]: {}", index, argument);
    }

    // For our mini_grep, we expect at least two arguments after the
program name.
    // So, arguments.len() should ideally be 3 or more.
    if arguments.len() < 3 {
        if arguments.len() > 0 { // Check if program name itself is
available
```

```
            eprintln!("\nUsage: {} <query> <file_path>", arguments[0]);
        } else {
            eprintln!("\nUsage: <program_name> <query> <file_path>");
        }
        eprintln!("Error: Not enough arguments provided.");
        std::process::exit(1); // Exit with an error code
    }

    // If we reach here, we assume we have at least the query and file_
path.
    // Note: arguments[0] is the program name.
    // So, arguments[1] would be the query, and arguments[2] the file_
path.
    if arguments.len() >= 3 {
        let query_arg = &arguments[1];
        let file_path_arg = &arguments[2];

        println!("\nIntended query: {}", query_arg);
        println!("Intended file path: {}", file_path_arg);
    }
}
```

- `use std::env;`: You need to import the env module to use `args()`.
- `env::args()`: This function returns an `std::env::Args` iterator, which yields String values.
- `.collect()`: We typically call `<<>> .collect::<Vec<String>>()` on the iterator to get all arguments into a vector for easier access by index.
- **Argument indexing**:
    - `arguments[0]` is usually the path that was used to run your program (e.g., `target/debug/my_cli_app` or just `my_cli_app` if it's in the PATH).
    - `arguments[1]` is the first actual argument provided by the user.
    - `arguments[2]` is the second, and so on.
- **Error handling**: The example includes a basic check for the number of arguments. If insufficient arguments are provided, it prints a usage message to standard error (`eprintln!`) and exits with a non-zero status code (`std::process::exit(1)`), which is a common convention for CLI tools to indicate an error.

- **Accessing arguments:** If enough arguments are present, `arguments[1]` and `arguments[2]` can be accessed. They are strings, so you might need to parse them further (e.g., if an argument is expected to be a number).

While `std::env::args()` is fine for very simple tools with a fixed number of positional arguments, it quickly becomes cumbersome for more complex scenarios involving optional arguments, named flags (such as `-i` or `--ignore-case`), subcommands, or automatic help message generation.

That's where dedicated argument parsing crates come in.

Introduction to argument parsing

Crates using clapFor any CLI tool that needs more than one or two simple positional arguments, using a dedicated argument parsing crate is highly recommended. These crates handle much of the boilerplate and provide a more robust and user-friendly experience.

clap (Command Line Argument Parser) is one of the most popular and powerful argument parsing libraries in the Rust ecosystem. It allows you to define your command-line interface using a declarative style (often by deriving a struct) and handles:

- Parsing arguments, flags (e.g., `-v`, `--verbose`), and options (e.g., `--output <file>`)
- Type conversion (e.g., parsing a string argument into a number)
- Generating help messages (`--help` or `-h`)
- Generating version information (`--version` or `-V`)
- Handling subcommands (such as `git add` ... or `git commit` ...)
- Validating arguments

While a full tutorial on clap is beyond the scope of this immediate section (it's a feature-rich library!), let's see a conceptual glimpse of how it simplifies things compared to manual parsing with `std::env::args()`.

You can learn more about the clap crate here:

`https://docs.rs/clap/latest/clap/`

First, you'd add clap to your `Cargo.toml` file, usually with the "derive" feature:

```
[dependencies]
clap = { version = "4.5", features = ["derive"] } # Check crates.io for
the latest version
```

Then, you could define your arguments as fields in a struct and derive clap::Parser:

```
use clap::Parser; // Import the Parser trait

/// A simple program to greet a person, demonstrating clap.
#[derive(Parser, Debug)]
#[command(author = "Your Name", version = "0.1.0", about = "Greets a
person - clap example", long_about = None)]
struct CliArgs {
    /// The name of the person to greet
    #[arg(short, long)] // Allows -n <NAME> or --name <NAME>
    name: String,

    /// Number of times to greet
    #[arg(short, long, default_value_t = 1)] // Allows -c <COUNT> or
--count <COUNT>, defaults to 1
    count: u8,

    /// Optional message to include in the greeting
    #[arg(long)] // Allows --message <MESSAGE>
    message: Option<String>,

    // For our mini_grep example, it might look more like:
    // query: String,
    // file_path: std::path::PathBuf,
    // #[arg(short, long, action = clap::ArgAction::SetTrue)] // for a
flag like -i
    // ignore_case: bool,
}

fn main() {
    // CliArgs::parse() will parse arguments from std::env::args(),
    // handle errors, and provide help/version messages automatically.
    let args = CliArgs::parse();

    for _ in 0..args.count {
        if let Some(ref msg) = args.message {
            println!("Hello, {}! Here's your message: {}", args.name,
```

```
msg);
        } else {
            println!("Hello, {}!", args.name);
        }
    }

    // If --help or --version was passed, clap handles it and exits before
this point.
    // If parsing failed, clap prints an error and exits.
}
```

To test the code:

```
cargo run -- --name Alice --count 3 --message "Welcome to Rust!"
```

- `#[derive(Parser)]`: This derive macro from clap automatically generates all the parsing logic for the `CliArgs` struct.
- `Struct-level attributes (#[command(...)])`: These configure the overall help message, author, version, and so on.
- **Field-level attributes (`#[arg(...)]`)**: These configure how each field is parsed from the command line:
    - `name: String`: A required positional argument (by default, or you'd specify how it's named).
    - `count: u8`: `#[arg(short, long, default_value_t = 1)]` makes it an option that can be specified with `-c <<value>>` or `--count <<value>>`, automatically parses it as a `u8`, and provides a default value if not given.
    - `message: Option<<String>>`: An optional argument. If `--message` "text" is provided, `message` will be `Some("text")`. Otherwise, it's `None`.
- `CliArgs::parse()`: This single line does all the work: it fetches arguments, parses them according to your struct definition, performs type conversions, handles errors (printing user-friendly messages), and populates an instance of `CliArgs`. If the user passes `--help` or `--version`, clap handles that and exits.

This is significantly more robust and user-friendly than manual parsing with `std::env::args()` for anything beyond the simplest cases. For our `mini_grep` tool, we'll stick with `std::env::args()` for now to focus on standard library features, but keep clap in mind for your real-world CLI projects!

With a way to get input from the user via command-line arguments, the next step for our `mini_grep` tool will be to interact with the file system to read the specified file.

Interacting with the file system

Most command-line tools, at some point, need to read from or write to files, or even interact with the directory structure. Our `mini_grep` tool, for example, needs to read the contents of a user-specified file. Rust's standard library, primarily through the `std::fs` and `std::io` modules, provides a comprehensive and safe way to perform these operations. We touched upon these in *Chapter 12, Managing System Resources*, but let's revisit them with a specific focus on their use within CLI applications.

Reading and writing files in a CLI context

When building a CLI tool that operates on files, robust error handling is paramount. The file specified by the user might not exist, your program might not have permission to access it, or other I/O errors could occur. Rust's `Result` type is central to managing these situations gracefully.

Reading files: For our `mini_grep` tool, we'll need to read the content of the target file. As discussed in *Chapter 12*, if we expect to process the file line by line (which is typical for a grep-like tool), using `File::open()` followed by `BufReader::new().lines()` is a good approach.

```
use std::fs::File;
use std::io::{self, BufRead, BufReader};
use std::path::Path;
use std::process; // For process::exit

// This function attempts to read and print lines from a file.
// It's similar to what our mini_grep will need to do before searching.
fn read_and_print_file_lines(file_path_str: &str) {
    let path = Path::new(file_path_str);

    // Attempt to open the file
    let file = match File::open(&path) {
        Ok(f) => f,
        Err(e) => {
            eprintln!("Error: Could not open file '{}': {}", path.
display(), e);
            process::exit(1); // Exit with error code
        }
```

```
    };

    // Use BufReader for efficient line-by-line reading
    let reader = BufReader::new(file);

    println!("--- Contents of '{}' ---", path.display());
    for (index, line_result) in reader.lines().enumerate() {
        match line_result {
            Ok(line_content) => {
                println!("Line {}: {}", index + 1, line_content);
            }
            Err(e) => {
                // Log error for a specific line but continue if possible,
                // or decide to exit if line read errors are critical.
                eprintln!("Error reading line {} from '{}': {}", index +
1, path.display(), e);
                // For a grep tool, we might want to skip unreadable lines
                // or halt. For now, we'll just report and continue.
            }
        }
    }
    println!("--- End of '{}' ---", path.display());
}

fn main() {
    // Simulate getting a file path from command-line arguments
    // In a real CLI, this would come from std::env::args() or a parsing
crate.
    let args: Vec<String> = std::env::args().collect();

    if args.len() < 2 {
        eprintln!("Usage: {} <file_path>", args.get(0).unwrap_
or(&"program_name".into()));
        process::exit(1);
    }
    let file_to_read = &args[1];
```

```
    // Create a dummy file for testing if it doesn't exist
    if !Path::new(file_to_read).exists() {
        if file_to_read == "sample_cli_read.txt" { // Only create if it's
our expected test file
            std::fs::write(file_to_read, "First line for CLI test.\nSecond
line, with a keyword.\nThird and final line.").expect("Failed to create
sample file.");
            println!("Created sample file: {}", file_to_read);
        } else {
            eprintln!("Specified file '{}' does not exist and won't be
auto-created for this generic example.", file_to_read);
            process::exit(1);
        }
    }

    read_and_print_file_lines(file_to_read);

    // Clean up the dummy file if we created it for the test
    if file_to_read == "sample_cli_read.txt" {
        std::fs::remove_file(file_to_read).ok();
    }
}
```

To test the code:

- Built-in test: '`cargo run -- sample_cli_read.txt`'
- Read specific file: '`cargo run -- my_notes.txt`'
- Test missing file: '`cargo run -- non_existent_file.txt`'
- Usage help: '`cargo run`'

Explanation:

- **Argument handling (simplified)**: `std::env::args().collect()` gets command-line arguments. We expect the file path as the first argument after the program name.
- **Error handling for File::open**: We use a `match` statement to handle the Result from `File::open()`. If an error occurs (e.g., file not found, no permissions), we print a message to standard error (`eprintln!`) and exit the program with a non-zero status code using `std::process::exit(1)`. This is standard practice for CLI tools to indicate failure.

- **BufReader and lines()**: As before, `BufReader` provides efficient line-by-line reading. `reader.lines()` returns an iterator over `io::Result<<String>>;`.
- **Line-specific errors**: Inside the loop, we again match on `line_result`. If an individual line cannot be read (perhaps due to encoding issues or an unexpected I/O error mid-file), we print an error for that line but allow the loop to continue to try and process subsequent lines. For a tool such as grep, this behavior (skipping unreadable lines or parts) might be desirable.
- **Dummy file**: The main function includes logic to create a `sample_cli_read.txt` file if it's specified and doesn't exist, just to make the example runnable. It also cleans it up.

Writing files: While our `mini_grep` primarily reads files, other CLI tools might need to write output to files (e.g., a log file, a processed data file, or if `mini_grep` had an option to save results). The principles are the same as discussed in *Chapter 12*:

- `File::create("path")` to create a new file (or truncate an existing one)
- `OpenOptions::new().append(true).open("path")` to append to a file
- `std::fs::write("path", content)` for simple, complete writes
- Always use `BufWriter` for buffered writing to improve performance if making multiple small writes
- Crucially, handle the Result returned by all write operations and inform the user (via `eprintln!`) if something goes wrong.

Directory traversal and manipulation

Some CLI tools need to work with directories – listing their contents, creating new ones, or even recursively processing a directory tree (such as `grep -r` or `find`). The `std::fs` module provides functions for these tasks.

Key functions we saw earlier include the following:

- `fs::read_dir("path")`: Returns an iterator over the entries in a directory
- `fs::create_dir("path") / fs::create_dir_all("path")`: Create directories
- `fs::remove_dir("path") / fs::remove_dir_all("path")`: Remove directories
- `entry.path()`: For a `DirEntry` from `read_dir`, this gives its full path
- `metadata.is_dir() / metadata.is_file()`: From `fs::metadata("path")`, tells you whether a path is a directory or a file

Let's write a small example that lists the contents of a directory specified on the command line, indicating whether each entry is a file or a directory.

```
use std::env;
use std::fs;
use std::path::Path;
use std::process;
use std::io;

fn list_directory_contents(dir_path_str: &str) -> io::Result<()> {
    let path = Path::new(dir_path_str);

    if !path.is_dir() {
        // Using eprintln! for error messages is good practice in CLI
tools
        eprintln!("Error: '{}' is not a directory or does not exist.",
path.display());
        // Return an error that can be handled by the caller if needed
        return Err(io::Error::new(io::ErrorKind::NotFound, "Path is not a
directory"));
    }

    println!("Contents of directory '{}':", path.display());

    // fs::read_dir returns a Result containing an iterator over DirEntry
results
    for entry_result in fs::read_dir(path)? { // '?' propagates I/O errors
from read_dir itself
        let entry = match entry_result {
            Ok(e) => e,
            Err(e) => {
                // Error accessing a specific entry, log it and continue
                eprintln!("Warning: Could not access an entry in '{}':
{}", path.display(), e);
                continue;
            }
        };
```

```
        let entry_path = entry.path();
        let entry_name = entry_path.file_name().unwrap_or_default().to_
string_lossy(); // Get just the name part

        // Get metadata to determine if it's a file or directory
        // This can also fail (e.g., permissions)
        match fs::metadata(&entry_path) {
            Ok(metadata) => {
                if metadata.is_dir() {
                    println!("  [DIR]  {}", entry_name);
                } else if metadata.is_file() {
                    println!("  [FILE] {} ({} bytes)", entry_name,
metadata.len());
                } else {
                    println!("  [OTHER] {}", entry_name); // Symlinks,
etc.
                }
            }
            Err(e) => {
                eprintln!("Warning: Could not get metadata for '{}': {}",
entry_path.display(), e);
            }
        }
    }
    Ok(())
}

fn main() {
    let args: Vec<String> = env::args().collect();
    let dir_to_list = if args.len() > 1 {
        args[1].clone() // Use the provided argument
    } else {
        // Default to the current directory if no argument is given
        String::from(".")
    };

    println!("Attempting to list contents of '{}'...", dir_to_list);
    if let Err(e) = list_directory_contents(&dir_to_list) {
```

```
        // Error was already printed in list_directory_contents if it was
path not being a dir.
        // This catches other potential errors from the function
signature.
        if e.kind() != io::ErrorKind::NotFound { // Avoid double printing
for "not a directory"
            eprintln!("An error occurred: {}", e);
        }
        process::exit(1);
    }
}
```

- **Argument or default**: The `main` function now defaults to listing the current directory (.) if no argument is provided.
- `path.is_dir()`: Before attempting to read a directory, it's good practice to check if the given path actually *is* a directory.
- `fs::read_dir(path)?`: This attempts to read the directory entries. The `?` handles errors such as "path not found" or "permission denied" for the directory itself.
- **Iterating entries:** `fs::read_dir` returns an iterator where each item is itself a `Result<<DirEntry, io::Error>>`. This is because even if you can open the directory, you might not have permission to access individual entries within it. Our loop uses `match entry_result` to handle such cases for each entry.
- `entry.path()` and `entry_path.file_name()`: `DirEntry` provides a `path()` method to get the full `PathBuf` of the entry. `file_name()` then extracts just the `name` component. `.to_string_lossy()` is useful as file names might not always be valid `UTF-8`.
- `fs::metadata(&entry_path)?`: For each entry, we fetch its metadata to determine whether it's a file (`metadata.is_file()`) or a directory (`metadata.is_dir()`) and to get its size (`metadata.len()` for files).
- **Error handling for entries:** If metadata for a specific entry cannot be retrieved, a warning is printed, but the program continues to list other entries.

This example demonstrates how a CLI tool might inspect directory structures.

For recursive operations (such as `find` or `grep -r`), you would combine `read_dir` with checks for `metadata.is_dir()` and then recursively call your processing function on subdirectories.

Interacting with the file system is a core part of many system utilities, and Rust provides the tools to do it safely and efficiently, provided you handle the results that these operations invariably return!

Handling standard input, output, and error streams

Command-line utilities don't just read from and write to files specified by path; they also frequently interact with three standard I/O streams provided by the operating system for every running process:

- **Standard input (stdin)**: This is the default input channel for a program. By default, it's usually connected to the keyboard in a terminal, but it can be redirected to read from a file or the output of another program using pipes (|).
- **Standard output (stdout)**: This is the default output channel for a program's normal results or data. By default, it's usually connected to the terminal display, but it can be redirected to a file or piped as input to another program. The `println!` macro writes to `stdout`.
- **Standard error (stderr)**: This is a separate output channel specifically intended for error messages and diagnostics. By default, it's also usually connected to the terminal display, but it can be redirected independently of `stdout`. This is useful because it allows users to redirect a program's normal output to a file while still seeing error messages on their screen. The `eprintln!` macro writes to `stderr`.

Effectively using these standard streams is key to making your CLI tools behave like good "Unix citizens", programs that can be easily composed with other tools in a command-line environment.

Writing to standard output and standard error:

We've already been using `println!` and `eprintln!` throughout our examples:

- `println!(...)`: Writes formatted text, followed by a newline, to standard output (`stdout`). Use this for the normal, successful output of your program.

  ```
  // println!("Processing complete. Found 10 matches.");
  ```

- eprintln!(...): Writes formatted text, followed by a newline, to standard error (stderr). Use this for error messages, warnings, or diagnostic information that isn't part of the primary program output.

  ```
  // eprintln!("Error: Input file not found at path '{}'", file_path);
  // eprintln!("Warning: Configuration value 'timeout' not set, using
  default.");
  ```

By directing errors and diagnostics to stderr, users can still redirect the useful output of your program to a file without cluttering it with error messages:

```
my_tool --input data.txt > results.txt # errors still go to screen
```

or

```
my_tool --input data.txt > results.txt 2> errors.log # redirect errors to
a log file
```

Reading from standard input (stdin):

If your CLI tool is designed to process data piped to it or typed directly by the user (when no file argument is given), you'll need to read from standard input. You can get a handle to `stdin` using `std::io::stdin()`.

This handle implements the `Read` trait, so you can use it with `BufReader` to read lines or chunks.

```
use std::io::{self, BufRead, BufReader};

fn main() -> io::Result<()> {
    println!("Please enter some lines of text. Press Ctrl+D (Unix) or
Ctrl+Z then Enter (Windows) to end input:");

    let stdin = io::stdin(); // Get a handle to standard input
    let reader = BufReader::new(stdin.lock()); // stdin() returns a Stdin,
lock() it for BufReader

    let mut line_count = 0;
    for line_result in reader.lines() {
        let line = line_result?; // Handle potential I/O errors from
reading stdin
        if line.trim().is_empty() && line.is_empty() { // Check if it was
just an empty line due to Ctrl+Z/D
            // Some terminals might send an empty line before EOF signal.
            // Depending on behavior, you might want to break or continue.
        }
        println!("You entered: {}", line);
        line_count += 1;
    }
```

```
    if line_count > 0 {
        println!("\nFinished reading from stdin. Total lines processed:
{}", line_count);
    } else {
        println!("\nNo input received from stdin, or input stream ended
immediately.");
    }

    Ok(())
}
```

- `io::stdin()`: This function returns a handle to the standard input stream of the current process (`std::io::Stdin`).
- `stdin.lock()`: `stdin` is globally synchronized. To use it with `BufReader` (which requires `Read`), you typically need to acquire a lock on it first using `.lock()`. This returns a `StdinLock`, which implements `Read` and `BufRead`. The lock is released when `StdinLock` goes out of scope.
- `BufReader::new(stdin.lock())`: We wrap the locked `stdin` in a `BufReader` for efficient line-by-line reading.
- `reader.lines()`: This works just like it did for files, returning an iterator over `io::Result<<;String>;`.
- **Ending input**: Users typically signal the end of input from the keyboard by pressing *Ctrl* + *D* on Unix-like systems (Linux, macOS) or *Ctrl* + *Z* followed by *Enter* on Windows. This sends an **EOF (End-of-File)** signal, which will cause `reader.lines()` to stop producing items (or `read()` to return `Ok(0)`).

Here's how to test this:

1. Compile the code: `cargo build`
2. Run it: `target/debug/your_program_name`
    - Type some lines and press *Enter* after each.
    - When done, press *Ctrl* + *D* (or *Ctrl* + *Z* then *Enter*).
3. You can also pipe input from another command:

```
ls -l | target/debug/your_program_name
echo -e "First line\nSecond line" | target/debug/your_program_name
```

Replace `your_program_name` with the actual name of your project! You will find it in the cargo.toml file at the key `name`. Many standard CLI tools (such as `grep`, `cat`, `sort`) are designed to read from `stdin` if no file arguments are provided, allowing them to be easily used in command pipelines. This is a powerful pattern in Unix-like environments. For our `mini_grep` tool, we could extend it to read from `stdin` if no file path is given.

Understanding and correctly using `stdin`, `stdout`, and `stderr` makes your CLI tools more versatile, conventional, and easier for users to integrate into their workflows.

Interfacing with C code: the Foreign Function Interface (FFI)

Rust is a powerful language for building new systems, but the reality of software development is that a vast amount of existing code, especially at the system level, is written in C (and C++, which often exposes a C-compatible interface).

Rewriting everything from scratch in Rust is often impractical or undesirable. This is where Rust's **Foreign Function Interface** (**FFI**) capabilities become incredibly important.

The FFI allows your Rust code to call functions written in other languages (primarily C, or languages that can export a C **Application Binary Interface** (**ABI**)) and, conversely, allows code written in those languages to call your Rust functions.

The "why" of FFI: leveraging existing C libraries

Why would you need to interface with C code from Rust??

There are several compelling reasons:

- **Reusing existing code**: There are countless mature, well-tested, and highly optimized C libraries available for virtually every imaginable task, from mathematical computations (such as BLAS, LAPACK) and image processing (libjpeg, libpng) to GUI toolkits (GTK, though Rust has its own GUI ecosystem emerging), operating system APIs (most OS kernels expose C APIs), and specialized hardware drivers. The FFI allows you to tap into this wealth of existing code without reinventing the wheel.
- **Performance-critical code**: While Rust is very fast, sometimes there are highly optimized C libraries for specific numerical or signal processing tasks that have been tuned over decades. Calling into these can be a pragmatic way to achieve peak performance for certain components of your application.

- **Interoperability with legacy systems:** You might be working on a project that involves integrating new Rust components into an existing C or C++ code base. The FFI provides the bridge to make these different parts of the system communicate.
- **Accessing hardware or OS features:** Many operating system functionalities and hardware interfaces are exposed via C APIs. The FFI is essential for writing Rust code that needs to interact at this low level (e.g., for device drivers or certain system utilities).

Rust's FFI is designed to be relatively straightforward. Still, it comes with a significant caveat: when you call into C code (or any external, non-Rust code), you are stepping outside the safety guarantees that the Rust compiler typically provides for your Rust code. The C code you call might have memory safety bugs, or you might misuse the C API in a way that leads to undefined behavior (such as passing invalid pointers). Therefore, FFI calls in Rust are almost always wrapped in `unsafe` blocks, signifying that you, the programmer, are responsible for upholding the safety contract of the C API you are calling.

Despite the unsafe aspect, FFI is a powerful and necessary feature that allows Rust to be a practical choice for a wide range of system programming tasks where interaction with existing C code bases is a reality.

The goal is usually to create safe Rust wrappers around the unsafe FFI calls, so the rest of your Rust application can interact with the C library through a safe and idiomatic Rust API.

Declaring and linking external C functions

To call a function written in C (or any language that exposes a C-compatible ABI), your Rust code needs two main things:

1. A **declaration** of that external function, telling the Rust compiler its name, arguments, and return type, and that it uses the C calling convention
2. A way to **link** against the compiled C library that actually contains the implementation of that function, so the linker can resolve the function call at compile time or runtime

Using extern "C" blocks

Rust uses `extern "C" { ... }` blocks to declare functions that are defined in external C libraries. The `"C"` part specifies the ABI to use, in this case, the C ABI. This is crucial because different languages (and even different C compilers on different platforms) might have different conventions for how function arguments are passed, how return values are handled, and how function names are represented (name mangling). Using `"C"` ensures Rust and the C library are speaking the same low-level language.

Inside an extern "C" block, you list the function signatures as they appear in the C header file, but translated into Rust types. Calling these declared functions is an unsafe operation because Rust cannot verify the safety of the external C code.

```
// Suppose a C library 'libmath_utils.so' (or .dylib or .dll) has these
functions:
// In C (e.g., math_utils.h):
//   int add_integers(int a, int b);
//   double get_pi();

// In your Rust code (e.g., src/main.rs or src/lib.rs):

// This block declares functions that Rust expects to find in an external
C library.
// We are telling Rust about their existence and their signatures.
extern "C" {
    // Maps to: int add_integers(int a, int b);
    fn add_integers(a: i32, b: i32) -> i32;

    // Maps to: double get_pi();
    fn get_pi() -> f64;

    // Example of a C function that takes a C string (const char*)
    // and doesn't return anything (void).
    // In C: void print_c_string(const char* s);
    fn print_c_string(s: *const std::os::raw::c_char);
}

fn main() {
    // Calling these external C functions is unsafe because Rust can't
guarantee
    // their safety or that they even exist at link/runtime if not linked
properly.
    unsafe {
        let sum = add_integers(5, 10);
        println!("Sum from C library (add_integers(5, 10)): {}", sum); //
Expected: 15
```

```
        let pi_val = get_pi();
        println!("Value of PI from C library (get_pi()): {}", pi_val); //
Expected: ~3.14159...

        // For print_c_string, we need to create a C-compatible string.
        let rust_str = "Hello from Rust to C!";
        // CString ensures null termination and gives us a pointer.
        match std::ffi::CString::new(rust_str) {
            Ok(c_str) => {
                print_c_string(c_str.as_ptr()); // as_ptr() gives *const
c_char
                // Output from C would depend on the C implementation of
print_c_string
            }
            Err(e) => {
                eprintln!("Error creating CString: {}", e);
            }
        }
    }

    println!("\nReminder: This code declares C functions. To run it
successfully,");
    println!("you would need an actual C library defining these
functions,");
    println!("and your Rust project would need to be configured to link
against it.");
}
```

- `extern "tC" { ... }`: This tells Rust that the functions declared inside follow the C ABI.
- **Function signatures**: Inside the block, you declare functions with Rust syntax, but their types must correspond to the C types. For example, C `int` usually maps to Rust `i32`, C `double` to Rust `f64`, and C `const char*` to Rust `*const std::os::raw::c_char` (a raw pointer to a C character). `std::os::raw` provides type aliases such as `c_char`, `c_int`, and so on, for platform-independent C type representation.

- **Unsafe calls**: Calling any function declared in an `extern "C"` block is an unsafe operation. You must wrap the call in an `unsafe { ... }` block. This is because Rust cannot verify the correctness or memory safety of the external C code. You are responsible for ensuring that you call the C function with valid arguments and handle its return values correctly according to its contract.
- `std::ffi::CString`: As seen in the `print_c_string` example, when passing strings from Rust to C functions expecting null-terminated `const char*`, you should use `std::ffi::CString`. `CString::new()` creates an owned, null-terminated byte string suitable for C. `c_string.as_ptr()` provides the `*const c_char` pointer.

The #[link] attribute and build scripts

Declaring `extern "C"` functions only tells the Rust *compiler* about their existence and signature. It doesn't tell the *linker* where to find their actual implementations. For that, you need to instruct Rust to link against the compiled C library (e.g., a `.so` file on Linux, `.dylib` on macOS, or `.dll` on Windows, or a static library such as `.a` or `.lib`).

There are two main ways to do this:

1. **Using the #[link] attribute (simpler, for common system libraries)**: For libraries that the linker already knows how to find (such as standard system libraries, e.g., libc's math library `m` on Linux), you can use the `#[link]` attribute directly above the `extern "C"` block.

```
    // This tells the linker to link against the system's math
library (libm)
    #[link(name = "m")] // On Linux; might be different or not
needed on other OS for basic math
    extern "C" {
        // double sin(double x);
        fn sin(x: f64) -> f64;
        // double sqrt(double x);
        fn sqrt(x: f64) -> f64;
    }

    fn main() {
        unsafe {
            let angle = std::f64::consts::PI / 2.0; // 90 degrees
            println!("sin(PI/2) from C libm: {}", sin(angle));   //
Expected: 1.0
```

```
            println!("sqrt(16.0) from C libm: {}", sqrt(16.0)); //
Expected: 4.0
        }
    }
```

`#[link(name = "m")]` instructs the linker to link with the library named `m` (which corresponds to `libm.so` or `libm.dylib`).

This method is often used for well-known system libraries.

You'll likely need a build script for custom C libraries or libraries in non-standard locations.

2. **Using a build script (build.rs) (more flexible and powerful)**: For more complex linking scenarios, especially with your own C libraries or third-party C libraries that aren't in standard system paths, the idiomatic Rust way is to use a **build script**.

    - Create a file named `build.rs` in the root of your Rust project (alongside `Cargo.toml`).
    - Cargo will compile and run `build.rs` *before* compiling your main crate.
    - Inside `build.rs`, you can write Rust code to do the following:
        - Compile C/C++ source files into a static library using crates such as `cc`.
        - Print special instructions to Cargo to tell it how to link against pre-compiled libraries (e.g., specifying library search paths and library names).

An example of `Cargo.toml` enabling a build script:

```
# Cargo.toml
# ...
[build-dependencies]
cc = "1.0" # For compiling C code, check latest version
```

Example `build.rs` to compile and link a local C file: Let's say you have a C file, `src/my_c_code.c`:

```
// src/my_c_code.c
int multiply_by_two(int x) {
    return x * 2;
}
```

Your `build.rs` could look like this:

```
    // build.rs
    extern crate cc; // Not needed for Rust 2018+ edition if listed in
[build-dependencies]

    fn main() {
        // Compile my_c_code.c and link it into our Rust executable/
library.
        // This will create a static library (e.g., libmy_c_code.a) and
link it.
        cc::Build::new()
            .file("src/my_c_code.c") // Path to your C source file
            .compile("my_c_code"); // Output library name will be libmy_c_
code.a (or .lib)

        // If you were linking against a pre-compiled library, you'd print
instructions:
        // For example, if libcustom.so is in /opt/custom_lib/lib:
        // println!("cargo:rustc-link-search=native=/opt/custom_lib/lib");
// Add search path
        // println!("cargo:rustc-link-lib=static=custom"); // Link against
libcustom.a
        // Or for a dynamic library:
        // println!("cargo:rustc-link-lib=dylib=custom"); // Link against
libcustom.so/dylib/dll
    }

Then, in your src/main.rs (or src/lib.rs if you are creating a library),
you would declare the external function and call it.
// src/main.rs
extern "C" {
    fn multiply_by_two(x: i32) -> i32;
}

fn main() {
    // Calling an external function is an unsafe operation
    // because the Rust compiler cannot guarantee its safety.
    unsafe {
```

```
        let number = 21;
        let result = multiply_by_two(number);
        println!("{} * 2 from C (via build.rs) = {}", number, result); //
Expected: 42
    }
}
```

A note on real-world build.rs scripts

The `cc` crate we used in our `build.rs` example is perfect for compiling simple C files that you've written as part of your Rust crate.

However, as your reviewer noted, `build.rs` scripts for the FFI in the real world can be much more complex. When you need to link against a C library that is *already installed* on the user's system (such as OpenSSL or a database driver), your build script is responsible for finding it.

This often involves the following:

- Using other build-time crates, such as `pkg-config`, to query the system for the library's location and linker flags.
- Checking environment variables to let users specify custom paths.
- Handling platform-specific logic (e.g., different library names for Windows, macOS, and Linux).

While these advanced scripts are beyond the scope of this introduction, it's important to know that `build.rs` is the fundamental tool Rust provides for handling all this complexity, making FFI possible in a robust, cross-platform way.

Build scripts are a powerful feature of Cargo that allow you to run custom code before your crate is compiled. They are conventionally placed in a file named `build.rs` at the root of your crate. Here's a breakdown of the elements often used when interfacing with C/C++ code:

- `[build-dependencies]` in `Cargo.toml`: Dependencies listed under this section are only compiled and made available to the `build.rs` script itself, not to your main crate. A common example is the `cc` crate, which helps in compiling C/C++ code.

  ```
  # Cargo.toml
  [package]
  name = "my_rust_project"
  ```

```
version = "0.1.0"
edition = "2021"
build = "build.rs" # Specifies the build script

[dependencies]
# Normal dependencies for your crate

[build-dependencies]
cc = "1.0" # Or the latest version
```

- Using the `cc` crate: The `cc` crate provides a convenient, cross-platform way to compile C, C++, or assembly code from your `build.rs` script.
    - `cc::Build::new()`: Creates a new build configuration.
    - `.file("src/c_code/multiply.c")`: Adds a C source file to the compilation. You can call this multiple times for multiple files.
    - `.compile("multiply_lib")`: Compiles the specified source files into a static library (e.g., `libmultiply_lib.a` on Linux/macOS, `multiply_lib.lib` on Windows). It also instructs Cargo to link this library into your Rust crate.
- `println!("cargo:...")` instructions: The `build.rs` script can communicate instructions to Cargo by printing specific commands to standard output, prefixed with `cargo:`. Some common instructions include the following:
    - `cargo:rustc-link-search=[KIND=]PATH`: Tells `rustc` to add `PATH` to the library search path. `KIND` can be `dependency`, `crate`, `native`, `framework`, or `all`. If omitted, `all` is assumed. For native libraries compiled by the build script, `native=path/to/your/lib` is common if you aren't using cc's automatic linking.
    - `cargo:rustc-link-lib=[KIND=]NAME`: Instructs `rustc` to link against the library named `NAME`. `KIND` can be `dylib` (for dynamic libraries) or `static` (for static libraries). If using the `cc` crate's `.compile()` method, it often handles these linking instructions for you.
    - `cargo:rerun-if-changed=PATH`: Tells Cargo to rerun the build script if the file or directory at `PATH` changes. This is crucial for ensuring that changes to your C code trigger a recompile.
    - `cargo:rerun-if-env-changed=VAR`: Tells Cargo to rerun the build script if the environment variable VAR changes.

Build scripts are incredibly versatile. Beyond the FFI, they can be used for tasks such as code generation, embedding resources, or any other pre-compilation setup your crate might require.

Using `extern "C"` blocks along with either `#[link]` or, more commonly for non-system libraries, a `build.rs` script, allows Rust to find and call functions from external C libraries successfully. The next step is understanding how to pass different types of data between Rust and C.

Passing data between Rust and C

Successfully calling C functions from Rust (and vice versa, though we're focusing on the former here) requires more than just declaring function signatures. You also need to ensure that the data types you're passing back and forth are compatible and understood by both languages.

Rust and C have different memory models, string representations, and struct layouts by default, so careful handling is essential.

Primitive types and their equivalents

For many basic numeric types, the mapping between Rust and C is quite direct, especially on common platforms. However, the exact size of C types such as `int`, `long`, and so on, can vary by platform and compiler. To ensure portability and correctness, Rust's `std::os::raw` module provides type aliases for C types. It's best practice to use these when defining your `extern "C"` function signatures.

Here's a common mapping:

C Type	Rust std::os::raw type	Typical Rust Equivalent (often the same size)
char	c_char	i8 (signed) or u8 (unsigned, depends on C char)
signed char	c_schar	i8
unsigned char	c_uchar	u8
short	c_short	i16
unsigned short	c_ushort	u16
int	c_int	i32
unsigned int	c_uint	u32
long	c_long	i32 or i64 (platform-dependent)
unsigned long	c_ulong	u32 or u64 (platform-dependent)

C Type	Rust std::os::raw type	Typical Rust Equivalent (often the same size)
long long	c_longlong	i64
unsigned long long	c_ulonglong	u64
float	c_float	f32
double	c_double	f64
size_t	usize (Rust equivalent)	usize
void*	*mut c_void or *const c_void	*mut () or *const () (or more specific raw pointers)

Tip: verify FFI type mappings across platforms

The sizes of C types (such as `int`, `long`, or `size_t`) can vary significantly across different architectures (e.g., 32-bit versus 64-bit) and operating systems (e.g., Windows versus Linux). Don't assume a C `long` is always a Rust `i64`!

- Verify sizes: Always check the actual byte size of types on your target platform. You can do this in your build script or tests using `std::mem::size_of::<T>()`.
- Compile conditionally: For robust code, use platform-specific conditional compilation (e.g., `#[cfg(target_arch = "x86_64")]` or `#[cfg(target_os = "windows")]`) to provide the correct type mappings for each target.

Example declaration:

```
use std::os::raw::{c_int, c_double, c_char};

extern "C" {
    fn process_data(input_val: c_int, scale_factor: c_double) -> c_int;
    fn get_version_char() -> c_char; // C char, might be signed or
unsigned
}
```

When calling C functions that take or return primitive types, if you use these `std::os::raw` types in your Rust `extern "C"` block, the Rust compiler will generally handle the conversions correctly for numeric types that have a direct size equivalent (such as `i32` for `c_int` on most platforms).

Working with C strings

Strings are a common source of complexity in the FFI because Rust strings and C strings are fundamentally different:

- Rust `String` / `&str` are UTF-8 encoded, store their length, and are *not* null-terminated
- C strings (`char*` / `const char*`) are typically sequences of bytes (often interpreted as ASCII or some locale-specific encoding), are *null-terminated* (a `\0` byte marks the end), and do not store their length explicitly.

The `std::ffi` module in Rust provides two key types for safely working with C strings: `CString` and `CStr`.

Passing strings from Rust to C (using CString): If a C function expects a `const char*` (a null-terminated string), you cannot pass a Rust `String` or `&str` directly.

You need to convert it to a `CString`. `CString::new()` takes a Rust string or byte slice and creates an owned, C-compatible, null-terminated byte string. It will return an error if the Rust string contains interior null bytes, as that's invalid for a C string.

```
use std::ffi::CString;
use std::os::raw::c_char;

// Assume this C function exists and prints a null-terminated string:
// extern "C" { fn c_puts(s: *const c_char); }
// For this example, let's simulate it in Rust to make it runnable.
#[cfg(target_os = "linux")] // Example for a system with puts from libc
#[link(name = "c")]
extern "C" {
    fn puts(s: *const c_char) -> std::os::raw::c_int;
}

// Fallback for other systems or if direct linking is complex for an
example
#[cfg(not(target_os = "linux"))]
unsafe extern "C" fn puts(s: *const c_char) -> std::os::raw::c_int {
```

```
    // This is a Rust reimplementation for example purposes
    // It's unsafe because we dereference a raw pointer.
    // A real FFI call wouldn't reimplement it.
    if s.is_null() { return -1; }
    let mut len = 0;
    while *s.add(len) != 0 { // Find null terminator
        len += 1;
    }
    let slice = std::slice::from_raw_parts(s as *const u8, len);
    match std::str::from_utf8(slice) {
        Ok(str_slice) => println!("{}", str_slice),
        Err(_) => eprintln!("[Simulated C puts] Invalid UTF-8 received"),
    }
    0 // Typically returns non-negative on success
}

fn main() {
    let rust_message = "Hello from Rust, C world!";

    // Convert the Rust string to a CString (null-terminated)
    match CString::new(rust_message) {
        Ok(c_message) => {
            // Call the C function, passing a pointer to the CString's
internal buffer.
            // c_message.as_ptr() returns a *const c_char.
            // This call must be in an unsafe block.
            unsafe {
                puts(c_message.as_ptr());
            }
            // c_message owns the C-compatible string data.
            // It will be freed when c_message goes out of scope.
        }
        Err(e) => {
            eprintln!("Error creating CString: {} (Likely an interior null
byte)", e);
        }
    }
```

```
    // Example of an interior null byte causing an error:
    let invalid_rust_str = "Hello\0World";
    if CString::new(invalid_rust_str).is_err() {
        println!("Correctly failed to create CString from: '{}' due to 
interior null byte.", invalid_rust_str);
    }
}
```

- `CString::new(rust_string)` attempts to create a new C-compatible string. It allocates memory, copies the Rust string's content, and appends a null terminator (`\0`). It returns `Result<;CString, NulError>;` because Rust strings can contain interior null bytes, which are invalid in C strings.
- `c_message.as_ptr()` returns a `*const c_char` raw pointer to the null-terminated byte sequence owned by the `CString`. This pointer can be safely passed to C functions.
- The `CString` instance owns the memory for the C-compatible string. When `c_message` goes out of scope, its `Drop` implementation frees this memory, preventing leaks. This is a key safety feature.

Receiving strings in Rust from C (using CStr): If a C function returns a `const char*` (or passes one to Rust via a callback), you get a raw pointer. Rust cannot assume this pointer is valid, correctly null-terminated, or that its contents are valid UTF-8. The `std::ffi::CStr` type is used to wrap such a raw pointer safely.

`CStr::from_ptr(raw_pointer)` creates a `&CStr` slice from a `*const c_char`. This operation is unsafe because `CStr` trusts that the provided pointer is valid and points to a null-terminated sequence of bytes. Once you have a `&CStr`, you can try converting it to a Rust `&str` or `String`.

```
use std::ffi::{CStr, CString};
use std::os::raw::c_char;
use std::str;

// Imagine this C function exists:
// const char* get_c_greeting();
// For this example, we'll simulate it by creating a CString in Rust
// and returning its raw pointer (which is what a C function might do).
fn simulate_get_c_greeting() -> *const c_char {
    // In a real scenario, this CString would live as long as C needs it,
    // or its ownership would be managed carefully.
```

```
    // For a simple return from a C function that allocates and returns a
string,
    // there would need to be a corresponding C function to free it.
    // Here, we leak it for simplicity of example, which is bad practice
in real code!
    // A better simulation would involve a static C string or careful
memory management.
    let c_string = CString::new("Hello from C!").unwrap();
    let ptr = c_string.as_ptr();
    std::mem::forget(c_string); // Intentionally leak for this example, DO
NOT DO THIS IN REAL CODE
                                // without a corresponding C-side free
mechanism.
    ptr
}

// A safer simulation of a C function returning a string literal
fn simulate_get_c_static_greeting() -> *const c_char {
    static GREETING: &str = "Static C Greeting!\0"; // Ensure null
termination
    GREETING.as_ptr() as *const c_char
}

fn main() {
    let c_char_ptr_leaked = simulate_get_c_greeting();
    let c_char_ptr_static = simulate_get_c_static_greeting();

    // Process the (conceptually) leaked C string
    // This is unsafe because we are trusting c_char_ptr_leaked is valid.
    unsafe {
        // Create a CStr slice from the raw pointer.
        let c_str_slice = CStr::from_ptr(c_char_ptr_leaked);

        // Attempt to convert the CStr to a Rust &str (UTF-8 validated)
        match c_str_slice.to_str() {
            Ok(rust_str) => println!("Received from (simulated) C
(leaked): '{}'", rust_str),
```

```
            Err(e) => eprintln!("CString from C was not valid UTF-8: {}",
e),
        }
        // In real FFI, if this memory was allocated by C, Rust should not
free it
        // unless C provides a specific free function. If we used our
simulated leak,
        // this memory is now leaked.
    }

    // Process the static C string
    unsafe {
        let c_str_slice = CStr::from_ptr(c_char_ptr_static);
        match c_str_slice.to_str() {
            Ok(rust_str) => println!("Received from (simulated) C
(static): '{}'", rust_str),
            Err(e) => eprintln!("CString from C was not valid UTF-8: {}",
e),
        }
    }
}
```

- **Simulating C Return**: The `simulate_get_c_greeting` and `simulate_get_c_static_greeting` functions mimic a C function returning a `const char*`. The `std::mem::forget` in the first simulation is a **dangerous hack** to prevent Rust from deallocating the CString's memory when it goes out of scope, which is **not** how you'd typically handle strings returned from real C functions (they usually return pointers to static memory, or memory you then own and must free with a C-provided deallocator). The static version is safer.
- `unsafe { CStr::from_ptr(c_char_ptr) }`: This is the crucial unsafe step. You are asserting that `c_char_ptr` is a valid, null-terminated C string whose memory will remain valid for the lifetime of the `CStr`.
- `c_str_slice.to_str()`: This attempts to convert `&;CStr` (which is a byte slice) into a Rust `&str`. It returns `Result<<&;str, Utf8Error>>;` because the C string might not be valid UTF-8.
- `c_str_slice.to_string_lossy()`: An alternative that converts to a `<>Cow<'_, str>`, replacing invalid UTF-8 sequences with U+FFFD. This is useful if you need a Rust string even if the C string isn't perfect UTF-8.

- **Memory management**: If the C string was allocated by C code (e.g., via malloc or returned from a C library function that allocates), Rust **must not** deallocate that memory using Rust's deallocators. The C library typically must provide a corresponding function to free that string (e.g., `free_c_string(ptr)`), which you would then call from Rust via the FFI. `CStr` itself does not manage the memory it points to; it's just a view.

Working with C strings requires careful attention to null termination, character encoding (UTF-8 versus others), and memory ownership.

`CString` and `CStr` provide the necessary tools to bridge these differences as safely as possible.

Representing C structs in Rust

When passing structs between Rust and C, you need to ensure that both languages agree on the memory layout of the struct (i.e., how its fields are ordered and padded in memory). By default, Rust does *not* guarantee a specific layout for structs; it might reorder fields for optimization.

To ensure C compatibility, you must annotate your Rust struct definition with `#[repr(C)]`.

```
// Suppose you have a C struct like this:
// typedef struct {
//     int id;
//     double value;
//     char active; // Assuming char is used as a boolean (0 or 1)
// } CItem;

// The equivalent Rust struct with #[repr(C)]
#[repr(C)] // Ensure C-compatible memory layout
#[derive(Debug, Copy, Clone)] // Optional, for convenience
pub struct RustItemEquivalent {
    id: std::os::raw::c_int,    // Use c_int for C int
    value: std::os::raw::c_double, // Use c_double for C double
    active: std::os::raw::c_char,  // Use c_char for C char
}

// Assume a C function:
// void process_c_item(const CItem* item_ptr);
// For this example, let's simulate it in Rust to make it runnable.
#[cfg(not(target_os = "some_os_where_this_is_real"))] // Avoid real link
errors
```

```
unsafe extern "C" fn process_c_item(item_ptr: *const RustItemEquivalent) {
    if item_ptr.is_null() {
        println!("[Simulated C] Received a null item_ptr!");
        return;
    }
    // In unsafe block because we dereference a raw pointer.
    let item_ref = &*item_ptr; // Dereference to get a Rust reference
    println!("[Simulated C] Processing item - ID: {}, Value: {}, Active:
{}",
             item_ref.id, item_ref.value, if item_ref.active != 0 { "yes"
} else { "no" });
}

fn main() {
    let my_item = RustItemEquivalent {
        id: 101,
        value: 3.14159,
        active: 1, // Representing true for C char
    };

    let my_item_inactive = RustItemEquivalent {
        id: 102,
        value: 2.718,
        active: 0, // Representing false
    };

    // Pass a pointer to our Rust struct to the (simulated) C function.
    // This must be in an unsafe block because process_c_item is extern
"C".
    unsafe {
        println!("Calling C function with my_item:");
        process_c_item(&my_item as *const RustItemEquivalent);

        println!("\nCalling C function with my_item_inactive:");
        process_c_item(&my_item_inactive as *const RustItemEquivalent);
    }
}
```

- #[repr(C)]: This attribute tells the Rust compiler to lay out the fields of RustItemEquivalent in memory in the same order and with the same padding rules that a C compiler would typically use for an equivalent C struct. This is essential for structs that will be passed to or received from C functions by value or by pointer.
- **Field types**: When defining the Rust struct, use the std::os::raw::c_* types (such as c_int, c_double, c_char) for fields that directly map to C primitive types to ensure size and signedness compatibility across platforms.
- **Passing by pointer**: In the main function, &my_item as *const RustItemEquivalent takes a reference to our Rust struct and casts it to a raw pointer (*const RustItemEquivalent), which is then passed to the (simulated) C function process_c_item. The C function would receive this as const CItem*.
- **Safety**: Because process_c_item is an extern "C" function, calling it requires an unsafe block. Inside the (simulated) C function (if it were real C, or if it's a Rust unsafe extern "C" function), dereferencing item_ptr also requires unsafe.

Using #[repr(C)] is fundamental when defining Rust structs that need to match the memory layout of C structs for the FFI.

Handling pointers and callbacks

Two more advanced FFI topics are handling arbitrary pointers and dealing with callbacks (where C code calls back into Rust functions).

Pointers to data:

- **Rust owning, C borrowing**: If Rust allocates data (e.g., with String, Vec, or Box) and passes a pointer to C, Rust is responsible for ensuring the data lives as long as C might use it. C should generally treat this pointer as borrowed and not try to free it. For Box<T>, you can use Box::into_raw(b) to get a raw pointer, *mut T, and transfer ownership responsibility (often to C, which must then have a way to give it back to Rust to be freed via Box::from_raw). This is advanced and requires careful lifetime management.
- **C owning, Rust borrowing**: If C allocates data and passes a pointer to Rust, Rust should treat this pointer as borrowed. Rust must not deallocate this memory. The C side is responsible for freeing it. If Rust needs to hold onto such a pointer, it must ensure the C data outlives the Rust pointer. The CStr type is an example of Rust borrowing a C-owned string.

- **Opaque pointers**: C APIs often use `void*` or pointers to incomplete types as "opaque handles" to resources managed by the C library. In Rust, these can be represented as `*mut std::os::raw::c_void` or a newtype struct wrapping such a pointer (e.g., `struct MyCHandle(*mut std::os::raw::c_void);`).

Callbacks (C calling Rust): It's possible for C code to call back into Rust functions. This typically involves the following:

- Defining a Rust function with the `extern "C"` ABI
- Getting a function pointer to this Rust function

Passing this function pointer to a C function that expects a callback. This is an advanced FFI topic because you must ensure the following:

- **Safety**: The Rust callback must be safe to call from C (e.g., it shouldn't panic across the FFI boundary without a catch mechanism, as panics unwinding into C are undefined behavior)
- **Lifetimes**: Any data the Rust callback accesses must be valid when C calls it
- **Data marshaling**: Data passed from C to the Rust callback, and vice versa, must be correctly converted
- **Thread safety**: If the C library might call the callback from a different thread, your Rust callback and any data it accesses must be thread-safe

```
// Rust function to be called by C
// It must have the C calling convention and be `unsafe` if it does unsafe
things,
// or be safe if its operations are all safe.
// For C to call it, it needs to be `extern "C"`.
#[no_mangle] // Prevents Rust from mangling the name, so C can find it
pub extern "C" fn rust_callback_function(value: i32) {
    println!("[Rust Callback] Called from C with value: {}", value);
}

// Assume a C function like this exists:
// typedef void (*rust_callback_t)(int);
// void register_and_call_rust_callback(rust_callback_t cb, int data_for_
cb);
```

```
extern "C" {
    // For this example, we'll only declare it conceptually.
    // fn register_and_call_rust_callback(
    //     callback: extern "C" fn(i32), // Type for a function pointer
    //     data: i32
    // );
}

fn main() {
    println!("Conceptual example of providing a Rust callback to C.");
    println!("To run this, you'd need a C side that calls 'register_and_
call_rust_callback'");
    println!("and links with this Rust code compiled as a library.");

    // unsafe {
    //     // This would pass our Rust function to the C function.
    //     // register_and_call_rust_callback(rust_callback_function, 42);
    // }
}
```

- `extern "C" fn rust_callback_function(...)`: This defines a Rust function that uses the C ABI, making it callable from C.
- `#[no_mangle]`: This attribute tells the Rust compiler not to change the name of the function during compilation, so the C linker can find it by the exact name, `rust_callback_function`.
- Function pointer type `extern "C" fn(i32)`: When passing a Rust callback to C, or receiving one from C, this is the type of the function pointer in Rust.
- **Real implementation**: Actually making C call this Rust function involves compiling the Rust code as a library, linking it with the C code, and having the C code get a pointer to `rust_callback_function` to call it. This is a more involved build setup.

Handling arbitrary pointers and callbacks correctly is one of the most complex parts of the FFI and requires a deep understanding of memory management and safety on both the Rust and C sides.

Creating safe Rust wrappers around unsafe C APIs

We've established that calling C functions via the FFI is an unsafe operation in Rust. This is because the Rust compiler cannot verify the memory safety or correctness of the external C code, nor can it ensure that you are upholding all the contracts (preconditions and postconditions) of the C API.

While using `unsafe` blocks is necessary to make the FFI calls, littering your entire Rust code base with `unsafe` blocks whenever you interact with a C library is undesirable. It reduces the areas where Rust's safety guarantees apply and makes the code harder to reason about.

The idiomatic and highly recommended approach is to **create safe Rust wrappers** around the unsafe FFI calls. The idea is to build a higher-level Rust API (functions, structs, methods) that internally handles the unsafe interactions with the C library but exposes a completely safe interface to the rest of your Rust application.

Here are the goals of a safe wrapper:

- **Encapsulate unsafety:** All `unsafe` blocks related to calling C functions and handling raw pointers should be contained within the wrapper module.
- **Uphold C API contracts:** The wrapper's internal unsafe code is responsible for ensuring that all preconditions of the C functions are met (e.g., pointers are not null if the C function doesn't expect them, string lengths are correct, resource handles are valid).
- **Manage resources:** If the C library allocates resources that need to be freed (e.g., memory allocated by malloc, file handles), the Rust wrapper should manage these resources, often by implementing the `Drop` trait on a Rust struct that represents the C resource. This ensures **RAII (Resource Acquisition Is Initialization)** and prevents leaks.
- **Convert data types:** The wrapper should handle conversions between Rust types and C-compatible types (e.g., Rust `String` to `CString` for C `const char*`, Rust `Result` for C error codes).
- **Provide an idiomatic Rust API:** The wrapper should feel natural to use for Rust developers. This might mean using Rust error handling (returning `Result`), using Rust strings and collections, and following Rust naming conventions.

A note on debugging across the FFI boundary

When bugs *do* occur, they can be much harder to diagnose than in pure Rust code. You are operating at the seam between two different languages, memory models, and calling conventions.

Because your safe wrapper contains an `unsafe` block, a bug might be in your C code, your Rust code, or (most commonly) in the *interaction* between them. A segmentation fault, for example, might be triggered by Rust passing a bad pointer, which only crashes deep inside the C library.

Standard Rust tools such as `cargo test` and `println!` debugging may not be enough. To be effective, you often need to use C-level tools:

- `gdb` (GNU Debugger) or `lldb`: These allow you to set breakpoints, step through the compiled C code, inspect C-level memory, and (most importantly) examine the full stack trace as it crosses from Rust into C and back.
- valgrind (on Linux): A powerful tool for detecting C-level memory errors. If your C library has a memory leak, reads from an invalid pointer, or has a use-after-free bug, valgrind can often pinpoint it.
- `strace` (on Linux) or `dtruss` (on macOS): Lets you trace the *system calls* your C library is making. This is invaluable if the bug involves file I/O, networking, or other OS interactions.

Debugging effectively at this level requires a deeper understanding of platform specifics, especially the ABI and calling conventions, the rules for how arguments are passed (e.g., on the stack or in registers) and how values are returned.

Let's consider our conceptual C library from before with `add_integers` and `print_c_string`, and build a slightly more structured safe wrapper.

```
use std::ffi::{CString, CStr};
use std::os::raw::c_char;
use std::fmt;

// --- Declarations for the conceptual C library ---
// Assume these functions are defined in an external C library
// and linked appropriately (e.g., via build.rs or #[link]).
//
```

```
// In C:
//   int c_add(int a, int b);
//   const char* c_get_static_message();
//   void c_free_string(char* s); // If C library allocates strings that
Rust needs to free
//   char* c_duplicate_string(const char* s); // C func that allocates &
returns a string

extern "C" {
    fn c_add(a: std::os::raw::c_int, b: std::os::raw::c_int) ->
std::os::raw::c_int;
    fn c_get_static_message() -> *const c_char; // Returns a pointer to a
C static string

    // For this example, we'll simulate c_duplicate_string and c_free_
string in Rust
    // to avoid needing an actual C library for this specific
demonstration.
    // In a real scenario, these would be true external C functions.
}

// --- Simulated C functions (for this example to be self-contained and
runnable) ---
// In a real FFI scenario, these would be in your C library.
#[no_mangle]
unsafe extern "C" fn simulated_c_add(a: i32, b: i32) -> i32 {
    a + b
}

#[no_mangle]
unsafe extern "C" fn simulated_c_get_static_message() -> *const c_char {
    static MESSAGE: &[u8] = b"Hello from simulated C!\0"; // Null-
terminated byte string
    MESSAGE.as_ptr() as *const c_char
}

// --- Safe Rust Wrapper Module ---
pub mod c_math_utils {
```

```
    use super::*; // To access CString, CStr, c_char, and the extern "C"
block if it were separate

    // Define a custom error type for our wrapper
    #[derive(Debug)]
    pub enum WrapperError {
        StringConversion(std::ffi::NulError), // For CString::new failures
        Utf8Conversion(std::str::Utf8Error),  // For CStr::to_str failures
        // Add other error types as needed
    }

    impl fmt::Display for WrapperError {
        fn fmt(&self, f: &mut fmt::Formatter<'_>) -> fmt::Result {
            match self {
                WrapperError::StringConversion(e) => write!(f, "CString
conversion error: {}", e),
                WrapperError::Utf8Conversion(e) => write!(f, "CStr to &str
UTF-8 conversion error: {}", e),
            }
        }
    }
    impl std::error::Error for WrapperError {
        fn source(&self) -> Option<&(dyn std::error::Error + 'static)> {
            match self {
                WrapperError::StringConversion(e) => Some(e),
                WrapperError::Utf8Conversion(e) => Some(e),
            }
        }
    }

    /// Safely adds two integers using the external C function.
    pub fn add_via_c(a: i32, b: i32) -> i32 {
        // The unsafe block is contained within this safe function.
        // The caller of add_via_c doesn't need to use unsafe.
        unsafe {
            // If we were using the real extern "C" c_add:
            // c_add(a as std::os::raw::c_int, b as std::os::raw::c_int)
as i32
```

```
            simulated_c_add(a,b) // Using our simulated version for this
example
        }
    }

    /// Safely gets a static message from the C library and converts it to
a Rust String.
    pub fn get_message_from_c() -> Result<String, WrapperError> {
        // Unsafe block to call the C function and handle the raw pointer.
        unsafe {
            let c_char_ptr = simulated_c_get_static_message(); // Or real
`c_get_static_message()`
            if c_char_ptr.is_null() {
                // C function might return NULL to indicate an error or no
message.
                // Decide how your wrapper should handle this.
                return Ok(String::from("<No message from C>")); // Or an
Err
            }
            // Create a CStr from the raw pointer. This itself is unsafe.
            let c_str_slice = CStr::from_ptr(c_char_ptr);
            // Attempt to convert the CStr (byte slice) to a Rust &str.
            // This can fail if the C string is not valid UTF-8.
            match c_str_slice.to_str() {
                Ok(rust_str_slice) => Ok(rust_str_slice.to_owned()), //
Convert &str to owned String
                Err(e) => Err(WrapperError::Utf8Conversion(e)),
            }
        }
    }
} // end of c_math_utils module

fn main() {
    // Users of our c_math_utils module call safe functions.
    let sum = c_math_utils::add_via_c(15, 27);
    println!("Safe wrapper call to add_via_c(15, 27) = {}", sum); //
Expected: 42
```

```
    match c_math_utils::get_message_from_c() {
        Ok(message) => println!("Safe wrapper call to get_message_
from_c(): '{}'", message),
        Err(e) => eprintln!("Error getting message from C via wrapper:
{}", e),
    }
}
```

- **Module encapsulation**: We create a module, `c_math_utils`, to house our safe Rust API. The unsafe FFI calls are hidden inside this module's implementation.
- `add_via_c` function:
    - This function is safe (`fn` not `unsafe fn`)
    - Internally, it has an `unsafe` block to call the (simulated) `c_add` function
    - It handles any necessary type conversions (such as `i32` to `c_int` if they were different, though often they are the same).
- `get_message_from_c` function:
    - This function is also safe and returns a `Result<String, WrapperError>` to handle potential errors idiomatically in Rust.
    - Inside its `unsafe` block, it does the following:
        - It calls the (simulated) `simulated_c_get_static_message()` C function, which returns a `*const c_char`.
        - It checks if the returned pointer is null, a common C pattern for indicating errors or no data.
        - `CStr::from_ptr(c_char_ptr)` creates a &`CStr` from the raw pointer. This step is unsafe because it relies on the promise that the pointer is valid and points to a null-terminated C string.
        - `c_str_slice.to_str()` attempts to convert the byte slice represented by &`CStr` into a UTF-8 Rust string slice (&`str`). This can fail if the C string is not valid UTF-8, so it returns a Result.
        - If successful, `to_owned()` creates a Rust string from the &`str`.

- Custom `WrapperError` enum: We define a simple error enum for our wrapper to represent different kinds of failures that can occur when interacting with the C library (e.g., string conversion issues). This enum implements `Debug`, `Display`, and `std::error::Error` for good error reporting.
- **Using the wrapper**: In `main`, we call `c_math_utils::add_via_c` and `c_math_utils::get_message_from_c` without needing any `unsafe` blocks. The complexity and unsafety of the FFI calls are hidden by the wrapper.

This pattern of creating safe Rust abstractions over unsafe FFI calls is fundamental to using C libraries in Rust effectively and safely.

It allows the majority of your Rust code base to remain within Rust's safety guarantees, while concentrating the unsafe responsibilities in a well-defined and well-documented wrapper layer.

Practical example: using a simple custom C library from Rust

Let's consolidate what we've learned about FFI by creating a very small C library, compiling it, and then writing a Rust program that calls functions from this C library using safe wrappers.

Our C library will provide two simple functions:

1. `int multiply(int a, int b);`
2. `void greet_person(const char* name);`

Prerequisite: installing a C compiler

Before `cargo build` can succeed, you must have a compatible C compiler (such as GCC, Clang, or MSVC) already installed on your system. The `cc` crate is smart and will automatically detect the one that's available.

Here's how to quickly get a C compiler on most systems:

- **On Linux** (Debian/Ubuntu): The `build-essential` package includes `gcc`, `make`, and other core build tools.

```
sudo apt install build-essential
```

- **On macOS**: Apple's command-line tools provide `clang`. This is the easiest way to get it:

```
xcode-select --install
```

- **On Windows**: The most common approach is to install the Visual Studio Build Tools.
    1. Go to the Visual Studio downloads page.
    2. Run the installer.
    3. Select the Desktop development with C++ workload. This will install the MSVC compiler, which `cc` will find.

Once you have one of these installed, `cargo build` will be able to find and use it to compile your C code.

Step 1: Create the C library

Create a file named `my_c_lib.c`:

```
// my_c_lib.c
#include <stdio.h> // For printf

int multiply(int a, int b) {
    return a * b;
}

void greet_person(const char* name) {
    if (name != NULL) {
        printf("[C Library] Hello, %s!\n", name);
    } else {
        printf("[C Library] Hello, (null name provided)!\n");
    }
}
```

Create a header file named `my_c_lib.h` (optional for this simple case, if we compile directly, but good practice):

```
// my_c_lib.h
#ifndef MY_C_LIB_H
#define MY_C_LIB_H

int multiply(int a, int b);
void greet_person(const char* name);

#endif // MY_C_LIB_H
```

Step 2: Compile the C library

You'll need a C compiler (such as GCC or Clang). Open your terminal in the directory where you saved `my_c_lib.c`.

- On Linux or macOS (creating a static library, `libmy_c_lib.a`):

```
gcc -c my_c_lib.c -o my_c_lib.o
ar rcs libmy_c_lib.a my_c_lib.o
```

- On Windows (creating a static library, `my_c_lib.lib`, with MinGW GCC):

```
gcc -c my_c_lib.c -o my_c_lib.o
ar rcs my_c_lib.lib my_c_lib.o
(If using MSVC, the commands would be cl /c my_c_lib.c and lib my_c_
lib.obj /OUT:my_c_lib.lib).
```

This creates a static library (`libmy_c_lib.a` or `my_c_lib.lib`) in the current directory.

Step 3: Create the Rust project and build.rs

Now, create a new Rust project:

```
cargo new rust_ffi_example --bin
cd rust_ffi_example
```

Copy the compiled C library (e.g., `libmy_c_lib.a`) into the root of your `rust_ffi_example` project (or a subdirectory such as `clib`).

Create a `build.rs` file in the root of your `rust_ffi_example` project:

```
// rust_ffi_example/build.rs
fn main() {
    // Get the current directory (where Cargo.toml and build.rs are)
    let project_dir = std::env::var("CARGO_MANIFEST_DIR").unwrap();

    // Tell Cargo to link against our C library.
    // Assumes libmy_c_lib.a (or .lib) is in the project root or a known
path.
    // For simplicity, let's assume it's in the project root.
    // If it's in a subdirectory like "clib", use:
    // println!("cargo:rustc-link-search=native={}/clib", project_dir);
    println!("cargo:rustc-link-search=native={}", project_dir); // Search
in project root
```

```
    // Link against the static library "my_c_lib"
    // Cargo will look for libmy_c_lib.a on Unix-like systems
    // or my_c_lib.lib on Windows.
    println!("cargo:rustc-link-lib=static=my_c_lib");

    // If your C library had other dependencies, you'd link them here too.
    // e.g., println!("cargo:rustc-link-lib=dylib=some_other_system_lib");

    // Tell Cargo to rerun this build script if build.rs changes
    println!("cargo:rerun-if-changed=build.rs");
    // Also, if your C library source changes, you might want to recompile
it here
    // using the `cc` crate if you weren't pre-compiling it manually.
}
```

You don't need `[build-dependencies]` in `Cargo.toml` for this simple `build.rs` that only prints linker flags.

If `build.rs` were *compiling* C code using the `cc` crate, then `cc` would be a build dependency.

Step 4: Write the Rust code with FFI declarations and safe wrappers

Now, edit `src/main.rs`:

```
use std::ffi::{CString, NulError};
use std::os::raw::{c_char, c_int};
use std::fmt;

// Declare the C functions we want to call
extern "C" {
    fn multiply(a: c_int, b: c_int) -> c_int;
    fn greet_person(name: *const c_char);
}

// Define a custom error type for our safe wrapper module
#[derive(Debug)]
pub enum CLibError {
    StringConversion(NulError), // Error from CString::new if string has
interior nulls
```

```
                                    // Add other potential C library error
types if needed
}

impl fmt::Display for CLibError {
    fn fmt(&self, f: &mut fmt::Formatter<'_>) -> fmt::Result {
        match self {
            CLibError::StringConversion(e) => write!(f, "Failed to convert
Rust string to C string: {}", e),
        }
    }
}

impl std::error::Error for CLibError {
    fn source(&self) -> Option<&(dyn std::error::Error + 'static)> {
        match self {
            CLibError::StringConversion(e) => Some(e),
        }
    }
}

// Safe Rust wrapper functions
mod my_c_lib_wrapper {
    use super::*; // To access extern "C" block, CString, CLibError

    pub fn safe_multiply(a: i32, b: i32) -> i32 {
        // The call to the extern "C" function must be in an unsafe block.
        // We assume that passing i32s (which usually match c_int) is
safe.
        unsafe {
            multiply(a as c_int, b as c_int) as i32
        }
    }

    pub fn safe_greet(name: &str) -> Result<(), CLibError> {
        // Convert Rust &str to CString (null-terminated)
        match CString::new(name) {
            Ok(c_name) => {
```

```
                // Call the C function within an unsafe block.
                // We are responsible for ensuring c_name.as_ptr() is
valid.
                unsafe {
                    greet_person(c_name.as_ptr());
                }
                Ok(())
            }
            Err(e) => Err(CLibError::StringConversion(e)),
        }
    }
}

fn main() {
    println!("--- Testing FFI with Custom C Library ---");

    let num1 = 12;
    let num2 = 7;
    let product = my_c_lib_wrapper::safe_multiply(num1, num2);
    println!("Rust calling C multiply({}, {}): {}", num1, num2, product);
// Expected: 84

    let name_to_greet = "Rustacean via FFI";
    match my_c_lib_wrapper::safe_greet(name_to_greet) {
        Ok(_) => println!("Greeting sent to C library successfully."),
        Err(e) => eprintln!("Error sending greeting: {}", e),
    }

    // Test with a name that would cause CString::new to fail (if it had
interior null)
    // let problematic_name = "Rust\0FFI";
    // if let Err(e) = my_c_lib_wrapper::safe_greet(problematic_name) {
    //     eprintln!("Correctly handled error for problematic name: {}",
e);
    // }
}
```

- C library (`my_c_lib.c`, `my_c_lib.h`): Contains the simple `multiply` and `greet_person` C functions.
- **Compiling C library**: We compile `my_c_lib.c` into a static library (`libmy_c_lib.a` or `my_c_lib.lib`). This library needs to be accessible to the Rust linker.
- `build.rs`: This script tells Cargo the following:
  - `println!("cargo:rustc-link-search=native={}", project_dir);`: Look for native libraries in the project's root directory (where we copied `libmy_c_lib.a`).
  - `println!("cargo:rustc-link-lib=static=my_c_lib");`: Link against the static library named `my_c_lib`. Cargo will automatically look for `libmy_c_lib.a` (Unix) or `my_c_lib.lib` (Windows).
- `src/main.rs`:
  - `extern "C" { ... }`: Declares the signatures of the `multiply` and `greet_person` C functions so Rust knows how to call them.
  - `CLibError`: A custom error type for our wrapper, specifically to handle potential errors from `CString::new`.
  - `my_c_lib_wrapper` module: This module provides safe Rust functions (`safe_multiply`, `safe_greet`) that internally call the unsafe C functions.
    - `safe_multiply` directly calls `multiply` within an `unsafe` block, casting Rust `i32` to `c_int` (often the same, but explicit casting is good practice for the FFI).
    - `safe_greet` converts the Rust `&str` to a `CString` (which can fail if the string contains interior null bytes, hence the Result), then calls `greet_person` with a pointer to the C-string's data.
  - `main()`: Calls the safe wrapper functions. No `unsafe` blocks are needed in `main` itself because the unsafety is encapsulated within the wrapper module.
- **Compilation and linking:** When you run `cargo build` or `cargo run`, the following happens:
  1. `build.rs` is compiled and run first. It prints the `cargo:rustc-link-search` and `cargo:rustc-link-lib` directives.
  2. Cargo then compiles `src/main.rs`.
  3. During the linking phase, Cargo uses the directives from `build.rs` to find and link `libmy_c_lib.a` with the compiled Rust code.

To run this example, do the following:

1. Save `my_c_lib.c` and `my_c_lib.h`.
2. Compile them into `libmy_c_lib.a` (or `.lib`) and place it in the root of your `rust_ffi_example` project.
3. Create `build.rs` and `src/main.rs` as shown.
4. Run `cargo run` from the `rust_ffi_example` directory.

You should see output from both Rust's `println!` and the C library's `printf` (via `greet_person`), demonstrating successful FFI calls. This example, while simple, covers the essential steps of declaring, linking, and safely wrapping calls to a custom C library.

Having covered user-space, we'll now see how Rust is used at a much deeper level: the OS kernel itself!

A glimpse into kernel module development with Rust

So far in our exploration of system programming, we've primarily dealt with user-space applications – programs that run under the supervision and protection of the operating system. Now, we're going to take a conceptual peek into a much deeper layer: **kernel module development**.

This involves writing code that runs directly within the operating system kernel itself. Rust, with its focus on safety and performance, is an increasingly interesting candidate for this demanding domain, traditionally dominated by C.

The unique environment of kernel space

Writing code for the kernel is fundamentally different from writing user-space applications. The kernel operates with the highest privileges and has direct access to hardware. This power comes with immense responsibility:

- **No safety net (almost)**: Unlike user-space programs, where the OS can often isolate and terminate a misbehaving process, a bug in a kernel module (such as a null pointer dereference or a buffer overflow) can crash the *entire system*. This is why memory safety is paramount.
- **Limited standard library**: Your typical `std` library, with its convenient abstractions for things such as strings, vectors, file I/O, and networking, is generally not available in the kernel. These features rely on OS services that the kernel *provides*, not consumes. Kernel code must often be written using `#![no_std]`, relying only on the Rust core library (`core`) and potentially a minimal allocation library (`alloc`).

- **Direct hardware interaction**: Kernel modules often need to interact directly with hardware registers, manage memory explicitly, and handle interrupts.
- **Concurrency is intrinsic**: The kernel is inherently concurrent. Multiple parts of the kernel can be executing simultaneously, and interrupt handlers can preempt regular kernel code. Synchronization primitives are even more critical here.
- **Different error handling**: Panicking in a kernel module is usually catastrophic. Error handling often involves returning error codes or using specific kernel mechanisms.
- **Resource management is manual and critical**: Memory allocation, if needed, is done via kernel-specific allocators, and all resources must be meticulously managed and released.

Despite these challenges, the desire to use Rust for kernel development is driven by its potential to bring greater memory safety to this critical layer of software, reducing the likelihood of common C vulnerabilities.

Essential setup for Rust kernel development

Developing kernel modules in Rust requires a more specialized setup than typical user-space applications. The exact steps can vary depending on the target operating system (Linux, macOS, Windows, though Linux is currently the most common target for Rust kernel experiments).

no_std and target specifications

As mentioned, kernel modules are typically built as `#![no_std]` crates. This means you don't have access to the Rust standard library, which depends on OS abstractions. You'll primarily use the following:

- `core`: The Rust core library, providing fundamental types (such as `Option`, `Result`, primitive types, and iterators) and macros that don't require an underlying OS.
- `alloc` (optional): If you need dynamic memory allocation (e.g., for `Box`, `Vec`, `String`), you can enable the `alloc` crate, but you'll also need to provide or link against a kernel-compatible memory allocator.

You'll also need to compile your Rust code for a specific **target triple** that matches the kernel's architecture and environment (e.g., `x86_64-unknown-linux-gnu` for a 64-bit Linux kernel, but often a custom target specification is needed for `#![no_std]` freestanding environments). This might involve using `rustup target add` or even creating a custom target JSON file.

Cross-compilation is common, meaning you compile the kernel module on your development machine (e.g., an x86_64 Linux desktop) for a different target architecture if necessary (e.g., an ARM-based embedded device).

Basic module structure (init/exit functions, logging)

Most operating systems (like Linux) expect kernel modules to have a specific structure, typically including the following:

- **Initialization function**: A function that is called when the module is loaded into the kernel. This function registers the module's functionality, allocates resources, and so on. In Linux, this is often equivalent to a function marked with `module_init()`. In Rust FFI terms, this might be an extern "C" `fn init_module() -> c_int`.
- **Exit (or Cleanup) Function:** A function that is called when the module is unloaded. This function unregisters functionality and frees any resources acquired by the init_module function. In Linux, this is often a function marked with `module_exit()`. In Rust FFI, this might be `extern "C" fn cleanup_module()`.
- **Licensing and metadata**: Information about the module's license (e.g., GPL), author, and description.

Kernel-level logging: Standard `println!` doesn't work in the kernel. Instead, you need to use the kernel's specific logging mechanism. For Linux, this is `printk`. To call `printk` from Rust, you'd typically declare it as an `extern "C"` function and call it within an `unsafe` block, often wrapping it in a safe Rust macro or function for convenience.

```
// --- STEP-BY-STEP: HOW TO RUN THIS KERNEL MODULE ---
//
// Since this is a specialized "no_std" library, you cannot just run it in
an existing bin crate.
// Follow these exact steps:
//
// 1. CREATE NEW CRATE:
//    Open your terminal and run:
//    $ cargo new --lib my_kernel_module
//    $ cd my_kernel_module
//
// 2. UPDATE Cargo.toml:
//    Open `Cargo.toml` and append these lines to handle panic/crate-type:
//
```

```
//    [lib]
//    crate-type = ["staticlib"]
//
//    [profile.dev]
//    panic = "abort"
//
//    [profile.release]
//    panic = "abort"
//
// 3. REPLACE CODE:
//    Replace the contents of `src/lib.rs` with the code below.
//
// 4. BUILD:
//    Run:
//    $ cargo build
//
//    (Success is seeing "Finished dev target(s)")

// We don't have the standard library in the kernel
#![no_std]

// Example feature for more detailed panics (requires nightly Rust)
// #![feature(panic_info_message)]

use core::ffi::{c_char, c_int}; // For C types
use core::panic::PanicInfo;

// --- Simulate printk via FFI ---
// FIXED: `extern` blocks must be marked `unsafe` in newer Rust versions
(Edition 2024+).
unsafe extern "C" {
    fn printk(fmt: *const c_char, ...) -> c_int;
}

// A safe wrapper for our simplified printk
fn kprint(message: &str) {
    // Create a fixed-size buffer for the message.
```

```
    let mut buffer = [0u8; 256];
    let mut len = 0;

    for (i, byte) in message.bytes().enumerate() {
        if i < buffer.len() - 1 { // Leave space for null terminator
            buffer[i] = byte;
            len = i + 1;
        } else {
            break; // Message too long for buffer
        }
    }

    buffer[len] = 0; // Null terminate

    unsafe {
        printk(buffer.as_ptr() as *const c_char);
    }
}

// --- Module Initialization and Exit ---

// FIXED: `#[no_mangle]` is unsafe in newer Rust. We use `#[unsafe(no_
mangle)]`.
#[unsafe(no_mangle)]
pub extern "C" fn my_rust_module_init() -> c_int {
    kprint("Hello from Rust Kernel Module! Init function called.\n");
    0
}

#[unsafe(no_mangle)]
pub extern "C" fn my_rust_module_exit() {
    kprint("Goodbye from Rust Kernel Module! Exit function called.\n");
}

// --- Panic Handler ---

#[panic_handler]
```

```
fn panic(info: &PanicInfo) -> ! {
    kprint("KERNEL PANIC in Rust module: ");

    if let Some(location) = info.location() {
        kprint("at file '");
        kprint(location.file());
        kprint("' line '...' ");
    }

    kprint("\n");

    loop {}
}
```

To test this code:

1. Create a new library: `$ cargo new --lib my_kernel_module $ cd my_kernel_module`
2. Configure Cargo.toml: Add these lines to `Cargo.toml` to support `no_std` (abort on panic):

   ```
   [lib] crate-type = ["staticlib"]

   [profile.dev] panic = "abort"

   [profile.release] panic = "abort"
   ```

3. Add the Code: `Replace src/lib.rs` with the provided code.
4. Build: Run `$ cargo` build. (You cannot use cargo run because this is a kernel library, not an executable).

- `#![no_std]`: Indicates that we are not linking against the Rust standard library.
- `extern crate alloc; (Optional)`: If you needed dynamic memory allocation (e.g., for `Box`, `Vec`, `String`), you'd include this and also need to provide a global memory allocator that is compatible with the kernel environment. For very simple modules, you might avoid `alloc`.
- `extern "C" { fn printk(...); }`: This is an FFI declaration for the kernel's `printk` function (or a similar logging function). The actual signature of `printk` is variadic and more complex; this is a simplification. In practice, you'd use a crate that provides safe bindings.

- `kprint` function: A simple safe wrapper around our FFI `printk` declaration. It attempts to convert a Rust `&str` to a null-terminated byte sequence suitable for `printk`. This is non-trivial without `alloc` for `CString`; the example uses a fixed-size buffer.
- `#[no_mangle] pub extern "C" fn my_rust_module_init() -> c_int`: This defines our module initialization function.
    - `#[no_mangle]`: Prevents the Rust compiler from changing the function's name, so it can be found by the kernel's module loader if it expects a C-style symbol name.
    - `extern "C"`: Specifies that this function should use the C calling convention.
    - It returns a `c_int` (typically 0 for success, non-zero for failure on Linux).
- `#[no_mangle] pub extern "C" fn my_rust_module_exit()`: This defines the module cleanup function.
- `#[panic_handler]`: A `#![no_std]` application (such as a kernel module) must define what happens when a Rust `panic!` occurs. This function is called by the Rust runtime when a panic is triggered. In a real module, you'd log detailed information using `printk` and then likely trigger a kernel oops or a safe halt. Looping indefinitely is a minimal "do nothing more" strategy.

Building, loading, and further considerations

Having sketched out the basic Rust code structure for a kernel module, the next steps involve actually compiling this Rust code into a loadable kernel object, getting it into the kernel, and being aware of the significant complexities and responsibilities that come with kernel development.

Compilation and loading process

Compiling Rust code into a format that a specific operating system kernel (such as Linux) can load as a module is more involved than a typical `cargo build`. It requires a specialized build process:

1. `cargo build` with a kernel target: You'd compile your Rust `#![no_std]` crate using `cargo build`, but you'd specify a target triple appropriate for the kernel environment (e.g., `x86_64-unknown-linux-gnu` with specific features disabled, or a custom bare-metal target). This produces an object file (e.g., `.o` or `.rlib`).
2. **Kernel build system integration (e.g., Makefile/Kbuild for Linux)**: The object file produced by Cargo usually isn't directly loadable as a kernel module. You typically need to integrate with the kernel's own build system. For Linux, this means creating a Makefile and a Kbuild file.

- The Makefile would invoke the kernel's build process, pointing it to your Rust object file(s).
- The Kbuild file tells the kernel build system which object files comprise your module. The kernel's build system then takes your Rust object file, links it against necessary kernel symbols, and produces the final loadable kernel module (e.g., a .ko file on Linux).

A Makefile is a classic build automation file used heavily in C and C++ projects. It's a text file (simply named `Makefile`) that tells the `make` command how to compile and link a program. You can think of it as a "recipe": it defines "targets" (like your final executable) and their "dependencies" (the source files). `make` then runs the specified commands (such as `gcc`) and is smart enough to only rebuild the parts of your program that have actually changed, saving a lot of time

Conceptual Makefile (for Linux):

```
# Makefile (Simplified)
# Assumes your Rust crate compiles to librust_kernel_module.a or
similar
# Or directly uses object files if configured properly

# Name of your kernel module object
obj-m += my_rust_module.o

# Specify the source files for your module object
# This might point to the .o file generated from your Rust lib.rs
my_rust_module-objs := path/to/your/rust_compiled_object.o
# Or, if linking a static library from Rust:
# my_rust_module-objs := main_loader.o # A small C stub
# EXTRA_LDFLAGS += path/to/your/librust_kernel_module.a

all:
	make -C /lib/modules/$(shell uname -r)/build M=$(PWD) modules

clean:
	make -C /lib/modules/$(shell uname -r)/build M=$(PWD) clean
```

This is highly simplified; real kernel Makefiles for Rust modules often involve more steps to correctly invoke Cargo and link the resulting static library or object files. Crates such as `kernel_module_builder` or established Rust-for-Linux project templates aim to simplify this.

3. **Loading the module**: Once you have a `.ko` file (on Linux), you load it into the running kernel, typically using the `insmod` command (as superuser):

```
sudo insmod ./my_rust_module.ko
```

If successful, your module's `init` function (e.g., `my_rust_module_init`) is called.

4. **Verifying and unloading**:

   - You can check if the module is loaded using `lsmod | grep my_rust_module`.
   - You can view kernel messages (including those from your module's `kprint` or `printk` calls) using `dmesg`.
   - To unload the module, you use `rmmod` (as superuser), which will call your module's `exit` function (e.g., `my_rust_module_exit`):

   ```
   sudo rmmod my_rust_module
   ```

This process requires correctly installed kernel headers for your running kernel version and often involves a bit of trial and error to get the build system and linker flags right.

Important caveats and next steps for exploration

Kernel module development, especially in a language newer to the space, like Rust, is an advanced topic with significant considerations:

- **Take extreme caution with unsafe**: While much of your Rust module logic can be safe, interactions with kernel APIs, direct memory manipulation, and hardware access will inevitably require `unsafe` blocks. These must be handled with extreme care, as errors can crash the entire system.
- **Kernel API stability**: Kernel internal APIs can change between versions, potentially breaking your module. Writing modules that rely only on stable kernel ABIs is preferred, but not always possible for deep integration.
- **Error handling**: Panicking in a kernel module is generally fatal to the system or at least the current operation. Errors must be handled gracefully, often by returning error codes understood by the kernel.

- **Concurrency**: The kernel is highly concurrent. Any shared data within your module must be protected by appropriate kernel synchronization primitives (spinlocks, mutexes, etc.), which you'd access via the FFI or Rust wrappers.
- **Memory allocation**: If you need dynamic memory, you must use kernel-specific allocators (e.g., `kmalloc`). The `alloc` crate in Rust can be used if a global allocator compatible with the kernel's mechanisms is provided.
- **Tooling and ecosystem**: While efforts such as Rust for Linux are rapidly maturing the ecosystem for kernel development in Rust, it's still a newer area compared to C. Tooling for debugging Rust kernel modules (beyond `printk`) might also be less mature than for C.
- **Specific OS**: The details provided here are heavily influenced by Linux kernel module development. Other operating systems (Windows, macOS) have different mechanisms and levels of support for kernel modules written in languages other than C/C++.

Further exploration: If you're serious about Rust kernel development, you should look into the following:

- The "Rust for Linux" project and its documentation
- Crates providing safe bindings to kernel APIs
- Examples of existing Rust kernel modules
- Detailed guides on setting up the build environment for your specific target kernel and architecture

This "glimpse" is intended to show that it's *possible* and increasingly practical to write kernel-level code in Rust, leveraging its safety features to reduce common bugs. However, it remains a challenging and advanced area of system programming requiring deep knowledge of both Rust and operating system internals.

Summary

And with that, we've reached the end of *Chapter 15*, our exploration into the world of system programming with Rust! We've seen how Rust's core features, designed for safety and performance, make it a strong contender for tasks that require low-level control and direct interaction with the operating system and even other programming languages. While system programming can be intricate, Rust provides tools that help manage this complexity with a degree of safety that is often hard to achieve elsewhere.

Let's recap what we've journeyed through in this chapter:

- **Rust for system-level tasks:** We began by defining system programming and highlighting why Rust's unique combination of memory safety without a garbage collector, C-level performance, fearless concurrency (though not the focus of this chapter), and low-level control makes it an excellent choice for this domain.
- **Low-level programming foundations**: We revisited Rust's memory model, emphasizing the importance of understanding ownership, borrowing, and the distinction between stack and heap allocation from a systems perspective. A crucial part of this was venturing into **unsafe Rust**. We discussed when and why unsafe is necessary, the "superpowers" it grants (such as dereferencing raw pointers and calling `unsafe` functions), and the added responsibility it places on the developer. We also touched upon best practices for encapsulating unsafe code to maintain overall program safety.
- **Building practical command-line utilities**: We then applied these concepts to a common system programming task: creating CLI tools. We covered designing a simple utility, parsing command-line arguments (using both the standard library's `std::env::args()` for basic needs and acknowledging powerful crates such as clap for more complex scenarios), interacting with the file system (`std::fs` for reading, writing, and directory operations), and handling standard input, output, and error streams.
- **Interfacing with C code (FFI)**: A significant portion of the chapter was dedicated to Rust's **Foreign Function Interface** (FFI). We learned why FFI is vital for leveraging existing C libraries and for interoperability. This included the following:
    - Declaring external C functions using `extern "C"` blocks
    - Linking against C libraries, either via the `#[link]` attribute or, more commonly for custom libraries, using `build.rs` scripts
    - The intricacies of **passing data between Rust and C**, covering primitive types, C-compatible strings (`CString`, `CStr`), and ensuring Rust structs match C struct layouts with `#[repr(C)]`
    - The importance of creating **safe Rust wrappers** around unsafe FFI calls to provide an idiomatic and secure interface for the rest of your Rust code
    - We walked through a practical example of building and using a simple custom C library from Rust

By working through these areas, you gained insight into how Rust enables you to write code that can operate close to the system, interact with existing C code bases, and build useful command-line tools, all while benefiting from Rust's modern features and safety emphasis. These are valuable skills for any developer looking to expand their capabilities beyond application-level programming.

We've now built powerful, low-level Rust applications; in the next chapter, we'll learn how to package and deploy them reliably to any machine using Docker.

Questions and assignments

Questions

1. What are the primary reasons a Rust programmer might need to use an `unsafe` block or an unsafe `fn`? Give two distinct scenarios.
2. List three key differences between Rust's safe references (`&T`, `&mut T`) and raw pointers (`*const T`, `*mut T`).
3. When you declare an external C function using `extern "C" { ... }`, why is calling that function from Rust considered an unsafe operation?
4. What is the purpose of the `#[repr(C)]` attribute when defining a Rust struct that needs to be passed to or received from C code?
5. Describe the basic mechanism for reading command-line arguments in Rust using the standard library. What are some limitations of this basic approach for more complex CLI tools?
6. Why is it a good practice for CLI tools to print error messages to standard error (`stderr`) and normal output to standard output (`stdout`)?
7. What is a `build.rs` script, and what role does it typically play when working with FFI to link against C libraries?
8. What is the main principle behind creating "safe Rust wrappers" around unsafe FFI calls?

Assignment

Enhanced command-line file analyzer

Goal: Extend a basic file analysis tool with more features, focusing on argument parsing and file system interaction.

Task: Building on the concepts of a `mini_grep`-like tool or the `wc`-like tool we discussed:

1. Create a new binary Rust project (e.g., `cargo new file_inspector --bin`).
2. Your tool should accept the following command-line arguments:
   - A mandatory file path.
   - An optional flag, say `-c` or `--chars`, to count only characters.
   - An optional flag, say `-w` or `--words`, to count only words.
   - An optional flag, say `-l` or `--lines`, to count only lines.
   - If no flags (`-c`, `-w`, `-l`) are provided, it should print all three counts (lines, words, characters). If one or more flags are provided, it should only print the counts corresponding to those flags.
3. Argument parsing:
   - For a basic implementation, try to parse these arguments using only `std::env::args()`. This will be a good exercise in manual parsing. You'll need to iterate through the arguments, check for your flags, and identify the file path.
   - (Optional challenge): If you're feeling adventurous, try using a crate such as clap to define and parse these arguments more robustly.
4. File processing:
   - Read the specified file line by line.
   - Implement the logic to count lines, words (simply split by whitespace), and characters (UTF-8 aware).
5. Output:
   - Print the requested counts to standard output.
   - Handle errors (e.g., file not found, invalid arguments) by printing messages to standard error and exiting with a non-zero status code.

Example usage:

```
./file_inspector my_document.txt # Prints lines, words, and chars
./file_inspector --lines my_document.txt # Prints only line count
./file_inspector -w -c my_document.txt # Prints word and char counts
```

What this practices: Manual command-line argument parsing (or using a crate), file reading, string manipulation, and standard CLI output/error handling.

16

Dockerization and Deployment of Rust Applications

We're now at the stage where you've likely built some impressive Rust applications, whether they are command-line tools, web servers, or system utilities. The next crucial step in the software life cycle is figuring out how to package, distribute, and run these applications reliably in different environments – from your development machine to testing servers and ultimately to production.

This is where **Docker** and the concept of **containerization** come into play, and they've become indispensable tools in modern software deployment.

What is Docker? An overview

At its core, Docker is an open source platform that automates the deployment, scaling, and management of applications by using **containers**. Think of a container as a standardized, lightweight, standalone, executable package of software that includes everything needed to run an application: the code, runtime, system tools, system libraries, and settings. It's like a neatly packed box where your application lives, isolated from the outside world.

Docker provides the ability to do the following:

- **Build** container images from a specification called a Dockerfile
- **Share** these images via registries such as Docker Hub
- **Run** these images as containers on any system that has Docker installed

This approach solves many common problems in software deployment and has revolutionized how developers build and ship applications.

A quick clarification: Do I need Docker for every project?

Before we dive in, it's important to set expectations. As a beginner, you might wonder whether you need to use Docker for every Rust program you write, even a simple `cargo run` application.

The short answer is: absolutely not!

Docker is a tool for deployment and environment management. It's incredibly powerful, but it *does* add a layer of complexity. You now have to think about images, containers, volumes, and networking, which isn't necessary when you're just learning or building a simple local tool.

So, when should you use it?

For learning: In this chapter, when you want to learn the *process* of shipping an application.

For complex setups: When your Rust app needs other services to run, such as the PostgreSQL database from our last chapter. Docker Compose makes this kind of setup easier.

For deployment: When you are ready to ship your application to a server, Docker is one of the best ways to ensure it runs the same way on the server as it did on your machine.

For all the simple CLI tools and basic examples in this book, just using `cargo run` is the perfect and correct way to build and run your code. Think of this chapter as the next step: preparing your application to be shared and run in the real world.

Key benefits of using Docker

So, why has Docker become so popular, and what are its main advantages, especially when we think about our Rust applications?

- **Consistency across environments**: This is a huge one. Docker containers ensure that your application runs in the exact same environment regardless of where it's deployed: be it your local development machine, a colleague's machine, a staging server, or the production cloud. The container packages all dependencies, so you can say goodbye to the classic "but it works on my machine!" problem.

- **Isolation and dependency management**: Each Docker container runs in its own isolated environment, with its own filesystem, processes, and network interface (if configured). This means your Rust application inside a container won't conflict with other applications or system libraries on the host machine, and its dependencies are self-contained. This makes managing complex dependency trees much simpler.
- **Resource efficiency and scalability**: Containers are much more lightweight than traditional **virtual machines (VMs)** because they share the host system's operating system kernel instead of emulating a full one. This efficiency means they consume fewer resources (CPU and memory) and generally start up significantly faster. It's important to remember, however, that startup time is not instant. The final "cold start" performance will still depend on the size of your container image and the time your Rust application needs to initialize; a large application with extensive setup will still take time to become ready. This overall efficiency makes it easier to scale your application up or down by simply starting or stopping container instances, allowing you to run a higher density of applications on the same hardware.
- **Portability and simplified deployment**: Once you've built a Docker image for your Rust application, that image can run on any system that has Docker installed – Windows, macOS, Linux, cloud servers, and so on. This "build once, run anywhere" capability greatly simplifies the deployment process. You're no longer deploying your application *and* its myriad dependencies; you're deploying a self-contained container.
- **Version control and rollback for images**: Docker images are typically built in layers and can be versioned using tags. This allows you to easily track changes to your application environment and, if something goes wrong with a new deployment, quickly roll back to a previous, stable version of your container image.

Why Dockerize Rust applications specifically?

While the general benefits of Docker apply to most languages, there are specific advantages when it comes to Rust:

- **Simplified deployment of compiled binaries**: Rust compiles to a native binary. Docker allows you to package this binary along with only the necessary runtime dependencies (which for Rust can be very minimal, especially with `musl` or static linking) into a small, efficient container. This avoids needing to install Rust toolchains or specific library versions on every server you deploy to.

- **Consistent build environment**: You can use Docker to create a consistent build environment for your Rust application itself. This ensures that your application is always compiled with the correct Rust version and build tools, regardless of the developer's local setup or the CI/CD server's configuration. We'll see this with multi-stage Dockerfiles.
- **Leveraging Rust's performance**: Rust's efficiency means your Docker containers can be very lean and performant. A well-optimized Rust application in a minimal Docker container can handle significant load with a small resource footprint.
- **Cross-compilation and targeting**: While Rust has good cross-compilation capabilities, Docker can sometimes simplify building for different target architectures (such as ARM for Raspberry Pi or cloud instances) by using base images or build tools specific to that architecture within the Docker build process.

Chapter objectives: What you'll learn

In this chapter, our goal is to get you comfortable with the fundamentals of Docker and how to apply it to your Rust projects. We will cover the following topics:

- Setting up Docker on your development machine
- Understanding basic Docker concepts such as images and containers, and common commands
- Writing a Dockerfile to package a Rust application into a Docker image
- Optimizing your Rust Docker images for size and build speed using techniques such as multi-stage builds
- Briefly looking at Docker Compose for managing multi-container applications (e.g., your Rust app and a database)
- An overview of deploying your Dockerized Rust applications, including using container registries and conceptual deployment to cloud platforms
- Key best practices for Dockerization and production deployments

By the end of this chapter, you should be able to take a Rust application you've built, package it into an efficient Docker container, and have a good understanding of how to get it running in various environments. Let's containerize!

Getting started with Docker

Before we can package our Rust applications into containers, we first need Docker installed and running on our system. We also need to understand a few fundamental Docker concepts and commands.

This section will guide you through the initial setup and introduce you to the basics of interacting with Docker.

Setting up your Docker environment

The first step is to get Docker onto your machine. The installation process varies slightly depending on your operating system, but it's generally quite straightforward.

Installing Docker Desktop (Windows, macOS, and Linux)

The most common way to use Docker on a personal computer is via **Docker Desktop**. It's an easy-to-install application that provides Docker Engine (the core runtime), the Docker **command-line interface** (**CLI**) tool, Docker Compose (for multi-container applications), and other helpful utilities:

1. **Visit the official Docker website**: Go to `www.docker.com` and navigate to the **Get Started** or **Downloads** section.
2. **Download Docker Desktop**: The website should automatically detect your operating system and offer the appropriate download for the following:
   - **Windows**: Docker Desktop for Windows.
   - **macOS**: Docker Desktop for Mac (available for both Intel and Apple Silicon chips).
   - **Linux**: Docker Desktop for Linux is available, but many Linux users opt to install Docker Engine and the Docker CLI directly using their distribution's package manager (e.g., `apt` for Debian/Ubuntu or `yum`/`dnf` for Fedora/CentOS). Detailed instructions for this are also available on the Docker website. If you choose Docker Desktop for Linux, it provides a nice GUI and integrates well.
3. **Follow installation instructions**: Once downloaded, run the installer and follow the on-screen prompts provided by Docker for your specific operating system. This usually involves a few clicks and potentially a system restart:
   - On Windows, Docker Desktop often uses **Windows Subsystem for Linux 2** (**WSL 2**) as its backend, which might require you to enable WSL 2 if you haven't already. The Docker installer usually guides you through this.

- On macOS, it's a standard application installation.
- On Linux, if using Docker Desktop, follow their specific instructions. If installing Docker Engine directly, consult the Docker documentation for your Linux distribution (e.g., *Install Docker Engine on Ubuntu*).

It's a good idea to ensure your system meets the minimum requirements listed on the Docker website before installation.

Verifying your Docker installation

After the installation is complete (and Docker Desktop is running, if applicable), you can verify that Docker is installed correctly and accessible from your command line.

Open your terminal or command prompt and type the following:

```
docker --version
```

If Docker is installed properly, this command should output the Docker version information, something like this (your version number will likely be different):

```
Docker version 26.x.x., build 123456
```

You can also check the Docker daemon (the background service) status with the following:

```
docker info
```

This command provides a lot of information about your Docker installation, including the number of containers and images, the storage driver, and the kernel version. If it runs without error, your Docker environment is likely ready to go!

If you encounter issues, the Docker documentation and community forums are excellent resources for troubleshooting installation problems. With Docker installed, we can now explore some of its essential concepts.

Essential Docker concepts

Docker is a powerful and extensive platform, and entire books and comprehensive courses are dedicated to mastering its intricacies. Its ecosystem covers everything from simple container execution to complex orchestration of microservices. For the purpose of this chapter, we're going to focus on just the very basics you need to get your Rust applications containerized and running.

This section will be a quick overview. If you're already quite familiar with Docker concepts such as images, containers, and registries, you might find this to be a review and could skim or skip ahead to the parts about Dockerizing Rust applications specifically. For everyone else, these are the core ideas we'll build upon.

Images and containers: The core building blocks

The two most fundamental concepts in the Docker world are **images** and **containers**:

- **Docker image**: Think of an image as a **blueprint** or a **template**. It's a lightweight, standalone, executable package that includes everything needed to run a piece of software, including the code (or compiled binary), a runtime, system tools, system libraries, and settings. Images are read-only. When you want to run your application, you use its image. You create images by writing a Dockerfile (which we'll do soon for our Rust app), or you can pull pre-built images from a registry such as Docker Hub (e.g., an image for a database such as PostgreSQL, or an image containing the Rust toolchain). Images are built in layers, which makes them efficient to store and share.
- **Docker container**: A container is a runnable instance of an image. If an image is the blueprint, a container is the actual house built from that blueprint. You can create many containers from the same image. Each container runs as an isolated process on your host machine's kernel, but it has its own filesystem, network interface, and process space, all derived from the image. It's important to remember that while containers are far more lightweight than full VMs, they are not free; each running container still consumes a portion of the host's memory and CPU. This means your system's available resources will ultimately limit how many containers you can run. Containers are where your application actually lives and executes, and they can be started, stopped, moved, and deleted. The relationship is often described as: an image is a class, and a container is an instance of that class.

Docker Hub and container registries

Once you've built a Docker image, you often need a place to store it and share it, especially if you want to deploy your application on other machines or collaborate with a team. This is where **container registries** come in:

- **Docker Hub**: This is the largest and most well-known public container registry, operated by Docker, Inc. It hosts a vast number of official images for popular software (e.g., operating systems such as Ubuntu, databases such as MySQL and PostgreSQL, and programming language runtimes such as Rust, Python, and Node). You can also create an account and push your own public or private images to Docker Hub.
- **Other registries**: Besides Docker Hub, many other container registries exist, both public and private. Cloud providers such as **Amazon Web Services Elastic Container Registry** (**AWS ECR**), **Google Container Registry** (**GCR**) and Artifact Registry, and Microsoft **Azure Container Registry** (**ACR**) offer their own managed registries. Companies often host private registries for their internal images.

When you run a command such as `docker run rust`, Docker first checks whether you have the Rust image locally. If not, it automatically tries to pull it from Docker Hub (by default). When we build our own Rust application image, we'll be able to "push" it to a registry to make it available for deployment.

Basic Docker commands for interaction

The Docker CLI is your primary way of managing Docker images, containers, volumes, and networks. Most commands start with `docker` followed by a subcommand (such as `run`, `ps`, and `images`). You can always run `docker --help` or `docker <subcommand> --help` for more details.

Running a container: docker run

The `docker run` command is used to create and start a new container from a specified image. It's one of the most versatile Docker commands with many options.

Its basic usage looks as follows: `docker run <image_name_or_id>`.

This will download the image if it's not already local (usually from Docker Hub by default) and then start a new container based on it.

The following are other common options:

- `-it` (or `-i -t`): Often used together:
    - `-i` (`--interactive`): Keeps `STDIN` open even if not attached.
    - `-t` (`--tty`): Allocates a pseudo-TTY (which stands for **teletype**), which gives you an interactive terminal session inside the container. This is essential if you want to run a shell or an interactive program inside the container.
- `-d` (`--detach`): Runs the container in the background (detached mode) and prints the new container ID. The container will keep running until its main process exits or it's stopped.
- `--name <container_name>`: Assigns a custom name to your container, making it easier to refer to later. If you don't provide a name, Docker assigns a random one.
- `-p <host_port>:<container_port>` (or `--publish <host_port>:<container_port>`): Publishes a container's port(s) to the host. This maps a port on your host machine to a port inside the container, allowing you to access services running in the container from your host (e.g., a web server).
- `-v <host_path>:<container_path>` (or `--volume <host_path>:<container_path>`): Mounts a volume from the host machine into the container. This is useful for persisting data or providing configuration files to the container.
- `--rm`: Automatically removes the container when it exits. Very handy for short-lived tasks or testing to avoid cluttering your system with stopped containers.
- `-e <VAR_NAME>=<value>` (or `--env <VAR_NAME>=<value>`): Sets environment variables inside the container.

For example, let's run a simple `hello-world` container (a very small image designed to test Docker installations) and then an interactive Ubuntu shell:

```
# 1. Run the basic "hello-world" container.
# It prints a message and exits.
docker run hello-world

# 2\. Run an interactive Ubuntu shell, assign a name, and automatically
remove it when done.

# This will pull the 'ubuntu:latest' image if you don't have it.

# You'll be dropped into a bash shell inside the Ubuntu container.
```

```
# Type 'exit' to leave the shell and stop/remove the container.

docker run -it --rm --name my\_ubuntu\_shell ubuntu:latest bash

# 3\. Run a detached Nginx web server, mapping port 8080 on your host

# to port 80 inside the container.

docker run -d --name my\_nginx\_server -p 8080:80 nginx:latest

# After this, you should be able to open http://localhost:8080 in your
browser

# to see the Nginx welcome page. We'll stop and remove this later.
```

- The first command runs `hello-world`. Docker downloads it (if needed) and runs it, then it prints a message and the container exits.
- The second command starts an Ubuntu container. `-it` gives you an interactive shell (Bash). `--rm` means when you type `exit` in the container's shell, the container is automatically removed. `--name` gives it a friendly name.
- The third command starts an Nginx web server in detached mode (`-d`), names it `my_nginx_server`, and maps port `8080` on your host machine to port `80` inside the Nginx container (which is Nginx's default port).

Listing containers: docker ps

The `docker ps` command is used to list containers:

- `docker ps`: Shows only currently *running* containers
- `docker ps -a` (or `--all`): Shows all containers, including stopped ones

```
# List currently running containers
docker ps

# List all containers (running and stopped)

docker ps -a
```

The output will show information such as container ID, image used, command being run, when it was created, its status (e.g., `Up 5 minutes` or `Exited (0) 2 hours ago`), ports mapped, and names. This is your go-to command for seeing what's happening with your containers.

Managing images: docker images, docker pull, and docker rmi

You'll also need to use commands to manage the Docker images stored on your local machine:

- `docker images`: Lists all Docker images you have locally.
- `docker pull <image_name>:<tag>`: Downloads an image (or a specific version/tag of an image) from a registry (Docker Hub by default) to your local machine. Examples are `docker pull rust:latest` or `docker pull postgres:15`.
- `docker rmi <image_name_or_id> (remove image)`: Deletes one or more images from your local machine. You usually can't remove an image if it's being used by any existing container (even a stopped one). You might need to remove the containers first.
- `docker rmi -f <image_name_or_id>`: Forces removal (use with caution).

```
# List local images
docker images

# Pull the latest Alpine Linux image

docker pull alpine:latest

# List images again to see alpine

docker images

# Remove the alpine image (assuming no containers are using it)

# You might need its ID if just 'alpine:latest' refers to multiple
things.

# docker rmi alpine:latest
```

These commands help you manage the storage used by Docker images and ensure you have the images you need for running containers.

Stopping and removing containers: docker stop and docker rm

When you're done with a container, you might want to stop it (if it's running) and then remove it (to free up resources):

- `docker stop <container_name_or_id>`: Stops one or more running containers gracefully (by sending a `SIGTERM` signal, then `SIGKILL` after a timeout)
- `docker start <container_name_or_id>`: Starts one or more stopped containers
- `docker rm <container_name_or_id>`: Removes one or more stopped containers
- `docker rm -f <container_name_or_id>`: Forces removal of a container (even if running, though it's better to stop it first)

```
# Let's assume our 'my_nginx_server' from the 'docker run' example
is still running.
# If not, you can start one: docker run -d --name my_nginx_server -p
8080:80 nginx:latest

# List running containers to find its name/ID

docker ps

# Stop the Nginx server container

# Replace 'my\_nginx\_server' with the actual name or ID if
different

docker stop my\_nginx\_server

# Verify it's stopped (it should now appear in 'docker ps -a' but
not 'docker ps')

docker ps
docker ps -a

# Remove the stopped container

docker rm my\_nginx\_server
```

```
# Verify it's removed

docker ps -a
```

It's good practice to clean up containers you no longer need to free up system resources and keep your Docker environment tidy. Remember, running `docker run --rm ...` is often useful for temporary containers as it handles removal automatically when the container exits.

These basic commands (`run`, `ps`, `images`, `stop`, `rm`, and `pull`) form the foundation of daily Docker interaction. As we move to Dockerizing our Rust application, we'll primarily focus on `docker build` (to create an image from a Dockerfile) and `docker run` (to run it).

Dockerizing your Rust application

We've set up Docker and learned some basic commands. Now, the core task is to create a **Dockerfile**. This special file is the recipe Docker uses to build an image containing your Rust application. It specifies everything from the base operating system and Rust toolchain to how your code should be compiled and how the final application should be run.

Once you have a Dockerfile, you can build a portable image that can be run consistently anywhere Docker is installed.

Understanding the Dockerfile

A Dockerfile (note the capitalization, with no file extension) is a simple text file that contains a sequence of instructions. Each instruction tells Docker how to build a layer of your image. When you run `docker build`, Docker reads these instructions, executes them one by one, and creates an image.

Think of a Dockerfile like a script for setting up an environment and installing/running your application, but in a standardized, reproducible way.

Core instructions: FROM, WORKDIR, COPY, RUN, CMD, and EXPOSE

While Dockerfiles can have many instructions, a few are fundamental and appear in almost every Dockerfile:

- `FROM <base_image>:<tag>`:
    - This *must* be the first instruction in a Dockerfile (unless preceded by `ARG`).

  - It specifies the **base image** upon which your image will be built. A base image could be a minimal operating system (such as `debian:buster-slim` or `alpine:latest`), an image with a specific programming language runtime pre-installed (such as `rust:latest` or `node:18`), or even another image you've built previously.
  - For example, `FROM rust:1.78` (uses a specific version of the official Rust image).
- `WORKDIR /path/to/workdir`:
  - Sets the working directory for any subsequent `RUN`, `CMD`, `ENTRYPOINT`, `COPY`, and `ADD` instructions. If the directory doesn't exist, Docker will create it.
  - It's good practice to set a `WORKDIR` early on.
  - For example, `WORKDIR /app`.
- `COPY <src_on_host> <dest_in_container>`:
  - Copies files or directories from your host machine (the build context, usually your project directory) into the filesystem of the Docker image
  - For example, `COPY . .` (copies everything from the current build context on the host to the current `WORKDIR` in the image)
  - For example, `COPY ./target/release/my_app /usr/local/bin/my_app`
- `RUN <command>`:
  - Executes any command in a new layer on top of the current image. This is typically used for installing software packages, compiling your application, creating directories, or setting up permissions. Each `RUN` instruction creates a new image layer, so it's often good to chain related shell commands together using && to reduce the number of layers.
  - For example, `RUN apt-get update && apt-get install -y libssl-dev pkg-config`.
  - For example, `RUN cargo build --release`.
- `CMD ["executable", "param1", "param2"]` (exec form, preferred) or `CMD command param1 param2` (shell form):
  - Specifies the default command to run when a container is started from this image.
  - There can only be one `CMD` instruction in a Dockerfile. If you list more than one `CMD` instruction, only the last one will take effect.

    - The `CMD` instruction can be overridden when you run a container using `docker run <image> <new_command>`.
    - The "exec form" (`CMD ["/usr/local/bin/my_app", "--port", "8080"]`) is generally preferred because it doesn't run in a shell, which avoids potential issues with signal handling or shell string processing.
    - For example, `CMD ["./target/release/my_rust_app"]`.
- `EXPOSE <port>/<protocol>`:
    - Informs Docker that the container listens on the specified network ports at runtime. This instruction does not actually publish the port; it functions as a type of documentation between the person who builds the image and the person who runs the container about which ports are intended to be published.
    - To actually make the port accessible from the host, you use the `-p` or `-P` flag with `docker run`.
    - For example, `EXPOSE 8080/tcp`.
- `ENV <key>=<value>`:
    - Sets an environment variable within the image. This variable will be available to subsequent `RUN` instructions and to the application when the container runs.
    - For example, `ENV APP_PORT=8080`.

These are some of the most common instructions you'll encounter. Understanding them is key to writing effective Dockerfiles for your Rust (or any other) applications. Next, we'll put them together to create a Dockerfile for a simple Rust program.

Creating a basic Dockerfile for a Rust application

The goal here is to create a Docker image that contains our compiled Rust application, ready to run. For this first pass, we'll focus on a simple, single-stage Dockerfile. We'll look at optimizations like multi-stage builds later.

Let's assume you have a simple Rust binary project. For instance, you might have created one with `cargo new my_rust_cli --bin` and have some code in `src/main.rs`. The Dockerfile will live in the root of this `my_rust_cli` project, alongside `Cargo.toml` and the `src` directory.

Choosing a base Rust image

The `FROM` instruction is the first thing in our Dockerfile. We need a base image that provides the Rust toolchain (the `rustc` compiler and the `cargo build` tool) so we can compile our Rust code *inside* the Docker image during the build process.

The official Rust images on Docker Hub are excellent for this. You can choose a specific version (e.g., `rust:1.78.0`) or use a tag such as `rust:latest` (for the latest stable version) or `rust:slim` (which might be a smaller variant of the Rust image). For reproducibility, specifying a version is often better than using `latest`.

So, our Dockerfile will start with the following:

```
FROM rust:1.78 # Or your preferred stable Rust version
```

This tells Docker to use an image that already has Rust 1.78 (or your chosen version) installed.

Copying your project and building

Next, we need to get our Rust project's source code into the image and then compile it:

1. **Set a working directory**: It's good practice to set a working directory inside the image for our application:

   ```
   WORKDIR /usr/src/app
   ```

   Subsequent commands will run relative to this directory.

2. **Copy project files**: We'll copy our `Cargo.toml` and `Cargo.lock` files first, then our `src` directory. Copying `Cargo.toml` and `Cargo.lock` first and running a command to download dependencies can leverage Docker's layer caching effectively (we'll refine this in the optimization section, but for a basic file, just copying everything is simpler to start). For now, let's keep it super simple and copy everything:

   ```
   COPY . .
   ```

   This copies all files and directories from the build context (your project root on the host) into the `/usr/src/app` directory inside the image.

3. **Build the application**: Now that our source code is in the image, we can use `cargo` (which is available from our Rust base image) to compile it. We'll build in release mode for a production-ready binary:

   ```
   RUN cargo build --release
   ```

This command runs `cargo build --release` inside the container.

The compiled binary will typically be placed in `/usr/src/app/target/release/your_app_name` (where `your_app_name` is the name of your crate from `Cargo.toml`).

Setting the CMD to run your compiled binary

Finally, we need to tell Docker what command to run when a container is started from our built image. This is done with the `CMD` instruction. We want to run our compiled Rust application:

```
# Assume your crate name is "my_rust_cli"
CMD ["./target/release/my_rust_cli"]
```

Note: The path is relative to the `WORKDIR` we set earlier (`/usr/src/app`).

Final Dockerfile

Create a file named Dockerfile (no extension) in the root of your `my_rust_cli` project with the following content:

```
# Stage 1: Use an official Rust image as a builder.
# Using a specific version is good for reproducibility.
FROM rust:1.78 AS builder
# You can replace 1.78 with the latest stable version or your project's
specific version.

# Set the working directory in the container.
WORKDIR /usr/src/app

# Copy the Cargo.toml and Cargo.lock files.
# This is done separately to leverage Docker's layer caching for
dependencies.
COPY Cargo.toml Cargo.lock ./

# Build dependencies. This will only rebuild if Cargo.toml or Cargo.lock
changes.
# Create a dummy src/main.rs or src/lib.rs if your project structure needs
it for this step.
# For a binary, we might need a minimal main.rs, or just build everything
after copying all src.
# For simplicity in this first pass, let's just build the target,
# a more optimized caching approach would involve building deps first.
```

```
# RUN cargo build --release --target-dir /usr/src/app/target_deps_only
--bin your_crate_name # (This is more advanced for caching)
# For a basic file, we'll copy all and build.

# Copy all your source code into the working directory.
COPY src ./src

# Build your application in release mode.
# The output will be in /usr/src/app/target/release/your_app_name
RUN cargo build --release

# (This basic Dockerfile is single-stage. Multi-stage for optimization
comes later)
# For a single-stage build like this, the final image will contain the
entire Rust toolchain,
# which makes it quite large. The CMD will run from this image.

# Set the command to run your application.
# Replace "my_rust_cli" with the actual name of your binary (usually your
crate name).
CMD ["./target/release/my_rust_cli"]

# (Optional) If your application is a web server, you might expose a port.
# EXPOSE 8080
```

- `FROM rust:1.78 AS builder`: We start with an official Rust image and name this build stage `builder`. Using a specific version (such as 1.78) is better for reproducible builds than `latest`.
- `WORKDIR /usr/src/app`: Sets the current directory inside the image for subsequent commands.
- `COPY Cargo.toml Cargo.lock ./`: Copies your dependency manifests. A more optimized Dockerfile would run `RUN cargo build --release` (perhaps with a dummy `main.rs`) after this step to cache dependencies separately from source code changes. For this first basic example, we'll simplify things.
- `COPY src ./src`: Copies your source code.

- `RUN cargo build --release`: This is the key step that compiles your Rust application. The `--release` flag ensures it's optimized for production. The output binary will be in `target/release/your_crate_name`.
- `CMD [""./target/release/my_rust_cli""]`: This specifies the command that will be run when a container starts from this image. Replace `my_rust_cli` with the actual name of your executable (which usually matches the name field in your `Cargo.toml`).
- **Image size note**: This basic, single-stage Dockerfile will result in a rather large image because the final image contains the entire Rust toolchain (compiler, `cargo`, source code, and build artifacts). In the *Optimizing Docker images for Rust* section, we'll use a *multi-stage build* to create a much smaller final image containing only the compiled binary and necessary runtime dependencies.
- **EXPOSE (optional)**: If your Rust application were a web server listening on a port (e.g., `8080`), you would add `EXPOSE 8080` to document this. It doesn't actually publish the port; that's done with `docker run -p`.

This simple Dockerfile provides a complete recipe for Docker to build an image containing your compiled Rust application.

Next, we'll see how to actually build the image and run it.

Building Your Docker Image

You've written your Dockerfile, which is the recipe for your application's container image. Now, you need to tell Docker to follow that recipe and create the actual image. This is done using the `docker build` command.

You run this command from your terminal, in the root directory of your Rust project (the same directory where your Dockerfile and `Cargo.toml` are located).

The basic syntax is docker build -t <image_name>:<tag>.

Let's break that down:

- `docker build`: The command to start the image-building process.
- -t <image_name>:<tag> (or --tag <image_name>:<tag>): This is very important. It assigns a **tag** to your image, which is a human-readable name, and optionally a version tag:
    - <image_name>: Usually, this is something such as `your_username/your_app_name` (if you plan to push it to Docker Hub), or just `your_app_name` for local use. Image names are typically lowercase.

    - `:<tag>`: This specifies a version or variant. Common tags are `latest`, `v1.0`, and `stable`. If you omit the tag, Docker defaults to `latest`.
    - For example, `-t my_rust_cli:0.1.0` or `-t myusername/my_rust_cli:latest`.
- `.` (a single dot at the end): This is crucial. It specifies the **build context**. The build context is the set of files and directories at the specified path that Docker can access during the image build process (e.g., for `COPY` instructions). The `.` character means "use the current directory as the build context." Docker will send the contents of this directory (respecting `.dockerignore` if present) to the Docker daemon to build the image.

Assuming your Dockerfile (like the one in the Canvas "Basic Dockerfile for a Rust Application") is in the current directory and your Rust project is named `my_rust_cli`, you would run the following:

```
# Navigate to the root of your Rust project (where Dockerfile and Cargo.
toml are)
# cd /path/to/your/my_rust_cli_project

# Build the Docker image and tag it as "my_rust_cli_app" with the tag
"latest"
docker build -t my_rust_cli_app:latest .
```

When you run `docker build`, you'll see Docker step through each instruction in your Dockerfile:

1. It will pull the base image (`FROM rust:1.78 AS builder` in our example) if it's not already on your system.
2. It will execute each subsequent instruction (`WORKDIR`, `COPY`, and `RUN`) in order, creating a new image layer for each one (or reusing cached layers if possible).
3. The `RUN cargo build --release` step will take the longest, as it involves compiling your entire Rust application. You'll see the `cargo build` output in your terminal.
4. Finally, if all steps succeed, Docker will report that the image was built successfully and tag it with the name you provided (e.g., `my_rust_cli_app:latest`).

After the build completes, you can verify that your image was created by running the following:

```
docker images
```

You should see `my_rust_cli_app` (with the `latest` tag) in the list of your local Docker images.

Docker is smart about caching. If you build an image and then make a small change to your source code (e.g., in `src/main.rs`) but *not* to `Cargo.toml` or `Cargo.lock`, and then run `docker build` again, Docker will reuse the cached layers for the steps that haven't changed (such as downloading the base image and potentially building dependencies if your `COPY` instructions were structured to enable that). This can significantly speed up subsequent builds. The order of instructions in your Dockerfile matters a lot for effective caching.

Running your Rust application inside a Docker container

You've created a Dockerfile and used `docker build` to produce a Docker image (e.g., `my_rust_cli_app:latest`) that packages your Rust application. Now, it's time to bring it to life by running it as a Docker container! The command for this is `docker run`.

The basic syntax to run a container from an image is `docker run <options> <image_name>:<tag> <optional_command_and_args_for_container>`.

Let's break down the key parts for running our Rust application:

- `docker run`: The command to create and start a new container.
- `<image_name>:<tag>`: You specify the image you want to run, using the name and tag you assigned during the `docker build` step (e.g., `my_rust_cli_app:latest`).
- `<options>`: `docker run` has many options. Some common ones for simple applications are as follows:
    - `--rm`: Automatically removes the container when it exits. This is very useful for CLI tools or tests to prevent cluttering your system with stopped containers.
    - `-it`: If your Rust application is interactive (e.g., reads from standard input or needs a TTY), you'd use `-i` (interactive, keep `STDIN` open) and `-t` (allocate a pseudo-TTY). For a non-interactive CLI that just prints output, these might not be strictly necessary, but often don't hurt.
    - If your Rust application were a web server and your Dockerfile included an `EXPOSE 8080` instruction, you would use `-p <host_port>:8080` (e.g., `-p 8000:8080`) to map a port on your host machine to the container's exposed port.

Assuming your Dockerfile (like the one in the *Creating a basic Dockerfile for a Rust application* section) has a `CMD` instruction pointing to your compiled Rust binary (e.g., `CMD ["./target/release/my_rust_cli"]`), running the container is straightforward.

If your `my_rust_cli` application simply prints `"Hello from Rust!"` to standard output, you could run it like this:

```
# Run a container from the image we built earlier (e.g., my_rust_cli_
app:latest)
# The --rm flag will automatically remove the container once the
application inside it finishes.
docker run --rm my_rust_cli_app:latest

# If your Rust CLI application expects command-line arguments,
# you can pass them after the image name. These will override the
Dockerfile's CMD
# if CMD was in shell form, or be passed as arguments to the CMD if it's
in exec form.
# For example, if your CMD was ["./target/release/my_rust_cli"]
# and your Rust app processed arguments:
# docker run --rm my_rust_cli_app:latest arg1 "another argument"
```

- `docker run --rm my_rust_cli_app:latest`:
    - Docker finds the `my_rust_cli_app:latest` image
    - It creates a new container based on this image
    - It executes the command specified by the `CMD` instruction in the Dockerfile (e.g., `./target/release/my_rust_cli`)
    - Any output from your Rust application (e.g., from `println!`) will be displayed in your terminal
    - Once your Rust application finishes (exits), the container will stop
    - Because of the `--rm` flag, Docker will then automatically remove the stopped container
- **Passing arguments**: If your Rust application (the binary defined in `CMD`) is designed to accept command-line arguments, you can provide them after the image name in the `docker run` command. For example, if your Dockerfile has `CMD [""./target/release/my_grep"]` and your `my_grep` Rust program expects a pattern and a file, you could run `docker run --rm my_grep_image:latest "search_pattern" /path/inside/container/file.txt` (note: `/path/inside/container/file.txt` would need to exist *inside* the container, perhaps copied in via the Dockerfile or mounted as a volume).

When you execute `docker run`, Docker creates an isolated environment based on your image. The `CMD` instruction from your Dockerfile is executed as the main process within this isolated environment. Standard output and standard error from your Rust application inside the container are, by default, connected to your terminal.

You've now successfully Dockerized a Rust application: you've written a Dockerfile, built an image from it, and run that image as a container! This is the fundamental workflow. The next step is to look at how to make these images more efficient, especially for production.

Optimizing Docker images for Rust

The basic Dockerfile we created in the previous section works, but it produces a rather large Docker image.

This is because it includes the entire Rust toolchain (compiler, `cargo`, source code, and intermediate build artifacts) in the final image, which isn't needed just to run our compiled binary.

Large images take longer to build, push to registries, and pull onto servers, and they consume more disk space.

In this section, we'll explore several key techniques to significantly reduce the size of your Rust Docker images and improve build times.

The importance of small and efficient images

Why all the fuss about small Docker images?

- **Faster deployment**: Smaller images are quicker to upload to container registries (such as Docker Hub) and faster for your servers or CI/CD systems to download and start. This speeds up your entire deployment pipeline.
- **Reduced storage costs**: Less disk space is used on your development machine, CI server, container registry, and production hosts. This can translate to real cost savings.
- **Improved security (reduced attack surface)**: Minimal images contain fewer packages and libraries. Fewer components mean fewer potential vulnerabilities and a smaller attack surface for your application.
- **Faster startup times (potentially)**: While the application binary size itself is a factor, smaller images generally mean less data for Docker to handle when starting a container.
- **Better resource utilization**: Especially in orchestrated environments such as Kubernetes, leaner images contribute to overall system efficiency.

For Rust applications, which compile to native binaries, we have a great opportunity to create very minimal runtime images.

Using multi-stage builds

This is perhaps the single most effective technique for reducing the size of Docker images for compiled languages such as Rust.

A **multi-stage build** allows you to use multiple `FROM` statements in a single Dockerfile. Each `FROM` instruction can use a different base image and starts a new "stage" of the build. You can selectively copy artifacts (such as your compiled binary) from one stage to another, discarding everything else from the earlier stages.

Separating the build environment from the runtime environment

The core idea is to have the following:

1. **A builder stage**: This stage uses a base image that contains the full Rust toolchain (e.g., `rust:1.78`). Its job is to compile your Rust application. It will be relatively large because it has all the build tools and source code.
2. **A runtime stage**: This stage uses a very minimal base image (e.g., `debian:buster-slim`, `alpine:latest`, or even `scratch` for truly minimal static binaries). Its only job is to run the compiled binary produced by the builder stage. It does *not* contain the Rust compiler, `cargo`, or your source code.

Copying artifacts

The `COPY --from=<stage_name_or_index> <src> <dest>` instruction is key to multi-stage builds. It lets you copy files from a previous stage (identified by its name given in `FROM ... AS <name>` or by its numerical index starting from 0) into the current stage.

Let's rewrite our basic Dockerfile for `my_rust_cli` using a multi-stage build:

```
# ----- Stage 1: Builder -----
# Use an official Rust image. We name this stage "builder".
FROM rust:1.78 AS builder
# (Using a specific version like 1.78 is good for reproducibility)

# Set the working directory for the build
WORKDIR /usr/src/app
```

```
# Copy Cargo.toml and Cargo.lock to leverage Docker cache for dependencies
COPY Cargo.toml Cargo.lock ./

# Build dependencies first. This layer is cached if manifests don't
change.
# Create a dummy main.rs or lib.rs to make `cargo build` work here if
needed,
# or just build the project target if your source is small.
# For a binary project, let's ensure we have a src directory for the next
step.
# If your project is simple, you might just run `cargo fetch` here,
# or build a dummy target.
# Let's assume a common pattern:
RUN mkdir src && echo "fn main() {println!(\"dummy main for dep build\")}"
> src/main.rs
RUN cargo build --release --bin my_rust_cli # Replace my_rust_cli with
your binary name
# Clean up the dummy main if you used one
RUN rm -f src/main.rs

# Now copy the actual source code
COPY src ./src

# Build the application, using cached dependencies if possible
# Ensure this matches the binary name in your Cargo.toml
RUN cargo build --release --bin my_rust_cli

# ----- Stage 2: Runtime -----
# Use a minimal base image for the final runtime environment.
# `debian:buster-slim` is a good small, general-purpose base.
# `alpine` is even smaller but uses musl libc, which might require changes
# to your Rust build if you have C dependencies.
FROM debian:buster-slim AS runtime
# Or: FROM alpine:latest AS runtime

# Set a working directory (optional, but good practice)
WORKDIR /app
```

```
# Copy *only* the compiled binary from the "builder" stage.
# The path in the builder stage is /usr/src/app/target/release/your_
binary_name
COPY --from=builder /usr/src/app/target/release/my_rust_cli /usr/local/
bin/my_rust_cli
# Replace "my_rust_cli" with your actual binary name.

# (Optional) If your Rust app needs system libraries like OpenSSL or libpq
at runtime,
# you would install them here using the OS package manager (e.g., apt-get
install ... for debian)
# RUN apt-get update && apt-get install -y libssl1.1 ca-certificates && rm
-rf /var/lib/apt/lists/*

# Set the command to run your application
CMD ["my_rust_cli"]
# Since it's in /usr/local/bin, it should be in the PATH.

# (Optional) If it's a web server
# EXPOSE 8080
```

- Stage 1 (named `builder`):
    - `FROM rust:1.78 AS builder`: Starts with the Rust toolchain image and names this stage `builder`.
    - `WORKDIR /usr/src/app`: Sets the working directory.
    - `COPY Cargo.toml Cargo.lock ./`: Copies manifest files.
    - `RUN mkdir src ... cargo build ...`: This sequence is an attempt to cache dependencies. First, it builds with minimal/dummy source. Then, `COPY src ./src` copies the actual source, and `RUN cargo build --release ...` rebuilds using already-downloaded/compiled dependencies if possible. (A more refined dependency caching strategy might involve `cargo fetch` or creating a dummy binary.)
    - The result of this stage is a compiled binary at `/usr/src/app/target/release/my_rust_cli`. This stage also contains all the source code, intermediate build files, and the Rust toolchain, making it large.

- Stage 2 (named `runtime`):
    - `FROM debian:buster-slim AS runtime`: Starts fresh with a very small Debian base image. This image does *not* have Rust or Cargo installed.
    - `WORKDIR /app`: Sets a working directory.
    - `COPY --from=builder /usr/src/app/target/release/my_rust_cli /usr/local/bin/my_rust_cli`: This is the magic! It copies *only* the compiled binary from the `target/release` directory of the builder stage into `/usr/local/bin/` in our new, minimal runtime stage. `/usr/local/bin/` is typically in the system's `PATH`.
    - **Runtime dependencies**: The commented-out `RUN apt-get install ...` line is crucial if your Rust binary dynamically links against system libraries (such as OpenSSL for HTTPS, or `libpq` for PostgreSQL) that are not present in the minimal base image. You must install them in this runtime stage.
    - `CMD ["my_rust_cli"]`: Sets the command to run your application.

The final image produced by this Dockerfile will only contain the layers from the *last* stage (the runtime stage). All the build tools, source code, and intermediate artifacts from the builder stage are discarded. This results in a dramatically smaller final image.

Choosing minimal base images for runtime

The choice of base image for your final runtime stage in a multi-stage build significantly impacts the final image size and its contents:

- `debian:<version>-slim` (e.g., `debian:buster-slim`, `debian:bullseye-slim`): These are official Debian images that are significantly smaller than the full Debian images because they omit many common packages and documentation. They are based on `glibc` (the GNU C Library), which is what Rust binaries dynamically link against by default on most Linux systems. This often makes them a good balance of small size and compatibility.
- `alpine:latest` (or specific versions): Alpine Linux is a distribution known for its extremely small size (the base image can be around 5 MB!). It uses `musl libc` instead of `glibc`.
- `scratch`: This is an empty image. It's the absolute smallest base possible. You can use `scratch` if your Rust binary is *fully statically linked* and has no external runtime dependencies at all. This is often achievable by compiling with a `*-unknown-linux-musl` target.

- **Distroless images (from Google)**: These images (e.g., `gcr.io/distroless/static-debian11` or `gcr.io/distroless/base-debian11`) contain only your application and its runtime dependencies, without package managers, shells, or other standard utilities. This further reduces the image size and attack surface. You'd copy your binary from a builder stage into a distroless base.

Considerations for Alpine and musl versus glibc

- **glibc (used by Debian, Ubuntu, Fedora, etc.)**: This is the standard C library on most Linux distributions. Rust binaries built with the default Linux targets (e.g., `x86_64-unknown-linux-gnu`) will dynamically link against `glibc` unless you specify otherwise. Using a `glibc`-based slim image (such as `debian:slim`) is often the easiest path for compatibility.
- **musl libc (used by Alpine)**: `musl` is an alternative, lightweight C library. To create Rust binaries that work well on Alpine, you typically need to compile your Rust code with a `musl`-based target, as follows:

  ```
  cargo build --release --target x86_64-unknown-linux-musl
  ```

  This creates a more statically linked binary (or one that links against `musl`).

  The following are the pros and cons of `musl`/Alpine:

  - **Pros**: Significantly smaller image sizes.
  - **Cons**:
    - Some Rust crates with C dependencies might have trouble compiling against `musl` or require extra configuration
    - DNS resolution can sometimes behave differently or require specific setup in Alpine
    - Performance characteristics can occasionally differ from `glibc`-based systems for certain workloads

  If you can easily compile your Rust app with a `musl` target and all your dependencies are compatible, Alpine can give you very small images. If you encounter issues or want broader compatibility with C dependencies that expect `glibc`, a `debian:slim` base is a good, still reasonably small, alternative.

Leveraging Docker build cache and cargo's build caching

Docker builds images in layers, and it caches these layers. If a Dockerfile instruction and the files it depends on haven't changed since the last build, Docker will reuse the cached layer instead of re-executing the instruction.

Similarly, `cargo` has its own build cache for dependencies.

Efficiently using these caches can drastically reduce your build times.

Structuring COPY and RUN commands effectively

The key to leveraging Docker's layer cache is to order your Dockerfile instructions so that the ones that change most frequently come *last*, and the ones that change infrequently come *first*.

For a Rust project, your `Cargo.toml` and `Cargo.lock` files (which define dependencies) usually change less often than your `src/` directory (your actual source code).

Here is an example of an optimized `COPY` and `RUN` sequence for dependency caching in the builder stage:

```
# ----- Stage 1: Builder -----
FROM rust:1.78 AS builder

WORKDIR /usr/src/app

# 1. Copy only the manifest files
COPY Cargo.toml Cargo.lock ./

# 2. Build dependencies.
# This step creates a dummy lib.rs or main.rs just to build dependencies.
# If Cargo.toml/Cargo.lock haven't changed, this layer will be cached.
RUN mkdir src && In less than 1 hour, starting from scratch and explaining
line by line what I am doing?``
    echo "fn main() {println!(\"Building dependencies...\");}" > src/main.
rs && \
    cargo build --release --bin my_rust_cli && \
    rm -rf src # Remove dummy src
```

```
# 3. Copy your actual source code
COPY src ./src

# 4. Build your application.
# This will now use the cached dependencies from the previous RUN step
# if only src code changed.
RUN cargo build --release --bin my_rust_cli

# ----- Stage 2: Runtime -----
FROM debian:buster-slim AS runtime
WORKDIR /app
COPY --from=builder /usr/src/app/target/release/my_rust_cli /usr/local/
bin/my_rust_cli
# (Potentially install runtime dependencies like libssl if needed)
# RUN apt-get update && apt-get install -y libssl1.1 ca-certificates && rm
-rf /var/lib/apt/lists/*
CMD ["my_rust_cli"]
```

- **Steps 1 and 2 (dependency caching):**
    - `COPY Cargo.toml Cargo.lock ./`: We copy *only* these files first.
    - `RUN mkdir src ... cargo build --release ... rm -rf src`: This is a common trick. We create a minimal `src/main.rs` (or `src/lib.rs` for a library) just so `cargo build` has something to compile. The key is that `cargo build` will resolve and compile all dependencies listed in `Cargo.toml`. This entire layer (including the compiled dependencies in `target/`) will be cached by Docker. If `Cargo.toml` and `Cargo.lock` don't change in subsequent builds, Docker reuses this layer, saving a lot of time. After dependencies are built, the dummy `src` is removed.
- **Step 3 (copy source):**
    - `COPY src ./src`: Now we copy our actual application source code. If only the source code changes (but not `Cargo.toml`/`Cargo.lock`), the previous dependency layer is reused, and only this `COPY` and the subsequent build need to run.
- **Step 4 (build application):**
    - `RUN cargo build --release --bin my_rust_cli`: This builds the final application. `cargo` itself will also try to reuse its own build cache for unchanged parts of your source code.

A quick note on Docker build efficiency

This `RUN cargo build` step is a simple, direct way to build your application, which is perfect for getting started.

Be aware that this single-step approach is not very efficient for development. Because all our source code was copied in one layer, any change to any `.rs` file will bust Docker's cache and force `cargo` to re-compile your entire project from scratch.

More advanced Dockerfiles use techniques such as multi-stage builds to first build dependencies (which rarely change) in a separate layer, and then build your application code (which changes often) in a later layer. This significantly speeds up day-to-day builds. Other tools, such as `sccache`, can also be integrated for even faster, shared compilation caching.

For our goal of getting a container running quickly, this simple method is perfectly fine.

This layering strategy means that if you only change your application logic in `src/` and not your dependencies in `Cargo.toml`, Docker can skip the potentially lengthy dependency compilation step on subsequent `docker build` runs.

Stripping debug symbols and binary compression

For even smaller binaries, especially for production, you can consider two more steps, usually performed in the builder stage just before copying the artifact to the runtime stage.

Using strip

When you compile with `cargo build --release`, the resulting binary still contains some debugging symbols and other information not strictly necessary for execution. The `strip` utility (common on Linux/macOS) can remove this information, reducing the binary size.

You can add this to your builder stage in the Dockerfile *after* `cargo build --release`:

```
# In the builder stage, after cargo build --release
RUN strip ./target/release/my_rust_cli
```

This can often shave off a noticeable percentage of the binary's size.

A quick note on the trade-off

Be aware that this is a trade-off. Stripping the binary makes debugging production crashes (such as analyzing a core dump) extremely difficult, as you are removing the very symbols the debugger needs to map memory addresses back to your function names and line numbers.

For simple projects or for achieving the absolute smallest image, `strip` is a quick win. For critical production applications, a more advanced approach is to keep these debug symbols in a separate file, giving you both a small binary and the ability to debug it.

Using tools such as UPX

Ultimate Packer for eXecutables (**UPX**) is a tool that can compress executables. The compressed executable then decompresses itself into memory when run:

- **Pros**: Can dramatically reduce the on-disk size of your binary, leading to even smaller Docker images.
- **Cons**:
    - **Slightly slower startup**: There's a small runtime cost for the initial decompression.
    - **Memory usage**: The decompressed program still takes up the same amount of memory when running.
    - **Antivirus issues**: Compressed executables are sometimes flagged by antivirus software (though this is less common for server-side deployments).
    - **Not always beneficial**: For very small binaries, the UPX overhead might not be worth it, or it might even make the file slightly larger. It's most effective on larger binaries.

If you choose to use UPX, you'd install it in your builder stage and run it on

```
# In the builder stage, after strip (if used)
# First, install upx (example for Debian/Ubuntu based builder like
'rust:latest')
RUN apt-get update && apt-get install -y upx-ucl && rm -rf /var/lib/apt/
lists/*
RUN upx --best --lzma ./target/release/my_rust_cli
```

Note

Always test the performance and behavior of UPX-compressed binaries carefully for your specific application. For many Rust applications where the binary size after stripping is already quite reasonable, UPX might be an unnecessary step unless an absolutely minimal image size is paramount.

By applying these optimization techniques, especially multi-stage builds and careful layer caching, you can create Docker images for your Rust applications that are lean, efficient, and fast to deploy.

In the next section, we will introduce a very important tool for running multiple services (containers): Docker Compose.

Managing multi-container apps with Docker Compose

So far, we've focused on Dockerizing a single Rust application. However, many real-world applications are more complex, consisting of multiple interconnected services. For example, your Rust web application might need a database (such as PostgreSQL), a caching service (such as Redis), or other backend microservices. Managing each of these as separate Docker containers with individual `docker run` commands, along with their networking and data persistence, can quickly become cumbersome and error-prone.

It's important to understand, however, that *Compose is fundamentally a single-host tool.* It is designed for managing multiple containers on *one* machine, which is perfect for development, testing, and simple production environments.

It *does not* handle multi-host deployments, automatic scaling across servers, or self-healing (e.g., restarting a container on a *different* machine if one server fails). For those more complex, distributed system challenges, you would need to move beyond Compose to a full-blown orchestration platform such as Kubernetes.

A quick note on commands: Historically, Docker Compose was a separate tool invoked with `docker-compose` (with a hyphen). Modern Docker versions (especially with Docker Desktop or when the Compose plugin is installed for Docker Engine) integrate Compose directly, and the command is now `docker compose` (with a space). We will be using this modern `docker compose` syntax. Similarly, while `docker-compose.yml` is still widely recognized, `compose.yml` or `compose.yaml` are now common default filenames for the configuration.

Introduction to Docker Compose: Why you need it

Imagine our Rust web application from *Chapter 14*, which we planned to connect to a PostgreSQL database. If we were to manage these two components (the Rust app and the Postgres database) using only basic Docker commands, we'd have to do the following:

1. Manually start a PostgreSQL container, ensuring we configure its ports, environment variables (for user, password, and database name), and set up a volume so its data persists if the container is removed.
2. Build the Docker image for our Rust application.
3. Manually run the Rust application container, making sure to do the following:
    - Link it to the same Docker network as the PostgreSQL container
    - Pass the correct database connection string (with the right hostname for the database container) as an environment variable
    - Map any necessary ports

If you add more services (a Redis cache or another microservice), this manual process becomes increasingly complex and error-prone. Docker Compose automates and simplifies all of this. By defining your entire application stack in a `compose.yml` file, you gain several key benefits:

- **Simplified multi-service management**: You can start, stop, and rebuild all your application's services with single, straightforward commands (e.g., `docker compose up` or `docker compose down`).
- **Isolated and connected environments**: By default, Compose sets up a dedicated network for your application's services. Services on this network can easily discover and communicate with each other using their service names as hostnames (e.g., your Rust app can connect to a database service named `db` using the `db` hostname).

- **Reproducibility and consistency**: Your entire multi-service application environment is defined declaratively in one file. This makes it easy to share your setup with team members or to replicate the environment consistently across different machines (development, testing, and staging).
- **Orchestration of startup order (basic)**: You can use the `depends_on` directive to specify basic startup dependencies between services (e.g., ensure a database container is started before your application container attempts to connect to it). For more robust readiness checks, health checks are often used in conjunction.
- **Configuration management**: Environment variables, port mappings, volume mounts, and network configurations for all services are centralized in the Compose file.

Docker Compose is an incredibly valuable tool for local development and testing of multi-container applications. It's also suitable for simpler production deployments, although for large-scale, complex production environments, more comprehensive orchestration tools such as Kubernetes are typically used (though Kubernetes can sometimes ingest Compose file definitions as a starting point).

Writing a compose.yml file

The heart of Docker Compose is its configuration file, typically named `compose.yml` (or `compose.yaml`; the older `docker-compose.yml` is also still common). This file is written in **YAML** (which stands for **YAML Ain't Markup Language**), a human-readable data serialization language. It's all about defining the structure and configuration of your application's services, networks, and volumes.

A quick note on the version string at the top of older `docker-compose.yml` files (e.g., `version: '3.8'`): this was used to specify the Compose file format version. With modern Docker Compose implementations that adhere to the *Compose Specification*, this top-level version property is generally deprecated or considered optional for most use cases. We'll omit it in our examples, which is common practice now, as features are generally tied to your Docker Engine version.

Let's break down the key parts of a `compose.yml` file.

Defining services

The most important top-level key in a `compose.yml` file is `services`. Under `services`, you list each component or microservice of your application. Each service will typically run in its own Docker container.

For each service, you can specify various configuration options, including the following:

- `image: <image_name>:<tag>`: If you're using a pre-built image from a registry such as Docker Hub (e.g., `postgres:15-alpine` or `redis:latest`).
- `build: <path_to_dockerfile_directory_or_context>`: If Docker Compose should build the image for this service from a local Dockerfile. You can provide a path to the directory containing the Dockerfile (e.g., `build: .` for the current directory, or `build: ./my_rust_app_service`). You can also provide more detailed build options here.
- `ports: ["<host_port>:<container_port>"]`: Maps ports from your host machine to ports inside the container. For example, `ports: ["8080:3000"]` would map port `8080` on your host to port `3000` in the container.
- `volumes: ["<host_path_or_named_volume>:<container_path>"]`: Mounts volumes for data persistence or for sharing files between the host and container.
- `environment: ["VAR_NAME=value", "ANOTHER_VAR=${HOST_VAR}"]` or a map: Sets environment variables inside the container.
- `depends_on: [<service_name>]`: Specifies other services that this service depends on. Compose will attempt to start dependent services in order.
- `command: ["executable", "param1"]`: Overrides the default command (from the Docker image's `CMD` instruction).
- `restart: <policy>`: Defines the restart policy (e.g., `no`, `always`, `on-failure`, `unless-stopped`).

The following is an example snippet:

```
# compose.yml
services:
  my_rust_backend:
    build: ./backend_app # Path to Dockerfile for the Rust backend
    ports:
      - "8000:8000" # Map host 8000 to container 8000
    environment:
      - RUST_LOG=info
      - DATABASE_HOST=db_service # Service name for the database

  db_service:
    image: postgres:15
    environment:
```

```
      POSTGRES_USER: myuser
      POSTGRES_PASSWORD: mypassword
      # ... other db configurations ...
```

Here, `my_rust_backend` and `db_service` are two distinct services defined in our application stack.

Linking services and managing networks

One of the most convenient features of Docker Compose is its automatic network setup:

- **Default network:** When you run `docker compose up`, Compose creates a default bridge network for your application stack. All services defined in your `compose.yml` file are automatically added to this network.
- **Service discovery via hostnames:** Crucially, services on this default network can discover and communicate with each other using their *service names as hostnames*. For example, if you have a service named `db` (for your database) and another service named `webapp` (for your Rust application) in the same `compose.yml`, your `webapp` container can connect to the `db` container using the `db` hostname. So, a database connection string within `webapp` might look like `postgres://user:pass@db:5432/dbname`. Compose handles the DNS resolution within this private network.
- **Custom networks:** For more complex scenarios, you can define your own custom networks under a top-level `networks:` key and then assign services to these networks. This gives you more control over network topology and isolation.

The following is an example snippet demonstrating implicit networking:

```
# compose.yml
services:
  api:
    build: ./api_service
    ports:
      - "3000:3000"
    environment:
      # The 'api' service can reach the 'database' service using hostname
'database'
      DATABASE_CONNECTION_STRING: "user:pass@database:5432/appdb"
    depends_on:
      - database
```

```
  database:
    image: some_database_image:latest
    # No 'ports' exposed to host here means database is only accessible
    # by other services on the same Docker Compose network (like 'api').
```

In this case, `api` can connect to `database:5432` because they are on the same Compose-managed network.

Using environment variables for configuration

Environment variables are a standard way to pass configuration to your containerized applications. Docker Compose provides several ways to set them for your services:

They can be set as a list:

```
services:
  myapp:
    image: myapp_image
    environment:
      - DEBUG_MODE=true
      - API_KEY=abcdef12345
```

They can be set as a dictionary:

```
services:
  myapp:
    image: myapp_image
    environment:
      DEBUG_MODE: "true"
      API_KEY: "abcdef12345"
      MAX_CONNECTIONS: "100" # Will be converted to string if not quoted
```

They can also be set from a .env file.

Docker Compose automatically looks for a file named `.env` in the same directory as your `compose.yml` file. Variables defined in this `.env` file are available for substitution in the `compose.yml` file (e.g., `POSTGRES_USER=${DB_USER_FROM_ENV}`) and can also be passed directly to containers if not explicitly overridden in the `environment` section of a service.

It's common practice to define default or development-specific environment variables in `.env` and keep this file out of version control if it contains secrets.

The following is an example `.env` file:

```
POSTGRES_USER=dev_user
POSTGRES_PASSWORD=dev_secret
RUST_APP_PORT=8080
```

The following is an example `compose.yml` file using these:

```
services:
  rust_app:
    build: .
    ports:
      - "${RUST_APP_PORT}:8080" # Variable substitution from .env
    environment:
      # These would be picked up by the rust_app if not defined here
      # but you can also explicitly pass them or override them.
      APP_DB_USER: ${POSTGRES_USER}
      APP_DB_PASS: ${POSTGRES_PASSWORD}

  db:
    image: postgres:15
    environment:
      # These are directly used by the postgres image
      POSTGRES_USER: ${POSTGRES_USER}
      POSTGRES_PASSWORD: ${POSTGRES_PASSWORD}
```

Managing persistent data with volumes

Containers are designed to be ephemeral. If a container is stopped and removed, any data written inside its filesystem (that wasn't part of the original image) is lost. For services such as databases, this is obviously not desirable! You need the data to persist. Docker **volumes** are the preferred mechanism for persisting data generated and used by Docker containers.

There are two main types of mounts for persisting data:

- Named volumes:
  - Docker manages the storage location on the host machine. You just give the volume a name.
  - They are the preferred way to persist data for production services such as databases.

    - They persist even if the container or the Compose stack is removed (unless explicitly removed with `docker compose down -v` or `docker volume rm <volume_name>`).
    - You define them under a top-level `volumes:` key in your `compose.yml` and then mount them into your services.

```
services:
  database:
    image: postgres:15
    volumes:
      - my_db_data:/var/lib/postgresql/data
        # Mount named volume 'my_db_data'
        # into the container's PG data directory.

volumes:
  my_db_data: {} # Declares the named volume (empty {} means
use default driver)
```

- Bind mounts:
    - Mounts a file or directory from your **host machine's filesystem** directly into a container. The path on the host is specified.
    - Useful for development, for example, mounting your source code into a container so changes are reflected live without rebuilding the image (though for compiled languages such as Rust, you'd still need to recompile inside the container or use a development server that watches for changes).
    - Less portable than named volumes, as they depend on the host's directory structure and can have permission issues.

```
services:
  webapp:
    build: .
    volumes:
      # Mount local ./src into /usr/src/app/src in the
container
      - ./src:/usr/src/app/src # Example for development
live-reloading (if app supports it)
```

For our Rust application with a PostgreSQL database, we'll definitely want to use a named volume for the PostgreSQL data.

Example: A Rust application with a PostgreSQL database

Let's define a `compose.yml` file for a common scenario: a Rust web application that needs to connect to a PostgreSQL database. We'll assume our Rust application will be built from a Dockerfile located in the current directory (or a specified subdirectory) and will be configured to connect to the database using an environment variable.

The following are assumptions for the Rust application (`rust_app` service):

- It's built using a Dockerfile in the current directory (or a path such as `./my_rust_app`)
- It listens for HTTP requests on port `8080` *inside* the container
- It expects a `DATABASE_URL` environment variable to know how to connect to PostgreSQL
- It will need Diesel CLI's migrations to be run against the database before it can fully operate (though Compose primarily starts services; migrations are often a separate step or an entrypoint script in more advanced setups)

The following are assumptions for the PostgreSQL database (`db` service):

- We'll use an official Postgres image
- We need to configure a user, password, and database name for our application to use
- Its data should be persisted using a named volume

Here's how the `compose.yml` file might look:

```
# compose.yml (or compose.yaml)

services:
  # Service for our Rust Web Application
  rust_app:
    build:
      context: . # Assumes Dockerfile is in the current directory along
with compose.yml
      # For a Rust project in a subdirectory, e.g., ./my_web_app:
      # context: ./my_web_app
    ports:
      - "8080:8080" # Map port 8080 on the host to port 8080 in the
container
    environment:
      # DATABASE_URL for the Rust app to connect to the 'db' service.
```

```
      # 'db' is the hostname of the postgres service on the Docker Compose
network.
      # The user, password, and db_name must match what's set for the 'db'
service.
      DATABASE_URL: "postgres://app_user:app_password@db:5432/app_db"
      RUST_LOG: "info,my_rust_app=debug" # Example app-specific logging
config
      # Other environment variables your Rust app might need
      # APP_SECRET_KEY: "${APP_SECRET_FROM_ENV_FILE}"
    depends_on:
      db: # Tells Compose to start the 'db' service before 'rust_app'.
        # For production, a healthcheck on 'db' is better for readiness.
        condition: service_started
        # For example, if db service had a healthcheck:
        # condition: service_healthy
    restart: unless-stopped # Optional: Restart policy for the container

  # Service for the PostgreSQL Database
  db:
    image: postgres:15-alpine # Using a specific version and a smaller
alpine variant
    ports:
      # Optionally expose the PostgreSQL port to the host for direct
access
      # with tools like psql or pgAdmin during development.
      # For security, you might not expose this in production directly.
      - "54321:5432" # Map host port 54321 to container's default
PostgreSQL port 5432
    environment:
      POSTGRES_USER: "app_user"
      POSTGRES_PASSWORD: "app_password" # Use strong passwords, preferably
from .env or secrets
      POSTGRES_DB: "app_db"
    volumes:
      # Mount a named volume to persist PostgreSQL data across container
restarts/recreations.
      # 'postgres_app_data' is the name of the volume (defined below).
```

```
      # '/var/lib/postgresql/data' is the standard directory where
PostgreSQL stores its data.
      - postgres_app_data:/var/lib/postgresql/data
    restart: always # Optional: Ensure database always tries to restart
    # healthcheck: # Example of a healthcheck for PostgreSQL
    #   test: ["CMD-SHELL", "pg_isready -U app_user -d app_db"]
    #   interval: 10s
    #   timeout: 5s
    #   retries: 5

# Named volume definition for PostgreSQL data persistence
volumes:
  postgres_app_data:
    driver: local # Specifies the local volume driver (usually default)
```

- `services:`: This is the top-level key where we define each independent part of our application stack.
- `rust_app: service:`
    - `build: context: .`: This tells Docker Compose to build an image for this service using the Dockerfile found in the current directory (where `compose.yml` resides). If your Rust app's Dockerfile is in a subdirectory, you'd change the context (e.g., `context: ./my_web_application`).
    - `ports: - "8080:8080"`: This maps port `8080` on your host machine to port `8080` inside the `rust_app` container. If your Rust application listens on a different port internally, adjust the container port accordingly (the second number).
    - `environment: DATABASE_URL: "..."`: This sets the `DATABASE_URL` environment variable *inside* the `rust_app` container:
        - Notice the `db` hostname: Docker Compose creates a network for these services, and services can reach each other using their service names as hostnames. So, `db` resolves to the IP address of the `db` service container.
        - The user (`app_user`), password (`app_password`), and database name (`app_db`) must match the `POSTGRES_*` environment variables set for the `db` service. In a real setup, passwords should come from a `.env` file or secrets management, not hardcoded here.

    - `depends_on: db: condition: service_started`: This tells Compose that the `rust_app` service depends on the `db` service. Compose will attempt to start `db` before `rust_app`. The `service_started` part means it waits until the `db` container has started. A more robust approach is `condition: service_healthy`, which requires the `db` service to have a health check defined (as shown in the commented-out example for the `db` service) that passes.
    - `restart: unless-stopped`: This is an optional policy that tells Docker to restart this container if it stops for any reason, unless it was explicitly stopped by an operator.

- `db: service`:

    - `image: postgres:15-alpine`: We use a pre-built official PostgreSQL image from Docker Hub, specifically version 15 based on Alpine Linux (which is smaller than full Debian-based images).
    - `ports: - "54321:5432"`: This *optionally* maps port `54321` on your host machine to the default PostgreSQL port `5432` inside the container. This is useful during development if you want to connect to the database directly from your host using tools such as `psql` or a database GUI (you'd connect to `localhost:54321`). For security, you might not expose the database port directly to the host in a production environment unless necessary and properly firewalled.
    - `environment: POSTGRES_USER...`: These environment variables are used by the official PostgreSQL image to initialize the database when it first starts: it creates the specified user, sets their password, and creates the specified database.
    - `volumes: - postgres_app_data:/var/lib/postgresql/data`: This is crucial for data persistence. It mounts a **named volume** called `postgres_app_data` into the `/var/lib/postgresql/data` directory inside the container (which is where PostgreSQL stores its data files).
    - `healthcheck: ...` (commented out): This shows an example of how you could define a health check for PostgreSQL. The `pg_isready` command is a utility that checks whether a PostgreSQL server is ready to accept connections. Using this with `depends_on: service_healthy` in `rust_app` would make `rust_app` wait until the database is truly ready.

- `volumes:` (top level):
    - `postgres_app_data: driver: local`: This declares the named volume `postgres_app_data`. Docker will manage its storage on your host system. The data in this volume will persist even if you remove and recreate the `db` container.

This `compose.yml` file now defines a complete, isolated environment for your Rust application and its PostgreSQL database. In the next part, we'll see the commands to bring this stack to life.

Running and managing your application stack

Once you have your `compose.yml` file (like the one in the Canvas defining your Rust app and PostgreSQL database) in the root of your project, you use `docker compose` commands from that same directory to manage your entire application stack. This makes controlling your multi-container setup much simpler than dealing with individual `docker run` commands for each service.

Here's an overview of the most common `docker compose` commands you'll use:

- **Building and starting your application stack**: The primary command to bring everything up is `docker compose up`.

  This command reads your `compose.yml` file. For any service with a `build:` instruction (such as our `rust_app`), it will build the Docker image if it doesn't exist or if the Dockerfile or source files have changed. It then creates and starts all the services defined, respecting any `depends_on` directives for startup order. By default, `docker compose up` attaches to the logs of all services and streams them to your terminal. Pressing *Ctrl* + *C* in the terminal will stop the services.

    - To force a rebuild of images before starting: `docker compose up -build`
    - To start services in detached (background) mode without attaching to logs: `docker compose up -d`

- **Stopping and removing your application stack**: When you're done, `docker compose down` is used to stop and remove the containers and networks created by your Compose project:
    - By default, named volumes (such as our `postgres_app_data`) are *not* removed by `docker compose down`. This is a safety feature to prevent accidental data loss.
    - If you want to remove the named volumes along with everything else, you must use the `-v` flag: `docker compose down -v`. Use this with caution!

- **Viewing the status of services**: To see which containers are running as part of your Compose project and their status: `docker compose ps`.
- **Viewing logs**: To view the aggregated logs from all services (if running detached) or logs for specific services:
    - `docker compose logs` (shows current logs from all services)
    - `docker compose logs -f` (follows new log output from all services)
    - `docker compose logs <service_name>` (e.g., `docker compose logs rust_app` or `docker compose logs db`)
    - `docker compose logs -f <service_name>` (follows logs for a specific service)
- **Building or rebuilding images**: If you've made changes to your Dockerfile or application source code for a service that's built by Compose and want to rebuild the image without necessarily starting the services:
    - `docker compose build` (builds images for all services with a build instruction)
    - `docker compose build <service_name>` (builds the image for a specific service, e.g., `docker compose build rust_app`)
- **Executing commands in a running service container**: To run a command inside an already-running container of a service (e.g., to open a shell or run a database CLI): `docker compose exec <service_name> <command_to_run_in_container>`.
    - Example for our database: `docker compose exec db psql -U app_user -d app_db`
    - Example for a shell in the app (if it has one): `docker compose exec rust_app /bin/sh`
- **Stopping, starting, and restarting services**: You can manage individual services without bringing down the entire stack:
    - `docker compose stop <service_name>` (stops a specific service, or all services if no name is specified)
    - `docker compose start <service_name>` (starts a previously stopped service)
    - `docker compose restart <service_name>` (restarts a service)

These commands provide a straightforward way to manage the life cycle of your multi-container application defined in `compose.yml`. For local development, `docker compose up --build` (to ensure your Rust app is rebuilt) and `docker compose down` will be your most frequent companions.

Deploying Dockerized Rust applications

Deployment is the process of taking your packaged application (in our case, a Docker image) and making it run on a server or platform where it can serve its purpose. Docker greatly simplifies deployment because your image already contains the application and its necessary runtime environment. This means you don't have to worry (as much) about whether the production server has the right version of Rust, system libraries, or other dependencies – they're all in your container!

This section will provide an overview of common strategies and platforms for deploying your Dockerized Rust applications.

Overview of deployment strategies

There's a wide spectrum of ways to deploy Docker containers, ranging from simple to highly complex, depending on your application's scale, availability requirements, and your team's operational capacity. Here are some general approaches:

- Single-server deployment:
    - **Concept:** The simplest approach. You have a single server (a **virtual private server (VPS)**, a dedicated server, or even a machine in your office), install Docker Engine on it, and then pull and run your Docker image(s) directly using `docker run` or `docker compose up`.
    - **Pros:** Easy to understand and set up, good for small projects, internal tools, or initial learning.
    - **Cons:** Single point of failure (if the server goes down, your app goes down), manual scaling (you have to provision a bigger server or more servers manually), and updates might involve some downtime unless carefully managed.
- Managed container platforms (PaaS-like):
    - **Concept:** Cloud providers offer services that abstract away much of the underlying server management. You provide your Docker image, and the platform handles running it, scaling it (often automatically), and sometimes even load balancing and SSL termination.
    - **Examples:** AWS App Runner, Google Cloud Run, Azure Container Apps, and Heroku (with Docker deploys).

    - **Pros**: Greatly simplified operations. Often has built-in auto-scaling. Easy integration with other cloud services. Good for developers who want to focus on code, not infrastructure.
    - **Cons**: Can be more expensive than managing your own VMs at a very large scale. Might have some limitations or vendor lock-in depending on the platform.
- Container orchestration platforms (e.g., Kubernetes or Docker Swarm):
    - **Concept**: For complex, large-scale applications with many microservices, high-availability needs, and sophisticated deployment requirements (such as rolling updates, canary releases, and self-healing), container orchestrators are the standard. Kubernetes is the dominant player here. Docker Swarm is simpler but less feature-rich.
    - **Pros**: Powerful control over scaling, deployment strategies, service discovery, load balancing, fault tolerance, and resource management for complex applications.
    - **Cons**: Significant learning curve and operational complexity. Kubernetes, in particular, is a very large system. Often overkill for simpler applications.
- Serverless functions (with containers):
    - **Concept**: Some serverless platforms (such as AWS Lambda, Google Cloud Functions, and Azure Functions) now support deploying custom Docker container images as the runtime for your functions. Your code only runs when triggered by an event, and you pay only for execution time.
    - **Pros**: Extreme scalability (scales to zero when not in use). Pay-per-use model.
    - **Cons**: Execution time limits. Statelessness requirements. Can be more complex for long-running tasks or applications with persistent connections.

The choice of deployment strategy depends heavily on your application's needs, your budget, your team's expertise, and your scalability requirements. For many Rust web applications or services, starting with a managed container platform or a simple server deployment can be a good entry point, with the option to move to orchestration platforms such as Kubernetes as your needs grow.

Regardless of the platform, a crucial first step after building your Docker image locally is making it accessible to your deployment environment. This usually involves a **container registry**.

Using container registries

Once you've built a Docker image for your Rust application using `docker build`, that image exists on your local machine. To deploy it to another server, a cloud platform, or share it with your team, you need to push it to a **container registry**. A container registry is a storage system for Docker images, acting like a central library from which images can be pulled.

Docker Hub is the most well-known public registry, and it's the default one Docker uses when you try to `docker pull` an image that isn't found locally (e.g., `docker pull rust:latest`). However, there are many other registries:

- **Cloud provider registries**: AWS has ECR, Google Cloud has GCR and Artifact Registry, and Azure has ACR. These integrate well with their respective cloud ecosystems.
- **Private registries**: Companies often host their own private registries (using tools such as Harbor, GitLab container registry, or JFrog Artifactory) for internal images.
- **GitHub Container Registry (GHCR)**: Allows you to host Docker images directly within your GitHub repositories.

For our examples, we'll focus on Docker Hub as it's easily accessible for personal projects. The general workflow of tagging, pushing, and pulling is similar across most registries.

If you don't have one already, you'll want to create a free account on **Docker Hub**. You'll get a Docker ID (your username), which will be part of your image names when you push to Docker Hub.

Tagging your Docker images for versioning

Before you can push an image to a registry such as Docker Hub, you need to tag it appropriately. A tag typically follows the format <registry_hostname_if_not_docker_hub>/<your_username_or_org>/<image_name>:<version_tag>.

- If you're using Docker Hub, the <registry_hostname_if_not_docker_hub>/ part is usually omitted
- <your_username_or_org> is your Docker Hub ID or organization name
- <image_name> is the name you want for your application's image
- :<version_tag> is crucial for versioning (e.g., `0.1.0`, `latest`, `stable`, `dev`)

Let's say you built your Rust application image locally and named it my_rust_cli_app:latest (as in our previous docker build -t my_rust_cli_app:latest . example). If your Docker Hub username is myrustdev, you would re-tag this image for pushing:

```
# First, list your local images to find the one you want to tag
# docker images

# Assume your locally built image is named 'my_rust_cli_app' and has tag
'latest'
# And your Docker Hub username is 'myrustdev'

# Tag the local image 'my_rust_cli_app:latest' with a new name suitable
for Docker Hub
# Format: docker tag <local_image_name>:<local_tag> <dockerhub_
username>/<repo_name>:<new_tag>
docker tag my_rust_cli_app:latest myrustdev/my_rust_cli_app:0.1.0

# You can also tag it as 'latest' for Docker Hub
docker tag my_rust_cli_app:latest myrustdev/my_rust_cli_app:latest

# Now if you run 'docker images', you'll see these new tags pointing to
the same image ID
# as your original 'my_rust_cli_app:latest'.
```

- The docker tag SOURCE_IMAGE[:TAG] TARGET_IMAGE[:TAG] command creates an alias (another name or tag) for an existing image. It doesn't create a new copy of the image layers; it just adds another pointer to them.
- To push to Docker Hub, your image name must be prefixed with your Docker Hub username (or organization name if you're pushing to an organization's repository).
- It's good practice to use specific version tags (such as 0.1.0) for your releases, in addition to potentially having a latest tag that points to your most recent stable build.

Pushing images to a registry

Once your image is correctly tagged (e.g., myrustdev/my_rust_cli_app:0.1.0), you can push it to Docker Hub. First, you'll need to log in to Docker Hub from your terminal:

```
# Log in to Docker Hub (it will prompt for your username and password/
access token)
docker login
```

```
# Enter your Docker Hub username and password (or an access token) when
prompted.

# Push the specifically versioned image
# Replace 'myrustdev' with your Docker Hub username and 'my_rust_cli_app'
with your image name.
docker push myrustdev/my_rust_cli_app:0.1.0

# Optionally, push the 'latest' tag as well
# docker push myrustdev/my_rust_cli_app:latest
```

- `docker login`: This command authenticates you with Docker Hub (or another specified registry). You'll need to provide your Docker ID and password (or, preferably, an access token generated from the Docker Hub website for better security, especially in CI/CD environments).
- `docker push <image_name_with_username_and_tag>`: This command uploads your tagged image and its layers to the specified repository on Docker Hub. If you have a free Docker Hub account, the repository will be public by default (meaning anyone can pull your image). Docker Hub also offers private repositories.

  The push process might take some time, especially for larger images or on slower connections, as it uploads all the layers that make up your image.

Once pushed, your image (`myrustdev/my_rust_cli_app:0.1.0`) is now available on Docker Hub for others (or your deployment servers) to use.

Pulling images in a deployment environment

On the server or platform where you want to deploy your application, you (or your deployment scripts/orchestrator) will need to *pull* the image from the registry before it can be run:

```
# On your deployment server (or any machine with Docker)

# Pull the image from Docker Hub
# Replace 'myrustdev' with the actual username and 'my_rust_cli_app' with
the image name.
docker pull myrustdev/my_rust_cli_app:0.1.0

# After pulling, you can run it:
# docker run --rm myrustdev/my_rust_cli_app:0.1.0
```

- `docker pull <image_name_with_username_and_tag>` downloads the specified image and its layers from Docker Hub (or another configured registry) to the local machine
- If the image (or specific layers) already exists locally, Docker will only download the missing or updated parts
- Once pulled, the image is available in the local image cache, and you can use `docker run` to start containers from it, just like you did with locally built images

This tag-push-pull workflow is fundamental to distributing Dockerized applications. Your **continuous integration/continuous deployment** (**CI/CD**) pipeline, which we'll touch on next, would typically automate the build, tag, push, and sometimes even the pull and deploy steps.

Summary

We've reached the end of *Chapter 16*, and with it, our journey into Dockerizing and deploying Rust applications!

This chapter aimed to take you from the fundamental concepts of containerization to the practical steps of packaging your Rust code into Docker images, optimizing them, and understanding how they can be run and managed, whether as single containers or as part of a multi-service application.

Docker is a transformative technology in modern software development, and being able to leverage it effectively with Rust can greatly enhance your development and deployment workflows.

Let's recap what we've covered in this chapter:

- **Introduction to Docker and containerization**: We started by defining Docker and its core benefits, such as providing consistent environments, isolating dependencies, enabling portability, and improving resource efficiency. We also specifically discussed why Dockerizing Rust applications is particularly advantageous, highlighting the simplified deployment of compiled binaries and consistent build environments.
- **Getting started with Docker**: We walked through setting up your Docker environment (installing Docker Desktop) and introduced essential Docker concepts such as **images** (the blueprints) and **containers** (the runnable instances). We also covered basic Docker commands for interacting with images and containers (`docker run`, `docker ps`, `docker images`, `docker stop`, and `docker rm`).
- **Dockerizing your Rust application**: The core of the chapter focused on creating a Dockerfile – the recipe for building your Rust application's image. We learned about fundamental Dockerfile instructions (`FROM`, `WORKDIR`, `COPY`, `RUN`, `CMD`, and `EXPOSE`) and constructed a basic Dockerfile to compile a Rust application and prepare it to run.

- **Optimizing Docker images for Rust**: We then explored crucial techniques to make our Rust Docker images smaller and more efficient, with a strong emphasis on **multi-stage builds**. This allows us to separate the build environment (with the Rust toolchain and source code) from the final runtime environment (which might only contain the compiled binary and minimal operating system dependencies). We also discussed choosing minimal base images (such as `debian:slim` or `alpine`) and leveraging Docker's build cache.
- **Managing multi-container applications with Docker Compose**: For applications consisting of multiple services (such as a Rust backend and a database), we introduced Docker Compose. We learned how to write a `compose.yml` file to define services, networks, environment variables, and volumes, and how to use `docker compose` commands (such as `up`, `down`, `logs`, and `exec`) to manage the entire application stack.
- **Deploying Dockerized Rust applications**: Finally, we provided an overview of how to get your Docker images out into the world. This included tagging images for versioning and pushing them to and pulling them from container registries (such as Docker Hub).

By now, you should have a solid understanding of how to package your Rust applications into Docker containers, making them portable, efficient, and easier to deploy across different environments. While we've covered a lot, the world of Docker and container orchestration is vast. This chapter provides a strong foundation for exploring more advanced topics, such as Kubernetes, detailed security hardening, and sophisticated CI/CD strategies, as your needs evolve.

The ability to containerize your applications is a valuable skill in today's software landscape!

Congratulations!

Congratulations! You've reached the end of this journey, and you've come a very long way.

You started with the basics of Rust's syntax and its unique ownership system, and you've since built concurrent programs, command-line utilities, and even a complete, database-backed web application with a WebAssembly frontend.

You now have a strong and practical set of skills for writing the safe, fast, and reliable software that Rust is known for.

This is a significant achievement, and you are now well equipped to explore the vibrant Rust ecosystem and create impressive projects. Well done, and happy coding!

Questions and assignments

This chapter has taken you through the essentials of Docker, from basic concepts to Dockerizing your Rust applications, optimizing images, managing multi-container setups with Docker Compose, and understanding deployment.

Now it's time to roll up your sleeves and apply what you've learned! These questions and assignments are designed to solidify your understanding and give you practical experience.

Questions

1. What is a Docker image, and how does it differ from a Docker container?
2. Explain the main purpose of a Dockerfile. List and briefly describe five common instructions you might find in one.
3. What is a multi-stage Docker build, and what is its primary benefit when Dockerizing compiled applications such as those written in Rust?
4. Why is it generally better to use `COPY Cargo.toml Cargo.lock ./` and run a dependency-focused `cargo build` step *before* copying the `src` directory in a Dockerfile for a Rust project?
5. What is Docker Compose used for? Describe a scenario where it would be more beneficial than just using `docker run` commands.
6. When would you use a named volume versus a bind mount in Docker Compose for persisting data?
7. What is a container registry (such as Docker Hub), and why is it important in the deployment workflow?

Assignments

Assignment 16.1: Dockerize an existing Rust CLI or web application

Goal: Get hands-on experience in writing an optimized Dockerfile for a Rust application.

Task:

1. **Choose a Rust project**: Pick a Rust project you've worked on previously in this book (such as the CLI tool from *Chapter 14*, or the Actix Web API from *Chapter 13* if you haven't done the database part yet, or even a simple new `cargo new my_app --bin` with a basic "Hello, World!" or a small calculation).

2. Write a Dockerfile:
    - Create a Dockerfile in the root of that project.
    - Implement a **multi-stage build.**
    - The first stage (the "builder" stage) should use a Rust base image (e.g., `rust:1.78` or your preferred version), copy your source code, and compile your application in release mode (`cargo build --release`).
    - The second stage (the "runtime" stage) should start from a minimal base image (e.g., `debian:buster-slim` or `alpine:latest`).
    - Copy *only* the compiled binary from the builder stage into the runtime stage.
    - If using Alpine, remember you might need to compile your Rust binary with a `musl` target (e.g., `cargo build --release --target x86_64-unknown-linux-musl`) in the builder stage for it to run correctly on Alpine. If using `debian:slim`, the default gnu target usually works.
    - Set the appropriate `CMD` to run your application.
3. **Build the image:** Use `docker build -t yourname/my_rust_app:0.1.0 .` to build your image.
4. **Run the container:** Run your application using `docker run --rm yourname/my_rust_app:0.1.0`. If it's a web application, remember to map ports using `-p`.
5. **Check image size:** Use `docker images` to see the size of your final image. Compare it to what it might have been with a single-stage build (if you want to experiment).

Deliverables (conceptual):

- Your Dockerfile
- A brief note on the base image you chose for the runtime stage and why
- The approximate size of your final Docker image

Assignment 16.2: Create a multi-container application with Docker Compose

Goal: Practice defining and running a multi-service application using Docker Compose.

Task:

1. **Choose or create a Rust web application**: You can use the Actix Web API project from *Chapter 13* (especially if you implemented the in-memory version or a version that can be configured to use a database via environment variables). If you don't have one, create a very simple Actix Web app with one or two endpoints (e.g., a `/ping` endpoint that returns `"pong"`).
2. **Dockerfile for the Rust app**: Ensure your Rust web app has a Dockerfile (preferably a multi-stage one from the previous exercise).
3. **Choose a database**: Select a simple database to run alongside your app, for example, PostgreSQL or Redis (if your app was designed for caching, or just as a second service example). For this exercise, let's assume PostgreSQL.
4. **Write a compose.yml file**:

    Define two services:

    - One for your Rust web application (let's call it `webapp`):
        - It should build from your Rust project's directory
        - Map the necessary port (e.g., `8080:8080`)
        - Set up any environment variables your app needs (e.g., `DATABASE_URL` pointing to the `db` service, `RUST_LOG`)
        - Make it depend on the `db` service
    - One for the PostgreSQL database (let's call it `db`):
        - Use an official Postgres image (e.g., `postgres:15-alpine`)
        - Set the required `POSTGRES_USER`, `POSTGRES_PASSWORD`, and `POSTGRES_DB` environment variables
        - Define a named volume to persist the PostgreSQL data
    - Declare the named volume at the top level of the `compose.yml` file.

5. Run with Docker Compose:
    - Use `docker compose up --build` to build your Rust app image and start both services
    - Test whether your Rust application can connect to the database (if you implemented that part) or at least that both services start up correctly
    - Use `docker compose logs webapp` and `docker compose logs db` to view their outputs
    - Use `docker compose down` (and `docker compose down -v` if you want to clear the database data) to stop and remove the application stack

Deliverables (conceptual):

- Your Dockerfile for the Rust web application
- Your `compose.yml` file
- A brief description of how you tested that the services were running and (if applicable) communicating

17

Unlock Your Exclusive Benefits

Your copy of this book includes the following exclusive benefits:

- Next-gen Packt Reader
- DRM-free PDF/ePub downloads

Follow the guide below to unlock them. The process takes only a few minutes and needs to be completed once.

Unlock this Book's Free Benefits in 3 Easy Steps

Step 1

Keep your purchase invoice ready for *Step 3*. If you have a physical copy, scan it using your phone and save it as a PDF, JPG, or PNG.

For more help on finding your invoice, visit `https://www.packtpub.com/unlock-benefits/help`.

Note: If you bought this book directly from Packt, no invoice is required. After *Step 2*, you can access your exclusive content right away.

Step 2

Scan the QR code or go to `packtpub.com/unlock`.

On the page that opens (similar to *Figure 17.1* on desktop), search for this book by name and select the correct edition.

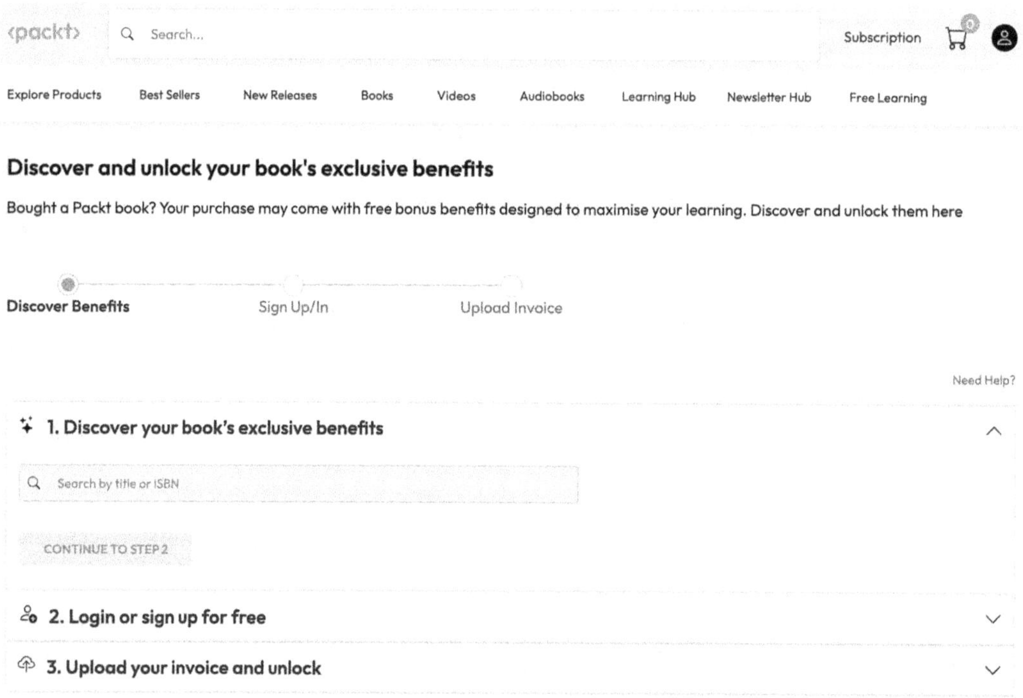

<packt> Search... Subscription

Explore Products Best Sellers New Releases Books Videos Audiobooks Learning Hub Newsletter Hub Free Learning

Discover and unlock your book's exclusive benefits

Bought a Packt book? Your purchase may come with free bonus benefits designed to maximise your learning. Discover and unlock them here

Discover Benefits Sign Up/In Upload Invoice

Need Help?

1. Discover your book's exclusive benefits

Search by title or ISBN

CONTINUE TO STEP 2

2. Login or sign up for free

3. Upload your invoice and unlock

Figure 17.1: Packt unlock landing page on desktop

Step 3

After selecting your book, sign in to your Packt account or create one for free. Then upload your invoice (PDF, PNG, or JPG, up to 10 MB). Follow the on-screen instructions to finish the process.

Need help?

If you get stuck and need help, visit `https://www.packtpub.com/unlock-benefits/help` for a detailed FAQ on how to find your invoices and more. This QR code will take you to the help page.

Note: If you are still facing issues, reach out to `customercare@packt.com`.

packtpub.com

Subscribe to our online digital library for full access to over 7,000 books and videos, as well as industry leading tools to help you plan your personal development and advance your career. For more information, please visit our website.

Why subscribe?

- Spend less time learning and more time coding with practical eBooks and Videos from over 4,000 industry professionals
- Improve your learning with Skill Plans built especially for you
- Get a free eBook or video every month
- Fully searchable for easy access to vital information
- Copy and paste, print, and bookmark content

At www.packtpub.com, you can also read a collection of free technical articles, sign up for a range of free newsletters, and receive exclusive discounts and offers on Packt books and eBooks.

Other Books You May Enjoy

If you enjoyed this book, you may be interested in these other books by Packt:

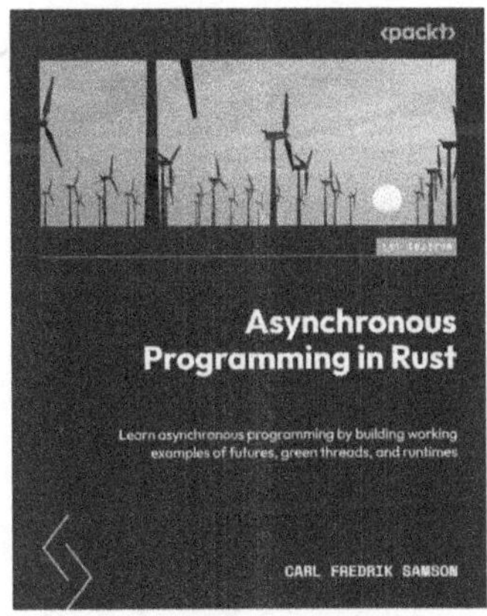

Asynchronous Programming in Rust

Carl Fredrik Samson

ISBN: 978-1-80512-662-1

- Explore the essence of asynchronous program flow and its significance
- Understand the difference between concurrency and parallelism
- Gain insights into how computers and operating systems handle concurrent tasks
- Uncover the mechanics of async/await
- Understand Rust's futures by implementing them yourself
- Implement green threads from scratch to thoroughly understand them

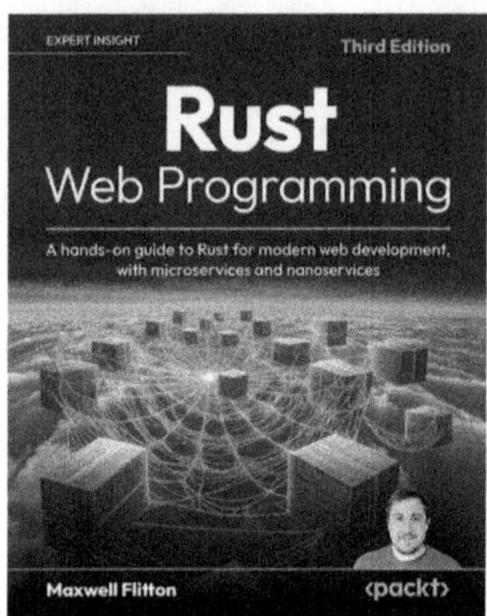

Rust Web Programming

Maxwell Flitton

ISBN: 978-1-83588-777-6

- Build scalable Rust web applications as monoliths or microservices
- Develop a deeper understanding of async Rust
- Get to grips with Rust language features like traits and the borrow checker
- Manage authentication and databases in Rust web apps
- Build app infrastructure on AWS using Terraform
- Learn how to package and deploy Rust servers
- Build unit tests and end-to-end tests for your Rust web apps with Python

Packt is searching for authors like you

If you're interested in becoming an author for Packt, please visit `authors.packt.com` and apply today. We have worked with thousands of developers and tech professionals, just like you, to help them share their insight with the global tech community. You can make a general application, apply for a specific hot topic that we are recruiting an author for, or submit your own idea.

Share your thoughts

Now you've finished *The Rust Programming Handbook*, we'd love to hear your thoughts! Scan the QR code below to go straight to the Amazon review page for this book and share your feedback or leave a review on the site that you purchased it from.

`https://packt.link/r/1836208871`

Your review is important to us and the tech community and will help us make sure we're delivering excellent quality content.

Index

Symbols

A

F

S

T

www.ingramcontent.com/pod-product-compliance
Lightning Source LLC
Chambersburg PA
CBHW[illegible]1208220326
4159[illegible]B00037B/6712